当代国外语言学与应用语言学文库（升级版）

语义学

第四版

Semantics (Fourth Edition)

John I. Saeed 著

张辉　杨琪 导读

外语教学与研究出版社
FOREIGN LANGUAGE TEACHING AND RESEARCH PRESS
北京 BEIJING

京权图字：01-2021-3956

图书在版编目（CIP）数据

语义学：第四版 = Semantics (Fourth Edition)：英文 /（英）约翰 · I. 萨伊德 (John I. Saeed) 著；张辉，杨琪导读. —— 北京：外语教学与研究出版社，2021.9
（当代国外语言学与应用语言学文库：升级版）
ISBN 978-7-5213-2980-3

Ⅰ. ①语… Ⅱ. ①约… ②张… ③杨… Ⅲ. ①语义学－英文 Ⅳ. ①H030

中国版本图书馆 CIP 数据核字 (2021) 第 173201 号

出 版 人　徐建忠
项目负责　姚　虹　李亚琦
责任编辑　李　鑫
责任校对　周渝毅
装帧设计　李　高
出版发行　外语教学与研究出版社
社　　址　北京市西三环北路 19 号（100089）
网　　址　http://www.fltrp.com
印　　刷　唐山市润丰印务有限公司
开　　本　650×980　1/16
印　　张　34
版　　次　2021 年 9 月第 1 版　2021 年 9 月第 1 次印刷
书　　号　ISBN 978-7-5213-2980-3
定　　价　85.00 元

购书咨询：（010）88819926　电子邮箱：club@fltrp.com
外研书店：https://waiyants.tmall.com
凡印刷、装订质量问题，请联系我社印制部
联系电话：（010）61207896　电子邮箱：zhijian@fltrp.com
凡侵权、盗版书籍线索，请联系我社法律事务部
举报电话：（010）88817519　电子邮箱：banquan@fltrp.com
物料号：329800001

当代国外语言学与应用语言学文库

（升级版）

出版前言

“当代国外语言学与应用语言学文库”（以下简称“文库”）从2000年至今已出版近200个品种，深受语言学与应用语言学专业师生和研究者的欢迎，大家既把“文库”视为进入语言学与应用语言学百花园的引路人，又把“文库”视为知识更新的源泉，还把“文库”当成点亮科研之路的明灯。

为了追踪相关领域的研究进程，并满足广大读者的需求，外语教学与研究出版社从2020年开始启动了“文库”的更新升级工作，与牛津大学出版社、剑桥大学出版社、劳特利奇出版社等世界知名出版机构合作，推出“文库”（升级版）。

“文库”升级的原则如下：

1. 对原有经典图书，若无新版，则予以保留，并予以必要修订；若有新版，则以新版代替旧版，并请相关领域学者撰写新版中文导读。

2. 引进语言学与应用语言学领域的新锐力作，进一步拓展学科领域。

3. 用二维码代替CD-ROM，帮助读者更加快捷地获取内容。

“文库”（升级版）定位为一套大型的、开放性的系列丛书，希望它能对我国语言学教学与研究和外语教学与研究起到积极的推动作用。外语教学与研究出版社亦将继续努力，力争把国外最新、最具影响力的语言学与应用语言学著作奉献给广大读者。

外语教学与研究出版社

2021年8月

当代国外语言学与应用语言学文库（升级版）

2021年出版书目

——Cognitive Linguistics 认知语言学

Cognitive Linguistics and Language Teaching
《认知语言学和语言教学》
Randal Holme

An Introduction to Cognitive Linguistics (Second Edition)
《认知语言学入门（第二版）》
F. Ungerer & H.-J. Schmid

——First Language Acquisition 第一语言习得

An Introduction to Child Language Development
《儿童语言发展引论》
Susan H. Foster-Cohen

——Functional Linguistics 功能语言学

Genre Relations: Mapping Culture
《语类关系与文化映射》
J. R. Martin & David Rose

An Introduction to Functional Grammar (Third Edition)
《功能语法导论（第三版）》
M. A. K. Halliday, revised by Christian Matthiessen

——General Linguistics 普通语言学

Course in General Linguistics
《普通语言学教程》
F. de Saussure

General Linguistics (Fourth Edition)
《普通语言学概论（第四版）》
R. H. Robins

An Introduction to Linguistics
《语言学入门》
Stuart C. Poole

—History of Linguistics 语言学史

A Short History of Linguistics (Fourth Edition)
《语言学简史（第四版）》
R. H. Robins

—Intercultural Communication 跨文化交际

Intercultural Interaction: A Multidisciplinary Approach to Intercultural Communication
《跨文化互动：跨文化交际的多学科研究》
Helen Spencer-Oatey & Peter Franklin

—Lexicography 词典学

Dictionary of Lexicography
《词典学词典》
R. R. K. Hartmann & Gregory James

—Philosophy of Language 语言哲学

How to Do Things with Words
《如何以言行事》
J. L. Austin

—Pragmatics 语用学

Meaning in Interaction: An Introduction to Pragmatics
《言谈互动中的意义：语用学引论》
Jenny Thomas

—Psycholinguistics 心理语言学

The Articulate Mammal: An Introduction to Psycholinguistics (Fourth Edition)
《会说话的哺乳动物：心理语言学入门（第四版）》
Jean Aitchison

—Research Method 研究方法

Research Perspectives on English for Academic Purposes
《学术英语的多维研究视角》
John Flowerdew & Matthew Peacock

—Second Language Acquisition 第二语言习得

Fossilization in Adult Second Language Acquisition
《成人二语习得中的僵化现象》
韩照红（Zhaohong Han）

Linguistics and Second Language Acquisition
《语言学和第二语言习得》
Vivian Cook

Strategies in Learning and Using a Second Language
《学习和运用第二语言的策略》
Andrew D. Cohen

Tasks in Second Language Learning
《第二语言学习中的任务》
Virginia Samuda & Martin Bygate

——Semantics 语义学

Meaning in Language: An Introduction to Semantics and Pragmatics (Third Edition)
《语言的意义：语义学与语用学导论（第三版）》
Alan Cruse

Semantics (Fourth Edition)
《语义学（第四版）》
John I. Saeed

——Sociolinguistics 社会语言学

The Handbook of Sociolinguistics
《社会语言学通览》
Florian Coulmas

An Introduction to Sociolinguistics (Seventh Edition)
《社会语言学引论（第七版）》
Ronald Wardhaugh & Janet M. Fuller

——Stylistics 文体学

A Linguistic Guide to English Poetry
《英诗学习指南：语言学的分析方法》
Geoffrey N. Leech

Patterns in Language: Stylistics for Students of Language and Literature
《语言模式：文体学入门》
Joanna Thornborrow & Shân Wareing

Style in Fiction: A Linguistic Introduction to English Fictional Prose
《小说文体论：英语小说的语言学入门》
Geoffrey N. Leech & Michael H. Short

Stylistics: A Practical Coursebook
《实用文体学教程》
Laura Wright & Jonathan Hope

——Syntax 句法学

Chomsky's Universal Grammar: An Introduction (Third Edition)
《乔姆斯基的普遍语法教程（第三版）》
V. J. Cook & Mark Newson

——Testing 语言测试

Language Testing and Validation: An Evidence-Based Approach
《语言测试与效度验证：基于证据的研究方法》
Cyril J. Weir

——Text Linguistics 语篇语言学

The Language of Evaluation: Appraisal in English
《评估语言：英语评价系统》
J. R. Martin & P. R. R. White

Metadiscourse
《元话语》
Ken Hyland

导　　读

张辉　杨琪

John I. Saeed撰写的教科书《语义学》是语义学领域经典著作之一，产生了广泛的影响，迄今为止已出版了第四版。本书结构脉络清晰，可读性较高。整本书分为三部分，第一部分介绍了语义学的基本概念，研究的进路以及语言、概念和思维的不同关系。第二部分介绍语义描写的不同方面，包括词义、句子关系与真值、句子语义学、语境与推理以及言语行为理论。第三部分介绍各种不同的语义学理论，包括成分分析法及其拓展、形式语义学和认知语义学。本书作者是爱尔兰都柏林大学的语言学教授，长期从事语义学的教学，具有扎实的功底。

第一章　语言学中的语义学

语义学研究的是语言交流的意义。Saeed撰写的这本语义学教科书是关于现代语言学中语义理论和实践的入门书。其基本的假设是，人的语言能力是基于其所拥有的知识，这种知识正是我们试图探讨的内容。语义学的定义非常简单，其研究的范围却非常广泛，涉及的话题不同，采用的研究方法也大相径庭。另外，语义学与哲学和心理学有千丝万缕的联系，哲学和心理学中提出的一些问题对语义学产生了重要的影响。

语义学的基本任务是探讨人们如何使用语言交流意义。理解意义（包括语言意义）不仅要知道包括任意性符号在内的语言意义或知识，还要知道包括基于因果关系的推理。语言的使用反映了人类普遍的识别能力和创造符号的习惯，即使用一事物替代另一事物。创造和解释符号的过程有时被称为意指（signification），比语言本身要宽广得多，研究语言意义是研究符号系统使用的一部分，后者是符号学（semiotics）。符号学家探讨符号与其所代表的物体之间的关系类型，即索绪尔所说的能指（signifier）和所指（signified）之间的关系，能指与所指的结合过程就是意指。皮尔斯（C. S. Peirce）区分了三种重要的意指：像似符号（icon）、指示符号（index）和规约符号（symbol）。像似符号是符号与所代表的事物之间具有相似性，如肖像与真人之间以及发动机的图片与真正的发动机之间的相似性；指示符号是符号紧密地与所指联系在一起，符号与所指之间具有因果关系，如冒烟预示火灾；规约符号是符号与所指只存在常规的连接，绝大部分的词汇都是规约符号。

分析说话人的语义是一个具有挑战性的工作。作者首先采用了一个简单且直观的理论，即定义理论（definitions theory），然后开始反驳这个理论，指出其缺陷。定义理论认为，我们必须首先建立词汇语义的定义，当说话人根据语法规则把词结合起来形成句子，词的定义也就结合起来形成了词组和句子的意义。

然而，定义理论存在以下三个问题：一是循环论证（circularity）的问题；二是词的定义准确性问题；三是语境问题。语境的特征是言语意义的一部分，其在很大程度上影响了我们对词义的理解，我们如何将语境纳入词义的定义中呢？为了克服这三个难点，我们不得不摒弃定义理论，而采用能解决上述问题的理论。本书写作的目的之一就是展示各种不同的理论是如何试图解决这三个难点的。就循环论证而言，一种解决办法是设计一个语义元语言（metalanguage）。元语言是描写语言的语言，是描写语言的工具。理想的元语言应该是中立、简洁、经济和一致的，但这种元语言几乎不存在，我们不得不使用日常语言描写意义。我们还要把解释语义置于非语言的知识层面上。建立元语言可以帮助我们解决语义知识与百科知识之间的关系，可真正的问题是：为了能使用词，我们要纳入多少知识，又会涉及哪些类型的知识。

为了解决第三个难点，传统的做法是严格区分局部语境效应和不受语境影响的意义。还有另一种做法，即探讨交际中语境信息的作用，试图解释说话人如何把语境知识和语言知识结合起来。这一探讨属于语用学。上面所简述的解决三个难点的办法在本书的章节中有不同程度的体现。

语法模式是否是模块化的观念起到分水岭的作用。一是语言学家通常把语法分成不同的模块，如音位、句法和语义等，即分为不同的分析层次，这就是语言知识的模块化。语义学该归为哪个模块，不同理论有不同的看法。二是有些语言学家反对在语言分析中采取模块化的思想，认为意义是所有语言层面的产品，不能被识别为一个独立、自主的层面，其中比较极端的语法理论就是认知语法（Cognitive Grammar）。

在本书中，有些语言学家提出的理论遵循模块化的思想，强调区分语言的和非语言的知识，而在语言知识内部，又区分关于语音、音位、语法知识、意义知识等不同的模式。与之形成鲜明对比的是，有一些语言学家则坚持非模块化的思想，强调语言的统一、整体分析和解释，不区分不同的模块。

首先掌握一种语言包括熟记和掌握单词，这些单词都储存在我们的记忆中，形成心理词库的一部分。与词义不同的是，句子也具有意义，句子与词之间的差异在于能产性（productivity）。说话人可以使用数量有限的词产出数量无限的句子，句子产出的规则是递归的（recursive），允许句子范畴的重复内嵌或并列。递归性对语义描写具有一定的启示。句子意义不可能像词库那样一一举列，必须由组合规则所创建。语义学家通过组构性（compositionality）描写句子意义。组构性指的是，表达的意义由其组成成分的意义和组成成分组合的方式来决定。

在语法模式中，意义存在于两个地方：一是在词库中——有一组稳定的词义；二是句子中——有无限组构的意义。关于词义和句子意义之间的关系，在不同的理论中是不一样的。在Chomsky的各种理论中，句法规则独立于语义规则而运作，两种规则在逻辑形式（Logical Form）上交叉，形成界面研究。然而在其他理论中，语义规则和句法规则不可分割地捆绑在一起，如Halliday的系统功能语法、van Valin的角色与参照语法以及认知语法等。

本书的第一章介绍了语义学的一些重要的假设：（1）指称与意义（reference and sense）。Saussure指出，语言表达的意义有两个来源：一是语言，二是语言所描写的世界。词让我们识别了世界的一部分，并对它们做出陈述，识别、选取或指称世界上的实体。词的价值来自于自身在语言系统中的位置。因此语言所“构筑”的世界的关系被称为指称（reference），而在词汇系统内各成分之间的语义连接的是意义（sense）。（2）言语、句子与命题。语言学家使用言语（utterance）、句子（sentence）和命题（proposition）来描写语言的不同层面。最具体的是言语，句子则是从实际语言使用中抽象或概括出来的；最抽象的是命题，命题是从各种句子类型中抽象出来，用于描写同一事态（state of affairs）。例如英语中的主动语态“Caesar invaded Gaul.”与被动语态“Gaul was invaded by Caesar.”是两种不同的句子，但其命题是一样的，描写的是同一事态。（3）字面义（literal meaning）与非字面义（non-literal meaning）。非字面义具有比喻性，包括隐喻、反语、转喻、提喻、夸张和曲言等。Lakoff 指出，词汇充满了石化隐喻，如 go viral，photobomb和chatroom等，而这一石化过程使我们很难确定词的哪些用法是字面义，哪些是比喻义。字面义与非字面义的区分存在两种观点：一种是Lakoff 等人的观点，认为在字面义与非字面义之间不存在原则性的差异。他们把隐喻看作人类范畴化不可分离的一部分，认为整个语义域围绕着一个被系统地组织起来的中心隐喻，隐喻的使用不是孤立的文体效应，而是反映了我们的思维方式。另一种是字面语言理论（literal language theory），认为字面义与非字面义的用法存在一定的差异，隐喻和非字面义用法需要与字面义语言采用不同的加工策略。（4）语义学与语用学。语义学和语用学之间很难划出一条清晰的界线，且备受争论。语用学探讨的是与说话人和听话人有关的意义，而语义学研究的是从语言使用者那里抽象来的意义。一些语义学家认为，存在着一些语言在使用中有共同的意义，这些共同且非具体语境的意义是语义学关注的焦点，而一些依赖语境的句子的使用则是语用学研究的目标。另一个区分是句子意义和说话人意义（speaker meaning），语义学关注句子意义，而语用学则探讨说话人意义。

区分语义学与语用学有好处，也有坏处。好处是，这一区分可以把语义学解放出来，避免包括所有类型的知识，可以使我们集中精力探讨言语理解中的语言成分，语用学则可以探讨听话人如何使用语境信息填补语义结构，并在语义结构的基础上做出推理。但有些学者质疑这一区分，指出我们很难从语言中削除语境的影响。在本书中，区分与不区分的观点都会得到体现，反映了不同理论的视角。

第二章 意义、思维与现实

在本章中，作者首先介绍了当代语义学的两种进路：指称进路

(referential/denotational approach)与表征进路(representational approach)。对语义学来说，采取指称进路意味着把词放入与世界的关系之中，这就是意义，因此对语言的语义进行描写就是表明语言表达如何“构筑”世界。

表征进路指的是，我们谈论世界的能力取决于我们所建立的关于这个世界的心理模式和概念结构。因此，依据这一进路，说话人可以选择不同方式来观察同一情景，不同的概念化影响我们对真实世界情景的描写。有些语义理论之所以称为表征，就是因为我们描写现实的方式受到语言中常规化的概念结构的影响。

这两个进路的侧重点不同，关注的是同一过程的不同方面。在指称进路中，意义来自根植于现实的语言，而在表征进程中，意义则来自体现概念结构的语言。这两种不同进路在本书都有体现。

指称分为不同的类型。名词可以是指称表达，也可以是非指称表达。在指称表达中存在常量指称(constant reference)和变量指称(variable reference)，常量指称指的是在不同的言语中总是指同一指称物，例如“天安门”或“南京”，而变量指称指的是其指称完全依靠语境，例如“I wrote to you.”中，我们必须根据语境来识别“I”和“you”的指称物。指示词(deixis)如“this”和“that”也是需要语境的变量指称。

除了个体和个体组群外，名词词组还可以指称物质、行为和抽象观念，例如“Who can afford coffee?”中“coffee”指的是物质，“Sleeping is his hobby.”中的“sleeping”指的是行为，“She has a passion for justice.”中的“justice”指的是抽象概念。有些包含量词的名词词组在指称上有歧义，例如“No students enjoyed the lecture.”中就有两种意义，一是“Of the students, not one enjoyed the lecture.”；二是“For each student X, X did not enjoy the lecture.”

指称作为意义的理论属于指称进路，语义就是指称，即为了给出词的意义，我们必须指出该词的指称是什么。这一简单的语义指称理论存在以下三个问题：一是许多词没有意义，因为我们很难为so，not，very，but，of等词找到真实世界的指称物；二是许多名词词组没有存在的或曾经存在的指称物，例如a unicorn，Father Christmas等；三是当谈论真实世界中的事物时，我们可以使用不同的名词词组指称同一指称物，即语言表达与其指称物之间不存在一对一的对应关系，例如“鲍里斯·约翰逊”和“英国首相”都指称同一指称物，前者是使用名称，后者使用限定摹状词或确定性描述（definite description）。以上两种语言表达都指称同一个体，但它们之间的意义是不同的。这就是为何Frege要区分指称和意义的原因。他指出，指称和意义是不同的事物，意义是基本的，因为它可以使指称成为可能。语言表达的语义不仅来自指称，还来自意义。简单的指称理论是错误的。

词义不仅仅指称真实世界中的实体或事物，还与说话者/听话者头脑中的心理表征或概念相关联。那么什么是心理表征或概念？心理学家对于概念是什么也存在分歧，这就使语义学家分为两派：一派怀疑心理学家的研究，如果指称是基于概念的，我们就不能把意义的理论基于指称，以形式而非心理的方式模拟意义；另一派则坚持心理表征的进路，试图建立概念模式，形成语义学研究的基础。

描写概念的理论有两种：一种是传统的充分必要条件（necessary and sufficient conditions），另一种是原型（prototype theory）。前者是，我们把一些特征看成条件，例如“woman”（女人）有以下特征，如“human（人类），adult（成年），雌性（female）”。如果必须具备这些特征或条件才能是“woman”（女人），那它们就是必要条件，而如果这些特征或条件足够界定“woman”，这就是充分条件。充分必要条件就是一个概念的界定必须符合所有的条件。后者是Rosch等学者提出的原型理论。他们发现界定概念的充分必要条件有问题，即一个概念并非符合所有的特征或条件，有些概念是范畴的中心或典型成员，而有些则逐渐滑向非典型或边缘成员，例如“sparrow”（麻雀）是鸟类的中心和典型成员，符合这一范畴所有的特征或条件，而“penguin”（企鹅）是鸟类的边缘和非中心成员，只符合部分的特征或条件。原型理论得到心理学实验的证实：说话人对典型成员同意程度比非典型成员高，典型成员容易被想起，等等，该实验的另一个结论是，概念之间的界限是不确定或模糊的。

心理学的文献中对原型性或典型性的解释有三种：（1）一些研究者指出，中心原型是抽象的，这一抽象可能是一组典型特征（characteristic features）。（2）其他学者则提出，我们通过样例（examplars）组织范畴，即记忆实际典型样例。（3）来自语言学内部的观点认为，说话人具有关于世界的通俗理论（folk theories），这些通俗理论被Fillmore称为框架，被Lakoff称为理想化的认知模式（Idealized Cognitive Models或ICM）。他们都认为，存在着我们关于词汇知识的划分，如“bachelor”，一部分是词典式的定义（没有结婚的男人），一部分是关于单身和婚姻文化知识的百科式的条目，即框架或ICM。前者称为语言或语义知识，而后者称为真实世界或一般知识，就是在后者的真实世界或一般知识的背景下制约着我们对“bachelor”的使用和理解。

概念的另一个重要问题是概念知识的关系本质（relational nature）。一个概念不在于知识的多少，而在于其与其他相关概念之间的关系，这一概念如何整合到现存的知识之中，以及如何与其他相关概念形成一个知识网络（knowledge network）。依据概念之间的这一关系，有学者提出概念层级模式（model of conceptual hierarchies）。Rosch等人探讨了概念层级，并建议这一层级包括三个层次：上位层次（superordinate level）、基本层次（basic level）和下位层次（subordinate level）。例如以家具为例，上位层次是furniture，基本层次是chair，下位层次是armchair和dining chair。其中的基本层次在认知上是重要的，因为这一层次在日常生活中使用最广泛，最早被儿童习得以及在实验中最快被识别和命名等。基本层次也会随着不同的认知域和不同人的专业知识而产生变化。概念的第三个问题是如何习得概念。最简单的理论是通过实指定义（ostensive definition）习得概念，即通过指明语词所指的对象或识别语词所指对象的典型例子习得概念。儿童初期大多数就是通过实指定义习得概念的。但明示（ostension）通常都是用语言表达，明示定义依赖于词义先前的知识，只有这样才能搞清楚它的交际意图是陈述、警告而不是指示等。因此习得概念是一个复杂的过程，而不仅仅是简单的明示。

语言与思维之间的关系存在着两种相对立的观点：语言相对论（linguistic relativity）和思维语言假设（language of thought hypothesis），前者认为词汇化的概念制约着我们可能的思维方式，而后者则指出，思维和说话虽然明显相关但包含了不同的表征层面。

语言相对论是Edward Sapir和Benjamin Lee Whorf提出的。Sapir提出，我们所说的某一语言决定了我们对世界的概念化，语言是"社会现实"的向导。Sapir的学生Whorf进一步强调了语言对思维的决定作用，提出了语言相对论，其基本前提是，我们思考世界的方式由我们的文化和语言背景决定。Whorf的观点并非仅局限于词义，他认为语言的语法系统更能塑造我们的思维。

许多语言学家和认知科学的研究者反对语言相对论，认为语言和思维之间的严格区分是一个谬论。心理学的研究表明，许多思维过程，如记忆和推理，都不需要语言。这一不包含语言的心理过程常被用来支持以下的观点：认知过程利用了思维中独立的计算系统，即思维语言（a language of thought）（Fodor，1975、1987、2008）。Stilling等人从心理学实验中找到了一系列支持思维语言观点的证据。其基本观点是，记忆和推理等认知过程好像利用了一种命题表征（propositional representation），这种命题表征与我们所说的语言的表层句法完全不同。

另一个支持思维语言假设的证据是，语言对意义的描写是不足的，换句话说，意义比语言丰富。说话人常压缩其思维，隐晦而不是明确地说出所要表达的内容，而听话人则从呈现出来的语言中填补说话人所意图表达的意义。这说明语言与思维是分离的，人们只是把思维放入语言中，把思维的内容“翻译”成语言，而不是仅仅直接用语言表达思维，语言思维仅仅是整个思维过程中的一部分。另外一种支持思维语言假设的证据来自认知科学，即心理语言（mentalese）。当说话时，我们把心理语言“翻译”成我们所说的语言，如英语或汉语。这一观点还认为，每个人的心理语言大概是一样的，即思维语言是普遍的，即使我们说不同的语言，人类本质上具有相同的认知架构和心理过程。

作者在本章中简要地论述了关于思维和现实之间关系的几种观点，这些观点都在某种程度上渗透在各种语义学理论之中。首先作者指出，研究语义学的不同学者都不免在本体论（ontology）和认识论（epistemology）上采取不同的立场。本体论是探讨存在（being）的本质和现实结构的哲学分支。认知论是探讨知识的本质的哲学分支。其中唯心主义（idealism）认为，现实无法独立于人类思维的运作而存在，而客观主义（objectivism）则认为，现实是独立于人类思维而存在的，现实的知识是可得到的，并来自于我们对世界的概念化和范畴化。另外还有一种关于现实和思维关系的立场叫心理建构主义（mental constructivism），它指出，我们从来不能感知世界的本来面目，只有过滤从生物和文化演变而来的概念，才能获取关于现实的知识。这两种关于思维和现实哲学的观点在某种程度上都与本书中提到的不同语义学理论相关。

语言、思维与现实之间的关系问题使语言学家采取三种探讨语义问题的立场：（1）把语言、思维和现实之间的问题留给哲学家和心理学家，只关注语言内部的意义关系(sense relations)或语言之间的关系;(2)采取指称进路，认为意义本质上是指称的，试图发展出一种探讨各种不同类型指称的理论，包括客观的情景和一些想象的情景;(3)采取表征进路，认为语义依靠概念结构。在本书中，我们可以看到以上三种立场的不同体现。

第三章　词义

本章聚焦于词义，即词汇语义学的研究。传统描述中，词汇语义学的目标是:(1)表示语言中每个词的意义;(2)说明一种语言中的词义是如何相互联系的。

现代语言学从句法和词法层面定义了语法范畴，不同语法范畴的词具有不同的语义，如代词I和you，只有在具体的语境中才具有意义，而逻辑词(如and和or)的意义始终如一，不受语境的影响。词与词之间的语义联系只在同一语义范畴内发生。语义学关注词素(lexeme)，即语义词(semantic word)的研究，但首先需要明确的是如何识别词。从书写的角度出发，由空格隔开的字就是词，又被称作正字词(orthographic word);从语音的角度出发，词就是一连串的声音;从语法角度出发，一个语义词由几个派生的语法词(grammatical word)表示。但问题是如何将上述从三种角度出发的观点结合起来，对词形成一个整体的定义。答案之一是从语义定义转换成语法定义，最著名的便是Bloomfield的最小自由词的定义和Lyon的语素黏合的定义，但是仍然存在两种定义不能囊括的边缘情况。

词义的理解会受到语境的影响，主要分为两类情况:第一类是限制性影响，比如出现频率高的单词会经历固化的过程，成为固定搭配;第二类是创造性影响，在不同的语境下，同一个词会有不同的意义。一词多义有两类:歧义(ambiguity)和模糊(vagueness)。歧义是由语境决定合适的语义，而模糊是语境的模糊性赋予词新的意义。本章介绍了三种区分歧义和模糊的方法：Kempson等人设计的测试、语义联系测试和共轭修辞（zeugma）测试。

词与词的关系有以下几种：（1）同音（形）异义词（homonym），如lap（跑道上的一圈）和lap（大腿）。（2）多义词（polysemy），即一个词素有多个密切相关的意义，如hook（钩、鱼钩、陷阱等）；“相关性”是识别多义词的标准。（3）同义词（synonym），不同读音的词有着相同或类似的意义，主要源于不同的方言、语言风格、情感态度和搭配。（4）反义词是意义相反的词，包括有简单反义词（simple antonym），又称互补反义词（complementary antonym）或二元对（binary antonym）；分级反义词（gradable antonymy）；逆向反义词（reverse）；换位反义词（converse）；分类姐妹词（taxonomic sisters）。（5）下位关系，一种蕴含关系，具有概括性的词被称为上位词，下位词则是更具体的词，并蕴含上位词的意义；下位关系是垂直关系，具有传递性。（6）部分－整体关系可以通过“X是Y的一部分”或“Y有X”这样的句子框架识别；与下位关系相比，部分－整体关系的层次结构并不清晰规则，且该关系既可能具有传递性，也可能不具有传递性。（7）派生关系通过举例让致使动词和施事名词得到说明。

词汇分类学是语义分类学的一个重要分支，得到了众多学者的关注，这是因为一种语言的词库能够反映语言结构、说话人的交际需要和他们所处的文化与自然环境的交互作用。研究有两种途径，一种是比较词的组织或原则，包括词汇关系的模式，如多义词的跨语言研究；另一种是比较词语和单独的词项，即跨语言研究概念映射到词的方式，其中最为人所知的是对色彩词的研究。此外，本文通过介绍核心词和普遍词汇的研究，探讨了一些词汇是否在世界上的大多数语言中存在对应关系。

第四章　句义关系和真实性

上一章探讨了词间的语义关系和其对词库的语义网络效应，本章中，作者继续讨论句间可能存在的语义关系。根据不同的情况，句义关系既可由句中特定的词汇决定，也取决于句法结构。为了表达句义关系，源于逻辑学的真值概念对其做出了系统的阐释：句义关系存在六种情况，即同义（A is synonymous with B）、蕴含（A entails B）、反义（A contradicts B）、预设（A presupposes B）、同义重复（tautology）和前后矛盾（contradiction）。

逻辑的研究起源于古希腊，本章简单介绍了四种逻辑原则的论证和推理：肯定前件论式、否定后件推理、假言三段论和选言三段论。逻辑中的真实性必须是语言对现实世界的正确描述。由于陈述的真实性是基于我们对现实世界事实的了解，因此在大多数情况下，真实性具有经验性（empirical）或偶然性（contingent）。语义学家把句子的真假称为真值（truth-value），句子描述符合事实为真，否则为假。真值条件（truth condition）是决定句子真值的事实依据。逻辑连接词（connective）对复合命题的真值条件有预测效应，一般由逻辑运算符（logical operator）研究其真值效应，并通过逻辑式（logical form）和真值表（truth table）来说明。作者主要介绍了六个逻辑连接词的真值效应，但仍存有无法解释的逻辑关系，这是因为真实语言的条件比逻辑连接词表示的真值效应更复杂。

前文提到句子命题的真伪取决于其和客观事实是否一致，但是我们发现在不确定客观事实的情况下，我们依然能够直接判断部分句子（如：My father is my father）的真伪。为了解释这种情况，哲学家和逻辑学家们分别从认识论（epistemological）、形而上学（metaphysical）和语义的角度区分了先验（priori）真实性与后验（posteriori）真实性、必然（necessary）真实性与偶然（contingent）真实性、分析（analytic）真实性与综合（synthetic）

真实性，这些概念紧密相连，但并不完全相同。

蕴含的真值效应可以让我们更清楚地了解蕴含关系：当p蕴含q时，若p为真，则q为真；若q为假，则p为假；若q为真，则p可能为真，也可能为假；若p为假，则q既可能为真，也可能为假。不依据客观事实也能推导出蕴含关系，这是因为它本身是由词法（如下义关系）和句法（如主动句和被动句这样的语言结构）赋予我们的。逻辑学中的真值关系可用于简洁地描述前文提到的几种句义关系，但预设是一个例外。

预设即假设，一直是语义学研究的焦点。在某些方面，预设类似于蕴含，不涉及推理，不受语境的影响；而在另一方面，预设对会话语境的事实敏感。作者分别从语义层面和语用层面讨论了预设的研究。语义学用真值关系描述预设：若p为真，则q为假；若p为假，则q为真；若q为假，则p可能为真，也可能为假。语用学预设被视为说话人组织信息的策略之一，目的是为了让听话人能最大程度地理解信息。通常，句中名字和限定摹状词的使用预设了现实世界里实体的存在，若名词指称不存在实体，就会产生问题。从会话交际互动的角度出发，则是若听话人不理解说话人的名称指代，即听话人无法在现实世界里找到对应的实体，则预设失灵。一些句法结构，如分裂结构（the cleft construction）、伪分裂结构（the pseudo-cleft）、从句和词汇，如事实动词（factual verb）、体态动词（aspectual verb），都能触发预设。预设还会受到语境的影响，如背景知识、会话主题、句法结构和语调都会影响预设的产生。

此外，本章还介绍了Stalnaker的"共同基础"、Lewis的"通用原则"和Sperber与Wilson的"关联原则"等语用学理论对预设的认识。

第五章 句义一：情景

第三章作者讨论了词义的相关研究，本章将围绕情景类型、时态、体、语态和言据性五个语义范畴探讨句义。

情景的分类需要从三个维度入手:情景类型、时态和体。情景类型是用语义区分情景的标签，不同的动词可以说明不同的情景类型。状态动词(stative verb)，如be,have,know等，说明的是无内部阶段或变化、处于稳定状态的情景。动态动词(dynamic verb)根据语义可分为四类:持续性(durative)动词、短暂性(punctual)动词、有界(telic)动词和无界(atelic)动词。持续性动词用于描述持续一段时间的情景或过程，而短暂性动词描述的是瞬间性事件。有界动词含有自然完成之意，而无界动词不包含此意。动词本身的内在语义属性描述了不同的情景类型，那么如何把动词内在的语义属性投射到具体的情景类型体系中呢? Vendler总结了四种情景类型:静态(state)、活动(activity)情景、成就(accomplishment)和完成(achievement)。Smith在此基础上增加了瞬时性(semelfactive)并描述了不同情景类型的语义特征，这可以帮助我们判断句子的情景类型。本章中，作者简介了一些常用的判断方法。

时态是对时间的标记，在英语中通常用时间副词提示。时态以说话行为的时间点为参照，具有指示性。大多数语法时态系统允许说话人以说话行为为参照，描述同时发生、在其之前或之后的情景，例如英语中，我们就有过去、未来和现在三个最基础的时态。体也和时间有关，但与时态不同的是体描述的是情景内部的时间特质。体分为进行体(progressive)和完成体(perfect)两类。印欧语系里的大部分语言通常由动词的屈折变化表现体，但仍然存在差异性。作者用英语、俄语和阿拉伯语的对比研究说明了体在不同语言中的共同点和差异。

情景的描述依赖于情景类型、时态和体。时态和体具有相互依赖的关系，二者的结合能够描述不同的情景，作者以英语为例，列举现在进行时、过去进行时、将来进行时和现在完成时、过去完成时、将来完成时对情景的描述。而情景类型和体则相互制约，这是因为情景类型本身带有的语义特征会限制其与体的结合。因此体的选择需要基于真实的情景、情景类型的语义特征和我们基于内在结构关注情景类型的方式，即选择关注事件的起点、过程，还是关注事件的结束。

情态是一个重要的语义范畴，用于表达说话人对命题的态度。情态可以由情态形容词或副词、描述说话人命题态度的动词或情态动词表达。情态动词主要用于标记两种情态：认知情态——用于推测，以说明事件发生的可能性；义务情态——用于表达道义上的请求、责任和义务。这种划分使得读者很难从形式上区分认知情态和义务情态。语义学家们开始思考二者是否具有共同点，两种情态是否可以互相转化。源于David Lewis等人的可能世界语义学的方法论认为两种情态具有共同点，都是对假设情景和现实世界进行匹配，这一方法论在以动词区分虚拟和现实的语言中得到验证。从区分现实和虚拟世界的功能出发，情态又可以分为现实（realis）情态和非现实（irrealis）情态。

语气是动词的语法特征，用以区分不同的情态。语气在各种语言中主要分为两大类：现实语气，如英语中的陈述语气，用于客观描述现实世界；非现实语气，如虚拟语气，用于标记特定语言中非真实的语气，表达愿望、劝诫、信仰等。需要注意的是在语义学中，语气还可用于表示命令、疑问等，主要通过词序和语调实现。

言据性（evidentiality）用于说明说话人对信息源的态度。在一些语言中，言据性的实现可以通过特殊的助词或动词的语法标记来完成。

第六章　句义二：参与成分

本章中，作者继续从句义层面入手，研究用于描述参与句中实体的语义成分。

语义学把各实体在句中所扮演的具体角色统称为题元角色。题元角色包括有：(1)施事(agent)，句中行动的发出者；(2)受事(patient)，句中行为动作的承受者，通常会发生状态上的变化；(3)主体(theme)，动作移动的实体或被描述的位置；(4)经验体(experiencer)，感知谓语描述的动作或状态但不控制该动作或状态的实体；(5)受益体(beneficiary)，受益于谓语动作的实体；(6)工具(instrument)，动作或事件发生的方式、手段；(7)处所(location)，某物所处或某事发生的位置；(8)目标(goal)，动作移动朝向的实体；(9)来源(source)，动作移动离开的实体；(10)刺激(stimulus)，对经验体造成影响(通常是心理上)的实体。文中作者介绍了一些语言学家识别句中实体所扮演的题元角色的测试方法，他们发现有的句子存在一个实体扮演多个题元角色的可能，这极大地引发了学者们的研究兴趣。Chomsky的题元准则主张实体和题元必须是一一对应的关系，即一个名词短语只能分配一个题元角色。而Jackendoff则认为一个实体可以匹配一个或多个题元角色，并在此基础上提出了题元阶层理论。

题元角色的确认还可以结合句法结构和动词的选择。首先，参与成分和语法关系间的匹配关系可以确认题元角色，以英语为例，通常情况下，主语多扮演施事，直接宾语一般是受事或主体，工具往往是句中的介词短语。但若有题元角色被忽略或说话人通过更改动词语态的方式变动题元角色和语法关系间的匹配，我们便无法根据之前的一般情况识别题元角色。尽管如此，学者们仍发现在大部分语言中，题元角色和语法关系的匹配蕴含等级，比如Fillmore提出题元角色充当主语的优先级，即施事>受益体>主体/受事>工具>处所，从左至右，题元角色充当主语的可能性依次递减。其次，不同的动词对题元角色有特殊的要求，能够决定题元角色的选择。乔姆斯基的生成语法提出了题元栅，用于研究谓语动词和题元角色的关系。题元栅用于描述动词的语义特征，即动词对论元（argument）数量的要求和其论元应当扮演的题元角色。需要注意的是，不是所有的名词都能充当动词的论元，这通常由题元栅决定。作者提到了两种确认论元的方式：语法测试和区分参与成分的角色与非参与成分的角色。

题元角色的研究依然存在着各种争论：第一个问题是如何界定特殊的题元角色，区分过细会使这一概念失去实用性，也无法概述题元角色和语法关系间的联系，而区分过粗会难以细辨差异性；第二个问题是表征角色的语义基础是什么。针对这些问题，Dowty指出题元角色并不是语义原语而是谓语的蕴含成分，我们不应把其视作不相关的、有界的类别。题元角色是原型，蕴含不同程度贴近原型的成员。这一观点使得题元角色的定义更具灵活性。

语态为题元角色和语法关系的联系提供了新的视角。和主动语态相反，被动语态让说话人从受事者角度出发描述事件，在句中的具体表现是前景化（foregrounding）受事、后景化（backgrounding）施事，目的是为了在会话中突出受事或是表现说话人对受事的共情。不同语言的被动语态结构具有差异性：有的语言除主动、被动语态外，还有中动语态，用于强调动词描述的动作对动词主语的影响，即受动性。受动性亦可分为几种，作者以古希腊语和索马里语为媒介重点阐释了四类受动性：中性不及物类、身体活动与情感类、反身类和自益类。

此外，文章还单独研究了名词短语在句中表征的语义特点，这是由其所指代实体的内在特质赋予的。大多数语言都有显性的系统，用于标记名词短语指代的实体融入语义分类系统的方式，常见于名词分类词和名词类。名词分类词是对名词指称的实体进行编码的词素或单词，允许说话人根据语义/概念范畴对指称分类；名词类是基于语义分类的一致性系统，如印欧语系里，根据性别分类的阴性词、阳性词和中性词。

第七章　语境和推理

作者在本章将考察说话人和听话人如何借助语境构建和理解话语意义，把研究重心从语言本身的意义转向语言实际的使用。

日常对话中，指示语的理解往往受语境的约束。指示语要求说话人围绕自己搭建参照框架，即以说话人为中心划分周围空间，根据说话人的说话动作划分时间，说话人通过人称代词指称参与会话的参与者。常见的指示语有空间指示语（spatial deixis）、人称指示语（person deixis）和社会指示语（social deixis）。除指示语外，还有许多指称的理解依赖于语境和对话参与人的背景知识，如缩写、转喻和提喻。因此，为了让听话人理解信息，说话人在选择指称前需要预估：听话人已有的知识，即听话人根据物理环境计算出的知识，如指示词；听话人能从话语中获取的知识；听话人具备的背景知识或常识。

那么如何推测听话人已有的知识的呢？说话人会"包装"自己的话语，这种包装又被称作信息结构，即用语言标记新信息和旧信息。比如，英语使用定冠词the标注说话人预设听话人已知的信息；其次，语调也可用于突显话语中的新信息，突显的部分又被称作"焦点"。有的语言会使用特定的词汇，它们和英语语调的功能相同，可以标记"焦点"。此外，英语里的一些句法结构如分裂结构、伪分裂结构可用于标记句中的信息结构，信息结构还可用于标记主题，即对话双方讨论的主要内容属于旧信息，往往放在开头，用于限定句子的陈述范围。语言不同，标记主题的方式也可能不同。

话语的语义构建和理解是双向的，为了理解说话人传达的信息，听话人会用推测填补信息空白，如利用回指推导信息。另一种是搭桥推理，听话人根据背景知识，把未知信息和前文联系起来，创造连贯性，理解信息。正是基于对听话人推理行为的了解，说话人在对话时往往会留有余地，而不是全盘托出，语用学把这种现象称为会话含义。

Grice认为这类交流的成功在于合作原则，即说话人和听话人之间都达成了积极交流的默契。合作原则包含四类准则：真实准则（The Maxim of Quality）、关联准则（The Maxim of Relevance）、适量准则（The Maxim of Quantity）和方式准则（The Maxim of Manner）。听话人会依据这四类准则预设说话人行为，推测说话人的话语意义。由于这些准则仅仅是假设而不是规定，所以说话人可以违背它们。Grice把违背合作原则的行为分为两类：说话人秘密地违背，如谎言；为了某种语言效果，说话人公然地违背，如利用隐喻、夸张等修辞手法。

但对Grice提出的合作原则的一个批评是它只适用于明确的、信息丰富的话语，而实际上大部分话语类型是含糊的、意义不明的，如诗歌、谜语等。合作原则在随后的理论研究中也得到了极大的发展，作者主要讨论了其中的两个分派。为了将Grice提出的合作原则普遍化，Horn把其概括为Q原则和R原则；而Sperber和Wilson则把合作原则和交流原则统一为关联原则，强调了话语的不确定性及其对语境和推理的依赖。

最后，作者从词义层面探讨了语境和推理对词义的影响，常见的现象如词义扩大、词义缩小等。

第八章　语言的功能：作为行动的言语

本章中，作者继续关注语言的使用，探讨话语意义的社会功能。说话人用语言交流时不仅要习得发音和语法，还需要学会用语言完成提问、建议、感谢、打招呼等社交行为，诸如此类的语言功能被称作言语行为。言语行为具有两个特征：交互性（interactivity），即语言的交流是说话人与其他话语参与者协调配合的活动；语境依赖性（context dependence），即许多言语行为依赖社会习俗的支持，同时受具体情境的限制。因此，讨论言语行为实际上是考察语言和社会行为的结合。

传统观点认为句子的基本类型是陈述句，主要用途是描述事件的状态，逻辑真值可用于表示其话语的意义。但Austin并不认同，为此他提出了两个重要的观察：并非所有的句子都是陈述句，大部分对话都是由疑问句、感叹句、命令和希望组成的；即使句子的语法形式是陈述句，也未必表示陈述，且无法用逻辑真伪说明其意义，这类句子被称为施为句（performative utterance），其自身就是某种话语行为。施为句的有效性取决于适切条件（felicity conditions），有效的施为句往往是贴切的、符合社会习俗的。施为句可分为显性施为句和隐性施为句。显性施为句通常以一般现在时、第一人称开始，谓语动词用于描述言语活动，并且句中可以插入hereby，用来强调其话语行为；而隐性施为句由动词语气、情态动词、声调等语言手段标记。

Austin最早的观点是施为句和表述句（constatives）有着明显的区别，但随后他发现二者并无明显区别，陈述也属于一种言语行为，因此他总结为所有话语都能构成某种话语行为。这一结论认为意义是由命题和说话人有意的言语行为构成的。言语行为分为三类：言内行为，即遵循语音、语法规则，表达话语字面意义的行为；言外行为，用来表达说话者意图；言后行为，关注施事话语行为后的结果或影响。Searle在Austin研究的基础上，把话语行为分为五类：断言类（representatives）、指令类（directives）、承诺类（commissives）、表达类（expressives）和宣告类（declaratives），任何有效的话语行为都必须满足前提条件（preparation conditions）、命题条件（propositional conditions）、真诚条件（sincerity conditions）和基本条件（essential conditions）。话语行为在其他研究中还有不同的分类，但基本达成一个共识，即预设句子类型和言语行为相匹配。但由此产生两个问题：第一，句子类型和其本身的言外行为存在不一致的情况；

第二，如何识别句子的类型。

句子类型和其本身言外行为相符是直接言语行为，而当句子类型表达的言语行为和其本身匹配的言语行为不一致时，我们称之为间接言语行为。那么如何确认间接言语行为呢？Searle认为间接言语行为的意义需要根据非字面信息推断。对于听话人而言，非文字信息是主要内容，而字面意义是背景信息或次要的。间接言语行为有效与否取决于其是否满足和它们相关的直接言语行为的一个适切条件。如何理解间接言语行为呢？Searle的观点是理解间接言语行为需要结合三类知识进行推断，即直接言语行为的适切条件、话语的语境和交流合作原则。但这个观点有一个问题，即没有考虑间接言语行为的习惯用法。Searle由此给出的回应是除推断外，间接言语行为的理解需要考虑不同程度的习惯规约的影响。Gordon和Lakoff则认为听话人使用了会话假设，减少了理解间接言语行为所涉及的推理，从而反映了某些间接言语行为的常规化。但是人们为什么会使用间接言语行为呢？礼貌可能是最主要的动机，说话人也会为了削弱威胁“面子”的行为而使用间接言语行为。

一般而言，我们是通过虚拟语气和句子的语气来识别句子类型的。在有的语言里，句子的类型还可以通过分类词识别，其中有的词用于标记疑问句，有的词用于标记陈述句，零标记（zero marking）则用于标记祈使句。但问题是这些标记可用于区分各种语义，那如何判断它们仅仅只是用于区分句子类型呢？针对这一问题，Sadock和Zwicky提出了区分句子类型的三个原则：第一，句子类型要形成一个系统，这样每个类型都应该有一个对应版本；第二，句子类型应该是互斥的，即在同一个句子中不应该有两个句子类型标记的组合；第三，句子类型和言语行为有约定俗成的联系。

第九章　意义成分

意义成分分析法（Componential Analysis或CA）是语义学中比较常用的研究方法。书中用成分分析法探讨了woman，bachelor，spinster和wife等名词。具体而言，使用[FEMALE]、[ADULT]、[HUMAN]和[MARRIED]来界定上面这些名词的意义，例如woman可以界定为[FEMALE] [ADULT] [HUMAN]。方括号中的成分如[FEMALE]称为语义成分（semantic components）或语义基元（semantic primitives）。采用语义成分分析法有三点原因：一是可以经济地描写词汇关系；二是识别这些语义成分可以使我们准确地描写一系列的句法和形态过程；三是语义成分成为我们心理架构的一部分，为我们提供概念结构的独特观点。

成分分析法经常使用二元特征（binary features）和冗余规则（redundancy rules）。二元特征是一个特征要么有，要么没有，例如在解释bachelor时，其成分是[-FEMALE] [+ADULT] [+HUMAN] [-MARRIED]，其中[FEMALE]和[MARRIED]这两个特征是负的，说明bachelor这个词不具备这两个特征。而wife的成分是[+FEMALE] [+ADULT] [+HUMAN] [+MARRIED]，对比bachelor的成分，只有[FEMALE]和[MARRIED]不同，这两个成分在wife中是正的，说明这个词的语义具备这两个特征。冗余规则指的是，在解释词义关系时，我们会遇到成分重叠和包含的现象，例如[ANIMATE]包含了[HUMAN]，也包含了[ADULT]，我们要避免使用重复的语义成分，这样可以使语义分析更加简洁和经济。例如当我们分析 wife的词义时，我们只使用[+FEMALE] [+ADULT] [+MARRIED]就可以了，删掉多余的语义成分如[+HUMAN]、[+ANIMATE]和[+CONCRETE]。

目前语义学存在四种语义成分分析法：Katz的语义理论、Talmy的关于运动事件的研究、Jackendoff的概念语义学（conceptual semantics）和Pustejovsky的生成词库（generative lexicon）。他们都进一步发展了语义成分分析法，不仅用来解释词义问题，更重要的是还可以解释许多语法和形态的问题。

Katz的语义学理论是生成语言学中最早对语义学进行研究的理论，其理论有两个主要观点：(1)语义规则应该是递归的，与句法规则是一样的；(2)句子与其语义之间的关系不是任意的和单一的，句法结构与词义相互作用，"John killed Fred." 和 "Fred killed John." 虽然包含同样的词汇，意义都大不相同，而 "The snake frightened Mary." 和 "The movie delighted Horace." 虽然具有同样的句法结构，但其意义由于词义不同而有所差别。

与句法结构平行的语义成分也有以下三个目的：(1)给出词项意义的具体描写；(2)给出词项意义组合成词组以及词组组合成句子的规则；(3)以一种普遍可应用的元语言做以上两种描写和给出规则。前两个目的通过两个成分实现：一是把词项与语义表征匹配在一起的词典；二是一组投射规则(projection rules)，它可以表明句子的意义是如何从词项意义中建构出来的。第三个目的通过语义成分的使用得到部分实现。

Katz的词典主要包括两个方面的信息：一是语法信息，用{i}表示；二是语言信息，包括两种语义成分类型，一个是语义标记语，表示把词汇捆绑在一起以及词汇之间的关系，用(i)表示，另一个是区别标记语，表示词项的特异性语义信息，用[i]表示。

投射规则研究句子的组合规则，利用树形图从下至上的方式建构词义，组合成词组义，进而词组义组合成句子义。这种组合过程的主要制约是选择性限制(selectional restrictions)，反映了语境对词义的影响，限制了词与词之间的共现和搭配，也制约着最后搭配的结果。从Katz对语义的探讨中，我们可以看到这一理论最基本的部分是试图通过语义成分的识别建立语义元语言，即这一理论是分解性的(decompositional)。Katz使用这些语义成分试图解释上下位、反义、同义和蕴含等。除了使用语义成分解释词义，语义成分也是正确解释句法过程所必需的，所以在本章中作者介绍了语法规则和语义成分之间的关系。

有些语言学家宣称，我们需要语义成分正确地描写语法过程。这要做到两点：一是建立动词类别（verb classes），如移动动词或致使动词（causative verb）等；二是抽取意义的共享成分，把它看作语义成分。Beth Levin的做法是通过考察四类动词的语法行为探讨其语义特征。她发现cut，break，touch和hit这四个动词的语法行为不同，例如cut和break可以用在中动构式（middle construction）中，如The bread cuts easily.和Crystal vases break easily.而touch和hit却不可以，如 * Cats touch easily. * Door frames hit easily. 另外cut和hit可以用在意欲构式（conative constructions）中，如Margaret cut at the bread. Carla hit at the door. 而break和touch却不可以，如 * Janet broke at the vase. * Terry touched at the cat. 另外cut，touch和hit可以用在身体部位上升（body part ascension）构式中，例如我们可以说Margaret cut Bill's arm.也可以说Margaret cut Bill on the arm. 后一句是身体部位上升构式，而break却不能用在这个构式中，例如我们可以说Janet broke Bill's finger.但不可以说 * Janet broke Bill on the finger. 因此依据这些动词的不同语法行为，语义学家假设这些动词属于不同类型的动词，进一步的分析发现CHANGE，MOTION，CONTACT和CAUSE这些语义成分导致这些动词产生不同的语法行为。换句话说，正确识别动词的语义成分可以帮助我们预测动词的语法行为，例如动词cut的语义成分包括CAUSE，CHANGE，CONTACT和MOTION，所以其语言行为比较灵活，可以用在中动构式、意欲构式和身体部位上升构式之中。而break的语义成分只包括CAUSE 和CHANGE，所以它只能用在中动构式之中，其语法行为受到较大的限制，其他两个动词touch和hit也是一样，受到语义成分的制约。

Leonard Talmy使用语义成分探讨移动事件（motion events）的跨语言类型学研究。他识别出四个与移动动词相关的语义成分，包括图形（figure）、移动（motion）、路径（path）和方式（manner）。图形是相对于另一物体（背景，ground）移动或所处的物体；移动指的是事件中位置或移动本身的存在；路径指的是相对于背景物体而言，图形物件所占据的方位或移动的路线；方式是指移动的类型。例如在Charlotte swam away from the crocodile.中，背景是the crododile，路径是away from，动词swam编码了移动本身和移动的方式。

Talmy（2000）指出语言之间的差异在于这些语义成分如何在动词和动词词组中被典型地组合或合并在一起。请看下面的例句：

1. He ran out of the house.
2. Salió de la casa corriendo.
（英语直译Lift from the house running.）

在英语句子中，移动的方式被合并在动词中，而移动的路径在外在的介词短语中被编码。但在西班牙的句子中，这些语义成分以不同的方式合并在一起，路径被合并在动词中，方式却在外在词组中被编码。

生活在美国加利福尼亚东北部部落里的人所说的Atsugewi的语言法则更加奇特，图形则与移动或移动动词合并在一起，图形的语义特征被编码在移动的动词之中，例如球形的图形和小而偏的图形与不同的动词搭配，也就是说，动词里编码了图形的语义特征。

根据以上的分析，世界上的语言大概可以分为三类：一类是像英语一样，动词合并模式是“移动+路径”，其被称为卫星框架语言（satellite-frame language），因为路径是由卫星或外在介词短语单独表达的;另一类，如西班牙语，动词合并模式是“移动+方式/原因”，它被称为动词框架语言（verb-framed language），因为路径被编码在动词中，方式反而用外在的表达来表示;还有一类像Atsugewi那样，动词合并模式是“移动+图形”，图形的语义特征被编码在动词之中。

Jackendoff在一系列的著作中发展了概念语义学。概念语义学的根本原则是，描写意义应包含描写心理表征，这被称为心理假定（Mentalist Postulate），即自然语言中的意义是心理上被人所编码的信息结构。因此句子的意义就是概念结构。

概念语义学的主要假设是，意义必须作为推理的基础。识别语义成分如CAUSE的主要目的是经济性，可以解释句子之间的关系。例如George killed the dragon.和dragon died之间是蕴含关系（entailment），因为如果第一句是真实的，第二句也是真实的。

Jackendoff的主要研究任务之一就是识别出一套普遍的语义范畴或概念，包括事件（Event）、事情或物体（Material Thing or Object）、路径（Path）、地点（Place）和特征（Property）。在概念结构层次上，句子由这些语义范畴构建而成。两个最基本的概念情景是事件和状态（State）。例如：

3. Bill went into the house.

4. The car is in the garage.

3a. $[_{s}\ [_{NP}$ Bill] $[_{VP}$ Went $[_{pp}[_{p}$ into$[_{NP}$ the house]]]]

3b. $[_{Event}$ Go $([_{Thing}$ Bill, $[_{Path}$ To $([_{Place}$ IN $([_{Thing}$ HOUSE])])]

4a. $[_{s}\ [_{NP}$ The car] $[_{VP}$ [V is] $[_{PP}[_{P}$ in] $[_{NP}$ the garage]]]]

4b. $[_{state}$ BE $([_{Thing}$ CAR], $[_{Place}$ IN$([_{Thing}$ GARAGE])])]

对于例3和例4来说，3a和4a是句法结构，而3b和4b是概念结构或语义结构.3b是移动的语义，这一移动事件包含了三个主要的语义范畴或语义成分:(1)移动本身,Go;(2)移动又包含了其他的语义成分，实体Thing与轨迹Path以及后面紧跟着另一个实体(HOUSE),Path可能有一个目的地Place。Jackendoff的概念结构有其自己的“句法”:语义范畴或语义成分通过组合规则由更简单成分建立起来,3b是由这样的组合规则建立起来的,GO、TO和IN这些成分描写移动、方向和方位，在语义“几何”中就像是函数一样，把这些成分组合起来，形成主要的语义范畴或语义成分，例如在3b中，整体的Event(事件)是由GO组合Thing(事物)和Path(路径)，从而形成某一具体类型的事件:某一物体向一个方向移动，其中语义范畴Path(路径)是由成分GO结合Place而形成的，用于描写物体移动的方向。Place(地点)由称为地点函数(Place-function)的IN结合实体(Thing)描写作为移动目的地之内的一个区域。

关于方位语义域,Jackendoff(1990)使用成分BE的下标，如BELoc表示方位BE(locational BE)，见例4和4b。同时他认为，语义成分BE可以用来表征状态的四个次范畴，这四个次范畴共同构成了一个语义域(semantic fields)，这样就可以把空间概念化(spatial conceptualization)拓展到非空间的域。除了表示空间关系外，还可以表示时间(BE temp)、表示特征(BE ident)以及占有关系(BE poss)。因此空间方位、时间方位、特征归属(property ascription)和所占有的关系(possession)对基本的本体范畴状态(STATE)和事件(EVENT)进行了交互分类。

通过对名词词组(nominals)的语义分类，我们可以看到语义成员(Thing)可被分解为更小和更简单的语义成分。Jackendoff使用语义特征“有界与无界”([±BOUNDED])来区分可数名词(count nouns)和不可数名词(mass nouns)，可数名词是[+BOUNDED]，不可数名词是[-BOUNDED]。Jackendoff又提出用语义特征内在结构[±INTERNAL STRUCTURE]来区分复数可数名词（[+INTERNAL STRUCTURE]）和不可数名词（[-INTERNAL STRUCTURE]）。

他进一步指出，语义特征[± BOUNDED]和[± INTERNAL STRUCTURE]可以对名词进行交互分类（cross-classify），例如集合名词government包含个体单位（其成员），是复数名词，因此语义特征是[+INTERNAL STRUCTURE]，但同时又有[+BOUNDED]的语义特征。另外语义特征[± BOUNDED]不仅交互分类名词，还可以用来描写情景。被描写为正进行的、时间无明确限制的情景是非完成的（atelic），因此语义特征是[-BOUNDED]，例如John is sleeping. 而有明确界定的开始和结束的情景是[+BOUNDED]。Jackendoff称之为情景类型（situation types）。

Pustejovsky提出了词汇语义学的组构性解释：生成词库。这一理论不仅拓展了某些领域的组构性表征，而且在解释中还并入了百科知识。这一理论的重点是计算，并指出词义最好由包括组合规则和推理的动态视角进行解释。Pustejovsky（1995）提出了词项语义表征的四个层次：（1）论元结构（argument structure），即词项的语义论元与句法的连接规则；（2）事件结构（event structure），即词项的情景类型；（3）物性结构（qualia structure），即对词项特征的分类；（4）词汇继承结构（lexical inheritance structure），即词汇如何与词库网络融为一体。在本书中，作者只集中讨论事件结构与动词、物性结构与名词。

Pustejovsky认为，事件结构可以用来表示情景类型，也就是说，用来表示动词中词汇上所编码的体区分（aspectual distinctions），这里事件包括状态，相当于Bach（1986）所说的术语事件类型（eventualities）。Pustejovsky提出的生成词库的主要特点是，事件是由更小的事件（次事件sub-event）组成的，这一事件/次事件的关系需要以清晰明了的方式，由句法的形式表征出来。他提出了三种事件类型:(1)状态(State或S)是单一的事件,不需要相对于其他事件来评估,例如静态动词如understand,love和betall。(2)过程(Processes或P)是识别同一语义表达的事件的序列,例如动词sing,walk和swim。(3)转变(Transitions或T)是识别语义表达的事件,是相对于其对立面来评估的,例如动词open,close和build。这些表征仅仅提供了事件结构的信息。这一事件的结构信息与其他两个层次上的语义信息联合起来,一个层次是逻辑谓词分解的层次,称为词汇概念结构(lexical conceptual structure或LCS),另一个层次是界面层次(interface level),包括词汇语义成分,但保留了事件结构。例如"The door closed."是转变事件类型(event type of transition),表征从没有关门到已经关门的转变。

物性结构是Pustejovsky处理名词多义特征的理论。Pustejovsky认为,名词存在多义变异,任何推理必须依靠与名词相伴的语言信息,另外词义的变异是系统的。词义变异是具体语义组合规则的产物,并与词项的系统特征相联系,这些系统特征称为物性结构。物性结构具有四个层面:(1)构成性(CONSTITUTIVE),物体与其构成成分之间的关系,如物质、重量、部分与组成成分;(2)形式(FORMAL),在更大的认知域内区别物体的特征,如方向、形状、颜色、位置和层级性;(3)表目的性(TELIC),物体的目的和功能,如施事实施一个行为的目的、内在的功能或目标;(4)施事性(AGENTIVE),物体来源和产生中所涉及的因素,如创造者、人工制品和因果链等。

举个例子说明一下,名词novel的物性结构包括:(1)构成性=叙事(narrative);(2)形式=书(book);(3)表目的性=阅读(read);(4)施事=写作(write)。

名词的物性结构可以用来解释一词多义现象,例如:

5. Joan baked the potato.

6. Joan baked the cake.

如何说明上面两句中对“bake”的不同解释呢？例5中的动词是改变状态的解释（change-of-state interpretation），而例6中的动词则是额外创造的意义，即创造一个原是不存在的物体。对于Pustejovsky来说，这种一词多义现象可由动词与名词之间的组合得到解释。例5和6的差异来自名词的物性结构，名词“cake”的施事角色是施事通过烘焙的行为产生了蛋糕，是一个人工制品，动词“bake”也具有这一施事角色，描写施事烘焙的行为。当动词与名词组合成动词短语时，名词的物性结构合并和联合了烘焙事件的两个表征，形成创造性的解释，这一拓展是由组合创造出来的，这就是生成词库对一词多义的动态解释观。

第十章　形式语义学

形式语义学是指称进路的语义理论，其在语义分析中使用逻辑学的相关知识，包括真值条件语义学（truth conditional semantics）、模型论语义学（model-theoretic semantics）和蒙塔古语法（Montague Grammar）。在本章中，作者介绍了从逻辑学中借用的真值概念以及命题逻辑的形式化，用来描写语义关系和句子语义。

形式语义学认为，语言的基本功能是可以让我们谈论我们周围的世界，寻求意义就是寻求语言符号如何与现实或客观世界相互关联。形式语义学使用真值符合论（correspondence theory of truth），认为说话人知道言语描写的是什么情景，能够说出的意义包含了理解这句话所匹配的世界情景。成功匹配就是真的；不成功匹配就是假的，换句话说，描写句子的另一方式就是理解这句话的听话人能够决定所说句子的真值条件（truth conditions）。

形式语义学是目前语义学中最重要的也是最灵活的研究进路之一，因为这一研究具有三个优势。最大的优势是用逻辑表达作为语义元语言，对语义的描写比较精确。另一个优势是避免循环论证的问题。形式语义学把自然语言翻译成逻辑语言，将逻辑语言与真实世界情景捆绑在一起，从而把语言与世界连接起来。第三个优势是形式语义学的研究让我们可以更清楚地看到人类语言与其他灵长类动物语言之间的联系。灵长类动物语言系统都是指称性的:灵长类动物都有不同的常规符号指称不同类型的猎食者，如老鹰、蛇或狮子等。符号与环境中的实体之间的基本匹配关系有可能是人类语言的起始点。

形式语义学分析的第一阶段是翻译，即把自然语言中的句子翻译成基于逻辑的普遍元语言表达式。这种元语言就是谓词逻辑（predicate logic）。谓词逻辑建立在对命题逻辑中的句子连词（sentence connectives）的研究之上，继而研究句子的内在结构。

命题逻辑中的连接词

连接词	句法	英语
$\neg$	$\neg p$	it is not the case that p（否定p）
$\wedge$	$p \wedge q$	p and q（p和q）
$\vee$	$p \vee q$	p and/or q（p和/或者q）
V_e	$p\ V_e\ q$	p or q but not both（p或者q，但不是两者）
$\rightarrow$	$p \rightarrow q$	if p, then q（如果p，然后q）
$\equiv$	$p \equiv q$	p if and only if q（当且仅当q，然后p）

依据真值符合理论，句子的指称是其与所描写情景是否匹配，匹配就是真实的（true或T），用数字1表示；不匹配就是不真实（false或T），用数字0表示。因此使用变量v表示情景，我们可以说，在情景v中一个句子p是真实的，用谓词表达式表示为$[p]^v=1$。

这里我们使用方括号表示表达的指称，所以$[x]^v$ 意思是在情景v中x的指称。与之形成对照的是$[p]^v=0$意思是在情景v中p的指称是不真实的。

个体常项是指某一情景中的个体和几组个体，通常用小写字母表示一个情景中的论元。谓词常项识别谓语所适用的一组或几组个体。一元谓语（one-place predicate），如be standing在某一情景中选择了站立的一组个体或一个个体；二元谓词（two-place predicate）可以选择一组有序的对子，即在既定顺序中有两个个体，如punch用集合理论可以表示为{ <x,y>: x punches y in v}。三元谓词也可以用同样的方式表示。

域是情景v中个体和关系的表征。指称的分配功能把逻辑表征的符号与域中的成分匹配起来，一是个体常项与情景v中的个体匹配；二是谓词常项与情景v中的一组或几组个体匹配。前者用F(x)表示，x在这里是论元，例如F(j)=John或F(p)=Paul，j和p分别表示不同的论文。后者也可用F(x)表示，但x在这里是谓词，例如F(B)=was a Beatle，B表示谓词was a Beatle。谓词逻辑的符号可以让我们建立一个模式，把域和指称的分配功能结合在一起。

我们可以使用上面讨论的谓词逻辑表达式检验句子的真值（truth-value）。检验句子真值的程序必须反映意义的组构性，也就是说，句子的组成成分对整个句子的真值是有所贡献的。我们以一个简单句“John sang.”为例来说明，这句话可以用$[S(j)]^{M1}=1$ iff $[j]^{M1}\in[S]^{M1}$表示，这个谓词逻辑表达式的意义是，“John sang.”这句话的意义是真的，当且仅当John的拓展是模式M1中的sang所界定的集合的一部分。在这个表达式中，S(j)表示John sang，$[\ ]^{M1}$表示某一事件发生在一个模式之中，而$[j]^{M1}$表示模式M_1中有一个John，$[S]^{M1}$表示在模式M1中存在sang（唱歌）这件事，而$\in$表示属于。

形式语义学还可以用来界定词汇关系，在第九章中作者介绍了词汇关系可以使用成分分析法来描写，在形式语义学中，我们使用逻辑表达式解释词汇关系，Carnap，Fodor和Kintsch等人提出使用来自逻辑学的意义公设（meaning postulates）来描写词汇关系。意义公设把词汇关系看作知识的一种形式，使用来自命题逻辑的连接词。例如dog和animal之间的关系，我们可以用下面的逻辑表达式表示：$\forall x(DOG(x) \rightarrow ANIMAL(x))$。这个表达式的意思是：对于所有的x来说，如果x是一条狗，那么x是一个动物。我们可以使用形式语义学解释同义和反词等词汇关系，也可以使用更高级的逻辑探讨自然语言的量词问题。

本章讨论的最后两个问题是内涵性（intensionality）和话语表征理论（Discourse Representation Theory或DRT）。指称进路的简单版本有一个劣势，它轻视了说话人–听话人的主观性（subjectivity），然而在自然语言中人们的交际大多涉及说话人和听话人之间的解释。例如句子Frank knows that S.中，Frank knows传递了说话人对S所表达的命题的态度，即命题态度（propostitional attitudes）。在下面的例句中也表现出同样的命题态度，例如Phil <u>probably</u> misrepresented his income. Phil <u>may have</u> misrepresented his income.在这两句中，probably和may have也表达了说话人的命题态度。这种揭示解释性或认知行为的句子是内涵性的，其特征称为内涵性。

在上面的例句中，我们需要通达说话人的信息内容或内涵。形式语言学试图丰富某些语言现象中体现内涵性的形式符号，这些语言现象包括情态（modality）、时体和命题态度等。情态涉及两个方面——认识情态（epistemic modality）和义务情态（deontic modality），前者关注的是说话人可以使用的表达事实判断和可能性的资源，就道德和法律而言，后者表达的是职责、义务和允许。所有的语言在认识情态和义务情态方面都有一系列不同的表达方式。例如在英语中，有以下例句I know that p. I am absolutely certain that p.以及I believe that p is probable.等。为了表达情态，形式语义学发展了情态逻辑（modality logic）。把认识情态分为事实和可能性或实际情景和可能情景。如何区分实际与非实际要用到Leibniz和Kripke提出的可能世界（possible worlds）。说话人在不确定的情况下可以设想两个或更多的可能场景，把真值看作是相对于可能情景或可能世界的。逻辑学家使用◇表示P可能发生（It is possible that P），□表示P必须发生（It is necessary that p），因此◇Φ=It is possible that Φ（Φ必须发生），□Φ=It is necessary that Φ（Φ必须发生）。这些逻辑符号表达式的语义定义都依靠可能世界的新的本体：□的意思是“在所有可能世界里是真实的”，◇的意思是“在一些可能世界里是真实的”。这就意味着我们的模式必须拓展，包括多种情景，即M={W,U,F}，在这个表达式中，U等于情景中个体的域，F是指称分配功能，而W是一组可能世界。

形式语义学研究的话语理论不少，其中最有名的是本书集中讨论话语表征理论时所涉及的三个语言现象——包括句内和跨句的回指、驴子句（donkey sentence）和话语回指。例如：

7. Joan bought a car and it doesn't start.
8. If a Teenager owns a Ferrari he races it.

在例7中，代词it回指名词a car，可以用下面的谓词逻辑表达式表示：$(\exists x{:}C(x))\ B(j,x) \wedge \neg S(x)$，其意思是，有一辆轿车，以致于Joan买了它，它不能发动。例8是一个驴子句，代词he的问题是，它不能是一个指称表达，因为没有它可指称的具体青少年。之所以叫做驴子句，是因为Geach曾讨论过下面的句子If a farmer owns a donkey, he beats it. 句中的it无法指称一个具体的驴子，具有这个指称问题的句子称为驴子句。我们可以用下面的谓词逻辑式表达:$\forall_x\forall_y((T(x)\wedge F(y)\wedge O(x,y)))\rightarrow R(x,y)$，这个表达式的意思是:对于所有的x和所有的y来说，如果x是一个青少年,y是法拉利，并且x拥有y，那么x会全速使y行进。

第十一章　认知语义学

认知语言学大概可以分为两大部分:认知语义学和语法的认知研究。前者是通过研究和分析语言从而发现人的概念结构，后者则利用学者们发现的概念结构探讨语法问题。这两者是相辅相成的，并非截然分离。在本章作者并没有做严格的区分。

认知语义学持有关于语言知识的独特观点，认为语言知识和一般思维与认知不是分离的，语言知识是认知的一部分。与Fodor和Chomsky具有广泛影响的观点相反的是，认知语义学家把语言行为看作一般认知能力的一部分。

认知语言学特别强调语言的形式学派和功能学派的区分。形式学派如生成语法常与语言和认知的某一观点相关联，即语言结构和规则的知识形成了自主的模块（或能力），独立于注意力、记忆和思维等其他心理过程。语言分析的不同层次如音位学、句法学和语义学等形成独立的模块。认知语言学属于功能主义，功能主义持有不同的语言观，语言使用原则体现一般的认知原则，对语言的解释必须横跨不同的分析层次。语言与其他的心理过程之间的差异只是一个程度，并没有本质的差异，对语法规则适当的解释必须参照语义才能进行。认知语义学的研究模糊了语言知识与百科知识之间的界限，认为区分不同的分析层次对语言学是有害的。

传统的语言学理论认可历时语言学和共时语言学这一区分，但认知语言学质疑这一区分，认为从功能的视角讲，语言结构经过长时间的使用深化而来，变化的过程是明显的，并与语言当前使用的理解相关联，例如语法化过程（processes of grammaticalization），语法化过程包含了词汇范畴，随着时间的推移逐渐发展成为功能范畴，因此独立的词变成了屈折变化。

就语义而言，认知语言学的特征是摒弃Lakoff提出的客观主义语义学（objectivist semantics）。客观主义语义学就是前面提到的指称进路，Lakoff在三个信条下对其进行了表征：（1）真值－条件意义的信条，即意义是基于指称和真值；（2）真值符合理论，即真值包括符号与世界上的事态（states of affairs）之间的对应关系；（3）客观指称的信条，即存在着把符号与世界上的事物关联起来的"客观的正确"方式。在拒绝客观主义语义学的基础上，认知语义学认为，我们无法通达独立于人类范畴化的现实，语言中反映的现实结构是人类心智的产物。因此认知语义学研究的焦点是概念框架以及语言如何反映这些概念框架。就语义本身而言，语义基于常规化的概念结构。基于这些认识，本书讨论了范畴化、一词多义、隐喻、转喻、意象图式、认知语法和构式语法等理论和概念。

在论述范畴化时，作者首先介绍了"经典"理论对范畴现象的传统认识，其中涉及范畴是否具有鲜明的结构及判定范畴成员时是否存在充分必要条件等问题。其次，综合论述"经典"范畴理论在定义（可定义性）、概念模糊性（范畴边界是否清晰）、典型性（范畴中心成员是否具有典型效应）、心理现实性（明确的范畴结构是否具有心理现实性）、无知和偏误（对概念的理解是否必须建立在对其特征和定义理解的基础之上）等方面存在的问题。

原型理论认为概念化过程应遵循以下两个基本原则：（1）认知经济性原则：和人类一样，任何生物都试图以最小认知努力或最少认知资源获得尽可能多的环境信息。（2）感知世界结构原则：世界上的任何事物都具有相互关联的结构。

理想认知模型理论之所以称之为"理想"，原因在于该理论提出的认知模型并不是特定的经验实例，而是对一系列经验实例抽象的结果。作者分别以最简类型、集群模型（如母亲）和转喻（如社会常规模式、典型事例、理想模型、模范、生成元、和凸显性事例等）等为例说明了典型效应的来源；其次，从中心实例（central case）和文化经验等方面论述了典型效应的另一来源——辐射范畴。

意象图式产生于人类与外部世界的互动体验过程之中，源于人类的运动和感知经验。意象图式具有涌现性特征。除此之外，意象图式还有以下特征：（1）意向图式在产生顺序上先于概念。因其来源于感知经验，所以在产生顺序上，意象图式先于概念生成，这决定了它在人类认知思维过程中的基础性地位。（2）意向图式为具体概念的产生提供了基础。（3）意象图式源自人类与外部世界的互动体验及其对世界的观察。（4）意象图式是有意义的。（5）意象图式是一种类比象征。此处的类比指的是意象图式与大脑中表征感知经验的概念系统之间存在类比关系。（6）意象图式具有复杂的内部结构。（7）意象图式和心智意象是两码事。（8）意象图式是多模态的。（9）意象图式具有可转换性。（10）意象图式的发生具有集群效应。

作者以"力"的图式为例，向读者证明了意象图式是如何为词项提供概念表征基础的。接着，作者列举了一些已有的意象图式，并对其进行了分类。另外，除为词项提供概念表征基础外，意象图式为抽象概念提供了认知基础，如它为隐喻映射提供具体的现实认知基础。作者认为语义结构（与语言单位相连的意义）能够通达大量详细的结构化知识（即概念系统），对词义甚至是任何语言单位意义的理解都离不开与其密切相关的百科知识，百科知识来源于人与人之间（社会体验）和人与世界之间（物质体验）的互动体验。

作者强调两个事实：一是一词多义指的是一个词汇形式对应两个及以上语义不同但相关的义项的现象；二是一词多义的概念性特征——一词多义是一种概念现象，为词义理论提供了概念基础。

作者以介词over为例详细介绍了全面详述方法的发展过程和操作方法，并强调意象图式转变和隐喻性引申在词义义项发展中所起的重要作用。

认知语言学认为，人类在理解隐喻和转喻性语言表达时与理解字面性语言所涉及的认知机制并无二致。关于隐喻的本质，认知语言学认为隐喻不仅仅是一种语言现象，更是一种思维方式。隐喻性语言表达了背后更为基础的概念层面的隐喻性思维系统，即概念隐喻。概念隐喻形成的基础在于两个概念域之间存在的规约性联系，之所以称之为概念是因为隐喻形成的动因存在于概念域层面。隐喻的经验基础是指概念隐喻植根于我们与外部世界的互动体验中。

作者首先从转喻的本质和动因等方面谈起，论述了其定义及主要种类并肯定了转喻的概念本质。随后探讨了意义建构和心理空间之间的关系，认为词语本身或脱离语境的词语并无意义可言。也就是说，词语并不是承载意义的容器，而是在心智通达大量百科知识的释义过程中发挥认知参照点或提示符作用。基于意义建构过程，语言为复杂程度不同的认知表征提供认知参照。认知语义学认为意义建构在本质上是一种概念现象，动态的意义建构过程即概念化过程。意义建构过程的基本单位是心理空间，它们之间彼此相连，为概念化提供概念基础。

作者介绍了心智空间的组成、结构及其在意义建构过程中发挥的基础作用，最后通过语言实例展示其解释力。认知语言学认为意义建构可分为两个部分：一是构建心理空间；二是建立起心理空间之间的映射关系。作者从空间构建器、构成元素、元素特征和元素间关系、心理空间网格、对应元素和连接器、通达原则以及角色和值等方面对心理空间的构架结构进行了详细介绍。以实际文本为例向读者演绎了心智空间建构的具体操作过程及其可行性和解释力。

概念整合理论由Gilles Fauconnier和Mark Turner等人提出。该理论的发展基于认知语义学的两大研究传统——概念隐喻理论和心理空间理论。概念整合理论的兴起源于对概念隐喻理论解释力的不满。比如对例9这句话，仅依靠概念隐喻理论所说的从源域到靶域的概念映射并不能得知对外科医生不称职的贬义评价来源何处。因此，概念整合理论提出的意义建构过程还包括了新创结构——意义大于其构成成分之和。

9. That surgeon is a butcher.

概念整合理论基于对应关系（时间、空间、表征、改变、角色–值关系、类比关系、部分–整体和因果关系等），将复杂、抽象的概念“降解”为人类可体验的尺度。概念整合过程并非局限于两个不同概念域之间的映射，而是基于整合网络，包括单一网络、镜像网络、单一输入域网络和双输入域网络等类型。概念整合中的不同映射过程存在层级性，即整合结果可以作为新的概念输入，进而引发新的整合或再整合过程。

Langacker提出的认知语法对认知语言学的发展起到非常重要的作用。他把词汇、形态和句法看作符号系统。在认知语法中，一个语言符号是语义结构和音位结构之间的映现和对应，Langacker不仅把词项看作符号，更重要的是，他还把语法看作符号，语法范畴和构式也都是符号。

Langacker认为语言范畴反映概念结构，提出典型的及物构式是桌球模式（billiard-ball model），其中包括空间、时间、能量和物质的概念。就名词而言，物理物体是典型的名词，其中关键的认知过程是从我们的经验中切分出一个有界部分，创建出一个与周围环境不同的事物，名词描写的是时间上稳定的状态，也可以描写动词所识别的过程。例如“his arrival among us”就是描写一个过程，这取决于我们对环境或经验的认知识解（construal）。对名词特征的描述让我们可以看到，名词不是客观存在的，而是认知和交际目的的产物。

Langacker从说话人或观察者的视角描写典型的及物构式。说话人或观察者的任务包括区分发生和背景，建立视角，决定什么类型的实体被解释为参与者，识别其相互作用的形式。

Goldberg的构式语法旨在将研究对象从不规则的习语性构式延伸到规则性构式研究中。为实现这一目标，Goldberg主要关注了动词－论元构式，也就是说，Goldberg的构式语法的研究对象是普通句子（如及物和不及物构式）。作者介绍了Goldberg提出的构式语法所坚持的重要假设，如词汇－语法连续统假设和基于使用的假设等，并着重介绍了Goldberg对构式的定义。Goldberg判断某一语言表达是否成为构式的关键在于该表达式是否具有可预测性。无论语言单位的层级如何，只要在其语音层或语义层的任意一层上，其构式内容就无法预测，该表达式便是构式。运用构式方法研究动词–论元结构的好处在于避免不合理的动词意义、循环释义等。在动词意义的本质认识上，Goldberg坚持框架观点；Goldberg认为构式之间存在相互关联且重合的意义，也就是说，构式没有特殊固定的意义，其表征方式并不是孤立的，而是与其他构式一起形成构式网络，且构式具有多义性。

本书在每一章后面都列出了参考文献，推荐了延伸阅读的书籍与论文。此外，作者不仅在每章后提供了供读者思考的练习题，还为练习题提供了参考答案，方便读者自学。

Contents

Figures and Tables

Figures

Table

Preface

This is an introduction to semantics for readers new to the subject. The aim of the book is not to propose a new theory of semantics, nor to promote any single current approach, but to give the reader access to some of the central ideas in the field and an introduction to some of its most important writers. Semantics, however, is a very broad and diverse field and keeping the book to a manageable size has involved a fairly firm selection of topics. Inevitably this selection will not please everyone but I hope readers will be able to gain a feel for what doing semantics is like, and gain the background to proceed to more advanced and specialized material in the primary literature.

The book assumes no knowledge of semantics but does assume a general idea of what linguistics is, and some familiarity with its traditional division into fields like phonetics, phonology, morphology, syntax, and so on. Thus it would be useful if the reader had already looked at a general introduction to linguistics.

The book is organized into eleven chapters, which are grouped into three main sections. Part I, **Preliminaries**, consists of the first two chapters and is concerned with the place of semantics within linguistics and its relations with the disciplines of philosophy and psychology, which share some of the same interests. Part II, **Semantic Description**, is the main part of the book and introduces central topics in the analysis of word and sentence meaning. Part III, **Theoretical Approaches**, reviews three important semantic theories: componential theory, formal semantics and cognitive semantics.

Each chapter includes a set of exercises to allow the reader to explore the issues raised, and suggestions for further reading. These will be a small selection of works which provide accessible investigations of the chapter's topics. In the text there are a large number of references to the semantics literature. These will frequently be works which are too specialized to attempt before the reader completes this book, but are given so that any particular interests may be followed up.

Examples from different languages are given in the transcription of the original source, and are commented on only when it is germane to the discussion. A list of symbols and abbreviations used in this text is given in the Abbreviations and Symbols list on pp. xix–xx.

I have used this book as a text in my courses in the Centre for Language and Communication Studies, Trinity College Dublin. I would like to thank my students for their responses and comments, which have been invaluable in getting the text into its present form. I am indebted to Philip Jaggar, Mark Keane, James Levine, and Feargal Murphy, who read the entire manuscript and made many suggestions, which improved the book and saved me from my worst mistakes. I am also grateful to those who have commented on particular sections, discussed specific language data, and provided me with source materials, in particular Abdullahi Dirir Hersi, Barbara Abbott, Martin Emms, Tim Fernando, Jim Jackson, Jeffrey Kallen, Ruth Kempson, Patricia Maguire, Cathal O Háinle, Sarah Smyth, Tadaharu Tanomura, Ib Ulbaek, Tony Veale, Carl Vogel, and Sheila Watts. None of the above is of course responsible for how the book turned out in the end; that is entirely my responsibility. The first draft of the book was written while I was enjoying the academic hospitality of the Department of African Languages and Cultures of the School of Oriental and African Studies, University of London. I would like to thank the members of that department, in particular Dick Hayward and Philip Jaggar, for making my time there so enjoyable and profitable. That visit was supported by the Trinity College Dublin Arts and Social Sciences Benefactions Fund. Later revisions were made while I was a visiting fellow at La Trobe University's Research Centre for Linguistic Typology and I would like to thank Bob Dixon and Sasha Aikhenvald and their colleagues for their generosity, hospitality, and for providing such a stimulating environment.

This fourth edition has been revised and updated, and now includes a glossary and suggested solutions to all exercises. I would once again like to thank the readers and users of the book, together with reviewers, who have kindly given me their comments and suggestions. I would like to thank the editorial team at Wiley-Blackwell for their enthusiasm and professionalism. Finally I would like to thank Joan, Alexander, and Isabel for their love and support.

J. I. S.

Abbreviations and Symbols

ACC	accusative case
ADJ	adjective
ADV	adverb
AG	agent
AP	adjectival phrase
ART	article
CAUSE	causative
CL or CLASS	classifier
DECL	declarative
DET	determiner
ERG	ergative
f	feminine gender
FOC	focus
FUT	future tense
GEN	genitive case
IMP	imperative
IMPERF	imperfective aspect
IMPERS	impersonal
INDIC	indicative mood
IN or INSTR	instrument
LO or LOC	location
m	masculine gender
N	noun
NOMIN	nominative case

NP	noun phrase
P	preposition
PA or PAT	patient
PAST	past tense
PERF	perfective aspect
pl	plural
PP	prepositional phrase
PRES	present tense
Q	interrogative
RE	recipient
S	sentence
sg	singular
SO	source
SUBJUN	subjunctive
TH	theme
V	verb
VP	verb phrase
1	first person
2	second person
3	third person
*	ungrammatical
?	semantically odd
#	pragmatically odd
[ ]	boundaries of a syntactic constituent
$[_{NP}]$	method of labeling a syntactic constituent, here an NP

Logical symbols:

¬	not (negation)
∧	and (conjunction)
∨	or (disjunction)
→	if . . . then (material implication)
⊻	exclusive or (exclusive disjunction, XOR)
≡	if and only if, truth-value equivalence
∃	existential quantifier
∀	universal quantifier

Less commonly known language names are introduced with the name of the large language family (phylum) they belong to and an indication of where the language is spoken, for example: Tiv (Niger-Congo; Nigeria).

part I

Preliminaries

chapter 1

Semantics in Linguistics

1.1 Introduction

Semantics is the study of meaning communicated through language. This book is an introduction to the theory and practice of semantics in modern linguistics. Although this is not an introduction to any single theory, we begin with a basic assumption: that a person's linguistic abilities are based on knowledge that they have. It is this knowledge that we are seeking to investigate. One of the insights of modern linguistics is that speakers of a language have different types of linguistic knowledge, including how to pronounce words, how to construct sentences, and about the meaning of individual words and sentences. To reflect this, linguistic description has different **levels of analysis**. So **phonology** is the study of what sounds a language has and how these sounds combine to form words; **syntax** is the study of how words can be combined into sentences; and **semantics** is the study of the meanings of words and sentences.

The division into levels of analysis seems to make sense intuitively: if you are learning a foreign language you might learn a word from a book, know what it means but not know how to pronounce it. Or you might hear a word, pronounce it perfectly but not know what it means. Then again, you might know the pronunciation and meaning of, say a noun, but not know how its plural is formed or what its genitive case looks like. In this sense knowing a word unites different kinds of knowledge, and this is just as true of your knowledge of how to construct phrases and sentences.

Since linguistic description is an attempt to reflect a speaker's knowledge, the semanticist is committed to describing semantic knowledge. This knowledge allows English speakers to know, for example, that both the following sentences describe the same situation:

1.1 In the spine, the thoracic vertebrae are above the lumbar vertebrae.

1.2 In the spine, the lumbar vertebrae are below the thoracic vertebrae.

that 1.3 and 1.4 below **contradict** each other:

1.3 Addis Ababa is the capital of Ethiopia.

1.4 Addis Ababa is not the capital of Ethiopia.

that 1.5 below has several possible meanings, that is it is **ambiguous**:

1.5 She gave her the slip.

and that 1.6 below **entails** 1.7:

1.6 Henry murdered his bank manager.

1.7 Henry's bank manager is dead.

We will look at these types of semantic knowledge in more detail a little later on; for now we can take **entailment** to mean a relationship between sentences so that if a sentence *A* entails a sentence *B*, then if we know *A* we automatically know *B*. Or alternatively, it should be impossible, at the same time, to assert *A* and deny *B*. Knowing the effect of inserting the word *not*, or about the relationships between *above* and *below*, and *murder* and *dead*, are aspects of an English speaker's semantic knowledge, and thus should be part of a semantic description of English.

As our original definition of semantics suggests, it is a very broad field of inquiry, and we find scholars writing on very different topics and using quite different methods, though sharing the general aim of describing semantic knowledge. As a result semantics is the most diverse field within linguistics. In addition, semanticists have to have at least a nodding acquaintance with other disciplines, like philosophy and psychology, which also investigate the creation and transmission of meaning. Some of the questions raised in these neighboring disciplines have important effects on the way linguists do semantics. In chapter 2 we discuss some of these questions, but we begin in this chapter by looking at the basic tasks involved in establishing semantics as a branch of linguistics.

1.2 Semantics and Semiotics

So we see our basic task in semantics as showing how people communicate meanings with pieces of language. Note, though, that this is only part of a larger enterprise of investigating how people understand meaning. Linguistic meaning is a special subset of the more general human ability to use signs, as we can see from the examples below:

1.8 Those vultures mean there's a dead animal up ahead.

1.9 His high temperature may mean he has a virus.

1.10 The red flag means it's dangerous to swim.

1.11 Those stripes on his uniform mean that he is a sergeant.

The verb *mean* is being put to several uses here, including inferences based on cause and effect, and on knowledge about the arbitrary symbols used in public signs. These uses reflect the all-pervasive human habit of identifying and creating signs: of making one thing stand for another. This process of creating and interpreting symbols, sometimes called **signification**, is far wider than language. Scholars like Ferdinand de Saussure (1974) have stressed that the study of linguistic meaning is a part of this general study of the use of sign systems, and this general study is called **semiotics**.[1] Semioticians investigate the types of relationship that may hold between a sign and the object it represents, or in Saussure's terminology between a **signifier** and its **signified**. One basic distinction, due to C. S. Peirce, is between **icon**, **index**, and **symbol**. An icon is where there is a similarity between a sign and what it represents, as for example between a portrait and its real life subject, or a diagram of an engine and the real engine. An index is where the sign is closely associated with its signified, often in a causal relationship; thus smoke is an index of fire. Finally, a symbol is where there is only a conventional link between the sign and its signified, as in the use of insignia to denote military ranks, or perhaps the way that mourning is symbolized by the wearing of black clothes in some cultures, and white clothes in others. In this classification, words would seem to be examples of verbal symbols.[2]

In our discussion of semantics we will leave this more comprehensive level of investigation and concentrate on linguistic meaning. The historical development between language and other symbolic systems is an open question: what seems clear is that language represents man's most sophisticated use of signs.

1.3 Three Challenges in Doing Semantics

Analyzing a speaker's semantic knowledge is an exciting and challenging task, as we hope to show in this book. We can get some idea of how challenging by adopting a simple but intuitively attractive theory of semantics, which we can call the **definitions theory**. This theory would simply state that to give the meaning of linguistic expressions we should establish definitions of the meanings of words. We could then assume that when a speaker combines words to form sentences according to the grammatical rules of her[3] language, the word definitions are combined to form phrase and then sentence definitions, giving us the meanings of sentences. Let us investigate putting this approach into practice.

As soon as we begin our task of attaching definitions to words, we will be faced with a number of challenges. Three in particular prove very tricky for our theory. The first is the problem of **circularity**. How can we state the meaning of a word, except in other words, either in the same or a different language? This is a problem that faces dictionary writers: if you look up a word like *ferret* in a monolingual English dictionary, you might find a definition like "Domesticated albino variety of the polecat, *Mustela putorius*, bred for hunting rabbits, rats, etc." To understand this, you have to understand the words in the definition. According to our aims for semantics, we have to describe the meanings of these words too, beginning with *domesticated*. The definition for this might be "of animals, tame, living with human beings." Since this definition is also in words, we have to give the meaning, for example, of *tame*. And so on. If the definitions of word meaning are given in words, the process might never end. The question is: can we ever step outside language in order to describe it, or are we forever involved in circular definitions?

A second problem we will meet is how to make sure that our definitions of a word's meaning are exact. If we ask where the meanings of words exist, the answer must be: in the minds of native speakers of the language. Thus meaning is a kind of knowledge. This raises several questions: for example, is there a difference between this kind of knowledge and other kinds of knowledge that people have? In particular: can we make a distinction between **linguistic knowledge** (about the meaning of words) and **encyclopedic knowledge** (about the way the world is)? For example, if I believe that a whale is a fish, and you believe that it is a mammal, do our words have different meanings when we both use the noun *whale*? Presumably you still understand me when I say *I dreamt that I was swallowed by a whale.*

There is another aspect to this problem: what should we do if we find that speakers of a language differ in their understanding of what a word means? Whose knowledge should we pick as our "meaning"? We might avoid the decision by picking just one speaker and limiting our semantic description to an **idiolect**, the technical term for an individual's language. Another strategy to resolve differences might be to identify experts and use their knowledge, but as we shall see, moving away from ordinary speakers to use a scientific definition for words has the danger of making semantics equivalent to all of science. It also ignores the fact that most of us seem to understand each other talking about, say animals, without any training in zoology. This is a point we will come back to in chapter 2.

A third type of challenge facing us comes from looking at what particular utterances mean in context. For example: if someone says to you *Marvelous weather you have here in Ireland*, you might interpret it differently on a cloudless sunny day than when the rain is pouring down. Similarly *He's dying* might mean one thing when said of a terminally ill patient, and another as a comment watching a stand-up comedian failing to get laughs. Or again: *It's getting late* if said to a friend at a party might be used to mean *Let's leave*. The problem here is that if features of context are part of an utterance's meaning then how can we include them in our definitions? For a start, the number of possible situations, and therefore of interpretations, is enormous, if not infinite. It doesn't seem likely that we could fit all the relevant information into our definitions.

These three issues: circularity; the question of whether linguistic knowledge is different from general knowledge; and the problem of the contribution of context to meaning, show that our definitions theory is too simple to do the job we want. Semantic analysis must be more complicated than attaching definitions to linguistic expressions. As we shall see in the rest of this book, semanticists have proposed a number of strategies for improving on this initial position. In the next section we discuss some initial ideas that will enable us to follow these strategies.

1.4 Meeting the Challenges

In most current linguistic theories, semantic analysis is as important a part of the linguist's job as, say, phonological analysis. Theories differ on details of the relationship between semantics and other levels of analysis like syntax and morphology, but all seem to agree that linguistic analysis is incomplete without semantics. We need, it seems, to establish a semantic component in our theories. We have to ask: how can we meet the three challenges outlined in the last section? Clearly we have to replace a simple theory of definitions with a theory that successfully solves these problems.

One of the aims of this book is to show how various theories have sought to provide solutions to these problems and we will return to them in detail over subsequent chapters. For now we will simply mention possible strategies which we will see fleshed out later. To cope with the problem of circularity, one solution is to design a semantic **metalanguage** with which to describe the semantic units and rules of all languages. We use metalanguage here with its usual meaning in linguistics: the tool of description. So in a grammar of Arabic written in French, Arabic is the *object language*, and French is the *metalanguage*. An ideal metalanguage would be neutral with respect to any natural languages, that is it would not be unconsciously biased toward English, French, and so on. Moreover it should satisfy scientific criteria of clarity, economy, consistency, and so on. We will see various proposals for such a metalanguage, for example to represent word meanings and the semantic relations between words, in chapters 9 and 10. We will also meet claims that such a metalanguage is unattainable and that the best policy is to use ordinary language to describe meaning.

For some linguists, though, translation into even a perfect metalanguage would not be a satisfactory semantic description. Such a line of reasoning goes like this: if words are symbols they have to relate to something; otherwise what are they symbols of? In this view, to give the semantics of words we have to ground them in something non-linguistic. In chapter 2 we will review the debate about whether the things that words signify are real objects in the world or thoughts.

Setting up a metalanguage might help too with the problem of relating semantic and encyclopedic knowledge, since designing meaning representations, for example for words, involves arguing about which elements of knowledge should be included. To return to our earlier example of *whale*: we assume that English speakers can use this word because they know what it means. The knowledge a speaker has of the meaning of words is often compared to a mental **lexicon** or dictionary. Yet if we open a real dictionary at the entry for *whale*, the definition is likely to begin "large marine mammal...." To rephrase our earlier question: does it follow that someone who doesn't know that whales are mammals fails to understand the meaning of the word *whale*? What if the speaker knows that it is a large animal that lives in the sea, but is hazy after that? The real issue is the amount of knowledge that it is necessary to have in order to use a word. We shall see aspects of this debate, which is really part of the general psychological debate about the representation of concepts and categories, in chapters 2, 3, 7, and 11.

In tackling the third problem, of context, one traditional solution has been to assume a split in an expression's meaning between the local contextual effects and a context-free element of meaning, which we might call **conventional** or **literal** meaning. We could perhaps try to limit our definitions to the literal part of meaning and deal with contextual features separately. As we shall see in chapter 3 though, it turns out to be no easy task to isolate the meaning of a word from any possible context. We discuss some aspects of this idea of literal meaning in 1.6.3 below. The other side of such an approach is to investigate the role of contextual information in communication, and try to establish theories of how speakers amalgamate knowledge of context with linguistic knowledge. As we shall see in chapter 7, it seems that speakers and hearers cooperate in using various types of contextual information. Investigating this leads us to a view of the listener's role that is quite different from the simple, but common, analogy of decoding a coded message. We shall see that listeners have a very active role, using what has been said, together with background knowledge, to make inferences about what the speaker meant. The study of these processes and the role in them of context, is often assigned to a special area of study called **pragmatics**. We discuss the relationship between semantics and pragmatics in 1.6.4 below. We shall see instances of the role of context in meaning throughout this book and this will give us the opportunity to review the division of labor between semantics and this newer field of pragmatics.[4]

Each of these strategies will be investigated in later chapters of this book: the creation of semantic metalanguages, the modeling of conceptual knowledge, the theory of literal language, and factoring out context into pragmatics. Meanwhile in the next section we look at how semantics might fit into a model of language.

1.5 Semantics in a Model of Grammar

1.5.1 Introduction

As has been suggested already, for many linguists the aim of doing semantics is to set up a component of the grammar that will parallel other components like syntax or phonology. Linguists like to draw flowchart-style diagrams of grammatical models, and in many of them there is a box labeled "semantics," as in figure 1.1.

Before we go on, it might be worthwhile to consider whether it is justified to view semantics as a component equal and parallel to, say, syntax.

Figure 1.1 Components of grammar

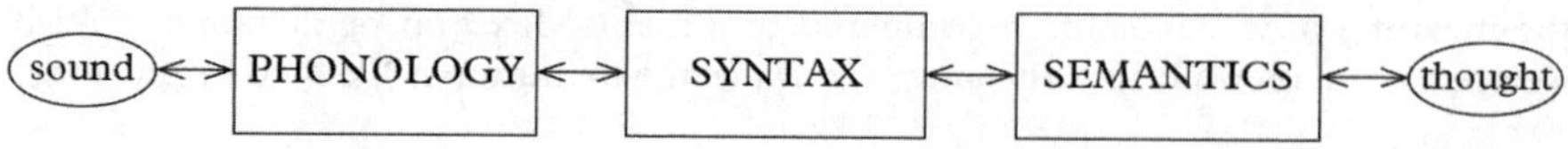

We saw earlier that linguists identify different levels of analysis. Another way of describing this is to say that linguistic knowledge forms distinct **modules**, or is **modularized**. As a result, many linguistic theories are themselves modularized, having something like our boxes in figure 1.1. Our question, though, remains: what kind of module is semantics? The answer varies from theory to theory. The real problem is of course that units at all linguistic levels serve as part of the general enterprise: to communicate meaning. This means that in at least one sense, meaning is a product of all linguistic levels. Changing one phoneme for another, one verb ending for another, or one word order for another will produce differences of meaning. This view leads some writers to believe that meaning cannot be identified as a separate level, autonomous from the study of other levels of grammar. A strong version of this view is associated with the theory known as **Cognitive Grammar**, advocated by linguists such as Ronald Langacker (e.g. Langacker 2008);[5] see, for example, this claim from a cognitive linguist:

1.12 the various autonomy theses and dichotomies proposed in the linguistic literature have to be abandoned: a strict separation of syntax, morphology and lexicon is untenable; furthermore it is impossible to separate linguistic knowledge from extra-linguistic knowledge. (Rudzka-Ostyn 1993: 2)

As we shall see in the course of this book, however, many other linguists do see some utility in maintaining both types of distinction referred to above: between linguistic and non-linguistic knowledge; and within linguistic knowledge, identifying distinct modules for knowledge about pronunciation, grammar, and meaning.

1.5.2 Word meaning and sentence meaning

If an independent component of semantics is identified, one central issue is the relationship between word meaning and sentence meaning. Knowing a language, especially one's native language, involves knowing thousands of words. As mentioned earlier, some linguists call the mental store of these words a **lexicon**, making an overt parallel with the lists of words and meanings published as dictionaries. In this view, the mental lexicon is a large but finite body of knowledge, part of which must be semantic. This lexicon is not completely static because we are continually learning and forgetting words. It is clear though that at any one time we hold a large amount of semantic knowledge in our memory.

Phrases and sentences also have meaning of course, but an important difference between word meaning on the one hand, and phrase and sentence meaning on the other, concerns **productivity**. It is always possible to create new words, but this is a relatively infrequent occurrence. On the other hand, speakers regularly create sentences that they have never used or heard before, confident that their audience will understand them. Noam Chomsky in particular has commented on the creativity of sentence formation (e.g. Chomsky 1965: 7–9). It is one of generative grammar's most important insights that a relatively small number of combinatory rules may allow speakers to use a finite set of words to create a very large, perhaps infinite, number of sentences. To allow this the rules for sentence formation must be **recursive**, allowing repetitive embedding or coordination of syntactic categories. To give a simple example, a compositional rule like 1.13 below, where elements in parentheses are optional and the asterisk means the optional group is repeatable, will allow potentially limitless expansions of S, as in 1.14:

1.13 S → [$_S$ S (and S)*]

1.14 a. [$_S$ S and S]
b. [$_S$ S and S and S]
c. [$_S$ S and S and S and S] etc.

The idea is that you can always add another clause to a sentence. Or as 1.15 and 1.16 below show, another nominal within a nominal:

1.15 NP → [$_{NP}$ NP (and NP)*]

1.16 a. I bought [$_{NP}$ a book]
b. I bought [$_{NP}$ [$_{NP}$ a book] and [$_{NP}$ a magazine]]
c. I bought [$_{NP}$ [$_{NP}$ a book] and [$_{NP}$ a magazine] and [$_{NP}$ some pens]] etc.

See Lyons (1968: 221–22) for discussion of such recursive rules in syntax.

This insight has implications for semantic description. Clearly, if a speaker can make up novel sentences and these sentences are understood, then they obey the semantic rules of the language. So the meanings of sentences cannot be listed in a lexicon like the meanings of words: they must be created by rules of combination too. Semanticists often describe this by saying that sentence meaning is **compositional**. This term means that the meaning of an expression is determined by the meaning of its component parts and the way in which they are combined.

This brings us back to our question of levels. We see that meaning is in two places, so to speak, in a model of grammar: a more stable body of word meanings in the lexicon, and the limitless composed meanings of sentences. How can we connect semantic information in the lexicon with the compositional meaning of sentences? It seems reasonable to conclude that semantic rules have to be compositional too and in some sense "in step" with grammatical rules. The relationship is portrayed differently in different theories of language. In the evolving forms of Noam Chomsky's generative grammar (e.g. Chomsky 1965, 1988) syntactic rules operate independently of semantic rules but the two types are brought together at a level of Logical Form.[6] In many other theories, semantic rules and grammatical rules are inextricably bound together, so each combination of words in a language has to be permissible under both. Such an approach is typical of functional approaches like Halliday's Functional Grammar (1994), and Role and Reference Grammar (Van Valin 2005), as well as variants of generative grammar like Head-Driven Phrase Structure Grammar (Sag et al. 2003).[7]

1.6 Some Important Assumptions

At this point we can introduce some basic ideas that are assumed in many semantic theories and that will come in useful in our subsequent discussion. In most cases the descriptions of these ideas will be simple and a little on the vague side: we will try to firm them up in subsequent chapters.

Figure 1.2 Reference and sense in the vocabulary

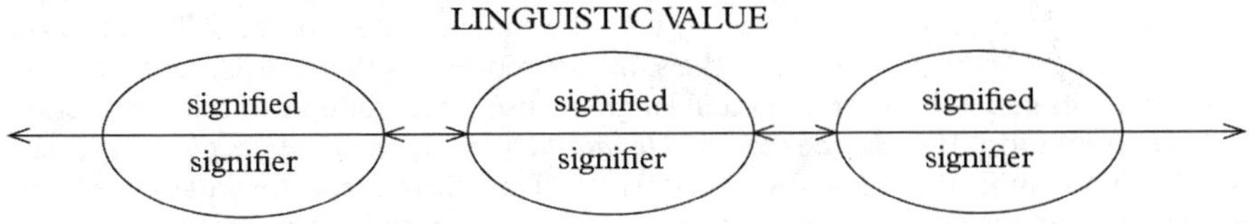

1.6.1 Reference and sense

One important point made by the linguist Ferdinand de Saussure (1974), whose ideas have been so influential in the development of modern linguistics, is that the meaning of linguistic expressions derives from two sources: the language they are part of and the world they describe. Words stand in a relationship to the world, or our mental classification of it: they allow us to identify parts of the world, and make statements about them. Thus if a speaker says *He saw Paul* or *She bought a dog*, the underlined nominals allow her to identify, pick out, or **refer** to specific entities in the world. However, words also derive their value from their position within the language system. The relationship by which language hooks onto the world is usually called **reference**. The semantic links between elements within the vocabulary system is an aspect of their **sense**,[8] or meaning.

Saussure (1974: 115) used the diagram in figure 1.2 to show this patterning. Each oval is a word, having its own capacity for reference, but each is also linked to other words in the same language, like a cell in a network. His discussion of this point is excellent and we cannot really do it justice here, except to recommend the reader to the original. His well-known examples include a comparison of English *sheep* and French *mouton*. In some cases they can be used to refer in a similar way but their meaning differs because they are in different systems and therefore have different ranges: in English there is an extra term *mutton*, used for meat, while the French word can be used for both the animal and the meat. Thus, the meaning of a word derives both from what it can be used to refer to and from the way its semantic scope is defined by related words. So the meaning of *chair* in English is partly defined by the existence of other words like *stool*. Similarly, the scope of *red* is defined by the other terms in the color system: *brown*, *orange*, *yellow*, and so on. The same point can be made of grammatical systems: Saussure pointed out that plural doesn't "mean" the same in French, where it is opposed to singular, as it does in Sanskrit or Arabic, languages which, in addition to singular, have **dual** forms, for exactly two entities. In the French system, plural is "two or more," in the other systems, "three or more."

1.6.2 Utterances, sentences, and propositions

These three terms are used to describe different levels of language. The most concrete is **utterance**: an utterance is created by speaking (or writing) a piece of language. If I say *Ontogeny recapitulates phylogeny*, this is one utterance. If another person in the same room also says *Ontogeny recapitulates phylogeny*, then we would be dealing with two utterances.

Sentences, on the other hand, are abstract grammatical elements obtained from utterances. Sentences are abstract because if a third and fourth person in the room also say *Ontogeny recapitulates phylogeny* with the same intonation, we will want to say that we have met four utterances of the same sentence. In other words, sentences are abstracted, or generalized, from actual language use. One example of this abstraction is direct quotation. If someone reports *He said "Ontogeny recapitulates phylogeny,"* she is unlikely to mimic the original speaker exactly. Usually the reporter will use her normal voice and thus filter out certain types of information: the difference in pitch levels between men, women, and children; perhaps some accent differences due to regional or social variation; and certainly those phonetic details which identify individual speakers. Speakers seem to recognize that at the level of the sentence these kinds of information are not important, and so discard them. So we can look at sentences from the point of view of the speaker, where they are abstract elements to be made real by uttering them; or from the hearer's point of view, where they are abstract elements reached by filtering out certain kinds of information from utterances.

One further step of abstraction is possible for special purposes: to identify **propositions**. In trying to establish rules of valid deduction, logicians discovered that certain elements of grammatical information in sentences were irrelevant; for example, the difference between active and passive sentences:

1.17 Caesar invaded Gaul.

1.18 Gaul was invaded by Caesar.

From a logician's perspective, these sentences are equivalent, for whenever 1.17 is true, so is 1.18. Thus the grammatical differences between them will never be significant in a chain of reasoning and can be ignored. Other irrelevant information (for these purposes) includes what we will in chapter 7 call **information structure**, that is the difference between the following sentences:

1.19 It was Gaul that Caesar invaded.

1.20 It was Caesar that invaded Gaul.

1.21 What Caesar invaded was Gaul.

1.22 The one who invaded Gaul was Caesar.

These sentences seem to share a description of the same state of affairs. Once again, if one is true all are true, and if one is false then all are false. To capture this fact, logicians identify a common proposition. Such a proposition can be represented in various special ways to avoid confusion with the various sentences that represent it, for example by using capitals:

1.23 CAESAR INVADED GAUL.

Thus the proposition underlying the sentence *The war ended* might be written:

1.24 THE WAR ENDED.

Logicians commonly use formulae for propositions in which the verb is viewed as a function, and its subject and any objects as arguments of the function. Such formulae often delete verb endings, articles, and other grammatical elements, so that corresponding to 1.23 and 1.24 we would get 1.25 and 1.26 below:

1.25 invade (caesar, gaul)

1.26 end (war)

Some semanticists have borrowed from logicians both this notion of proposition and the use of logical formulae. We will see various applications of such formulae in later chapters.[9] As we shall see, some linguists employ this notion of proposition in their semantic analysis, often to identify a description of an event or situation that might be a shared element in different sentences. So, for example the statement *Joan made the sorbet*, the question *Did Joan make the sorbet?*, and the command: *Joan, make the sorbet!* might be seen to share a propositional element: JOAN MAKE THE SORBET. In this view, these different sentences allow the speaker to do different things with the same proposition: to assert it as a past event; to question it; or to request someone to bring it about.

Propositions then can be a way of capturing part of the meaning of sentences. They are more abstract than sentences because, as we saw in examples 1.17–22 above, the same proposition can be represented by several different statements. Moreover, in non-statements like questions, orders, and so on, they cannot be the complete meaning since such sentences include an indication of the speaker's attitude to the proposition. We will come back to the linguistic marking of such attitudes in chapter 8.

To sum up: **utterances** are real pieces of speech. By filtering out certain types of (especially phonetic) information we can get to abstract grammatical elements, **sentences**. By going on to filter out certain types of grammatical information, we can get to **propositions**, which are descriptions of states of affairs and which some writers see as a basic element of sentence meaning. We will get some idea of the different uses to which these terms are put in the remainder of this book.[10]

1.6.3 Literal and non-literal meaning

This distinction is assumed in many semantics texts but attempting to define it soon leads us into some difficult and theory-laden decisions. The basic distinction seems a common-sense one: distinguishing between instances where the speaker speaks in a neutral, factually accurate way, and instances where the speaker deliberately describes something in untrue or impossible terms in order to achieve special effects. Thus if one afternoon you are feeling the effects of missing lunch, you might speak literally as in 1.27, or non-literally as in 1.28–30:

1.27 I'm hungry.

1.28 I'm starving.

1.29 I could eat a horse.

1.30 My stomach thinks my throat's cut.

Non-literal uses of language are traditionally called **figurative** and are described by a host of rhetorical terms including **metaphor**, **irony**, **metonymy**, **synecdoche**, **hyperbole**, and **litotes**. We will meet examples of these terms later on. On closer examination, though, it proves difficult to draw a firm line between literal and non-literal uses of language. For one thing, one of the ways languages change over time is by speakers shifting the meanings of words to fit new conditions. One such shift is by metaphorical extension, where some new idea is depicted in terms of something more familiar. For a while the new expression's metaphorical nature remains clear, as for example in the expressions *go viral* or *photobomb*. Older coinings might include *chatroom* or *fiscal cliff*. After a while such expressions become fossilized and their metaphorical quality is no longer apparent to speakers. It is doubtful, for example, whether anyone discussing the prospects for a new space shuttle thinks of looms or sewing machines when they utter the word *shuttle*. The vocabulary of a language is littered with fossilized metaphors such as these, and this continuing process makes it difficult to decide the point at which the use of a word is literal rather than figurative. Facts such as these have led some linguists, notably George Lakoff (Lakoff and Johnson 1980; Lakoff 1987), to claim that there is no principled distinction between literal and metaphorical uses of language. Such scholars see metaphor as an integral part of human categorization: a basic way of organizing our thoughts about the world. Lakoff and Johnson identify clusterings of metaphoric uses, giving them labels such as "Time is money" to explain clusters such as 1.31 (Lakoff and Johnson 1980: 7):

1.31 You're **wasting** my time.
This gadget will **save** you hours.
I don't have the time to **give** you.
How do you **spend** your time these days?
That flat tire **cost** me an hour.
I've **invested** a lot of time in her.

Their claim is that whole semantic fields are systematically organized around central metaphors such as these, and that their use is not just an isolated stylistic effect: that we think, culturally, of time as a commodity.

Clearly, if sentences like *How do you spend your time these days?* are identified as metaphorical, then it will prove difficult to find any uses of language that are literal. Many linguists, however, would deny that this use of *spend* is metaphorical. The position adopted by many semanticists is that this is an example of a faded or dead metaphor. The idea is that metaphors fade over time, and become part of normal literal language, much as we described for *shuttle* above. In this approach, there *is* a valid distinction between literal and non-literal language. In what we can call the **literal language theory**, metaphors, and other non-literal uses of language require a different processing strategy than literal language. One view is that hearers recognize non-literal uses as semantically odd, that is factually nonsensical, like "eating a horse" in 1.29 earlier, but then are motivated to give them some interpretation by an assumption that speakers generally are trying to make sense. The hearer then makes inferences in order to make sense out of a non-literal utterance. Clearly some figurative expressions like *eat a horse* are quite conventionalized (i.e. well on their way to being "dead") and do not require much working out. Other examples of non-literal language might require a little more interpretative effort, as when a reader gets to this exchange in Sean O'Faolain's novel *And Again?* (1972: 82):

1.32 "Of course," my host said with a sigh, "the truth is he didn't get on with the wife."
"Really?"
"She flew her kite a bit too often. All Dublin knew it."

In the literal language theory, the reader's task here is firstly to reject the literal interpretation, that the husband had a phobia about kite flying, and then to work out what kind of behavior is being referred to so obliquely here.

We discuss hearers' assumptions about speakers' intentions in chapter 7, when we also investigate the inferences hearers routinely make to interpret utterances. In chapter 11 we discuss arguments from writers in **cognitive semantics**, like Lakoff (1987), that the literal language theory is mistaken in viewing metaphor as something extra to, and different from, ordinary literal language.

1.6.4 Semantics and pragmatics

A similarly difficult distinction is between **semantics** and **pragmatics**. These terms denote related and complementary fields of study, both concerning the transmission of meaning through language. Drawing the line between the two fields is difficult and controversial but as a preliminary we can turn to an early use of the term **pragmatics** in Charles Morris's division of semiotics:

1.33 syntax: the formal relation of signs to each other;
semantics: the relations of signs to the objects to which the signs are applicable;
pragmatics: the relation of signs to interpreters.
(adapted from Morris 1938, 1955)

Narrowing signs to *linguistic* signs, this would give us a view of pragmatics as the study of the speaker's/hearer's interpretation of language, as suggested by Rudolph Carnap (1942: 9, cited in Morris 1955: 218) below:

1.34 If in an investigation explicit reference is made to the speaker, or, to put it in more general terms, to the user of a language, then we assign it to the field of pragmatics. (Whether in this case reference to designata is made or not makes no difference for this classification.) If we abstract from the user of the language and analyze only the expressions and their designata, we are in the field of semantics. And if, finally, we abstract from the designata also and analyze only the relations between the expressions, we are in (logical) syntax. The whole science of language, consisting of the three parts mentioned, is called semiotic.

We might interpret this, rather crudely, as:

1.35 meaning described in relation to speakers and hearers = pragmatics
meaning abstracted away from users = semantics

Let's investigate what this might mean, using a simple example. A speaker can utter the same sentence to a listener, for example *The place is closing*, and mean to use it as a simple statement, or as a warning to hurry and get that last purchase (if they're in a department store) or drink (if in a bar). It could also be an invitation or command to leave. In fact we can imagine a whole series of uses for this simple sentence, depending on the speaker's wishes and the situation the participants find themselves in. Some semanticists would claim that there is some element of meaning common to all of these uses and that this common, non-situation-specific meaning is what semantics is concerned with. On the other hand the range of uses a sentence can be put to, depending on context, would be the object of study for pragmatics.

One way of talking about this is to distinguish between **sentence meaning** and **speaker meaning**. This suggests that words and sentences have a meaning independently of any particular use, which meaning is then incorporated by a speaker into the particular meaning she wants to convey at any one time. In this view semantics is concerned with sentence meaning and pragmatics with speaker meaning. We can see how this distinction might be used when we consider the use of pronouns, which as we mentioned earlier are very dependent on contextual support. For example if someone says to a listener *Is he awake?* we would say that the listener has to understand two things, among others, to get the meaning: the first is that in English sentence meaning, *he* means something like "male entity referred to by the speaker, not the speaker and not the person spoken to" and the second is how to work out who right now the speaker is referring to by *he*. In this view knowing the first is part of semantic knowledge and working out the second is a task for one's pragmatic competence.

The advantage of such a distinction is that it might free the semanticist from having to include all kinds of knowledge in semantics. It would be the role of pragmaticists to investigate the interaction between purely linguistic knowledge and general or encyclopedic knowledge, an issue we touched on earlier. As we shall see in chapter 7, in order to understand utterances, hearers seem to use both types of knowledge along with knowledge about the context of the utterance and common-sense reasoning, guesses, and so on. A semantics/pragmatics division enables semanticists to concentrate on just the linguistic element in utterance comprehension. Pragmatics would then be the field that studies how hearers fill out the semantic structure with contextual information (e.g., work out who the speaker is referring to by pronouns, etc.) and make inferences that go beyond the meaning of what was said to them (e.g. that *I'm tired* might mean *Let's go home*).

The semantics/pragmatics distinction seems then to be a useful one. The problems with it emerge when we get down to detail: precisely which phenomena are semantic and which pragmatic? As discussed in chapters 3 and 7, much of meaning seems to depend on context: it is often difficult, for example, to identify a meaning for a word that does not depend on the context of its use. Our strategy in this book will be not to try too hard to draw a line along this putative semantics/pragmatics divide. Some theorists are skeptical of the distinction (e.g. Lakoff 1987; Langacker 2008) while others accept it but draw the line in different places. The reader is referred to the discussion in Birner (2012) for detail. What will become clear as we proceed is that it is very difficult to shake context out of language and that the structure of sentences minutely reveals that they are designed by their speakers to be uttered in specific contexts and with desired effects. Chapter 7 is largely devoted to providing examples of these contextual aspects of meaning.

1.7 Summary

In this chapter we have taken a brief look at the task of establishing semantics as a branch of linguistics. We identified three challenges to doing this: circularity, context, and the status of linguistic knowledge. We will see examples of these problems and proposed solutions as we proceed through this book. We noted that establishing a semantics component in linguistic theory involves deciding how to relate word meaning and sentence meaning. Finally, we introduced some background ideas that are assumed in many semantic theories and which we will examine in more detail in subsequent chapters: reference and sense; utterance, sentence, and proposition; literal and non-literal meaning; and semantics and pragmatics. We turn to reference and sense in the next chapter.

EXERCISES

1.1 We made the claim that meaning is **compositional**, that is that the meaning of complex linguistic expressions is built up from the meaning of their constituent parts. However, there are a number of areas where compositionality is restricted and one of these is compound words. Below is a list of English compound nouns. One very common pattern is for the second element to identify the type of thing the compound is, while the first is some kind of qualifier. The qualification can identify a subtype, be what the thing is used for, what the thing is made of, where or when the thing happens, etc. So a *teacup* is a cup used for tea. Divide the list below into two types: one where the meaning is predictable from the meaning of the two parts and a second type where the meaning is not predictable in this way. For the first type, which shows a certain compositionality, how would you characterize the type of qualification made by the first part of the compound? Check your explanations against a dictionary's entries.

agony aunt	eye candy	houseboat	shopping list
blackmail	firsthand	housewife	software
boyfriend	flea market	human being	speed limit
businessman	foxhound	mailbox	spin doctor
bus stop	gravy train	monkey business	sunglasses
climate change	greenhouse	mousetrap	sweatshop
daydream	horseshoe	nightmare	taste bud
doormat	hotdog	redhead	video game

1.2 We raised the issue of a speaker's **linguistic** and **encyclopedic knowledge**. Most English speakers will have encountered the words below, which we partly define below by their part of speech and some indication of context of use. Try to give an exact definition of their meanings, as if you were writing your own dictionary:

sabre	(noun: a weapon)
yew	(noun: a tree)
copper	(noun: a metal)
vodka	(noun: a drink)
hay	(noun: farming product)

How would you distinguish between the following pairs, using your original definitions as a basis?

sabre/rapier yew/oak copper/bronze vodka/gin hay/straw

When you have done this exercise, you may like to compare your definitions against a dictionary.

1.3 We used the term **reference** for the use of nominals (noun phrases and names) and pronouns to identify or pick out individuals in the world. For each of the following, imagine the sentence being spoken in an average kind of situation. Discuss which elements would be used to **refer** in your situation.

a. This schedule is crazy.
b. She enjoyed herself at the party.
c. There's a policeman looking at your car.
d. The script calls for a short fat guy.
e. You asked for a ham sandwich; this is a ham sandwich.

1.4 Discuss the importance of contextual information in understanding an utterance of the following sentences:

a. Take another shot.
b. The Tigers beat the Bulldogs again.
c. Isabel is tall.
d. It's too hot in here.
e. Everyone has gone home.

1.5 Discuss the use of **figurative** language in the following newspaper headlines:[11]

a. Women still face a glass ceiling.
b. UK faces debt time bomb from ageing population.
c. One last push and a pointless bill is born, to no joy but to the relief of all involved.

[On the passage of a bill of law through the Irish parliament]
d. US report puts Indian IT in the dock.
e. Spain thrown lifeline by Brussels with extra year to cut deficit.

FURTHER READING

A concise general history of linguistics is Robins (1990) and the influence of the ideas of Saussure on modern linguistics is described in Lepschy (1982). Matthews (1993) describes American linguistics from Bloomfield to Chomsky. Two very detailed surveys of semantics, which include the topics mentioned in this chapter and others we will cover later, are Lyons (1977) and Allan (1986). These both consist of two volumes and are very useful as works of reference. An introduction to the areas covered by pragmatics is given by Birner (2012).

NOTES

1 For an accessible introduction to semiotics, see Sebeok (1994). A more advanced discussion is in Eco (1976).
2 There are however iconic elements to language, as for example the use of **onomatopoeia**, or sound symbolism, as in the English words *tick-tock*, *cuckoo*, *ratatat*, and *sizzle*. Onomatopoeic words are a subset of **ideophones** (Voeltz and Kilian 2001), words that involve sound symbolism and often evoke sensory stimuli, as in English *twinkle* and *higgledy-piggledy*. Some writers claim that iconicity is a much more extensive feature of language than this; see Haiman (1985) for example.
3 To avoid cumbersome devices like "s/he," we will when discussing simple conversations use "he" and "she" at random.
4 For an introduction to pragmatics see Birner (2012).
5 We look at semantics within this Cognitive Grammar approach in chapter 11.
6 For an introductory account of Chomskyan syntax see Carnie (2013).
7 As mentioned earlier, in Cognitive Grammar (Langacker 2008), discussed later in chapter 11, no distinction is made between semantic and grammatical rules.
8 This distinction between sense and reference is a translation of Frege's distinction between *Sinn* and *Bedeutung*; see Frege (1980), especially the section "On Sense and Reference" (originally published in 1892). We discuss these notions further in chapter 2.
9 See Allwood, Andersson, and Dahl (1977) for details of translating from English sentences into such logical formulae. We will look at this strategy again in chapter 10.
10 For simplicity this section has concentrated on the relationship between propositions and the utterance of full sentences. In fact as we can see from examples 1 and 2 below, in the right context propositions can be communicated by less than full sentences:
1 What's the longest river in the world?
2 a. The Nile is the longest river in the world.
b. The Nile is.
c. The Nile.
It seems reasonable to say that in the context of the question in 1 above, each of 2a–c can communicate the proposition THE NILE IS THE LONGEST RIVER IN THE WORLD, even though only 2a is a full sentence: 2b is a reduced or elliptical sentence,

while 2c is of course just a noun phrase. This is another example of the possible indirectness of the relationship between utterances, sentences and propositions: a proposition can be communicated by the utterance of various grammatical units, one of which is a sentence. See Lyons (1981: 195ff) for discussion of this point. We assume here that grammatical units like sentence (S), noun phrase (NP), verb phrase (VP), etc. are defined and specified at the level of syntax.

11 The headlines are from articles in the following newspapers: a. *The Guardian*, 21 February 2011, by Graham Snowdon; b. *The Daily Telegraph*, 29 October 2014, by Szu Ping Chan; c. *The Irish Times*, 24 July 2013, by Miriam Lord; d. *The Times of India*, 30 October 2014, by Shilpa Phadnis; e. *The Independent*, 31 May 2012, by Russell Lynch.

REFERENCES

Allan, Keith 1986: *Linguistic Meaning*, 2 vols. London: Routledge & Kegan Paul.

Allwood, Jens, Lars-Gunnar Andersson and Östen Dahl 1977: *Logic in Linguistics*. Cambridge: Cambridge University Press.

Birner, Betty J. 2012: *Introduction to Pragmatics*. Oxford: Wiley-Blackwell.

Carnap, Rudolf 1942: *Introduction to Semantics*. Cambridge, MA: Harvard University Press.

Carnie, Andrew 2013: *Syntax: A Generative Introduction*, third edition. Oxford: Wiley-Blackwell.

Chomsky, Noam 1965: *Aspects of the Theory of Syntax*. Cambridge, MA: MIT Press.

Chomsky, Noam 1988: *Language and Problems of Knowledge. The Managua Lectures*. Cambridge, MA: MIT Press.

Eco, Umberto 1976: *A Theory of Semiotics*. Bloomington: Indiana University Press.

Frege, Gottlob 1980: *Translations from the Philosophical Writings of Gottlob Frege*, edited by Peter Geach and Max Black. Oxford: Blackwell.

Haiman, John 1985: *Iconicity in Syntax*. Amsterdam: John Benjamins.

Halliday, M. A. K. 1994: *An Introduction to Functional Grammar*. London: Edward Arnold.

Lakoff, George 1987: *Women, Fire, and Dangerous Things: What Categories Reveal about the Mind*. Chicago: University of Chicago Press.

Lakoff, George and Mark Johnson 1980: *Metaphors We Live By*. Chicago: University of Chicago Press.

Langacker, Ronald W. 2008: *Cognitive Grammar: A Basic Introduction*. Oxford: Oxford University Press.

Lepschy, Giulio C. 1982: *A Survey of Structural Linguistics*, new edition. London: Deutsch.

Lyons, John 1968: *Introduction to Theoretical Linguistics*. Cambridge: Cambridge University Press.

Lyons, John 1977: *Semantics*, 2 vols. Cambridge: Cambridge University Press.

Lyons, John 1981: *Language, Meaning and Context*. London: Fontana.

Matthews, Peter H. 1993: *Grammatical Theory in the United States from Bloomfield to Chomsky*. Cambridge: Cambridge University Press.

Morris, Charles 1938: *Foundations of the Theory of Signs: International Encyclopedia of Unified Science*, vol. 1, no. 2. Chicago: University of Chicago Press.

Morris, Charles 1955: *Signs, Language and Behavior*. New York: George Braziller. (First published 1946 Prentice-Hall.)

O'Faolain, Sean 1972: *And Again?* London: Penguin Books.

Robins, Robert H. 1990: *A Short History of Linguistics*, third edition. London: Longman.

Rudzka-Ostyn, Brygida 1993: Introduction. In Richard A. Geiger and Brygida Rudzka-Ostyn (eds.) *Conceptualizations and Mental Processing in Language*, 1–20. Berlin: Mouton de Gruyter.

Sag, Ivan A., Thomas Wasow and Emily M. Bender 2003: *Syntactic Theory: A Formal Introduction*, second edition. Stanford, CA: Center for the Study of Language and Information.

Saussure, Ferdinand de 1974: *Course in General Linguistics*. Edited by Charles Bally and Albert Sechehaye, translation by Wade Baskin. Glasgow: Fontana/Collins. (First published 1915 as *Cours de Linguistique Générale*. Paris: Pyot.)
Sebeok, Thomas A. 1994: *An Introduction to Semiotics*. London: Pinter.
Van Valin, Robert D. 2005: *Exploring the Syntax–Semantics Interface*. Cambridge: Cambridge University Press.
Voeltz, F. K. E. and Christa Kilian-Hatz (eds.) 2001: *Ideophones*. Amsterdam: John Benjamins.

chapter 2

Meaning, Thought, and Reality

2.1 Introduction

In this chapter we look at the basic question of how it is that we can use language to describe the world. How is it possible, for example, that by uttering strings of sounds I can convey information to a listener about what is happening in a scene, say, outside my window? Clearly all languages allow speakers to describe, or as we might say model, aspects of what they perceive. We routinely pick out, for example, individual entities or locations, as with the elements in bold in:

2.1 **That dog** looks vicious.

2.2 We've just flown back from **Paris**.

where *that dog* and *Paris* are expressions allowing us to do this. In semantics this action of picking out or identifying with words is often called **referring** or **denoting**. Thus one can use the word *Paris* to **refer** to or **denote** the city. The entity referred to, in this case the city, is usually called the **referent** (or more awkwardly, the **denotatum**). Some writers, like John Lyons (1977: 396–409), separate the terms **refer** and **denote**. For these writers **denote** is used for the relationship between a linguistic expression and the world, while **refer** is used for the action of a speaker in picking out entities in the world. We will adopt this usage, so that if I say *A sparrow flew into the room*, I am using the two noun phrases *a sparrow* and *the room* to refer to things in the world, while the nouns *sparrow* and *room* denote certain classes of items. In other words, referring is what speakers do, while denoting is a property of words. Another difference, which follows from these definitions, is that denotation is a stable relationship in a language that is not dependent on any one use of a word. Reference, on the other hand, is a moment-by-moment relationship: what entity somebody refers to by using the word *sparrow* depends on the context.

As we shall see, there are different views of how semanticists should approach this ability to talk about the world. Two of these are particularly important in current semantic theories: we can call them the **referential** (or **denotational**) approach and the **representational** approach. For semanticists, adopting the first approach, this action of putting words into relationship with the world *is* meaning, so that to provide a semantic description for a language we need to show how the expressions of the language can "hook onto" the world.

Thus theories of meaning can be called **referential** (or **denotational**) when their basic premise is that we can give the meaning of words and sentences by showing how they relate to situations. Nouns, for example, are meaningful because they denote entities in the world and sentences because they denote situations and events.[1] In this approach, the difference in meaning between the sentences

2.3 There is a casino in Grafton Street.

2.4 There isn't a casino in Grafton Street.

arises from the fact that the two sentences describe different situations. If we assume the sentences were spoken at the same time about the same street, then they can be said to be incompatible: that is, one of them is a false description of the situation.

For semanticists adopting the second approach our ability to talk about the world depends on our mental models of it. In this view a language represents a theory about reality, about the types of things and situations in the world. Thus, as we shall see in later chapters, a speaker can choose to view the same situation in different ways. Example 2.5 below shows us that in English we can view the same situation as either an activity (2.5a) or a state (2.5b):

2.5 a. Joan is sleeping.
b. Joan is asleep.

Such decisions are influenced by each language's conventional ways of viewing situations. We can compare the three ways of saying that someone has a cold in 2.6–8 below:

2.6 English
You have a cold.

2.7 Somali
Hargab baa ku haya
a.cold FOCUS you has
"A cold has you." i.e. "You have a cold."

2.8 Irish
Tá slaghdán ort.
is a.cold on.you
"A cold is on you." i.e. "You have a cold."

In English and Somali, 2.6 and 2.7, we see the situation viewed as **possession**: in English the person possesses the disease; in Somali the disease possesses the person. In Irish, 2.8, the situation is viewed as **location**: the person is the location for the disease. We shall look at such differences in later chapters. The point here is that different conceptualizations influence the description of the real-world situations. Theories of meaning can be called **representational** when their emphasis is on the way that our reports about reality are influenced by the conceptual structures conventionalized in our language.

We can see these two approaches as focusing on different aspects of the same process: talking about the world. In referential theories, meaning derives from language being attached to, or grounded in, reality. In representational approaches meaning derives from language being a reflection of our conceptual structures. This difference of approach will surface throughout this book and we outline a specific referential theory in chapter 10, and versions of representational theories in chapters 9 and 11. These two approaches are influenced by ideas from philosophy and psychology and in this chapter we review some of the most important of these. We begin, however, with language, by looking at the different ways linguistic expressions can be used to refer. We then go on to ask whether reference is indeed all of meaning and examine arguments that reference relies on conceptual knowledge. Here we review some basic theories about concepts from the philosophical and psychological literature. Finally we discuss how these ideas from philosophy and psychology have influenced the ways that semanticists view the task of describing meaning.

2.2 Reference

2.2.1 Types of reference

We can begin our discussion by looking briefly at some major differences in the ways that words may be used to refer. For the introductory purposes of this chapter we will for the most part confine our discussion to the referential possibilities of names and noun phrases, which together we can call **nominals**, since the nominal is the linguistic unit which most clearly reveals this function of language. Later, in chapter 10, we look at a more fully fledged theory of denotation and discuss the denotations of other linguistic elements like verbs and sentences. In this section we discuss some basic distinctions in reference.

Referring and non-referring expressions

We can apply this distinction in two ways. Firstly there are linguistic expressions which can never be used to refer, for example the words *so, very, maybe, if, not, all.* These words do of course contribute meaning to the sentences they occur in and thus help sentences denote, but they do not themselves identify entities in the world. We will say that these are intrinsically non-referring items. By contrast, when someone says the noun *cat* in a sentence like *That cat looks vicious*, the noun is a referring expression since it is being used to identify an entity. So nouns are potentially referring expressions.

The second use of the distinction *referring/non-referring* concerns potentially referring elements like nouns: it distinguishes between instances when speakers use them to refer and instances when they do not. For example, the indefinite noun phrase *a cholecystectomy* is a referring expression in the following sentence:

2.9 They performed a cholecystectomy this morning.

where the speaker is referring to an individual operation but not in:

2.10 A cholecystectomy is a serious procedure.

where the nominal has a generic interpretation. Some sentences can be ambiguous between a referring and a non-referring reading, as is well-known to film writers. Our hero, on the trail of a missing woman, is the recipient of leers, or offers, when he tells a barman *I'm looking for a woman*. We know, but the barman doesn't, that our hero won't be satisfied by the non-referring reading.

Constant versus variable reference

One difference among referring expressions becomes clear when we look at how they are used across a range of different utterances. Some expressions will have the same referent across a range of utterances, for example *the Eiffel Tower* or *the Pacific Ocean*. Others have their reference totally dependent on context, for example the items in bold below, where to identify the referents we need to know who is speaking to whom, etc.:

2.11 **I** wrote to **you**

2.12 **She** put **it** in **my office**.

Expressions like *the Pacific Ocean* are sometimes described as having **constant reference**, while expressions like *I*, *you*, *she*, etc. are said to have **variable reference**. To identify who is being referred to by pronouns like *she*, *I*, *you*, etc. we obviously need to know a lot about the context in which these words were uttered. We look at such context-dependent elements in chapter 7, where we will use the term **deixis**, a term from Greek meaning roughly "pointing," as a label for words whose denotational capability so obviously needs contextual support.

In fact, though, our examples so far turn out to be the extreme cases. As we shall see in chapter 7, most acts of referring rely on some contextual information: for example, to identify the referent of the nominal *the President of the United States* we need to know when it was uttered.

Referents and extensions

So far we have been looking at referential differences between expressions. We can also make useful distinctions among the things referred to by expressions. We use the term **referent** of an expression for the thing picked out by uttering the expression in a particular context; so the referent of *the capital of Nigeria* would be, since 1991, the city of Abuja. Similarly, the referent of *a toad* in *I've just stepped on a toad* would be the unfortunate animal on the bottom of my shoe.

The term **extension** of an expression is the set of things which could possibly be the referent of that expression. So the extension of the word *toad* is the set of all toads. As mentioned earlier, in the terminology of Lyons (1977), the relationship between an expression and its extension is called **denotation**.

As we mentioned, names and noun phrases, which together we can call nominals, are the paradigmatic case of linguistic elements used to refer. In the next sections we outline some of the main ways that nominals are used to refer. The referential uses of different nominals have, of course, been an important area of investigation in the philosophy of language and there is a large literature on names, common nouns, definite nominals, and so on. We won't attempt to cover the philosophical arguments in detail here: we will just touch on some major aspects of nominal reference.[2]

2.2.2 Names

The simplest case of nominals which have reference might seem to be names. Names after all are labels for people, places, and so on and often seem to have little other meaning. It does not seem reasonable to ask what the meaning of *Karl Marx* is, other than helping us to talk about an individual.

Of course, context is important in the use of names: names are definite in that they carry the speaker's assumption that her audience can identify the referent. So if someone says to you:

2.13 He looks just like Brad Pitt.

the speaker is assuming you can identify the American actor.

But even granting the speaker's calculation of such knowledge, how do names work? This, like most issues in semantics, turns out to be not quite as simple a question as it seems and we might briefly look at a couple of suggestions from the philosophical literature.

One important approach can be termed the **description theory**, associated in various forms with Russell (1967), Frege (1980) and Searle (1958). Here a name is taken as a label or shorthand for knowledge about the referent, or in the terminology of philosophers, for one or more definite descriptions. So for *Christopher Marlowe*, for example, we might have such descriptions as *The writer of the play Dr Faustus* or *The Elizabethan playwright murdered in a Deptford tavern*. In this theory understanding a name and identifying the referent are both dependent on associating the name with the right description.

Another, very interesting, explanation is the **causal theory** espoused by Devitt and Sterelny (1987), and based on the ideas of Kripke (1980), and Donnellan (1972). According to this theory, the names are socially inherited, or borrowed. At some original point, or points, a name is given, let us say to a person, perhaps in a formal ceremony. People actually present at this begin to use this name, and thereafter, depending on the fate of the named person and this original group, the name may be passed on to other people. In the case of a person who achieves prominence, the name might be used by thousands or millions of people who have never met or seen the named person, or know very much about him. So the users of the name form a kind of chain back to an original naming or **grounding**. This is a very simplified sketch of this theory: for example, Devitt and Sterelny (1987: 61ff.) argue that in some cases a name does not get attached by a single grounding. It may arise from a period of repeated uses. Sometimes there are competing names and one wins out; or mistakes may be made and subsequently fixed by public practice. The great advantage of this causal theory is that it recognizes that speakers may use names with very little knowledge of the referent. It is easy to think of examples of historical figures whose names we might bandy about impressively, but, sadly for our education, about whom we might be hard pressed to say anything factual.

So where the causal theory stresses the role of social knowledge in the use of names, the description theory emphasizes the role of identifying knowledge. See Devitt and Sterelny (1987) for a detailed discussion of these proposals. The importance of this debate is that the treatment chosen for names can be extended to other nominals like **natural kinds**, a term in the philosophy of language for nouns referring to classes which occur in nature, like *giraffe* or *gold* (see S. Schwartz 1979, 1980, Churchland 1985). We will look at this proposal later in this chapter.

2.2.3 Nouns and noun phrases

Nouns and noun phrases (NPs) can be used to refer: indefinite and definite NPs can operate like names to pick out an individual, for example

2.14 a. I spoke to *a woman* about the noise.
b. I spoke to *the woman* about the noise.

where of course the difference between the nominals hangs on whether the woman to whom the speaker refers is known to the listener and/or has been identified earlier in the conversation.

Definite noun phrases can also form definite descriptions where the referent is whoever or whatever fits the description, as in:

2.15 She has a crush on *the captain of the hockey team*.

An account of reference has to deal with cases where there is no referent to fit the definite description, as in Bertrand Russell's famous example:

2.16 *The King of France* is bald.

or where the referent is not real, for example *the man in the iron mask* or *the wizard of Oz*. We look at the problematic status of such sentences in chapter 4, when we discuss the semantic notion, **presupposition**.

NPs can also be used to refer to groups of individuals, either **distributively**, where we focus on the individual members of the group as in 2.17, or **collectively**, when we focus on the aggregate as in 2.18:

2.17 *The people in the lift* avoided each other's eyes.

2.18 *The people in the lift* proved too heavy for the lift motor.

As well as individuals and groups of individuals, nominals can of course denote substances, actions and abstract ideas, for example:

2.19 Who can afford *coffee*?

2.20 *Sleeping* is his hobby.

2.21 She has a passion for *justice*.

One important referential distinction is between mass and count nouns, which is marked grammatically. Count nouns, for example *hat*, can occur with the article *a* (*a hat*), as plurals (*hats*), can be quantified by counting quantifiers like *many* (*many hats*), and be counted by numerals (*three hats*). Mass nouns, for example *furniture*, typically do none of these (**a furniture*, **furnitures*, **many furnitures*, **three furnitures*) and occur with non-counting quantifiers like *much*, as in *how much furniture*? Count nouns seem to denote discrete units that can be counted while mass nouns denote stuff that is not individuated and cannot therefore be counted. However, mass nouns can be counted if there is a unit of measure, for example *a container of furniture*, which can sometimes be implicitly supplied by context, as in *Two milks please!* Many mass nouns can be used with a kind or type interpretation, for example the mass noun *oil* used in *They manufacture two or three great oils*. Some count nouns, on the other hand, can in certain contexts be used as mass nouns, for example the count noun *banana* in *There's banana in this sandwich*. Finally, some nouns regularly occur with both mass and count senses, often in abstract and concrete versions, for example *light* in *There was a lot of light in the room* (mass) and *There were three lights in the room* (count). So rather than being strictly a property of items in the world the count/mass distinction is a way of conceptualizing items in order to refer to them through language. Such referential decisions are conventionalized within a speech community, so that for example *advice* is a mass noun in English but corresponds to a count noun in Spanish, *un consejo* "an advice, a piece of advice." We will see some attempts to set up semantic classes of nominals to reflect their features of reference in chapter 9.

Some nominals are tricky in their denotational behavior: for example the nominal *no student* in 2.22 below:

2.22 No student enjoyed the lecture.

where *no student* does not of course denote an individual who enjoyed the lecture. The meaning of this sentence can be paraphrased as in 2.23a, or in a logical framework we will investigate in chapter 10, as in 2.23b:

2.23 a. Of the students, not one enjoyed the lecture.
b. For each student x, x did not enjoy the lecture.

This complex denotational behavior is characteristic of **quantifiers**: a class of words that in English includes *each*, *all*, *every*, *some*, *none*, *no*. These allow a speaker, among other things, the flexibility to predicate something of a whole class of entities, or of some subpart, for example:

2.24 *Every Frenchman* would recognize his face.

2.25 *Some Frenchmen* voted for him twice.

2.26 *A few Frenchmen* voted for him.

Speakers can combine quantifiers with negative words to produce some subtle effects; for example, the sentence

2.27 Every American doesn't drink coffee.

which has an interpretation which is not "The class of Americans does not drink coffee" but rather "Not every American drinks coffee." We will look at some proposals for describing the use of quantifiers in chapter 10. Having taken this brief look at the referential properties of nominals, in the next section we take up the more general issue of the role of reference in a theory of meaning.

2.3 Reference as a Theory of Meaning

As we observed earlier, perhaps the simplest theory of meaning is to claim that semantics *is* reference, that is, to give the meaning of a word one shows what it denotes. In its simplest form this theory would claim that reference picks out elements in the real world. As described by Ruth Kempson (1977: 13) such an approach might claim the following:

2.28	proper names	denote	individuals
	common names	"	sets of individuals
	verbs	"	actions
	adjectives	"	properties of individuals
	adverbs	"	properties of actions

As she points out, there are a number of problems with this simplest version as a theory of semantics. Firstly it seems to predict that many words have no meaning, for, as we mentioned earlier, it is very difficult to find a real-world referent for words like *so*, *not*, *very*, *but*, *of*. A second problem is that many nominal expressions used by speakers do not have a referent that exists or has ever existed, as the elements in bold in 2.29–31 below:

2.29 In the painting **a unicorn** is ignoring a maiden.

2.30 **World War III** might be about to start.

2.31 **Father Christmas** might not visit you this year.

We would have to make the rather odd claim that expressions like *unicorn*, *World War III*, and *Father Christmas* are meaningless if meaning is taken to be a relation between words and items in the real world. If a speaker using these expressions is not referring to anything in reality, and such reference *is* meaning, how do sentences 2.29–31 have meaning? Since they clearly do, it seems that we must have a more sophisticated theory of meaning.

A further problem is that even when we are talking about things in the real world, there is not always a one-to-one correspondence between a linguistic expression and the item we want to identify. To take a simple example, we can refer to the same individual in different ways, as in:

2.32 Then in 1981 Anwar El Sadat was assassinated.

2.33 Then in 1981 the President of Egypt was assassinated.

In 2.32 and 2.33 the same individual is referred to by a **name**, Anwar El Sadat, and by a **definite description**, the President of Egypt. These two expressions would share the same referent but we probably want to say they have different meanings. If so, there is more to meaning than reference. One might object that names do not really have any meaning. This is often so in English, where we commonly use names derived from other languages like Hebrew, Greek, etc., but is not necessarily true of other cultures. Still, even if we allow this objection, the phenomenon is not restricted to names. You might refer to the woman who lives next door to you by various descriptions like *my neighbor*, *Pat's mother*, *Michael's wife*, *the Head of Science at St Helen's School*, etc. It seems clear that while these expressions might all refer to the same individual, they differ in meaning. Indeed it is possible to know that some nominal expressions refer to an individual but be ignorant of others that do. We might understand expressions like *the President of the United States* and *the Commander-in-chief of the United States Armed Forces* but not know that they both refer to the same person. This has traditionally been an issue in the philosophical literature where we can find similar but more complicated examples: the logician Gottlob Frege (1980) pointed out that a speaker might understand the expressions *the morning star* and *the evening star* and use them to refer to two apparently different celestial bodies without knowing that they both refer to sightings of Venus. For such a speaker, Frege noted, the following sentence would not be a tautology:

2.34 The morning star is the evening star.

and might have a very different meaning from the referentially equivalent sentence (but for our hypothetical speaker, much less informative):

2.35 Venus is Venus.

If we can understand and use expressions that do not have a real-world referent, and we can use different expressions to identify the same referent, and even use two expressions without being aware that they share the same referent, then it seems likely that meaning and reference are not exactly the same thing. Or to put it another way, there is more to meaning than reference. How should we characterize this extra dimension? One answer is to follow Frege in distinguishing two aspects of our semantic knowledge of an expression: its **sense** (Frege used the German word *Sinn*) and its **reference** (Frege's *Bedeutung*). In this division, sense is primary in that it allows reference: it is because we understand the expression *the President of Ireland* that we can use it to refer to a particular individual at any given time. Other ways of describing this same person will differ in sense but have the same reference.[3]

If we follow this line of argument, then our semantic theory is going to be more complicated than the simple referential theory: the meaning of an expression will arise both from its sense and its reference. In the next section, we discuss some suggestions of what this sense element may be like.

2.4 Mental Representations

2.4.1 Introduction

In the last section we concluded that although reference is an important function of language, the evidence suggests that there must be more to meaning than simply denotation. We adopted the convention of calling this extra dimension **sense**.[4] In the rest of this chapter we explore the view that sense places a new level between words and the world: a level of mental representation.[5] Thus, a noun is said to gain its ability to denote because it is associated with something in the speaker's/hearer's mind. This gets us out of the problem of insisting everything we talk about exists in reality, but it raises the question of what these mental representations are. One simple and very old idea is that these mental entities are images. Presumably the relationship between the mental representation (the image) and the real-world entity would then be one of resemblance; see Kempson (1977) for discussion. This might conceivably work for expressions like *Paris* or *your mother*; it might also work for imaginary entities like *Batman*. This theory however runs into serious problems with common nouns. This is because of the variation in images that different speakers might have of a common noun like *car* or *house* depending on their experience. One example often cited in the literature is of the word *triangle*: one speaker may have a mental image of an equilateral triangle, another's might be isosceles or scalene. It is difficult to conceive of an image which would combine the features shared by all triangles, just as it is difficult to have an image which corresponds to all cars or dogs. This is to ignore the difficulties of what kind of image one might have for words like *animal* or *food*; or worse *love*, *justice*, or *democracy*. So even if images are associated with some words, they cannot be the whole story.

The most usual modification of the image theory is to hypothesize that the sense of some words, while mental, is not visual but a more abstract element: a concept. This has the advantage that we can accept that a concept might be able to contain the non-visual features which make a dog a dog, democracy democracy, and so on. We might also feel confident about coming up with a propositional definition of a triangle, something corresponding to "three-sided polygon, classifiable by its angles or sides." Another advantage for linguists is that they might be able to pass on some of the labor of describing concepts to psychologists rather than have to do it all themselves. Some concepts might be simple and related to perceptual stimuli –like SUN,[6] WATER, and so on. Others will be complex concepts like MARRIAGE OF RETIREMENT which involve whole theories or cultural complexes.

This seems reasonable enough but the problem for many linguists is that psychologists are still very involved in investigating what concepts might be like. Unless we have a good idea of what a concept is, we are left with rather empty definitions like "the sense of the word *dog* is the concept DOG."

It is at this point that different groups of linguists part company. Some, like Kempson in the quotation below (1977: 16–17) have seemed skeptical of psychologists' success and do not see much point in basing a theory of meaning on reference, if reference is based on concepts:

2.36 What is involved in this claim that a word has as its meaning a "convenient capsule of thought" [Edward Sapir's definition of meaning]? If this is a retraction from an image theory of meaning, as it is, then it is a retraction from a specific, false claim to one that is entirely untestable and hence vacuous. It does no more than substitute for the problem term *meaning* the equally opaque term *concept*.

Kempson makes this point as part of an argument for a denotational semantics and in favor of modeling sense in a formal, rather than psychological way. Linguists who favor a representational approach have gone on to set up models of concepts to form the basis of semantics, throwing linguistic light onto a traditional line of research in cognitive psychology. There are a number of proposals for conceptual structure in the semantics literature; we shall look at some details of these later, especially in chapters 9 and 11. For now we can follow this representational line of inquiry and briefly examine some basic approaches from the psychological literature to the task of describing concepts.

2.4.2 Concepts

If we adopt the hypothesis that the meaning of, say, a noun is a combination of its denotation and a conceptual element, then from the point of view of a linguist, two basic questions about the conceptual element are:

1. What form can we assign to concepts?
2. How do children acquire them, along with their linguistic labels?

We can look at some answers to these questions. In our discussion we will concentrate on concepts that correspond to a single word, that is, they are **lexicalized**. Of course not all concepts are like this: some concepts are described by phrases, as with the underlined concept in 2.37 below:

2.37 On the shopping channel, I saw a tool for compacting dead leaves into garden statuary.

We can speculate that the reason why some concepts are lexicalized and others not is **utility**. If we refer to something enough it will become lexicalized. Possibly somebody once said something like 2.38 below:

2.38 We're designing a device for cooking food by microwaves.

describing something that for a while was given the two-word label *microwave oven*, but is now usually called just a *microwave*. Presumably if every home ends up having a tool to turn leaves into statues, a name for it will be invented and catch on. We see this process happening all the time of course as new concepts are invented and new words or new senses of old words given to them. An example of such a recent introduction is *selfie*, a self-portrait photograph, a notion brought to prominence by the ubiquity of *smartphones*, the latter itself a relatively new word in English. For the rest of this chapter we deal only with such lexicalized concepts.

When we talk of children acquiring concepts we have to recognize that their concepts may differ from the concepts of adults. Work in developmental psychology has shown that children may operate with concepts that are quite different: students of child language describe children both **underextending** concepts, as when for a child *dog* can only be used for their pet, not the one next door; and **overextending** concepts, where a child uses *daddy* for every male adult, or *cat* for cats, rabbits, and other pets. Or the concepts may be just different, reflecting the fact that items in a child's world may have different salience than for an adult. See Mervis (1987), Keil (1989), and Markman (1989) for discussion of the relationship between child and adult categorization.

2.4.3 Necessary and sufficient conditions

One traditional approach to describing concepts is to define them by using sets of **necessary and sufficient conditions**. This approach comes from thinking about concepts as follows. If we have a concept like WOMAN, it must contain the information necessary to decide when something in the world is a woman or not. How can this information be organized? Perhaps as a set of characteristics or attributes, that is:

2.39 *x* is a woman if and only if *L*.

where *L* is a list of attributes, like:

2.40 *x* is human;
x is adult;
x is female, etc.

One can see these attributes as conditions: if something must have them to be a woman, then they can be called necessary conditions. In addition, if we can find the right set, so that just that set is enough to define a woman, then they can be called sufficient conditions, that is, we have identified the right amount of information for the concept.

So this theory views concepts as lists of bits of knowledge: the necessary and sufficient conditions for something to be an example of that concept. One major problem with this approach has been that it seems to assume that if speakers share the same concept they will agree on the necessary and sufficient conditions: if something has them, it is an X; if not, it is not. But it has proved difficult to set these up even for nouns which identify concrete and natural kinds like *dog* or *cat*. Let us take as an example the noun *zebra*. We might agree on some attributes:

2.41 is an animal,
has four legs,
is striped,
is a herbivore, etc.

The problem we face though is: which of these is necessary? The first obviously; but the rest are more problematic. If we find in a herd of zebra, one that is pure white or black, we might still want to call it a zebra. Or if by some birth defect, a three-legged zebra came into the world, it would still be a zebra. Similarly, if a single zebra got bored with a grass diet and started to include a few insects, would it cease to be a zebra? These, you might think, are rather whimsical questions, perhaps problems for philosophers rather than linguists, and indeed this zebra example is just a version of Saul Kripke's example about tigers (Kripke 1980: 119–21), or Putnam's fantasy about cats (Putnam 1962). If we suddenly discovered that cats had always been automata rather than animals, would the meaning of the word *cat* be different? Questions such as these have important consequences for our ideas about concepts: if we cannot establish a mutual definition of a concept, how can we use its linguistic label?

Another argument against necessary and sufficient conditions as the basis for linguistic concepts is Putnam's (1975) observations about ignorance. Speakers often use words to refer despite knowing very little, and sometimes nothing, about the identifying characteristics of the referent. Putnam's examples include the tree names *beech* and *elm*: like Putnam, many English speakers cannot distinguish between these two trees yet use the words regularly. Such a speaker would presumably be understood, and be speaking truthfully, if she said:

2.42 In the 1970s Dutch elm disease killed a huge number of British elms.

Perhaps as Putnam suggests, we rely on a belief that somewhere there are experts who do have such knowledge and can tell the difference between different species of tree. In any case it seems, as with other natural kind terms like *gold* or *platinum*, we can use the words without knowing very much about the referent. It seems unlikely then that a word is referring to a concept composed of a set of necessary and sufficient conditions, or what amounts to the same thing, a **definition**. This approach is often termed the **definitional theory** of concepts.

This is reminiscent of our earlier discussion of the use of names. There we saw that one of the advantages claimed for the causal theory of names over the description theory is that it allows for speaker ignorance: we can use a name for a person or place knowing little or nothing about the referent. This parallel is overtly recognized by writers such as Putnam (1975) and Kripke (1980), who have proposed that the causal theory be extended to natural kind terms. The idea is that natural kind terms, like names, are originally fixed by contact with examples of the kind. Thereafter, speakers may receive or borrow the word without being exposed to the real thing, or knowing very much about its characteristics. As we have seen, philosophers like to use examples of metals like gold or silver. Any inability to identify correctly or define the substance silver does not prevent one from using the word *silver*. We assume that someone once had the ability or need to recognize the individual metal and that somewhere there are experts who can identify it empirically. The latter is Putnam's "division of labor" in a speech community: between "expert" and "folk" uses of a term. Only the expert or scientific uses of a word would ever be rigorous enough to support necessary and sufficient conditions, but speakers happily go on using the word.

2.4.4 Prototypes

Because of problems with necessary and sufficient conditions, or definitions, several more sophisticated theories of concepts have been proposed. One influential proposal is due to Eleanor Rosch and her co-workers (e.g. Rosch 1973, 1975, Rosch and Mervis 1975, Rosch et al. 1976, Mervis and Rosch 1981) who have suggested the notion of **prototypes**. This is a model of concepts which views them as structured so that there are central or typical members of a category, such as BIRD or FURNITURE, but then a shading off into less typical or peripheral members. So *chair* is a more central member of the category FURNITURE than *lamp*, for example. Or *sparrow* a more typical member of the category BIRD than *penguin*. This approach seems to have been supported by Rosch's experimental evidence: speakers tend to agree more readily on typical members than on less typical members; they come to mind more quickly, and so on. Another result of this and similar work (e.g. Labov 1973) is that the boundaries between concepts can seem to speakers uncertain, or "fuzzy," rather than clearly defined.

This approach allows for borderline uncertainty: an item in the world might bear some resemblance to two different prototypes. Here we might recall our hypothetical example in chapter 1 of an English speaker being able to use the word *whale* yet being unsure about whether a whale is a mammal or a fish. In the prototype theory of concepts, this might be explained by the fact that whales are not typical of the category MAMMAL, being far from the central prototype. At the same time, whales resemble prototypical fish in some characteristic features: they live underwater in the oceans, have fins, and so on.

There are a number of interpretations of these typicality effects in the psychology literature: some researchers for example have argued that the central prototype is an abstraction. This abstraction might be a set of **characteristic features**, to which we compare real items; see Smith and Medin (1981) for discussion. These characteristic features of BIRD might describe a kind of average bird, small perhaps, with wings, feathers, the ability to fly, and so on, but of no particular species. Other researchers have proposed that we organize our categories by **exemplars**, memories of actual typical birds, say sparrows, pigeons and hawks, and we compute the likelihood of something we meet being a bird on the basis of comparison with these memories of real birds. An overview of this area of investigation is given by Medin and Ross (1992).

There is another approach to typicality effects from within linguistics, which is interesting because of the light it sheds on the relationship between linguistic knowledge and encyclopedic knowledge, a topic we discussed in chapter 1. Charles Fillmore (1982) and George Lakoff (1987) both make similar claims that speakers have folk theories about the world, based on their experience and rooted in their culture. These theories are called **frames** by Fillmore and **idealized cognitive models** (ICMs) by Lakoff.[7] They are not scientific theories or logically consistent definitions, but collections of cultural views. Fillmore gives an example of how these folk theories might work by using the word *bachelor*. It is clear that some bachelors are more prototypical than others, with the Pope, for example, being far from prototypical. Fillmore, and Lakoff in his discussion of the same point (1987: 68–71), suggest that there is a division of our knowledge about the word *bachelor*: part is a **dictionary**-type definition (perhaps simply "an unmarried man") and part is an **encyclopedia**-type entry of cultural knowledge about bachelorhood and marriage – the frame or ICM. The first we can call linguistic or semantic knowledge and the second real-world or general knowledge. Their point is we only apply the word *bachelor* within a typical marriage ICM: a monogamous union between eligible people, typically involving romantic love, and so on. It is this idealized model, a form of general knowledge, which governs our use of the word *bachelor* and restrains us from applying it to celibate priests, or people living in isolation like Robinson Crusoe on his island or Tarzan living among apes in the jungle. In this view then using a word involves combining semantic knowledge and encyclopedic knowledge, and this interaction may result in typicality effects.

Prototype theory,[8] frame, and ICMs are just a few of the large number of proposals for conceptual structure. We will look at some suggestions from the specifically linguistics literature in later chapters.

2.4.5 Relations between concepts

One important issue that our discussion has bypassed so far is the **relational** nature of conceptual knowledge. We will see in chapter 3 that words are in a network of semantic links with other words and it is reasonable to assume that conceptual structures are similarly linked. Thus if all you know about *peccary* is that it is a kind of wild pig and of *pecorino* that it is a kind of Italian cheese, then your knowledge of these concepts "inherits" knowledge you have about pigs and cheese. This has implications for our earlier discussion of how much knowledge a speaker has to have in order to use a word. It suggests that the crucial element is not the amount of knowledge but its integration into existing knowledge. Thus, knowing that a peccary is a kind of pig, together with what you know about pigs, is perhaps enough to begin to understand the meaning of sentences containing the word, and thereby to start to gain extra knowledge about the concept.

Such relations between concepts have been used to motivate models of **conceptual hierarchies** in the cognitive psychology literature. Research has shown the importance of such hierarchies in reasoning and learning, for example Gelman and Markman (1986), Osherson et al. (1990), Coley et al. (2004), Shafto et al. (2008). In a conceptual hierarchy for living things the concept BIRD, for example, will have such attributes as *has wings*, *can fly*, *has feathers*, *lays eggs*, *has a beak*. It does not have to specify attributes such as *living organism*, *has senses*, because it will inherit these from a higher concept in the hierarchy, ANIMAL. Concepts lower in the hierarchy such as ROBIN and EAGLE need not specify any of these attributes. The concept PENGUIN however will specify *cannot fly*. Such hierarchical conceptual structure allows individuals to perceive entities as examples of types and to make predictions about their nature and behavior without direct observation.

If the attributes in this model are taken to be the equivalent of the necessary and sufficient conditions we discussed earlier then it suffers from the disadvantages of that approach. Proponents of prototype theory, for example Rosch et al. (1976), have also investigated conceptual hierarchies and have proposed that such hierarchies contain three levels of generality: a superordinate level, a basic level, and a subordinate level. The idea is that the levels differ in their balance between informativeness and usefulness. If we take one of Rosch et al.'s (1976) examples, that of furniture, the superordinate level is FURNITURE, which has relatively few characteristic features; the basic level would include concepts like CHAIR, which has more features, and the subordinate level would include concepts like ARMCHAIR, DINING CHAIR, and so on, which have still more features and are thus more specific again. The basic level is identified as cognitively important: it is the level that is most used in everyday life; it is acquired first by children; in experiments it is the level at which adults spontaneously name objects; such objects are recognized more quickly in tests; and so on.

This model has proved to be very robust in the psychological literature, though the simple picture we have presented here needs some modifications. It seems that the relationship between the basic level and the intermediate term might vary somewhat from domain to domain: man-made categories like FURNITURE differ somewhat from natural kind terms, and the relationship may vary depending on the person's experience of the categories. So a person's expert knowledge of a domain might influence the relationship between the basic and subordinate levels. See for example Tanaka and Taylor (1991) for a study suggesting that experts on dogs and birds might have a different, richer structure at subordinate levels for these categories from the average person.

2.4.6 Acquiring concepts

Our second basic issue was: how do we acquire concepts? One simple and intuitively satisfying theory is that we do it by **ostensive definition**. This is the idea that children (and adults) acquire concepts by being directed to examples in the world. So if you are walking with a child and you see a dog, you say *That's a dog* or *Look at the doggie!* and the child begins to acquire the concept DOG, which is filled out by subsequent experience of dogs.

This common-sense picture cannot be the whole story, however. The philosopher W. V. O. Quine has pointed out that ostension (defining by example) is usually couched in language. Quine's (1960) famous example is of walking with someone whose language you do not know who, when a rabbit runs past, says *Gavagai*. You do not know whether it is a warning or an instruction, or what the content might be: "They are a menace," "They are good to eat," "Wow, that scared me," and so on. To understand that you are being given a name you need to know something about the language that the ostension takes place in. So in English, a sentence frame like "*It's a*" tells you this. Similarly, you cannot even tell what is being pointed to without some linguistic support: is it the whole rabbit, its tail, or the way it is running? The point is that even ostensive definition depends on prior knowledge of some word meanings. Where, we may ask, do these come from? Are we forced to admit that we may be born with certain basic concepts innately within us? See J. A. Fodor (1975, 1980, 1981b) and Samet and Flanagan (1989) for discussion of these ideas. Once again, we will not try to deal with these issues in detail here; we can merely point out that the acquisition of concepts must be a more complicated process than simple ostension.

Our discussion in this section has focused on the relationship between words and concepts; in the next section we discuss the relationship between words and thinking in general.

2.5 Words, Concepts, and Thinking

In our discussion so far, we have assumed a straightforward association between words and concepts: that is, that a speaker has a store of lexicalized concepts which is of course smaller than the larger set that she is capable of thinking about or talking about, using phrases or sentences. There are though a number of positions that can be taken on the issue of the relationship between these lexicalized concepts and general thinking and reasoning. In this section we discuss two opposing views: the first, **linguistic relativity**, is that lexicalized concepts impose restrictions on possible ways of thinking; the second, the **language of thought** hypothesis, maintains that thinking and speaking, while obviously related, involve distinct levels of representation. There are strong and weak versions of both of these positions, but we will for clarity outline fairly strong versions.

2.5.1 Linguistic relativity

The notion of **linguistic relativity**, associated with Edward Sapir and Benjamin Lee Whorf, is an idea that has spread far outside the fields of anthropology and linguistics where it began. One reason perhaps is that it provides an explanation for a common experience when dealing with different languages. Writers translating between languages have often remarked on the lack of fit between words in two languages. For example, color words might not have exactly the same range: does French *pourpre* describe the same range as English *purple*?[9] Similarly, while the English verbs for putting on clothes (*put on*, *don*, etc.) make no distinction about the part of the body the clothing goes on, other languages like Japanese (as discussed by E. V. Clark 1983) and Korean (Choi and Bowerman 1992) have separate verbs for putting clothes on various parts of the body. It seems obvious too that words for social institutions and customs will vary between cultures. There is no easy translation in English for the Somali verb *maddooyeyso*, except the approximation: "to play the children's game called *maddooyamaddooyo*, where an object is hidden in the hand and a special kind of rhyme is recited."

The fact that language mirrors cultural differences became an important issue in the school of American anthropological linguistics which followed the work of the distinguished anthropologist Franz Boas. In one line of thought this idea of language as a mirror of culture developed into a much stronger idea: that people's thoughts are *determined* by the categories available to them in their language. We can follow this line of development, starting with the following famous quotation where we find Boas suggesting that different languages, reflecting their speakers' cultural practices, might embody different conceptual classifications of the world:

2.43 As an example of the manner in which terms that we express by independent words are grouped together under one concept, the Dakota language may be selected. The terms *naxta'ka* TO KICK, *paxta'ka* TO BIND IN BUNDLES, *yaxta'ka* TO BITE, *ic'a'xtaka* TO BE NEAR TO, *boxta'ka* TO POUND, are all derived from the common element *xtaka* TO GRIP, which holds them together, while we use distinct words for expressing the various ideas.

It seems fairly evident that the selection of such simple terms must to a certain extent depend upon the chief interests of a people; and where it is necessary to distinguish a certain phenomenon in many aspects, which in the life of the people play each an entirely independent role, many independent words may develop, while in other cases modifications of a single term may suffice.

Thus it happens that each language, from the point of view of another language, may be arbitrary in its classifications; that what appears as a single simple idea in one language may be characterized by a series of distinct phonetic groups in another. (Boas 1966: 22)

Boas observed that the effect of this was largely unconscious because the use of language is mostly an automatic process which we do not normally pause to reflect on.

These observations open the debate in this literature about the relationship between language, culture and thought. To what extent does the particular language we speak determine the way that we think about the world? Perhaps Boas's most famous student is the anthropologist and linguist Edward Sapir; in the following quotation, we see him proposing the view that the particular language we speak conditions our conceptualization of the world:

2.44 Language is a guide to "social reality"... Human beings do not live in the objective world alone, nor alone in the world of social activity as ordinarily understood, but are very much at the mercy of the particular language which has become the medium of expression for their society... the "real world" is to a large extent unconsciously built up on the language habits of the group. No two languages are ever sufficiently similar to be considered as representing the same social reality. The worlds in which different societies live are distinct worlds, not merely the same world with different labels attached...

We see and hear and otherwise experience very largely as we do because the language habits of our community predispose certain choices of interpretation... From this standpoint we may think of language as the *symbolic guide* to culture. (Sapir 1949: 162)

It seems fair to say that Sapir had a stronger view of the determining role of language than Boas. Stronger still are the views of Benjamin Lee Whorf, a linguist well known for his work on native American languages, especially the Uto-Aztecan languages of the south west United States and Mexico. Whorf strengthened this idea of the link between language and thought into the notion he called **linguistic relativity**. Its basic premise is that the way we think about the world is determined by our cultural and linguistic background:

2.45 We cut nature up, organize it into concepts, and ascribe significances as we do, largely because we are parties to an agreement to organize it in this way – an agreement that holds through our speech community and is codified in the patterns of our language. The agreement is, of course, an implicit and unstated one, BUT ITS TERMS ARE ABSOLUTELY OBLIGATORY; we cannot talk at all except by subscribing to the organization and classification of data which the agreement decrees. (Whorf 1956: 213–14)

Whorf's observation is not restricted to word meaning; indeed, he believed that meanings derived from grammatical systems (e.g. notions of number and space in nouns, or aspect and tense in verbs)[10] were even stronger determinants of thought. The idea is that speakers can reflect on word meanings but grammatical systems are largely unavailable to conscious reflection.

If this view is correct then our own language predisposes us to see both reality and other languages through its own filter. This would have serious implications for the prospects of a universal semantic theory. It might mean that we could always, with some difficulty and inexactitude, translate from one language to another. But if speaking different languages means that we think in different ways, how could we ever step outside our own language to set up a neutral metalanguage which does not privilege any particular language or language family? Such metalanguages are of course the basis for theories in other areas of linguistics like syntax or phonology.

2.5.2 The language of thought hypothesis

The idea of linguistic relativity is rejected by many linguists and researchers in **cognitive science**, the interdisciplinary study of intelligence which draws on cognitive psychology, computer science, and linguistics. A typical response is to dismiss as a fallacy such a strict identification of thought and language. We can identify two main types of argument used to support this view. The first is that there is evidence of thinking without language; and the second is that linguistic analysis has shown us that language underspecifies meaning. We can look briefly at these two types of argument. A succinct presentation of the first type of argument is given by Pinker (1994, 59ff.), who presents various kinds of evidence that thinking and language are not the same thing. He gives examples of evidence of thought processes, such as remembering and reasoning, which have been identified in psychological studies of human babies and of primates, both providing examples of creatures without language. He also recounts the various reports of artists and scientists who claim that their creativity sometimes derives from ideas which are non-linguistic images. There is also evidence from psychological experiments of visual thinking: subjects seem able to manipulate images mentally, rotating them, scanning them, zooming in and out, and so on, exhibiting a variety of mental processes which do not seem to involve language. Finally Pinker casts doubt on the various attempts in psychological experiments to suggest that people from different linguistic communities perform reasoning or other cognitive tasks in any very different ways.[11]

Such evidence for mental processes not involving language is often used to argue that cognitive processes do not employ a spoken language like English or Arabic but make use of a separate computational system in the mind: a **language of thought**. For a philosophical defense of this position see for example Fodor (1975, 1987, 2008) and Fodor and Pylyshyn (1988). Stillings et al. (1995) provide a range of evidence from psychological experiments to support the same view. The basic idea is that memory and processes such as reasoning seem to make use of a kind of propositional representation that does not have the surface syntax of a spoken language like English.

Turning to the second type of argument – that language underspecifies meaning – some indirect support for this position emerges from the characteristic view of the communication of meaning that has emerged from research in semantics and pragmatics, as we shall see in the course of this book. It has become clear that meaning is richer than language at both ends, so to speak, of the communication process. Speakers compress their thoughts, and often imply rather than state explicitly what they mean, while hearers fill out their own version of the intended meaning from the language presented to them. This idea, that language underspecifies meaning and has to be enriched by hearers, would seem to fit naturally with the idea that speakers are putting their thoughts into language, that is translating into the spoken language, rather than simply voicing their thoughts directly. This does not of course provide direct evidence for this view: we could equally imagine English speakers thinking in English and still compressing their thoughts when speaking, on some grounds of economy and social cooperation.

Nonetheless these different types of argument are often taken, especially in cognitive science, to support the view that we think in a language of thought, sometimes called **Mentalese**. When we want to speak, we translate from Mentalese into our spoken language, be it Mohawk or Russian. One natural extension of this view is the proposal that everybody's Mentalese is roughly the same, that is, that the language of thought is universal. Thus we arrive at a position diametrically opposed to linguistic relativity: human beings have essentially the same cognitive architecture and mental processes, even though they speak different languages.[12]

2.5.3 Thought and reality

If we leave this question of the relation between words and thinking for the time being, we might ask whether semanticists must also consider questions of the relationship between thought and reality. We can ask: must we as aspiring semanticists adopt for ourselves a position on traditional questions of **ontology**, the branch of philosophy that deals with the nature of being and the structure of reality, and **epistemology**, the branch of philosophy concerned with the nature of knowledge? For example, do we believe that reality exists independently of the workings of human minds? If not, we are adherents of **idealism**. If we do believe in an independent reality, can we perceive the world as it really is? One response is to say yes. We might assert that knowledge of reality is attainable and comes from correctly conceptualizing and categorizing the world. We could call this position **objectivism**. On the other hand we might believe that we can never perceive the world as it really is: that reality is only graspable through the conceptual filters derived from our biological and cultural evolution. We could explain the fact that we successfully interact with reality (run away from lions, shrink from fire, etc.) because of a notion of ecological viability. Crudely: that those with very inefficient conceptual systems (not afraid of lions or fire) died out and weren't our ancestors. We could call this position **mental constructivism**: we can't get to a God's-eye view of reality because of the way we are made. These are of course very crude characterizations of difficult philosophical issues. By now any philosophers chancing on this text will have thrown it into the back of their own fire. But the relevance of these issues to semantics is that, as we shall see in later chapters, different theories of semantics often presuppose different answers to these very basic questions.

Still, for the linguist keen to describe the semantics of Swahili or English these are a heavy set of issues to deal with before getting on with the job, especially when added to the complex issues of conceptual representation that we discussed a little earlier. One understandable response is to decide that only language is the proper object of study for linguists and issues of mental representations and the existence of reality are best left to psychologists and philosophers. See for example the following comment by Charles Hockett:

2.46 We can leave to philosophers the argument whether the abstract relationships themselves have any sort of existence in the world outside of speech. Whatever they may decide, it is clear that the "meaning" of a word like *and* or *the*... is a very different thing from the meaning of a word like *morning* or *sunbeam*. (Hockett 1958: 263) and we can see a similar sentiment in John Lyons's (1968) discussion of semantics:

2.47 the view that semantics is, or ought to be, an empirical science, which as far as possible avoids commitment with respect to such philosophical and psychological disputes as the distinction of "body" and "mind" and the status of "concepts." This view will be accepted in the discussion of semantics given in this chapter. It should be stressed, however, that the methodological renunciation of "mentalism" does not imply the acceptance of "mechanism," as some linguists have suggested... The position that should be maintained by the linguist is one that is neutral with respect to "mentalism" and "mechanism"; a position that is consistent with both and implies neither. (1968: 408)

Thus some linguists have decided to leave the philosophical high ground to other disciplines, to put aside discussion of the reality of the world, and the nature of our mental representations of it, and to concentrate instead on the meaning relations between expressions within a language, or to try to compare meanings across languages. As we will see, this turning inward toward language, a position we could call **linguistic solipsism,**[13] leads to an interest in describing semantic relations like **ambiguity, synonymy, contradiction, antonymy**, and so on, which we will look at in chapter 3. The decision is that it is more the task of linguists to describe, for example, how the meaning of the word *dog* is related to the words *animal* or *bitch*, than to discuss what the mental concept of DOG might look like, or how this relates to the real dogs running around in the world.

2.6 Summary

In this chapter we have seen that though it seems true that through language we can identify or refer to real-world entities, it is difficult to use reference as the whole of a theory of meaning. We have seen that our semantic knowledge seems to include both **reference** and **sense**. We have seen that there are two different approaches to our ability to talk about the world: a **denotational** approach which emphasizes the links between language and external reality; and a **representational** approach which emphasizes the link between language and conceptual structure. Each approach has to answer certain key questions. For example, how do denotational approaches cope with our ability to talk about imaginary or hypothetical entities? Of representational approaches we might ask: do we need to establish a theory of conceptual structure in order to describe meaning? In this chapter we have seen some aspects of such a task.

These issues of the relationship between language, thought and reality have typically led linguists to adopt one of three positions:

1. to leave these issues to philosophers and psychologists and decide that linguists should concentrate on **sense relations** within a language, or between languages;
2. to decide that meaning *is* essentially denotation and try to develop a theory to cope with the various types of reference we looked at earlier in 2.4, including the ability to talk about imagined situations;

3. to decide that meaning *does* rely on a theory of conceptual structure and go on to try to determine the nature of linguistic concepts.

We will see examples of each of these approaches in this book. The first is characteristic of traditional semantics and especially of lexical semantics, with its concentration on semantic relations like ambiguity, synonymy, and so on. We turn to these topics in chapter 3. The second approach, beefing up denotational theories to cope with the referential characteristics of different linguistic categories and the problems of mental entities, is characteristic of **formal semantics**, as we will describe in chapter 10. The third approach is characteristic of much recent work, as in Jackendoff's (2002) **conceptual semantics**, described in chapter 9, or **cognitive semantics**, which we turn to in chapter 11. Before we look in detail at these theories, in Part II of this book we identify key areas of semantic description that any theory must come to terms with.

EXERCISES

2.1 Imagine the sentences below being spoken. Decide, for each of the nominal expressions in bold, whether the speaker would be using the nominal to **refer**.

a. We waited for twelve hours at **Nairobi airport**.
b. They had **no food**.
c. Edward opened the cupboard and **a pair of shoes** fell out.
d. Henry is going to make **a cake**.
e. Doris passed through the office like **a whirlwind**.
f. He was run over by **a bus** in Donnybrook.
g. What we need is **an army of volunteers**.

2.2 Try to devise alternative descriptions for the **referents** of the nominals in bold below:

a. The Senator paid a visit to **the Ukrainian capital**.
b. **The British Prime Minister** refused to comment.
c. They arrived on **Christmas Day**.
d. Craig took a bus to **Washington, DC**.
e. He had reached the summit of **the tallest mountain in the world**.

2.3 In section 2.2.3 we noted the grammatical differences between **mass** and **count** nouns in English. Using these, decide whether the nouns below are basically mass nouns (with possible count uses as described earlier), count nouns, or words that can occur equally as both. Note that it helps to use the nouns in example sentences.

table, milk, dog, difficulty, weather, hand, warmth, talk, word, blood

2.4 We discussed the traditional proposal that a concept can be defined by a set of **necessary and sufficient conditions**, where the right set of attributes might define a concept exactly. If words are labels for concepts these attributes might also define word meaning. Lehrer (1974) discusses the definitions of words associated with cooking. Some of her examples are in the two groups below. For each word try to establish sets of attributes that would distinguish it from its companions in the group.

a.	cake	biscuit/cookie	bread	roll	bun	cracker	
b.	boil	fry	bake	sauté	simmer	grill	roast

2.5 We discussed the **prototype** theory of concepts. Assume that each of the following is a label for a concept and suggest a list of **characteristic attributes** for the concept's prototype. Discuss some actual examples of members of the category and assess them for typicality.

a. FRUIT
b. MAMMAL
c. FOOD
d. TOY
e. SPORT

FURTHER READING

Devitt and Sterelny (1987) is an accessible overview of philosophical approaches to reference. Lycan (2008) provides an accessible introduction to the philosophy of language that includes the topics in this chapter. For an accessible introduction to Frege's distinction between sense and reference and its place in his philosophy see Kenny (1995). Stillings et al. (1995) review the issue of mental representations from the perspective of **cognitive science**, the name used for an interdisciplinary approach to mental representations and processes, drawing on research in cognitive psychology, computer science, philosophy of mind, and linguistics. Taylor (2003) is a comprehensive discussion of the implications of prototype theory for linguistics. Eysenck and Keane (2010) give an introduction to cognitive psychology which includes discussion of the nature of concepts. Murphy (2002) provides an overview of psychological research on concepts. An interesting collection of papers on the linguistic relativity hypothesis is Gumperz and Levinson (1996), which has useful introductory sections.

NOTES

1 In chapter 10, Formal Semantics, we outline a Fregean-style denotational semantics, where nouns denote entities, predicates denote sets of entities, and sentences denote a truth-value, a true or false match with a situation.
2 For a comprehensive survey on the topics of naming and reference see Abbott (2010).

3 See the articles in Frege (1980) for discussion.

4 In cognitive psychology and formal semantics a term **intension** is used for a similar notion. In this usage the intension of a concept or a word is the set of criteria for identifying the concept together with the properties that relate it to other concepts.

5 Note that this implies that the sense of a word is a conceptual representation in an individual's mind. This is somewhat different from Frege's emphasis on sense as a means of determining reference that is objective, public, and independent of any one individual mind. See Kenny (1995) for a brief discussion and Dummett (1981) for a detailed exposition.

6 Since in this section we will be talking about words, concepts, and things in the world, and the relation between them, we will adopt a typographical convention to help us keep them apart: words will be in italics (*dog*); concepts in small capitals (DOG); and things in the world in plain type (dog).

7 These proposals are similar to a number of suggestions within cognitive science for representing knowledge: an example is Minsky's (1977) frames. See Stillings et al. (1995) for an overview of such proposals. The idea that concepts are based on knowledge and theories about the world has been discussed in psychology by several writers, for example Murphy and Medin (1985), and Keil (1987).

8 See Taylor (2003) for a detailed discussion of prototype theory and a suggestion that this structure is not limited to word meaning but is characteristic of all linguistic categories, even in syntax and phonology.

9 We discuss the comparison of color words in different languages in 3.7 later.

10 We will discuss these notions of tense, aspect, etc. in later chapters.

11 Such a study is Kay and Kempton's (1984) experiment comparing speakers of English and Tarahumara (a Uto-Aztecan language of Mexico) and their abilities to sort and compare colored chips in color ranges where the two languages differ.

12 This view also fits in well with the influential hypothesis of the **modularity of mind**: i.e. that there are separate and self-contained faculties of mind, of which language is one. In this view, these faculties function independently from one another and from general cognition; they are dedicated to only one kind of input (e.g. language; facial recognition); and they are not under conscious control. See J. A. Fodor (1983) for discussion.

13 Here we are borrowing and adapting Putnam's (1975) term **methodological solipsism**, as discussed in Fodor (1981a). Putnam applies the term to psychological research: here we use the term **linguistic solipsism** to describe a decision to focus on language-internal issues, ignoring the connections to thought and/or to the world.

REFERENCES

Abbott, Barbara 2010: *Reference*. Oxford: Oxford University Press.

Boas, Franz 1966: *Introduction to the Handbook of American Indian Languages*, vol. 1. Washington, DC: Smithsonian Institution. (First published 1911.)

Choi, Soonja and Melissa Bowerman 1992: Learning to express motion events in English and Korean: the influence of language-specific lexicalization patterns. In Beth Levin and Steven Pinker (eds.) *Lexical and Conceptual Semantics*, 83–121. Oxford: Blackwell.

Churchland, Paul 1985: Conceptual progress and word/world relations: in search of the essence of natural kinds. *Canadian Journal of Philosophy* 15: 1, 1–17.

Clark, Eve V. 1983: Meanings and concepts. In John H. Flavell and Ellen M. Markman (eds.) *Cognitive Development*, 787–840. Vol. 3 of Paul H. Mussen (ed.) *Handbook of Child Psychology*, fourth edition. New York: John Wiley & Sons, Inc.

Coley, John D., Brett Hayes, Christopher Lawson and Michelle Moloney 2004: Knowledge, expectations, and inductive reasoning within conceptual hierarchies. *Cognition* 90.3: 217–53.

Devitt, Michael and Kim Sterelny 1987: *Language and Reality: An Introduction to the Philosophy of Language*. Oxford: Blackwell.
Donnellan, Keith S. 1972: Proper names and identifying descriptions. In Donald Davidson and Gilbert Harmon (eds.) *Semantics of Natural Language*, 356–79. Dordrecht: Reidel.
Dummett, Michael 1981: *Frege: Philosophy of Language*, second edition. London: Duckworth.
Eysenck, Michael W. and Mark T. Keane 2010: *Cognitive Psychology: A Student's Handbook*, sixth edition. Hove: Psychology Press.
Fillmore, Charles J. 1982: Frame semantics. In Linguistic Society of Korea (ed.), *Linguistics in the Morning Calm*, 111–38. Seoul: Hanshin.
Fodor, Jerry A. 1975: *The Language of Thought*. New York: Thomas Crowell.
Fodor, Jerry A. 1980: Fixation of belief and concept acquisition. In Massimo Piatelli-Palmarini (ed.) *Language and Learning*, 143–49. Cambridge, MA: Harvard University Press.
Fodor, Jerry A. 1981a: Methodological solipsism considered as a research strategy. In Jerry A. Fodor *Representations: Philosophical Essays on the Foundations of Cognitive Science*, 225–53. Cambridge, MA: MIT Press/Bradford Books.
Fodor, Jerry A. 1981b: The present status of the innateness controversy. In J. A. Fodor *Representations: Philosophical Essays on the Foundations of Cognitive Science*, 257–316. Cambridge, MA: MIT Press/Bradford Books.
Fodor, Jerry A. 1983: *The Modularity of Mind*. Cambridge, MA: MIT Press.
Fodor, Jerry A. 1987: *Psychosemantics: The Problem of Meaning in the Philosophy of Mind*. Cambridge, MA: MIT Press.
Fodor, Jerry A. 2008: *LOT 2: The Language of Thought Revisited*. Oxford: Oxford University Press.
Fodor, Jerry A. and Zenon W. Pylyshyn 1988: Connectionism and cognitive architecture: a critical analysis. *Cognition* 28: 3–71.
Frege, Gottlob 1980: *Translations from the Philosophical Writings of Gottlob Frege*, edited by Peter Geach and Max Black. Oxford: Blackwell.
Gelman, Susan A. and Ellen M. Markman 1986: Categories and induction in young children. *Cognition* 23.3: 183–209.
Gumperz, John J. and Stephen C. Levinson (eds.) 1996: *Rethinking Linguistic Relativity*. Cambridge: Cambridge University Press.
Hockett, Charles F. 1958: *A Course in Modern Linguistics*. New York: Macmillan.
Jackendoff, Ray 2002: *Semantic Structures*. Cambridge, MA: MIT Press.
Kay, Paul and Willett Kempton 1984: What is the Sapir-Whorf hypothesis? *American Anthropologist* 86.1: 65–79.
Keil, Frank C. 1987: Conceptual development and category structure. In Ulric Neisser (ed.) *Concepts Reconsidered: The Ecological and Intellectual Bases of Categorization*, 175–200. Cambridge: Cambridge University Press.
Keil, Frank C. 1989: *Concepts, Kinds and Conceptual Development*. Cambridge, MA: MIT Press.
Kempson, Ruth M. 1977: *Semantic Theory*. Cambridge: Cambridge University Press.
Kenny, Anthony 1995: *Frege*. London: Penguin Books.
Kripke, Saul 1980: *Naming and Necessity*. Oxford: Blackwell.
Labov, William 1973: The boundaries of words and their meanings. In Charles-James N. Bailey and Roger W. Shuy (eds.) *New Ways of Analyzing Variation in English*, 340–73. Washington, DC: Georgetown University Press.
Lakoff, George 1987: *Women, Fire, and Dangerous Things: What Categories Reveal about the Mind*. Chicago: University of Chicago Press.
Lehrer, Adrienne 1974: *Semantic Fields and Lexical Structure*. Amsterdam: North-Holland.
Lycan, William G. 2008: *Philosophy of Language: A Contemporary Introduction*. London: Routledge.

Lyons, John 1968: *Introduction to Theoretical Linguistics*. Cambridge: Cambridge University Press.
Lyons, John 1977: *Semantics*, 2 vols. Cambridge: Cambridge University Press.
Markman, Ellen M. 1989: *Categorization and Naming in Children*. Cambridge, MA: MIT Press.
Medin, Douglas L. and Brian H. Ross 1992: *Cognitive Psychology*. San Diego, CA: Harcourt Brace Jovanovich.
Mervis, Carolyn 1987: Child-basic object categories and early lexical development. In Ulric Neisser (ed.) *Concepts Reconsidered: The Ecological and Intellectual Bases of Categorization*, 201–33. Cambridge: Cambridge University Press.
Mervis, Carolyn. B. and Eleanor Rosch 1981: Categorization of natural objects. *Annual Review of Psychology* 32: 89–115.
Minsky, Marvin L. 1977: Frame-system theory. In Philip N. Johnson-Laird and Peter C. Wason *Thinking: Readings in Cognitive Science*, 355–77, Cambridge: Cambridge University Press.
Murphy, Gregory 2002: *The Big Book of Concepts*. Cambridge, MA: MIT Press.
Murphy, Gregory L. and Douglas L. Medin 1985: The role of theories in conceptual coherence. *Psychological Review* 92: 289–316.
Osherson, Daniel N., Edward E. Smith, Ormond Wilkie, Alejandro López and Eldar Shafir 1990: Category-based induction. *Psychological Review* 97.2: 185–200.
Pinker, Steven 1994: *The Language Instinct*. London: Penguin Books.
Putnam, Hilary 1962: It ain't necessarily so. *Journal of Philosophy* 59.22: 658–71.
Putnam, Hilary 1975: The meaning of *meaning*. In Keith Gunderson (ed.) *Language, Mind, and Knowledge*, 131–93. Minneapolis: University of Minnesota Press.
Quine, W. V. 1960: *Word and Object*. Cambridge, MA: MIT Press.
Rosch, Eleanor 1973: Natural categories. *Cognitive Psychology* 4, 328–50.
Rosch, Eleanor 1975: Cognitive reference points. *Cognitive Psychology* 7, 532–34.
Rosch, Eleanor and Carolyn Mervis 1975: Family resemblances: studies in the internal structure of categories. *Cognitive Psychology* 7, 573–605.
Rosch, Eleanor, Carolyn Mervis, Wayne Gray, David Johnson and Penny Boyes-Braem 1976: Basic objects in natural categories. *Cognitive Psychology* 8: 382–439.
Russell, Bertrand 1967: *The Problems of Philosophy*. London: Oxford Paperbacks. (First published 1917.)
Samet, Jerry and Owen Flanagan 1989: Innate representations. In Stuart Silvers (ed.) *Representation: Readings in the Philosophy of Mental Representation*, 189–210. Dordrecht: Kluwer.
Sapir, Edward 1949: *Selected Writings in Language, Culture and Personality*. Edited by David G. Mandelbaum. Berkeley: University of California Press.
Schwartz, Stephen 1979: Natural kind terms. *Cognition* 7, 301–15.
Schwartz, Stephen 1980: Natural kinds and nominal kinds. *Mind* 89, 182–95.
Searle, John R. 1958: Proper names. *Mind* 67, 166–73.
Shafto, P., C. Kemp, E. B. Bonawitz, J. D. Coley and J. D. Tenenbaum 2008: Inductive reasoning about causally transmitted properties. *Cognition* 109.2: 175–92.
Smith, Edward E. and Douglas L. Medin 1981: *Categories and Concepts*. Cambridge, MA: Harvard University Press.
Stillings, Neil A., Steven W. Weisler, Christopher H. Chase, Mark H. Feinstein, Jay L. Garfield and Edwina L. Rissland 1995: *Cognitive Science: An Introduction*. Cambridge, MA: MIT Press.
Tanaka, James W. and Marjorie Taylor 1991: Object categories and expertise: is the basic level in the eye of the beholder? *Cognitive Psychology* 23: 457–82.
Taylor, John R. 2003: *Linguistic Categorization*, third edition. Oxford: Oxford University Press.
Whorf, Benjamin Lee 1956: *Language, Thought, and Reality. Selected Writings of Benjamin Lee Whorf*. Edited by John B. Carroll. Cambridge, MA: MIT Press.

[illegible] Cambridge: Cambridge University Press.
[illegible]
[illegible]
[illegible]
[illegible] Cambridge University Press.
[illegible]
[illegible]
[illegible]
[illegible]
[illegible]
[illegible]
[illegible]
[illegible]
Quine, W. V. 1960. *Word and Object*. Cambridge, MA: MIT Press.
[illegible]
[illegible]
[illegible]
[illegible]
[illegible]
[illegible]
[illegible]
[illegible]
[illegible]
[illegible]
[illegible]
[illegible]
[illegible]
[illegible]

part II

Semantic Description

chapter 3

Word Meaning

3.1 Introduction

In this chapter we turn to the study of word meaning, or **lexical semantics**.[1] The traditional descriptive aims of lexical semantics have been: (a) to represent the meaning of each word in the language; and (b) to show how the meanings of words in a language are interrelated. These aims are closely related because, as we mentioned in chapter 1, the meaning of a word is defined in part by its relations with other words in the language. We can follow structuralist thought and recognize that as well as being in a relationship with other words in the same sentence, a word is also in a relationship with other, related but absent words.[2] To take a very simple example, if someone says to you:

3.1 I saw my mother just now.

you know, without any further information, that the speaker saw a woman. As we will see, there are a couple of ways of viewing this: one is to say that this knowledge follows from the relationship between the uttered word *mother* and the related, but unspoken word *woman*, representing links in the vocabulary. Another approach is to claim that the word *mother* contains a semantic element WOMAN[3] as part of its meaning.

Whatever our particular decision about this case, it is easy to show that lexical relations are central to the way speakers and hearers construct meaning.[4] One example comes from looking at the different kinds of conclusions that speakers may draw from an utterance. See, for example, the following sentences, where English speakers would probably agree that each of the b sentences below follows automatically from its a partner (where we assume as usual that repeated nominals have the same reference), whereas the c sentence, while it might be a reasonable inference in context, does not follow in this automatic way:

3.2 a. My bank manager has just been murdered.
b. My bank manager is dead.
c. My bank will be getting a new manager.

3.3 a. Rob has failed his statistics exam.
b. Rob hasn't passed his statistics exam.
c. Rob can't bank on a glittering career as a statistician.

3.4 a. This bicycle belongs to Sinead.
b. Sinead owns this bicycle.
c. Sinead rides a bicycle.

The relationship between the a and b sentences in (3.2–4) was called **entailment** in chapter 1, and we look at it in more detail in chapter 4. For now we can say that the relationship is such that if we believe the a sentence, then we are automatically committed to the b sentence. On the other hand, we can easily imagine situations where we believe the a sentence but can deny the associated c sentence. As we shall see in chapters 4 and 7, this is a sign that the inference from a to c is of a different kind from the entailment relationship between a and b. This entailment relationship is important here because in these examples it is a reflection of our lexical knowledge: the entailments in these sentences can be seen to follow from the semantic relations between *murder* and *dead*, *fail* and *pass*, and *belong* and *own*.

As we shall see, there are many different types of relationship that can hold between words, and investigating these has been the pursuit of poets, philosophers, writers of laws, and others for centuries. The study of word meanings, especially the changes that seem to take place over time, are also the concern of philology, and of lexicology. As a consequence of these different interests in word meaning there has evolved a large number of terms describing differences and similarities of word meaning. In this chapter we begin by discussing the basic task of identifying words as units, and then examine some of the problems involved in pinning down their meanings. We then look at some typical semantic relations between words, and examine the network-like structure that these relations give to our mental lexicon. Finally we discuss the search for lexical universals. The topics in this chapter act as a background to chapter 9, where we discuss some specific theoretical approaches to word meaning.

3.2 Words and Grammatical Categories

It is clear that grammatical categories like noun, preposition, and so on, though defined in modern linguistics at the level of syntax and morphology, do reflect semantic differences: different categories of words must be given different semantic descriptions. To take a few examples: names, common nouns, pronouns, and what we might call **logical words** (see below and chapter 4) all show different characteristics of reference and sense:

3.5	a.	names	e.g. Fred Flintstone
	b.	common nouns	e.g. dog, banana, tarantula
	c.	pronouns	e.g. I, you, we, them
	d.	logical words	e.g. not, and, or, all, any

Looking at these types of words, we can say that they operate in different ways: some types may be used to refer (e.g. names), others may not (e.g. logical words); some can only be interpreted in particular contexts (e.g. pronouns), others are very consistent in meaning across a whole range of contexts (e.g. logical words); and so on. It seems too that semantic links will tend to hold between members of the same group rather than across groups. So that semantic relations between common nouns like *man*, *woman*, *animal*, and so on, are clearer than between any noun and words like *and*, *or*, *not*, and vice versa.

Note too that this is only a selection of categories: we will have to account for others like verbs, adjectives, adverbs, prepositions, and so on. Having said this, we deal mainly with nouns and verbs in this chapter; the reader should bear in mind that this is not the whole story.

3.3 Words and Lexical Items

We will follow general linguistic tradition and assume that we must have a list of all the words in a language, together with idiosyncratic information about them, and call this body of information a **dictionary** or **lexicon**. Our interest in semantics is with **lexemes** or **semantic words**, and as we shall see there are a number of ways of listing these in a lexicon. But first we should examine this unit **word**. Words can be identified at the level of writing, where we are familiar with them being separated by white space, where we can call them **orthographic words**. They can also be identified at the levels of phonology, where they are strings of sounds that may show internal structuring which does not occur outside the word, and syntax, where the same semantic word can be represented by several grammatically distinct variants. Thus *walks, walking, walked* in 3.6 below are three different **grammatical** words:

3.6 a. He walks like a duck.
 b. He's walking like a duck.
 c. He walked like a duck.

However, for semantics we will want to say these are instances of the same lexeme, the verb **walk**. We can then say that our three grammatical words share the meaning of the lexeme. This abstraction from grammatical words to semantic words is already familiar to us from published dictionaries, where lexicographers use abstract entries like **go**, **sleep**, **walk**, and so on for purposes of explaining word meaning, and we don't really worry too much what grammatical status the reference form has. In Samuel Johnson's *A Dictionary of the English Language*, for example, the infinitive is used as the entry form, or **lemma**, for verbs, giving us entries like *to walk*, *to sleep*, and so on (Johnson 1983), but now most of us are used to dictionaries and we accept an abstract dictionary form to identify a semantic word.

Our discussion so far has assumed an ability to identify words. This doesn't seem too enormous an assumption in ordinary life, but there are a number of well-known problems in trying to identify the word as a well-defined linguistic unit. One traditional problem was how to combine the various levels of application of word, mentioned above, to an overall definition: what is a word? As Edward Sapir noted, it is no good simply using a semantic definition as a basis, since across languages speakers package meaning into words in very different ways:

3.7 Our first impulse, no doubt, would have been to define the word as the symbolic, linguistic counterpart of a single concept. We now know that such a definition is impossible. In truth it is impossible to define the word from a functional standpoint at all, for the word may be anything from the expression of a single concept – concrete or abstract or purely relational (as in *of* or *by* or *and*) – to the expression of a complete thought (as in Latin *dico* "I say" or, with greater elaborateness of form, as in a Nootka verb form denoting "I have been accustomed to eat twenty round objects [e.g. apples] while engaged in [doing so and so]"). In the latter case the word becomes identical with the sentence. The word is merely a form, a definitely molded entity that takes in as much or as little of the conceptual material of the whole thought as the genius of the language cares to allow. (Sapir 1949: 32)

Why bother then attempting to find a universal definition? The problem is that in very many languages, words do seem to have some psychological reality for speakers; a fact also noted by Sapir from his work on native American languages:

3.8 Linguistic experience, both as expressed in standardized, written form and as tested in daily usage, indicates overwhelmingly that there is not, as a rule, the slightest difficulty in bringing the word to consciousness as a psychological reality. No more convincing test could be desired than this, that the naive Indian, quite unaccustomed to the concept of the written word, has nevertheless no serious difficulty in dictating a text to a linguistic student word by word; he tends, of course, to run his words together as in actual speech, but if he is called to a halt and is made to understand what is desired, he can readily isolate the words as such, repeating them as units. He regularly refuses, on the other hand, to isolate the radical or grammatical element, on the ground that it "makes no sense." (Sapir 1949: 33–4)

One answer is to switch from a semantic definition to a grammatical one, such as Leonard Bloomfield's famous definition:

3.9 A word, then, is a free form which does not consist entirely of (two or more) lesser free forms; in brief, a word is a *minimum free form*.

Since only free forms can be isolated in actual speech, the word, as the minimum of free form, plays a very important part in our attitude toward language. For the purposes of ordinary life, the word is the smallest unit of speech. (Bloomfield 1984: 178)

This distributional definition identifies words as independent elements, which show their independence by being able to occur in isolation, that is to form one-word utterances. This actually works quite well for most cases, but leaves elements like *a*, *the*, and *my* in a gray area. Speakers seem to feel that these are words, and write them separately, as in *a car*, *my car*, and so on, but they don't occur as one word utterances, and so are not words by this definition. Bloomfield was of course aware of such problem cases:

3.10 None of these criteria can be strictly applied: many forms lie on the borderline between bound forms and words, or between words and phrases; it is impossible to make a rigid distinction between forms that may and forms that may not be spoken in absolute position.[5] (Bloomfield 1984: 181)

There have been other suggestions for how to define words grammatically: Lyons (1968) for example, discusses another distributional definition, this time based on the extent to which morphemes stick together. The idea is that the attachments between elements within a word will be firmer than will the attachments between words themselves. This is shown by numbering the morphemes as in 3.11, and then attempting to rearrange them as in 3.12:

3.11 Internal cohesion (Lyons 1968: 202–04)
$\text{the}_1 + \text{boy}_2 + \text{s}_3 + \text{walk}_4 + \text{ed}_5 + \text{slow}_6 + \text{ly}_7 + \text{up}_8 + \text{the}_9 + \text{hill}_{10}$

3.12 a. $\text{slow}_6 + \text{ly}_7 + \text{the}_1 + \text{boy}_2 + \text{s}_3 + \text{walk}_4 + \text{ed}_5 + \text{up}_8 + \text{the}_9 + \text{hill}_{10}$
b. $\text{up}_8 + \text{the}_9 + \text{hill}_{10} + \text{slow}_6 + \text{ly}_7 + \text{walk}_4 + \text{ed}_5 + \text{the}_1 + \text{boy}_2 + \text{s}_3$
c. $^*\text{s}_3 + \text{boy}_2 + \text{the}_1$
d. $^*\text{ed}_5 + \text{walk}_4$

This works well for distinguishing between the words *walked* and *slowly*, but as we can see also leaves *the* as a problem case. It behaves more like a bound morpheme than an independent word: we can no more say **boys the* than we can say just *the* in isolation.

We can leave the debate at this point: that words seem to be identifiable at the level of grammar, but that there will be, as Bloomfield said, borderline cases. As we said earlier, the usual approach in semantics is to try to associate phonological and grammatical words with semantic words or lexemes. Earlier we saw an example of three grammatical words representing one semantic word. The inverse is possible: several lexemes can be represented by one phonological and grammatical word. We can see an example of this by looking at the word *foot* in the following sentences:

3.13 a. He scored with his left **foot**.
b. They made camp at the **foot** of the mountain.
c. I ate a **foot**-long hot dog.

Each of these uses has a different meaning and we can reflect this by identifying three lexemes in 3.13. Another way of describing this is to say that we have three **senses** of the word *foot*. We could represent this by numbering the senses:

3.14 **foot**^{1}: part of the leg below the ankle;
foot^2: base or bottom of something;
foot^3: unit of length, one third of a yard.

Once we have established our lexemes, the lexicon will be a listing of them with a representation of:

1. the lexeme's pronunciation;
2. its grammatical status;
3. its meaning;
4. its meaning relations with other lexemes.[6]

Traditionally, each entry has to have any information that cannot be predicted by general rules. This means that different types of information will have to be included: about unpredictable pronunciation; about any exceptional morphological behavior; about what syntactic category the item is, and so on, and of course, the semantic information that has to be there: the meaning of the lexeme, and the semantic relations it enters into with other lexemes in the language.

One point that emerges quite quickly from such a listing of lexemes is that some share a number of the properties we are interested in. For example the three lexemes in 3.13 all share the same pronunciation ([fʊt]), and the same syntactic category (noun). Dictionary writers economize by grouping senses and listing the shared properties just once at the head of the group, for example:

3.15 **foot** [fʊt] noun. **1**. part of the leg below the ankle. **2**. base or bottom of something. **3**. unit of length, one third of a yard.

This group is often called a **lexical entry.** Thus a lexical entry may contain several lexemes or senses. The principles for grouping lexemes into lexical entries vary somewhat. Usually the lexicographer tries to group words that, as well as sharing phonological and grammatical properties, make some sense as a semantic grouping, either by having some common elements of meaning, or by being historically related. We will look at how this is done in section 3.5 below when we discuss the semantic relations of **homonymy** and **polysemy**. Other questions arise when the same phonological word belongs to several grammatical categories, for example the verb *heat*, as in *We've got to heat the soup*, and the related noun *heat*, as in *This heat is oppressive*. Should these belong in the same entry? Many dictionaries do this, sometimes listing all the nominal senses before the verbal senses, or vice versa. Readers can check their favorite dictionary to see the solution adopted for this example.

There are traditional problems associated with the mapping between lexemes and words at other levels, which we might mention but not investigate in any detail here. One example, which we have already mentioned, is the existence of multi-word units, like **phrasal verbs**, for example: *throw up* and *look after*; or the more complicated *put up with*. We can take as another example **idioms** like *kick the bucket*, *spill the beans*, and so on. Phrasal verbs and idioms are both cases where a string of words can correspond to a single semantic unit.

3.4 Problems with Pinning Down Word Meaning

As every speaker knows if asked the meaning of a particular word, word meaning is slippery. Different native speakers might feel they know the meaning of a word, but then come up with somewhat different definitions. Other words they might have only the vaguest feel for and have to use a dictionary to check. Some of this difficulty arises from the influence of context on word meaning, as discussed by Firth (1957), Halliday (1966) and Lyons (1963). Usually it is easier to define a word if you are given the phrase or sentence it occurs in. These contextual effects seem to pull word meanings in two opposite directions. The first, restricting influence is the tendency for words to occur together repeatedly, called **collocation**. Halliday (1966), for example, compares the collocation patterns of two adjectives *strong* and *powerful*, which might seem to have similar meanings. Though we can use both for some items, for instance *strong arguments* and *powerful arguments*, elsewhere there are collocation effects. For example we talk of *strong tea* rather than *powerful tea*; but a *powerful car* rather than a *strong car*. Similarly *blond* collocates with *hair* and *addle* with *eggs*. As Gruber (1965) notes, names for groups act like this: we say a *herd of cattle*, but a *pack of dogs*.

These collocations can undergo a fossilization process until they become fixed expressions. We talk of *hot and cold running water* rather than *cold and hot running water*; and say *They're husband and wife*, rather than *wife and husband*. Such fixed expressions are common with food: *salt and vinegar*, *fish and chips*, *curry and rice*, *bangers and mash*, *franks and beans*, and so on.[7] A similar type of fossilization results in the creation of **idioms**, expressions where the individual words have ceased to have independent meanings. In expressions like *kith and kin* or *spick and span*, not many English speakers would be able to assign a meaning here to *kith* or *span*.

Contextual effects can also pull word meanings in the other direction, toward creativity and semantic shift. In different contexts, for example, a noun like *run* can have somewhat different meanings, as in 3.16 below:

3.16 a. I go for a run every morning.
b. The tail-end batsmen added a single run before lunch.
c. The ball-player hit a home run.
d. We took the new car for a run.
e. He built a new run for his chickens.
f. There's been a run on the dollar.
g. The bears are here for the salmon run.

The problem is how to view the relationship between these instances of *run* above. Are these seven different senses of the word *run*? Or are they examples of the same sense influenced by different contexts? That is, is there some sketchy common meaning that is plastic enough to be made to fit the different context provoked by other words like *batsmen*, *chickens*, and *the dollar*? The answer might not be simple: some instances, for example 3.16b and c, or perhaps, a, b, and c, seem more closely related than others. Some writers have described this distinction in terms of **ambiguity** and **vagueness**. The proposal is that if each of the meanings of *run* in 3.16 is a different sense, then *run* is seven ways ambiguous; but if 3.16a–g share the same sense, then *run* is merely vague between these different uses. The basic idea is that in examples of vagueness the context can add information that is not specified in the sense, but in examples of ambiguity the context will cause one of the senses to be selected. The problem, of course, is to decide, for any given example, whether one is dealing with ambiguity or vagueness. Several tests have been proposed, but they are difficult to apply. The main reason for this is once again context. Ambiguity is usually more potential than real since in any given context one of the readings is likely to fit the context and be automatically selected by the participants; they may not even be aware of readings that they would naturally prefer in other contexts. This means that we have to employ some ingenuity in applying ambiguity tests: usually they involve inventing a sentence and a context where both readings could be available. We can briefly examine some of the tests that have been proposed.

One test proposed by Zwicky and Sadock (1975) and Kempson (1977) relies on the use of abbreviatory forms like *do so, do so too, so do*. These are short forms used to avoid repeating a verb phrase, for example:

3.17 a. Charlie hates mayonnaise and **so does** Mary.
b. He took a form and Sean **did too**.

Such expressions are understandable because there is a convention of **identity** between them and the preceding verb phrase: thus we know that in 3.17a Mary hates mayonnaise and in 3.17b Sean took a form. This test relies on this identity: if the preceding verb phrase has more than one sense, then whichever sense is selected in this first full verb phrase must be kept the same in the following *do so* clause. For example 3.18a below has the two interpretations in 3.18b and 3.18c:

3.18 a. Duffy discovered a mole.
b. Duffy discovered a small burrowing mammal.
c. Duffy discovered a long-dormant spy.

This relies of course on the two meanings of *mole*, and is therefore a case of **lexical ambiguity**. If we add a *do so* clause as in 3.18d:

d. Duffy discovered a mole, and so did Clark.

whichever sense is selected in the first clause has to be repeated in the second, that is, it is not possible for the first clause to have the *mammal* interpretation and the second the *spy* interpretation, or vice versa. By contrast where a word is vague, the unspecified aspects of meaning are invisible to this *do so* identity. Basically, they are not part of the meaning and therefore are not available for the identity check. We can compare this with the word *publicist* that can be used to mean either a male or female, as 3.19 below shows:

3.19 a. He's our publicist.
b. She's our publicist.

Is *publicist* then ambiguous? In a sentence like 3.20 below:

3.20 They hired a publicist and so did we.

it is quite possible for the publicist in the first clause to be male and in the second, female. Thus this test seems to show that *publicist* is unspecified, or "vague," for gender. We can see that vagueness allows different specifications in *do so* clauses, but the different senses of an ambiguous word cannot be chosen.

This *do so* identity test seems to work, but as mentioned earlier, its use relies on being able to construct examples where the same sentence has two meanings. In our *run* examples earlier, the different instances of *run* occur in different contexts and it is difficult to think of an example of a single sentence that could have two interpretations of *run*, say the cricket interpretation and the financial one.

A second type of test for ambiguity relies on one sense being in a network of relations with certain other lexemes and another sense being in a different network. So, for example, the *run* of 3.16a above might be in relation of near synonymy to another noun like *jog*, while *run* in 3.16e might be in a similar relation to nouns like *pen*, *enclosure*, and so on. Thus while the b sentences below are fine, the c versions are bizarre:

3.21 a. I go for a run every morning.
b. I go for a jog every morning.
c. ?I go for an enclosure every morning.

3.22 a. He built a new run for his chickens.
b. He built a new enclosure for his chickens.
c. ?He built a new jog for his chickens.

This **sense relations test** suggests that *run* is ambiguous between the 3.16a and 3.16e readings.

A third test employs **zeugma**, which is a feeling of oddness or anomaly when two distinct senses of a word are activated at the same item, that is in the same sentence, and usually by conjunction, for example ?*Jane drew a picture and the curtains*, which activates two distinct senses of *draw*. Zeugma is often used for comic effect, as in *Joan lost her umbrella and her temper*. If zeugma is produced, it is suggested, we can identify ambiguity, thus predicting the ambiguity of *run* as below:

3.23 ?He planned a run for charity and one for his chickens.

This test is somewhat hampered by the difficulty of creating the appropriate structures and because the effect is rather subjective and context-dependent.

There are a number of other tests for ambiguity, many of which are difficult to apply and few of which are uncontroversially successful; see Cruse (1986: 49–83) for a discussion of these tests. It seems likely that whatever intuitions and arguments we come up with to distinguish between contextual coloring and different sense, the process will not be an exact one. We'll see a similar problem in the next section, when we discuss **homonymy** and **polysemy**, where lexicographers have to adopt procedures for distinguishing related senses of the same lexical entry from different lexical entries.

In the next section we describe and exemplify some of the semantic relations that can hold between lexical items.

3.5 Lexical Relations

There are a number of different types of lexical relation, as we shall see. A particular lexeme may be simultaneously in a number of these relations, so that it may be more accurate to think of the lexicon as a **network**, rather than a listing of words as in a published dictionary.

An important organizational principle in the lexicon is the **lexical field**. This is a group of lexemes that belong to a particular activity or area of specialist knowledge, such as the terms in cooking or sailing; or the vocabulary used by doctors, coal miners, or mountain climbers. One effect is the use of specialist terms like *phoneme* in linguistics or *gigabyte* in computing. More common, though, is the use of different senses for a word, for example:

3.24 **blanket**[1] verb. to cover as with a blanket.

blanket[2] verb. *Sailing.* to block another vessel's wind by sailing close to it on the windward side.

3.25 **ledger**[1] noun. *Bookkeeping.* the main book in which a company's financial records are kept.

ledger[2] noun. *Angling.* a trace that holds the bait above the bottom.

Dictionaries recognize the effect of lexical fields by including in lexical entries labels like *Banking*, *Medicine*, *Angling*, and so on, as in our examples above.

One effect of lexical fields is that lexical relations are more common between lexemes in the same field. Thus **peak**[1] "part of a mountain" is a near synonym of *summit*, while **peak**[2] "part of a hat" is a near synonym of *visor*. In the examples of lexical relations that follow, the influence of lexical fields will be clear.

3.5.1 Homonymy

Homonyms are unrelated senses of the same phonological word. Some authors distinguish between **homographs**, senses of the same written word, and **homophones**, senses of the same spoken word. Here we will generally just use the term homonym. We can distinguish different types depending on their syntactic behavior, and spelling, for example:

1. lexemes of the same syntactic category, and with the same spelling: e.g. *lap* "circuit of a course" and *lap* "part of body when sitting down";
2. of the same category, but with different spelling: e.g. the verbs *ring* and *wring*;
3. of different categories, but with the same spelling: e.g. the verb *bear* and the noun *bear*;
4. of different categories, and with different spelling: e.g. *not*, *knot*.

Of course variations in pronunciation mean that not all speakers have the same set of homonyms. Some English speakers for example pronounce the pairs *click* and *clique*, or *talk* and *torque*, in the same way, making these homonyms, which are spelled differently.

3.5.2 Polysemy

There is a traditional distinction made in lexicology between homonymy and **polysemy**. Both deal with multiple senses of the same phonological word, but polysemy is invoked if the senses are judged to be related. This is an important distinction for lexicographers in the design of their dictionaries, because polysemous senses are listed under the same lexical entry, while homonymous senses are given separate entries. Lexicographers tend to use criteria of "relatedness" to identify polysemy. These criteria include speakers' intuitions, and what is known about the historical development of the items. We can take an example of the distinction from the *Collins English Dictionary* (Treffry 2000: 743) where, as 3.26 below shows, various senses of *hook* are treated as polysemy and therefore listed under one lexical entry:

3.26 **hook** (hʊk) *n.* **1**. a piece of material, usually metal, curved or bent and used to suspend, catch, hold, or pull something. **2**. short for fish-hook. **3**. a trap or snare. **4**. *Chiefly U.S.* something that attracts or is intended to be an attraction. **5**. something resembling a hook in design or use. **6.a**. a sharp bend or angle in a geological formation, esp. a river. **b**. a sharply curved spit of land. **7**. *Boxing.* a short swinging blow delivered from the side with the elbow bent. **8**. *Cricket.* a shot in which the ball is hit square on the leg side with the bat held horizontally. **9**. *Golf.* a shot that causes the ball to swerve sharply from right to left. **10**. *Surfing.* the top of a breaking wave, etc.

Two groups of senses of *hooker* on the other hand, as 3.27 below shows, are treated as unrelated, therefore a case of homonymy, and given two separate entries:

3.27 **hooker^1** ('hʊkə) *n.* **1**. a commercial fishing boat using hooks and lines instead of nets. **2**. a sailing boat of the west of Ireland formerly used for cargo and now for pleasure sailing and racing.

hooker^2 ('hʊkə) *n.* **1**. a person or thing that hooks. **2**. *U.S. and Canadian slang.* **2a**. a draft of alcoholic drink, esp. of spirits. **2b**. a prostitute. **3**. *Rugby.* the central forward in the front row of a scrum whose main job is to hook the ball.

Such decisions are not always clear-cut. Speakers may differ in their intuitions, and worse, historical facts and speaker intuitions may contradict each other. For example, most English speakers seem to feel that the two words *sole* "bottom of the foot" and *sole* "flatfish" are unrelated, and should be given separate lexical entries as a case of homonymy. They are however historically derived via French from the same Latin word *solea* "sandal." So an argument could be made for polysemy. Since in this case, however, the relationship is really in Latin, and the words entered English from French at different times, dictionaries side with the speakers' intuitions and list them separately. A more recent example is the adjective *gay* with its two meanings "lively, light-hearted, carefree" and "homosexual." Although the latter meaning was derived from the former, for current speakers the two senses are quite distinct, and are thus homonyms.

3.5.3 Synonymy

Synonyms are different phonological words that have the same or very similar meanings. Some examples might be the pairs below:

3.28 couch/sofa boy/lad lawyer/attorney toilet/lavatory large/big

Even these few examples show that true or exact synonyms are very rare. As Palmer (1981) notes, the synonyms often have different distributions along a number of parameters. They may have belonged to different dialects and then become synonyms for speakers familiar with both dialects, like Irish English *press* and British English *cupboard.* Similarly the words may originate from different languages, for example *cloth* (from Old English) and *fabric* (from Latin). An important source of synonymy is taboo areas where a range of euphemisms may occur, for example in the English vocabulary for sex, death, and the body. We can cite, for example, the entry for *die* from Roget's *Thesaurus*:

3.29 *die*: cease living: decease, demise, depart, drop, expire, go, pass away, pass (on), perish, succumb. *Informal:* pop off. *Slang:* check out, croak, kick in, kick off. *Idioms*: bite the dust, breathe one's last, cash in, give up the ghost, go to one's grave, kick the bucket, meet one's end (or Maker), pass on to the Great Beyond, turn up one's toes. (Roget 1995)

As this entry suggests, the words may belong to different **registers**, those styles of language, colloquial, formal, literary, and so on, that belong to different situations. Thus *wife* or *spouse* is more formal than *old lady* or *missus.* Synonyms may also portray positive or negative attitudes of the speaker: for example *naive* or *gullible* seem more critical than *ingenuous.* Finally, as mentioned earlier, one or other of the synonyms may be collocationally restricted. For example the sentences below might mean roughly the same thing in some contexts:

3.30 She called out to the young lad.

3.31 She called out to the young boy.

In other contexts, however, the words *lad* and *boy* have different connotations; compare:

3.32 He always was a bit of a lad.

3.33 He always was a bit of a boy.

Or we might compare the synonymous pair 3.34 with the very different pair in 3.35:

3.34 a big house: a large house

3.35 my big sister: my large sister.

As an example of such distributional effects on synonyms, we might take the various words used for the police around the English-speaking world: *police officer*, *cop*, *copper*, and so on. Some distributional constraints on these words are regional, like Irish English *the guards* (from the Irish *garda*), British English *the old Bill*, or American English *the heat.* Formality is another factor: many of these words are of course slang terms used in colloquial contexts instead of more formal terms like *police officer.* Speaker attitude is a further distinguishing factor: some words, like *fuzz*, *flatfoot*, *pigs*, or *the slime*, reveal negative speaker attitudes, while others like *cop* seem neutral.

Finally, as an example of collocation effects, one can find speakers saying *a police car* or *a cop car*, but not very likely are ?*a guards car* or ?*an Old Bill car*.

3.5.4 Opposites (antonymy)

In traditional terminology, **antonyms** are words which are opposite in meaning. It is useful, however, to identify several different types of relationship under a more general label of **opposition**. There are a number of relations that seem to involve words which are at the same time related in meaning yet incompatible or contrasting; we list some of them below.

Complementary antonyms

This is a relation between words such that the negative of one implies the positive of the other. The pairs are also sometimes called **contradictory, binary,** or **simple antonyms**. In effect, the words form a two-term classification. Examples would include:

3.36 dead/alive (of e.g. animals)
pass/fail (a test)
hit/miss (a target)

So, using these words literally, *dead* implies *not alive*, and so on, which explains the semantic oddness of sentences like:

3.37 ?My pet python is dead but luckily it's still alive.

Of course speakers can creatively alter these two-term classifications for special effects: we can speak of someone being *half dead*; or we know that in horror films the *undead* are not alive in the normal sense.

Gradable antonyms

This is a relationship between opposites where the positive of one term does not necessarily imply the negative of the other, for example *rich/poor, fast/slow, young/old, beautiful/ugly*.[8] This relation is typically associated with adjectives and has two major identifying characteristics: firstly, there are usually intermediate terms so that between the gradable antonyms *hot* and *cold* we can find:

3.38 hot (warm tepid cool) cold

This means of course that something may be neither hot nor cold. Secondly, the terms are usually relative, so *a thick pencil* is likely to be thinner than *a thin girl*; and *a late dinosaur fossil* is earlier than *an early Elvis record*. A third characteristic is that in some pairs one term is more basic and common, so for example of the pair *long/short*, it is more natural to ask of something *How long is it?* than *How short is it?* For other pairs there is no such pattern: *How hot is it?* and *How cold is it?* are equally natural depending on context. Other examples of gradable antonyms are: *tall/short, clever/stupid, near/far, interesting/boring*.

Reverses

The characteristic **reverse** relation is between terms describing movement, where one term describes movement in one direction, →, and the other the same movement in the opposite direction, ←; for example the terms *push* and *pull* on a swing door, which tell you in which direction to apply force. Other such pairs are *come/go*, *go/return*, *ascend/descend*. When describing motion the following can be called reverses: (go) *up/down*, (go) *in/out*, (turn) *right/left*.

By extension, the term is also applied to any process that can be reversed: so other reverses are *inflate/deflate*, *expand/contract*, *fill/empty*, or *knit/unravel*.

Converses

These are terms which describe a relation between two entities from alternate viewpoints, as in the pairs:

3.39 own/belong to
above/below
employer/employee

Thus if we are told *Alan owns this book* then we know automatically *This book belongs to Alan*. Or from *Helen is David's employer* we know *David is Helen's employee*. Again, these relations are part of a speaker's semantic knowledge and explain why the two sentences below are **paraphrases**, that is can be used to describe the same situation:

3.40 My office is above the library.

3.41 The library is below my office.

Taxonomic sisters

The term antonymy is sometimes used to describe words which are at the same level in a taxonomy. Taxonomies are hierarchical classification systems; we can take as an example the color adjectives in English, and give a selection at one level of the taxonomy as below:

3.42 red orange yellow green blue purple brown

We can say that the words *red* and *blue* are sister-members of the same taxonomy and therefore incompatible with each other. Hence one can say:

3.43 His car isn't red, it's blue.

Other taxonomies might include the days of the week: *Sunday*, *Monday*, *Tuesday*, and so on, or any of the taxonomies we use to describe the natural world, like types of dog: *poodle*, *setter*, *bulldog*, and so on. Some taxonomies are **closed**, like days of the week: we can't easily add another day, without changing the whole system. Others are **open**, like the flavors of ice cream sold in an ice cream parlor: someone can always come up with a new flavor and extend the taxonomy.

In the next section we see that since taxonomies typically have a hierarchical structure, we will need terms to describe vertical relations, as well as the horizontal "sisterhood" relation we have described here.

3.5.5 Hyponymy

Hyponymy is a relation of inclusion. A **hyponym** includes the meaning of a more general word, for example:

3.44 *dog* and *cat* are hyponyms of *animal*
sister and *mother* are hyponyms of *woman*

The more general term is called the **superordinate** or **hypernym** (alternatively **hyperonym**). Much of the vocabulary is linked by such systems of inclusion, and the resulting semantic networks form the hierarchical taxonomies mentioned above. Some taxonomies reflect the natural world, like 3.45 below, where we only expand a single line of the network:

3.45

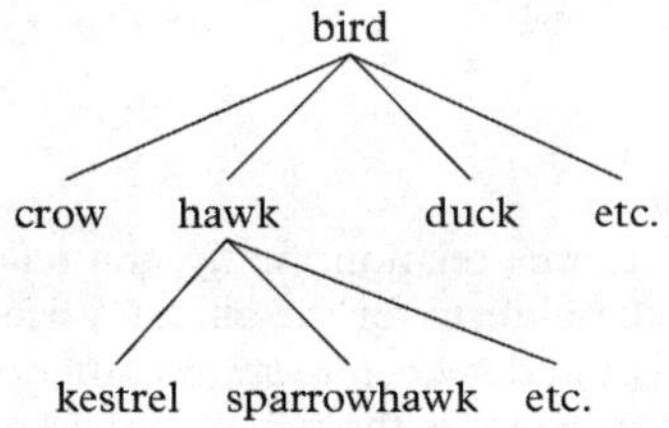

Here *kestrel* is a hyponym of *hawk*, and *hawk* a hyponym of *bird*. We assume the relationship is transitive so that *kestrel* is a hyponym of *bird*. Other taxonomies reflect classifications of human artifacts, like 3.45 below:

3.46

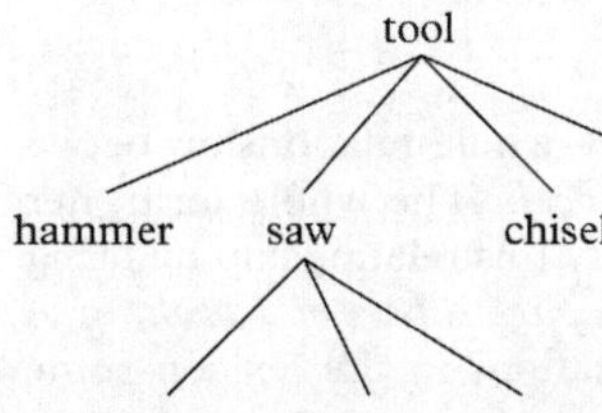

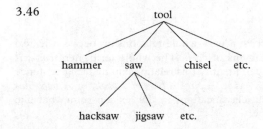

From such taxonomies we can see both hyponymy and the taxonomic sisterhood described in the last section: hyponymy is a vertical relationship in a taxonomy, so *saw* is a hyponym of *tool* in 3.46, while taxonomic sisters are in a horizontal relationship, so *hacksaw* and *jigsaw* are sisters in this taxonomy with other types of saw. Such classifications are of interest for what they tell us about human culture and mind. Anthropologists and anthropological linguists have studied a range of such folk taxonomies in different languages and cultures, including color terms (Berlin and Kay 1969, Kay and McDaniel 1978), folk classifications of plants and animals

(Berlin, Breedlove, and Raven 1974, Hunn 1977) and kinship terms (Lounsbury 1964, Tyler 1969, Goodenough 1970). The relationship between such classifications and the vocabulary is discussed by Rosch et al. (1976), Downing (1977), and George Lakoff (1987).

Another lexical relation that seems like a special sub-case of taxonomy is the ADULT–YOUNG relation, as shown in the following examples:

3.47	dog	puppy
	cat	kitten
	cow	calf
	pig	piglet
	duck	duckling
	swan	cygnet

A similar relation holds between MALE–FEMALE pairs:

3.48	dog	bitch
	tom	?queen
	bull	cow
	boar	sow
	drake	duck
	cob	pen

As we can see, there are some asymmetries in this relation: firstly, the relationship between the MALE–FEMALE terms and the general term for the animal varies: sometimes there is a distinct term, as in *pig–boar–sow* and *swan–cob–pen*; in other examples the male name is general, as in *dog*, while in others it is the female name, for example *cow* and *duck*. There may also be gaps: while *tom* or *tomcat* is commonly used for male cats, for some English speakers there doesn't seem to be an equivalent colloquial name for female cats (though others use *queen*, as above).

3.5.6 Meronymy

Meronymy[9] is a term used to describe a part–whole relationship between lexical items. Thus *cover* and *page* are meronyms of *book*. The whole term, here *book*, is sometimes called the **holonym**. We can identify this relationship by using sentence frames like *X is part of Y*, or *Y has X*, as in *A page is part of a book*, or *A book has pages*. Meronymy reflects hierarchical classifications in the lexicon somewhat like taxonomies; a typical system might be:

3.49

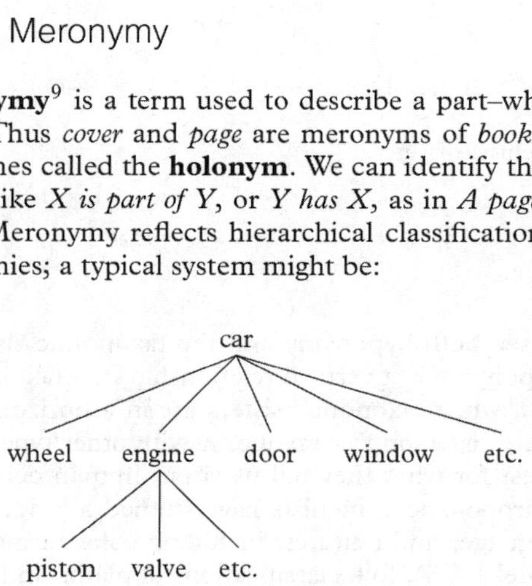

Meronymic hierarchies are less clear cut and regular than taxonomies. Meronyms vary for example in how necessary the part is to the whole. Some are necessary for normal examples, for example *nose* as a meronym of *face*; others are usual but not obligatory, like *collar* as a meronym of *shirt*; still others are optional like *cellar* for *house*.

Meronymy also differs from hyponymy in transitivity. Hyponymy is always transitive, as we saw, but meronymy may or may not be. A transitive example is: *nail* as a meronym of *finger*, and *finger* of *hand*. We can see that *nail* is a meronym of *hand*, for we can say *A hand has nails*. A non-transitive example is: *pane* is a meronym of *window* (*A window has a pane*), and *window* of *room* (*A room has a window*); but *pane* is not a meronym of *room*, for we cannot say *A room has a pane*. Or *hole* is a meronym of *button*, and *button* of *shirt*, but we wouldn't want to say that *hole* is a meronym of *shirt* (*A shirt has holes!*).

One important point is that the networks identified as meronymy are lexical: it is conceptually possible to segment an item in countless ways, but only some divisions are coded in the vocabulary of a language. There are a number of other lexical relations that seem similar to meronymy. In the next sections we briefly list a couple of the most important.

3.5.7 Member–collection

This is a relationship between the word for a unit and the usual word for a collection of the units. Examples include:

3.50	ship	fleet
	tree	forest
	fish	shoal
	book	library
	bird	flock
	sheep	flock
	worshipper	congregation

3.5.8 Portion–mass

This is the relation between a mass noun and the usual unit of measurement or division. For example in 3.51 below the unit, a count noun, is added to the mass noun, making the resulting noun phrase into a count nominal. We discuss this process further in chapter 9.

3.51	drop	of	liquid
	grain	of	salt/sand/wheat
	sheet	of	paper
	lump	of	coal
	strand	of	hair

3.6 Derivational Relations

As mentioned earlier, our lexicon should include derived words when their meaning is not predictable. In the creation of real dictionaries this is rather an idealized principle: in practice lexicographers often find it more economical to list many derivatives than to attempt to define the morphological rules with their various irregularities and exceptions. So while in principle we want to list only unpredictable forms in individual entries, in practice the decision rests on the aims of the lexicon creators.

We can look briefly at just two derivational relations as examples of this type of lexical relation: causative verbs and agentive nouns.

3.6.1 Causative verbs

We can identify a relationship between an adjective describing a state, for example *wide* as in *the road is wide*; a verb describing a beginning or change of state, *widen* as in *The road widened*; and a verb describing the cause of this change of state, *widen*, as in *The City Council widened the road.* These three semantic choices can be described as a **state, change of state** (or **inchoative**), and **causative.**

This relationship is marked in the English lexicon in a number of different ways. There may be no difference in the shape of the word between all three uses as in: *The gates are* ***open***; *The gates* ***open*** *at nine*; *The porters* ***open*** *the gates.* Despite having the same shape, these three words are grammatically distinct: an adjective, an intransitive verb, and a transitive verb, respectively. In other cases the inchoative and causative verbs are morphologically derived from the adjective as in: *The apples are* ***ripe***; *The apples are* ***ripening***; *The sun is* ***ripening*** *the apples.*

Often there are gaps in this relation: for example we can say *The soil is* ***rich*** (state) and *The gardener* ***enriched*** *the soil* (causative) but it sounds odd to use an inchoative: ?*The soil is* ***enriching***. For a state adjective like *hungry*, there is no colloquial inchoative or causative: we have to say *get hungry* as in *I'm getting hungry*; or *make hungry* as in *All this talk of food is making me hungry.*

Another element in this relation can be an adjective describing the state that is a result of the process. This **resultative** adjective is usually in the form of a past participle. Thus we find examples like: *closed, broken, tired, lifted.* We can see a full set of these relations in: *hot* (state adjective)–*heat* (inchoative verb)–*heat* (causative verb)–*heated* (resultative adjective).

We have concentrated on derived causatives, but some verbs are inherently causative and not derived from an adjective. The most famous English example of this in the semantics literature is *kill*, which can be analysed as a causative verb "to cause to die." So the semantic relationship state–inchoative–causative for this example is: *dead–die–kill.* We can use this example to see something of the way that both derivational and non-derivational lexical relations interact. There are two senses of the adjective *dead*: **dead^1**: not alive; and **dead^2**: affected by a loss of sensation. The lexeme **dead^1** is in a relationship with the causative verb *kill*; while **dead^2** has a morphologically derived causative verb *deaden.*

3.6.2 Agentive nouns

There are several different types of agentive nouns.[10] One well-known type is derived from verbs and ends in the written forms *-er* or *-or.* These nouns have the meaning "the entity who/which performs the action of the verb." Some examples are: *skier*, *walker*, *murderer*, *whaler*, *toaster*, *commentator*, *director*, *sailor*, *calculator*, *escalator*. The process of forming nouns in *-er* is more productive than *-or*, and is a good candidate for a regular derivational rule. However, dictionary writers tend to list even these forms, for two reasons. The first is that there are some irregularities: for instance, some nouns do not obey the informal rule given above: *footballer*, for example, is not derived from a verb *to football*. In other cases, the nouns may have several senses, some of which are quite far from the associated verb, as in the examples in 3.52 below:

3.52	**lounger**	a piece of furniture for relaxing on
	undertaker	mortician
	muffler	*US* a car silencer
	creamer	*US* a jug for cream
	renter	*Slang*. a male prostitute

A second reason for listing these forms in published dictionaries is that even though this process is quite regular, it is not possible to predict for any given verb which of the strategies for agentive nouns will be followed. Thus, one who depends upon you financially is not a **depender* but a *dependant*; and a person who cooks is a *cook* not a *cooker*. To cope with this, one would need a kind of default structure in the lexical entries: a convention that where no alternative agentive noun was listed for a verb, one could assume that an *-er* form is possible. This kind of convention is sometimes called an **elsewhere condition** in morphology: see Spencer (1991: 109–11) for discussion.

Other agentive nouns which have to be listed in the lexicon are those for which there is no base verb. This may be because of changes in the language, as for example the noun *meter* "instrument for making measurements" which no longer has an associated verb *mete*.[11]

3.7 Lexical Typology

Our discussion so far has concentrated on the lexicon of an individual language. As we mentioned in chapter 2, translating between two languages highlights differences in vocabulary. We discussed there the hypothesis of linguistic relativity and saw how the basic idea of language reflecting culture can be strengthened into the hypothesis that our thinking reflects our linguistic and cultural patterns. **Semantic typology** is the cross-linguistic study of meaning and, as in other branches of linguistic typology, scholars question the extent to which they can identify regularities across the obvious variation. One important branch is **lexical typology**, which is of interest to a wide range of scholars because a language's lexicon reflects interaction between the structures of the language, the communicative needs of its speakers and the cultural and physical environment they find themselves in. We can identify two important avenues of inquiry. One is the comparison of lexical organization or principles, and the other is the comparison of lexical fields and individual lexical items. The former includes patterns of lexical relations, for example the cross-linguistic study of polysemy: how related senses of a lexeme can pattern and change over time. We look briefly at this in the next section. The latter can be seen as the investigation of the ways in which concepts are mapped into words across languages. Cross-language comparisons have investigated words for kinship (Read 2001, Kronenfeld 2006), number (Gordon 2004), spatial relations (Majid et al. 2004), and time (Boroditsky 2001, Boroditsky, Fuhrman, and McCormick 2010). Perhaps the best-known area of investigation however has been of color terms and we look at this in section 3.7.2 below. A related issue is whether some lexemes have correspondences in all or most of the languages of the world. We discuss two proposals in this area in 3.7.3 and 3.7.4.

3.7.1 Polysemy

It seems to be a universal of human language that words have a certain plasticity of meaning that allows speakers to shift their meaning to fit different contexts of use. In this chapter we have used the term **polysemy** for a pattern of distinct but related senses of a lexeme. Many writers have identified this polysemy as an essential design feature of language: one that aids economy.[12] Such shifts of meaning also play an important role in language change as they become conventionalized. In chapter 1 we briefly discussed how metaphorical uses can over time change the meaning of words by adding new senses. There have been a number of cross-linguistic studies of polysemy, for example Fillmore and Atkins (2000), Viberg (2002), Riemer (2005), Vanhove (2008), which investigate regularities in the patterns of word meaning extensions. Some studies have focused on specific areas of the lexicon, for example Viberg (1984) investigates perception verbs in fifty-two languages, studying extensions of meanings from one sense modality to another, such as when verbs of seeing are used to describe hearing. In a related area other writers such as Sweetser (1990) and Evans and Wilkins (2000) have discussed cross-linguistic patterns of verbs of perception being used for comprehension, as in the English *I see what you mean* or when speakers say *I hear you* for *I understand/I sympathize*. Boyeldieu (2008) investigates cross-linguistic pattern where animal lexemes have animal and meat senses, as in English when speakers use a count noun to refer to the animal (*He shot a rabbit*) and a mass noun to refer to its meat (*She doesn't eat rabbit*). Newman (2009) contains studies of cross-linguistic polysemy with verbs of eating and drinking, for example in languages that use the verb of drinking for voluntarily inhaling cigarette smoke as in the Somali example below:

3.53	Sigaar	ma	cabtaa?
	cigarette(s)	Q	drink+you.SING.PRES
	"Do you smoke?" (lit. Do you drink cigarettes?)		

This use of a verb of drinking is reported for Hindi, Turkish, and Hausa among other languages.

Other systematic patterns of polysemy seem to show cross-linguistic consistency, such as when words for containers are used for their contents, as in English *I will boil a kettle*, or places used for the people that live there, such as *Ireland rejects the Lisbon Treaty*. These along with lexical meaning shifts such as animal/meat have traditionally been termed metonymy, which we mentioned in chapter 1. Metonymy along with metaphor has been identified as an important producer of polysemy across languages, as when the word for a material becomes used for an object made from it, as in English *iron* (for smoothing clothes), *nylons* (stockings), and *plastic* (for credit cards). We shall discuss attempts to characterize metonymy in more detail in chapter 11.

3.7.2 Color terms

One of the liveliest areas of discussion about cross-language word meaning centers on color terms. While we might readily expect differences for words relating to things in the environment such as animals and plants, or for cultural systems like governance or kinship terms, it might be surprising that terms for colors should vary. After all we all share the same physiology. In an important study Berlin and Kay (1969) investigated the fact that languages vary in the number and range of their basic color terms. Their claim is that though there are various ways of describing colors, including comparison to objects, languages have some lexemes which are basic in the following sense:

3.54 Basic color terms (Berlin and Kay 1969)

a. The term is monolexemic, i.e. not built up from the meaning of its parts. So terms like *blue-gray* are not basic.
b. The term is not a hyponym of any other color term, i.e. the color is not a kind of another color. Thus English *red* is basic, *scarlet* is not.
c. The term has wide applicability. This excludes terms like English *blonde*.
d. The term is not a semantic extension of something manifesting that color. So *turquoise*, *gold*, *taupe*, and *chestnut* are not basic.

The number of items in this basic set of color terms seems to vary widely from as few as two to as many as eleven; examples of different systems reported in the literature include the following:

3.55 Basic color term systems[13]

Two terms: Dani (Trans-New Guinea; Irin Jaya)
Three: Tiv (Niger-Congo; Nigeria), Pomo (Hokan; California, USA)
Four: Ibibio (Niger-Congo; Nigeria), Hanunóo (Austronesian; Mindoro Island, Philippines)
Five: Tzeltal (Mayan; Mexico), Kung-Etoka (Khoisan; Southern Africa)
Six: Tamil (Dravidian; India), Mandarin Chinese
Seven: Nez Perce (Penutian; Idaho, USA), Malayalam (Dravidian; India)
Ten/eleven: Lebanese Arabic, English[14]

While this variation might seem to support the notion of linguistic relativity, Berlin and Kay's (1969) study identified a number of underlying similarities which argue for universals in color term systems. Their point is that rather than finding any possible division of the color spectrum into basic terms, their study identifies quite a narrow range of possibilities, with some shared structural features. One claim they make is that within the range of each color term there is a basic focal color that speakers agree to be the best prototypical example of the color. Moreover, they claim that this focal color is the same for the color term cross-linguistically. The conclusion drawn in this and subsequent studies is that color naming systems are based on the neurophysiology of the human visual system (Kay and McDaniel 1978). A further claim is that there are only eleven basic categories; and that these form the implicational hierarchy below (where we use capitals, WHITE etc., to show that the terms are not simply English words):

3.56 Basic color term hierarchy (Berlin and Kay 1969)

$$\begin{Bmatrix}\text{WHITE}\\ \text{BLACK}\end{Bmatrix} < \text{RED} < \begin{Bmatrix}\text{GREEN}\\ \text{YELLOW}\end{Bmatrix} < \text{BLUE} < \text{BROWN} < \begin{Bmatrix}\text{PURPLE}\\ \text{PINK}\\ \text{ORANGE}\\ \text{GRAY}\end{Bmatrix}$$

This hierarchy represents the claim that in a relation A < B, if a language has B then it must have A, but not vice versa. As in implicational hierarchies generally, leftward elements are seen as more basic than rightward elements.[15] A second claim of this research is that these terms form eight basic color term systems as shown:

3.57 Basic systems

System	*Number of terms*	*Basic color terms*
1	Two	WHITE, BLACK
2	Three	WHITE, BLACK, RED
3	Four	WHITE, BLACK, RED, GREEN
4	Four	WHITE, BLACK, RED, YELLOW
5	Five	WHITE, BLACK, RED, GREEN, YELLOW
6	Six	WHITE, BLACK, RED, GREEN, YELLOW, BLUE
7	Seven	WHITE, BLACK, RED, GREEN, YELLOW, BLUE, BROWN
8	Eight, nine, ten, or eleven	WHITE, BLACK, RED, GREEN, YELLOW, BLUE, BROWN, PURPLE +/ PINK +/ ORANGE +/ GRAY

Systems 3 and 4 show that either GREEN or YELLOW can be the fourth color in a four-term system. In system 8, the color terms PURPLE, PINK, ORANGE, and GRAY can be added in any order to the basic seven-term system. Berlin and Kay made an extra, historical claim that when languages increase the number of color terms in their basic system they must pass through the sequence of systems in 3.57. In other words the types represent a sequence of historical stages through which languages may pass over time (where types 3 and 4 are alternatives).

In her experimentally based studies of Dani (Heider 1971, 1972a, 1972b) the psychologist Eleanor Rosch investigated how speakers of this Papua New Guinea language compared with speakers of American English in dealing with various color memory tasks. Dani has just two basic color terms: *mili* for cold, dark colors and *mola* for warm, light colors; while English has eleven. Both groups made similar kinds of errors and her work suggests that there is a common, underlying conception of color relationships that is due to physiological rather than linguistic constraints. When Dani speakers used their kinship terms to learn a new set of color names they agreed on the best example or focal points with the English speakers. This seems to be evidence that Dani speakers can distinguish all the focal color distinctions that English speakers can. When they need to, they can refer to them linguistically by circumlocutions, the color of mud, sky, and so on and they can learn new names for them. The conclusion seems to be that the perception of the color spectrum is the same for all human beings but that languages lexicalize different ranges of the spectrum for naming. As Berlin and Kay's work shows, the selection is not arbitrary and languages use the same classificatory procedure. Berlin and Kay's work can be interpreted to show that there are universals in color naming, and thus forms a critique of the hypothesis of linguistic relativity.

This universalist position has been challenged by scholars who have investigated other languages with small inventories of color terms, for example Debi Roberson and her colleagues' work on Berinmo, spoken in Papua New Guinea, which has five basic color terms (Roberson and Davidoff 2000, Roberson et al. 2005, Roberson and Hanley 2010). Berinmo's color terms divide up the blue/green area differently than English and experiments showed that speakers' perception and memory of colors in this zone are influenced by differences in the lexical division. Thus words seem to influence speakers' perception of colors. However, other studies, for example Kay et al. (2005) and Regier et al. (2010), have supported the important idea of universal focal colors or universal best examples. Research continues in this area, and it seems a more complicated picture may emerge of the relationship between the perception of colors and individual languages' systems of naming them.

3.7.3 Core vocabulary

The idea that each language has a core vocabulary of more frequent and basic words is widely used in foreign language teaching and dictionary writing. Morris Swadesh, a student of Edward Sapir, suggested that each language has a core vocabulary that is more resistant to loss or change than other parts of the vocabulary. He proposed that this core vocabulary could be used to trace lexical links between languages to establish family relationships between them. The implication of this approach is that the membership of the core vocabulary will be the same or similar for all languages. Thus comparison of the lists in different languages might show **cognates**, related words descended from a common ancestor language. Swadesh originally proposed a 200-word list that was later narrowed down to the 100-word list below:

3.58 Swadesh's (1972) 100-item basic vocabulary list

1. I
2. you
3. we
4. this
5. that
6. who
7. what
8. not
9. all
10. many
11. one
12. two
13. big
14. long
15. small
16. woman
17. man
18. person
19. fish
20. bird
21. dog
22. louse
23. tree
24. seed
25. leaf
26. root
27. bark
28. skin
29. flesh
30. blood
31. bone
32. grease
33. egg
34. horn
35. tail
36. feather
37. hair
38. head
39. ear
40. eye
41. nose
42. mouth
43. tooth
44. tongue
45. claw
46. foot
47. knee
48. hand
49. belly
50. neck
51. breasts
52. heart

53. liver	65. walk	77. stone	89. yellow
54. drink	66. come	78. sand	90. white
55. eat	67. lie	79. earth	91. black
56. bite	68. sit	80. cloud	92. night
57. see	69. stand	81. smoke	93. hot
58. hear	70. give	82. fire	94. cold
59. know	71. say	83. ash	95. full
60. sleep	72. sun	84. burn	96. new
61. die	73. moon	85. path	97. good
62. kill	74. star	86. mountain	98. round
63. swim	75. water	87. red	99. dry
64. fly	76. rain	88. green	100. name

To give one example, the Cushitic language Somali has for number 12 "two" the word *laba* and for 41 "nose" *san* while the Kenyan Cushitic language Rendille has 12 *lama* and 41 *sam*. Other cognates with consistent phonological alternations in the list will show that these two languages share a large proportion of this list as cognates. Swadesh argued that when more than 90 percent of the core vocabulary of two languages could be identified as cognates then the languages were closely related. Despite criticisms, this list has been widely used in comparative and historical linguistics.

The identification of semantic equivalences in this list is complicated by semantic shift. Cognates in two languages may drift apart because of historical semantic processes, including narrowing and generalization. Examples in English include *meat*, which has narrowed its meaning from "food" in earlier forms of the language and *starve*, which once had the broader meaning "die." The problem for the analyst is deciding how much semantic shift is enough to break the link between cognates. The idea that this basic list will be found in all languages has been contested. Swadesh's related proposal that change in the core vocabulary occurs at a regular rate and therefore can be used to date the splits between related languages has attracted stronger criticism.[16]

3.7.4 Universal lexemes

Another important investigation of universal lexical elements is that undertaken by Anna Wierzbicka and her colleagues (Wierzbicka 1992, 1996, Goddard and Wierzbicka 1994, 2002, 2013, Goddard 2001). These scholars have analyzed a large range of languages to try and establish a core set of universal lexemes. One feature of their approach is the avoidance of formal metalanguages. Instead they rely on what they call "reductive paraphrase in natural language." In other words they use natural languages as the tool of their lexical description, much as dictionary writers do. Like dictionary writers they rely on a notion of a limited core vocabulary that is not defined itself but is used to define other lexemes. Another way of putting this is to say that these writers use a subpart of a natural language as a natural semantic metalanguage, as described below:

3.59 Natural Semantic Metalanguage (Goddard 2001: 3)
... a "meaning" of an expression will be regarded as a paraphrase, framed in semantically simpler terms than the original expression, which is

> substitutable without change of meaning into all contexts in which the original expression can be used... The postulate implies the existence, in all languages, of a finite set of indefinable expressions (words, bound morphemes, phrasemes). The meanings of these indefinable expressions, which represent the terminal elements of language-internal semantic analysis, are known as "semantic primes."

A selection of the semantic primes proposed in this literature is given below, informally arranged into types:

3.60 Universal semantic primes (from Wierzbicka 1996, Goddard 2001)

Substantives:	I, you, someone/person, something, body
Determiners:	this, the same, other
Quantifiers:	one, two, some, all, many/much
Evaluators:	good, bad
Descriptors:	big, small
Mental predicates:	think, know, want, feel, see, hear
Speech:	say, word, true
Actions, events, movement:	do, happen, move, touch
Existence and possession:	is, have
Life and death:	live, die
Time:	when/time, now, before, after, a long time, a short time, for some time, moment
Space:	where/place, here, above, below, far, near, side, inside
"Logical" concepts:	not, maybe, can, because, if
Intensifier, augmentor:	very, more
Taxonomy:	kind (of), part (of)
Similarity:	like

About sixty of these semantic primes have been proposed in this literature. They are reminiscent of Swadesh's notion of core vocabulary but they are established in a different way: by the in-depth lexical analysis of individual languages. The claim made by these scholars is that the semantic primes of all languages coincide. Clearly this is a very strong claim about an admittedly limited number of lexical universals.

3.8 Summary

In this chapter we have looked at some important features of word meaning. We have discussed the difficulties linguists have had coming up with an airtight definition of the unit *word*, although speakers happily talk about them and consider themselves to be talking in them. We have seen the problems involved in divorcing word meaning from contextual effects and we discussed lexical ambiguity and vagueness. We have also looked at several types of lexical relations: homonymy, synonymy, opposites, hyponymy, meronymy, and so on; and seen two examples of derivational relations in the lexicon: causative verbs and agentive nouns. These represent characteristic examples of the networking of the vocabulary that a semantic description must reflect.[17] Finally we discussed how lexical typology investigates cross-linguistic patterns of word meaning. In chapter 9 we will look at approaches that try to characterize the networking of the lexicon in terms of semantic components.

EXERCISES

3.1 We saw that lexicographers group **lexemes**, or **senses**, into **lexical entries** by deciding whether they are related or not. If they are related (i.e. **polysemous**) then they are listed in a single lexical entry. If they are not related (i.e. **homonymous**) they are assigned independent entries. Below are groups of senses sharing the same phonological shape; decide for each group how the members should be organized into lexical entries.

port^{1}	noun. a harbor.
port^{2}	noun. a town with a harbor.
port^{3}	noun. the left side of a vessel when facing the prow.
port^{4}	noun. a sweet fortified dessert wine (*originally from Oporto in Portugal*).
port^{5}	noun. an opening in the side of a ship.
port^{6}	noun. a connector in a computer's casing for attaching peripheral devices.
mold^{1} (*Br.* **mould**)	noun. a hollow container to shape material.
mold^{2} (*Br.* **mould**)	noun. a furry growth of fungus.
mold^{3} (*Br.* **mould**)	noun. loose earth.
pile^{1}	noun. a number of things stacked on top of each other.
pile^{2}	noun. a sunken support for a building.
pile^{3}	noun. a large impressive building.
pile^{4}	noun. the surface of a carpet.
pile^{5}	noun. *Technical.* the pointed head of an arrow.
pile^{6}	noun. the soft fur of an animal.
ear^{1}	noun. organ of hearing.
ear^{2}	noun. the ability to appreciate sound (*an ear for music*).
ear^{3}	noun. the seed-bearing head of a cereal plant.
stay^{1}	noun. the act of staying in a place.
stay^{2}	noun. the suspension or postponement of a judicial sentence.
stay^{3}	noun. *Nautical.* a rope or guy supporting a mast.
stay^{4}	noun. anything that supports or steadies.
stay^{5}	noun. a thin strip of metal, plastic, bone, etc. used to stiffen corsets.

When you have done this exercise, you should check your decisions against a dictionary.

3.2 In the chapter we noted that **synonyms** are often differentiated by having different **collocations**. We used the examples of *big/large* and *strong/powerful*. Below is a list of pairs of synonymous adjectives. Try to find a collocation for one adjective that is impossible for the other. One factor you should be aware of is the difference between an **attributive** use of an adjective, when it modifies a noun, e.g. *red* in *a red face*, and a **predicative** use where the adjective follows a verb, e.g. *is red*, *seemed red*, *turned red*, etc. Some adjectives can only occur in one of these positions (*the man is unwell*, **the unwell man*), others change meaning in the two positions (*the late king*, *the king is late)*, and synonymous adjectives may differ in their ability to occur in these two positions. If you think this is the case for any of the following pairs, note it.

safe/secure	quick/fast	near/close	dangerous/perilous	wealthy/rich
fake/false	sick/ill	light/bright	mad/insane	correct/right

3.3 In section 3.4 we discussed three tests for ambiguity: the ***do so* identity**, **sense relations**, and **zeugma** tests. Try to use these tests to decide if the following words are ambiguous:

case (noun) fair (adjective) file (verb)

3.4 Below is a list of incompatible pairs. Classify each pair into one of the following types of relation: **complementary antonyms**, **gradable antonyms**, **reverses**, **converses**, or **taxonomic sisters**. Explain the tests you used to decide on your classifications and discuss any shortcomings you encountered in using them.

temporary/permanent	monarch/subject	advance/retreat
strong/weak	buyer/seller	boot/sandal
assemble/dismantle	messy/neat	tea/coffee
clean/dirty	open/shut	present/absent

3.5 Using nouns, provide some examples to show the relationship of **hyponymy**. Use your examples to discuss how many levels of hyponymy a noun might be involved in.

3.6 Try to find examples of the relationship of **hyponymy** with verbs. As in the last exercise, try to establish the number of levels of hyponymy that are involved for any examples you find.

3.7 Give some examples of the relationship of **meronymy**. Discuss the extent to which your examples exhibit **transitivity**.

3.8 Below are some nouns ending in *-er* and *-or*. Using your intuitions about their meanings, discuss their status as **agentive nouns**. In particular, are they derivable by regular rule or would they need to be listed in the lexicon? Check your decisions against a dictionary's entries.

author, blazer, blinker, choker, crofter, debtor, loner, mentor, reactor, roller

3.9 How would you describe the semantic effect of the suffix *-ist* in the following sets of nouns?

a.		b.	
	socialist		artist
	Marxist		scientist
	perfectionist		novelist
	feminist		chemist
	optimist		dentist
	humanist		satirist

For each example, discuss whether the derived noun could be produced by a general rule.

3.10 For each sentence pair below discuss any meaning relations you identify between the verbs marked in bold:

1 a. Freak winds **raised** the water level.
  b. The water level **rose**.
2 a. Fred **sent** the package to Mary.
  b. Mary **received** the package from Fred.
3 a. Ethel **tried** to win the cookery contest.
  b. Ethel **succeeded** in winning the cookery contest.
4 a. She didn't **tie** the knot.
  b. She **untied** the knot.
5 a. Vandals **damaged** the bus stop.
  b. The women **repaired** the bus stop.
6 a. Harry didn't **fear** failure.
  b. Failure didn't **frighten** Harry.
7 a. Sheila **showed** Klaus her petunias.
  b. Klaus **saw** Sheila's petunias.

FURTHER READING

John Lyons's *Semantics* (1977) discusses many of the topics in this chapter at greater length. Cruse (1986) is a useful and detailed discussion of word meaning and lexical relations. Lipka (2002) provides a survey of English lexical semantics. Lehrer and Kittay (1992) contains applications of the concept of lexical fields to the study of lexical relations, and Aitchison (2012) introduces current ideas on how speakers learn and understand word meanings. Nerlich et al. (2003) brings together studies on polysemy from a number of theoretical approaches. Lakoff (1987) is an enjoyable and stimulating discussion of the relationship between conceptual categories and words. Landau (2001) is an introduction to the practical issues involved in creating dictionaries. Fellbaum (1998) describes an important digital lexicon project: WordNet. Malt and Wolff (2010) contains cross-linguistic studies of word meanings, including kinship and color terms.

NOTES

1 In this chapter we talk only of whole-word meaning. Strictly speaking, lexical semantics is wider than this, being concerned both with the meaning of **morphemes** and **multi-word units**. Morphemes are the minimal meaningful units that make up words and larger units. So we can identify the word *hateful* as being composed of the two morphemes *hate* and *ful*, each of which has meaning. Some morphemes are words, traditionally called **free morphemes**, like *sleep*, *cat*, *father*. Others are **bound morphemes**: parts of word like *un-*, *re-*, and *pre-* in *unlikely*, *reanalyze*, and *prebook*. These elements exhibit a consistent meaning but do not occur as independent words. For reasons of space, we ignore here the question of the status of bound morphemes in the lexicon. See Aronoff and Fudeman (2005) and Booij (2007) for very accessible descriptions of morpheme theory. Lexical semanticists must also account for multi-word units: cases where a group of words have a unitary meaning which does not correspond to the compositional meaning of their parts, like the idiomatic phrases: *pass away*, *give up the ghost*, *kick the bucket*, *snuff it*, *pop one's clogs*, all of which mean *die*. Again, for reasons of space we won't pursue discussion of these multi-word semantic units here; see Cruse (1986) for discussion.

2 Ferdinand de Saussure called the relationship between a word and other accompanying words a **syntagmatic** relation, and the relationship between a word and related but non-occurring words, an **associative** relationship. This latter is also sometimes called a **paradigmatic** relationship. So the meaning of a phrase like *a red coat*, is partly produced by the syntagmatic combination of *red* and *coat*, while *red* is also in a paradigmatic relationship with other words like *blue*, *yellow*, etc.; and *jacket* is in a relationship with words like *coat*. The idea is that these paradigmatically related words help define the meaning of the spoken words. See Saussure (1974: 122–34) for discussion.

3 Here we follow the convention of writing postulated semantic elements in small capitals to distinguish them from real words. We discuss the hypothesis that words are composed of such semantic elements in chapter 9.

4 It is also possible to argue that this knowledge is not linguistic at all but knowledge about the world. Such an approach is consistent with the view that there is no distinction between linguistic and factual knowledge: it is all knowledge about the world. See Wilson (1967) for similar arguments and Katz (1972: 73ff.) for counterarguments. One of Katz's arguments is that you still have to have a division among knowledge to distinguish what would be the two following facts or beliefs:

a. Women are female.

b. Women are under fifty-feet tall.

We know both a and b from our experience of the world but there is a difference between them. If you met a fifty-foot woman, you would probably say that you had met a woman, albeit an unusual one. However if you meet a woman who is not female, there is some doubt: did you meet a woman at all? This difference is evidence for a conceptual/linguistic category of *woman*. See our earlier discussion of concepts and necessary and sufficient conditions in chapter 2.

5 By "absolute position" here Bloomfield means in isolation.

6 It is often proposed that the ideal lexicon would also include a fifth point: the lexical rules for the creation of new vocabulary, e.g. for just about any adjective X ending in *-al*, you can form a verb meaning "to cause to become X" by adding *-ize*: *radical* → *radicalize*; *legal* → *legalize*. However, it is clear that the results of derivational morphology are often semantically unpredictable: e.g. as Allan (1986, 1: 223) points out, this *-ize*

morpheme sometimes doesn't have this "cause to become" meaning, as in *womanize*, "to chase women." It seems that some forms formed by derivational processes, including compounding, are predictable in meaning, like *dog food*, *cat food*, *fish food*, etc., while others are not, like *fullback* or *night soil*. The latter type will have to be listed in the lexicon. See Allan (1986, 1: 214–56) for discussion.

7 These pairs are called *irreversible binomials* by Cruse (1986: 39), after Malkiel (1959). Cruse discusses their fossilization in terms of increasing degrees of *semantic opacity*, where the constituent elements begin to lose their independent semantic value.

8 Some authors use the term **antonymy** narrowly for just this class we are calling **gradable antonyms**. Cruse (1986), for example, calls this class **antonyms** and uses the cover term **opposites** for all the relations we describe in section 3.5.4.

9 This term should not be confused with **metonymy**. Metonymy, as will see briefly later in this chapter and in more detail in chapter 7, describes a referential strategy where a speaker refers to an entity by naming something associated with it. If, for example, in a mystery novel, one detective at a crime scene says to another: *Two uniforms got here first*, we might take the speaker to be using the expression *two uniforms* to refer to two uniformed police officers. This is an example of metonymy. Note that since a uniform could by extension be seen as part of a police officer, we can recognize some resemblance between metonymy and the part–whole relation **meronymy**. However we can distinguish them as follows: metonymy is a process used by speakers as part of their practice of referring; meronymy describes a classification scheme evidenced in the vocabulary.

10 We discuss the semantic role of AGENT in chapter 6. As we shall see there, AGENT describes the role of a voluntary initiator of an action, while ACTOR describes an entity that simply performs an action. Since the *–er/-or* nouns are used both for people, e.g. *teacher*, *actor*, and for machines, e.g. *blender*, *refrigerator*, a term like **actor nouns** would be more suitable than **agentive nouns**. Since this latter is well established though, we continue to use it here.

11 Of course a noun may just coincidentally have the appearance of an agentive noun, and not contain a productive English *-er* or *-or* suffix at all, like *butler*, *porter*, or *doctor*, which were borrowed as units already possessing French or Latin agentive endings.

12 See for example Ullmann's comment: "polysemy is an indispensable resource of language economy. It would be altogether impracticable to have separate terms for every referent" (Ullmann 1959: 18).

13 The source for these languages' color systems is Berlin and Kay (1969), except Dani (Heider 1971, 1972a, 1972b). This research became the World Color Survey project (Kay et al. 2009).

14 English has ten or eleven items depending on whether *orange* is included as a basic term. Wierzbicka (1990) noted that twelve-term systems exist in Russian, which has two terms corresponding to BLUE, and in Hungarian, which has two for RED.

15 See Croft (1990) for discussion of such hierarchies in typological studies.

16 This counting of percentages of cognates between languages is known as **lexicostatistics**, while the attempt to date languages by lexical changes is called **glottochronology**. See Swadesh (1972), Anttila (1989), and Trask (1996) for discussion.

17 There are differing views in the literature on how many lexical relations we should identify. For a very full list of relations, see Mel'čuk and Zholkovsky (1988).

REFERENCES

Aitchison, Jean 2012: *Words in the Mind: An Introduction to the Mental Lexicon*, fourth edition. Oxford: Wiley-Blackwell.

Allan, Keith 1986: *Linguistic Meaning*, 2 vols. London: Routledge & Kegan Paul.

Anttila, Raimo 1989: *Historical and Comparative Linguistics*. Amsterdam: John Benjamins.

Aronoff, Mark and Kirsten Fudeman. 2005: *What is Morphology?* Oxford: Blackwell.
Berlin, Brent and Paul Kay 1969: *Basic Color Terms: Their Universality and Evolution*. Berkeley: University of California Press.
Berlin, Brent, Dennis E. Breedlove and Peter H. Raven 1974: *Principles of Tzeltal Plant Classification*. New York: Academic Press.
Bloomfield, Leonard 1984: *Language*. Chicago: University of Chicago Press. (Originally published 1933.)
Booij, Geert 2007: *The Grammar of Words: An Introduction to Linguistic Morphology*, second edition. Oxford: Oxford University Press.
Boroditsky, Lera 2001: Does language shape thought? English and Mandarin speakers' conceptions of time. *Cognitive Psychology* 43.1: 1–22.
Boroditsky, Lera, Orly Fuhrman and Kelly McCormick 2010: Do English and Mandarin speakers think about time differently? *Cognition* 118: 123–29.
Boyeldieu, P. 2008: From semantic change to polysemy. In Vanhove (ed.), 303–15.
Croft, William 1990: *Typology and Universals*. Cambridge: Cambridge University Press.
Cruse, D. Alan 1986: *Lexical Semantics*. Cambridge: Cambridge University Press.
Downing, Pamela A. 1977: On "basic levels" and the categorization of objects in English discourse. *Proceedings of the Berkeley Linguistics Society* 3: 475–87.
Evans, Nick and David Wilkins 2000: In the mind's ear: the semantic extensions of perception verbs in Australian. *Language* 76: 546–92.
Fellbaum, Christiane (ed.) 1998: *WordNet: An Electronic Lexical Database*. Cambridge, MA: MIT Press.
Fillmore, Charles J. and B. T. S. Atkins 2000: Describing polysemy: the case of 'crawl'. In Yael Ravin and Claudia Leacock (eds.) *Polysemy*, 91–110. Oxford: Oxford University Press.
Firth, J. R. 1957: Modes of meaning. In J. R. Firth, *Papers in Linguistics 1934–1951*. London: Oxford University Press.
Goddard, Cliff 2001: Lexico-semantic universals: a critical overview. *Linguistic Typology* 5.1: 1–65.
Goddard, Cliff and Anna Wierzbicka (eds.) 1994: *Semantic and Lexical Universals*. Amsterdam: John Benjamins.
Goddard, Cliff and Anna Wierzbicka (eds.) 2002: *Meaning and Universal Grammar: Theory and Empirical Findings* (2 vols). Amsterdam/Philadelphia: John Benjamins.
Goddard, Cliff and Anna Wierzbicka 2013: *Words and Meanings: Lexical Semantics Across Domains, Languages, and Cultures*. Oxford: Oxford University Press.
Goodenough, Ward H. 1970: *Description and Comparison in Cultural Anthropology*. Chicago: Aldine.
Gordon, P. 2004: Numerical cognition without words: Evidence from Amazonia. *Science* 306: 496–99.
Gruber, J. S. 1965: Studies in lexical relations. PhD dissertation, MIT, Cambridge, MA. Reprinted by Indiana University Linguistics Club, Bloomington, Indiana.
Halliday, M. A. K. 1966: Lexis as a linguistic level. In C. E. Bazell, J. C. Catford, M. A. K. Halliday and R. H. Robins (eds.) *In Memory of J. R. Firth*. London: Longman.
Heider, E. 1971: Focal color areas and the development of color names. *Developmental Psychology* 4: 447–55.
Heider, E. 1972a: Probabilities, sampling, and the ethnographic method: the case of Dani colour names. *Man* 7.3: 448–66.
Heider, E. 1972b: Universals in color naming and memory. *Journal of Experimental Psychology* 93.1: 10–20.
Hunn, Eugene S. 1977: *Tzeltal Folk Zoology: The Classification of Discontinuities in Nature*. New York: Academic Press.
Johnson, Samuel 1983: *A Dictionary of the English Language*. London: Times Books. (First published 1755.)
Katz, Jerrold J. 1972: *Semantic Theory*. New York: Harper and Row.

Kay, Paul and Chad McDaniel 1978: The linguistic significance of the meanings of basic color terms. *Language* 54.3: 610–46.
Kay, Paul, Terry Regier and Richard S. Cook 2005: Focal colors are universal after all. *Proceedings of the National Academy of Science* 102: 8386–91.
Kay, Paul, Brent Berlin, William Merrifield and Richard Cook 2009: *The World Color Survey.* Stanford, CA: Center for the Study of Language and Information.
Kempson, Ruth M. 1977: *Semantic Theory.* Cambridge: Cambridge University Press.
Kronenfeld, David B. 2006: Issues in the classification of kinship terminologies. Toward a new typology. *Anthropos* 101.1: 203–19.
Lakoff, George 1987: *Women, Fire, and Dangerous Things: What Categories Reveal about the Mind.* Chicago: University of Chicago Press.
Landau, Sidney I. 2001: *Dictionaries: The Art and Craft of Lexicography,* second edition. Cambridge: Cambridge University Press.
Lehrer, Adrienne and Eva F. Kittay (eds.) 1992: *Frames, Fields, and Contrasts: New Essays in Semantic and Lexical Organization.* Hillsdale, NJ: Lawrence Erlbaum.
Lipka, Leonhard 2002: *English Lexicology: Lexical Structure, Word Semantics and Word Formation.* Tübingen: Gunter Narr.
Lounsbury, Floyd 1964: A formal account of the Crow- and Omaha-type kinship terminologies. In Ward H. Goodenough (ed.) *Explorations in Cultural Anthropology: Essays in Honor of George Peter Murdock,* 351–94. New York: McGraw-Hill. Reprinted in Stephen A. Tyler (ed.) 1969: *Cognitive Anthropology,* 212–45. New York: Holt, Rinehart & Winston.
Lyons, John 1963: *Structural Semantics.* Oxford: Blackwell.
Lyons, John 1968: *Introduction to Theoretical Linguistics.* Cambridge: Cambridge University Press.
Lyons, John 1977: *Semantics,* 2 vols. Cambridge: Cambridge University Press.
Majid, A., M. Bowerman, S. Kita, D. B. M. Haun, and S. C. Levinson 2004: Can language restructure cognition? The case for space. *Trends in Cognitive Science* 8: 108–14. Mahwah, NJ: Lawrence Erlbaum Associates.
Malkiel, Yakov 1959: Studies in irreversible binomials. *Lingua* 8: 113–60.
Malt, Barbara C. and Philip M. Wolff (eds.) 2010: *Words and the Mind: How Words Capture Human Experience.* Oxford: Oxford University Press.
Mel'čuk, Igor and Alexander Zholkovsky 1988: The explanatory combinatorial dictionary. In Martha Walton Evens (ed.) *Relational Models of the Lexicon: Representing Knowledge in Semantic Networks,* 41–74. Cambridge: Cambridge University Press.
Nerlich, Brigitte, Zazie Todd, Vimala Herman, and David D. Clarke (eds.) 2003: *Polysemy: Flexible Patterns of Meaning in Mind and Language.* Berlin: Mouton de Gruyter.
Newman, John (ed.) 2009: *The Linguistics of Eating and Drinking.* Amsterdam: John Benjamins.
Palmer, Frank R. 1981: *Semantics,* second edition. Cambridge: Cambridge University Press.
Read, Dwight W. 2001: Formal analysis of kinship terminologies and its relationship to what constitutes kinship. *Anthropological Theory* 1.2: 239–67.
Regier, Terry, Paul Kay, Aubrey L. Gilbert and Richard B. Ivry 2010: Language and thought: Which side are you on, anyway? In Malt and Wolff (eds.), 165–82.
Riemer, Nick 2005: *The Semantics of Polysemy: Meaning in English and Warlpiri.* Berlin: Mouton de Gruyter.
Roberson, Debi and Jules B. Davidoff 2000: The categorical perception of colors and facial expressions: The effect of verbal interference. *Memory & Cognition,* 28.6: 977–86.
Roberson, Debi, Jules B. Davidoff, Ian R. L. Davies, and Laura Shapiro 2005: Color categories: Evidence for the cultural relativity hypothesis. *Cognitive Psychology,* 50.4: 378–411.
Roberson, Debi and J. Richard Hanley 2010: Relatively speaking: An account of the relationship between language and thought in the color domain. In Malt and Wolff (eds.), 183–98.

Roget, Peter Mark 1995: *Roget's II: The New Thesaurus*, third edition. Boston: Houghton Mifflin. www.bartleby.com/110/, accessed 23 March 2015.
Rosch, Eleanor, Carolyn Mervis, Wayne Gray, David Johnson and Penny Boyes-Braem 1976: Basic objects in natural categories. *Cognitive Psychology* 8: 382–439.
Sapir, Edward 1949: *Language: An Introduction to the Study of Speech*. New York: Harcourt Brace. (First published 1921.)
Saussure, Ferdinand de 1974: *Course in General Linguistics*. Edited by Charles Bally and Albert Sechehaye, translation by Wade Baskin. Glasgow: Fontana/Collins. (First published 1915 as *Cours de Linguistique Générale*. Paris: Pyot.)
Spencer, Andrew 1991: *Morphological Theory*. Oxford: Blackwell.
Swadesh, Morris 1972: What is glottochronology? In Morris Swadesh, *The Origin and Diversification of Languages*, 271–84. Edited by Joel Sherzer. London: Routledge & Kegan Paul. (Article originally published in 1960.)
Sweetser, Eve E. 1990: *From Etymology to Pragmatics*. Cambridge: Cambridge University Press.
Trask, Robert Lawrence 1996: *Historical Linguistics*. London: Arnold.
Treffry, Diane (ed.) 2000: *Collins English Dictionary*, fifth edition. London and Glasgow: HarperCollins.
Tyler, Stephen A. (ed.) 1969: *Cognitive Anthropology*. New York: Holt, Rinehart & Winston.
Ullmann, Stephen 1959: *Semantics: An Introduction to the Science of Meaning*. Oxford: Blackwell.
Vanhove, Martine (ed.) 2008: *From Polysemy to Semantic Change: Towards a Typology of Lexical Semantic Associations*. Amsterdam: John Benjamins.
Viberg, Åke 1984: The verbs of perception: a typological study. In Brian Butterworth, Bernard Comrie and Östen Dahl (eds.) *Explanations for Language Universals*, 123–62. Berlin: Mouton.
Viberg, Åke 2002: Polysemy and disambiguation cues across languages: the case of Swedish *få* and English *get*. In Bengt Altenberg and Sylviane Granger (eds.) *Lexis in Contrast*, 3–30. Amsterdam: John Benjamins.
Wierzbicka, Anna 1990: The meaning of color terms: semantics, culture and cognition. *Cognitive Linguistics* 1: 99–150.
Wierzbicka, Anna 1992: *Semantics, Culture, and Cognition: Universal Concepts in Culture-Specific Configurations*. Oxford: Oxford University Press.
Wierzbicka, Anna 1996: *Semantics: Primes and Universals*. Oxford: Oxford University Press.
Wilson, N. L. 1967: Linguistic butter and philosophical parsnips. *Journal of Philosophy* 64: 55–67.
Zwicky, Arnold and Jerrold Sadock 1975: Ambiguity tests and how to fail them. In John P. Kimball (ed.) *Syntax and Semantics 4*, 1–36. New York: Academic Press.

chapter 4

Sentence Relations and Truth

4.1 Introduction

In the last chapter we looked at some of the semantic relations which hold between words and at the network effect that this gives to the lexicon. In this chapter we move on to semantic relations that may hold between sentences of a language. As we shall see, sometimes these relations are the result of particular words in the sentences, but in other cases the relations are the result of syntactic structure. As an example of an attempt to represent these relations, we will look at an approach to meaning based on the notion of **truth**, which has grown out of the study of logic. In particular we examine how successfully a truth-based approach is in characterizing the semantic relations of **entailment** and **presupposition**. We begin by going back to our early, deceptively simple question: what is meaning?

Many linguists would argue (see for example J. D. Fodor 1983) that there is no answer to this question and that in this it is like the question "what is a number?" in mathematics; or "what is grammaticality?" in syntax. The only true answer to such questions, it is argued, are whole theories: so one has to have a syntactic theory to give a substantive answer to the question: "what is grammaticality?" Otherwise, it is claimed, we are reduced to empty answers like: "Grammaticality is a property assigned to sentences by a grammar" (J. D. Fodor 1983). One way around this problem is to identify the kinds of phenomena a theory of semantics must cover. As we have seen, generative linguists orient their explanation in terms of a native speaker's competence. In this approach, the question then becomes: what kind of knowledge about the meaning of his or her language does the native speaker have? Answers to this question differ but there is a consensus in the literature that for sentence meaning, a semantic theory should reflect an English speaker's knowledge:[1]

4.1 That a and b below are **synonymous**:
  a. My brother is a bachelor.
  b. My brother has never married.

4.2 That a below **entails** b:
  a. The anarchist assassinated the emperor.
  b. The emperor is dead.

4.3 That a below **contradicts** b:
  a. My brother Sebastian has just come from Rome.
  b. My brother Sebastian has never been to Rome.

4.4 That a below **presupposes** b, as c does d:
  a. The Mayor of Manchester is a woman.
  b. There is a Mayor of Manchester.
  c. I regret eating your sandwich.
  d. I ate your sandwich.

4.5 That a and b are necessarily true, i.e. **tautologies**:
  a. Ireland is Ireland.
  b. Rich people are rich.

4.6 That a and b are necessarily false, i.e. **contradictions**:
  a. ?He is a murderer but he's never killed anyone.
  b. ?Now is not now.

We shall be looking at some of these relations in more detail in this chapter but for now we can give a rough characterization of each, as follows:

4.7 A is synonymous with B: A has the same meaning as B.

4.8 A entails B: we know that if A then automatically B.

4.9 A contradicts B: A is inconsistent with B.

4.10 A presupposes B: B is part of the assumed background against which A is said.

4.11 A is a tautology: A is automatically true by virtue of its own meaning, but informationally empty.

4.12 A is a contradiction: A is inconsistent with itself, i.e. asserts and denies the same thing.

The problem for semantics is to provide a more rigorous account of these and similar notions. In the following sections we look at how a notion of truth might be used to do this.

4.2 Logic and Truth

In this section, we take a brief excursion into the realm of logic. In doing this we are following a number of writers, like Richard Montague (1974), who have hypothesized that the tools of logic can help us to represent sentence meaning. We won't be going very far on this excursion and the interested reader is referred to an excellent introduction to logic in Allwood et al. (1977). We will go on to look at logic-based semantics in more detail ourselves in chapter 10.

The study of logic, of course, comes down to us from the classical Greek world, most famously from Aristotle. The beginnings of logic lie in a search for the principles of valid argument and inference. A well-known example is Aristotle's **modus ponens**, a type of argument in three steps, like the following:

4.13 a. If Arnd left work early, then he is in the pub.
b. Arnd left work early.
c. Arnd is in the pub.

If steps a and b (called the premises) are true then step c (the conclusion) is also guaranteed to be true. Here we follow the tradition of separating the premises from the conclusion by a horizontal line. Other rules of valid inference include the **modus tollens** exemplified in 4.14 below, the **hypothetical syllogism** in 4.15 and the **disjunctive syllogism** in 4.16:

4.14 a. If Arnd has arrived, then he is in the pub.
b. Arnd is not in the pub.
c. Arnd has not arrived.

4.15 a. If Arnd is in the pub, then he is drinking beer.
b. If Arnd is drinking beer, then he is drinking Guinness.
c. If Arnd is in the pub, then he is drinking Guinness.

4.16 a. Arnd is in the public bar or he is in the lounge.
b. Arnd isn't in the public bar.
c. Arnd is in the lounge.

A part of this study is a concern for the truth of statements and whether truth is preserved or lost by putting sentences into different patterns. Truth here is taken to mean a correspondence with facts, or in other words, correct descriptions of states of affairs in the world.[2] For the most part this truth is said to be **empirical** (or **contingent**), because we have to have some access to the facts of the world to know whether a statement is true or not. Thus the truth or otherwise of the sentence

4.17 My father was the first man to visit Mars.

depends on facts about the life of the speaker's father: if her father did go to Mars and was the first man there, then the sentence is true; otherwise it is false. In the same way the empirical truth of 4.18 below:

4.18 The earth revolves around the sun.

depends upon the facts of the universe.

Semanticists call a sentence's being true or false its **truth-value**, and the facts that would have to obtain in reality to make a sentence true or false, its **truth conditions**. A simple example of a linguistic effect on truth-value comes from negating a sentence. If we have a sentence like a below in English, adding *not* will reverse its truth-value:

4.19 a. Your car has been stolen.
b. Your car has not been stolen.

If a is true then b is false; also if a is false then b is true. To show that this relationship works for any statement, logicians use a schema called **logical form**, where a lower case letter (**p**, **q**, **r**, etc.) stands for the statement and a special symbol for negation: ¬. So the logical form for 4.19a is 4.20a and for 4.19b is 4.20b:

4.20 a. **p**
b. **¬p**

The effect of negation on the truth-value of a statement can be shown by a truth table, where T represents "true" and F "false," as below:

4.21

p	**¬p**
T	F
F	T

This table shows that when **p** is true (T), **¬p** is false (F); when **p** is false (F), **¬p** is true (T). This is then a succinct way of describing the truth effect of negation.

The truth-value of other linguistic elements is studied in logic in the same way. A number of connectives are especially important to logicians because they have a predictable effect on the truth conditions of compound statements. For example the truth-value of a compound formed by using *and* to join two statements is predictable from the truth of the constituent statements. See, for example:

4.22 a. The house is on fire.
b. The fire brigade are on the way.
c. The house is on fire and the fire brigade are on the way.

If 4.22a and b above are true, then the compound c is also true. If however either of a or b is false then the compound will be false. This can be shown by designing a truth table for *and*, and representing it by a special symbol ∧:

4.23

p	**q**	**p ∧ q**
T	T	T
T	F	F
F	T	F
F	F	F

This table tells us that only when both statements connected by ∧ are true will the compound be true. So 4.22c above will be false if the house is on fire but the fire brigade are not on the way, and also false if the fire brigade are on their way but to a false alarm: the house is not on fire. Most obviously of all, 4.22c is false if there is no fire and no fire brigade on the way. This connective is called **logical conjunction**.

The study of the truth effects of connectives like ¬ and ∧, also called **logical operators**, is called **propositional logic**, and logicians have studied the truth effects of a number of other connectives, for example those corresponding to the English words *or* and *if . . . then*. We can look briefly at these here and we will come back to them again in chapter 10.

There are two logical connectives which can correspond to English *or*. The first is called **disjunction** (or alternatively **inclusive or**) and is symbolized as ∨, thus giving logical forms like **p** ∨ **q**. The truth table for this connective is as follows:

4.24

p	q	p ∨ q
T	T	T
T	F	T
F	T	T
F	F	F

Thus a compound created with ∨ is true if one or both of the constituent sentences is true. This connective corresponds to the use of English *or* in sentences like the following:

4.25 I'll see you today or tomorrow.

Sentence 4.25 is true if either *I'll see you today* or *I'll see you tomorrow* is true, or both. It is only false if both are false.

The second connective which can correspond to English *or* is called **exclusive or**, or **XOR** for short, which we can symbolize as ⊻. This connective has the truth table in 4.26 below:

4.26

p	q	p ⊻ q
T	T	F
T	F	T
F	T	T
F	F	F

From 4.26 we can see that **p** ⊻ **q**. This connective corresponds to the use of English *or* in sentences like 4.27 below:

4.27 You will pay the fine or you will go to jail.

This use of *or* in English seems to have an implicit qualification of "but not both." Thus if a judge said sentence 4.27 to a defendant, it would seem very unfair if the defendant paid the fine and then was still sent to jail, as would be consistent with disjunction represented by the inclusive *or*. Thus the use in 4.27 seems to correspond more closely to exclusive *or*.

The next connective we will look at here is the **material implication**, symbolized as →. This connective has the truth table in 4.28

4.28

p	**q**	**p → q**
T	T	T
T	F	F
F	T	T
F	F	T

As 4.28 shows, the expression **p → q** is only false when **p** (the **antecedent**) is true and **q** (the **consequent**) is false. This connective is something like my use of English *if . . . then* if I utter a sentence like 4.29:

4.29 If it rains, then I'll go to the movies.

We can identify the *if*-clause in 4.29 as the antecedent and the *then*-clause as the consequent. This conditional sentence can only be false if it rains and I don't go to the movies, that is **p** = T, **q** = F. If it doesn't rain (**p** = F), my conditional claim cannot be invalidated by whatever I do: whether I go to the movies (**q** = T) or not (**q** = F). We can describe this relation by saying that **p** is a **sufficient condition** for **q** (rain will cause me to go) but not a **necessary condition** (other things might make me go; it might snow!).

This relation is a little hard to grasp and the reason is because we intuitively try to match it with our ordinary use of conditional sentences in English. However, conditionals in real languages often have more to them than this truth-conditional connective shows. For example, there is often an assumption of a causal connection between the antecedent clause (the *if*-clause) and the consequent (the *then*-clause), as in 4.30 below:

4.30 If Patricia goes to the party, then Emmet will go too.

A natural implication of sentence 4.30 is that Emmet is going **because** Patricia is. This is partly like our connective → because if Patricia goes to the party but Emmet doesn't (**p** = T, **q** = F) then the conditional sentence 4.30 is false, as the truth table for → suggests. However, because of the causal implication, we might feel that if Patricia doesn't go (**p** = F) the conditional 4.30 implies that Emmet won't go. Thus we might feel that if he does go (**q** = T), the claim is invalidated. The logical connective, however, doesn't work like this: as 4.28 shows, if the antecedent is false, the compound is true, whatever the truth-value of the consequent.

This truth-conditional relation also seems to miss our intuitions about another ordinary language use of conditional *if . . . then* constructions: **counterfactuals**, where the speaker overtly signals that the antecedent is false, for example:

4.31 If wishes were money, then we'd all be rich.[3]

The lack of fit here with our intuitions can be shown by the sentences in 4.32 below:

4.32 a. If I were an ostrich, then I would be a bird.
b. If I were an ostrich, then I would not be a bird.

Let us interpret each of these conditionals as the **p** → **q** relation: since I am not in fact an ostrich, we might take **p** in 4.32a to be false, and if we follow the reasoning of the conditional then **q** might seem to be true. Thus, by the truth table in 4.28 the sentence 4.32a is true. This seems a reasonable fit with our intuition about 4.32a. The problem is that assuming the same antecedent **p** in 4.32b to be false means that 4.32b also has to be true, according to our truth table 4.28. Even if we accept the less likely 4.32b as true, it is uncomfortable to try and hold both 4.32a and b to be true for the same speaker in the same context. It seems likely that the material implication relation simply doesn't fit our use of counterfactuals. We will not follow this issue any further here; for a discussion of logical implication and ordinary language conditionals, see Lewis (1973) and the overview in Haack (1978). What we can say is that the logical relation of material implication captures some but not all aspects of our use of *if . . . then* in English.

There is one other related connective we might mention here, the **bi-conditional**, symbolized by ≡ (or alternatively ↔). This connective has the truth table in 4.33 below:

4.33

p	q	p ≡ q
T	T	T
T	F	F
F	T	F
F	F	T

As 4.33 shows, a statement **p ≡ q** is true when **p** and **q** have the same truth-value. The name "bi-conditional" reflects the fact that the **p ≡ q** is equivalent to the compound conditional expression (**p** → **q**) ∧ (**q** → **p**), which we can paraphrase as "if **p** then **q** and if **q** then **p**." This connective corresponds to the English words *if and only if* as in 4.34:

4.34 We'll leave if and only if we're forced to.

If we reverse the English clause order and identify the condition *if and only if we are forced to* as **p,** and the consequent *We'll leave* as **q,** then we can say that **p** is a **necessary condition** for **q**, that is, **p** is the only possible cause for **q**. Given this, this connector is a plausible translation of the intended meaning of our earlier example 4.30 with *if... then.* In logic this relation "**p** if and only if **q**" is often abbreviated to "**p** iff **q**."

This has been just a brief look at logical connectives and their English counterparts. As we have mentioned, in logic these connectives are important for the establishment of valid arguments and correct inductive reasoning. Using the symbols we have introduced in this section, we can represent the types of valid inference exemplified earlier in 4.13–16, as follows:

4.35 Modus ponens

p → **q**
p
———
q

4.36 Modus tollens

$$\begin{array}{l} \mathbf{p} \rightarrow \mathbf{q} \\ \neg \mathbf{q} \\ \hline \neg \mathbf{p} \end{array}$$

4.37 Hypothetical syllogism

$$\begin{array}{l} \mathbf{p} \rightarrow \mathbf{q} \\ \mathbf{q} \rightarrow \mathbf{r} \\ \hline \mathbf{p} \rightarrow \mathbf{r} \end{array}$$

4.38 Disjunctive syllogism

$$\begin{array}{l} \mathbf{p} \lor \mathbf{q} \\ \neg \mathbf{p} \\ \hline \mathbf{q} \end{array}$$

For our current purposes, what we need to hold onto are these ideas from logic: that statements have a truth-value; that this truth-value depends upon a correspondence to facts, and that different ways of connecting statements have different effects on the truth-value of the compounds produced.

4.3 Necessary Truth, *A Priori* Truth, and Analyticity

As we have seen, the notion of empirical truth depends on a correlation to states of affairs in reality. Philosophers and logicians have identified another type of truth which seems instead to be a function of linguistic structure. For example, we know that the tautology

4.39 My father is my father.

is always true (in its literal meaning) without having to refer to the facts of the world, as is a sentence like:

4.40 Either he's still alive or he's dead.

We do not have to check a pulse to find out whether this sentence is true.

In the same way, contradictions are false simply by virtue of their own meaning, for example:

4.41 ?She was assassinated last week but fortunately she's still alive.

This second kind of truth has been the focus of much investigation. The question of how it is that we might know a statement to be true without checking the facts of the world has been discussed by many philosophers[4] and various distinctions of truth have been made. For example, we started out by characterizing this type of truth in epistemological terms, that is in terms of what the speaker knows (or needs to know before making a judgment about truth). From this perspective, truth that is known before or without experience has traditionally been called ***a priori***. This *a priori* truth is contrasted with ***a posteriori*** truth: truth which, as in our examples 4.17 and 4.18 earlier, can only be known on the basis of empirical testing.

Another related concept is Leibniz's distinction between **necessary** truths, which cannot be denied without forcing a contradiction, for example the arithmetical statement *Two and two make four*, and **contingent** truths which can be contradicted, depending on the facts, for example the sentence *The dodo is extinct*. If someone unexpectedly found a dodo in a forest on Mauritius, this latter sentence would become false. It is difficult, on the other hand, to imagine circumstances in which *Two and two make four* would unexpectedly become false. This is similar to our *a priori/a posteriori* distinction but comes at truth from another viewpoint: not in terms of what the speaker knows but in terms of what the world is like. We can say that it is hard to think how our sentence about two and two making four could not be true without changing our view of the present facts of the world.[5] From this perspective a sentence like 4.40 is also **necessarily true** and a contradiction like 4.41 is **necessarily false**.

In another, related terminology tautologies like 4.39 are **analytic** while a sentence like *My father is a sailor* is **synthetic**. Analytic statements are those where the truth follows from the meaning relations within the sentence, regardless of any relationship with the world, while a synthetically true statement is true because it accords with the facts of the world.

Thus we have three related distinctions of truth: between *a priori* and *a posteriori*, necessary and contingent, and analytic and synthetic. These notions are closely linked, yet not quite identical. As noted by Kripke (1980), part of their difference comes from the concerns of the analyst: the *a priori/a posteriori* distinction is an epistemological one: it concerns the source of what the speaker knows. If just knowing a language is enough to know the truth of a proposition then it is *a priori*. If the knowledge has to be based on experience of the world it is *a posteriori*. The necessary/contingent distinction on the other hand is really a metaphysical one, where we are philosophically questioning the nature of reality. We can hypothesize that it is the nature of reality that ensures that a sentence like *Two and two make four* is a necessary truth. Finally, the analytic/synthetic distinction is semantic in orientation. The traditional claim has been that analytic sentences are true because of the meaning of the words within them: for example, the meaning of the predicate might somehow be included in the meaning of the subject: it might not add anything new.[6] This certainly seems to be true of our tautology *My father is my father*.

We can see that the three notions are related because under the kind of definitions we have introduced so far, our example sentence *My father is my father* is an *a priori* truth, it is necessarily true and it is analytic. As we have mentioned, this classification of truth has been the subject of much debate in the philosophical literature and it has been argued by some philosophers, for example Kripke (1980), that the terms do not characterize exactly the same set of statements, for example that a statement might be a necessary truth but not an *a priori* truth. To parallel a standard example, a statement of identity like *Mogadishu is Hamar* is necessarily true because these are two names for the same city, the capital of Somalia. Clearly, though, it is possible for a person not to know this, and therefore for this person our sentence is not an *a priori* truth. The person might have to ask people or look it up in a book, making the knowledge *a posteriori*.[7]

This sketch is enough for our present purposes. In our discussion we will informally use necessary truth and analytic truth as synonymous terms to describe sentences which are true by virtue of their meaning, and which therefore are known to be true by a speaker of the language without any checking of the facts. See Grayling (1982) for further discussion of the relations of these notions.

We can provide further examples of sentences that are analytic or necessarily true in this sense if we imagine logically minded sports fans looking forward to the next World Cup Final and saying the following:

4.42 a. Either Germany will win the World Cup or Germany won't win the World Cup.
b. If Germany are champions and Brazil are runners-up then Germany are champions.
c. All teams who win are teams.
d. If Germany beat Brazil then Brazil lose to Germany.

Sentences like 4.42 a–c above have been important in the development of logic. This is because their truth can be predicted from their logical form. Take 4.42a for example: if, as before, we replace each clause by an arbitrary letter, we produce a logical form, for example:

4.43 Either **p** or not-**p**

This formula will be true for any clause, as long as each clause is the same, represented above by using the same letter. For example:

4.44 Either we'll make it on time, or we won't make it on time.

Similarly, sentence 4.42b above can be given the logical form:

4.45 If **p** and **q** then **p**

Once again whatever clauses we use for **p** and **q** the formula will be true, for example:

4.46 If the house is sold and we aren't there, the house is sold.

Sentence 4.42c is also necessarily true because of its logical form, but in this case the truth behavior is caused by the presence within the clause of the quantifier *all*. To find its logical form we have to go inside the clause and replace the subject and predicate by variables, for example:

4.47 All *X*'s that *Y* are *X*'s.

Again, this form will be true whatever subject and predicate we insert for *X* and *Y*, for example:

4.48 All birds that fly are birds.[8]

The study of the truth behavior of such sentences with quantifiers like *all*, *every*, *each*, *some*, *one* gave rise to a second type of logic usually called **predicate logic**. Once again, good introductions to this logic can be found in Allwood et al.

(1977). We will come back to both propositional and predicate logic again in chapter 10.

The important point here is that, as we have seen, there are certain words like the connectors *and*, *or*, *if . . . then*, the negative word *not*, and quantifiers like *all*, *some*, *one*, which influence the truth behavior of sentences. For this reason these are sometimes called **logical words**. So the sentences 4.42a–c are necessarily true because of the presence of logical words, which means that their truth behavior is predictable from their logical form.

The truth of sentence 4.42d (*If Germany beat Brazil then Brazil lose to Germany*), however, depends on the meaning of individual words like *beat* and *lose*, and not any logical form we might give the sentence, like 4.49:

4.49 If *G X B* then *B Y G*.

We can see this because, if we replace the verbs with other verbs, we cannot predict that the resulting sentence will also be analytically true, for example:

4.50 If Germany attack Brazil then Brazil outscore Germany.

This sentence might be true, or not: we cannot tell just from the sentence. It seems that sentence 4.42d is necessarily true because of the semantic relationship in English between the verbs *beat* and *lose*. This kind of necessary truth has not traditionally been a concern of logicians, because its effects cannot easily be reduced to general rules or schemas: it relies on the very varied and individual lexical relations we looked at in chapter 3. Thus such necessarily true sentences can derive from synonymy as in 4.51a below; from simple **antonymy** as in 4.51b; from converse pairs as in 4.51c; or **hyponymy** as in 4.51d:[9]

4.51 a. My bachelor brother is an unmarried man.
b. If Elvis is dead then he is not alive.
c. If she's his sister then he's her brother.
d. A cat is an animal.

So our examples have shown us that sentences can be analytically true because of the behavior of logical words (connectors, quantifiers) or because of the meaning of individual nouns and verbs. In each case we know that the sentences are true without having to check any facts about the world.

4.4 Entailment

Using this special meaning of "truth" that we have been looking at, some semanticists have claimed that the meaning relations discussed in section 4.1 can be given a more rigorous definition. The claim is that there are fixed **truth relations** between sentences which hold regardless of the empirical truth of the sentences. We can examine this claim by looking at the semantic relation of **entailment**. Let's take as an example the relationship between sentences 4.52a and b below, where a is said to entail b:

4.52 a. The anarchist assassinated the emperor.
b. The emperor died.

Assuming as usual that the same individual is denoted by *the emperor* here, there are a number of ways of informally describing this relationship. We could say that if somebody tells us 4.52a and we believe it, then we know 4.52b without being told any more. Or we could say that it is impossible for somebody to assert 4.52a but deny b. What such definitions have to try to capture is that entailment is not an inference in the normal sense: we do not have to reason to get from 4.52a to b, we just know it instantaneously because of our knowledge of English. A truth-based definition of entailment might allow us to state the relationship more clearly and would be something like 4.53 below:

4.53 Entailment defined by truth:
A sentence **p** entails a sentence **q** when the truth of the first (**p**) guarantees the truth of the second (**q**), and the falsity of the second (**q**) guarantees the falsity of the first (**p**).

We can see how this would work for our examples:

4.54 Step 1: If **p** (The anarchist assassinated the emperor) is true, is **q** (The emperor died) automatically true? Yes.
Step 2: If **q** (The emperor died) is false, is **p** (The anarchist assassinated the emperor) also false? Yes.
Step 3: Then **p** entails **q**. Note if **p** is false then we can't say anything about **q**; it can be either true or false.

We can try to show this relation in an accessible form if we take the logician's truth tables, seen earlier, and adapt them somewhat. We can continue to use the symbols **p** and **q** for our two sentences, and T and F for true and false, as in normal truth tables, but we will add arrows (→ and ←) to show the direction of a relation "when … then." So the first line of 4.55 below is to be read "When **p** is true, **q** is true," and the last line is to be read "when **q** is true, **p** can be either true or false." By taking these liberties with traditional truth tables, we can show the truth relations of entailment in 4.55, a composite truth table:

4.55 Composite truth table for entailment

p		**q**
T	→	T
F	→	T or F
F	←	F
T or F	←	T

When this set of relations hold between **p** and **q**, **p** entails **q**. From this table we can see that only the truth of the entailing sentence or the falsity of the entailed sentence has consequences for the other sentence. When **p** is false, **q** can be either true or false: if all we were told was that the anarchist didn't assassinate the emperor, we wouldn't know whether the emperor was dead or alive. When **q** is true, **p** can be either true or false: if we just know that the emperor is dead, that doesn't tell us anything about whether the anarchist assassinated him or not.[10]

We have said that an entailment relation is given to us by linguistic structure: we do not have to check any fact in the world to deduce the entailed sentence from the entailing sentence. The source may be lexical or syntactic. In our example above it is clearly lexical: the relationship of entailment between 4.52a and b derives from the lexical relationship between *assassinate* and *die*. In some sense the meaning of *assassinate* contains the meaning of *die*. In chapter 3 we called a similar relationship of meaning **hyponymy**; and indeed hyponymy between lexical items is a regular source for entailment between sentences. For example, the noun *dog* is a hyponym of *animal*, so it follows that sentence 4.56 below entails sentence 4.57:

4.56 I bought a dog today.

4.57 I bought an animal today.

Other sources for entailment are syntactic: for example, active and passive versions of the same sentence will entail one another. Sentence 4.58 below entails 4.59, and vice versa:

4.58 The Etruscans built this tomb.

4.59 This tomb was built by Etruscans.

In fact, the relationship of entailment allows us to define **paraphrase**. Paraphrases, like 4.58 and 4.59, are sentences which have the same set of entailments, or, to put it another way, **mutually entail** each other.

This truth-based definition does seem to capture our basic intuitions about entailment and semanticists have gone on to characterize other semantic relations in terms of truth relations. For example, we could very simply characterize synonymy with the table:

4.60 Composite truth table for synonymy

p		**q**
T	→	T
F	→	F
T	←	T
F	←	F

This table simply says, of course, that **p** and **q** always have the same truth-value, that is, if **p** describes a situation so will **q**, and vice versa; while if either incorrectly describes a situation so will the other. We can see this is true for examples like:

4.61 Alice owns this book.

4.62 This book belongs to Alice.

where again we observe the convention that it is the same Alice and the same book in the two sentences.[11]

The opposite of this relation of synonymy would be contradiction, with the truth table below:

4.63 Contradiction

p		q
T	→	F
F	→	T
T	←	F
F	←	T

where the simplest examples involve negation, as below:

4.64 Mr Jones stole my car.

4.65 Mr Jones did not steal my car.

but other examples might also include the lexical relation of simple or binary antonymy, as in our earlier examples with *beat/lose to*.

So thus far it seems that recasting semantic relations as truth relations allows us to describe neatly the relations we listed in section 4.1 as being the focus of our investigations. In the next section, however, we look at one of these relations, presupposition, which seems to lend itself less well to a truth-based description.

4.5 Presupposition

4.5.1 Introduction

In ordinary language, of course, to presuppose something means to assume it, and the narrower technical use in semantics is related to this. In the following examples the a sentence is said to presuppose the b sentence:

4.66 a. He's stopped turning into a werewolf every full moon.
b. He used to turn into a werewolf every full moon.

4.67 a. Her husband is a fool.
b. She has a husband.

4.68 a. I don't regret leaving London.
b. I left London.

4.69 a. The Prime Minister of Malaysia is in Dublin this week.
b. Malaysia has a prime minister.

4.70 a. I do regret leaving London.
b. I left London.

Presupposition has been an important topic in semantics: the 1970s in particular saw lively debates in the literature. Books devoted largely to the subject include

Kempson (1975), D. Wilson (1975), Boer and Lycan (1976), Gazdar (1979) and Oh and Dinneen (1979); and important papers include J. D. Fodor (1979) and Wilson and Sperber (1979). In retrospect this interest in presupposition can be seen as coinciding with the development of pragmatics as a subdiscipline. The basic idea, mentioned in chapter 1, is that semantics would deal with conventional meaning, those aspects which do not seem to vary too much from context to context, while pragmatics would deal with aspects of individual usage and context-dependent meaning.

The importance of presupposition to the pragmatics debate is that, as we shall see, it seems to lie at the borderline of such a division. In some respects presupposition seems like entailment: a fairly automatic relationship, involving no reasoning, which seems free of contextual effects. In other respects though, presupposition seems sensitive to facts about the context of utterance. We will look at this sensitivity to context in section 4.5.5.

For now we can begin by identifying two possible types of approach to presupposition, arising from different ways of viewing language.

4.5.2 Two approaches to presupposition

In the first approach, rather in the philosophical tradition, sentences are viewed as external objects: we don't worry too much about the process of producing them, or the individuality of the speaker or writer and their audience. Meaning is seen as an attribute of sentences rather than something constructed by the participants. Semantics then consists of relating a sentence-object to other sentence-objects and to the world. When in the last section we characterized sentence relations in terms of truth relations we adopted this perspective. The second approach views sentences as the utterances of individuals engaged in a communication act. The aim here is about modeling the strategies that speakers and hearers use to communicate with one another. So we might look at communication from the speaker's viewpoint and talk about presupposition as part of the task of packaging an utterance; or adopt the listener's viewpoint and see presupposition as one of a number of inferences that the listener might make on the basis of what the speaker has just said. The first approach is essentially semantic and the second pragmatic.

Let's use 4.71 below and its presupposition 4.72 as an example to show these different views.

4.71 John's brother has just got back from Texas.

4.72 John has a brother.

We can adopt the sentences-as-external-objects approach and try to identify a semantic relationship between these two sentences. One obvious way is to cast this as a truth relation, as we did for entailment and other relations in the last section. To do this we might reason as in 4.73, to set up the partial truth table in 4.74:

4.73 Presupposition as a truth relation.
Step 1: If **p** (the presupposing sentence) is true then **q** (the presupposed sentence) is true.
Step 2: If **p** is false, then **q** is still true.
Step 3: If **q** is true, **p** could be either true or false.

4.74 A first composite truth table for presupposition

p		**q**
T	→	T
F	→	T
T or F	←	T

At the risk of being longwinded, we can work through 4.73. If it is true that John's brother has come back from Texas, it must be true that John has a brother. Similarly, if it is false that John's brother has come back from Texas (if he is still there, for example), the presupposition that John has a brother still survives. Finally, if is true that John has a brother, it doesn't tell us anything about whether he has come back from Texas or not: we just don't know.

So viewing presupposition as a truth relation allows us to set up a truth table like 4.74, and allows us to capture an important difference between entailment and presupposition. If we negate an entailing sentence, then the entailment fails; but negating a presupposing sentence allows the presupposition to survive. Take for example the entailment pair in 4.75:

4.75 a. I saw my father today.
b. I saw someone today.

If we negate 4.75a to form 4.76a then it no longer entails 4.75b, repeated as 4.76b:

4.76 a. I didn't see my father today.
b. I saw someone today.

Now 4.76b no longer automatically follows from the preceding sentence: again it might be true, we just don't know. Compare this with the presupposition pair:

4.77 a. The mayor of Liverpool is in town.
b. There is a mayor of Liverpool.

If we negate 4.77a to form 4.78a the resulting sentence still has the presupposition, shown as 4.78b:

4.78 a. The mayor of Liverpool isn't in town today.
b. There is a mayor of Liverpool.

So negating the presupposing sentence does not affect the presupposition, whereas, as we saw, negating an entailing sentence destroys the entailment. So it seems that viewing presupposition as a truth relation allows us to capture one interesting difference between the behavior of presupposition and entailment under negation.

By comparison, we can sketch an idea of how an alternative, interactional view of presupposition might work for our original example; *John's brother has just got back from Texas.* This approach views presupposition as one aspect of a speaker's strategy of organizing information for maximum clarity for the listener. Let us say roughly that the speaker wants to inform the listener that a particular individual has returned from Texas. The way she does this will depend on what she estimates about her listener's knowledge. If she thinks he knows John but not his brother, we can see in her use of 4.64 an ordering of the assertions in 4.79–80:

4.79 Assertion 1: John has a brother X.

4.80 Assertion 2: X has come back from Texas.

In our example 4.71 the first assertion is downgraded or backgrounded by being placed in a noun phrase [*John's brother*] while the second assertion is highlighted or foregrounded by being given the main verb. Why foreground one assertion rather than another? The answer must depend on the speaker's intentions and her guesses about the knowledge held by the participants. For example the speaker might judge that the listener knows 4.79 but that 4.80 is new information, and therefore needs to be foregrounded. Here we could speculate that the speaker decides to include the old information 4.79 to help the listener to identify the individual that the new information is about. Note too that a speaker can use 4.71 even if the listener does not know John has a brother. In such a case both assertions are new but the speaker has decided to rank them in a particular order.

4.5.3 Presupposition failure

One phenomenon which has traditionally caused problems for a truth relations approach but may be less problematic in an interactional approach is **presupposition failure**. It has been observed that using a name or a definite description to refer presupposes the existence of the named or described entity:[12] so the a sentences below presuppose the b sentences:

4.81 a. Ronald is a vegetarian.
b. Ronald exists.

4.82 a. The King of France is bald.
b. There is a King of France.

Example 4.82 is of course the subject of Bertrand Russell's discussion of the problem (Russell 1905), and is by now one of the most discussed examples in this literature. The problem arises when there exists no referent for the nominal. If there's no Ronald or King of France, that is if the b sentences above are false, what is the status of the a sentences? Are they false, or are they in a gray area, neither true nor false? In a truth-based approach, on a gray-area analysis, we need to add a line to our truth table, but what does the line look like?

4.83 A second truth table for presupposition

p		**q**
T	→	T
F	→	T
T or F	←	T
?(T or F)	←	F

What this table tries to show is that if **q** is false, the status of **p** is dubious, possibly neither true nor false. This is a problem for truth-based theories, known as a **truth-value gap**. If a statement can be neither true nor false, it opens a nasty can of worms. How many degrees in between are possible? A good deal of the attractive simplicity of the truth-based approach seems in danger of being lost. It is a problem that has generated a number of solutions in the philosophical literature; see McCulloch (1989) for discussion, and for a solution in the linguistics literature, J. D. Fodor (1979). Russell's famous solution was to analyze definite descriptions as complex expressions roughly equivalent to 4.84 (adapted from McCulloch 1989: 47):

4.84 The King of France is bald is true if and only if:
 a. at least one thing is the king
 b. at most one thing is the king
 c. whatever is the king is bald.

From 4.84, it follows that sentence 4.82a is false if there is no king of France, and that there is no gray area between true and false, no truth-value gap. The cost however is a large discrepancy between the surface language and the semantic representation. Do we really want to say that a name is underlyingly a cluster of three statements?

For an interactional approach, there is less of a problem. Such an approach would claim that a speaker's use of definite NPs like names and definite descriptions to refer is governed by conventions about the accessibility of the referents to the listener. In some obvious way, I have made a communication error if I say to you:

4.85 Heronymous is bringing us a crate of champagne.

if you don't know any person called Heronymous. Your most likely response would be to ask "Who's Heronymous?," thus signaling the failure. So we can hypothesize that there is an interactional condition on referring: a speaker's use of a name or definite description to refer usually carries a guarantee that the listener can identify the referent.[13]

So in an interactional approach the issue of presuppositional failure shifts attention from the narrow question of the truth-value of statements about non-existent entities to the more general question of what conventions license a speaker's referring use of definite nominals.

4.5.4 Presupposition triggers

We have seen that the use of a name or definite description gives rise to a presupposition of existence. Other types of presupposition are produced by particular words or constructions, which together are sometimes called **presupposition triggers**. Some of these triggers derive from syntactic structure, for example the cleft construction in 4.86 and the pseudo-cleft in 4.87 share the presupposition in 4.88:

4.86 It was his behavior with frogs that disgusted me.

4.87 What disgusted me was his behavior with frogs.

4.88 Something disgusted me.

Other forms of subordinate clauses may produce presuppositions, for example, time adverbial clauses and comparative clauses. In the following sentences, the a sentence has the presupposition in b:

4.89 a. I was riding motorcycles before you learned to walk.
b. You learned to walk.

4.90 a. He's even more gullible than you are.
b. You are gullible.

Many presuppositions are produced by the presence of certain words. Many of these **lexical triggers** are verbs. For example, there is a class of verbs like *regret* and *realize* that are called **factive** verbs because they presuppose the truth of their complement clause. Compare sentences 4.91 and 4.92 below: only the sentence with the factive *realize* presupposes 4.93. There is no such presupposition with the non-factive verb *think*.

4.91 Sean realized that Miranda had dandruff.

4.92 Sean thought that Miranda had dandruff.

4.93 Miranda had dandruff.

Similarly compare 4.94–6:

4.94 Sheila regretted eating the banana.

4.95 Sheila considered eating the banana.

4.96 Sheila ate the banana.

Some verbs of judgment produce presuppositions. Compare 4.97–9 below:

4.97 John accused me of telling her.

4.98 John blamed me for telling her.

4.99 I told her.

Once again one verb, *blame*, produces the presupposition in 4.99, while another, *accuse*, does not.

For a final example of lexical triggers, consider so-called aspectual verbs, like *start*, *begin*, *stop*. These verbs have a kind of switch presupposition: the new situation is both described and is presupposed not to have held prior to the change; see for example 4.100–1 below, where again the a sentences presuppose the b sentences:

4.100 a. Judy started smoking cigars.
b. Judy used not to smoke cigars.

4.101 a. Michelle stopped seeing werewolves.
b. Michelle used to see werewolves.

4.5.5 Presuppositions and context

As mentioned earlier, one problem for a simple truth-based account of presupposition is that often the presuppositional behavior seems sensitive to context. While a given sentence always produces the same set of entailments, it seems that this is not true of presuppositions. Levinson (1983) gives as an example the type of presupposition usually triggered by time adverbial clauses, for instance 4.102a presupposing 4.102b below:

4.102 a. She cried before she finished her thesis.
b. She finished her thesis.

However, if we change the verb, as in 4.103a below, the presupposition 4.103b is no longer produced:

4.103 a. She died before she finished her thesis.
b. She finished her thesis.

Why is this? It is argued that in 4.103 the presupposition is blocked or canceled by our general knowledge of the world: quite simply we know that dead people do not normally complete unfinished theses. This characteristic is sometimes known as **defeasibility**, that is the canceling of presuppositions. If presuppositions arise or not depending on the context of knowledge, this suggests that we need an account of them that can make reference to what the participants know, as in an interactional approach, rather than an account limited to formal relations between sentences.

Another example of context sensitivity, pointed out by Strawson (1950), occurs with sentences like 4.104 and 4.105 below:

4.104 It was Harry who Alice loved.

4.105 It was Alice who loved Harry.

These sentences seem to describe the same essential situation of Alice loving Harry; or, to put it another way, we might say that they embody the same proposition. The difference between them is that they belong to different conversational contexts: whether the participants have been discussing Harry or Alice. As Strawson points out, they seem to give rise to different presuppositions, with 4.104 producing 4.106 and 4.105 producing 4.107:

4.106 Alice loved someone.

4.107 Someone loved Harry.

The same phenomenon is found with **intonation** in English, where stressing different parts of the sentence can produce different presuppositions. Using capitals to show the position of this stress, we can produce the presupposition in 4.106 above with 4.108 below, and 4.107 above with 4.109 below:

4.108 Alice loved HARRY.

4.109 ALICE loved Harry.

Such phenomena are discussed by Jackendoff (1972) and Allan (1986) among others. So these examples seem to provide another case where presuppositional behavior is related to context: in this case the context of the discourse.

Another, narrower, contextual feature is traditionally called the **projection problem**, and is discussed by a number of writers, including Gazdar (1979), Karttunen and Peters (1979), Levinson (1983), Soames (1989), and Heim (1992). Sometimes the presupposition produced by a simple clause does not survive when the clause is incorporated into a complex sentence. Levinson (1983: 191ff.) gives the example of conditional clauses. Sentence 4.110a contains the factive verb *regret* and would normally produce the presupposition in 4.110b:

4.110 a. John will regret doing linguistics.
b. John is doing/will do linguistics.

However, in the context of a conditional clause like 4.111 below, the presupposition 4.110b disappears:

4.111 If John does linguistics, he'll regret it.

The context here is the syntactic one provided by the adjoining clause.

So we can see that different levels of context can cause fluctuations in presuppositional behavior. At the most general level, the context provided by background knowledge; then, the context provided by the topic of conversation; and finally, the narrower linguistic context of the surrounding syntactic structures – all can affect the production of presuppositions. Simply giving a truth table of fixed relations between presupposing and presupposed sentences cannot adequately describe this complicated behavior. Some more sophisticated account is required which takes account of how what participants know forms a background to the uttering of a sentence.

4.5.6 Pragmatic theories of presupposition

There have been a number of responses in the semantics literature to the features of presupposition we have outlined. Some writers (for example Leech 1981) have divided presuppositions into two types: one, **semantic presupposition**, amenable to a truth-relations approach; another, **pragmatic presupposition**, which requires an interactional description. In contrast, Stalnaker (1974) argued that presupposition is essentially a pragmatic phenomenon: part of the set of assumptions made by participants in a conversation, which he termed the **common ground**. This set of assumptions shifts as new sentences are uttered. In this view a speaker's next sentence builds on this common ground and it is pragmatically odd to assert something which does not fit it. Presumably cases of presuppositional failure like *The king of France is bald* would be explained in terms of the speaker assuming something (*There is a king of France*) that is not in the common ground.

This type of approach can cope with cases where presuppositions are not necessarily already known to the hearer, as when a speaker says *My sister just got married* (with its presupposition *I have a sister*) to someone who didn't know she had a sister. To capture this ability Lewis (1979: 127) proposes a principle of **accommodation**, where: "if at time *t* something is said that requires presupposition *p* to be acceptable, and if *p* is not presupposed just before *t* then – ceteris paribus – presupposition *p* comes into existence." In other words presuppositions can be introduced as new information.[14]

A pragmatic view of presupposition is also proposed by Sperber and Wilson (1995) who argue that presupposition is not an independent phenomenon but one of a series of effects produced when the speaker employs syntactic structure and intonation to show the hearer how the current sentence fits into the previous background. These writers integrate presupposition with other traditional discourse notions like **given** and **new** information, and **focus**. They propose (1995: 215) that the same principle of relevance to contextual assumptions covers both presupposition and the choice of the different word orders and intonations in 4.112 below:

4.112 a. It rained on MONDAY.
b. On Monday it RAINED.
c. On MONDAY it rained.

These sentences belong to different contexts of use in a similar way to our presupposition examples in 4.104–9, that is, the preceding context will naturally lead a speaker to choose one of the sentences in 4.112 over another. In Sperber and Wilson's view a general theory of conversational cooperation will explain all such cases. We will look at further examples of this in chapter 7.

4.6 Summary

In this chapter we have identified a number of semantic relations that hold between sentences: **synonymy**, **contradiction**, **entailment** and **presupposition**; and the sentential qualities of **tautology** and **contradiction**. We have reviewed an approach which characterizes these in terms of truth relations, using a notion of linguistic or analytic **truth**. We have seen that while this approach provides an attractive account of a number of properties, including synonymy, contradiction, tautology, and most importantly entailment, it fails to account for the full range of presuppositional behavior, in particular presupposition's sensitivity to contextual features. We contrasted this purely semantic approach with accounts which assume a pragmatic approach: describing presupposition in terms of a speaker's strategies to package her message against her estimate of what her audience knows. We will come back to this idea of processes of packaging information again in chapter 7.

EXERCISES

4.1 Take three sentences, **p**, **q**, and **r** as follows:

p: The sun is shining.
q: The day is warm.
r: The sun is shining and the day is warm.

Let's make the working assumption that we can represent sentence **r** by the logical formula $\mathbf{p} \wedge \mathbf{q}$. Use the truth table for $\wedge$ given in 4.23 in this chapter to show the truth-value of **r** in the three situations (S1–3) below:

S1. **p** is true; **q** is false
S2. **p** is true; **q** is true
S3. **p** is false; **q** is true
S4. **p** is false; **q** is false

4.2 In propositional logic is it assumed that $\mathbf{p} \wedge \mathbf{q}$ and $\mathbf{q} \wedge \mathbf{p}$ are logically equivalent, that is the order of the elements is irrelevant. Discuss how the following examples show that this is not true for the way that speakers use English *and*.

a. He woke up and saw on TV that he had won the lottery.
b. Combine the egg yolks with water in a bowl and whisk the mixture until foamy.
c. He made two false starts and was disqualified from the race.
d. Move and I'll shoot!

4.3 Take three sentences, **p**, **q**, and **r** as follows:

p: Peter is drinking.
q: Aideen is driving home.
r: It is not the case that Peter is drinking or Aideen is driving home.

Let's make the working assumption that sentence **r** is ambiguous: in one reading the whole sentence is negated; in the other, just the first disjunct is negated. Thus the sentence may be given the two logical forms in a and b below:

a. $\neg (\mathbf{p} \vee \mathbf{q})$
b. $\neg \mathbf{p} \vee \mathbf{q}$

Use the truth tables for $\neg$ given in 4.21 and $\vee$ in 4.24 in this chapter to show the truth-values of a and b above in the four situations (S1–4) below:

S1. **p** is true; **q** is false
S2. **p** is true; **q** is true
S3. **p** is false; **q** is true
S4. **p** is false; **q** is false

4.4 To begin with, assume a general rule of **disjunction reduction**, by which any phrasal or clausal disjunction is derived from the disjunction of full sentences, that is, assume that a sentence like *You can say yes or no* is equivalent to *You can say yes or you can say no*. For each of the sentences below, decide whether the use of *or* corresponds to inclusive (∨) or exclusive ($\underline{\vee}$) disjunction. Discuss your reasoning. Do any of these sentences have meanings that you feel are not captured by assuming disjunction reduction; or by the truth table characterization of the two logic connectors in 4.24 and 4.26 earlier?

a. We spend the afternoons swimming or sunbathing.
b. They can resuscitate him or allow him to die.
c. If the site is in a particularly sensitive area, or there are safety considerations, we can refuse planning permission.
d. You can take this bus or wait till the next one.
e. Beffni is a man's name or a woman's name.
f. The base camp is five or six days' walk from here.
g. He doesn't smoke or drink.
h. She suffers from agoraphobia, or fear of open places.
i. Stop or I'll shoot!

4.5 Decide which of the following sentences are **analytically true**. Discuss the reasons for your decision.

a. If it rains, we'll get wet.
b. The train will either arrive or it won't arrive.
c. Every doctor is a doctor.
d. If Albert killed a deer, then Albert killed an animal.
e. Madrid is the capital of Spain.
f. Every city has pollution problems.

4.6 Below are some paired sentences. Use the composite truth table for **entailment** given in 4.55 in this chapter to decide whether the a sentence **entails** its b partner. Note any cases of mutual entailment and the difference in truth relations this involves. (As usual, assume that repeated nouns, names and pronouns refer to the same entity twice, and that the b sentences are uttered immediately after the a sentences.)

1 a. Olivia passed her driving test.
  b. Olivia didn't fail her driving test.
2 a. Cassidy inherited a farm.
  b. Cassidy owned a farm.
3 a. Cassidy inherited a farm.
  b. Cassidy owns a farm.
4 a. Arnold poisoned his wife.
  b. Arnold killed his wife.
5 a. We brought this champagne.
  b. This champagne was brought by us.

6 a. Not everyone will like the show.
b. Someone will like the show.

4.7 We noted that factive predicates, like English *regret*, presuppose the truth of their clausal complements, as in *He regretted that he didn't move to Melbourne*. Using your own examples, identify the factive predicates from the following list: *announce, assume, be aware, believe, be fearful, be glad, realize, be sorry, be worried, know, reason, report*.

4.8 Using the different behavior of entailment and presupposition under negation as a test, decide whether the a sentences below **entail** or **presuppose** their b counterparts. (Again, assume that repeated nouns, names and pronouns refer to the same entity twice, and that the b sentences are uttered immediately after the a sentences.)

1 a. Dave knows that Jim crashed the car..
b. Jim crashed the car.
2 a. Zaire is bigger than Alaska.
b. Alaska is smaller than Zaire.
3 a. The minister blames her secretary for leaking the memo to the press.
b. The memo was leaked to the press.
4 a. Everyone passed the examination.
b. No-one failed the examination.
5 a. Mr Singleton has resumed his habit of drinking stout.
b. Mr Singleton had a habit of drinking stout.

FURTHER READING

A very clear introduction to logic for linguists is given by Allwood, Andersson, and Dahl (1977). Grayling (1982) contains a very readable discussion of the different notions of truth used in logic and the philosophy of language. Chierchia and McConnell-Ginet (2000) propose a truth-based account of entailment and other sentential relations which is probably best approached after reading chapter 10 below. Levinson (1983) has an accessible discussion of approaches to presupposition, and Allan (1986) has as its basic principle the kind of interactional approach we have discussed in this chapter. Beaver (2001) discusses the role of presupposition in the dynamic updating of context. Stalnaker (2002) discusses his pragmatic approach to presupposition.

NOTES

1 In 4.1–4 we assume, as in other examples, that pairs of sentences are uttered by the same speaker, in sequence and that repeated nominals identify the same individual.

2 We assume here a simple **correspondence** theory of truth; see Grayling (1982) for a discussion of this and other theories of truth. For many semanticists employing truth conditions to investigate meaning it is in fact the proposition expressed by a sentence (uttered in a particular context) that, depending on the facts of the world, may be true or false. In Chapter 10 we review the proposal that this truth-evaluable proposition is the essential part of the meaning of sentences and therefore the object of study in semantics. For simplicity, in the present discussion we continue to talk of sentences being true or false.

3 Logicians sometimes distinguish between two types of what we are here calling counterfactuals: **subjunctive conditionals**, which set up a hypothetical situation in the antecedent, as in *If Liverpool were to win the championship, he'd be a happy man*; and **counterfactual conditionals**, where the antecedent is implied to be false, as in *If Liverpool had won the championship, he would have been a happy man*. For the rest of this book, we will use the term **counterfactual** as a cover term for both types. See Lewis (1973) and Haack (1978) for discussion.

4 Including for example Leibniz (1981), Kant (1993), Quine (1953), Carnap (1956), and Kripke (1980).

5 Another definition of necessary truth uses the notion of **possible worlds**, due originally to Leibniz. Possible worlds in the work of, for example, Lewis (1973, 1986), is a notion used to reflect the way speakers use language to do more than describe the world as it is. Speakers can, for example, hypothesize situations different from reality, as in **counterfactuals** like *If Ireland was a Caribbean island, we'd all be drinking rum*. Such situations that are not asserted as real are called possible worlds, the idea being that the world where Ireland is a Caribbean island is linguistically set up as a possible world, not the actual world. One definition of necessary truth uses this notion as follows: A statement is necessarily true if it is true in all possible worlds. However, since the constraints on setting up hypothetical worlds and their possibilities of difference from the real world are far from easy to ascertain, such a definition needs some work to establish. See Grayling (1982: 43–95) for introductory discussion and Kripke (1971), Lewis (1973) and the papers in Loux (1979) for more detailed discussion. We come back to this idea of possible worlds again in chapters 5 and 10.

6 This idea, often known as **concept containment**, derives from Leibniz. See the papers in Jolley (1995) for discussion.

7 An anonymous reviewer has suggested that an example like *Whales are mammals* brings out the difference between necessary and *a priori* truth. Following Kripke, this sentence is a necessary truth, but it is not an *a priori* truth for our hypothetical speaker who thinks that whales are fish. Similarly *Water is* H_2O might be a reasonable candidate for a necessary truth but might only be learned by experimental inquiry and thus be *a posteriori*.

8 This assumes that we rule out self-reference to avoid paradoxes. For example by choosing to instantiate Y as "are not Xs," we would get the necessarily false statement *All Xs that are not Xs are Xs*.

9 We discuss a formal approach to these lexical relations, **meaning postulates**, in chapter 10.

10 Another, more strictly logical way of describing this entailment relation is to say that **p** entails **q** when an argument that takes **p** as a premise and **q** as a conclusion must be valid, for example the argument:

The anarchist assassinated the emperor.
∴ The emperor died.
is valid.

11 Since this relation is clearly similar to the bi-conditional connective described earlier, we could give a logical definition of synonymy as in: **p** and **q** are synonymous when the expression $\mathbf{p} \equiv \mathbf{q}$ is always true.

12 Of course not all definite nominals are used to refer: so, for example, the definite NP in bold in the following sentence is traditionally described as being predicative and not referential: *Stuart is* ***the answer to our prayers.***

13 As we will note later, in chapter 8, Austin (1975) suggested that this condition is a **felicity condition** on the making of statements.

14 See Heim (1983) for a development of this idea of presuppositions as a set of assumptions forming part of the context for a sentence being uttered. A dynamic account of how participants update the context of assumptions is also given by Discourse Representation Theory (DRT), which we discuss in chapter 10. See Beaver (2002) for a DRT account of presupposition.

REFERENCES

Allan, Keith 1986: *Linguistic Meaning*, 2 vols. London: Routledge & Kegan Paul.

Allwood, Jens, Lars-Gunnar Andersson and Östen Dahl 1977: *Logic in Linguistics*. Cambridge: Cambridge University Press.

Austin, J. L. 1975: *How to Do Things with Words*, second edition. Oxford: Clarendon Press. (First published 1962.)

Beaver, David I. 2001: *Presupposition and Assertion in Dynamic Semantics*. Stanford, CA: Center for the Study of Language and Information.

Beaver, David I. 2002: Presupposition projection in DRT. In David I. Beaver, Luis D. Casillas Martínez, Brady Z. Clark and Stefan Kaufmann (eds.) *The Construction of Meaning*, 23–43. Stanford, CA: Center for the Study of Language and Information.

Boer, Steven E. and William G. Lycan 1976: *The Myth of Semantic Presupposition*. Bloomington: Indiana University Linguistics Club.

Carnap, Rudolf 1956: *Meaning and Necessity: A Study in Semantics and Modal Logic*, second edition. Chicago: University of Chicago Press.

Chierchia, Gennaro and Sally McConnell-Ginet 1990/2000: *Meaning and Grammar: An Introduction to Semantics*, second edition. Cambridge, MA: MIT Press. (First edition 1990.)

Fodor, Janet Dean 1979: The King of France is false. In Choon-Kyu Oh and David A. Dinneen (eds.) *Syntax and Semantics, Vol. 11: Presupposition*, 200–20. New York: Academic Press.

Fodor, Jerry A. 1983: *The Modularity of Mind*. Cambridge, MA: MIT Press.

Gazdar, Gerald 1979: *Pragmatics: Implicature, Presupposition, and Logical Form*. New York: Academic Press.

Grayling, Anthony C. 1982: *An Introduction to Philosophical Logic*. Brighton: Harvester Press.

Haack, Susan 1978: *Philosophy of Logics*. Cambridge: Cambridge University Press.

Heim, Irene 1983: On the projection problem for presupposition. In Michael Barlow, Daniel P. Flickinger and Michael T. Westcoat (eds.) *Proceedings of the West Coast Conference on Formal Linguistics*, vol. 2, 114–26. Stanford, CA: Stanford Linguistics Association.

Heim, Irene 1992: Presupposition projection and the semantics of attitude verbs. *Journal of Semantics* 9: 183–221.

Jackendoff, Ray 1972: *Semantic Interpretation in Generative Grammar*. Cambridge, MA: MIT Press.

Jolley, Nicholas (ed.) 1995: *The Cambridge Companion to Leibniz*. Cambridge: Cambridge University Press.

Kant, Immanuel 1993: *Critique of Pure Reason*. Revised and expanded translation by Vasilis Politis. London: Everyman. (First published 1781.)

Karttunen, Lauri and Stanley Peters 1979: Conventional implicature. In Choon-Kyu Oh and David A. Dinneen (eds.) *Syntax and Semantics, Vol. 11: Presupposition*, 1–56. New York: Academic Press.

Kempson, Ruth M. 1975: *Presupposition and the Delimitation of Semantics*. Cambridge: Cambridge University Press.
Kripke, Saul 1971: Identity and necessity. In Milton K. Munitz (ed.) *Identity and Individuation*, 135–64. New York: New York University Press.
Kripke, Saul 1980: *Naming and Necessity*. Oxford: Blackwell.
Leech, Geoffrey N. 1981: *Semantics*, second edition. Harmondsworth: Penguin.
Leibniz, Gottfried Wilhelm 1981: *New Essays Concerning Human Understanding*. Translated and edited by Peter Remnant and Jonathan Bennett. Cambridge: Cambridge University Press. (First published 1765.)
Levinson, Stephen C. 1983: *Pragmatics*. Cambridge: Cambridge University Press.
Lewis, David K. 1973: *Counterfactuals*. Oxford: Blackwell.
Lewis, David K. 1979: Scorekeeping in a language game. *Journal of Philosophical Logic* 8: 339–59.
Lewis, David K. 1986: *The Plurality of Worlds*. Oxford: Blackwell.
Loux, Michael J. (ed.) 1979: *The Possible and the Actual: Readings in the Metaphysics of Modality*. Ithaca, NY: Cornell University Press.
McCulloch, G. 1989: *The Game of the Name*. Oxford: Clarendon Press.
Montague, Richard 1974: *Formal Philosophy: Selected Papers of Richard Montague*. Edited and with an introduction by Richmond H. Thomason. New Haven: Yale University Press.
Oh, Choon-Kyu and David A. Dinneen (eds.) 1979: *Syntax and Semantics, Vol. 11: Presupposition*. New York: Academic Press.
Quine, W. V. 1953: *From a Logical Point of View*. Cambridge, MA: Harvard University Press.
Russell, Bertrand 1905: On denoting. *Mind* 14: 479–93.
Soames, S. 1989: Presupposition. In Dov A. Gabbay and Franz Guenther (eds.) *Handbook of Philosophical Logic. Vol. 4: Topics in the Philosophy of Language*, 553–616. Dordrecht: Reidel.
Sperber, Dan and Deirdre Wilson 1995: *Relevance: Communication and Cognition*, second edition. Oxford: Blackwell.
Stalnaker, Robert 1974: Pragmatic presuppositions. In Milton K. Munitz and Peter K. Unger (eds.) *Semantics and Philosophy*, 197–213. New York: New York University Press.
Stalnaker, Robert 2002: Common ground. *Linguistics and Philosophy* 24.5–6: 701–21.
Wilson, Deidre 1975: *Presupposition and Non-Truth Conditional Semantics*. New York: Academic Press.
Wilson, Deidre and Dan Sperber 1979: Ordered entailments: an alternative to presuppositional theories. In Choon-Kyu Oh and David A. Dinneen (eds.) *Syntax and Semantics. Vol. 11: Presupposition*, 299–323. New York: Academic Press.

chapter 5

Sentence Semantics 1
Situations

5.1 Introduction

In chapter 3 we discussed aspects of word meaning. In this chapter we investigate some aspects of meaning that belong to the level of the sentence. One aspect is the marking of time, known as **tense**. How this is marked varies from language to language: it might be marked on a verb in languages like English or by special time words as in Chinese, as shown in 5.1a–c below:[1]

5.1 a. Tā xiànzài yǒu kè.
he now have classes
"He now has classes."

b. Tā zuótiān yǒu kè.
he yesterday have classes
"He had classes yesterday."

c. Tā míngtiān yǒu kè.
he tommorrow have classes
"He will have classes tomorrow."

(Tiee 1986: 90)

Here the verb *yǒu* "has/have" does not change form: the time reference is given by the time words, *xiànzài* "now," *zuótiān* "yesterday," and *míngtiān* "tomorrow." We can compare this with the English translations where the verb *have* changes for tense to give the forms, *have*, *had*, and *will have*.

However it is marked, the location in time identified by tense belongs not to a single word but to the whole sentence. Take for example the English sentence 5.2 below:

5.2 Hannibal and his armies brought elephants across the Alps.

Though it is the verb *bring* which carries the morphological marker of tense, it seems sensible to say that the whole event described belongs in the past. In this chapter we will look at a number of semantic categories which, like tense, belong at the sentence level and which can be seen as ways that languages allow speakers to construct different views of situations. We begin by looking in section 5.2 at how languages allow speakers to classify situations by using semantic distinctions of **situation type**, **tense**, and **aspect**. Then in section 5.3 we look at how the system of **mood** allows speakers to adopt differing attitudes toward the factuality of their sentences; and how **evidentiality** systems allow them to identify the source of their belief. Each of these are sentence-level semantic systems which enable speakers to organize descriptions of situations.

5.2 Classifying Situations

5.2.1 Introduction

We can identify three important dimensions to the task of classifying a situation in order to talk about it. These dimensions are **situation type**, **tense**, and **aspect**. Situation type, as we shall see in section 5.2.2, is a label for the typology of situations encoded in the semantics of a language. For example, languages commonly allow speakers to describe a situation as static or unchanging for its duration. Such **states** are described in the following examples:

5.3 Robert loves pizza.

5.4 Mary knows the way to San Jose.

In describing states the speaker gives no information about the internal structure of the state: it just holds for a certain time, unspecified in the above examples. We can contrast this with viewing a situation as involving change, for example:

5.5 Robert grew very quickly.

5.6 Mary is driving to San Jose.

These sentences describe **dynamic** situations. They imply that the action has subparts: Robert passed through several sizes and Mary is driving through various places on the way to San Jose.

This distinction between static and dynamic situations is reflected in the choice of lexical items. In English, for example, adjectives are typically used for states and verbs for dynamic situations. Compare the states in the a examples below with the dynamic situations in the b sentences:

5.7 a. The pears are ripe.
b. The pears ripened.

5.8 a. The theatre is full.
b. The theatre filled up.

This is not an exact correlation however: as we saw above there are a number of **stative verbs** like *be*, *have*, *remain*, *know*, *love* that can be used to describe states, for example:

5.9 The file **is** in the computer.

5.10 Ann **has** red hair.

5.11 You **know** the answer.

5.12 The amendment **remains** in force.

5.13 Jenny **loves** to ski.

We will say that adjectives and stative verbs are inherently static, that is, it is part of their lexical semantics to portray a static situation type.

Some writers (for example Carlson 1977, Diesing 1992, Kratzer 1994) distinguish two types of state: stage-level predicates (SLPs), which are predicates that hold of temporal stages of an individual, and individual-level predicates (ILPs), which simply hold of individuals. The idea is that SLPs are tied to specific intervals of time while ILPS are atemporal. Such a distinction would distinguish between the states in *Mary is tired* and *Mary is intelligent*. This seems to have grammatical reflexes in some languages, for example the distinction between the Spanish verbs *ser* "be" and *estar* "be" as in 5.14 and 5.15 below: [2]

5.14 Pedro es inteligente
"Pedro is intelligent."

5.15 Pedro está cansado esta mañana.
Pedro is tired this morning
"Pedro is tired this morning."

We have already briefly mentioned the dimension of **tense**. As we will describe in section 5.2.3, many languages have grammatical forms, such as verb endings, which allow a speaker to locate a situation in time relative to the "now" of the act of speaking or writing. **Aspect** is also a grammatical system relating to time, but here the speaker may choose how to describe the internal temporal nature of a situation. If the situation is in the past, for example, does the speaker portray it as a closed completed event, as in 5.16 below, or as an ongoing process, perhaps unfinished, as in 5.17?

5.16 David wrote a crime novel.

5.17 David was writing a crime novel.

This is a difference of aspect, usually marked, like tense, by grammatical devices. Tense and aspect are discussed in sections 5.2.3–6 and we discuss the problems of comparing the aspectual systems of different languages in 5.2.7. Finally section 5.2.8 is a brief look at how these dimensions combine to allow speakers to portray different situations.

5.2.2 Verbs and situation types

We saw in the last section that certain lexical categories, in particular verbs, inherently describe different situation types. Some describe states, others are dynamic and describe processes and events. In this section we describe elements of the meaning of verbs, which correlate to differences of situation type.

Stative verbs

In the last section we saw examples of inherently stative verbs like *be*, *have*, *know*, and *love*. These verbs allow the speaker to view a situation as a steady state, with no internal phases or changes. Moreover the speaker does not overtly focus on the beginning or end of the state. Even if the speaker uses a stative in the past, for example:

5.18 Mary loved to drive sports cars.

no attention is directed to the end of the state. We do not know from 5.18 if or how the state ended: whether Mary's tastes changed, or she herself is no longer around. All we are told is that the relationship described between Mary and sports cars existed for a while. We can contrast this with a sentence like 5.19 below, containing a dynamic verb like *learn*:

5.19 Mary learned to drive sports cars.

Here the speaker is describing a process and focusing on the end point: at the beginning Mary didn't know how to drive sports cars, and at the end she has learned. The process has a conclusion.

Stative verbs display some grammatical differences from dynamic verbs. For example in English progressive forms can be used of dynamic situations like 5.20a below but not states like 5.20b:

5.20 a. I am learning Swahili.
b. *I am knowing Swahili.

As noted by Vlach (1981) this is because the progressive aspect, marked by *-ing* above, has connotations of dynamism and change which suits an activity like *learn* but is incompatible with a stative verb like *know.* We discuss the English progressive in sections 5.2.4 and 5.2.6 below.

Similarly it usually sounds odd to use the imperative with statives; we can compare the following:

5.21 a. Learn Swahili!
b. ?Know Swahili!

Once again, we can speculate that imperatives imply action and dynamism, and are therefore incompatible with stative verbs.

It may be, however, that the distinction between state and dynamic situations is not always as clear-cut. Some verbs may be more strongly stative than others; *remain* for example, patterns like other stative verbs in not taking the progressive, as in 5.22 b below, but it does allow the imperative, as in 5.22c:

5.22 a. The answer remains the same: no!
b. *The answer is remaining the same: no!
c. Remain at your posts!

It is important too to remember that verbs may have a range of meanings, some of which may be more stative than others. We can contrast the stative and non-stative uses of *have*, for example, by looking at how they interact with the progressive:[3]

5.23 a. I have a car.
b. *I am having a car.
c. I am having second thoughts about this.

5.24 a. She has a sister in New York.
b. *She is having a sister in New York.
c. She is having a baby.

Dynamic verbs

Dynamic verbs can be classified into a number of types, based on the semantic distinctions **durative/punctual** and **telic/atelic,** which we will discuss below.

The first distinction is between **durative** and **punctual**: **durative** is applied to verbs that describe a situation or process which lasts for a period of time, while **punctual** describes an event that seems so instantaneous that it involves virtually no time. A typical comparison would be between the punctual 5.25 and the durative 5.26:

5.25 John coughed.

5.26 John slept.

What matters of course is not how much time an actual cough takes but that the typical cough is so short that conventionally speakers do not focus on the internal structure of the event.

In Slavic linguistics the equivalent of verbs like *cough* are called **semelfactive** verbs, after the Latin word *semel*, "once." This term is adopted for general use by C. S. Smith (1991), Verkuyl (1993), and other writers. Other semelfactive verbs in English would include *flash*, *shoot*, *knock*, *sneeze* and *blink*. One interesting fact is that in English a clash between a semelfactive verb and a durative adverbial can trigger an **iterative** interpretation, that is where the event is assumed to be repeated for the period described, for example:

5.27 Fred coughed all night.

5.28 The drunk knocked for ten minutes.

5.29 The cursor flashed until the battery ran down.

In each of these examples the action is interpreted as being iterative: 5.27 is not understood to mean that Fred spent all night uttering a single drawn-out cough!

The second distinction is between **telic** and **atelic**. **Telic** refers to those processes that are seen as having a natural completion. Compare for example:

5.30 a. Harry was building a raft.
b. Harry was gazing at the sea.

If we interrupt these processes at any point then we can correctly say:

5.31 Harry gazed at the sea.

but we cannot necessarily say:

5.32 Harry built a raft.

Another way of looking at this distinction is to say that *gaze* being atelic can continue indefinitely, while *build* has an implied boundary when the process will be over. Alternative terms are **bounded** for telic and **unbounded** for atelic.

It is important to recognize that while verbs may be inherently telic or atelic, combining them with other elements in a sentence can result in a different aspect for the whole, as below:

5.33 a. Fred was running. (atelic)
b. Fred was running in the London Marathon. (telic)

5.34 a. Harry was singing songs. (atelic)
b. Harry was singing a song. (telic)

This telic/atelic distinction interacts with aspectual distinctions: for example a combination of either the English perfect or simple past with a telic verb will produce an implication of completion. Thus, as we have seen, both 5.35 and 5.36 entail 5.37:

5.35 Mary painted my portrait.

5.36 Mary has painted my portrait.

5.37 The portrait is finished.

However, the combination of a progressive aspect and a telic verb, as in 5.38 below does not produce this implication: 5.38 does not entail 5.36 above:

5.38 Mary was painting my portrait.

Comrie (1976) gives examples of derivational processes that can create telic verbs from atelic verbs, for example the German pairs in 5.39:

5.39 a. *essen* "eat," *aufessen* "eat up"
b. *kämpfen* "fight," *erkämpfen* "achieve by fighting"

He contrasts the following sentences:

5.40 a. Die Partisanen haben für die Freiheit ihres Landes gekämpft.
b. Die Partisanen haben die Freiheit ihres Landes erkämpft.
"The partisans have fought for the freedom of their country."
(Comrie 1976: 46–47)

where 5.40b implies that their fight was successful while 5.40a does not.

We can draw together some of the main semantic distinctions among situation types into the diagram below, where we include a single example of adjectives and verbs for each:

5.41 Semantic distinctions among situation types

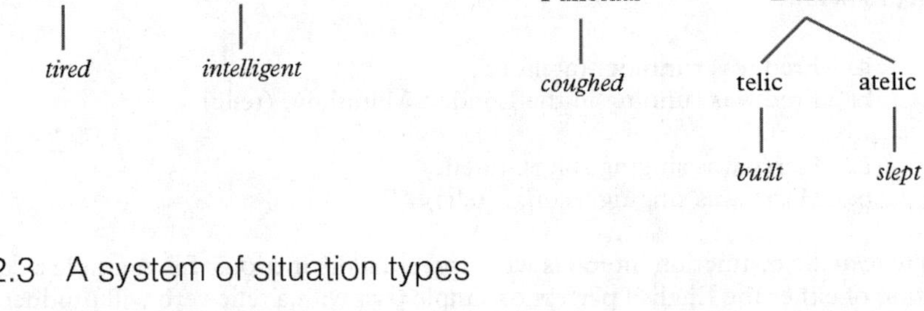

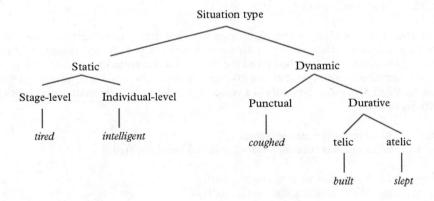

5.2.3 A system of situation types

Speakers use their knowledge of these semantic distinctions – stative/dynamic, durative/punctual, telic/atelic – to draw distinctions of situation type. We have seen that some verbs, like *paint*, *draw*, and *build*, are inherently telic while others like *talk*, *sleep*, and *walk* are atelic. Similarly some verbs are inherently stative like *know*, love, and *resemble*, while others like *learn*, *die*, and *kill* are non-stative. We have also seen from examples like 5.33 and 5.34 above that while these distinctions are principally associated with verbs, combining a verb with other elements in a sentence, like object noun phrases and adverbials, can alter the situation type depicted.

The task for the semanticist is to show how the inherent semantic distinctions carried by verbs, and verb phrases, map into a system of situation types. One influential attempt to do this is Vendler (1967). Below are the four kinds of situations he identified, together with some English verbs and verb phrases exemplifying each type (Vendler 1967: 97–121):

5.42 a. States
desire, want, love, hate, know, believe
b. Activities (unbounded processes)
run, walk, swim, push a cart, drive a car
c. Accomplishments (bounded processes)
run a mile, draw a circle, walk to school, paint a picture, grow up, deliver a sermon, recover from illness
d. Achievements (point events)
recognize, find, stop, start, reach the top, win the race, spot someone

Smith (1991), building on Vendler's system, adds the situation type **semelfactive**, distinguishing it from achievements as follows:

5.43 *Semelfactives* are instantaneous atelic events, for example [knock], [cough]. *Achievements* are instantaneous changes of states, with an outcome of a new state, for example [reach the top], [win a race]. (Smith 1991: 28)

She identifies three semantic categories or features: [stative], [telic], and [duration], with roughly the characteristics we have already described, and uses these to classify five situation types, as follows (1991: 30):

5.44

Situations	Static	Durative	Telic
States	[+]	[+]	n.a.
Activity	[−]	[+]	[−]
Accomplishment	[−]	[+]	[+]
Semelfactive	[−]	[−]	[−]
Achievement	[−]	[−]	[+]

We can provide examples of each situation type, as follows:

5.45 She hated ice cream. (State)

5.46 Your cat watched those birds. (Activity)

5.47 Her boss learned Japanese. (Accomplishment)

5.48 The gate banged. (Semelfactive)

5.49 The cease-fire began at noon yesterday. (Achievement)

As we noted in the last section the situation type communicated by a clause results from the combination of the verb and other elements. So the addition of a locational prepositional phrase to the verb *cycle* in 5.50a below produces an activity while a directional prepositional phrase in 5.50b produces an accomplishment:

5.50 a. Frankie cycled in the park.
b. Frankie cycled to the park.

As noted by Verkuyl (1972) accomplishment verbs like *eat*, *write*, and *build* produce different situation types depending on their objects. With a count expression as in 5.51a below the result is an accomplishment, while with a mass noun or a bare plural as in 5.51b the result is an activity:

5.51 a. Alexander built a bridge.
b. Alexander built bridges.

A semantic account of situation type has to provide an account of such combinatorial effects, as discussed for example by Rothstein (2004).

It is important to remember that these situation types are interpretations of real situations. Some real situations may be conventionally associated with a situation type; for example it seems unlikely that the event described in 5.52 below would be viewed other than as an accomplishment:

5.52 Sean knitted this sweater.

Other situations are more open, though: 5.53 and 5.54 below might be used of the same real-world situation, but give two different interpretations of it: 5.53 as an activity and 5.54 as a state:

5.53 Sean was sleeping.

5.54 Sean was asleep.

5.2.4 Tests for situation types

The semantic characteristics of the situation types we have described permit the use of certain tests or diagnostics to help decide which type a clause belongs to. In this section we outline some of the most commonly used tests. Each of these tests needs to be used with care. They are helpful in identifying typical uses but speakers can sometimes shift verbs and their clauses across situation types for special effects and thus counter examples can be found or imagined, as mentioned below. We begin with tests for statives, and for brevity we focus on English.

Statives

- The progressive verb form, discussed in section 5.6 below, can be used as a (negative) test for statives since, as shown in example 5.20 earlier, only non-statives occur in the progressive, so that the stative **I am knowing Swahili* is ungrammatical. We noted though that some verbs like English *have* include both stative and non-stative senses so care is needed distinguishing these. Similarly the dynamism of the progressive, discussed below, is sometimes used to give dynamic senses to a stative verb, as in *I'm loving it*.

- Imperative verb forms also provide a negative test since, as shown in 5.21 earlier, only non-statives occur as imperatives, so that ?*Know Swahili!* is odd.
- Simple present verb forms can be used as a test since they refer to the current time of speaking with statives but have a habitual reading with non-statives, as in the examples below:

5.55 a. Isabel knows Cannes.
b. Isabel visits Cannes.

Sentence b cannot be used to mean that Isabel is visiting Cannes now. Again special uses can provide counterexamples to this test as when the simple present is used in forms of narrative, such as jokes, *An elephant goes into a bar...*, or sports commentary, *He shoots and scores!*

- If a situation type can occur in the frame *What happened was...* it is non-stative, as shown below:

5.56 a. What happened was that Alice left the school.
b. ?What happened was that Alice was intelligent.

Other tests have been proposed, for example that statives cannot occur as complements of the verb *finish* (Dowty 1979). However, while this is true, so that ?*She finished knowing Swahili* is odd, some classes of dynamic verbs are also excluded, reducing the value of this test. Thus 5.57 below is odd with the dynamic verb *lose*:

5.57 ?Fred finished losing his car keys.[4]

Duratives

Dowty (1979) suggests using different types of temporal adverbial expressions as tests for activity, accomplishment, and achievement situation types. These tests work best using sentences with simple past tense forms. The temporal adverbial *in (a period)* only occurs with telic situation types and so distinguishes between the telic achievement in 5.58a below and the atelic activity in 5.58b:

5.58 a. They reached the school in half an hour. (Achievement)
b. ?They played cards in half an hour. (Activity)

The durational time adverbial *for (a period)* does not occur with telic situation types, so distinguishes between the atelic activity in 5.59a and the telic achievement in 5.59b:

5.59 a. They played cards for half an hour. (Activity)
b. ?They reached the school for half an hour. (Achievement)

The test with *finish* mentioned above for statives in fact picks out situation types that are durative and telic. Thus *finish* naturally occurs with accomplishments, as in 5.60a below, but not with activities (which are not telic) or achievements (which are not durative), as in 5.60b–c:

5.60 a. Joan finished fixing the car. (Accomplishment)
b. ?Joan finished fixing cars. (Activity)
c. ?Joan finished recognizing her old boss. (Achievement)

Finally, Dowty (1979) also proposed a test using the adverb *almost*. When an accomplishment is modified by *almost* as in 5.61 below it has two readings: one where the described event has occurred but not been completed and one where it has not occurred at all:

5.61 John almost wrote a novel.

In this example *almost* can refer to the whole process or just the end point. Activity and achievement types on the other hand, which do not have this combination of process and end point, only have the second reading, as in 5.62 below:

5.62 a. John almost played. (Activity)
b. John almost noticed the mistake. (Achievement)

Thus this test identifies accomplishments.

When using such tests it is important to recall the point made earlier: situation type is a characteristic of clauses rather than individual verbs. We can see this especially clearly when verbs shift types. One example, as discussed by Hay et al. (1999), is when verbs derived from gradable adjectives, called "degree achievements" by Dowty (1979), switch between activity and accomplishment with the two temporal adverbials we have been using as tests:

5.63 a. The soup cooled for ten minutes. (Activity)
b. The soup cooled in ten minutes. (Accomplishment)

5.2.5 Tense

Tense and aspect systems both allow speakers to relate situations to time, but they offer different slants on time. Tense allows a speaker to locate a situation relative to some reference point in time, most likely the time of speaking. Sometimes in English this information is given by a temporal adverb; compare the following:

5.64 Yesterday they cut the grass.

5.65 Tomorrow they cut the grass.

Here, because the shape of the verb *cut* does not change, the temporal information is given by the adverbs *yesterday* and *tomorrow*. Usually in English, though, tense is

Figure 5.1 Simple tenses

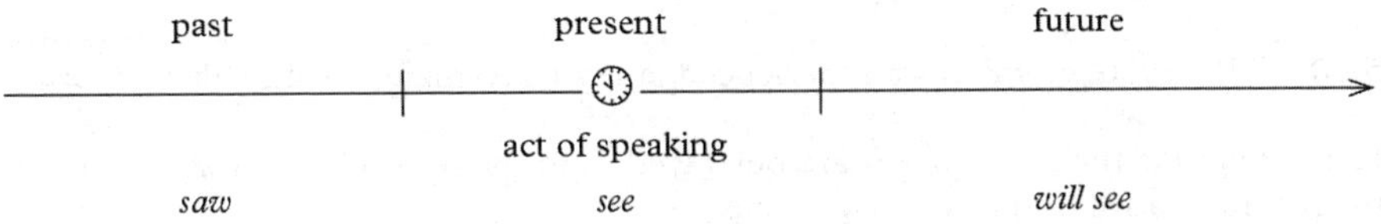

marked on the verb by endings and the use of special **auxiliary verbs**, as in the forms of *speak* below:

5.66 She spoke to me.

5.67 She will speak to me.

5.68 She is speaking to me.

Tense is said to be a **deictic** system, since the reference point for the system is usually the act of speaking. As we shall see in chapter 7, deictic systems are the ways in which a speaker relates references to space and time to the "here and now" of the utterance. Most grammatical tense systems allow the speaker to describe situations as prior to, concurrent with, or following the act of speaking. So in English, we have the three tenses: past, future, and present, as in 5.66–8 above. These are basic tenses and we could use a diagram like figure 5.1 to represent them, metaphorically representing time as line moving left to right, and using the clock symbol for the time of the act of speaking.

More complicated time references are possible. For example the speaker can locate an event in the past or future and use that event as the reference point for its own past, present and future. To do this in English complex tenses are used. If a speaker in 1945 said, for example:

5.69 By 1939 my father had seen several arrests.

the verb *had seen* is one of these complex tenses, called the **past perfect** or **pluperfect**. The year 1939 is in the past of the utterance of course, but the speaker has made it the anchoring point for its own past. The father's acts of seeing are marked as being in this secondary past, as well as in the past relative to the act of speaking. Again we could represent this in a simple diagram as in figure 5.2.

Figure 5.2 Complex past tense

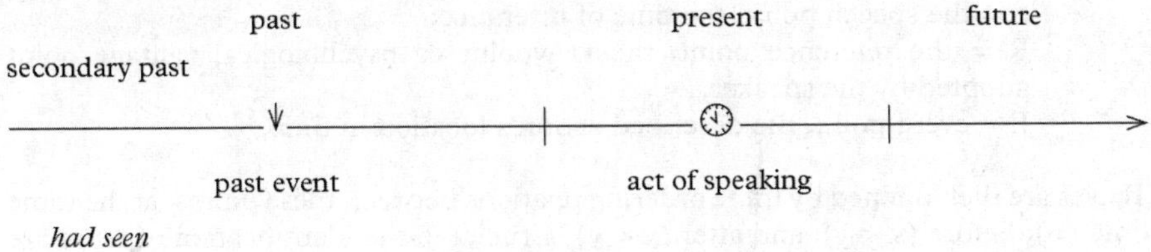

Complex future tenses like *will have seen* allow a similar creation of a past-of-a-future-event, as in an utterance now of 5.70:

5.70 By 2050 we will have experienced at least two major earthquakes.

Here of course the earthquakes are portrayed as in the past relative to 2050, but in the future relative to the act of speaking.

Since tense is a deictic system it may vary from language to language. Some languages, like the Bantu language Chibemba (Sharman 1956, Givón 1972) have more complicated systems of divisions than English:

5.71 Chibemba past tense system (Givón 1972)
  a. Remote past:
     Ba-àlí-bomb-ele "They worked (before yesterday)"
  b. Removed past:
     Ba-àlíí-bomba "They worked (yesterday)"
  c. Near past:
     Ba-àcí-bomba "They worked (earlier today)"
  d. Immediate past:
     Ba-á-bomba "They worked (in the past few hours)"

5.72 Chibemba future tense system
  a. Immediate future:
     Ba-áláá-bomba "They'll work (in the next few hours)"
  b. Near future:
     Ba-léé-bomba "They'll work (later today)"
  c. Removed future:
     Ba-kà-bomba "They'll work (tomorrow)"
  d. Remote future:
     Ba-ká-bomba "They'll work (after tomorrow)"

Here we see marked four degrees of remoteness from the act of speaking (Givón 2001): a few hours from now; within today; within the day adjacent to today; and beyond the day adjacent to today. Each of these projects backwards into the past and forwards into the future. Since this system includes not only intervals relative to the act of speaking but an implied measurement of the intervals, it is termed a **metrical tense** system by Chung and Timberlake (1985: 207).

An influential system of representing the deictic nature of tense is Reichenbach's (1947) reference point theory of tense which, as shown in 5.73, identifies three reference points in time:

5.73 Reichenbach's (1947: 290) tense reference points
  S = the speech point, the time of utterance;
  R = the reference point, the viewpoint or psychological vantage point adopted by the speaker;
  E = event point, the described action's location in time.

Tenses are then defined by three ordering relations between these points: at the same time (=); before (**x** < y); and after (x < **y**). Crucial to the identification of tense are the relations (i) between reference time and speech time, and (ii) between event and reference time. We can show this with the examples in (5.74–6):

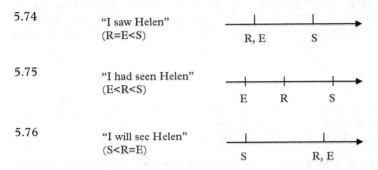

5.74 "I saw Helen"
(R=E<S)

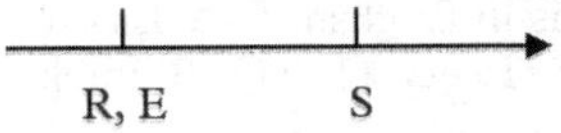

5.75 "I had seen Helen"
(E<R<S)

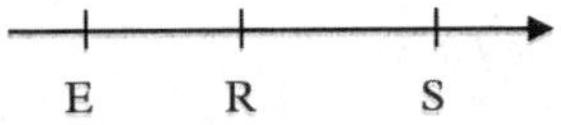

5.76 "I will see Helen"
(S<R=E)

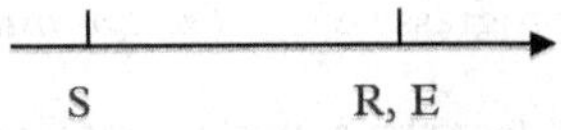

In 5.74 the vantage point and the event are situated before the act of speaking, the speech time, which then corresponds to the simple past tense in the sentence "I saw Helen." In 5.75, as in example 5.69 above, the reference time is in the past of the speech time, setting up a secondary past, corresponding to the past perfect form. In 5.76 the vantage point and event are in the future of the speech time, giving the simple future "I will see Helen."

It is difficult to go much further than these brief remarks about tense without discussing aspect. This is because in many languages, including English, aspect and tense interact in subtle ways and are marked on verbs in similar ways, often sharing composite endings. We discuss aspect in the next section.

5.2.6 Aspect

Aspect systems allow speakers to relate situations and time, but instead of fixing situations in time relative to the act of speaking, like tense does, aspect allows speakers to view an event in various ways: as complete, or incomplete, as so short as to involve almost no time, as something stretched over a perceptible period, or as something repeated over a period. As Charles Hockett (1958: 237) describes it:

5.77 *Aspects* have to do, not with the location of an event in time, but with its temporal distribution or contour.

We can compare the sentences 5.78 and 5.79 below for example:

5.78 Ralph was building a fire escape last week.

5.79 Ralph built a fire escape last week.

Both sentences describe a situation in the past but they differ: 5.79 views the fire escape as completed, while 5.78 gives no information about whether the fire escape ever got finished. The difference arises, of course, because the verb forms are each at a different intersection of the tense and aspect systems of English: *was building* is in a **past progressive** tense/aspect form in 5.78 and *built* is in a **simple past** tense/aspect form in 5.79.

We can look at this interdependence between aspect and tense by outlining some of the main forms in English. Discussion of each will necessarily be brief and readers are referred to Leech (1971), Binnick (1991), and Declerck (2006) for detailed descriptions.

English progressive forms

5.80	Present progressive	*I am listening*
	Past progressive	*I was listening*
	Future progressive	*I will be listening*

The progressives describe action as ongoing and continuing. As mentioned earlier, progressives are used with dynamic situations rather than states and provide a way of describing processes as being extended through time without any implication of completion. In the past and future, progressives can be used to provide a background activity against which another event occurs, for example:

5.81 She was hiding the money when the doorbell rang.

5.82 She'll be washing the car when you arrive.

Aside from this central use there are a number of subsidiary uses of the progressive, for example for intentions or plans in the immediate future as in 5.83:

5.83 I'm catching the midnight train tonight.

This use is sometimes called the **proximate future**. Reference grammars of English like Jespersen (1931), Quirk et al. (1985), and Huddleston and Pullum (2002) provide comprehensive descriptions of these uses.

English perfect forms

5.84	Present perfect	*I have listened*
	Past perfect	*I had listened*
	Future perfect	*I will have listened*

The perfect aspect allows a speaker to emphasize the relevance of events in the past to the "present." In the simplest case, the present perfect, this "present" is the time of speaking, what we could call the unmarked anchoring point. This relevance can be of different types: one is to give a "just now" sense of the immediate past, compare:

5.85 Don't run. The train has left.

5.86 ?Don't run. The train left.

Another interpretation of a sentence like 5.87

5.87 The train has left.

is that the speaker is focusing interest on the consequences now of the event described, that is that the train is no longer here. This sense of "relevance to now" is reflected by the fact that the perfect is often used with the adverb *already*, which means of course "by now, by then," for example:

5.88 I've already eaten.

In fact in some dialects of English this adverb can do the same job as the perfect aspect, thus making it redundant and allowing sentences like:

5.89 I already ate.

With the past and future perfect the connection, or relevance, relies on a secondary location in time, an anchoring point in the past or future of the time of speaking. See for example the past perfect in 5.90:

5.90 The train had left.

Here the anchoring point is in the past relative to the act of speaking and the verb form links the time prior to the anchoring point with the anchoring point itself. Though the locations in time are different, the same interpretations are possible as with the present perfect: a sense of immediacy, that is, a "just then" sense; or an emphasis on consequences, at that point the train was no longer there:

5.91 He was too late. The train had left.

The future perfect allows the same interpretations with an anchoring point in the future:

5.92 The train will have left.

So the perfect aspect is a relative aspect: it allows a speaker to emphasize the relevance to an anchoring point of an event in its past. This anchoring point can be the time that the speaker is speaking, or a time she chooses in the past or future. The economy allowed by such verbal forms as we find in 5.92 is clear as soon as we try to paraphrase such meanings as "events in the past of a future time but in the future of now."

English simple forms

5.93	Simple present	*I listen*
	Simple past	*I listened*
	Simple future	*I will listen*

These forms are simple tense forms which can be seen as basically neutral with respect to aspect: depending on other elements in the sentence, and on context, they are compatible with a number of aspects. Take for example the simple past form in 5.94:

5.94 I watched the six o'clock news.

This is compatible with a couple of interpretations: referring to one occasion in the past or describing a habitual action. As we will see below, when a simple past like 5.94 refers to a single occasion it portrays the action as completed.

The simple present is more restricted than the past. For most verbs, the use of the simple present to describe present events has largely been supplanted by the use of the present progressive: in an exchange like 5.95:

5.95 a. What are you doing?
b. I'm looking for my ticket.

the present progressive is used where many other languages would use a simple present, e.g. French:

5.96 a. Que'est-ce que tu fais?
b. Je cherche mon billet.

However, the English simple present is used as an ordinary present tense with stative verbs, as in 5.97:

5.97 a. He knows the answer.
b. *He is knowing the answer.

With non-stative verbs the simple present has other uses: it is used for habitual action, as in 5.98; for general or universal statements, as in 5.99, and in some instances for the future, as in 5.100:

5.98 She reads *The Independent*.

5.99 Earthworms belong to the phylum Annelida.

5.100 The ship departs tomorrow at dawn.

These then are examples of some basic tense and aspect forms in English. We have concentrated on the intersection of three tenses and three aspects, but we haven't of course exhausted the system: as learners of English know, more complex forms like *they will have been listening* are possible. See Quirk et al. (1985) and Huddleston and Pullum (2002) for a more complete listing of the forms.

The Reichenbach system for tenses that we discussed earlier attempts to reflect the aspectual meanings of verb forms, especially the relevance effects, by linking the reference point, which is the viewpoint or psychological vantage point adopted by the speaker, to the other points. We can expand earlier examples in 5.74–6 to the fuller selection in 5.101:

5.101 Reichenbach tenses for English:

a.	Simple past	(R=E<S)	"I saw Helen"
b.	Present perfect	(E<S=R)	"I have seen Helen"
c.	Past perfect	(E<R<S)	"I had seen Helen"
d.	Simple present	(S=R=E)	"I see Helen"
e.	Simple future	(S<R=E)	"I will see Helen"
f.	Proximate future	(S=R<E)	"I'm going to see Helen"
g.	Future perfect	(S=E<R)	"I will have seen Helen"

In this system, the present perfect in 5.101b and the proximate future in 5.101f have their meaning of "relevance to the present" reflected by linking the reference point and the speech point, that is S=R.

However, as foreign language learners also know, it is one thing to learn the verbal tense and aspect forms of a language and quite another to learn to use them correctly. One example of difficulty is that there are often restrictions on sequences of tense and aspect within complex sentences: for example, while the a sentence sequences below are possible, the b versions with a complex sentence sound very strange:

5.102 a. Joan walked out. She has left her bag.
b. ?Joan walked out and has left her bag.

5.103 a. You will get your results next Thursday. Come over for a drink.
b. ?When you will get your results next Thursday, come over for a drink.

See Comrie (1985:102–21) and Binnick (1991: 339ff.) for discussion of sequencing constraints on tense and aspect forms.[5]

Speakers may also employ unusual tenses and aspects in narratives to add freshness to the telling. For example, in many languages, including English, speakers and writers may narrate past events in the present tense, sometimes known as the **historical present**, to give immediacy to a description. See for example the following extract from John le Carré's novel *The Night Manager*:

5.104 Jonathan is in the bedroom of the little flat in Luxor, with the moonlight sloping between the half-closed curtains. Sophie is lying on the bed in her white nightgown, eyes closed and face upward. Some of her drollness has returned. She has drunk a little vodka. So has he. The bottle stands between them. (1993: 122)

Within the novel this scene is a flashback, situated in time before the main action of the novel, which itself is often described in the past tense. Since the description is in the present, the whole tense/aspect system is shifted, with the present perfect replacing the expected past perfect in, for example, "She has drunk a little vodka." See Schiffrin (1981) for a discussion of such effects.

5.2.7 Comparing aspect across languages

Although aspect is a sentential feature, we expect, especially in Indo-European languages, that it will be marked on verbs. Many languages, most famously Slavic languages, have inflectional affixes that give aspectual information, for example Russian:

5.105	On	čital	pis'mo.	(imperfective)
	he	read.PAST.IMPERF	a letter	
	"He was reading a letter."			

5.106	On	pročital	pis'mo.	(perfective)
	he	read.PAST.PERF	a letter	
	"He read a letter."[6]			

This **perfective/imperfective** distinction of aspect is very widespread among the languages of the world: Dahl (1985) and Bybee (1985) identify it as the most commonly found and in many senses the most basic distinction. Some writers view the difference as being one of viewpoint: Comrie (1976) describes perfectivity as viewing a situation externally, from outside, with no reference to its internal temporal structure, while imperfectivity allows the viewing of a situation from within, making explicit reference to the internal temporal structure. C. S. Smith (1991) proposes a similar definition: perfectivity includes the viewing of the beginning and end of a situation, while imperfectivity focuses on the middle phase, leaving especially the end unspecified. She supports this with examples from Russian, where the oddity of 5.108 below comes from taking a situation described in 5.107 in the perfective, and therefore ended, and trying to extend it into the present (1991: 302):

5.107	On	napisal	pis'mo.
	He	wrote.PERF	a letter
	"He wrote^{perf} a letter."		

5.108	?On	napisal	pis'mo	i	ešče	pišet	ego.
	he	wrote.PERF	a letter	and	still	writes.IMPERF	it
	"He wrote^{perf} the letter and is still writing^{imperf} it."						

However, with a situation described in the imperfective, like 5.109 below, the end point is unspecified and is thus compatible with an extension into the present as in 5.110 (Smith 1991: 304):

5.109	My	pisali	pis'mo.
	we	wrote.IMPERF	a letter
	"We were writing^{imperf} a letter."		

5.110	My	pisali	pis'mo	i	ešče	pišem	ego.
	we	wrote.IMPERF	a letter	and	still	write.IMPERF	it
	"We were writing^{imperf} a letter and are still writing^{imperf} it."						

These definitions allow us to correlate the imperfective/perfective system with the distinction we saw earlier in English between the simple past and the past progressive. Returning to an earlier example:

5.111 John was building a fire escape.

5.112 John built a fire escape.

we can identify the simple past verb form *built* in 5.112 as an English representative of the perfective aspect, with *was building* in 5.111 representing the imperfective. As we have seen, the perfective focuses on the end points of a situation while the imperfective does not, producing a distinction between complete and incomplete action. This helps explain why we can interleave another event into the progressive of example 5.111 but not the simple past of 5.112, as 5.113 and 5.114 below show:

5.113 John was building a fire escape last week, when Rosemary came to stay.

5.114 John built a fire escape last week, when Rosemary came to stay.

In 5.113 Rosemary interrupts the building process, while in 5.114 Rosemary's arrival can only be placed outside the closed event, that is before or after the building of the fire escape, perhaps most naturally the latter. Though the added clause is the same in both sentences, we understand different sequences of events: indeed the sequence understood in 5.114 can lead to the implication that Rosemary's arrival was the cause of Ralph building the fire escape.

We can parallel Smith's examples from Russian with similar examples from English: 5.115 below is odd because the second clause contradicts the perfective nature of the first clause, while 5.116 is fine:

5.115 ?I baked a cake and I'm still baking it.

5.116 I was baking a cake, and I am still baking it.

What this brief comparison of English and Russian disguises is that while we can compare the aspectual systems of different languages, it is very difficult to characterize a typical aspectual system. Firstly, of course, the means of marking aspects differ: Russian, as we saw, uses prefixes on the verb, while English tends to use combinations of verbal endings and auxiliary verbs like *be*, *have*, *use to*, for example:

5.117 a. He read *The Irish Times*.
b. He has read *The Irish Times*.
c. He used to read *The Irish Times*.
d. He was reading *The Irish Times*.

A second and more serious problem in trying to come up with universal aspectual distinctions is that the aspectual systems of different languages tend not to correspond very closely. As we noted, it has been claimed that the aspectual distinction between perfective and imperfective aspects is very widespread: forty-five of the sixty-four languages in Dahl's (1985) worldwide sample possess an aspectual distinction of this type. However, there are numerous differences between uses of these two aspects among these languages. For example, the perfective in Arabic is only used with reference to the past, for example:

5.118	Harbat	al-bint	min	al-madrasa.
	run away.3f.sg.PERF	the-girl	from	the-school
	"The girl ran/has run away from the school."			

In Russian, on the other hand, a perfective can occur with past and non-past tenses: a perfective non-past is understood to refer to the future, for example:

5.119	Ja	napišu	pis'mo.
	I	write.PERF.NON-PAST	a letter
	"I'll write a letter."		

(Dahl 1985: 80)

The examples we have seen of tense and aspect have been marked grammatically, for example by verbal affixes and auxiliary verbs. As mentioned earlier, a speaker's characterization of a situation derives from combining a choice from the situation types encoded in the verbal semantics with forms from the grammatical systems of tense and aspect. We end discussion of aspect by looking briefly at the interaction of situation types and aspect in the next section.

5.2.8 Combining situation type and aspect

We saw in section 5.2.2 that situation type and aspect interact: for example, certain verb forms such as progressives are used with some situation types but not with others. In fact the options for describing situations in any language are constrained by natural combinations of situation type, aspect and tense. Inherent features of a verb's meaning fit in with the meaning of certain tense and aspect forms, but not with others. Speakers know the valid combinations and the semanticist's task is to reflect this knowledge. The difficulty is that the combinations are very language specific. For example, in the last section we saw that the English progressive aspect has features of the cross-linguistic aspect imperfective. However, it also has connotations of activity, dynamism, and volition. C. S. Smith (1991: 224) gives examples of contrasts between simple and progressive forms which show this:

5.120 a. She blinked her eyes.
b. She was blinking her eyes.

5.121 a. The ship moved.
b. The ship was moving.

The observation is that the b sentences have a vividness missing from the a sentences. Additionally, 5.120b has connotations of willful behavior missing from 5.120a; and in 5.121b the description of motion is more vivid than in 5.121a because of the progressive's focus on internal successive phases. As we saw earlier, these connotations of dynamism mean that the progressive does not combine with stative situation types in English:

5.122 a. *He was understanding the problem.
b. He understood the problem.

5.123 a. *She was having long legs.
b. She had long legs.

However in French the **imparfait** aspect, which might be seen as a corresponding imperfective,[7] does not have these connotations of dynamism and therefore does occur with statives, as below (Rand 1993: 39):

5.124 L'air sentait le jasmin.
the-air smell.IMP-PAST the jasmine
"The air smelled of jasmine."

5.125 Je vous entendais bien.
I you hear.IMP-PAST well
"I heard you well."

Part of the semantic description of particular languages then is to reflect which aspectual viewpoints are available on a particular situation type. Thus for English we need to recognize that a speaker can choose to view an accomplishment from a perfective viewpoint as in 5.126a below or from an imperfective viewpoint as in 5.126b:

5.126 a. Rory painted a seascape.
b. Rory was painting a seascape.

Thus the interaction between situation type and aspect is a complex area of semantics, but what seems clear is that in describing a speaker's aspectual choices we must distinguish between three dimensions: real situations, the situation types lexically coded in languages, and ways of viewing these situations types in terms of their internal structure (the choice of whether or not to focus on their beginning, middle, and end phases). There are some differences in the terminology applied across these three dimensions. Some writers use **aspect** for both the second and third dimensions, which we have termed situation type and aspect. Others use opposing terms for these two dimensions: **situation type** vs. **viewpoint aspect**, **lexical aspect** vs. **grammatical aspect**, and **inner aspect** vs. **outer aspect**. Still others reserve **aspect** for viewpoint and borrow foreign language terms like ***modes d'action*** or ***Aktionsarten*** for the situation types, or the real situations, or both. Binnick (1991) picks a very detailed path through the terminology.

5.3 Modality and Evidentiality

5.3.1 Modality

Another important semantic category which operates at the sentence level is **modality**. Modality is a cover term for devices which allow speakers to express varying degrees of commitment to, or belief in, a proposition. Let us take a simple assertion like 5.127:

5.127 Niamh has gone to the airport.

It seems that when being told 5.127, we assume a certain commitment on the behalf of the speaker to its truth. The speaker may be wrong of course, or be lying in order to mislead us. Our conversational practice, however, seems to be built upon an assumption that speakers generally try to tell the truth, as they know it. If we discover that Niamh hasn't gone to the airport then our reactions will be very different depending on whether we think the speaker was simply wrong in her belief, or intentionally misleading us. We discuss this assumption of truthfulness as part of the more general issue of conversational conventions in chapter 7. We might take the opposite of the assertion 5.127 to be the denial 5.128:

5.128 Niamh hasn't gone to the airport.

However, without any further spoken qualification, both 5.127 and its negation 5.128 seem to carry an unspoken guarantee of "to the best of my knowledge."

Modal systems allow speakers to modulate this guarantee: to signal stronger and weaker commitment to the factuality of statements. There are a number of possible linguistic strategies: for example, the sentence can be embedded under a higher clause with an adjective or adverb of modality, as in (where S represents our sentence):

5.129
a. It is certain that S
b. It is probable that S
c. It is likely that S
d. It is possible that S

Here versions 129a–d move from strong to weak commitment to S. Another strategy is to put into the higher clause a verb which describes the extent of the speaker's belief – what is often called in the philosophical literature her **propositional** attitude:

5.130
a. I know that S
b. I believe that S
c. I think that S
d. I don't know that S
e. I doubt that S
f. I know that not S

In 5.130 we have a gradient from the certainty of the truth of the proposition expressed by S through to the certainty of its falsity.

A third strategy we find in English is to employ auxiliary verbs: in 5.132 below these mark the variations of commitment toward the assertion in 5.131:

5.131 She has left by now.

5.132 a. She must have left by now.
b. She might have left by now.
c. She could have left by now.
d. She needn't have left by now.
e. She couldn't have left by now.

Auxiliary verbs in this role are called **modal verbs**.

These modal verbs have other functions. The examples so far have been of **epistemic modality**, so called because the speaker is signaling degrees of knowledge. A second major use is to signal **deontic modality**, where the verbs mark the speaker's attitude to social factors of obligation, responsibility and permission. Take for example 5.133 below:

5.133 You can drive this car.

A speaker can use this to mean either of the following:

5.134 It is possible for you to drive this car.

5.135 You have my permission to drive this car.

The first is another example of epistemic modality; the second is an example of deontic modality. Deontic modals communicate two types of social information: **obligation** as in 5.136 and **permission** as in 5.137:

5.136 a. You must take these books back.
b. You should take these books back.
c. You need to take these books back.
d. You ought to take these books back.

5.137 a. You can leave them there.
b. You could leave them there.
c. You might leave them there.

Deontic modals, like epistemic modals, signal a speaker's judgments, but while with epistemics the judgment is about the way the real world is, with deontics it is about how people should behave in the world. This means that the use of deontics is tied in with all sorts of social knowledge: the speaker's belief systems about morality and legality; and her estimations of power and authority. The sentences in 5.136 and in 5.137 step down in modal strength. Thus 5.136a is a stronger statement of obligation than 5.136d, and while 5.137a for example is a bald granting of permission, 5.137c is a weaker and politer version. We can imagine that deciding which of 5.137a–c to use would depend on different judgments by the speaker of her authority over the listener and the degree of formality of their relationship.

Sometimes the relationship between epistemic and deontic modality is more complicated than an ambiguity resolvable in context, like 5.133 earlier. Speakers can use an epistemic modal to imply a deontic interpretation as in 5.138:

5.138 You could have told me you were coming.

Here the possibility of telling is used to imply a missed obligation, turning 5.138 into a reproof.

Other types of non-epistemic modality have been identified including **abilitive**, **teleological**, and **bouletic** modality. These are expressed by the same forms, for example modal verbs in English, italicized in the examples below. Abilitive modality reflects possibility based on the speaker's view of a subject's abilities, as in 5.139 below:

5.139 a. Alexander *can* play cricket.
b. This bridge *can* support the trucks' weight.

Teleological modality expresses strengths of possibility and necessity relative to the speaker's view of a subject's goals, as in 5.140:

5.140 [Context: In order to get the job...] He *can*/*has to* improve his Irish.

Bouletic modality reflects possibility and necessity relative to the speaker's view of a subject's desires, for example:

5.141 [Context: Since Isabel wants to go on a world cruise...] She *can*/*should* start saving now.

Some scholars identify a third category distinct from epistemic and deontic modality. Palmer (2003), for example, assigns examples like 5.139 to a category called **dynamic modals**. Deontic and dynamic modals share the characteristic of being concerned with actions and behavior but Palmer suggests the difference is one of control. In deontic modals the event is controlled by people or circumstances other than the subject of the sentence, as in the deontic reading of example 5.133 above. In dynamic modals the control belongs to the subject, as in example 5.139 where the possibilities derive from the subjects' own abilities. Other scholars suggest different classifications: Coates (1983) for example places such examples into a group with deontic modality called **root** modality as distinct from epistemic modality. The term "root" is rather opaque but is used by Leech (2004) for example to reflect the assumption that non-epistemic modality is more basic and common.

We have seen that epistemic and deontic modality can be marked by the same means, for example modal verbs, and indeed that some sentences are ambiguous in form between an epistemic and deontic reading. This has led semanticists to ask what they have in common, and to speculate whether one type of modality has developed out of the other. One suggestion is that modality in general allows us to compare the real world with hypothetical versions of it. This approach derives from work on **possible world semantics** by David Lewis (1973, 1986) and others;[8] some of its grammatical implications are discussed by Chung and Timberlake (1985) and Palmer (1986). In this view, epistemic modals allow us to set up hypothetical situations and express different strengths of prediction of their match with the real world. Thus if a speaker says:

5.142 It might be raining in Belfast.

she is setting up a hypothetical situation (rain in Belfast) and predicting a reasonable match with reality. If on the other hand she says:

5.143 It must be raining in Belfast.

she is proposing a very strong match between her prediction and reality.

This approach views deontic modality in the same way. Here though the speaker is proposing a match between an ideal moral or legal situation and the real world of behavior. So if a speaker says:

5.144 You should pay for that doughnut.

she is proposing a match between the ideal situation and the real situation; a match more strongly proposed in 5.145:

5.145 You must pay for that doughnut.

This approach would relate modality to **conditional sentences** like 5.146 and 5.147 below, which also set up hypothetical situations:

5.146 If I were rich, I would be living somewhere hotter.

5.147 You would sleep all day, if we let you.

We can call the *if*-clause in sentences like 5.146–7, the **condition**, and the other clause, the **consequent**. This view of conditionals as part of the modal system neatly explains why we also find modal verbs used in consequent clauses, like *would* in 5.146–7 above, or *should* in the condition clauses below:

5.148 If you should go to Paris, stay near the river.

5.149 Should you meet Christy, there's something I would like you to ask him.

This approach to modality is also supported by the existence of languages that have verb forms which regularly distinguish between events in the real world and events in future or imaginary worlds. This two-term modal distinction is often called a **realis/irrealis modality** (i.e. a reality/unreality distinction): for example, Palmer

(1986: 47) describes a distinction between realis and irrealis moods in the Australian language Ngiyambaa:

5.150 a. yuruŋ-gu ŋidja-a.[9]
rain-ERG rain-PRES
"It is raining." (realis)
b. yuruŋ-gu ŋidja-l-aga.
rain-ERG rain-CM-IRREALIS
"It might/will rain." (irrealis)

In this section we have looked briefly at the semantic system of modality; in the next we look at how modality distinctions are encoded in the grammar, in particular, at mood.

5.3.2 Mood

Thus far we have seen modality distinctions in English being marked by various means including adverbs and modal verbs. When such distinctions are marked by verb endings that form distinct conjugations, there is a grammatical tradition of calling these moods. Thus the distinction in the Ngiyambaa verb in 5.151 would be described as a distinction between a realis mood and an irrealis mood. In the verbal inflection of the Cushitic language Somali we find, in addition to the basic indicative mood in 5.151, a conditional mood, as in 5.152, and a potential mood as in 5.153:

5.151 Wuu sameeyey.
he make.PAST
"He made it."

5.152 Wuu sameyn lahaa.
he make.INFINITIVE have
"He would make it, he would have made it."

5.153 Show sameyee.
possibly make.POTENTIAL
"Maybe he'll make it, it's possible he will make it."

The indicative in 5.151, which is a *realis* form, and the potential in 5.153 are marked by specific verb endings, while the conditional in 5.152 uses an the infinitive with an auxiliary verb "have," rather like English.[10]

A more familiar example of mood is the **subjunctive** mood found in many European languages. The label subjunctive is applied somewhat differently in different languages, but we can identify two opposite poles of use, with an area of mixing and overlap between them. One pole is the grammatical one of syntactic subordination, that is, subjunctive verb forms show that a verb is in a subordinate clause. The other pole is semantic, where the subjunctive marks language-specific types of irrealis mood, and is thus used for wishes, beliefs, exhortations, commands and so on. At the syntactic pole, we can cite the example of Somali again where subordinate clause verbs are always differentiated from their main clause equivalents by a combination of tone and endings; compare 5.154 and 5.155 below:

5.154 Lacágta way kéenaysaa.[11]
lacág-ta waa-ay kéenaysaa
'money-the CLASS-she bring.PROGRESSIVE
"She is bringing the money."

5.155 ínay lacágta kéenaysó
ín-ay lacág-ta kéenaysó
that-she money-the bring.SUBJUNCTIVE
"that she is bringing the money"

In 5.154 the classifier *waa* identifies a main clause, while in 5.155 the complementizer *in* "that" identifies a subordinate clause. As is clear, the main clause and subordinate clause forms of the verb *keen* "bring" have different tonal shapes and a different endings.[12]

If such subordinate verb forms are termed "subjunctive," then this use of the term does not seem to have anything to do with the semantic system of modality. However, in classical Greek and in Latin, the subjunctive describes a verbal form that occurs in both main and subordinate clauses, though with somewhat different applications in each. Palmer (1986: 39–43), citing R. T. Lakoff (1968), gives six meanings of the subjunctive in Latin main clauses: imperative, optative (for wishes), jussive, concessive, potential and deliberative. Each of these can be identified with descriptions of unreal situations, and thus be examples of our semantic pole of unreality. They contrast with the **indicative** mood used for descriptions of factual, or real, situations.

In-between positions are very common, especially in modern European languages. In many languages, the subjunctive is most commonly found in subordinate clauses, but often with some special meaning: following verbs of wishing and preference, as in the Spanish example 5.156 below (Butt and Benjamin 1994: 246) and the French 5.157; for the future in Spanish 5.158 (Butt and Benjamin 1994: 241); or indirect speech as in German 5.159 (Hammer 1991: 310):

5.156 Quiero que estudies más.
want.INDIC.PRES.1sg that study.SUBJUN.PRES.2sg more
"I want you to study more."

5.157 Il vaut mieux qu'elle le sache.
it worth better that+she it know.SUBJUN.PRES.3sg
"It's better that she know it."

5.158 Iremos allí cuando haga buen tiempo
go.INDIC.FUT.1p there when have.SUBJUN.PRES.3sg good weather
"We'll go there when the weather's good."

5.159 Sie sagte sie schreibe den Brief.
she said she write.SUBJUN.IMPERF.3sg the letter
"She said she was writing the letter."

While there seems to be some shared element of modality in these uses, that is of non-factuality,[13] the range of use of subjunctives is usually both complex and language-specific. Often the choice between indicative and subjunctive moods allows speakers to make subtle semantic distinctions, as for example between the different degrees of possibility marked by the French indicative and subjunctive in 5.160 and 5.161 below (Judge and Healey 1985: 141):

5.160 Je pense qu'il viendra.
I think.INDIC.PRES that-he come.INDIC.FUT
"I think that he'll come."

5.161 Je doute qu'il vienne.
I doubt.INDIC.PRES that-he come.SUBJUN.PRES
"I doubt that he'll come."

Before we close this section on mood, we should point out that there is another quite distinct use of the term in semantics. This applies to changes in verbal morphology associated with the different social functions or **speech acts** that a speaker may intend. For example a speaker may intend a sentence as a statement, a question, a command or a wish. Depending on the language, these different functions may be marked by different word orders or special intonation tunes. Some languages mark this information by particular verb forms: for example, some languages have special **optative** verb conjugations to express wishes like the English phrases "may he get well," "I hope he gets well," "if only he would get well," for example. See for example the Nahuatl sentence (Bybee 1985: 171):

5.162 mā choca. "If only he would weep."

Such special speech act verbal forms are often called moods: the example above would therefore be in the optative mood, and in some languages this would contrast with an imperative mood (for commands), an interrogative mood (for questions) or a declarative mood (for statements). We will discuss this grammaticalization of speech functions in chapter 8 on speech acts. See Foley and Van Valin (1984) for discussion of the relationship between this use of mood and the epistemic and deontic modality we have been concerned with here.

5.3.3 Evidentiality

Under epistemic modality we looked at ways in which a speaker can mark different attitudes toward the factuality of a proposition. There is a further semantic category **evidentiality** which allows a speaker to communicate her attitude to the source of her information. This is possible in English of course by the use of a separate clause or by parenthetic adverbials. Compare the bare assertion in 5.163 with the various evidentially qualified versions in 5.164a–g:

5.163 She was rich.

5.164 a. I saw that she was rich.
b. I read that she was rich.
c. She was rich, so they say.
d. I'm told she was rich.
e. Apparently she was rich.
f. She was rich, it seems.
g. Allegedly, she was rich.

These qualifications allow the speaker to say whether the statement relies on personal first-hand knowledge, or was acquired from another source; and if the latter, perhaps to say something of the source.

Some languages routinely mark such information grammatically, by special particles or specific verb forms, so that in these languages evidentiality is coded in the morphology. A collection of descriptions of such languages is Chafe and Nichols (1986), which contains articles both on the North and South American languages where such systems were first described and also on evidential systems in European and Asian languages. Aikhenvald (2004) provides a comparative overview of such evidential systems. We can take as an example Tariana, an Arawak language spoken in northern Amazonia, whose verbal morphology distinguishes several different sources for information (Aikhenvald 2004: 2–3):

5.165 a. Juse iɾida di-manika-**ka**
José football 3sgnf-play-REC.P.VIS
"José has played football (we saw it)"
b. Juse iɾida di-manika-**mahka**
José football 3sgnf-play-REC.P.NONVIS
"José has played football (we heard it)"
c. Juse iɾida di-manika-**nihka**
José football 3sgnf-play-REC.P.INFR
"José has played football (we infer it from visual evidence)"
d. Juse iɾida di-manika-**sika**
José football 3sgnf-play-REC.P.ASSUM
"José has played football (we assume this on the basis of what we already know)"
e. Juse iɾida di-manika-**pidaka**
José football 3sgnf-play-REC.P.REP
"José has played football (we were told)"

We follow Aikhenvald in marking the evidential morphemes in bold, giving us the five-fold evidential distinction between these reports of a recent past event. In a the speaker has seen the event; in b the speaker heard the noise of the football game; in c the report is an inference from visual evidence;[14] in d the assumption is based on previous knowledge about José's habits; and finally in e, the speaker has learned the information from someone else.

What emerges from these studies of evidential systems are differences among languages in whether the evidential markers are obligatory in ordinary speech or an optional resource for speakers. Hardman, for example, reports that among the Jaqi languages of Peru, Bolivia, and Chile the identification of what she calls "data source" (i.e. the use of evidentials) is a central part of knowing how to communicate (1986: 114):

5.166 Accuracy on the part of the speaker is a crucial element in the public reputation of individuals; misuse of data-source is somehow somewhat less than human, or is insulting to the listener.

Speakers of Jaqi languages, which include Jaqaru, Aymara, and Kakwi, have obligatorily to signal whether the source of information for their statements is personal experience, or knowledge gained from other individuals by language, or comes from the remote past where no witnesses are available, that is from myths, history, and religion. In other languages the use of evidentials is more voluntary, providing a speaker with creative resources to structure a point of view in a discourse, or perhaps to argue more convincingly. See Chafe (1986) for a description of evidentials in English.

5.4 Summary

In this chapter we looked at aspects of sentence meaning that allow the speaker to classify situations. The category of **situation type**, for example, incorporating semantic distinctions like **static/dynamic**, **durative/punctual**, and **telic/atelic**, allows a basic classification of situations into **states**, **activities**, **accomplishments**, and so on. The categories of **tense** and **aspect** interact with situation type to allow a speaker to relate a situation to time in two ways: to locate it relative to the act of speaking, and to portray its internal temporal shape. We saw something of how these choices are reflected in grammar. We also saw that the distinctions available to speakers may be very subtle and language specific.

We also looked at the semantic categories of **modality** and **evidentiality**, which allow the speaker to assume various attitudes toward a proposition. **Epistemic** modality reflects various judgments of factuality and **deontic** modality communicates judgments of moral and legal obligation. Both can be seen as implying a comparison between the real world and hypothetical versions of it. **Evidentiality** is a term for the ways in which a speaker qualifies a statement by referring to the source of the information. We saw that in some languages this information is grammaticalized and therefore obligatory, implying that in these communities, calculation of evidence is assumed of speakers by their hearers. We look at the role of similar hearer assumptions, for example that the speaker is estimating and updating her audience's state of knowledge, in chapter 7.

EXERCISES

5.1 **Stative verbs** typically do not occur in the progressive aspect nor as imperatives. Use these two facts as tests to decide which of the following verbs are stative. If you identify stative and non-stative uses for a verb give examples of the two uses.

seem	think	imitate	possess	know	resemble	lack
seize	last	comprise	lose	prefer		

5.2 As we saw, some verbs can have distinct **stative** and **dynamic** senses. For each of the following verbs, provide two sentences: one with the verb in a stative sense and the other a dynamic sense. You can use the progressive test, as in the last exercise, to distinguish between the senses.

admire equal appear hold contain reach cost smell

5.3 We noted that adding a **durative** adverb like *all night* or *for three hours* to a **punctual** verb like *cough* results in an **iterative** or repetitive interpretation (i.e. "again and again"). Thus in *The patient coughed all night* we interpret the activity as a sequence of individual coughs throughout the night. Use this behavior to identify the punctual verbs among the following:

read drive ring tap sigh fly twitch sob float

5.4 We saw that some verbs may describe **bounded** (**telic**) or **unbounded** (**atelic**) processes, depending on the form of their complements. Thus while *build a bridge* is a bounded process, *build bridges* is an unbounded process. Below is a list of verb phrases. For each one decide whether it is bounded or unbounded, then see if you can change this value by altering the verb's complement.

ate oranges	ripen
swim	direct movies
rig an election	walk to the station
put out fires	

5.5 In this chapter, we identified a number of English tense/aspect forms, e.g. the past perfect form in *she had realized*. Identify the tense/aspect forms of the italicized verbs below:

a. They *founded* a school of medicine.
b. A guy *was telling* them a joke.
c. Who *decides*?
d. They'*ve eaten* a lot of peanuts.
e. She *will bring* the money.

f. You'*re treating* me like a child.
g. They *will have reached* the warehouse by now.
h. I'*m sitting* here.

5.6 Below are paired examples containing **simple present** and **present progressive** verb forms. Explain what semantic differences you detect (if any) between the pairs.

1 a. My brother works in France.
  b. My brother is working in France.
2 a. We leave tomorrow.
  b. We are leaving tomorrow.
3 a. You look good.
  b. You're looking good.
4 a. She lives near the airport.
  b. She's living near the airport.
5 a. You eat too much meat.
  b. You're eating too much meat.
6 a. You always laugh at me.
  b. You're always laughing at me.

5.7 We described the use of **modal verbs** to convey **epistemic modality**. In the following sentences discuss what the modal verbs (in bold) tell us about the speaker's attitude.

a. This **could** be our bus now.
b. They **would** be very happy to meet you.
c. You **must** be the bride's father.
d. The bus **should** be here soon.
e. It **might** freeze tonight.
f. He **will** be home by now.

5.8 Some sentences with modal verbs are ambiguous between an **epistemic** and a **deontic** reading. For each of the sentences below, try to imagine two contexts: one where the sentence might be used with an epistemic reading and the other a deontic reading. Once again modal verbs appear in bold type.

a. Alcohol **may** not be served to persons under twenty-one.
b. You **can** go home now.
c. We **could** take the examination early.
d. You **will** not leave this island.
e. We **should** be at the hotel by nine.

5.9 One use of the **subjunctive** mood in English is in *that*-clauses which report a suggestion or proposal, as in 1 below. As is shown by 2 below, this use is paralleled by clauses with the modal verb *should*:

1 Subjunctive
   a. He proposed *that the meeting come to a close.*
   b. She agreed *that the house be sold.*

2 Modal verb
   a. He proposed *that the meeting should come to a close.*
   b. She agreed *that the house should be sold.*

As 1 shows, the form of the subjunctive in English is the base (or bare stem) form of the verb. Decide which of the following verbs may take a subjunctive *that*-clause by constructing example sentences:

urge demand beg remember command report tell warn deny
insist decide request promise suggest

5.10 Chafe (1986), discussing **evidentiality** in English, identifies five sources for information. In the following the marker of evidentiality is shown in bold.

1	belief:	the information is already held by the speaker, who makes no overt reference to evidence, e.g. ***I think that*** *democracy means more than just one person one vote*;
2	induction:	the speaker concludes the information from evidence, without specifying the type of evidence, e.g. *The exit* ***must*** *be blocked*;
3	sensory evidence:	information from perceptual evidence, e.g. ***It smells like*** *they're having a barbecue next door.*
4	hearsay evidence:	information acknowledged as being told to the speaker by others, e.g. *They're* ***supposed*** *to be having an affair*;
5	deduction:	the speaker uses a hypothesis to predict a fact, e.g. *The snow* ***should*** *melt more quickly near the sea.*

Below are some sentences containing markers of evidentiality. For each sentence identify the marker and say which of these five sources of information you think is involved. Some markers may be appropriate with more than one type of source; if you think this is the case, please note it.

a. Apparently Fred doesn't like skiing.
b. Electrons should flow through the wire from Fe^{2+} to MnO_{4-}.
c. You look like you need a stiff drink.
d. Evidently we're no longer welcome here
e. He sounds a bit unsure of himself.
f. You must be very tired after your journey.
g. The jeweler was the ringleader, allegedly.
h. I suppose that I'd better go to the lecture.

FURTHER READING

Comrie's *Aspect* (1976) and *Tense* (1985) are concise monographs, using examples from a range of languages. Smith (1991) discusses universals of situation type and aspect and gives brief descriptions of the aspectual systems of English, French, Russian, Mandarin Chinese, and Navajo. Rothstein (2004) is a detailed discussion of the semantics of situation type. Binnick (2012) is a collection of articles covering recent research on tense and aspect. Palmer (1986) and Bybee and Fleischman (1995) contain discussions of modality systems in various languages. Bybee et al. (1994) contains a large cross-linguistic survey of tense, aspect and modality. The marking of these semantic categories on the English verb can be seen in Leech (1971), and the comprehensive reference grammar Quirk et al. (1985). Aikhenvald (2004) provides a survey of evidential systems in a wide range of languages.

NOTES

1 Transcription as in the original, where tone is marked as follows: ō (macron) = high level tone, ó = rising; ǒ= fall-rise, ò = falling.

2 Though see Schmitt and Miller (2007) for some arguments that this is too simple a characterization.

3 See Dowty (1979) for a discussion of stativity and English verbs, especially verbs like *sit* and *stand*, which act like statives in many ways but allow progressive forms.

4 It is important to remember that the interpretation of a situation type depends on context. So example 5.57 is fine if we imagine a situation where Fred had the task of losing his keys. This changes the situation type to an accomplishment, which may occur with *finish*, as discussed later in this section.

5 See also Ogihara (1989).

6 Note that our translations here are meant to be suggestive: in fact, as my colleague Sarah Smyth has pointed out to me, the contrast between the English past progressive and past simple doesn't exactly capture the Russian distinction between imperfective and perfective. Thus 5.105 can also mean *He read a letter* or *He has read a letter*. The perfective form in 5.106 is more likely to mean *He read a letter (and then threw it away)*, for perfective verbs in Russian suggest continuation of narrative.

7 The French *imparfait* does not of course correspond to the Russian imperfective: for example, the French perfective *Tu as vu ce film?* would be translated into Russian as an imperfective *Ty videl etot fil'm?*.

8 We discuss this notion of possible worlds in chapter 10.

9 In this transcription CM = "conjugation marker," ERG = ergative case.

10 We have glossed *show* in 5.153 as "possibly" but in fact it is a sentence type indicator, or **classifier**, which can only be used with verbs in the potential mood. See Saeed (1993) for more details, and chapter 8, section 8.5, where we discuss these classifiers in Somali and their status as sentence type markers.

11 The tone markings used here are *á* = high tone, and *a* (i.e. unmarked) = low tone. They are only marked on the first vowel of long vowels, e.g. *ée*.

12 Note that such subordinate clause verbs are finite, showing inflectional marking of person, tense, and aspect.

13 Another way of viewing what these uses of the subjunctive have in common comes from the modality of speech acts, to be discussed in chapter 8. This to recognize a common element of *non-assertion* in these clauses.

14 Aikhenvald gives a possible licensing context as follows: "If one sees that the football is not in its usual place in the house, and José and his football boots are gone, with crowds of people coming back from the football ground, this is enough for us to infer that José is playing football" (2004: 2).

REFERENCES

Aikhenvald, Alexandra Y. 2004: *Evidentiality*. Oxford: Oxford University Press.

Binnick, Robert I. 1991: *Time and the Verb: A Guide to Tense and Aspect*. Oxford: Oxford University Press.

Binnick, Robert I. (ed.) 2012: *The Oxford Handbook of Tense and Aspect*. Oxford: Oxford University Press.

Butt, John and Carmen Benjamin 1994: *A New Reference Grammar of Modern Spanish*, second edition. London: Edward Arnold.

Bybee, Joan 1985: *Morphology*. Amsterdam: John Benjamins.

Bybee, Joan and Suzanne Fleischman (eds.) 1995: *Modality in Grammar and Discourse*. Amsterdam: John Benjamins.

Bybee, Joan, Revere Perkins and William Pagliuca 1994: *The Evolution of Grammar: Tense, Aspect, and Modality in the Languages of the World*. Chicago: University of Chicago Press.

Carlson, G. 1977: Reference to kinds in English. PhD dissertation. University of Massachusetts at Amherst.

Chafe, Wallace 1986: Evidentiality in English conversation and academic writing. In Wallace Chafe and Johanna Nichols (eds.) *Evidentiality: The Linguistic Coding of Epistemology*, 261–72. Norwood, NJ: Ablex.

Chafe, Wallace and Johanna Nichols (eds.) 1986: *Evidentiality: The Linguistic Coding of Epistemology*. Norwood, NJ: Ablex.

Chung, Sandra and Alan Timberlake 1985: Tense, aspect and mood. In Timothy Shopen (ed.) *Language Typology and Syntactic Description. Vol. 3: Grammatical Categories and the Lexicon*, 202–58. Cambridge: Cambridge University Press

Coates, Jennifer 1983: *The Semantics of Modal Auxiliaries*. London: Croom Helm

Comrie, Bernard 1976: *Aspect*. Cambridge: Cambridge University Press.

Comrie, Bernard 1985: *Tense*. Cambridge: Cambridge University Press.

Dahl, Östen 1985: *Tense and Aspect Systems*. Oxford: Blackwell.

Declerck, Renaat. 2006: *The Grammar of the English Tense System: A Comprehensive Analysis*. (Grammar of the English Verb Phrase, Vol. 1). Berlin: Mouton de Gruyter.

Diesing, Molly. 1992. *Indefinites*. Cambridge, MA: MIT Press.

Dowty, David R. 1979: *Word Meaning and Montague Grammar*. Dordrecht: Reidel.

Foley, William and Robert Van Valin 1984: *Functional Syntax and Universal Grammar*. Cambridge: Cambridge University Press.

Givón, Talmy 1972: Studies in ChiBemba and Bantu grammar. *Studies in African Linguistics*, supplement 3.

Givón, Talmy 2001: *Syntax: An Introduction*, 2 vols. Amsterdam: John Benjamins.

Hammer, A. E. 1991: *Hammer's German Grammar and Usage*, second edition revised by Martin Durrell. London: Edward Arnold.

Hardman, Martha James 1986: Data-source marking in the Jaqi languages. In Wallace Chafe and Johanna Nichols (eds.) *Evidentiality: The Linguistic Coding of Epistemology*, 113–36. Norwood, NJ: Ablex.

Hay, Jennifer, Christopher Kennedy and Beth Levin 1999: Scalar structure underlies telicity in "degree achievements." In T. Mathews and D. Strolovitch (eds.) *Proceedings of Semantics and Linguistic Theory (=SALT) IX*, 127–44. Ithaca, NY: CLC Publications, Cornell University.

Hockett, Charles F. 1958: *A Course in Modern Linguistics*. New York: Macmillan.
Huddleston, Rodney and Geoffrey K. Pullum 2002: *The Cambridge Grammar of the English Language*. Cambridge: Cambridge University Press.
Jespersen, Ottto 1931: *A Modern English Grammar on Historical Principles*, 4 vols. London: George Allen & Unwin.
Judge, Ann and F. G. Healey 1985: *A Reference Grammar of Modern French*. London: Edward Arnold.
Kratzer, Angelika 1994: The Event Argument and the Semantics of Voice. Manuscript, University of Massachusetts at Amherst.
Lakoff, Robin T. 1968: *Abstract Syntax and Latin Complementation*. Cambridge, MA: MIT Press.
Leech, Geoffrey N. 1971: *Meaning and the English Verb*. London: Longman.
Leech, Geoffrey 2004: *Meaning and the English Verb*, third edition. London: Longman.
Lewis, David K. 1973: *Counterfactuals*. Oxford: Blackwell.
Lewis, David K. 1986: *The Plurality of Worlds*. Oxford: Blackwell.
Ogihara, Toshi 1989: Temporal Reference in English and Japanese. PhD dissertation, University of Texas at Austin. (Distributed by Indiana University Linguistics Club, 1992.)
Palmer, Frank R. 1986: *Mood and Modality*. Cambridge: Cambridge University Press.
Palmer, F. R. 2003: Modality in English. In R. Facchinetti, M. Krug and F.R. Palmer *Modality in Contemporary English*, 1–17. Berlin: Mouton de Gruyter.
Quirk, Randolph, Sidney Greenbaum, Geoffrey Leech, and Jan Svartvik 1985: *A Comprehensive Grammar of the English Language*. London: Longman.
Rand, Sharon R. 1993: *The French Imparfait and Passé Simple in Discourse*. Arlington, TS: Summer Institute of Linguistics and the University of Texas at Arlington.
Reichenbach, Hans 1947: *Elements of Symbolic Logic*. London: Macmillan.
Rothstein, Susan 2004: *Structuring Events: A Study in the Semantics of Lexical Aspect*. Oxford: Blackwell.
Saeed, John Ibrahim 1993: *Somali Reference Grammar*, second edition. Kensington, MD: Dunwoody Press.
Schiffrin, Deborah 1981: Tense variations in narration. *Language* 57: 45–62.
Schmitt, Cristina and Karen Miller 2007: Making discourse dependent decisions: The case of the copulas *ser* and *estar* in Spanish. *Lingua* 117.11: 1907–929.
Sharman, John C. 1956: The tabulation of tenses in a Bantu language (Bemba: Northern Rhodesia). *Africa: Journal of the International African Institute* 26.1: 29–46.
Smith, Carlotta S. 1991: *The Parameter of Aspect*. Dordrecht: Kluwer.
Vendler, Zeno 1967: *Linguistics in Philosophy*. Ithaca, NY: Cornell University Press.
Verkuyl, Henk J. 1972: *On the Compositional Nature of the Aspects*. FLSS, Vol. 15. Dordrecht: Reidel.
Verkuyl, Henk J. 1993: *A Theory of Aspectuality: The Interaction betweeen Temporal and Atemporal Structure*. Cambridge: Cambridge University Press.

chapter 6

Sentence Semantics 2

Participants

6.1 Introduction: Classifying Participants

In the last chapter we looked at aspects of sentence-level semantics: how speakers may choose to characterize situations and express various degrees of commitment to the portrayal. In this chapter we examine some of the semantic options through which speakers may characterize the entities involved in the situation. We begin with the notion of thematic roles. Take for example 6.1 below:

6.1 Gina raised the car with a jack.

This sentence identifies an event with three entities, *Gina*, *the car*, and *a jack*, related by the action described by the verb *raise*. The sentence portrays these entities in specific roles: Gina is the entity responsible for initiating and carrying out the action, the car is acted upon and has its position changed by the action, and the jack is the means by which Gina is able to cause the action. Such roles have a number of labels in semantics, including participant roles (Allan 1986), deep semantic cases (Fillmore 1968), semantic roles (Givón 1990), thematic relations (Jackendoff 1972, Gruber 1976) and thematic roles (Dowty 1986, 1989, 1991, Jackendoff 1990). Given its wide usage in recent work, we will use the last term here: **thematic roles**.

We begin by sketching the basic picture of these roles that seems to be assumed by much of the syntax and semantics literature. Thus in sections 6.2–6.4 we outline the main contenders for individual types of roles, look at the relationship between thematic roles and grammatical relations, and discuss the idea that verbs must have their thematic role requirements listed in the lexicon. In section 6.5 we review criticisms that have been made of the notion of thematic roles and then in 6.6 we review the job these roles do in linguistic description. Section 6.7 discusses causation, which reminds us that although we are discussing them in separate chapters thematic roles are intimately linked to the semantics of situation type.

In the second part of the chapter, section 6.8, we investigate **voice** systems and see how they allow speakers some flexibility in the relationship between thematic roles and grammatical structure: we focus on **passive** voice and **middle** voice. In the final part of the chapter we turn our attention to semantic classification systems that are based on the inherent features of nominal rather than their roles within a predication. In section 6.9.1 we discuss **classifiers** and in 6.9.2 **noun classes.** Each of these semantic systems reflects the speaker's decisions about how to characterize entities involved in a situation.

6.2 Thematic Roles

Each of the writers mentioned above, and others, for example Andrews (1985) and Radford (1988), have proposed lists of thematic roles. From this extensive literature we can extract a list of thematic roles like the following (where the relevant role-bearing nominal is in bold):

AGENT: the initiator of some action, capable of acting with volition, e.g.

6.2 **David** cooked the rashers.

6.3 **The fox** jumped out of the ditch.

PATIENT: the entity undergoing the effect of some action, often undergoing some change in state, e.g.

6.4 Enda cut back **these bushes**.

6.5 The sun melted **the ice**.

THEME: the entity which is moved by an action, or whose location is described, e.g.

6.6 Roberto passed **the ball** wide.

6.7 **The book** is in the library.

EXPERIENCER: the entity which is aware of the action or state described by the predicate but which is not in control of the action or state, e.g.:

6.8 **Kevin** felt ill.

6.9 **Mary** saw the smoke.

6.10 **Lorcan** heard the door shut.

BENEFICIARY: the entity for whose benefit the action was performed, e.g.

6.11 Robert filled in the form for **his grandmother**.

6.12 They baked **me** a cake.

INSTRUMENT: the means by which an action is performed or something comes about, e.g.

6.13 She cleaned the wound with **an antiseptic wipe**.

6.14 They signed the treaty with **the same pen**.

LOCATION: the place in which something is situated or takes place, e.g.

6.15 The monster was hiding **under the bed**.

6.16 The band played **in a marquee**.

GOAL: the entity toward which something moves, either literally as in 6.17 or metaphorically as in 6.18:

6.17 Sheila handed her license **to the policeman**.

6.18 Pat told the joke **to his friends**.

SOURCE: the entity from which something moves, either literally as in 6.19 or metaphorically as in 6.20:

6.19 The plane came back **from Kinshasa**.

6.20 We got the idea **from a French magazine**.

STIMULUS: the entity causing an effect (usually psychological) in the EXPERIENCER, e.g.

6.21 John didn't like **the cool breeze.**

6.22 **The noise** frightened the passengers.

Thus to return to our first example, repeated below:

6.23 Gina raised the car with a jack.

we can describe the thematic roles by calling *Gina* the AGENT of the action, *the car* the THEME, and *the jack* the INSTRUMENT.

There is some variation in the use of these terms: for example Radford (1988) treats PATIENT and THEME as different names for the same role. Here we adopt the distinction that PATIENT is reserved for entities acted upon and changed by the verb's action while THEME describes an entity moved in literal or figurative space by the action of the verb, but constitutionally unchanged. Thus the noun phrase *the rock* would be a PATIENT in 6.24 below but a THEME in 6.25:

6.24 Fred shattered **the rock**.

6.25 Fred threw **the rock**.

A number of tests for identifying thematic roles have been suggested. Jackendoff (1972) for example provides a test for AGENT: whether the phrases like *deliberately*, *on purpose*, *in order to*, and so on can be added to the sentence. This reflects the fact that an AGENT characteristically displays animacy and volition. The contrast between 6.26 and 6.27 below identifies John as an AGENT in 6.26 but not 6.27:

6.26 **John** took the book from Bill in order to read it.

6.27 ?**John** received the book from Bill in order to read it.

Some writers (e.g. Foley and Van Valin 1984, Jackendoff 1990) have suggested that AGENT is a particular type of a more general thematic role ACTOR, where ACTOR "expresses the participant which performs, effects, instigates, or controls the situation denoted by the predicate" (Foley and Van Valin 1984: 29). So every AGENT is an ACTOR, but not the other way round: in 6.28 below *the car* is an ACTOR but not an AGENT since it presumably is neither in possession of a wish to kill nor animate:

6.28 **The car** ran over the hedgehog.

Other simple tests suggested by Jackendoff (1990) include predicting that for an ACTOR (X) it will make sense to ask 6.29 below, and for a PATIENT (Y) that it will be able to occur in the frames in 6.30:

6.29 What did X do?

6.30 a. What happened to Y was …
b. What X did to Y was …

So for example in 6.31 below, the tests would give 6.32–3 identifying *Robert* as the ACTOR and *the golf club* as PATIENT:

6.31 Robert snapped the golf club in half.

6.32 What Robert did was to snap the golf club in half.

6.33 a. What happened to the golf club was that Robert snapped it in half.
b. What Robert did to the golf club was snap it in half.

Some writers have suggested other thematic roles in addition to those we have discussed. For example a role of FORCE is sometimes used for an inanimate entity that causes something, for example

6.34 a. **The wind** flattened the crops.
b. The sea wall was weakened by **the waves**.

A role of RECIPIENT is sometimes identified, for example by Andrews (1985), as a type of GOAL involved in actions describing changes of possession, such as

6.35 a. He sold **me** this wreck.
b. He left his fortune **to the church**.

While these roles, ACTOR, AGENT, PATIENT, EXPERIENCER, THEME, INSTRUMENT, and so on may seem intuitively clear, in practice it is sometimes difficult to know which role to assign to a particular noun phrase. For example, in a sentence like 6.36 below *to the lighthouse* is clearly a GOAL, and in 6.37 *him* is a BENEFICIARY, but in 6.38 below is *Margarita* the GOAL/RECIPIENT, or the BENEFICIARY, or both?

6.36 Fergus carried the bag **to the lighthouse**.

6.37 Sylvie bought **him** a sports car.

6.38 **Margarita** received a gift of flowers.

Examples like these raise the difficult question of whether a single entity can fulfill two or more thematic roles at the same time; for example in 6.39 below, are we to say that Mr Wheeler is both AGENT and THEME?

6.39 **Mr Wheeler** jumped off the cliff.

These issues are still under investigation in various theoretical approaches. A central claim of Chomsky's Principles and Parameters theory, for example, is the **Theta-Criterion**, which states that there must be a one-to-one correspondence between noun phrases and thematic roles (see Chomsky 1988, Haegeman 1994). Jackendoff (1972), on the other hand, suggested that one entity might fulfill more than one role. In Jackendoff (1990) the idea that one nominal might fulfill more than one role is elaborated into a theory of tiers of thematic roles: a **thematic tier**, which describes spatial relations, and an **action tier**, which describes ACTOR–PATIENT type relations. His examples include the following (1990: 126–27):

6.40	a.	Sue hit	Fred.	
		Theme	Goal	(thematic tier)
		Actor	Patient	(action tier)
	b.	Pete threw	the ball.	
		Source	Theme	(thematic tier)
		Actor	Patient	(action tier)

c.	Bill entered	the room.	
	Theme	Goal	(thematic tier)
	Actor		(action tier)
d.	Bill received	a letter.	
	Goal	Theme	(thematic tier)
			(action tier)

Thus *Fred* in 6.40a is simultaneously the GOAL and the PATIENT of the action. The gaps in a tier reflect instances where the nominal has only one thematic role: thus *the room* in 6.40c has no role in the action tier. Presumably these tiers would divide thematic roles into two types, perhaps as follows:

6.41 a. Action tier roles: ACTOR, AGENT, EXPERIENCER, PATIENT, BENEFICIARY, INSTRUMENT.
b. Thematic tier roles: THEME, GOAL, SOURCE, LOCATION.

To these dimensions of action and space, Jackendoff also proposes a dimension of time, which we will not investigate here. The basic insight is clear: the roles that speakers assign to entities may be more complicated than a single thematic role label. For a detailed discussion of this proposal, see Jackendoff (1990: 125–51).

Having identified these thematic roles, the next question we might ask is: how are such roles identified in the grammar? For our English examples above, the answer is by a combination of syntactic structure and the choice of verb. There are typical matchings between participant roles and grammatical relations. As in our original example 6.23, the subject of the sentence often corresponds to the AGENT, the direct object to the THEME, while the INSTRUMENT often occurs as a prepositional phrase. Though this is the typical case, it is not necessarily so: for example it is possible to omit the AGENT from the sentence and as a result have the INSTRUMENT occupy subject position, for example:

6.42 **The jack** raised the car.

We can see the effect of the choice of verb if we try to describe this same situation without either the AGENT or the INSTRUMENT. We cannot simply allow the THEME to occupy subject position as in 6.43; we have to change the verb as in 6.44:

6.43 *The car raised.

6.44 The car rose.

This is because the verb *raise* requires an ACTOR. The verb *rise* however describes a change of state without any slot for an ACTOR so that while 6.44 above is fine, 6.45 and 6.46 below are not possible:

6.45 *Gina rose the car.

6.46 *The jack rose the car.

What this simple example shows is that a speaker's choice of participant roles has two aspects: the choice of a verb with its particular requirements for thematic roles, and within the limits set by this, the choice of grammatical relations for the roles. We look at these choices next, beginning with the relationship between thematic roles and grammatical relations: first we describe how various thematic roles may occupy subject position, then we look briefly at the selection of thematic roles as part of a verb's lexical semantics.

6.3 Grammatical Relations and Thematic Roles

We have seen that while in English there is a tendency for subjects to be AGENTS, direct objects to be PATIENTS and THEMES, and INSTRUMENTS to occur as prepositional phrases, this need not always be the case. There are two basic situations where this is not the case: the first is where roles are simply omitted, and the grammatical relations shift to react to this, as we will discuss in this section; and the second is where the speaker chooses to alter the usual matching between roles and grammatical relations, a choice often marked by an accompanying change of verbal *voice*. We deal with voice later on in section 6.7.

We can begin with a simple example of thematic role omission in 6.47–49 below:

6.47 Ursula broke the ice with a pickaxe.

6.48 The pickaxe broke the ice.

6.49 The ice broke.

This is similar to our example 6.23 earlier: in 6.47 Ursula is the AGENT and subject, the ice is PATIENT and direct object, and the pickaxe, the INSTRUMENT, is in a prepositional phrase. In 6.48 the AGENT is omitted and now the INSTRUMENT is subject; and finally in 6.49 with no AGENT or INSTRUMENT expressed, the PATIENT becomes subject. The verb *break*, unlike *raise* earlier, allows all three thematic roles to occupy subject position. Several writers have suggested that this process of different roles occupying the subject position is a hierarchical process, not only in English but across many languages. The observation is that when speakers are constructing a sentence, they tend to place an AGENT into subject position, the next preference being for a RECIPIENT or BENEFICIARY, then THEME/PATIENT, then other roles. From our English examples, it seems that INSTRUMENT is then preferred to LOCATION. This is sometimes described as an *implicational hierarchy.* There are various versions of such a hierarchy proposed in the literature, for example in Fillmore (1968) and Givón (1984b), but we can construct a simple example of a universal subject hierarchy like 6.50 below:

6.50 AGENT > RECIPIENT/BENEFICIARY > THEME/PATIENT > INSTRUMENT > LOCATION

This diagram can be read in two equivalent ways: one is that the leftmost elements are the preferred, most basic and expected subjects, while moving rightward along the string gives us less expected subjects. A second way to read this diagram is as a kind of rule of expectation, going from right to left: if a language allows the LOCATION role to be subject, we expect that it will allow all the rest. If, however, it allows the role INSTRUMENT to be subject, we expect that it allows those roles to the left, but we don't know if it allows the LOCATION role as subject. The idea is that languages can differ in what roles they allow to occur as subject but they will obey this sequence of preference, without any gaps. So, for example, we should not find a language that allows AGENT and INSTRUMENT to be subject but not THEME/PATIENT.

It is a little difficult to think of English examples with LOCATION as subject, unless we include sentences like 6.51a–b below:

6.51 a. **This cottage** sleeps five adults.
b. **The table** seats eight.[1]

but the other positions on the hierarchy occur regularly, as we can see from the following examples:

6.52 AGENT subjects:
The thief stole the wallet.
Fred jumped out of the plane.

6.53 EXPERIENCER subjects:
I forgot the address.
Your cat is hungry.

6.54 RECIPIENT subjects:
She received a demand for unpaid tax.
The building suffered a direct hit.

6.55 PATIENT subjects:
The bowl cracked.
Una died.

6.56 THEME subjects:
Joan fell off the yacht.
The arrow flew through the air.

6.57 INSTRUMENT subjects:
The key opened the lock.
The scalpel made a very clean cut.

See Comrie (1981) and Croft (1990) for discussion of this and other implicational hierarchies.

6.4 Verbs and Thematic Role Grids

As we saw earlier with the verbs *raise*, *rise*, and *drive*, verbs have particular requirements for their thematic roles. Since this is part of a speaker's semantic knowledge about a verb, we might expect it to be part of the lexical information stored for verbs. Thus we need to know not only how many arguments a verb requires (i.e. whether it is intransitive, transitive, etc.) but also what thematic roles its arguments may hold.

In the generative grammar literature, this listing of thematic roles is often called a **thematic role grid**, or **theta-grid** for short.[2] A simple example might be:

6.58 **put** V: <<u>AGENT</u>, THEME, LOCATION>

This entry tells us that *put* is a three-argument, or ditransitive, verb and spells out the thematic roles the three arguments may carry. Here we show Williams's (1981) suggestion of underlining the AGENT role to reflect the fact that it is this role that typically occurs as the subject of the verb (or "external argument" in Williams's terminology). Clearly this is just the start of the job that a grammatical description must do of mapping between thematic roles and grammatical categories and structures. Our thematic grid for *put* in 6.58 predicts that this verb, when saturated with the correct arguments, might form a sentence like 6.59:

6.59 John$_{\text{AGENT}}$ put the book$_{\text{THEME}}$ on the shelf$_{\text{LOCATION}}$.[3]

Of course, not all nominals in a sentence are arguments of a verb and thus specified in verbal theta-grids in the lexicon. We will make the assumption that one can employ grammatical tests to identify arguments: for example, to distinguish between the role of argument played by the prepositional phrase *in the bathroom* in 6.60 below and its status as an non-argument in 6.61:

6.60 $[_S$ Roland $[_{VP}$ put $[_{NP}$ the book] $[_{PP}$ in the bathroom]]]

6.61 $[_S$ Roland $[_{VP}$ read $[_{NP}$ the book]] $[_{PP}$ in the bathroom]]

The square brackets in 6.60–1 reflect the fact that while *in the bathroom* is an argument of the verb *put*, explaining why it cannot be omitted:

6.62 *Roland put the book.

it is not an argument of the verb *read*, on the other hand, which can form a sentence without it:

6.63 Roland read the book.

In grammatical terms, while *in the bathroom* is an argument in 6.60, it is an **adjunct** in 6.61. As well as not being required by the verb, adjuncts are seen as less structurally attached to the verb, explaining why 6.64 below is a much more unusual word order than 6.65, and usually requires a marked intonation pattern:

6.64 In the bathroom Roland put a book.

6.65 In the bathroom Roland read a book.

See Radford (1988) and Haegeman (1994) for discussion of the grammatical status of arguments and adjuncts. We will assume that all verbs may co-occur with adjuncts (usually adverbials of time, place, manner, etc.) and that requirements need only be listed in the lexicon for arguments.

Another way of making this distinction is to distinguish between **participant roles** and **non-participant roles**. The former correspond to our arguments: they are needed by the predication, in the sense we have been discussing; the latter are optional adjuncts which give extra information about the context, typically information about the time, location, purpose, or result of the event. Of course only participant roles will be relevant to verbal thematic grids, and our discussion in this chapter focuses on these participant roles.

Listing thematic grids soon reveals that verbs form classes which share the same grids. For example English has a class of TRANSFER, or GIVING, verbs which in one subclass includes the verbs *give*, *lend*, *supply*, *pay*, *donate*, *contribute*. These verbs encode a view of the transfer from the perspective of the AGENT. They have the thematic grid in 6.66; 6.67 is an example:

6.66 V: <AGENT, THEME, RECIPIENT>

6.67 Barbara$_{AG}$ loaned the money$_{TH}$ to Michael$_{RE}$.[4]

Another subclass of these TRANSFER verbs encodes the transfer from the perspective of the RECIPIENT. These verbs include *receive*, *accept*, *borrow*, *buy*, *purchase*, *rent*, *hire*. Their thematic grid is in 6.68, with an example in 6.69, paralleling 6.67 above:

6.68 V: <RECIPIENT, THEME, SOURCE>

6.69 Michael$_{RE}$ borrowed the money$_{TH}$ from Barbara$_{SO}$.

Thematic grids such as these are put to use in the literature for a variety of descriptive jobs. We can look at some of these in section 6.6, when we ask more generally: what purpose do thematic roles serve in linguistic analysis? First though, we discuss some of the problems associated with the simple picture of thematic roles we have outlined so far.

6.5 Problems with Thematic Roles

In our introductory discussion, we mentioned that the lists of roles given in the literature have varied from author to author. Authors disagree about what if any distinctions are to be made between PATIENT and THEME, for example, or between AGENT and related roles like ACTOR, EXPERIENCER, and so on.

We can see these debates as reflections of two general problems with thematic roles (usually abbreviated to "theta-roles," sometimes also called θ-roles). The first problem is really about delimiting particular roles. The extreme case would be to identify individual thematic roles for each verb: thus we would say that a verb like *beat* gives us two theta-roles, a BEATER-role and a BEATEN-role. This would of course reduce the utility of the notion: if we lose the more general role-types like AGENT, PATIENT, and so on, then we cannot make the general statements about the relations between semantic roles and grammatical relations discussed earlier, nor put theta-roles to any of the uses we describe in the next section.

But if we are to classify individual theta-roles roles like BEATER and BEATEN into theta-role types like AGENT and PATIENT, we will have to find some way of accommodating variation within the role type. Let us take the example of PATIENT in a typical grid:

6.70 V: <<u>AGENT</u>, PATIENT, INSTRUMENT>

A typical example would be 6.71:

6.71 The child$_{AG}$ cracked the mirror$_{PA}$ with his toy$_{IN}$.

Earlier we defined the PATIENT as the entity affected by the action of the verb. However, attempts to examine particular verbs, such as Dixon (1991), reveal that both the type of "affectedness" and the role of the INSTRUMENT vary between verb types. For example, Dixon (1991: 102–13) identifies eight types of affectedness: a range including the minimal contact of the verb *touch* in 6.72, where possibly no change occurs in the PATIENT, through *rub* in 6.73, where the surface of the PATIENT might be affected, and *squeeze* in 6.74 where a temporary change of shape in the PATIENT occurs, to *smash* in 6.75, where the PATIENT loses its physical integrity:

6.72 John touched the lamp with his toe.

6.73 The captain rubbed the cricket ball with dirt.

6.74 Henry squeezed the rubber duck in his hands.

6.75 Alison smashed the ice cube with her heel.

The questions which face semanticists here are: do the differences between the affectedness of the PATIENT reduce the usefulness of this label, or can the differences be explained in some way?[5]

The second problem is more general: how do we define theta-roles in general? That is, what semantic basis do we have for characterizing roles? Facing both of these problems, Dowty (1991) proposes a solution where theta-roles are not semantic primitives but are defined in terms of **entailments** of the predicate. In this view a theta-role is a cluster of entailments about an argument position, which are shared by some verbs. He gives examples like *x murders y*, *x nominates y*, *x interrogates y*, where:

6.76 entailments they all share include that *x* does a volitional act, that *x* moreover intends this to be the kind of act named by the verb, that *x* causes some event to take place involving *y* (*y* dies, *y* acquires a nomination, *y* answers questions – or at least hears them), and that *x* moves or changes externally (i.e. not just mentally). (1991: 552)

Such a set of shared entailments about *x* will serve to define the nominal which denotes *x* as AGENT. Thus theta-roles are defined in terms of shared verbal entailments about nominal referents.[6] We will see something of how these entailments are used in this approach in the rest of this section.

In this view of theta-roles as clusters of entailments, we can see a solution to the problem of the fuzziness of roles. Dowty proposes that we view the roles not as discrete and bounded categories but instead as **prototypes**, where there may be different degrees of membership. He suggests that there are two basic prototypes: Proto-Agent and Proto-Patient,[7] each of which would contain characteristic lists of entailments such as those in 6.77 and 6.78 below:

6.77 Properties of the Agent Proto-Role (Dowty 1991: 572):
- a. volitional involvement in the event or state
- b. sentience (and/or perception)
- c. causing an event or change of state in another participant
- d. movement (relative to the position of another participant)

6.78 Properties of the Patient Proto-Role (Dowty 1991: 572):
- a. undergoes change of state
- b. incremental theme[8]
- c. causally affected by another participant
- d. stationary relative to movement of another participant

The idea is that these clusters of entailments would allow various kinds of shading. For example some arguments might have more of the entailments than others. So, for example, *John* in *John cleaned the house* would include all four of the entailments in 6.77 above: volition, sentience, causation and movement. By contrast *John* as an argument of *drop* in *John fainted and dropped the vase* would involve no volition, and *the storm* in *The storm destroyed the house* would involve neither sentience nor volition. We can see that this approach allows variation among AGENTS: some will be more typical and involve a greater number of characteristic entailments; others will be more marginal. Similar variation would hold for PATIENTS.

This approach would also allow other forms of fuzziness: some entailments might be viewed as more important than others; or each entailment itself might be fuzzy-edged. As several commentators have pointed out, speakers sometimes blur the distinction between sentient and non-sentient when they talk about computers, saying things like *The computer thinks these are the same file* or *This program doesn't realize that the memory is full.*

These proposals by Dowty to view thematic roles in terms of prototypical clusters of entailments allow flexibility in defining thematic roles. One result of his classification is that traditional role-types fall out as more-or-less prototypical versions of the two main categories. Thus, as we have seen, a centrally prototypical AGENT like *Maggie* in 6.79a below involves all four entailments in 6.77, while an EXPERIENCER, like *Joan* in 6.79b can be seen as a more marginal AGENT, including sentience but not volition or causation; and an INSTRUMENT like *the scalpel* in 6.79c includes causation and movement but not volition or sentience:

6.79
- a. **Maggie** pruned the roses.
- b. **Joan** felt the heat as the aircraft door opened.
- c. **The scalpel** cut through the muscle.

Similarly a centrally prototypical PATIENT, like *the roses*, in 6.79a and repeated in 6.80a below, will involve all four entailments in 6.78 above, but a STIMULUS like *the game* in 6.80b does not undergo a change of state nor is causally affected:

6.80 a. Maggie pruned **the roses**.
b. Roberto watched **the game**.

Having seen something of an attempt to cope with the problem of defining thematic roles on a more systematic basis, in the next section we examine some of the uses of such roles.

6.6 The Motivation for Identifying Thematic Roles

From our discussion so far it is clear that linguists employ thematic roles to describe aspects of the interface between semantics and syntax, in particular to characterize the links between the semantic classification of its participants that is inherent in a verb's meaning and the grammatical relations it supports. Thus, to recap our discussion in its simplest terms, when we use an English verb like *feel* in *Joan felt the heat as soon as the aircraft door was opened*, we identify a relationship between an EXPERIENCER and a PERCEPT. This can be viewed as one of many conventional ways of viewing relations that are coded in the language. Grammatically of course the verb *feel* is transitive, taking a subject and direct object. As we have seen, one fact we have to account for is that there is a conventional linkage between the participant roles and the grammatical relations, such that in this case the EXPERIENCER will be subject and the PERCEPT, direct object.[9]

Predicting such linkages, and more general patterns among individual cases, is one of the primary functions of thematic roles. To take one example, in Dowty's prototype and entailments approach described in the last section, this linkage is described as below by an argument selection principle (1991: 576) (together with a couple of ancillary principles and the characteristics in 6.81d):

6.81 a. *Argument Selection Principle*: In predicates with grammatical subject and object, the argument for which the predicate entails the greatest number of Proto-Agent properties will be lexicalized as the subject of the predicate; the argument having the greatest number of Proto-Patient entailments will be lexicalized as the direct object.
b. *Corollary 1*: If two arguments of a relation have (approximately) equal numbers of entailed Proto-Agent and Proto-Patient properties, then either or both may be lexicalized as the subject (and similarly for objects).
c. *Corollary 2*: With a three-place predicate, the non-subject argument having the greater number of entailed Proto-Patient properties will be lexicalized as the direct object and the non-subject argument having fewer entailed Proto-Patient properties will be lexicalized as an oblique or prepositional object (and if two non-subject arguments have approximately equal numbers of entailed Proto-Patient properties, either or both may be lexicalized as direct object).

d. *Non-discreteness*: Proto-roles, obviously, do not classify arguments exhaustively (some arguments have neither role) or uniquely (some arguments may share the same role) or discretely (some arguments could qualify partially but equally for both proto-roles).

Though the phrasing of these principles makes it sound as if theta-roles are in competition for grammatical slots in the formation of each sentence, Dowty intends these observations as a set of constraints on verbal linking rules. As the term *lexicalized* in the above suggests, these principles are viewed as constraints on possible verbs.

We can give an idea of how such principles might work by looking again at the type of example we have already discussed: the relations between subject position and theta-roles in the sentences in 6.82 below:

6.82 a. Captain Nemo sank the ship with a torpedo.
b. The torpedo sank the ship.
c. The ship sank.

In 6.82a *Captain Nemo* has the Proto-Agent properties of volition, sentience, causation and movement and is thus linked to subject position, as predicted by the selection principles. In 6.82b *the torpedo* has the Proto-Agent properties of causation and movement, and thus, in the absence of an entity with a stronger cluster of such properties, becomes subject. Finally in 6.82c *the ship* has just the property of movement, but in this sentence that is enough for it to become the subject.

This idea of stronger and weaker candidates for subject, and other grammatical roles, leads naturally to the idea of a hierarchy, as we discussed in section 6.3. Dowty's version of a subject hierarchy is as in 6.83 (1991: 578):[10]

6.83 $$\text{Agent} > \left\{\begin{matrix}\text{Instrument}\\ \text{Experiencer}\end{matrix}\right\} > \text{Patient} > \left\{\begin{matrix}\text{Source}\\ \text{Goal}\end{matrix}\right\}$$

As before, the candidates move from left to right in decreasing strength of linkage to the subject position. In this version, though, the roles themselves are not primitives but convenient labels for clusterings of the Proto-role entailments.

So far we have been talking about theta-roles as explanatory devices in accounting for linkage between semantic and syntactic argument structure. A second justification for using thematic roles is to help characterize semantic verbal classes. For example we can identify in English two classes of psychological verbs both of which take two arguments (i.e. are transitive), one of which is an EXPERIENCER and the other a STIMULUS.[11] The classes differ however in their linking between these roles and subject and object position. The first class has the theta-grid in 6.84a below, and can be exemplified by the verbs in 6.84b, while the second class has the theta-grid in 6.85a and includes verbs like those in 6.85b:

6.84 Psychological verbs type 1
a. V: <EXPERIENCER, STIMULUS>
b. *admire, enjoy, fear, like, love, relish, savor*

6.85 Psychological verbs type 2
  a. <STIMULUS, EXPERIENCER>
  b. *amuse, entertain, frighten, interest, please, surprise, thrill*[12]

Thus we say *Claude liked the result* but *The result pleased Claude.*

Such classifications of verbs can help predict the grammatical processes individual verbs will undergo. Thus, though the motivation for grammatical rules is often multifactorial, theta-role grids have been used to describe argument-changing processes like **passive**, as we shall see shortly, or argument structure alternations like those in 6.86–7 below, where in each case the example sentences are in a, the link between theta-grids and syntactic arguments is given in b, and some example verbs in c:

6.86 a. He banged the broom-handle on the ceiling.
He banged the ceiling with the broom-handle.
She tapped the can against the window.
She tapped the window with the can.
  b. V: <AGENT, INSTRUMENT & THEME,[13] LOCATION>
NP NP PP
V: <AGENT, LOCATION, INSTRUMENT & THEME>
NP NP PP
  c. *bang, bash, beat, hit, knock, pound, rap, tap, whack*[14]

6.87 a. The whole community will benefit from the peace process.
The peace process will benefit the whole community.
  b. V: <BENEFICIARY, SOURCE>
NP PP
V: <SOURCE, BENEFICIARY>
NP NP
  c. *benefit, profit*[15]

These alternations are just two of a large range identified for English in Levin (1993). The conditional factors for such alternations are often a mix of semantic information, such as the verb's meaning and its theta-grid (as shown above), and its syntactic environment.

We can look at one further type of justification for thematic roles which comes from another area of grammar: the claim that in some languages they play a role in the morphology of verbal agreement. Mithun (1991: 514) gives examples of the pronominal verbal prefixes in Lakhota (Siouan; USA, Canada). In the transitive verbs in 6.88a below we see a prefix *wa* which marks an AGENT argument and in 6.88b a prefix *ma*, which marks a PATIENT:

6.88 a. a**wá**ʔu "**I** brought it."
waktékte "**I**'ll kill him."
  b. a**má**ʔu "He brought **me**."
maktékte "He'll kill **me**."

We can see that these prefixes do not mark subject or object agreement because a subject, for example, can take either prefix depending on whether it is an AGENT (as in 6.89a below) or a PATIENT (as in 6.89b) (Mithun 1991: 514):

6.89 a. AGENT subjects
wapsíca "**I** jumped."
wahí "**I** came."
b. PATIENT subjects
mak^{h}úže "**I**'m sick."
maxwá "**I**'m sleepy."

In other words, what would be a subject pronoun in English corresponds to either an AGENT or a PATIENT pronoun affix in Lakhota. Thus Lakhota morphological marking is sensitive to theta-roles rather than grammatical relations. Mithun gives similar examples from Guaraní (Tupi; Paraguay, Bolivia), and the Pomoan languages of California. The implication for our discussion is clear: if we need theta-roles to explain morphological patterns, this is strong evidence that they are significant semantic categories. We have seen then in this section a number of different motivations for identifying thematic roles: to explain linking rules in verbal argument structure, to reflect semantic classes of verbs, to predict a verb's participation in argument structure alternations, and finally to describe morphological rules adequately. For many linguists this utility motivates their continuing use, despite the definitional problems discussed in the last section. The notion has also been used in related disciplines, for example in the psycholinguistic investigation of language comprehension (Gross and White-Devine 1998, Ferreira 2003, Price and Grossman 2005, Manouilidou et al. 2009, Cohn and Paczynski 2013), in research on language acquisition (Alishahi and Stevenson 2010). Semantic role labeling has been an important element in the creation of computer lexicons, used in applications such as machine translation and question answering systems (Palmer et al. 2005, Giuglea and Moschitti 2006, Kipper et al. 2008). In the next section we look at the semantic category of **causation**, which is an important element in the linking between thematic roles, verbs and situation type.

6.7 Causation

We saw that Dowty's (1991) prototypical thematic roles in 6.77 and 6.78 are defined by properties of the situation, in particular causation and change. We can see the importance of causation to thematic role selection if we look at the English causative-inchoative verb alternation, briefly mentioned in chapter 3 earlier. In this alternation the same verb can occur in an intransitive form where the one argument is an entity undergoing a change of state, as in 6.90a below, or a transitive form which adds a causer role as in 6.90b:

6.90 a. The water boiled.
b. Helen boiled the water.

This pattern allows the speaker to either select or omit a causing entity. In terms of thematic roles such verbs allow the cause to be an AGENT as in 6.90b above, a non-volitional cause (or FORCE) as in 6.91b below, or an instrument as in 6.92b:

6.91 a. The ice melted.
b. The sun melted the ice.

6.92 a. The door opened.
b. The key opened the door.

This type of alternation is very common across the languages of the world, as discussed by Haspelmath (1993). In English not all change of state intransitives allow a corresponding causative transitive, as 6.93 below shows, nor all causative transitives an intransitive inchoative, as shown by 6.94:

6.93 a. The fruit trees blossomed.
b. ?The early spring blossomed the fruit trees.

6.94 a. The buyers demolished the house.
b. ?The house demolished.

The factors governing the occurrence of this alternation have been much discussed in the literature, for example in Levin and Rappaport Hovav (1995) and Rappaport Hovav and Levin (2012).

In English the same form of the verb occurs in both alternants, leading scholars to label the causatives in 6.91b and 6.92b **lexical causatives.**[16] In other languages special affixes signal causative readings, producing **morphological causatives**, as in the examples in 6.95 below from Somali:

6.95 a. Waan toosay.
waa-aan toos-ay
CLASS-I awake-PAST
"I awakened," "I woke up"
b. Wuu i toosiyey.
Waa-uu i toos-iy-ey
CLASS+he me awake-CAUSE-PAST
"He caused me to awaken," "He woke me up"

In this example the causative affix, here in the form *iy*, creates a transitive causative verb from an intransitive inchoative, thus adding an AGENT role.[17] Somali also has a decausative affix that when added to a lexical causative verb removes the AGENT, as in example 6.96 below:

6.96 a. Cali albaabkii buu furay.
Cali albaab-kii ba-uu fur-ay
Ali door-the FOC+he open-PAST
"Ali opened the door."
b. Albaabkii baa furmay.
albaab-kii baa fur-m-ay
door-the FOC open-DECAUSATIVE-PAST
"The door opened."

The verb *fur* "open" is transitive and causative; adding the decausative affix, here in the form *-m-*, creates an intransitive inchoative verb and thus removes a thematic role of AGENT.

These alternations and derivations show how speakers can signal their selections within what some writers (for example Talmy 2000, Langacker 2008, Croft 2012) have termed the **causal chain**, which is an analysis of events as segments of a causal network where individuals act on other individuals asymmetrically. Causation itself is of course an important part of human thinking and of interest to many disciplines. However, here we are concerned with how the semantic frame for an event is profiled by the verb and its thematic roles. Some writers have characterized the expression of causation in language as a selective merging of sub-events: for example Talmy (2000, 2: 271) uses the term **causal chain windowing** to describe the speaker's portrayal of the sub-events. Thus a sentence like *Joan broke the photocopier* focuses on the AGENT's responsibility for causing the event and on the result, the broken photocopier, but misses out other intermediate information about the actions involved. Speakers have a number of options in characterizing the connection between these sub-events, for example in portraying the unity of the cause and effect between the events. So for example in English we can compare the inchoative in 6.97a with the causatives in 6.97b–d:

6.97 a. The car stopped.
b. I stopped the car.
c. I made the car stop.
d. I had the car stopped.

The lexical causative in b implies, depending on context, that the speaker stopped the car in the normal way that this is done, perhaps by as a driver braking or by some other direct action. The versions in c and d are often termed **periphrastic causatives** because they employ two verbs in a complex clause construction. The version with *make* in c suggests that the speaker caused the car to stop in an unusual way or perhaps had to overcome resistance, while d with *have* implies the presence of other implicit actors in the event. In chapter 9 we will discuss some theoretical proposals for characterizing the relationship between verbs, thematic roles and causation. In the next section we look at the category of **voice**, which, as we shall see, adds new dimensions to the relationship between thematic roles and grammatical relations.

6.8 Voice

6.8.1 Passive voice

The grammatical category of *voice* affords speakers some flexibility in viewing thematic roles. Many languages allow an opposition between *active voice* and *passive voice*. We can compare for example the English sentences in 6.98 below:

6.98 a. Billy groomed the horses.
b. The horses were groomed by Billy.

In the active sentence 6.98a *Billy*, the AGENT, is subject and *the horses*, the PATIENT, is object. The passive version 6.98b, however, has the PATIENT as subject and the AGENT occurring in a prepositional phrase, the structure often associated with INSTRUMENT, as we saw in the last section. This is a typical active-passive voice alternation: the passive sentence has a verb in a different form – the past participle with the auxiliary verb *be* – and it allows the speaker a different perspective on the situation described. This passive sentence (6.98b) allows the speaker to describe the situation from the point of view of the PATIENT rather than that of the AGENT. In some cases indeed passive constructions are used to obscure the identity of an AGENT, as in 6.99 below:

6.99 The horses were groomed.

Here the AGENT is so far backgrounded that it becomes merely an implied participant. Many writers describe this foregrounding of the PATIENT and backgrounding of the AGENT in terms of promoting the PATIENT and demoting the AGENT in terms of discourse or topic prominence (e.g. Givón 1990, 1994), or as reflecting the speaker's greater empathy with the PATIENT rather than the AGENT (Kuno 1987). There are other lexical and syntactic strategies that alter perspective in this way. For example in 6.100 below the alternation relies in part on the lexical relation between *in front of* and *behind*; while in 6.101 it is accomplished by the syntactic patterns known as **pseudo-cleft** in a and **cleft** in b:

6.100 a. The house stood in front of the cliff.
b. The cliff stood behind the house.

6.101 a. What Joan bought was a Ferrari.
b. It was Joan who bought the Ferrari.

In 6.101 above the same situation is described but in a the speaker is interested in Joan's purchase, while in b she is interested in the Ferrari's purchaser. This kind of choice of perspective presumably depends on a speaker's judgments of conversational salience. We can use the terms **Figure** and **Ground**[18] to describe this kind of linguistic perspective: if we call the situation described a **scene**, then the entity that the speaker chooses to foreground is the figure, and the background is the ground. So in 6.100a above *the house* is the figure and *the cliff* the ground, and vice versa in 6.100b.

Passive constructions allow the foregrounding of roles other than PATIENT. In 6.102–4 we see English examples of THEME, PERCEPT, and RECIPIENT roles occurring as the subject of passives:

6.102 **This money** was donated to the school. (THEME)

6.103 **The UFO** was seen by just two people. (PERCEPT)

6.104 **He** was given a camera by his grandmother. (RECIPIENT)

The qualifications for foregrounding in a passive in English are complex: partly grammatical, partly semantic and partly due to the flow of discourse and the speaker's choice of viewpoint. The importance of grammatical information can be shown by observing that each of the roles occurring as passive subjects in 6.103–4 above occurs in object position in a corresponding active sentence:

6.105 Someone donated **this money** to the school.

6.106 Just two people saw **the UFO**.

6.107 His grandmother gave **him** a camera.

The typical pattern is that a nominal occupying object position is fronted to subject in passives. When a theta-role normally occurs as a prepositional phrase in an active sentence, this is less likely to be foregrounded in a passive. Neither moving the full prepositional phrase nor extracting just the nominal seems to work, as shown below:

6.108 a. This house stood **on the corner**. (LOCATION)
b. ***On the corner** was stood by this house.
c. ?**The corner** was stood **on** by this house.

6.109 a. John built a garage for **her**. (BENEFICIARY)
b. ***For her** was built a garage by John.
c. ?**She** was built a garage by John.

6.110 a. He opened the door **with this key**. (INSTRUMENT)
b. ***With this key** was opened the door by him.
c. ***This key** was opened the door **with**.

Some apparent exceptions to this rule are possible however, for example:

6.111 a. Three monarchs lived in **this house**. (LOCATION)
b. **This house** was lived in by three monarchs.[19]

To further underline this grammatical aspect of passives, that it is the object position that is relevant to passivization, we can look at a class of English verbs called the *spray/load* verbs. These verbs allow the speaker to select either their THEME role (as in 6.112a and 6.113a) below, or the GOAL (as in 6.112b and 6.113b), to be the verb's direct object and thus be the focus of the effect of the action:

6.112 a. He sprayed paint on the car.
b. He sprayed the car with paint.

6.113 a. He loaded hay onto the tractor.
b. He loaded the tractor with hay.

We can easily show that whichever argument occupies object position can be passivized, while the argument in the prepositional phrase cannot: corresponding to 6.112 above we find the patterns:

6.114 a. Paint was sprayed on the car.
b. *The car was sprayed paint on.
c. The car was sprayed with paint.
d. *Paint was sprayed the car with.

See Rappaport and Levin (1985, 1988), Jeffries and Willis (1984), and Levin (1993) for further discussion of these *spray/load* verbs.[20]

The discourse factors affecting passives have been described in a number of frameworks: for example, as mentioned above, Kuno (1987: 209–16) employs the notion of speaker empathy. He gives an example of a person relating a story about their friend Mary and her experiences at a party. In the narrative the speaker's empathy is with Mary and thus events are viewed from her perspective. This explains why a passive is fine in 6.115b below but not in 6.116b (treating these as two independent reports of events):

6.115 Mary had quite an experience at the party she went to last night.
a. An eight-foot-tall rowdy harassed her.
b. She was harassed by an eight-foot-tall rowdy.

6.116 Mary had quite an experience at the party she went to last night.
a. She slapped an eight-foot-tall rowdy in the face.
b. *An eight-foot-tall rowdy was slapped in the face by her.

The passive construction works in 6.115b because the fronted nominal refers to the entity the speaker empathizes with, but not in 6.116b where the other participant is fronted.

Passive constructions have received a great deal of attention in the linguistics literature. This is not surprising: even from our brief discussion, we can see that while the general effect of passives is to allow a shift in linkage between thematic roles and grammatical relations, the process is subject to a complex of grammatical and discourse factors. It is this interdependence of different levels of analysis that makes passives an interesting arena for theoretical debate.

6.8.2 Comparing passive constructions across languages

While many languages have passive-type constructions, the comparison of passives across languages reveals that there is considerable variation around the pattern of the English passive outlined in the last section, that is where the AGENT is demoted from subject position, a non-AGENT role is promoted to subject, and the verb shows a distinct form which agrees with the promoted subject: the total package being what we have called **passive voice**. Often languages have more than one passive construction: in English for example, it is possible to distinguish between *be*-passives and *get*-passives, as in 6.117 (R. Lakoff 1971, Givón and Yang 1994):

6.117 a. Mary was shot on purpose.
b. Mary got shot on purpose.

As noted by Lakoff these sentences differ in the amount of control over the event associated with Mary.[21]

Other languages have a special type of passive, often called the **impersonal passive**, which does not allow the AGENT to be mentioned in the sentence. In Irish, for example, we can distinguish between one type of passive associated with verbal noun constructions as shown in the active/passive pair in 6.118 below, and another, the impersonal passive, with verbs, as is shown in 6.119 (Noonan 1994: 282–86):

6.118 a. Bhí sí ag bualadh Sheáin.
was she at hit-NOMIN John-GEN
"She was hitting John."
b. Bhí Seán á bhualadh aici.
was John to+his hit-NOMIN at-her
"John was being hit by her."

6.119 a. Thug siad Siobhán abhaile inniu.
brought they Joan home today
"They brought Joan home today."
b. Tugadh Siobhán abhaile inniu.
brought-IMPERS Joan home today.
"Joan was brought home today."

This impersonal passive in 6.119 does not straightforwardly correspond to the translation given: that is to an English passive where no AGENT is expressed. In 6.119b we can see how both in Irish and in the English translation the passive verb form is differentiated from the active, and how in both the AGENT is often omitted. However, the Irish passive in 6.119b differs from its English translation because the THEME, *Siobhán*, remains in its original position as an object while in the English passive *Joan* becomes subject. In other words, the PATIENT is not promoted to subject in the Irish impersonal passive in 6.119b, but the AGENT is omitted. See Noonan (1994) for discussion.

This example from Irish is of a transitive impersonal passive. In many languages the term *impersonal passive* is used to describe passives of intransitive verbs: Kirsner (1976: 387) gives the following pair of examples from Dutch:

6.120 a. De jongens fluiten.
the boys whistle.
"The boys whistle/are whistling."
b. Er wordt door de jongens gefloten.
there becomes by the boys whistling
"By the boys (there) is whistling."

In 6.120b the AGENT is backgrounded, but there is no other argument to be foregrounded and subject position is taken by the word *er* "there," which does not refer directly to any entity and which has no theta-role. It is also possible to delete the AGENT altogether in this passive, giving:

6.121 Er wordt gefloten.
there becomes whistling
"There is whistling/People whistle/Someone whistles."

Similar impersonal passives have been reported for other languages, including German, Welsh and Latin; see Perlmutter (1978) and Perlmutter and Postal (1984) for discussion.

These impersonal passives imply that in comparing languages we need to separate out the two functions of the passive: firstly, the demotion of AGENTS, and secondly, the promotion of non-AGENTS. Thus an English passive like *Spike was arrested by the police* combines both functions: the AGENT argument is demoted to a prepositional phrase, and the PATIENT is promoted to subject. We can see the related sentence *Spike was arrested* as a special case of this, where demotion reaches its extreme in the suppression of the AGENT. In the Dutch impersonal passives in 6.120b on the other hand we see a passive strategy which just embodies the first function: demotion of AGENT, with no concomitant promotion function. Since this example has an intransitive verb, the further step of suppressing the AGENT leaves a sentence with no theta-role bearing nominal as in 6.121.

The third characteristic of English passives described in the last section was a special verb form and associated verbal agreement with the promoted subject. This too is subject to cross-linguistic variation. Passive verbs are often semantically distinguished from their active counterparts, for example by being more **stative**, though this is not always so, and they may show agreement with the promoted non-AGENT nominal (as in English), or the demoted-AGENT, or neither, since agreement inflections may be neutralized; see Givón (1990: 563–644) for discussion of variations along this parameter as well as along the parameters of AGENT demotion and non-AGENT promotion.

One conclusion from comparing passives across languages seems to be that the phenomenon is typically a cluster of functions: in each case following the general pattern of allowing the speaker planning her discourse some variation in the linkage between thematic and grammatical roles, but with considerable variation in the associated semantic and grammatical elements of the cluster.

In most active-passive systems the active form is usually grammatically simpler and we may ask why this should be so. It has been argued that we as humans naturally view situations from the point of view of any human beings involved, and if there are none, of other living creatures. This preference, sometimes called an **animacy hierarchy** (see e.g. Dixon 1979, Hopper and Thompson 1980), is coded into the lexical semantics of a language so that a verb like *drive*, for example, in 6.122 sets up a thematic role frame which requires an AGENT as the subject:

6.122 Ann drove the truck across the field.

and since agency, as we have seen, requires willful action, AGENTS are typically people, or higher animals. It is difficult to think of a verb which describes the action in 6.122 from the point of view of the truck. We might say:

6.123 The truck carried Ann across the field.

but this sentence has a different meaning: we have not specified that Ann was driving. So it seems that the meaning of the verb *drive* is set up to prioritize the role of any human or volitional agent. Passive voice allows the speaker to get around this in-built bias, so that to switch the viewpoint from Ann to the truck, or to the field, she can use passive constructions as in 6.124–5:

6.124 The truck was driven across the field by Ann.

6.125 The field was driven across by a truck (*by Ann).

We can see that in 6.125 there is no longer a slot for the AGENT, Ann. So passive constructions do allow a change of perspective but the conventional bias toward animate subjects means that the active *drive* is grammatically simpler than the passive *was driven*.

6.8.3 Middle voice

While very many languages display this active/passive voice contrast, some languages have a three-way distinction between active, passive and **middle voice**. As we might expect, the use of middle voice varies from language to language, but a central feature is that middle forms emphasize that the subject of the verb is affected by the action described by the verb. This **affectedness**, as it is often termed (e.g. Klaiman 1991), can be of several types, and we can select four typical uses as examples: neuters, bodily activity, and emotions, reflexives, and autobenefactives. Though we will use examples from several languages, to keep the discussion brief we will concentrate on two unrelated languages, well separated in space and time: classical Greek and the modern Cushitic language Somali.[22] In both these languages middle voice is marked by verbal inflection.

Neuter intransitives

This type of middle is where the subject undergoes a non-volitional process or change of state. The external cause is not represented but can often be shown in a related active form, as shown in 6.126 below, an example from Sanskrit (Klaiman 1991: 93):

6.126 a. So namati daṇḍam.
he-NOM bends-3sg ACTIVE stick-ACC
"He bends the stick."

b. Namate daṇḍaḥ.
bends-3sg MIDDLE stick-NOM
"The stick bends."

Middle voice verb forms of this neuter type, where the subject undergoes a process over which it has no control, occur in classical Greek, as shown in 6.127 (Bakker 1994: 30) and Somali,[23] as in 6.128:

6.127 phú-e-**sthai** "grow"
tréph-e-**sthai** "grow up"
sêp-e-**sthai** "rot"
têk-e-**sthai** "melt"
rhêgnu-**sthai** "break"

6.128	kab-**o**	"recover, set (of a bone)"
	qub-**o**	"fall (of leaves and fruit)"
	dhim-**o**	"die"
	haf-**o**	"drown"
	garaads-**o**	"reach maturity"

Bodily activity and emotions

In some languages the verb occurs in a middle voice when the activity involves the body or emotions of the subject. These would seem to be clear cases of affectedness since the subject is so overtly involved. Examples of such middle voice verbs are in 6.129–30:

6.129 Classical Greek (Bakker 1994)

klín-e-**sthai**	"lean"
hêd-e-**sthai**	"rejoice"

6.130 Somali (Saeed 1999)

fadhiis-**o**	"sit down"
baroor-**o**	"mourn, wail"

Reflexives

In some languages the middle is used where the subject's action affects the subject himself, or a possession or body part of the subject. To take another example from classical Greek (Barber 1975: 18–19):

6.131 Loú-omai.
wash-1sg.MIDDLE
"I wash myself."

This use means that in many languages verbs of grooming occur in the middle voice, with no need for a reflexive pronoun as object; see 6.132 for some further examples from Somali, and examples from other languages in 6.133 from Kemmer (1994: 195):

6.132	feer-**o**	"comb one's hair"
	maydh-**o**	"wash oneself, bathe"
	labbis-**o**	"dress up, put on one's best clothes"

6.133	Latin	orno-**r**	"adorn oneself"
	Quechua	arma-**ku**-y	"bathe"
	Turkish	giy-**in**	"dress"
	Hungarian	mosa-**kod**-	"wash oneself"

Autobenefactives

This type of middle is used to signify that the action of the subject is done for his or her own benefit. Once again this use occurred in classical Greek as in 6.134 (Barber 1975: 18), and is a regular process is Somali, as 6.135 shows (Saeed 1993: 58):

6.134	a.	hair-o	moiran.
		take-1sg-ACTIVE	share
		"I take a share."	
	b.	hari-oumai	moiran.
		take-1sg-MIDDLE	share
		"I take a share for myself."	

6.135	Active verbs:		Middle verbs:	
	wad	"to drive"	wad-**o**	"to drive for oneself"
	beer	"to cultivate"	beer-**o**	"to cultivate for oneself"
	qaad	"to take"	qaad-**o**	"to take for oneself"
	sid	"to carry"	sid-**o**	"to carry for oneself"

In the examples so far, middle voice has been marked by verbal inflection. In some languages a pronoun marks middle forms, often the same form as a reflexive pronoun, for example German *sich*, French *se*, Spanish *se*, or a closely related form, for example Russian reflexive *sebja*, middle *-sja*, Dutch reflexive *zichzelf*, middle *-zelf* (Kemmer 1994). In such languages the overlap between middle voice and reflexivity, seen in examples 6.129–35 above, becomes overt. In French and Spanish for example, we might identify our first three types of middle:

6.136	French middle reflexives			
	a.	neuter:	s'écrouler	"collapse"
			s'évanouir	"vanish"
	b.	bodily activity:	s'asseoir	"sit down"
		emotion:	se plaindre	"complain"
	c.	reflexive:	s'habiller	"dress oneself"
			se peigner	"comb one's hair"

6.137	Spanish middle reflexives			
	a.	neuter:	helarse	"freeze (intr.)"
			recuperarse	"get well"
	b.	bodily activity:	tirarse	"jump"
		emotion:	enamorarse (de)	"fall in love (with)"
	c.	reflexive:	afeitarse	"shave"
			quitarse	"take off (clothes)"

However, even in languages where the middle and reflexives are marked by the same pronoun, there are usually clear cases where the meaning distinguishes between true reflexives and the middle, for example in German (Kemmer 1994: 188):

6.138	Er sieht **sich**	"He sees himself"	(Reflexive)
	Er fürchtet **sich**	"He is afraid"	(Middle – emotion)

In English there is no inflectional or pronominal marker of the middle: the distinction is only shown by alternations between transitive active verbs and intransitive middle verbs, where the agent is omitted, for example:

6.139 a. They open the gates very smoothly. (Active)
b. The gates open very smoothly. (Middle – neuter)

These intransitive middles in English are often used to describe the success of a non-AGENT in some activity, for example:

6.140 a. These clothes wash well.
b. This model sells very quickly.
c. These saws don't cut very efficiently.

See Dixon (1991: 322–35) for more examples of this type of construction in English. Because of the similar suppression of the AGENT in this type of middle and in the passive, some writers use the term **medio-passive** to cover both.

6.9 Classifiers and Noun Classes

So far in this chapter we have been exploring the ways that participants may be assigned semantic roles relative to the action or situation described by the verb. In this section we look at semantic characterizations that are based on inherent properties of the entities referred to by noun phrases. Many languages have overt systems for marking how referents fit into a semantic classification system. We divide our brief discussion of these into, first, classifiers, and then noun classes.

6.9.1 Classifiers

Noun classifiers are morphemes or lexical words that code characteristics of the referent of the noun, allowing the speaker to classify the referent according to a system of semantic/conceptual categories. They may show up grammatically in different guises. Some, termed **noun classifiers**, occur with nouns. Dixon (1977) describes the noun classifiers of the Australian language Yidiŋ as a closed set of around twenty members, which he divides into two general types, each containing several subtypes. The first type, inherent nature classifiers, includes as subtypes of classifiers: human; animals; vegetation; natural objects (like the classifier *walba* "stone"); and artifacts (like the classifier *baji* "canoe"). The second type, functional classifiers, divides entities into: meat food; non-meat food; drinkable things; movable; habitable; and "purposeful noise." Dixon (1982) reports that two classifiers can be used with the same nominal as long as they come from the two different general types, for example (where CL = classifier):

6.141 bulumba walba malan
CL:HABITABLE CL:STONE flat.rock
"a flat rock for camping" (Dixon 1982: 200)

In many languages classifiers occur in specific grammatical constructions or locations, for example **numeral classifiers**, which occur when the entity is being counted, and **possessive classifiers**, which occur in constructions describing possession. Numeral classifiers occur in Japanese as shown in the table in 6.142 below:

6.142 Classifiers in a Japanese shopping list (cited in Aikhenvald 2000:2)

Shopping list	Numeral	Classifier	Meaning of classifier
nasu (eggplant)	*nana* (7)	*-ko*	CL:SMALL. EQUIDIMENSIONAL
kyuuri (cucumber)	*hachi* (8)	*-hon*	CL:ELONGATED
hamu (ham)	*juu* (10)	*-mai*	CL:SHEETLIKE

As we can see, these classifiers relate to a classification based on shape.

Possessive (or genitive) classifiers may characterize the possessed item, as in the Fijian example in 6.143 below; or classify the type of possession relation involved, as in 6.144 from Hawaiian:

6.143 Fijian possessive classifiers (Lichtenberk 1983: 157–58)

a. na me-qu yaqona
ART CL:DRINKABLE-my kava
"my kava (which I intend to drink)"

b. na no-qu yaqona
ART CL:GENERAL-my kava
"my kava (that I grew, or that I will sell)"

6.144 Hawaiian possessive classifiers (Lichtenberk 1983: 163)

a. k-o-'u inoa
ART-CL-my name
"my name (that represents me)"

b. k-a-'u inoa
ART-CL-my name
"my name (that I bestow on someone)"

A further type is **verbal classifiers**, where the classifier occurs as a morpheme attached to the verb and serves to classify (intransitive) subjects or objects: see for example:

6.145 Dogrib (Athapaskan) (cited in Allan 2001: 309)

a. let'e niyeh-tši
bread I.pick.up-PERF.CL:FLAT.FLEXIBLE.ENTITY
"I pick up a slice of bread"

b. let'e niyeh-ʔa
bread I.pick.up-PERF.CL:ROUND.ENTITY
"I pick up a loaf of bread"

Wherever they are marked grammatically classifiers tend to exploit a fixed set of semantic distinctions. Though there is large variation, it is possible to identify some prototypical distinctions, as Allan (2001) does below:

6.146 Prototypical classifier categories (Allan 2001: 307)

a. *Material make-up*: e.g. human (-like), animate, female, tree (-like)
b. *Function*: e.g. piercing, cutting, or writing instruments; for eating, drinking
c. *Shape*: e.g. long (saliently one-dimensional), flat, round
d. *Consistency*: e.g. rigid, flexible, mass
e. *Size*: including diminutives and augmentatives
f. *Location*: inherently locative entities such as towns
g. *Arrangement*: e.g. a row of, a coil of, a heap of
h. *Quanta*: e.g. head of cattle, pack of cigarettes

6.9.2 Noun classes

Noun classes are agreement-based noun systems that seem, at least historically, to be based on semantic classifications somewhat similar to those we have seen for classifiers. One famous example occurs in the Bantu languages of Africa, where nouns belong to a pattern of classes, related variously in the modern languages to an ancestral system that is characterized by Aikhenvald (2000) as follows, (where class pairs *1/2* etc. are singular and plural):[24]

6.147 Noun classes in Proto-Bantu (Aikhenvald 2000: 282)

CLASS	SEMANTICS
1/2	Humans, a few other animates
3/4	Plants, plant parts, foods, non-paired body parts, miscellaneous
5/6	Fruits, paired body parts, miscellaneous inanimates
7/8	Miscellaneous inanimates
9/10	Animals
11/10	Long objects, abstract entities
12/13	Small objects, birds
6	Masses
14	Abstract qualities, states, masses, collectives
15	Infinitives

The key feature of noun class systems is that other elements in the sentence agree with the noun in terms of its class. See for example (6.148) below from the modern Bantu language Swahili:

6.148 Swahili class 8 (Allan 2001: 310):

Vi-su	**vi**dogo	**vi**wili	hi-**vi**	amba-**vy**-o	nili-**vi**-nunua	ni	**vi**-kali	sana
vi-knife	*vi*-small	*vi*-two	this-*vi*	which-*vi*	1.s-*vi*-buy	be	*vi*-sharp	very

"These two small knives which I bought are very sharp"

Here the noun class prefix, marked in bold, is copied as an agreement feature by other elements in the noun phrase headed by *visu* "knife" and in the sentence in which the noun phrase is subject.

In the modern Bantu languages the assignment of nouns to classes is not always as semantically transparent as the classes in 6.147 suggest. Often the classes are much more heterogeneous and membership may be more conventionalized.

Gender systems, familiar from Indo-European languages, in which nouns are assigned to two or thee classes: male, female and perhaps neuter, are a type of noun class system. Indeed Corbett (1991) extends the term *gender* to cover all noun class systems. As may be the case with more complex noun class systems, gender in languages like German or Hindi is a grammatical distinction only loosely connected to biological sex. Humans and animals may be typically (though not exclusively) assigned to genders on the basis of biological sex, but other nouns are assigned by a mixture of criteria, some of which have no semantic basis, for example phonological shape.

Noun class systems may be differentiated from classifiers by a number of features, some of which are summarized by Dixon (1986) as follows:

6.149 Differences between noun classes and classifiers (Dixon 1986)

	NOUN CLASSES	CLASSIFIERS
Size	Small finite set	Large number
Realization	Closed grammatical system	Free forms
Scope	Marking is never entirely within the noun word	Never any reference outside the noun phrase

However, the large degree of variation within both types of system means that any simple characterization is only suggestive of typical cases.

6.10 Summary

In this chapter our main focus has been on the ways in which a speaker may portray the roles of participants in a situation. We outlined a classification of such semantic roles, termed **thematic roles** or **theta-roles**, including AGENT, PATIENT, THEME, and so on, and described the relationship between these roles and grammatical relations like **subject** and **object**. It has been claimed that as part of its inherent lexical specification a verb requires its arguments to be in specific thematic roles, and that this can be reflected by formulating thematic role **grids**, or **theta-grids**. We discussed the difficulties there are in fixing tight definitions for individual thematic roles, and presented one approach, from Dowty (1991), which seeks to provide a solution in terms of fuzzy categories. This difficulty with precision notwithstanding, it seems that the notion of thematic roles has proved a useful descriptive tool in a number of areas of the semantics–grammar interface. We also discussed **causation**, which is an important element in how speakers characterize a situation and identify participants.

The grammatical category of **voice** allows speakers different strategies for relating thematic roles and grammatical relations. We concentrated on relations with **subject** position, in particular the way in which **passive voice** allows the foregrounding of non-AGENT roles to subject and the backgrounding of AGENT roles away from subject. We also looked at **middle voice**, which reflects the **affectedness** of the subject in the action of the verb, thus offering a different view of the relationship between subject and verb from the **active voice**.

Finally we looked at **classifiers** and **noun classes**: systems where nouns identifying entities are classified by inherent semantic features, though membership of the relevant classes may be only partially semantically determined.

EXERCISES

6.1 On the basis of the informal definitions in section 6.2, try to assign a single **thematic role** label to each of the expressions in bold in the following sentences:

a. **Helen** drove **to the party**.
b. **He** swatted **the fly** with **a newspaper**.
c. **The baboon** was asleep **on the roof of my car**.
d. **Joan** drank **the yard of ale**.
e. **Campbell** saw **the gun** first.
f. **George** gave **the doorman a tip**.

6.2 For each of the **theta-roles** below, construct an English sentence where an argument bearing that role occurs as **subject**. Use simple active sentences, avoiding for the present exercise passive constructions and complex sentences.

a. EXPERIENCER
b. PATIENT
c. THEME
d. INSTRUMENT
e. RECIPIENT

6.3 For each of the **theta-roles** below, construct an English sentence where an argument bearing that role occurs as **object**.

a. PATIENT
b. THEME
c. BENEFICIARY
d. RECIPIENT
e. STIMULUS

6.4 As we saw, Jackendoff (1990) proposes a distinction between a **thematic tier** of thematic roles (relating to movement and location) and an **action tier** (relating to ACTOR–PATIENT type relations). An argument may have a role at each level and thus fulfill two roles. For example the underlined argument in *The car smashed into* <u>*the shop window*</u> can be analyzed as both PATIENT and GOAL. For each of the combinations of roles below, try to invent a sentence where a single argument fulfills the combination:

a. AGENT and GOAL
b. PATIENT and THEME
c. AGENT and SOURCE
d. AGENT and THEME

6.5 In sections 6.5 and 6.6 we discussed proposals from Dowty (1991) to characterize thematic roles in terms of clusters of **entailments**, and to describe the rules linking thematic roles and grammatical relations like subject and object in terms of **argument selection principles**. Using the selection principles in 6.81 in the chapter and the properties of Proto-roles in 6.77 and 6.78, discuss the selection of subject and object positions in the following sentences:

a. The butler is polishing the silverware.
b. The dogs will smell the food.
c. The train hit the cow.

What problems are posed for these principles by the selection of subject and objects in the pairs of sentences below?

1 a. He fears AIDS.
  b. AIDS frightens him.
2 a. Patricia resembles Maura.
  b. Maura resembles Patricia.
3 a. Joan bought a sports car from Jerry.
  b. Jerry sold a sports car to Joan.

6.6 We saw how **passive** allows the foregrounding of non-AGENT theta-roles into subject position. Compare for example the active sentence 1 below with the passive equivalent in 2:

1 Craig$_{\text{AG}}$ devoured the ice cream$_{\text{PA}}$.
2 The ice cream$_{\text{PA}}$ was devoured by Craig$_{\text{AG}}$.

Assume 2 is formed from 1 by a simple rule: (a) place the non-AGENT argument at the beginning of the sentence; (b) change the active verb to a passive verb (e.g. *devoured* → *was devoured*); (c) place the word *by* in front of the AGENT and place the AGENT at the end of the sentence. Below are some active sentences with a non-subject argument underlined. For each one, use our simple rule to try to create a corresponding passive where the underlined non-AGENT argument becomes subject.

a. The court fined Emma five hundred francs.
b. Aliens abducted me in the middle of my examination.
c. The professor mailed the answer to the student.
d. The professor mailed the answer to the student.
e. The professor mailed the student the answer.
f. The professor mailed the student the answer.

Were any of the resulting passives ungrammatical? If so, what explanation can you give?

6.7 In section 6.7 we described the English **causative-inchoative verb alternation**. In the list of verbs below try to identify those verbs that undergo this alternation and those that do not. Of the latter divide them into inchoative-only and causative-only types. Note: In making your decisions try to avoid using examples with passive and middle voice constructions since this alternation relates to the argument structure of verbs in basic active voice sentences.

break, open, dirty, melt, disappear, bend, erupt, mow, dissolve, dry, decay, tilt, crush

6.8 As we saw, in some languages (e.g. Somali) when a speaker describes a reflexive act of grooming, say for example the equivalent of *I wash myself*, the verb occurs in a **middle voice** form with no object. In others (e.g. French) a **reflexive pronoun** is used as the object. In English we find another strategy: some verbs which are normally transitive allow the speaker to omit the object in order to convey a reflexive meaning. For example, we know that *hide* is normally a transitive verb because of sentences like *She hid the money*; however *She hid* means of course *She hid herself*. So English has verbs like *hide*, which by omitting an argument can convey an **understood reflexive object**. Unlike Somali though, the English verbs in these constructions do not have a special middle voice ending. Below are some verbs which describe what we could call acts of grooming. Decide which of these allow an understood reflexive object.

undress	towel
wash	bathe
brush	shampoo
soap	shave
strip	lather

Is there any semantic differences between those verbs which allow this understood reflexive object and those which do not? If you think there is, test your hypothesis with other verbs from this semantic field of grooming.

6.9 Design **lexical theta-grids** for the verbs in bold in the sentences below. For example a theta-grid for *buy* in *Dee-dee* **bought** *the car for his mistress* would be: **buy** <AGENT, THEME, BENEFICIARY>.

a. Brenda **reported** the incident to her boss.
b. Frogs **fell** from the sky.
c. Our headquarters will **remain** in London.
d. Batman **received** a commendation from the mayor.
e. Harvey **noticed** a strange smell.

FURTHER READING

An important study of thematic roles is Dowty's (1991) article. Palmer (1994) is a survey of thematic roles, the different ways they are grammaticalized and the role of passive and middle voice. Bornkessel et al. (2006) is an interdisciplinary collection of articles on thematic roles. Dixon (2005) discusses the ways in which the grammar of English verbs reflects semantic distinctions, and includes sections on semantic/thematic roles, and the English passive. Levin and Rappaport Hovav (2005) provides further discussion of the problems with thematic roles identified in this chapter. Màrquez et al. (2008) provides a brief introduction to semantic role labeling. Shibatani (2002) is a collection of studies of causatives across a range of languages. Lyngfelt and Solstad (2006) contains articles on argument structure changing processes, including passive. Klaiman (1991) explores middle voice in a number of languages. Corbett (1991) discusses noun classes, Aikhenvald (2000) provides a comprehensive cross-linguistic overview of classifier systems, and Grinevald (2002) discusses the relationship between the two types of system.

NOTES

1 One might also think of examples like: *In the village stands a pump*. But here the subject still seems to be *a pump* rather than *in the village*, as can be shown by the pattern of agreement in: *In the village stand several pumps*. But see Levin and Rappaport Hovav (1995: 261–64) for arguments, couched in the theory of Lexical-Functional Grammar (e.g. Bresnan 1994), that the preverbal PP is, at some level of analysis, a subject.

2 See the introductory discussion of theta-grids in Haegeman (1994: 33–73).

3 Hereafter we will use just the two first letters of a thematic role with this subscript notation, e.g. Joan_{AG} for $\text{Joan}_{\text{AGENT}}$.

4 In Jackendoff's (1990) two-tier representation described earlier, these "transfer" verbs would have a more complicated thematic grid: e.g. we could assign both AGENT and SOURCE roles to *Barbara* in 6.67.

5 In Dixon (2005: 110–19) the affected entity in examples 6.72–5 is called a Target and a verb class called AFFECT is sub-classified according to the type of interaction with the Target.

6 Note that in this view, theta-roles convey a speaker's classifications of things in the world: in other words, the roles are borne by real-world entities rather than grammatical elements like NPs. See for instance the following example and comment from Laduslaw and Dowty (1988: 63):

 1 a. Fido chased Felix.
 b. Felix was chased by Fido.

 … The only sense in which it is reasonable to think of the subject NP of (1a) as the Agent is the sense in which it is shorthand for saying that the object (in the world) referred to by the subject is the Agent in the action described by the sentence. What makes Fido an agent in the event described by (1a) and (1b) is information about Fido and his role in the event, not about the grammatical category or function of anything in the sentence.

7 For a related idea, see Foley and Van Valin's (1984) theory of **macro-roles**, where all thematic roles fall into two main categories: **actor** and **undergoer**.

8 This term arises from Dowty's (1991) examination of different types of what he calls THEME roles, some of which would be PATIENT roles in our classification. He proposes a class of **incremental themes** for the THEME/PATIENT roles of achievement and

accomplishment verbs, e.g. *mow the lawn, eat an egg, build a house, demolish a building*. The observation is that the action (for example, the mowing action) and the state of the associated THEME/PATIENT (e.g. the lawn) are in a proportional relationship: some mowing cuts some of the grass, more mowing, more of the grass, etc., until completing the action cuts all of the grass. Dowty extends this idea of incremental themes to other types of role, e.g. *swim from England to France*, where the path is incrementally affected, and *memorize a poem*, where there is a similar incremental relationship between the action and a representation of the THEME entity. See Dowty (1991) for further details.

9 In our discussion we focus on languages like English which have the grammatical relations, **subject** and **object**. We therefore leave aside the different pattern of mapping between theta-roles and grammatical relation shown by **ergative** languages. Briefly, in a typical ergative system one grammatical relation, called **absolutive**, is used for the single argument of an intransitive verb, whatever its theta-role (and in this resembles English subject), but is also used in ditransitive verbs for the PATIENT argument (and here resembles English object). A second grammatical relation, called **ergative**, is used for the AGENT/EXPERIENCER in ditransitive verbs (as is English subject). There is therefore no correspondence between the absolutive/ergative distinction and the subject/object distinction. They represent two different strategies for mapping between theta-roles and grammatical relations. See the following simple example of an ergative system from Tongan (Austronesian: Tonga), given by Anderson (1976):

a. na'e lea **'a** etalavou.
PAST speak ABS young.man
"The young man spoke."

b. na'e alu **'a** Tevita ki Fisi.
PAST go ABS David to Fiji
"David went to Fiji."

c. na'e tamate'i **'a** Kolaiate **'e** Tevita.
past kill ABS Goliath ERG David
"David killed Goliath."

d. na'e ma'u **'e** siale **'a** e me'a'ofa.
past receive ERG Charlie ABS DEF gift
"Charlie received the gift."

Note that in these Tongan sentences the verb comes first in the sentence, and the case-marking particles (in bold) precede their nominals. Sentences a and b have intransitive verbs and the verb's only argument is in the absolutive case. Sentences c and d have transitive verbs. Here the AGENT in c and the RECIPIENT in d are in the ergative case. The PATIENT in c and the THEME in d are in the absolutive case. The reader may compare this with the mapping for subject-object languages like English. Ergative languages are found all over the world and include Basque in southern Europe, the Australian language Dyirbal, Tongan from the Pacific, and the Inuit languages of Canada, Greenland, etc. See Dixon (1979) for discussion and Croft (1990) and Palmer (1994) for cross-linguistic overviews.

10 Note that Dowty's hierarchy here has INSTRUMENT and PATIENT in reverse order to our earlier hierarchy. We won't try to arbitrate between these claims here: compare the discussion in Dowty (1991) and Croft (1990).

11 These are labels commonly used in the literature for the thematic roles associated with these verbs. We leave aside discussion of how these roles would correlate with the Agent-properties and Patient-properties in a Dowty-style approach.

12 See Grimshaw (1990) and Levin (1993) for discussion of these classes of psychological verbs.

13 Here we follow Jackendoff (1990) in allowing one argument to have two theta-roles, as described earlier.

14 See Dowty (1991: 594–95), Levin (1993: 67–68).

15 See Levin (1993: 83).

16 Since the same form occurs there has been debate in the literature about whether the causative is derived from the inchoative (as suggested by Dowty 1979, Pesetsky 1995 among others), the inchoative from the causative (Chierchia 1989, Levin and Rappaport 1995, Reinhart 2002), or both from a common source (Piñón 2001, Alexiadou et al. 2006).

17 See Saeed (1999) for details of causative affixes in Somali.

18 This is similar to the use of "Figure" and "Ground" in the analysis of motion verbs by Talmy (1975), and others, as discussed in chapter 9. There the *figure* is the entity in motion and the background is called the *ground*.

19 But only under some special conditions, which have been much debated in the literature. Levin and Rappaport Hovav (1995: 143–44), for example, discuss examples of this type like *This platform has been stood on by an ex-president* under the label **prepositional passives**. They provide a restriction on the construction in English that mixes grammatical and semantic factors: that it is only possible with **unergative verbs** which take an animate subject. **Unergative** is a term introduced by Perlmutter (1978) for intransitive verbs like *sit* and *stand* whose single argument is an AGENT and whose grammatical behavior contrasts with **unaccusative verbs** which are intransitive verbs like *grow* or *drown* and whose single argument is essentially a PATIENT. Dixon (1991: 298–321) on the other hand proposes syntactic restrictions, which include the absence of a direct object in the active sentence, and a lack of an alternative active construction in which the passivized NP could occur as direct object. For an in-depth study of these prepositional passive constructions, see Couper-Kuhlen (1979).

20 Other English verbs allow alternations into object position, e.g.:

1 a. He wrapped cling-film around the food.
b. He wrapped the food in cling-film.

2 a. David gave the keys to Helen.
b. David gave Helen the keys.

3 a. She bought some flowers for her husband.
b. She bought her husband some flowers.

Alternations like 2 and 3 are often called *Dative Shift*. Givón (1984a) describes these, and similar alternations in other languages, as *promotion to object*, a process paralleling passive. By comparison with passive, though, the process is more restricted to particular verbs and is less likely to be marked on the verb by a distinct inflection of voice.

21 Though this is less true of pairs like:

1 Mary was killed.
2 Mary got killed.

See Givón and Yang (1994) for a discussion of the English *get*-passive; and Weiner and Labov (1983) for a sociolinguistic approach.

22 For a survey of the meanings of middle voice in Somali, see Saeed (1995).

23 Note that not all neuter middles in Somali have an active form: the verbs *jabo*, *qubo*, *hafo* do, but *garaadso* does not, and the middle verb *dhimo* "to die" has as its active equivalent a different lexical verb *dil* "to kill." It seems that all languages which have a middle voice have some verbs that are inherently middle and have no morphologically related active forms. See Klaiman (1991) for discussion.

24 See Denny and Creider (1986) for a detailed discussion of the semantics of the Proto-Bantu noun classes.

REFERENCES

Aikhenvald, Alexandra Y. 2000. *Classifiers: A Typology of Noun Categorization Devices*. Oxford: Oxford University Press.

Alexiadou, Artemis, Elena Anagnostopoulou, and Florian Schäfer 2006: The properties of anti-causatives crosslinguistically. In Mara Frascarelli (ed.) *Phases of Interpretation*, 187–211. Berlin: Mouton de Gruyter.

Alishahi, A. and S. Stevenson 2010: A computational model of learning semantic roles from child-directed language. *Language and Cognitive Processes* 25.1: 50–93.

Allan, Keith. 1986: *Linguistic Meaning*, 2 vols. London: Routledge & Kegan Paul.

Allan, Keith. 2001: *Natural Language Semantics*. Oxford: Blackwell.

Anderson, John R. 1976: *Language, Memory and Thought*. Hillsdale, NJ: Lawrence Erlbaum.

Andrews, A. 1985: The major functions of the noun phrase. In Timothy Shopen (ed.) *Language Typology and Syntactic Description. Vol. 1: Clause Structure*, 2–154. Cambridge: Cambridge University Press.

Bakker, Egbert J. 1994: Voice, aspect and aktionsart: middle and passive in Ancient Greek. In Barbara Fox and Paul J. Hopper (eds.) *Voice: Form and Function*, 23–48. Amsterdam: John Benjamins.

Barber, Elizabeth J. Wayland 1975: Voice: beyond the passive. *Berkeley Linguistics Society* 1: 16–23.

Bornkessel, I., M. Schlesewsky, A. D. Friederici and B. Comrie (eds.) 2006: *Semantic Role Universals and Argument Linking: Theoretical, Typological and Psycholinguistic Perspectives*. Berlin: Mouton de Gruyter.

Bresnan, Joan 1994: Locative inversion and the architecture of universal grammar. *Language* 70: 72–131.

Chierchia, Gennaro. 1989. A semantics for unaccusatives and its syntactic consequences. Manuscript, Cornell University, Ithaca.

Chomsky, Noam 1988: *Language and Problems of Knowledge. The Managua Lectures*. Cambridge, MA: MIT Press.

Cohn, Neil and Martin Paczynski 2013: Prediction, events, and the advantage of Agents: the processing of semantic roles in visual narrative. *Cognitive Psychology* 67.3: 73–97.

Comrie, Bernard 1981: *Language Universals and Linguistic Typology*. Oxford: Blackwell.

Corbett, G. 1991: *Gender*. Cambridge: Cambridge University Press.

Couper-Kuhlen, E. 1979: *The Prepositional Passive in English*. Tübingen: Niemeyer.

Croft, William 1990: *Typology and Universals*. Cambridge: Cambridge University Press.

Croft, William 2012: *Verbs: Aspect and Causal Structure*. Oxford: Oxford University Press.

Denny, J. Peter and Chet A. Creider 1986: The semantics of noun classes in Proto-Bantu. In C. G. Craig (ed.) *Noun Classes and Categorization*, 217–39. Amsterdam: John Benjamins.

Dixon, Robert M. W. 1977: *A Grammar of Yidiɲ*. Cambridge: Cambridge University Press.

Dixon, Robert M. W. 1979: Ergativity. *Language* 55.1: 59–138.

Dixon, Robert M. W. 1982: *Where Have All the Adjectives Gone? And Other Essays in Semantics and Syntax*. Berlin: Mouton.

Dixon, Robert M. W. 1986: Noun classes and noun classification in typological perspective. In C. G. Craig (ed.) *Noun Classes and Categorization: Proceedings of a Symposium on Categorization and Noun Classification, Eugene, Oregon, October 1983*, 105–12. Amsterdam: John Benjamins.

Dixon, Robert M. W. 1991: *A New Approach to English Grammar on Semantic Principles*. Oxford: Oxford University Press.

Dixon, R. M. W. 2005: *A Semantic Approach to English Grammar*. Oxford: Oxford University Press.

Dowty, David R. 1979: *Word Meaning and Montague Grammar*. Dordrecht: Reidel.

Dowty, David R. 1986: Thematic roles and semantics. *Berkeley Linguistics Society* 12: 340–54.

Dowty, David R. 1989: On the semantic content of the notion "thematic role." In Barbara H. Partee, Gennaro Chierchia, and Raymond Turner (eds.) *Properties, Types and Meanings*, vol. 2, 69–130. Dordrecht: Kluwer.

Dowty, David R. 1991: Thematic proto-roles and argument selection. *Language* 67: 574–619.

Ferreira, F. 2003: The misinterpretation of noncanonical sentences. *Cognitive Psychology* 47.2: 164–203

Fillmore, Charles J. 1968: The case for Case. In Emmon Bach and Robert T. Harms (eds.) *Universals in Linguistic Theory*, 1–88. New York: Holt, Rinehart & Winston.

Foley, William and Robert Van Valin 1984: *Functional Syntax and Universal Grammar*. Cambridge: Cambridge University Press.

Giuglea, Ana-Maria and Alessandro Moschitti 2006: Semantic role labeling via FrameNet, Verb-Net and PropBank. In N. Calzolari, C. Cardie, and P. Isabelle (eds.) *Proceedings of the 21st International Conference on Computational Linguistics and 44th Annual Meeting of the Association for Computational Linguistics (COLING/ACL-06)*, 929–36. Sydney, Australia: Association for Computational Linguistics.

Givón, Talmy 1984a: Direct object and dative shifting: semantic and pragmatic case. In Frans Plank (ed.) *Objects: Towards a Theory of Grammatical Relations*, 151–82. London: Academic Press.

Givón, Talmy 1984b: *Syntax: A Functional-Typological Introduction*, Vol. 1. Amsterdam: John Benjamins.

Givón, Talmy 1990: *Syntax: A Functional-Typological Introduction*, Vol. 2. Amsterdam: John Benjamins.

Givón, Talmy and Lynne Yang 1994: The rise of the English GET-passive. In Barbara Fox and Paul J. Hopper (eds.) *Voice: Form and Function*, 120–49. Amsterdam: John Benjamins.

Grimshaw, Jane 1990: *Argument Structure*. Cambridge, MA: MIT Press.

Grinevald, Colette 2002: Making sense of nominal classification systems. In I. Wischer and G. Diewald (eds.) *New Reflections on Grammaticalization*, 259–75. Amsterdam: John Benjamins.

Grossman, M. and T. White-Devine 1998: Sentence comprehension in Alzheimer's disease. *Brain and Language* 62.2: 186–201.

Gruber, Jeffrey S. 1976: *Lexical Structure in Syntax and Semantics*. Amsterdam: North-Holland.

Haegeman, Liliane 1994: *Introduction to Government and Binding Theory*, second edition. Oxford: Blackwell.

Haspelmath, Martin 1993: More on the typology of inchoative/causative verb alternations. In B. Comrie and M. Polinsky (eds.) *Causatives and Transitivity*, 87–120. Amsterdam: John Benjamins.

Hopper, Paul J. and Sandra A. Thompson 1980: Transitivity in grammar and discourse. *Language* 56: 251–399.

Jackendoff, Ray 1972: *Semantic Interpretation in Generative Grammar*. Cambridge, MA: MIT Press.

Jackendoff, Ray 1990: *Semantic Structures*. Cambridge, MA: MIT Press.

Jeffries, Lesley and Penny Willis 1984: A return to the spray paint issue. *Journal of Pragmatics* 8: 715–29.

Kemmer, Suzanne 1994: Middle voice, transitivity, and the elaboration of events. In Barbara Fox and Paul J. Hopper (eds.) *Voice: Form and Function*, 179–230. Amsterdam: John Benjamins.

Kipper, Karin, Anna Korhonen, Neville Ryant, and Martha Palmer 2008: A large-scale classification of English verbs. *Language Resources and Evaluation Journal* 42.1: 21–40.

Kirsner, Robert S. 1976: On the subjectless "pseudo-passive" in Dutch and the semantics of background agents. In Charles N. Li (ed.) *Subject and Topic*, 385–415. New York: Academic Press.

Klaiman, Miriam H. 1991: *Grammatical Voice*. Cambridge: Cambridge University Press.

Kuno, Susumu 1987: *Functional Syntax: Anaphora, Discourse and Empathy*. Chicago: University of Chicago Press.

Laduslaw, William A. and David R. Dowty 1988: Toward a nongrammatical account of thematic roles. In Wendy Wilkins (ed.) *Syntax and Semantics. Vol. 21: Thematic Relations*, 61–73. New York: Academic Press.

Lakoff, Robin T. 1971: Passive resistance. *CLS* 7, University of Chicago, Chicago Linguistics Society.

Langacker, Ronald W. 2008: *Cognitive Grammar: A Basic Introduction*. Oxford: Oxford University Press.

Levin, Beth 1993: *English Verb Classes and Alternations*. Chicago: University of Chicago Press.

Levin, Beth and Malka Rappaport Hovav 1995: *Unaccusativity: At the Syntax–Lexical Semantics Interface*. Cambridge, MA: MIT Press.

Levin, Beth and Malka Rappaport Hovav 2005: *Argument Realization*. Cambridge: Cambridge University Press.

Lichtenberk, Frantisek 1983: Relational classifiers. *Lingua* 60: 147–76.

Lyngfelt, Benjamin and Torgrim Solstad (eds.) 2006: *Demoting the Agent: Passive, Middle and Other Voice Phenomena*. Amsterdam: John Benjamins.

Manouilidou, C., R. G. de Almeida, G. Schwartz, and N. Nair 2009: Thematic roles in Alzheimer's disease: hierarchy violations in psychological predicates. *Journal of Neurolinguistics* 22.2: 167–86.

Màrquez, Lluís, Xavier Carreras, Kenneth C. Litkowski, and Suzanne Stevenson 2008: Semantic role labeling: an introduction to the special issue. *Computational Linguistics* 34.2: 145–59.

Mithun, Marianne 1991: Active/agentive case marking and its motivations. *Language* 67.3: 510–46.

Noonan, Michael 1994: A tale of two passives in Irish. In Barbara Fox and Paul J. Hopper (eds.) *Voice: Form and Function*, 279–311. Amsterdam: John Benjamins.

Palmer, Frank R. 1994: *Grammatical Roles and Relations*. Cambridge: Cambridge University Press.

Palmer, Martha, Daniel Gildea, and Paul Kingsbury 2005: The Proposition Bank: an annotated corpus of semantic roles. *Computational Linguistics* 31.1: 71–106.

Perlmutter, David M. 1978: Impersonal passives and the unaccusative hypothesis. *Berkeley Linguistics Society* 4: 157–89.

Perlmutter, David M. and Paul M. Postal 1984: Impersonal passives and some relational laws. In David M. Perlmutter and Carl G. Rosen (eds.) *Studies in Relational Grammar*, vol. 2, 126–70. Chicago: University of Chicago Press.

Pesetsky, David 1995: *Zero Syntax: Experiencers and Cascades*. Cambridge, MA: MIT Press.

Piñón, Christopher. 2001: A finer look at the causative-inchoative alternation. In R. Hastings, B. Jackson, and Z. Zvolenszky (eds.) *Proceedings of Semantics and Linguistic Theory 11*, 346–64. Ithaca, NY: CLC Publications, Cornell University.

Price, C. and M. Grossman 2005: An on-line study of verb knowledge in individuals diagnosed wirh AD and FTD. *Brain and Language* 92.2: 217–32.

Radford, Andrew 1988: *Transformational Grammar*. Cambridge: Cambridge University Press.

Rappaport, Malka and Beth Levin 1985: A case study in lexical analysis: the locative alternation. Unpublished manuscript: MIT Center for Cognitive Science.

Rappaport, Malka and Beth Levin 1988: What to do with theta-roles. In Wendy Wilkins (ed.) *Syntax and Semantics. Vol. 21: Thematic Relations*, 7–36. New York: Academic Press.

Rappaport Hovav, Malka and Beth Levin 2012: Lexicon uniformity and the causative alternation. In M. Everaert, M. Marelj, and T. Siloni (eds.) *The Theta System: Argument Structure at the Interface*, 150–176. Oxford: Oxford University Press.

Reinhart, Tanya 2002: The theta system: an overview. *Theoretical Linguistics* 28: 229–90.

Saeed, John Ibrahim 1993: *Somali Reference Grammar*, second edition. Kensington, MD: Dunwoody Press.

Saeed, John Ibrahim 1995: The semantics of middle voice in Somali. *African Languages and Cultures* 8.1: 61–85.

Saeed, John Ibrahim 1999: *Somali*. London Oriental and African Language Library. Amsterdam: John Benjamins.

Shibatani, Masayoshi (ed.) 2002: *The Grammar of Causation and Interpersonal Manipulation*. Amsterdam: John Benjamins.

Talmy, Leonard 1975: Semantics and syntax of motion. In John P. Kimball (ed.) *Syntax and Semantics 4*, 181–238. London: Academic Press.
Talmy, Leonard. 2000: *Toward a Cognitive Semantics*, 2 vols. Cambridge, MA: MIT Press.
Weiner, E. Judith and William Labov 1983: Constraints on the agentless passive. *Journal of Linguistics* 19: 29–58.
Williams, Edwin 1981: Argument structure and morphology. *The Linguistic Review* 1.1: 81–114.

chapter 7

Context and Inference

7.1 Introduction

In this chapter we examine how speakers and hearers rely on context in constructing and interpreting the meaning of utterances. We have already seen instances of this: in chapter 2 we mentioned the role of assumed knowledge in the use of proper names and definite noun phrases. The use of the names in bold in 7.1–2 below is only licensed by an assumption that the hearer can identify the individuals:

7.1 It'll take more than a pair of Levis to make you into **James Dean**.

7.2 Her mistake was to hire an **Elvis** impersonator.

We discuss this kind of assumed or background knowledge in section 7.6. Sometimes this kind of knowledge is called **non-linguistic knowledge** because it is argued that knowing who James Dean or Elvis is does not form part of one's knowledge of English, in the same way as knowing the meaning of *pair* or *talk*. For of course, knowledge about film stars or music personalities is not restricted to speakers of any single language in the way that knowledge of a particular noun or verb's meaning is.

We will see though that this non-linguistic knowledge about the world does perform an important role in understanding utterances.

Of course to understand these sentences the hearer also has to be able to identify the *you* of 7.1 and the *her* of 7.2. This information is normally instantly understood from the context, but if we provide an odd enough situation, for example finding these sentences written on pieces of paper, we can clearly see the essential role of knowing contextual information like who wrote the sentence, to whom it is addressed, and so on. The reason of course is that, as we have seen in earlier chapters, pronouns like *I*, *you*, *her*, and so on are shorthand devices which need various forms of contextual support. Elements of language that are so contextually bound are called **deictic**, from the noun **deixis** (from classical Greek *deiknymi* "to show, point out"). In chapter 5 we called tense a deictic category because, for example, past tense and future tense identify time phases relative to the "now" of utterances. We noted how commonly references to time are oriented toward the time of speaking, as in 7.3 below:

7.3 We'll put the letters in the post later.

In this sentence both the future tense of the verb and the temporal adverb *later* set up a division of time which is "in the future of now," where "now" is whenever the sentence is uttered.

In chapter 1 we discussed the relationship between semantics and pragmatics. One proposal we reviewed suggested that while both areas of study are concerned with meaning, semantics is the study of conventional, linguistic meaning and pragmatics is the study of how we use this linguistic knowledge in context. In this view, pragmatics is the study of how hearers, for example, have to combine semantic knowledge with other types of knowledge and make inferences in order to interpret a speaker's meaning. In this chapter we focus on areas of meaning where there is very clear evidence of this combination of different types of knowledge. By doing this we move our attention to the study of language use and to what are therefore, for many linguists, pragmatic aspects of meaning. We begin with deixis.

7.2 Deixis

7.2.1 Spatial deixis

The deictic devices in a language commit a speaker to set up a frame of reference around herself. As we will see, every language carries an implicit division of the space around the current speaker, a division of time relative to the act of speaking, and, via pronouns, a shorthand naming system for the participants involved in the talk. To take a simple example, adverbs of location can be used deictically as in 7.4:

7.4 It's too hot **here** in the sun, let's take our drinks into the shade over **there**.

The adverbs *here* and *there* pick out places according to their proximity to the location of the speaker. We can see this because, of course, if the speaker moves, the interpretation of the adverbs will change. When the speaker and her addressee in

7.4 have moved, they can call the shade *here* and their original place in the sun *there*, as in 7.5:

7.5 I'm glad we moved **here,** I was melting **over there**.

Demonstratives work in a similar way: English has a two-term opposition between *this/these* and *that/those*. Once again the current speaker occupies the reference point: items closer to her will be described as *this/these*, items further away as *that/those*. While languages contain such deictic divisions of space, their use has to be calculated by the participants in actual contexts. For example, how big an area is meant by *here* depends on context: a speaker might use *here* to refer to a country, a city, a room, a part of a room, and so on. This plasticity is inherent: the use of *here* does not even always have to include the location of the speaker. We can use *here* pointing to locations on a map, but there will be an actual or implicit contrast with *there*, a place further away from the speaker.

Other languages vary in the number of deictic divisions of space available to the speaker. We can compare English's two-term adverbial distinction between *here* and *there* with Spanish's three-term *aquí* "here," *ahí* "(just) there," and *allí*, "(over) there." Spanish parallels this with a three-term demonstrative system: *este* "this," *ese* "that (just there)," and *aquel* "that (over there)."[1] These demonstratives can be used to give three zones of proximity to the speaker as shown in 7.6. They can also be used to relate to the position of an addressee as in 7.7:

7.6

	near speaker	further away	furthest from speaker
* speaker	———	———	———→
	este	*ese*	*aquel*

7.7 *este* "close to speaker"
ese "close to addressee"
aquel "distant from both"

Languages differ in both how many divisions of space are coded in their demonstratives and what other information is obligatorily included. We can look at some examples. In the West African language Hausa (Afroasiatic; Nigeria, Niger), as 7.8 below shows, the demonstrative and adverbial systems include terms which obligatorily make reference to the location of the addressee (Jaggar 2001: 323–30, 645–47):

7.8 (SP = speaker; ADR = addressee, â = falling tone; a = high tone)
nân "here" (near the SP)
nan "there" (near the ADR)
cân "there" (away from both)
can "there" (further away from both)

The English translation "there" for *nan* in 7.8 is of course inaccurate: as Jaggar and Buba (1994) observe, *nan* has to relate to the vicinity of the addressee and thus a sentence like 7.9 below is impossible:[2]

7.9 ?jèe-ka nan!
"OFF you go there!"

Similar reference to the addressee is reported for Japanese demonstratives and adverbs by Kuno (1973).

Other languages incorporate more complex divisions of space in their demonstratives, for example Malagasy (Austronesian; Madagascar), as shown in 7.10 (Anderson and Keenan 1985: 294):

7.10 Near SP Increasingly far from SP
→
ity *io* *itsy* *iny* *iroa* *iry*

More unusual is the addition of a vertical dimension as is described by Anderson and Keenan (1985: 291) for Daga (Trans-New Guinea; Papua New Guinea), shown in 7.11:

7.11	*oea*	"overhead"	*ea*	"underneath"	*ata*	"same level"
	ao	"up, high"	*ae*	"down, low"	*ase*	"same level, far"
	uta	"higher (near)"	*ita*	"lower (near)"	*ma*	"near SP, this"
	utu	"higher (far)"	*isi*	"lower (far)"	*ame*	"near ADR, that"
	use	"higher (remote)"	*ise*	"lower (remote)"		

As 7.11 shows, these Daga demonstratives distinguish locations in space above, below, and on the same level as the speaker's position.

The examples so far have been of deictic elements relating to location and proximity relative to the speaker. Deictic elements may also include information about motion toward and away from the speaker. We can see this in English: the comparison between *come* and *go* in 7.12 and 7.13 below tells us something about the location of the speaker:

7.12 Don't come into my bedroom.

7.13 Don't go into my bedroom.

This explains why the sentences in 7.14 and 7.15 below sound odd at first:

7.14 ?Fred went to me.

7.15 ?Fred came from me.

We have to interpret the situations described in a rather complicated way to accept these sentences. Some languages have specific deictic motion morphemes: Somali for example has two: *soo* "toward the speaker" and *sii* "away from the speaker," which combine freely with verbs, as in 7.16:

7.16 a. Soo soco!
DEIC walk
"Come this way!, Approach!"

b. Sii soco!
DEIC walk
"Go on over there!, Go away!"

Finally we can end this look at spatial deixis with an example of a very complex system, and one which includes information other than distance and position: Yup'ik (Eskimo-Aleut; Alaska) in 7.17 (Anderson and Keenan 1985: 295):

7.17	**Extended**	**Restricted**	**Obscured**	
	man'a	*una*		"this (near SP)"
	tamana	*tauna*		"that (near ADR)"
			imna	"the aforementioned one"
	ukna			"the one approaching the speaker"
	au͡gna	*ingna*	*amna*	"the one going away from the speaker"
	agna	*ikna*	*akemna*	"the one across there"
	qau͡gna	*kiu͡gna*	*qamna*	"the one inland, inside, upriver"
	qagna	*keggna*	*qakemna*	"the one outside"
	un'a	*kan'a*	*camna*	"the one below, toward river"
	unegna	*ugna*	*cakemna*	"the one downriver, by the exit"
	pau͡gna	*pingna*	*pamna*	"the one up there, away from river"
	pagna	*pikna*	*pakemna*	"the one up above"

The headings in 7.17 describe a semantic classification of the objects to which the demonstratives refer: "extended" forms are for either large expanses of land or water, or objects that are lengthy or moving; "restricted" applies to objects that are stationary, or moving within a confined area, and fairly small in extent, relatively near, and visible; and "obscured" describes objects that are farther away and not clearly in sight. See Anderson and Keenan (1985) for details.

7.2.2 Grammaticalization of context

We can see from the Yup'ik example above that languages vary in the type of semantic information that is obligatorily included in deictic terms. When semantic distinctions are obligatory in this way we will say that they are **grammaticalized**. We can make an informal distinction between, on the one hand, the obligatory "wired-in" ways a language divides up space and time in its function words (like demonstratives and pronouns) or its morphology, and, on the other hand, the ability which seems to exist in all languages to talk about any division of space and time by paraphrase. Thus we can use the latter ability to provide English translations for the Yup'ik demonstratives above. To use a different example: a language like Arabic obligatorily includes information about the gender of the addressee. If, for example, one wants to refer to a single addressee, the choice is as in 7.18 below:

7.18 *'anta* "you (masculine, singular)"
'anti "you (feminine, singular)"

These pronouns have corresponding verbal forms. There is no "you (singular)" pronoun which does not include a gender specification. English on the other hand does not distinguish the gender of the addressee in its pronouns and verbal morphology. To come back to our distinction, this does not mean, of course, that English speakers cannot make reference to the gender of an addressee, merely that this information is not obligatory, that is grammaticalized. In our discussion of deixis we are concerned with cases where contextual features are grammaticalized in language.

7.2.3 Extensions of spatial deixis

Systems of spatial deixis are also used in other domains. For example they are often used as a form of orientation within a discourse, in what we could therefore call **discourse** or **textual deixis,**[3] as when we say ***Here*** *our argument runs into some difficulties* or ***At this point*** *we have to look back to our initial premises*. In many languages too, spatial deixis terms, such as demonstratives, are extended to refer to time.[4] An example of this use of the demonstratives is below:

7.19 **That** year was much hotter than **this** one is.

This transference is often described as a metaphorical shift from the more concrete domain of physical space to the more abstract domain of time. The belief that there is a general human tendency to extend spatial terms in this way to a range of other linguistic domains is sometimes called **localism** (as in for example Lyons 1977). A commonly used example is languages where semantic notions like possession and states are expressed spatially, as in the Irish examples below:

7.20 Tá Porsche agam.
is Porsche at.me
"I have a Porsche."

7.21 Tá slaghdán orm.
is cold on.me
"I have a cold."

7.22 Tá gliondar orm.
is delight on.me
"I am delighted."

In 7.20 possession is expressed spatially, while in 7.21 and 7.22 physical and emotional states are so expressed.[5] A more complicated example which is sometimes quoted is the use of the verb *go* in English and other languages for immediate future tenses as in the future tense reading of *He is going to leave the country*, where the idea of spatial movement away from the speaker is mapped into time as a future event. See Fleischman (1982, 1989) for discussion of these ideas.

7.2.4 Person deixis

Thus far we have concentrated on deictic divisions of space. A further deictic system grammaticalizes the roles of participants: the current speaker, addressee(s), and others. This information is grammaticalized by pronouns: typically a first person singular pronoun is used for the speaker, second person pronouns for addressee(s), and minimally, a third person category for a category "neither-speaker-nor-addressee(s)." This basic three-way system is the basis of most pronoun systems but once again languages differ in the amount of other contextual information that is included in pronouns. We can show this by continuing our comparison of Arabic and English, using just subject pronouns for brevity:

7.23	**Singular**	**Plural**	**Singular or Plural**
	I	we	you
	he	they	
	she		
	it		

7.24	**Singular**	**Dual**	**Plural**
	'anaa "I"		*naḥnu* "we"
	'anta "thou (m)"	*'antumaa* "you (two)"	*'antum* "you (m)"
	'anti "thou (f)"		*'antunna* "you (f)"
	huwa "he, it"	*humaa* "they (two)"	*hum* "they (m)"
	hiya "she, it"		*hunna* "they (f)"

We can see that the Arabic pronouns in 7.24 encode more information about number than the English pronouns in 7.23: there is an extra category *dual*, which is used for "exactly two." The coding of gender is also different: English has a neuter pronoun "it" which does not occur in Arabic, where all third persons have to have either masculine or feminine gender. On the other hand Arabic pronouns encode gender more widely: English only distinguishes between *he* and *she*. So both languages have an economic and "portable" reference system for participants that can be used in any context, but we can see that the packaging of information about participants differs.

One point worth mentioning here is that for obvious reasons there is a difference between the notion of plurality applied to the role of speaker and to non-speaker roles. Since (in normal situations) the speaker is singular, what are called first person plural pronouns actually encode information about some form of identification between the speaker and others. In English it is as simple as that; other languages are more specific. The Ethiopian Omotic language Zayse, for example, has two distinct first person plural pronouns, as shown below (again in subject forms) (Hayward 1990):

7.25 *núy* "we" (including the addressee(s))
níi "we" (not including the addressee(s))

Thus in Zayse, saying the equivalent of "We're going to the party" overtly communicates whether the addressee is included, whereas English speakers have to rely on the context.

7.2.5 Social deixis

The pronoun systems of some languages also grammaticalize information about the social identities or relationships of the participants in the conversation. Some writers, for example Levinson (1983), call this phenomenon **social deixis**. The most obvious example is the distinction in many European languages between "familiar" and "polite" pronouns, for example *tu/vous* in French, *tú/usted* in Spanish, *du/Sie* in German. Speakers of these languages are committed to revealing their calculations of relative intimacy and formality to their addressees. If we identify this category of social deixis, then Asian languages like Japanese, Korean, and Balinese have much richer systems for grammaticalizing social relations. In Japanese, for example, distinctions are marked by the speaker not only in relation to an addressee but also to third persons referred to, as in 7.26 and 7.27 below (Kuno 1973):

7.26 a. *Tanaka-san ga kudasaimashita.*
"Mr Tanaka gave it to me."
[where hearer is on a somewhat formal basis with speaker]
b. *Tanaka-san ga kudasatta.*
"Mr Tanaka gave it to me."
[where hearer is a friend of speaker]

According to Kuno (1973), in both the sentences above Mr Tanaka is in a higher social position than the speaker; we can see the effect of changing the relationship between the speaker and the third person in 7.27 below:

7.27 a. *Jiroo-kun ga kuremashita.*
"Jiro gave it to me."
[where hearer is in a semi-formal relationship with speaker]
b. *Jiroo-kun ga kureta.*
"Jiro gave it to me."
[where hearer is a friend of speaker]

In these sentences Jiro is in a lower social position than the speaker. Comparing 7.26 and 7.27 we can see that distinctions of social relationship have a marked effect on the form of sentences: the speaker's judgments of these are encoded by the choice of verb "to give" and by the verbal endings.

7.3 Reference and Context

Deictic expressions have been extensively studied, but it would be wrong to see their context-dependence as exceptional, as a special part of language. Much of reference involves reliance on context, together with some calculation on the part of the speaker and hearers. A clear example of this is what Clark (1978) calls **shorthands**. Turning on the radio once, I heard this sentence:

7.28 It's a struggle keeping the barnacles from off the crops.

After a while it became clear that *barnacles* was a shorthand for *barnacle geese*. The reference would have been clear, of course, if I had listened from the beginning of the program. This simple example is characteristic of normal language use: speakers calculate how much information their hearers need to make successful references, and where they can, they economize. To give another personal example, I once overheard 7.29 below in a bookshop:

7.29 I'm looking for the new wolf (i.e. Wolfe).

where the speaker obviously felt that *the new Wolfe* was sufficient for the bookseller to identify *the new book by Tom Wolfe*. Another example might be 7.30 below, said during a snooker game:

7.30 He's got two reds left.

Shorthands are sometimes grouped with the notion of **metonymy**, which we briefly discussed in chapter 3, and **synecdoche**. The former is where we identify the referent by something associated with it, as in 7.31 below:

7.31 a. The cover-up extends to **the Oval Office**.
b. Who were all **those suits** drinking in the pub last night?
c. Have you cleared this deal with **the top floor**?

Synecdoche is a form of reference where the part stands for the whole, as in 7.32:

7.32 a. All of his cattle are affected; he'll lose more than fifty **head**.
b. It's good to see some new **faces** in here.

The use of technical terms like shorthands, metonymy, and synecdoche has the disadvantage that it suggests that these are rhetorical devices, special uses of language, whereas they are just specific examples of the routine calculation involved in making reference. We can see this use of context and calculation if we parallel examples from Clark (1978) with a hypothetical situation where someone wants to buy two bottles of Heineken lager. In a pub, they might say *Two bottles of Heineken, please!* In a theatre bar, where only bottled beer is available, their order might be: *Two Heinekens, please!* At a sponsor's stall at an open-air concert, which only serves Heineken beer, in bottle and on draft, they could say: *Two bottles, please!* If the stall only sold bottles, they might say just *Two please!* The point here is that the ordinary use of referring expressions involves calculations of retrievability, which take account of contextual information.

7.4 Knowledge as Context

These calculations of retrievability are really guesses about knowledge: a speaker choosing how to make reference to an entity must make estimations of what her hearers know. So if someone were to rush up to you and shout:

7.33 The baby's swallowed the canary!

their choice of words reveals that they think you can identify both the baby and the canary involved. To discuss the role of knowledge it is useful to divide it into different types. This is not a scientific classification but just a way of organizing our discussion. We might, for example, distinguish between three different sources for the knowledge a speaker has to estimate:

1. that computable from the physical context;
2. that available from what has already been said;
3. that available from background or common knowledge.

Under the first heading we can put the knowledge gained from filling in the deictic expressions, as described in 7.2, that is who is speaking to whom, the time and location of the conversation. Let us examine what might come under the second and third headings.

7.4.1 Discourse as context

Under the second heading, we might view the talk itself, often called the **discourse**, as a kind of context. One clear example of this is the interpretation of sentence fragments. In isolation, fragments like *Ronan did* or *Me too* cannot be interpreted, but in the right conversational context they are meaningful:

7.34 a. Who moved these chairs?
b. Ronan did.

7.35 a. I'm starving.
b. Me too.

Participants would have no difficulty interpreting *Ronan did* as *Ronan moved these chairs*; or *Me too* as *I'm starving too*. Clearly the preceding discourse licenses these interpretations.

We can see another example of the role of the discourse itself as context when we look at the notion of **discourse topic**. It seems clear that in conversing, participants construct a notion of what the discourse is about – a kind of current topic. This topic is a form of knowledge which then influences the way they interpret the meaning of what they subsequently hear. There have been a number of experiments which support this picture. One simple one is described by Brown and Yule (1983: 139–40), from a study by Anderson et al. (1977). Subjects were asked to read the story in 7.36 below, with the "Prisoner" title, then asked questions about it.

7.36 **A Prisoner Plans His Escape**
Rocky slowly got up from the mat, planning his escape. He hesitated a moment and thought. Things were not going well. What bothered him was being held, especially since the charge against him had been weak. He considered his present situation. The lock that held him was strong, but he thought he could break it.

It was generally agreed "that Rocky was alone, that he had been arrested by the police, and that he disliked being in prison" (p. 139). When the same text was presented under another title, the "Wrestler" title in 7.37 below, other subjects agreed that "Rocky was a wrestler who was being held in some kind of wrestling hold and was planning to get out of this hold." (p. 140). In this interpretation there is no prison-cell and no police.

7.37 **A Wrestler in a Tight Corner**
Rocky slowly got up from the mat, planning his escape. He hesitated a moment and thought. Things were not going well. What bothered him was being held, especially since the charge against him had been weak. He considered his present situation. The lock that held him was strong, but he thought he could break it.

The main point here is that listeners add their own inferences when they interpret utterances, fleshing out the material in ways that depend on knowledge provided by the discourse topic. We look at these inferences in more detail a little later in sections 7.6 and 7.7.

7.4.2 Background knowledge as context

Our third type of knowledge has been called many things, including background, common sense, encyclopedic, sociocultural, and real-world knowledge. What is usually meant is the knowledge a speaker might calculate others would have before, or independently of, a particular conversation, by virtue of membership in a community. We are all of course members of many overlapping communities: speakers of our native language, citizens of the same state, city or neighborhood, members of the same sports teams, churches, or political groups, fellow university students, co-workers, and so on. Each community implies certain types of knowledge which might be shared with other members and which conversationalists must seek to calculate as they interact. We can use an example that is so obvious that we may not notice its reliance on cultural knowledge:

7.38 A: I'm hungry.
B: I'll lend you some money.

This exchange gains coherence from the knowledge that money can be exchanged for food, which is cultural knowledge not present in any reasonable dictionary entry for the words *food* or *money*. Much of the fleshing out of an utterance via inference that we mentioned above relies on this kind of background knowledge. To take another invented exchange, in 7.39:

7.39 A: Shall we go and get some ice cream?
B: I'm on a diet.

Here speaker A might reasonably infer that B's reply is a refusal; that B's reply implies "No." We will look at the use of such implications in section 7.7, but what's important here is that the implication and inference both rely on cultural knowledge about diets and ice cream. The fact that it is cultural knowledge which is providing the basis for the inference can be shown by using an example that is less familiar to English speakers, like the exchange in 7.40 below:

7.40 A: Come over next week for lunch.
B: It's Ramadan.

If A knows that B is a Muslim then A will probably infer that B's reply means "No."[6]

In chapter 4 we discussed Stalnaker's (1974) use of the term **common ground** for the presuppositions in a discourse. Clark (1994) adopts this term and distinguishes between **communal** common ground for the knowledge shared by co-members of communities and **personal** common ground for the knowledge two people share from their past experience of each other.

Some slightly different evidence for the importance of background knowledge comes from a study by Kess and Hoppe (1985) on how listeners detect and resolve ambiguity. It is a well-known fact about English sentence structure that adding a prepositional phrase to a verb phrase can cause ambiguity, as in 7.41 below:

7.41 a. John chased the dog.
b. John chased the dog with a stick.

The ambiguity in 7.41b is in whether John or the dog has the stick. Kess and Hoppe provide a list of similar sentences, as in 7.42:

7.42 John chased the dog with the stick.
John chased the dog with the bone.
John chased the dog with the broom.
John chased the dog with the trombone.
John chased the dog with the white tail.
John chased the dog with the pointed ears.
John chased the dog with the black spot.
John chased the dog with the wound.

They suggest that while, structurally, ambiguity should be present in all of these sentences, in fact background knowledge about dogs and people will mean that for most people there is no ambiguity in any but the first sentence in the list. Of course these sentences are given without a context: since "background knowledge" here is a prediction of how typically dogs and people behave, based on experience, the "normal" interpretation can be overruled in a particular context.

7.4.3 Mutual knowledge

One important point about this background knowledge is that while the speaker makes guesses about the knowledge her listeners have, there is no certainty. It is probably a mistake to identify this background knowledge with **mutual knowledge.**[7] This is a topic that has been heavily debated in the philosophical and semantic literature; see for example the collection of papers in N. V. Smith (1982). As linguists have pointed out (e.g. Gibbs 1987), the problem is that if we take from philosophers a tight definition like 7.43 below, the notion is too strong (Gibbs 1987: 565):

7.43 (where S = speaker, A = addressee)
S and A mutually know a proposition P, if and only if:
S knows that P
A knows that P
S knows that A knows that P
A knows that S knows that A knows that P,
... and so on, *ad infinitum*.

For an example of a proposition that might be mutual knowledge in this sense, we can go back to our example 7.39, and extend it slightly below:

7.44 A: Shall we go and get some ice cream?
B: I'm on a diet.
A: Oh, okay.

We could take the mutually known proposition P to be something like "Diets usually prohibit ice cream (because it's too fattening)." So B knows this, and relies for her implication on A knowing it. Since A seems to understand the refusal correctly, then A did know P, and also knows that for B to imply it, A must have known it, and so on.

While there doesn't seem to be a principled way of stopping this chain of reciprocal knowledge as in 7.43, this is obviously not a promising definition for linguists, leading as it does to at least the two following problems:

7.45 a. How can speakers and hearers compute an infinite series of propositions in a finite (actually very small) piece of time?
b. How do S and A ever coordinate what they mutually believe if there's always one more belief statement to be established?

It seems that a plausible pragmatic theory of how participants use background knowledge will have to employ a weaker form of knowledge than this philosophical notion of mutual knowledge. We will not pursue this issue any further here, but see Wilson and Sperber (2012) and Blakemore (1992) for discussions of solutions to this problem. What seems intuitively clear is that the participants' access to background knowledge must be based on guesswork rather than certain knowledge and must involve relatively quick and economic calculations.

7.4.4 Giving background knowledge to computers

The importance of background knowledge to language understanding was quickly recognized in the field of Artificial Intelligence (AI). One typical application is the design of computer programs to process and store information from texts, for example newspaper articles, so that users can later interrogate the databases. These programs quickly revealed the extent to which human readers make inferences to gain an understanding of a text; inferences that are often based on background knowledge. Various forms of knowledge representation have been proposed to model this background information. Roger Schank and his colleagues (Schank and Abelson 1977, Cullingford 1978) devised **scripts** to do this. Scripts are descriptions of what typically goes on in various social settings. One well-known example is a restaurant script of which 7.46 below is a simplified version (written in English rather than a computer language) (Schank and Kass 1988: 190):

7.46
1 Actor goes to a restaurant.
2 Actor is seated.
3 Actor orders a meal from waiter.
4 Waiter brings meal to the actor.
5 Actor eats the meal.
6 Actor gives money to the restaurant.
7 Actor leaves the restaurant.

In this very basic script the underlined elements are variables that have to be filled in from any specific restaurant text the script is applied to. A fuller script than 7.46, with more details of what goes on in a typical restaurant, allowed the computer program Script Applier Mechanism (SAM) to interpret a text about a restaurant visit by using inferences to fill in the gaps in the text. Such a text is in 7.47 below with an interpretation 7.48 (both based on Schank and Abelson 1977), which includes inferences based on the script in 7.46:

7.47 John went to a restaurant. The waiter gave John a menu. The waiter came to the table. John ordered a lobster. John was served quickly. John left a large tip.

7.48 John went to a restaurant. John looked for a table. John went to the table. John sat down in the chair. John got the menu from the waiter. John read the menu. The waiter went to the table. John ordered lobster. The cook prepared the lobster. The waiter got the lobster from the cook. The waiter served John the lobster. John ate the lobster. John indicated to the waiter he would like to get the bill from him. John got the bill from the waiter. John left the waiter a large tip. John paid the bill. John left the restaurant.

As can be seen, inferences based on a script allow a much fuller version of what went on in the visit than is explicit in the text, and SAM is then able to respond to questions about the visit, as shown in an example interrogation 7.49 (based on Schank and Abelson 1977):

7.49
Q: What did John eat?
A: LOBSTER.
Q: Who gave John the menu?
A: THE WAITER.
Q: Who gave John the lobster?
A: PROBABLY THE WAITER.

Q: Who paid the Bill?
A: PROBABLY JOHN.
Q: What happened when John went to the table?
A: JOHN SAT DOWN AND THE WAITER GAVE HIM A MENU.
Q: Why did John get a menu?
A: SO HE COULD ORDER.
Q: Why did John give the waiter a large tip?
A: BECAUSE HE WAS SERVED QUICKLY.

In subsequent work Schank and his colleagues developed this approach further, replacing scripts with knowledge representations which are more flexible and which share components more easily; see Schank and Kass (1988) for a brief overview. This research was influential in the development of case-based reasoning (Kolodner 1992) and knowledge representation in the field of Artificial Intelligence (AI).

7.5 Information Structure

We have been looking at how different types of knowledge provide a contextual background for understanding utterances, and at how speakers routinely make guesses about the knowledge accessible to their listeners. In this section we briefly examine how linguistic structure reflects these guesses, or to put it another way: how these estimates of knowledge are grammaticalized. We will see that speakers "package" their utterances to take account of these estimates of knowledge. This packaging is often called **information structure** or, alternatively, **thematic structure**.

Perhaps the most universally grammaticalized distinction is the basic one between the information which the speaker assumes her hearers already know and the information that the speaker is presenting as additional or new. This distinction is so ubiquitous and grammaticalized in so many different ways that there are a number of different terminologies describing it, as we shall see in the following sections. As a starting point it is simplest to call the already present knowledge **given**, and the additional information **new**.[8] In the next sections we look at some linguistic markers of this distinction.

7.5.1 The information status of nominals

One basic way for a speaker to convey her assumption that something is given is to use a definite nominal. One way to do this in English is to use the definite article *the*; compare for example:

7.50 a. I'm going to the party.
b. I'm going to a party.

The definite article in 7.50a signals that the speaker assumes the hearer can identify the referent, the party. The normal conversation pattern is for items to be introduced by an indefinite nominal, remain conversationally salient for a time, then fade from salience, perhaps later to be reintroduced. This is a very complicated and little-understood process but a simple sketch might go as follows: a nominal will be introduced with a marker that it is new, perhaps an indefinite noun phrase, as in 7.51 below:

7.51 I'm going to **a party** tonight.

Thereafter a definite article can be used to show that it is now given:

7.52 **The party** begins at eleven.

If the party is not mentioned again, it fades from salience and will need to be referred to by various support structures: *that party, that party you mentioned*, and so on. While an entity is accessible, it can be referred to by pronouns, for example

7.53 The party begins at eleven and **it**'ll go on for hours.

The sensitivity of nominal types to information structure has been described in various approaches. Gundel et al. (1993), for example, identify a Givenness Hierarchy for English nominals as below:

7.54 Givenness hierarchy (Gundel et al. 1993)[9]

in focus >	activated >	familiar >	uniquely identifiable >	referential >	type identifiable
{*it*}	{*that* / *this* / *this* N}	{*that* N}	{*the* N}	{indefinite *this* N}	{*a* N}

This hierarchy identifies different information states of a referent, moving left to right from most given to most new. Beneath each states are examples of English nominals typically used for it. These writers use examples like 7.55–6 below (from Gundel et al. 2000), where 7.55 is the sentence that provides the context and 7.56 provides different continuations appropriate in different information states, with the relevant nominal in bold:

7.55 I couldn't sleep last night.

7.56
a. **A dog next door** kept me awake.
b. **This dog next door** kept me awake.
c. **The dog next door** kept me awake.
d. **That dog next door** kept me awake.
e. **This dog/that/this** kept me awake.
f. **It** kept me awake.

In this approach the indefinite article *a* used with the nominal in 7.56a signals the rightmost end of the Givenness Hierarchy: its use just assumes that the hearer can identify the type of thing referred to. The referentially indefinite use of *this* in the b version signals an extra message: that the speaker intends to refer to a particular dog subsequently. The definite article *the* in c signals the assumption that the hearer can identify the referent. The demonstrative *that* in d assumes previous familiarity with the referent from the hearer's part. The demonstrative article *this* and the pronominal versions *this* and *that* in e signal that the referent has been mentioned, or "activated" in the discourse.[10] Finally the pronoun *it* in f shows that the referent is both activated and currently under discussion. Other hierarchies of informational status have been discussed by Ariel (1988) and Prince (1981, 1992).

In a sentence like 7.53 above, *The party begins at eleven and* ***it'll*** *go on for hours*, the reference of *it* is supported by the preceding nominal *the party*. This relationship of indirect reference is called **anaphora**. The nominal *the party* is termed the antecedent and the pronoun *it* is termed an **anaphoric pronoun**. Of course there are constraints on how far apart the antecedent and the anaphoric pronouns may be;[11] moreover, if they are in the same sentence, there are complicated structural conditions on their co-occurrence: see Chomsky (1988) for proposals for describing the latter within generative grammar. We will not pursue these issues here, simply recognizing that the use of anaphoric pronouns is part of this process of grammaticalizing the information status of nominals. As seen in the hierarchy in 7.54 above, for hearers to be able to make reference on the basis of such abbreviatory forms as pronouns, they have to be maximally accessible. We can see the parallel between the anaphoric use of pronouns, where the referents have been introduced into the discourse, and the **deictic** use of pronouns, where the referents are also maximally accessible because they are physically present in the context of the utterance, for example if I point to someone and say:

7.57 That's **him**.

Another way of viewing this process of using indefinite nominals, definite nominals and pronouns to refer to entities is to see it as a kind of filing system, a way of tracking entities through the discourse. We might think of it as a spoken version of the colored lines some novelists are said to use for keeping track of characters and plotlines in their stories. See Givón (1983), Tomlin (1987), and Lambrecht (1994) for studies of the grammaticalization of referential accessibility and the knowledge base of discourse participants.

7.5.2 Focus and topic

Another marker of information structure in English is intonation, where the assignment of primary stress can be used to bring parts of the sentence into prominence. One of the main functions of this prominence is to mark new information. In the following examples, capitals show this primary stress, and we divide the given and new elements of the sentence:

7.58 a. HENRY cleaned the kitchen.
b. Given: Someone cleaned the kitchen.
c. New: It was Henry.

7.59 a. Henry cleaned THE KITCHEN.
b. Given: Henry cleaned something.
c. New: It was the kitchen.

7.60 a. Henry CLEANED the kitchen.
b. Henry did something to the kitchen.
c. He cleaned it.

For a detailed discussion of this use of intonation see Allan (1986, II: 59–163). What the English intonation system is doing here is to allow the speaker to partition the sentence into two elements: a prominent part and the rest.[12] This prominent part is usually called the **focus**. As we see here, one function of focus is to mark new information. Another function allows the speaker to pick out one of a number of alternatives, as in:

7.61 a. Did HARRY take the car?
b. No, GEORGE did.

Here both nominals may be activated in the conversation and the focus now has a **contrastive** function.

In other languages this function of intonation is taken over by specific, otherwise meaningless, words which mark elements of the sentence as in focus or not. Somali, for example, has focus words which include the nominal focus particle *baa*, as shown in 7.62a and b:

7.62 a. *Amina baa wargeyskii keentay.*
Amina FOCUS newspaper brought
"AMINA brought the newspaper, It was AMINA who brought the newspaper."

b. *Amina wargeyskii bay keentay.*
baa + ay
Amina newspaper FOCUS + she brought
"Amina brought THE NEWSPAPER, It was THE NEWSPAPER Amina brought."

This word *baa* follows a nominal and places it in focus. Once again one of the primary uses of this focus system is to mark new information: sentence 7.62a fits a conversational context where it was known that someone brought the newspaper and the sentence asserts it was Amina, while in 7.62b it was known that Amina brought something, and the sentence asserts that it was the newspaper she brought.

These Somali focus words also have the contrastive function described above, as we can see from the proverb below:

7.63 *Libàax yeedháy iyo libàax aammusáy, libàax aammusáy bàa xún.*
lion roared and lion kept:silent lion roared FOCUS bad
"(Of) a roaring lion and a silent lion, A SILENT LION is worse."[13]

As indicated by the English glosses to the examples 7.62a and b above, another way of marking information structure in English is by syntactic constructions. Certain constructions serve to place parts of the sentence in focus, for example the constructions known as **clefts** in 7.64, and the **pseudo-cleft** in 7.65, where the focus elements are underlined:

7.64 a. It was yesterday that Bob came.
b. It was Bob who came yesterday.

7.65 What we want is a living wage.

Once again we can see that focus is part of information structure: in 7.64a and b the basic situation described is the same: *Bob came yesterday*, but the information is packaged differently to fit different states of participants' knowledge at the specific point in the conversation.

There is another important information structure role that is marked in languages, that of **topic**. We discussed in section 7.4.1 the notion of discourse topic; that is, a general idea among participants of what the current topic of discussion is. As Halliday and Hasan (1976) pointed out, such discourse topics are maintained by a battery of conversational devices, including anaphora, using related lexemes, repetition of lexemes, all of which create a cohesion to discourses that make them more than a collection of unrelated sentences. In addition some languages have **sentence topics**: see for example the Japanese sentences below, from Kuno (1973: 44):

7.66 *Kuzira* *wa* *honyuu-doobutu* *desu*
whale TOPIC mammal is
"Speaking of whales, they are mammals, A whale is a mammal."

7.67 *John* *wa* *watakusi* *no* *tomodati* *desu*
John TOPIC I 's friend is
"Speaking of John, he is my friend."

In these examples the topic occurs at the beginning of the sentence and identified by a following particle *wa*. In the following Mandarin Chinese example from Li and Thompson (1976: 468) the topic is again initial but there is no special morpheme:

7.68 *Nèikē* *shù* *yèzi* *dà*
that tree leaves big
"That tree (topic), the leaves are big."

The major characteristic of topics is that they must be "entered into the registry of the present discourse" as Kuno (1973: 45) put it. The function of this kind of topic is characterized by Chafe (1976: 50) as limiting the applicability of the rest of the sentence:

7.69 Typically, it would seem, the topic sets a spatial, temporal, or individual framework within which the main predication holds.

As the translations in 7.66–7 show, there is no exact correspondence in English to these sentence topics. Many of the features of topics are typical of subjects in English, for example: that they are typically given information, often activated elements; that they tend to occur at the beginning of sentences; and that they are in some sense what the sentence is "about." There are also, especially in spoken English, sentences like those below:

7.70 As for the referendum, it's a foregone conclusion.

7.71 Me, I've been a Liverpool fan all my life.

In such sentences the first part, before the comma, seems rather like a topic. These though are rather marginal constructions in the language and speakers tend to avoid using them in writing. Li and Thompson (1976) argue that languages differ systematically in their use of sentence topics and subjects. They identify four types: subject prominent languages (like English); topic-prominent languages (like Chinese); languages where both topics and subjects are important (like Japanese); and finally, languages where neither is important. For this last type they suggest as an example Tagalog (Austronesian; Philippines). Traditionally observers speak of the first type having a subject-predicate structure to their sentences, while the second type have a topic-comment structure. In each case the claim is that the basic organization of the sentence is related to the speaker's decisions about its information structure.

7.5.3 Information structure and comprehension

Brown and Yule (1983: 128) cite an example from a talk by M. A. K. Halliday which demonstrates the importance of information structure to comprehension. Halliday, who has written detailed studies of discourse structure, (e.g. Halliday and Hasan 1976), quoted a US radio report describing an official welcome for astronauts, as in 7.72 below:

7.72 The sun's shining, it's a perfect day. Here come the astronauts. They're just passing the Great Hall; perhaps the President will come out to greet them. No, it's the admiral who's taking the ceremony...

Halliday then altered the markers of information structure to produce the text in 7.73:

7.73 It's the sun that's shining, the day that's perfect. The astronauts come here. The Great Hall they're just passing; he'll come out to greet them the President. No, it's the ceremony that the admiral's taking...

As can be seen, the use of inappropriate markers of information structure, in effect disregarding the reader's evolving state of knowledge, makes the text incoherent and difficult to read. The point is of course that in reality speakers continually assess their audience's knowledge, and package their utterances accordingly.

7.6 Inference

Throughout our discussion of the role of context, we have seen examples of the way that listeners actively participate in the construction of meaning, in particular by using inferences to fill out the text toward an interpretation of speaker meaning. We now turn to look at examples of conversational inference, first with a general discussion in this section, then with a look at one important approach to inference, conversation implicature, in section 7.7.

We can begin our examples of inference with anaphora. As described above, this is a special subtype of **coreference**, a referential relation between expressions where they both refer to the same entity. There are many types of coreference: a nominal may be repeated as in 7.74; there may be an independent nominal, used as an epithet as in 7.75, or very commonly, an anaphoric pronoun may be used as in 7.76. As mentioned earlier, anaphoric pronouns differ from full nominals in that they have no independent reference and must rely on an antecedent.

7.74 I fell down a hole yesterday. **The hole** was very deep.

7.75 I saw your brother this morning. **The old fool** still doesn't recognize me.

7.76 I trod on a slug this morning. **It** died.

Very commonly interpreting anaphora across sentences involves inference. Take for example the interpretation of the pronoun **it** (shown in bold) in 7.77 below:

7.77 The plane was late, the hotel wasn't fully built, there were crowds everywhere she went. I think **it** really disappointed her.

If we are to look for a nominal antecedent for the pronoun *it* in 7.77, possible candidates are *the plane*, *the hotel*, *crowds*. It seems more likely though that it is the whole situation that *it* refers back to: a kind of composite antecedent we could call something like *the holiday*. This cumulative antecedent has to be constructed by the listener. This kind of "sloppy" use of pronouns is very common, but seems to cause listeners no difficulty.[14]

There are other inferential links routinely made between sentences. Some were called **bridging inferences** by Clark (1977). Below are a few of his examples:

7.78 a. I looked into the room. **The ceiling** was very high.
b. I walked into the room. **The windows** looked out to the bay.
c. I walked into the room. **The chandeliers** sparkled brightly.
d. John went walking out at noon. **The park** was beautiful.

In each of these examples, the nominal in bold occurs with a definite article, showing that the speaker assumes that referent is accessible to the listener, that is, it is given. In each case the question is: how, if it has not been mentioned earlier, nor is physically present at the utterance, did this nominal become part of given information? The answer seems to be that the listener makes a bridging inference which links the nominal to the preceding sentence and creates coherence. In these examples the basis for the inferences seems to be background knowledge. People know that rooms usually have ceilings, commonly have windows, may have chandeliers, and that one of the conventional places to go for a walk is in a park. With this knowledge, the listener can infer, for example, that the park referred to in 7.78d is the one that John went walking in.

What the listeners seem to be doing here is making inferences to preserve a notion of coherence in what they are told. Speakers seem confident that their listeners will do this and they take advantage of it to speak less explicitly than they might. The following are examples of where the speaker seems to rely on listener inferences:

7.79 I left early. I had a train to catch.
INFERENCE: Speaker left **because** of having to catch the train.

7.80 A: Did you give Mary the money?
B: I'm waiting for her now.
INFERENCE: B did not give Mary the money.

Knowing that their listeners will flesh out their utterances with inferences gives speakers the freedom to imply something rather than state it. In the next section we look at one particular type of implication identified in the pragmatics literature, **conversational implicature**.

7.7 Conversational Implicature

The term conversational implicature was introduced by the philosopher H. Paul Grice. In lectures and a couple of very influential articles (Grice 1975, 1978, 1989), he proposed an approach to the speaker's and hearer's cooperative use of inference. As we suggested above, there seems to be enough regularity in the inference-forming behavior of listeners for speakers to exploit this by implying something, rather than stating it. Grice, investigating the gap between what a speaker explicitly says and what her intended meaning is understood to be, suggested that the success of this type of communication could be explained by postulating a **cooperative principle**, as below:

7.81 Grice's Co-operative Principle (Grice 1989: 26)
Make your contribution such as is required, at the stage at which it occurs, by the accepted purpose or direction of the talk exchange in which you are engaged.

This principle is a kind of tacit agreement by speakers and listeners to recognize and participate in events of interactive communication. The principle allows participants to make assumptions about each other's goals and conversational strategies. In this view it supports the use of inferences for communication, such as the inference communicated in 7.80 above, which would be termed a conversational implicature.[15]

It would be a mistake to interpret this too widely: we may assume that Grice is not identifying in human interaction a utopian ideal of rational and egalitarian cooperation. As sociolinguists have shown us, people use language as an integral part of their social behavior, whether competing, supporting, expressing solidarity, dominating, or exploiting. Grice's observations are focused at a different, more micro-level: if I am in conflict with you, I still may want to communicate my intentions to you, and assume you will work out the implications of my utterances. The proposal is that shared assumptions license the exploitation of inference as part of linguistic communication.

7.7.1 Grice's maxims of conversational cooperation

The assumptions that hearers make about a speaker's conduct seemed to Grice to be of several different types, giving rise to different types of inference, or, from the speaker's point of view, implicatures. In identifying these, Grice called them **maxims**, and phrased them as if they were injunctions: Do *thus*! This can be misleading: it is important to realize that the conversational principles that Grice proposed are not rules, like phonological or morphological rules, which people have to follow to speak a language; nor are they moral principles. Perhaps the best way to interpret a maxim *Do X!* is to translate it into a descriptive statement: the hearer seems to assume that the speaker is doing *X* in communicating. We can see this by looking at the maxims and some examples.

Grice's four main maxims are as follows (Grice 1975, 1978):

7.82 *The Maxim of Quality*
Try to make your contribution one that is true, i.e.
1. Do not say what you believe is false
2. Do not say that for which you lack adequate evidence.

The Maxim of Quantity
1. Make your contribution as informative as is required (for the current purposes of the exchange)
2. Do not make your contribution more informative than is required.

The Maxim of Relevance (Relation)
Make your contributions relevant.

The Maxim of Manner
Be perspicuous, and specifically:
1. Avoid ambiguity
2. Avoid obscurity
3. Be brief
4. Be orderly.

As suggested above, these maxims can be viewed as follows: the listener will assume, unless there is evidence to the contrary, that a speaker will have calculated her utterance along a number of parameters: she will tell the truth, try to estimate what her audience knows and package her material accordingly, have some idea of the current topic, and give some thought to her audience being able to understand her. To repeat: these are assumptions the listener starts out with; any or all may be wrong, and he may realize this or not, but this is a kind of baseline for talking.

We can look at a couple of examples of how these maxims help the hearer arrive at implicatures; we focus on the maxims of relevance and quantity:

7.83 Relevance
A: Can I borrow ten euros?
B: My purse is in the hall.
(Implicature: Yes.)

Here it is A's assumption that B's reply is intended to be relevant that allows the inference: yes. The implicature in 7.83 has three characteristics: firstly, that it is implied rather than said; secondly, that its existence is a result of the context, the specific interaction – there is, of course, no guarantee that in other contexts *My purse is in the hall* will mean "yes"; the third characteristic is that such implicatures are cancellable, or **defeasible** in the terminology we used in chapter 4, without causing a contradiction. Thus the implicature "yes" in 7.83 can be cancelled in 7.84 below by the addition of extra clauses:

7.84 Defeasibility of implicature
A: Can I borrow ten euros?
B: My purse is in the hall. But don't you dare touch it. I'm not lending you any more money.

This behavior contrasts with the semantic relation of entailment discussed earlier in chapter 4, as shown in 7.85 below. The sentence 7.85a has the entailment in 7.85b, assuming constancy of reference; and 7.85c shows that canceling it produces anomaly:

7.85 a. The president was assassinated yesterday.
b. The president is dead.
c. ?The president was assassinated yesterday but he's not dead.

Our next example involves the maxim of quantity:

7.86 Quantity
A: Did you do the reading for this week's seminar?
B: I intended to.
(Implicature: No.)

Here B's answer would of course be true if B intended to do the reading and then did, but then the answer would violate the maxim of quantity. A, assuming the maxim to be observed, is likely to infer the answer no. Once again the implicature is implied, contextual, and cancelable. Another typical example is 7.87 below:

7.87 Quantity
A: Did you drink all the bottles of beer in the fridge?
B: I drank some.
(Implicature: B didn't drink them all.)

Once again, logically if B drank all of the beer, then B drank some of the beer. So B's reply would be true in this case. However, the maximum of quantity would lead A to the implicature above, assuming that B would otherwise make the more informative reply.

A further property of Gricean conversational implicatures is that they are reinforceable without causing redundancy, so the sentence 7.88a below may communicate the implicature in 7.85b and explicitly stating this does not cause redundancy in 7.88c.

7.88 a. Some of her friends are musicians.
b. Not all of her friends are musicians.
c. Some of her friends are musicians but not all of them.

Once again this contrasts with entailment where the sentence *The president was assassinated yesterday and he is dead* seems to involve redundancy.

Grice made a distinction between **particularized conversational implicatures** (PCIs) and **generalized conversational implicatures** (GCIs). The former are instances, like 7.83 above, where the implicature is entirely context dependent. The latter are instances like 7.85 above where the implicature is more predictable and less context dependent. The word *some* may imply *not all* across a range of contexts. However, it is still cancelable, as in 7.88. A GCI can be seen as a form of default that can be overridden in context. See Levinson (2000) for an extended discussion of this phenomenon.

As mentioned above, these maxims are basic assumptions, not rules, and they can be broken. Grice distinguished between the speaker secretly breaking them, for example by lying, which he termed **violating** the maxims; and overtly breaking them for some linguistic effect, which he called **flouting**. We take an example of the creative flouting of the maxim of manner from Flann O'Brien's novel *At-Swim-Two-Birds* (1967: 38):

7.89 The three of us were occupied in putting glasses of stout into the interior of our bodies and expressing by fine disputation the resulting sense of physical and mental well-being.

From a linguist's point of view cases of flouting are more interesting than violations of maxims. Irony, for example, can be seen as a flouting of the maxim of quality, as for example, if you say to a friend who has done something terrible to you: *You're a fine friend.* Indeed the cooperative principle often forms an important part of the **literal language theory** described in chapter 1. In this theory the principle is often viewed as the engine which drives the interpretation of non-literal utterances. The explanation goes like this: if a listener interprets an utterance as literally untrue or nonsensical, the principle may lead him to search for a further level of meaning, **figurative** language, which preserves the maxim of quality. Thus the listener will be led to interpret rather than reject as impossible the **metaphors** in 7.90 below, or the **hyberbole** in 7.91:

7.90 a. He lit the stage with his talent.
b. She just lapped up all the compliments.

7.91 a. I've read this millions of times.
b. You're the only woman in my life.

One possible criticism of these maxims, for example the maxim of manner, is that they contain a built-in assumption of one type of language use: one that is clear and informative. By contrast, most cultures have types of language use where obscurity and ambiguity are expected and valued: perhaps poetry and riddles, or, more mundanely, advertising. One solution might be to relativize the maxims to some classification of talk interaction, such as is discussed in studies in the ethnography of communication; see, for example, Gumperz and Hymes (1972).

A number of writers have proposed cooperative principles like the ones we have been discussing. Brown and Levinson (1978), for example, have identified a politeness principle, as discussed in Leech (1983) and Allan (1986), which we will return to in the next chapter. Meanwhile, Grice's cooperative principle and maxims have been much developed in subsequent work; we discuss two strands of this work in the next two sections.

7.7.2 Generalizing the Gricean maxims

Subsequent writers have attempted to reduce Grice's original four maxims (and eight sub-maxims). In one tradition the Quality maxim is elevated to a higher level than the others and seen as a prerequisite for all others. Thereafter Horn (1984, 1989, 1996), for example, collapses several maxims into two general principles: a Q-principle and an R-principle, which are held to be in tension with each other. The Q-principle draws together Grice's first Quantity maxim and the first two sub-maxims of Manner. It is a kind of guarantee of informational adequacy to the hearer. It is may be informally characterized as:

7.92 Q-principle: Say as much as you can, balancing against the R-principle.

The R-principle is a principle of speaker economy; it subsumes the Relevance maxim and the last two maxims of Manner, and can be represented as:

7.93 R-principle: Say no more than you must, balancing against the Q-principle.

One area where the Q-principle is held to operate is in scalar implicatures (Gazdar 1979, Horn 1989). This is the claim that certain linguistic expressions form a scale of strength, <*x*, *y*>, where *x* is stronger than *y*, for example:

7.94 Q-principle scales
- a. <all, some>
- b. <be certain that, think that>
- c. <succeed in, try to>

Strength here is a notion of informational content and also involves an asymmetrical relation of entailment, the semantic relation discussed in chapter 4. The stronger expression *x* entails *y* but *y* does not entail *x*. Thus *all* entails *some* but *some* does not entail *all*. The idea is that when a speaker utters a weaker expression from a scale, the Q-principle ensures that the hearer infers that the speaker believes the stronger expression does not hold. This explains the following implicatures:

7.95
- a. Jane ate some of the biscuits IMPLICATES Jane didn't eat all of them.
- b. I think she's at home IMPLICATES I'm not certain she's home.
- c. I tried to buy you some flowers IMPLICATES I didn't buy you some flowers.

In simple terms, though if Jane in 7.95a did eat all the biscuits she surely ate some of them, to use *some* when *all* would apply is held to be a violation of the Q-principle and therefore uncooperative, in Gricean terms.

The R-principle is used to explain why longer forms have different interpretation than shorter ones, when they seem to be paraphrases of each other. See for example the pairs:

7.96 a. Leonora caused her husband to die.
b. Leonora killed her husband.

7.97 a. I don't not like you.
b. I like you.

In 7.96a the periphrastic use of two clauses weakens the chain of cause and effect relative to 7.96b. It would be odd to use 7.96a if for example Leonora stabbed her husband to death in a violent rage. The sentences in 7.97 show that a double negative often has a different interpretation than a corresponding positive: in ordinary use 7.97a doesn't quite mean the same as 7.97b. In both these examples the shorter form is assumed to be the expected form because of the R-principle; the longer forms, as violations, will therefore carry extra levels of meaning.[16]

7.7.3 Relevance Theory

A more radical development of Grice's maxims is Relevance Theory (Sperber and Wilson 1995, Wilson and Sperber 2012). This approach seeks to unify the Gricean cooperative principle and conversational maxims into a single principle of relevance that will motivate a hearer's inferential strategy:

7.98 Principle of relevance
Every act of ostensive communication communicates the presumption of its own optimal relevance. (Sperber and Wilson 1995: 158)

For these writers the term **ostensive communication** describes a situation where there is interaction: the communicator wants to signal something and create a mutual environment of communication and this intention is recognized by her hearers. This is the situation of ordinary conversation.

This principle follows Grice in recognizing that hearers can assume a speaker has a communicative intent. In this theory it is this intent that leads her to calculate the relevance of her utterance with the hearer's role in mind. In Relevance Theory this is often described as a speaker calculating a balance between communicative profit and loss from the hearer's point of view. The profit is the extent to which the communication produces cognitive effects (e.g. changing existing knowledge); the loss is the processing cost where the closer the new information is to already existing knowledge, the less "expensive" it is to assimilate it. The hearer takes this speaker calculation for granted when making his inferences.

One characteristic of Relevance Theory is the argument that the inferential processes that we identify as leading from the basic meaning of an utterance to its conversational implicatures are also involved in getting to the "basic" meaning in the first place. Blakemore (1992: 58) discusses a traditional example of implicature in 7.99 below, where B's answer produces the implicature shown.

7.99 A: Did you enjoy your holiday?
B: The beaches were crowded and the hotel was full of bugs.
(B's implicature: No, I didn't enjoy my holiday)

Blakemore argues that pragmatic processes of another more basic sort are involved in the interpretation of B's utterance. The hearer A has a number of problems to solve because of the sketchiness of the linguistic input. For example, what were the beaches crowded with? Which hotel is referred to? Which meaning of the word bug is involved, for example electronic listening device, or insect? She argues that we get the answers to these by pragmatic processes, and that these processes necessarily produce an intervening phase which underlies the production of implicatures. This two-phase interpretation gives us 7.100a and b from B's reply in 7.99:

7.100 a. The beaches at the holiday resort that the speaker went to were crowded with people and the hotel he stayed at was full of insects.
b. The speaker did not enjoy his holiday.

To get to 7.100a the hearer must perform certain tasks, including for example determining which hotel is referred to. In this theory the correct target for reference will be the one that makes the resulting proposition maximally relevant to the accessible context. Clearly the most relevant hotel to B's holiday story is the one he stayed in. This information being accessible in the context relies on the real-world knowledge that beach holidays often involve staying in hotels. Other tasks involve expanding elliptical expressions: that the beaches were crowded with people; and resolving lexical ambiguity: that the bugs are insects. Clearly in a context where A and B are spies, the most accessible interpretation might have bugs as listening devices. These interpretations, which are expansions of the original underspecified linguistic input, are called **explicatures** in this theory. They too are licensed by the principle of relevance and they form the basis for further inferential steps to arrive at the conversational implicature in 7.100b.

In their account of implicature, writers in this theory make a distinction between **implicated premises** and **implicated conclusions**. We can illustrate these terms by modifying an example from Sperber and Wilson (1995: 194):

7.101 a. Peter: Would you drive a Saab?
b. Mary: I wouldn't drive ANY Swedish car.
(Mary's implicature: I would not drive a Saab.)

Mary's implicature is called an implicated conclusion and fits what is traditionally called a conversational implicature. However, for it to be derived, Mary has introduced into the context the linking assumption:

7.102 A Saab is a Swedish car.

In this theory 7.102 is called an implicated premise. It is not directly stated and therefore is implicated but it is provided as an inferential support for the final implicature, or implicated conclusion. Note that the implicated premise 7.102 need not be known by the hearer; in 7.101 if Peter doesn't know a Saab is Swedish he will infer it in order to preserve the relevance of Mary's reply in 7.101b.

In summary, in this theory one overarching principle of relevance is used to describe a whole range of inferential behavior. The theory stresses the underdetermination of meaning and its reliance on context and inference. Through the notion of explicatures these writers take the process of inference in understanding deep into traditional areas of semantics and reduce the importance of literal or context-free meaning.

7.8 Lexical Pragmatics

In the last section we saw the view that linguistic form underdetermines meaning and that contextual processes are required to derive explicit content. One application of this idea at word level is **lexical pragmatics** (Blutner 1998, 2004, Wilson and Carston 2006, 2007), which seeks to investigate how the meanings of words reflect or are adjusted to specific contexts. Though the currency of the term is relatively new the issues addressed have long been a concern of semantics. We saw in chapter 3 how the notion of polysemy is invoked to account for distinct but related senses of the same semantic word or lexeme. We saw too that a major problem in identifying polysemy is judging the extent to which meaning differences in uses of a word are fixed or derived in context. The verb *open* for example seems to describe different actions depending on what is being opened:

7.103 Verb *open*
- a. Joan opened the door.
- b. Joan opened the wine.
- c. Joan opened the curtains.
- d. Joan opened the box.
- e. Joan opened her eyes.
- f. Joan opened the book.

Rather than assuming that there are many distinct senses of *open* we could instead assume that there is a basic semantic specification that is modulated in context to access the intended specific meaning. In Relevance Theory (Wilson and Carston 2006, 2007), for example, this contextual modulation is seen as an inferential process governed by the principle of relevance.

Several such inferential processes have been identified in the literature, including **broadening** (Wilson and Carston 2006, Vega-Moreno 2007), which is a process where the concept expressed by use of a lexical item is more general than that usually assumed to be linguistically encoded.[17] Examples include words for shapes as in (7.104), where the sense of the words *rectangular* and *square* are extended:

7.104
- a. Bornholm Island is rectangular.
- b. His father has a square face too.

In these examples it is unlikely that the speaker intends the strictly geometric sense of the word.

Other uses identified as broadening are **hyperbole** and **category extension**. Examples (7.105a–b) below for example might exemplify hyperbole in certain contexts: if (7.105a) is uttered in a restaurant it is likely that the speaker means "not cooked enough for me to enjoy," while (7.105b) uttered in an everyday context might broaden *freezing* to *very cold*:

7.105 a. This steak is raw.
b. Your hands are freezing.

One type of category extension is exemplified in (7.106) below, where brand names are used to denote a broader category of items or activities:

7.106 a. She can just google the restaurant.
b. It's not a serious cut: a band aid will do.

A further process of lexical adjustment is **narrowing**, as in Wilson and Carston's (2006: 409) example:

7.107 All politicians drink.

Here the meaning of drink has been narrowed from the meaning "drinks liquid" to mean "drinks alcohol" and possibly further, to "drinks alcohol in sufficient quantities to be worth commenting on." In Relevance Theory terms, drinking liquid is clearly necessary for staying alive and in most contexts the fact that a person drinks liquid has no obvious relevance. Thus in many contexts the expected interpretation of 7.108 below:

7.108 Brian doesn't drink.

is that Brian doesn't drink alcohol.

Within Relevance Theory the derivation of contextual lexical meaning from minimal lexical forms is explained by work from psychology on the process of **ad hoc concept** construction (Barsalou 1983, 1987, 1993, Rubio Fernandez 2008), where individuals form novel categories relevant to their current interest, such as *tourist activities to perform in Dublin*. Wilson and Carston (2007) quote Murphy's (1997) experimental work on evidence for distinct word senses by respondents' supplied antonyms. For the English word *fresh* when used with different nouns these include those in 7.109:

7.109 Antonyms of fresh (Murphy 1997: 237–39)

fresh	ANTONYMS
shirt	dirty
vegetables	rotten
fish	frozen
sheets	recently slept-in

water	dirty/salt
bread	stale
air	polluted
outlook	tired
assistant	experienced
idea	old

They argue that the variation in meaning, reflected in the different antonyms, is typical of the process by which a general lexical concept, here FRESH, gets "tailored" to individual contexts. In this approach the localized concept is conventionally shown starred, that is FRESH* for this example. One important aspect of this approach is the claim that lexical pragmatic processes like broadening and narrowing can be used to explain metaphorical extension in examples like (7.110), an idea discussed in a different framework by Glucksberg and Keysar (1990):

7.110 His boss is a shark.

Here the ad hoc concept SHARK* would be seen as a contextually adjusted version of the encyclopedic lexical entry SHARK. In this Relevance Theory approach the word *boiling* in example 7.111 below could be intended and interpreted as literal, approximation, hyperbole, or metaphor, depending on the contextual features and inferential process involved (Wilson and Carston 2007: 248–49):

7.111 The water is boiling.

7.9 Summary

One basic conclusion from this chapter is that to understand an utterance hearers have to access and use contextual information of different types. We have seen, for example, that a hearer has to be able to perform the interpretative tasks in 7.112:

7.112
a. Fill in deictic expressions.
b. Fix the reference of nominals.
c. Access background knowledge.
d. Make inferences.

Each of these tasks involves calculation. Hearers have to create meaning by combining linguistic and contextual information; in doing so, they make inferences as a matter of course. We have seen several examples of this, including shorthand expressions and conversational implicature. These tasks draw upon different types of knowledge, which we can classify as in 7.113:

7.113
a. the language used (e.g. English, French, Arabic),
b. the local contextual information (e.g. when and where uttered, and by whom),
c. background knowledge (e.g. cultural practices).

In this chapter we have concentrated on fleshing out the second and third types of knowledge. For the first of course the hearer needs to know linguistic facts, for example that the activity of writing is described by the verb *kataba* in Arabic and *escribir* in Spanish, or that the current speaker calls herself *je* in French or *ég* in Icelandic.

This distinction between types of knowledge brings us back to the issue of the division between semantics and pragmatics, discussed in chapter 1. Is only the use of the first type of knowledge in 7.113 above properly part of semantics, leaving the use of the second and third types to pragmatics? If so, and many linguists would accept this, many of the processes of interpreting meaning that we have discussed in this chapter, for example interpreting deictic expressions and forming conversational implicatures, are part of pragmatics. One related problem is what to call this first type of knowledge: if we call it "meaning," then what do we call the result of combining it with contextual information to get the final message?

One response is to distinguish between three types of meaning: the conventional meaning of words and sentences in the language, the speaker's intended meaning, and the hearer's constructed meaning. Another possibility is to call the linguistically encoded sentence meaning, simply **meaning**; the speaker meaning, **content**; and the hearer meaning, **interpretation**.[18] If we use these latter terms, then our basic observation in this chapter has been that meaning underrepresents content and that the hearer must enrich meaning to get an interpretation. The extent to which this interpretation corresponds to content will determine the success of the communication. As pointed out by the American linguist W. D. Whitney over a hundred years ago, communication is a process of interpretation (1867: 14–15):

7.114 Sentences are not images of thoughts, reflected in a faultless mirror; or even photographs, needing only to have the color added: they are but imperfect and fragmentary sketches, giving just outlines enough to enable the sense before which they are set up to seize the view intended, and to fill it out to a complete picture; while yet, as regards the completeness of the filling out, the details of the work, and the finer shades of coloring, no two minds will produce pictures perfectly accordant with one another, nor will any precisely reproduce the original.

The balance in spoken communication between learned, conventional meaning, and contextual inference is at issue in current semantic and pragmatic theories.

EXERCISES

7.1 Give two examples of each of the following:

a. shorthand expressions
b. metonymy
c. synecdoche

For the shorthands you should give the contextual information that would allow their use.

7.2 Underline the deictic expressions in the following sentences and describe which type of deixis (**person, time, space**) is involved.

a. She is sitting over there.
b. This is the biggest room in the house.
c. Bring him in whenever you're ready.
d. I'll see you tomorrow.
e. They were here, looking at this painting.

7.3 We discussed how the use of **a definite nominal** reflects a speaker's confidence that the referent is **accessible** to her audience. We saw that this confidence can derive from several sources, including the referent being unique in the wider discourse (e.g. *the sun, the Pope, the President*); being physically present in the context (i.e. via **deixis**); being already talked about (e.g. **anaphora**); being available from lexical relations like **meronymy** (e.g. *the kitchen* when talking about a house), or being **inferable**.

In the following pairs of sentences, the definite nominal (marked in bold) in the second sentence is accessible because of the first sentence. We could say that its definiteness is **licensed** by the first sentence. Decide whether this licensing relationship is due to:

1 **anaphora**
2 **hyponymy**
3 **meronymy**
4 none of these and the link must be based on an **inference** by the listener.

a. I chose a dog for her. **The animal** turned out to be vicious.
b. He made a sandwich for me. **It** was delicious.
c. I went sailing last week and I hated it. **The motion** made me really sick.
d. She walked into the cinema. **The seats** had all been removed.
e. Don't buy this car. **The engine** is useless.
f. He drove the car very erratically. I kept **the vehicle** in sight.
g. They drove me to the airport. I couldn't believe **the traffic jams**.

7.4 We saw that the **information structure** of a sentence reflects its context in the conversation. The examples below consist of a sentence followed by several candidates for a continuing sentence. In each case the candidates describe the same basic situation but have the information packaged differently in their information structure. Choose the continuation sentences (there may be more than one) which best fit the previous sentence. Discuss how differences in earlier sentences, not given below, might influence your choice.

1 Was it Henry who brought in the groceries?
 a. No, Fred brought the groceries in.
 b. No, it was the groceries that Fred brought in.
 c. No, what Fred brought in was the groceries.
 d. No, it was Fred who brought the groceries in.

2 Watching the house, Maguire saw a car arrive.
 a. The car turned into the driveway.
 b. It was the driveway the car turned into.
 c. What turned into the driveway was the car.
 d. It was the car that turned into the driveway.

3 I just want to know who made this coffee.
 a. I made the coffee.
 b. The coffee was made by me.
 c. What was made by me was the coffee.
 d. What I made was the coffee.

4 Kelly picked up her jacket and walked out of the kitchen.
 a. The hall was dark.
 b. What was dark was the hall.
 c. It was the hall that was dark.
 d. It was dark, the hall.

7.5 Below are a series of invented exchanges. Using Grice's notion of conversational implicature, give for each a likely implicature of B's reply. Discuss, firstly, the contextual information you have to supply in order to support your proposal, and secondly, the reasons B might have for using an implicature rather than a simple statement.

a. A: Are you coming out for a pint tonight?
 B: My in-laws are coming over for dinner.

b. A: How did United play this afternoon?
 B: Well, eleven guys wearing United shirts ran out onto the pitch.

c. A: I'm going to tell those young thugs to stop smoking in this compartment.
 B: Do you have life insurance?

d. A: Are you going to wear those trousers?
 B: They're brand new. I just bought them.

e. A: A lot of people's livelihoods depend on your performance today.
 B: Thanks, that really takes the pressure off.

f. A: Does my smoking bother you?
 B: I can't say that it doesn't.

g. A: Where are you going?
 B: Out.

h. A: Would you like a beer?
 B: Is the Pope a Catholic?

7.6 Speakers, aware that they are going to violate a Gricean maxim, often use **hedges** to introduce their utterance; thereby signaling their awareness of the coming violation. For the following hedges, say what Gricean maxim you think is about to be violated:

a. I may have got it all wrong but I thought...
b. I don't quite know how to say this, but...
c. This is what the papers are saying; I haven't heard it myself...
d. I can't say too much about this, it's still *sub judice*...
e. This may sound like a stupid question, but...

7.7 In discussing Horn's notion of Q-principle scales in section 7.7.2 we noted that in a scale <*x*, *y*>, where *x* is a stronger term, uttering *y* implicates "not *x*." Thus *some* implicates *not all*. Use this behavior to discuss whether the following are valid scales in this sense:

a. <always, sometimes>
b. <certainly, possibly>
c. <hot, warm>
d. <more than, as many as>
e. <five, four>
f. <none, not all>

7.8 In section 7.8 we discussed the process of **broadening** where the concept expressed by use of a lexical item is more general than that we might assume to be the dictionary definition. Find or invent your own examples of lexical broadening using the words and phrases below:

a. starving
b. a thousand
c. painless
d. genius
e. flat

7.9 In section 7.8 we also discussed lexical **narrowing**, where the intended meaning is narrower than the conventional meaning of a word. Find or invent your own examples of lexical narrowing using the words below:

a. bird
b. color
c. money
d. body
e. reputation

FURTHER READING

Levinson (2004) provides an overview of deixis, while Fillmore (1997) is a lively discussion of topics in deixis. Brown and Yule (1983) include discussions of information structure, discourse topic, and coherence. Culicover and McNally (1998) have a number of papers on the influence of information structure on grammar. Levinson (2000) presents a development of Grice's approach to conversational implicature similar to that described in 7.7.2. Clark (2013) is an accessible introduction to Relevance Theory, while an authoritative account is in Wilson and Sperber (2012). Finally, Birner (2012) is a general introduction to pragmatics.

NOTES

1 These are the masculine singular forms of the demonstratives.

2 In this transcription, ` = low tone, e.g. *è*.

3 Lyons (1977, 2: 668ff.) distinguishes between **textual deixis**, where reference is made to the surface form of words and sentences and **impure textual deixis**, where reference is made to some underlying unit of discourse like a point made, or an argument. He gives an example of the former involving an anaphoric use of **it**:

A: That's a rhinoceros.
B: A what? Spell **it** for me.

where B is using **it** to refer not to a real rhinoceros but to the word *rhinoceros* just used by A. In this distinction, our examples here are of the impure variety.

4 In chapter 5 we saw that **tense** is a deictic system too: dividing zones of time around the current act of speaking, i.e. the speaker's position in time.

5 Other examples of such spatial metaphors include the one below which is the normal Irish equivalent to English *I enjoyed it*:

Bhain	mé	taitneamh	as.
took	I	enjoyment	out of.it

"I enjoyed it."

6 The study of the role of cultural or common-sense knowledge is an important focus of investigation in the field of study known as the **ethnography of communication**. See Schiffrin (1994: 137–89) for an introductory survey.

7 The term **mutual knowledge** is often used as a more inclusive term than our use of background knowledge, i.e. to cover knowledge gained from all the sources mentioned above, including deixis, the discourse, and background knowledge. However, the problems discussed below apply to any application of the term.

8 Other labels for given information have included **old information**, the **theme**, or the **presupposition**; and new information has been called the **rheme**, or **focus** (in a sense related to but distinct from how we shall use the term in 7.5.2 below).

9 Note the use of the term **focus** here is consistent with the psychology and psycholinguistics literature, where it signifies a notion of current topic and therefore given information. This is diametrically opposed to the use in general linguistics, as discussed in 7.5.2 below, where focus is used for elements given prominence in some way because they represent new information or for contrast. We follow the general linguistic use in this chapter. The hierarchy in 7.53 is treated as a kind of scale: a nominal may be used for the status conventionally associated with it, or for any status to the left, i.e. higher

in familiarity. The explanation for why there is a tendency to use an expression for its minimal status and not for higher points on the scale is usually given in terms of Gricean scalar implicatures, discussed in 7.7 below.

10 See Chafe (1976) and Dryer (1996) for discussion of activation in discourse.

11 See Givón (1983) for quantitative studies of the distances between coreferential elements in discourse.

12 As is well known, English intonation does not always uniquely identify the focused constituent. When the sentential nuclear stress falls on the final constituent, e.g. the scope of the focus (marked [$_{FOC}$] below), is ambiguous:

1a What is he drinking?
 b He's drinking [$_{FOC}$ BEER].
2a What's he doing?
 b He's [$_{FOC}$ drinking BEER].

See Vallduví and Engdahl (1996) for discussion.

13 Saeed (1984) and (2000) are studies of these markers of informational structure in Somali.

14 See Kuno (1987) and Levinson (1991) for discussions of anaphora in discourse.

15 Grice proposed another kind of inference that he called **conventional implicature**. This inference aims, for example, to explain the interpretations of contrast and surprise associated with English *but* in a and b below:

a. He is Brazilian but he hates soccer.
b. But you don't drink alcohol!

Grice's motivation for treating this as inference comes from his adherence to truth conditions to define meaning. The difference between *and* and *but*, for example, never makes a difference to the truth conditions of sentences and from this perspective, it follows, cannot be semantic. However, it is regular and conventional; hence the term. The question this raises is whether an inference can be part of the linguistic meaning of a word: see Blakemore (1989) and Bach (1999) for different answers to this. We leave aside discussion of this kind of implicature.

16 This discussion is based on Horn's development of Gricean implicature. A related approach is outlined by Levinson (2000), which presents a slightly different systematization of the maxims.

17 Broadening is termed *loosening*, *approximation*, or *generalization* by various writers.

18 See Barwise (1988) for a discussion of the role of context in meaning which includes proposals for terms similar to these.

REFERENCES

Allan, Keith. 1986: *Linguistic Meaning*, 2 vols. London: Routledge & Kegan Paul.

Anderson, Richard C., Ralph E. Reynolds, Diane L. Schallert, and Ernest T. Goetz 1977: Frameworks for comprehending discourse. *American Educational Research Journal* 14: 367–81.

Anderson, Stephen R. and Edward L. Keenan 1985: Deixis. In Timothy Shopen (ed.) *Language Typology and Syntactic Description. Vol. 3: Grammatical Categories and the Lexicon*, 259–308. Cambridge: Cambridge University Press.

Ariel, Mira 1988: Referring and accessibility. *Journal of Linguistics* 24: 67–87.

Bach, Kent. 1999: The myth of conventional implicature. *Linguistics and Philosophy* 22: 327–66.

Barsalou, L.W. 1983: Ad hoc categories. *Memory & Cognition* 11: 211–227.
Barsalou, L.W. 1987: The instability of graded structure: implications for the nature of concepts. In U. Neisser (ed.) *Concepts and Conceptual Development: Ecological and Intellectual Factors in Categorization*, 101–140. Cambridge: Cambridge University Press.
Barsalou, L.W. 1993: Flexibility, structure, and linguistic vagary in concepts: manifestations of a compositional system of perceptual symbols. In A. C. Collins, S. E. Gathercole, & M. A. Conway (eds.) *Theories of Memory*, 29–101. London: Lawrence Erlbaum Associates.
Barwise, Jon 1988: On the circumstantial relation between meaning and content. In Umberto Eco, Marco Santambrogio and Patrizia Violi (eds.) *Meaning and Mental Representations*, 23–40. Bloomington and Indianapolis: Indiana University Press.
Birner, Betty J. 2012: *Introduction to Pragmatics*. Oxford: Wiley-Blackwell.
Blakemore, Diane 1989. Denial and contrast: a relevance theoretic account of *but*. *Linguistics and Philosophy* 12: 15–37.
Blakemore, Diane 1992: *Understanding Utterances: An Introduction to Pragmatics*. Oxford: Blackwell.
Blutner, R. 1998. Lexical pragmatics. *Journal of Semantics* 15.2: 115–62.
Blutner, R. 2004. Pragmatics and the lexicon. In L. R. Horn and G. L. Ward (eds.) *Handbook of Pragmatics*, 488–514. Oxford: Blackwell.
Brown, Gillian and George Yule 1983: *Discourse Analysis*. Cambridge: Cambridge University Press.
Brown, Penelope and Stephen C. Levinson 1978: Universals in language usage: politeness phenomena. In Esther N. Goody (ed.) *Questions and Politeness: Strategies in Social Interaction*, 56–310. Cambridge: Cambridge University Press.
Chafe, Wallace 1976: Givenness, contrastiveness, definiteness, subjects, topics, and points of view. In Charles N. Li (ed.) *Subject and Topic*, 25–55. New York: Academic Press.
Chomsky, Noam 1988: *Language and Problems of Knowledge. The Managua Lectures*. Cambridge, MA: MIT Press.
Clark, Billy 2013: *Relevance Theory*. Cambridge: Cambridge University Press.
Clark, Herbert H. 1977: Bridging. In Philip N. Johnson-Laird and Peter C. Wason (eds.) *Thinking: Readings in Cognitive Science*, 411–20. Cambridge: Cambridge University Press.
Clark, Herbert H. 1978: Inferring what is meant. In W. J. M. Levelt and G. B. Flores d'Arcais (eds.) *Studies in the Perception of Language*, 295–322. Chichester: John Wiley & Sons, Ltd.
Clark, Herbert H. 1994: Discourse in production. In Morton A. Gernsbacher (ed.) *Handbook of Psycholinguistics*, 985–1021. San Diego, CA: Academic Press.
Culicover, Peter and Louise McNally (eds.) 1998: *Syntax and Semantics. Vol. 29: The Limits of Syntax*. New York: Academic Press.
Cullingford, R. 1978: Script Application: Computer Understanding of Newspaper Stories. PhD dissertation, Yale University.
Dryer, Matthew S. 1996: Focus, pragmatic presupposition, and activated propositions. *Journal of Pragmatics* 26: 475–523.
Fillmore, Charles J. 1997: *Lectures on Deixis*. Stanford, CA: Center for the Study of Language and Information.
Fleischman, Suzanne 1982: The past and future: are they coming or going? *Proceedings of the Eighth Annual Meeting of the Berkeley Linguistics Society*, 322–24.
Fleischman, Suzanne 1989: Temporal distance: a basic linguistic metaphor. *Studies in Language* 13.1: 1–50.
Gazdar, Gerald 1979: *Pragmatics: Implicature, Presupposition, and Logical Form*. New York: Academic Press.
Gibbs, Raymond W. 1987: Mutual knowledge and the psychology of conversational inference. *Journal of Pragmatics* 11: 561–88.
Givón, Talmy (ed.) 1983: *Topic Continuity in Discourse: A Quantitative Cross-Language Study*. Amsterdam: John Benjamins.

Glucksberg, S. and B. Keysar 1990. Understanding metaphorical comparisons: beyond similarity. *Psychological Review* 96: 3–18.
Grice, H. Paul 1975: Logic and conversation. In Peter Cole and Jerry Morgan (eds.) *Syntax and Semantics. Vol. 3: Speech Acts*, 43–58. New York: Academic Press.
Grice, H. Paul 1978: Further notes on logic and conversation. In Peter Cole (ed.) *Syntax and Semantics. Vol. 9: Pragmatics*, 113–28. New York: Academic Press.
Grice, H. P. 1989: *Studies in the Way of Words*. Cambridge, MA: Harvard University Press.
Gumperz, John J. and Dell Hymes (eds.) 1972: *Directions in Sociolinguistics: The Ethnography of Communication*. New York: Holt, Rinehart & Winston.
Gundel, Jeanette K., Nancy Hedberg and Ron Zacharski 1993: Cognitive status and the form of referring expressions in discourse. *Language* 69: 274–307.
Gundel, Jeanette K., Nancy Hedberg and Ron Zacharski 2000: Status cognitif et forme des anaphoriques indirects. *Verbum* 22: 79–102.
Halliday, M. A. K. and R. Hasan 1976: *Cohesion in English*. London: Longman.
Hayward, R. J. 1990: Notes on the Zayse language. In R. J. Hayward (ed.) *Omotic Language Studies*, 210–355. London: School of Oriental and African Studies.
Horn, Laurence R. 1984: Towards a new taxonomy for pragmatic inference: Q- and R-based implicature. In Deborah Schiffrin (ed.) *Meaning, Form and Use in Context*, 11–42. Washington, DC: Georgetown University Press.
Horn, Laurence R. 1989: *A Natural History of Negation*. Chicago: University of Chicago Press.
Horn, Laurence R. 1996: Presupposition and implicature. In Shalom Lappin (ed.) *The Handbook of Contemporary Semantic Theory*, 299–320. Oxford: Blackwell.
Jaggar, Philip J. 2001: *Hausa*. London Oriental and African Language Library. Amsterdam: John Benjamins.
Jaggar, Philip J. and Malami Buba 1994: The space and time adverbials NAN/CAN in Hausa: cracking the deictic code. *Language Sciences* 16 3/4, 327–421.
Kess, Joseph F. and Ronald A. Hoppe 1985: Bias, individual preferences and "shared knowledge" in ambiguity. *Journal of Pragmatics* 9: 21–39.
Kolodner, Janet L. 1992. An introduction to case-based reasoning. *Artificial Intelligence Review* 6: 3–34.
Kuno, Susumu 1973: *The Structure of the Japanese Language*. Cambridge, MA: MIT Press.
Kuno, Susumu 1987: *Functional Syntax: Anaphora, Discourse and Empathy*. Chicago: University of Chicago Press.
Lambrecht, Knud. 1994. *Information Structure and Sentence Form: Topic, Focus, and the Mental Representation of Discourse Referents*. Cambridge: Cambridge University Press.
Leech, Geoffrey N. 1983: *Principles of Pragmatics*. London: Longman.
Levinson, Stephen C. 1983: *Pragmatics*. Cambridge: Cambridge University Press.
Levinson, Stephen C. 1991: Pragmatic revision of the binding conditions revisited. *Journal of Linguistics* 27: 107–61.
Levinson, Stephen C. 2000: *Presumptive Meanings: The Theory of Generalized Conversational Implicature*. Cambridge, MA: MIT Press.
Levinson, Stephen C. 2004. Deixis. In L. R. Horn and G. Ward (eds.) *The Handbook of Pragmatics*, 97–121. Oxford: Blackwell.
Li, Charles N. and Sandra A. Thompson 1976: Subject and topic: a new typology of language. In Charles N. Li (ed.) *Subject and Topic*, 457–89. New York: Academic Press.
Lyons, John 1977: *Semantics*, 2 vols. Cambridge: Cambridge University Press.
Murphy, G. 1997: Polysemy and the creation of novel word meanings. In T. Ward, S. Smith and J. Vaid (eds.) *Creative Thought: An Investigation of Conceptual Structures and Processes*, 235–65. Washington, DC: American Psychological Society.
O'Brien, Flann 1967: *At-Swim-Two-Birds*. London: Penguin Books.
Prince, Ellen F. 1981: Towards a taxonomy of given-new information. In Peter Cole (ed.) *Radical Pragmatics*, 223–55. New York: Academic Press.

Prince, Ellen F. 1992: The ZPG letter: subjects, definiteness, and information-status. In William C. Mann and Sandra A. Thompson (eds.) *Discourse Description: Diverse Linguistic Analyses of a Fund-Raising Text*. Amsterdam: John Benjamins.

Rubio Fernandez, P. 2008. Concept narrowing: the role of context-independent information. *Journal of Semantics* 25.4: 381–409.

Saeed, John Ibrahim 1984: *The Syntax of Focus and Topic in Somali*. Hamburg: Helmut Buske.

Saeed, John Ibrahim 2000: The functions of focus in Somali. *Lingua Posnaniensis* 42: 133–43.

Schank, Roger C. and Robert P. Abelson 1977: *Scripts, Plans, Goals and Understanding*. Hillsdale, NJ: Lawrence Erlbaum.

Schank, Roger C. and Alex Kass 1988: Knowledge representation in people and machines. In Umberto Eco, Marco Santambrogio and Patrizia Violi (eds.) *Meaning and Mental Representations*, 181–200. Bloomington and Indianapolis: Indiana University Press.

Schiffrin, Deborah 1994: *Approaches to Discourse*. Oxford: Blackwell.

Smith, N. V. (ed.) 1982: *Mutual Knowledge*. London: Academic Press.

Sperber, Dan and Deirdre Wilson 1995: *Relevance: Communication and Cognition*, second edition. Oxford: Blackwell.

Stalnaker, Robert 1974: Pragmatic presuppositions. In Milton K. Munitz and Peter K. Unger (eds.) *Semantics and Philosophy*, 197–213. New York: New York University Press.

Tomlin, Russell. (ed.) 1987. *Coherence and Grounding in Discourse*. Amsterdam: John Benjamins.

Vallduví, Enric and Elisabet Engdahl 1996: The linguistic realization of information packaging. *Linguistics* 34: 459–519.

Vega-Moreno, R. 2007. *Creativity and Convention: The Pragmatics of Everyday Figurative Speech*. Amsterdam: John Benjamins.

Wilson, Deirdre and Robyn Carston 2006: Metaphor, relevance and the emergent property issue. *Mind and Language* 21.23: 404–33.

Wilson, Deirdre and Robyn Carston 2007: A unitary approach to lexical pragmatics: relevance, inference and ad hoc concepts. In N. Burton-Roberts (ed.) *Pragmatics*, 230–59. Basingstoke: Palgrave Macmillan.

Wilson, Deirdre and Dan Sperber 2012: *Meaning and Relevance*. Cambridge: Cambridge University Press.

Whitney, William Dwight 1867: *Language and the Study of Language*. London and New York: Charles Scribner & Sons. Extracted in Michael Silverstein (ed.) 1971: *Whitney on Language*, 7–110. Cambridge, MA: MIT Press.

chapter 8

Functions of Language

Speech as Action

8.1 Introduction

In this chapter we maintain our focus on language use and we look at the idea that part of the meaning of an utterance is its intended social function. It seems clear that learning to communicate in a language involves more than acquiring the pronunciation and grammar. We need to learn how to ask questions, make suggestions, greet, and thank other speakers. In other words we need to learn the uses to which utterances are conventionally put in the new language community and how these uses are signaled, if we are to use the language in a realistic way. Similarly, as hearers, part of understanding the meaning of an utterance is knowing whether we have been asked a question, invited to do something, and so on. In a terminology introduced by J. L. Austin which we discuss in section 8.2, such functions of language are called *speech acts*.

In the last chapter we discussed areas of meaning which highlight the role of context and speaker–hearer interpretation. We recognized that if we admit a distinction between semantics and pragmatics, some of these topics, for example conversational implicature, seem to fall under pragmatics, while others, like reference and deixis, seem to straddle the semantics–pragmatics divide. The study of speech acts occupies a similar border area. In many cases the intended function is linguistically coded: languages often have, for example, specific morphemes, intonation and sentence patterns to mark questions, wishes, orders, and so on. However, as we shall see, communicating functions also relies on both general knowledge of social conventions and specific knowledge of the local context of utterance. This area, then, reveals the pattern we saw in the last chapter: hearers have to coordinate linguistic and non-linguistic knowledge to interpret a speaker's intended meaning.

We can begin our discussion by identifying two important characteristics of speech acts: **interactivity** and **context dependence**. The first is a crucial feature: communicating functions involves the speaker in a coordinated activity with other language users. For some uses of language this interactivity is more explicit than others. We can take as an example Akindele's description of a typical afternoon greeting between persons of equal age and status in the Nigerian language Yoruba (1990: 4):[1]

8.1	Greetings:		Gloss:	
	F:	Ẹ káàsán.	F:	Good afternoon.
	MT:	Ẹ káàsán.	MT:	Good afternoon.
	F:	Ṣ'álàáfíà ni?	F:	How are you?
	MT:	A dúpẹ́.	MT:	We thank (God).
	F:	Ilé ńkọ́?	F:	How is your house(hold)?
	MT:	Wọ́n wà.	MT:	They are (in good health).
	F:	Ọmọ nkọ́?	F:	How are your children?
	MT:	Wọ́n wà.	MT:	They are (in good health).
	F:	Bá mi kí wọn.	F:	Help me to greet them.
	MT:	Wọ́n á gbọ́.	MT:	They will hear.

A similar, if less extended, interactivity is characteristic of one of Austin's well-known examples: bets in English. As Austin described, a bet only comes into existence when two or more parties interact. If I say to someone *I bet you five pounds he doesn't get elected*, a bet is not performed unless my addressee makes some response like *Okay* or *You're on*. While other speech acts like asking a question or greeting someone do not need explicit responses to make them questions or greetings, they nonetheless set up the expectation for an interactive response. Studies in the discourse analysis approach known as **conversational analysis** (for example, Schegloff 1972, 1979, Schegloff and Sacks 1973, Goodwin 1979, Atkinson and Heritage 1984), have revealed that failure to respond to a question, say by silence, triggers certain types of compensatory behavior: the speaker may repeat the question, seek to evade the perceived rejection, or others may try to repair the lapse.[2] Similarly, Akindele (1990: 3) says of Yoruba greetings like 8.1 above:

8.2 Another factor is the Yoruba ethical code in which it is a duty to greet people engaged in different activities. Hence there is a salutation for every conceivable occasion and situation ... Greeting persons at work is regarded as a matter of respect in one's occupation. Failure to offer such greetings in the appropriate context usually gives rise to bad feelings especially among close friends and relatives to the extent that it can lead to suspicion of sorcery or witchcraft.

The second feature, context dependence, has two aspects. The first is that many speech acts rely on social conventions to support them. Sometimes this is very explicit, where the speech act is supported by what Searle (1969) called **institutional facts**. Thus every society has procedures and ceremonies where some participants' words carry a special function. Examples commonly used in the literature include a judge saying *I sentence you to hang by the neck until dead*, a priest in the marriage ceremony saying *I now pronounce you man and wife*, a country's president announcing *I declare a state of national emergency*, and so on. These speech acts of sentencing prisoners, pronouncing a couple married, and so on can only be performed by the relevant people in the right situations, where both are sanctioned by social laws and conventions. Again, though these are just the most explicit cases, it is clear that social conventions also govern ordinary uses of language in society. Sociolinguistic and ethnographical studies have shown us how the forms of asking questions, making greetings, and so on are influenced by a particular society's conventions for the participants' age, gender, relative social status, degree of intimacy, and so on.[3]

The second aspect of context dependence is the local context of a speech act. An utterance may signal one speech act in one situation and another elsewhere. Questions in English are notoriously flexible in this way. If the asker already knows the answer then an utterance with the form of a question can be, for example, a request, as if I see you are wearing a watch and I say *Can you tell me the time?* Or the question might have the force of a statement *No* as in B's possible replies in the invented exchange in 8.3 below:

8.3 A: Are you going to buy his car?
B: a. Are you crazy?
b. Do you think I'm crazy?

We can find a parallel use of questions with known answers in the popular use of sentences like *Is the Pope a Catholic?*, *Do dogs have fleas?* or *Do bears shit in the woods?* as livelier and more informal ways of saying *Yes of course.*[4]

Because of this flexibility, we have to be careful about terminology. Some sentences have a particular grammatical form which is conventionally associated with a certain speech act. Thus questions in English, which of course include several types, usually have a special rising intonation pattern and an inverted subject-verb word order which differentiates them from statements, as 8.4b and c below are distinguished from 8.4a:

8.4 a. He is leaving.
b. Is he leaving?
c. When is he leaving?

When there is a conventional match between grammatical form and speech act function we can identify a **sentence type**. We need to use separate terms for sentence types and speech acts though, so that we can identify cases where the matching does not hold. Thus we might identify the sentence types in 8.5 below:

8.5 a. declarative, e.g. *Siobhán will paint the anaglypta.*
b. interrogative, e.g. *Will Siobhán paint the anaglypta?*
c. imperative, e.g. *Siobhán, paint the anaglypta!*
d. optative, e.g. *If only Siobhán would paint the anaglypta!*

The conventional, or literal, use of these sentence types will be to perform the speech acts with the corresponding letter in 8.6 below:

8.6 a. assertions
 b. questions
 c. orders
 d. wishes

However, as we have already seen, interrogatives can be used for other speech acts than asking questions, and the same is true to a greater or lesser degree of the other sentence types. We discuss this variability in section 8.4.

Both of the features we have outlined, interactivity and context dependence, emphasize that in discussing speech acts we are examining the union of linguistic and social behavior. We will begin our discussion of this behavior by reviewing J. L. Austin's theory of speech acts in section 8.2, then go on to examine revisions of the theory by J. R. Searle and others in 8.3. Thereafter in section 8.4 we look at an interesting and difficult area for the theory: variability and indirect speech acts. Finally, in section 8.5 we come back to the identification of sentence types.

8.2 Austin's Speech Act Theory

8.2.1 Introduction

Speech act theory was developed by the Oxford philosopher J. L. Austin whose 1955 lectures at Harvard University were published posthumously as *How to Do Things with Words* (1975). The approach has been greatly developed since so that there is a large literature. One of the most important writers on speech acts has been the philosopher John R. Searle (for example: 1969, 1975, 1976, 1999) and the theory has been of interest to many philosophers, for example Strawson (1964), Recanati (1987), Vanderveken (1990), Alston (2000), and Green (2013). Within linguistics, studies have included Sadock (1974, 1994), Cole and Morgan (1975), Bach and Harnish (1979), Gazdar (1981), Sadock and Zwicky (1985), Wierzbicka (1985, 1987), Croft (1994), Zaefferer (2001), Allan (2006), and Jucker and Taavitsainen (2008). We look at Austin's proposals in this section and discuss subsequent developments in section 8.3.

Austin's work is in many respects a reaction to some traditional and influential attitudes to language. We can risk simplifying these as a starting point. The attitudes can be said to involve three related assumptions, as follows:

8.7 a. that the basic sentence type in language is declarative (i.e. a statement or assertion);
 b. that the principal use of language is to describe states of affairs (by using statements);
 c. that the meaning of utterances can be described in terms of their truth or falsity.

Some of these assumptions are discernible in recent formal approaches to semantics, as we shall see in chapter 10. Among Austin's contemporaries these assumptions are associated with the philosophers known as **logical positivists**, a term originally applied to the mathematicians and philosophers of the Vienna Circle; see Ayer (1959) for discussion. An important issue for logical positivist approaches is how far the meaning of a sentence is reducible to its verifiability, that is, the extent to which, and the means by which, it can be shown to be true or false.

Austin's opposition to these views is the "common-sense" one that language is used for far more than making statements and that for the most part utterances cannot be said to be either true or false. He makes two important observations. The first is that not all sentences are statements and that much of conversation is made up of questions, exclamations, commands, and expressions of wishes like the examples in 8.8 below:

8.8 a. Excuse me!
b. Are you serving?
c. Hello.
d. Six pints of stout and a packet of peanuts, please!
e. Give me the dry roasted ones.
f. How much? Are you serious?
g. *O tempora! O mores!*

Such sentences are not descriptions and cannot be said to be true or false.

Austin's second observation was that even in sentences with the grammatical form of declaratives, not all are used to make statements. Austin identified a subset of declaratives that are not used to make true or false statements, such as the examples in 8.9 below:

8.9 a. I promise to take a taxi home.
b. I bet you five pounds that he gets breathalyzed.
c. I declare this meeting open.
d. I warn you that legal action will ensue.
e. I name this ship *The Flying Dutchman*.

Austin claimed of these sentences that they were in themselves a kind of action: thus by uttering 8.9a a speaker makes a promise rather than just describing one. This kind of utterance he called **performative** utterances: in these examples they perform the action named by the first verb in the sentence, and we can insert the adverb *hereby* to stress this function, for example *I hereby request that you leave my property*. We can contrast performative and non-performative verbs by these two features. A speaker would not for example expect the uttering of 8.10a below to constitute the action of cooking a cake, or 8.11a the action of starting a car. These sentences describe actions independent of the linguistic act. Accordingly the use of *hereby* with these sentences as in 8.10b and 8.11b sounds odd.

8.10 a. I cook this cake.
b. ?I hereby cook this cake.

8.11 a. I start this car.
b. ?I hereby start this car.

8.2.2 Evaluating performative utterances

Austin argued that it is not useful to ask whether performative utterances like those in 8.9 are true or not, rather we should ask whether they work or not: do they constitute a successful warning, bet, ship naming and so on? In Austin's terminology a performative that works is called **felicitous** and one that does not is **infelicitous**. For them to work, such performatives have to satisfy the social conventions that we mentioned in section 8.1: for a very obvious example, I cannot rename a ship by walking up to it in dock and saying *I name this ship the Flying Dutchman*. Less explicitly, there are social conventions governing the giving of orders to co-workers, greeting strangers, and so on. Austin's name for the enabling conditions for a performative is **felicity conditions**.

Examining these social conventions that support performatives, it is clear that there is a gradient between performatives that are highly institutionalized, or even ceremonial, requiring sophisticated and very overt support, like the example of a judge pronouncing sentence, through to less formal acts like warning, thanking, and so on.[5] To describe the role of felicity conditions, Austin (1975: 25–38) wrote a very general schema:

8.12 A1 There must exist an accepted conventional procedure having a certain conventional effect, the procedure to include the uttering of certain words by certain persons in certain circumstances ...
A2 The particular persons and circumstances must be appropriate for the invocation of the particular procedure invoked ...
B1 The procedure must be executed by all the participants correctly ...
B2 ... and completely....

Austin went on to add **sincerity** clauses: firstly that participants must have the requisite thoughts, feelings and intentions, as specified by the procedure, and secondly, that if subsequent conduct is called for, the participants must so conduct themselves. If the speech act is unsuccessful by failing the A or B conditions in 8.12, then he described it as a **misfire**. Thus my casually renaming any ship visiting Dublin docks is a misfire because A2 above is not adhered to. If the act is insincerely performed, then he described it as an **abuse** of a speech act, as for example saying *I bet ...* with no intention to pay, or *I promise ...* when I already intend to break the promise. Linguists, as opposed to philosophers, have tended not to be so interested in this second type of infelicity, since the primary speech act has, in these cases, been successfully communicated.

8.2.3 Explicit and implicit performatives

Looking at examples of performative utterances like those in 8.9 earlier, we can say that they are characterized by special features, as in 8.13:

8.13 a. They tend to begin with a first person verb in a form we could describe as simple present: *I bet*, *I warn*, etc.
b. This verb belongs to a special class describing verbal activities, for example: *promise*, *warn*, *sentence*, *name*, *bet*, *pronounce*.
c. Generally their performative nature can be emphasized by inserting the adverb *hereby*, as described earlier, thus *I hereby sentence you to...*

Utterances with these characteristics we can call **explicit** performatives. The importance of speech act theory lies in the way that Austin and others managed to extend their analysis from these explicit performatives to other utterances. The first step was to point out that in some cases the same speech act seems to be performed but with a relaxation of some of the special characteristics mentioned in 8.13 above. We regularly meet utterances like those in 8.14 below, where this is so:

8.14 a. You are (hereby) charged with treason.
b. Passengers are requested to avoid jumping out of the aircraft.
c. Five pounds says he doesn't make the semifinal.
d. Come up and see me sometime.

We can easily provide the sentences in 8.14 above with corresponding explicit performatives, as below:

8.15 a. I (hereby) charge you with treason.
b. We request that passengers avoid jumping out of the aircraft.
c. I bet you five pounds that he doesn't make the semifinal.
d. I invite you to come up and see me sometime.

It seems reasonable to say that the sentences in 8.14 could be uttered to perform the same speech acts as those in 8.15. In fact it seems that none of the special characteristics of performative utterances is indispensable to their performance. How then do we recognize these other performatives, which we can call **implicit** performatives? Answers to this have varied somewhat in the development of the theory but Austin's original contention was that it was an utterance's ability to be expanded to an explicit performative that identified it as a performative utterance. Austin discussed at length the various linguistic means by which more implicit performatives could be marked, including the mood of the verb, auxiliary verbs, intonation, and so on. We shall not follow the detail of his discussion here; see Austin (1975: 53–93). Of course we soon end up with a situation where the majority of performatives are implicit, needing expansion to make explicit their force. One positive advantage of this translation strategy is that it focuses attention on the task of classifying the performative verbs of a language, a task we shall take up in section 8.3. For now, the basic claim is clear: explicit performatives are seen as merely a specialized subset of performatives whose nature as speech acts is more unambiguous than most.

8.2.4 Statements as performatives

Austin's original position was that performatives, which are speech acts subject to felicity conditions, are to be contrasted with declarative sentences, which are potentially true or false descriptions of situations. The latter were termed **constatives**. However, as his analysis developed, he collapsed the distinction and viewed the making of statements as just another type of speech act, which he called simply **stating**. Again, we needn't follow his line of argument closely here: see Austin (1975: 133–47) and the discussion in Schiffrin (1994: 50–54). In simple terms, Austin argued that there is no theoretically sound way to distinguish between performatives and constatives. For example, the notion of felicity applies to statements too: statements which are odd because of presupposition failure, like the sentence *The king of France is bald* discussed in chapter 4, are infelicitous because the speaker has violated the conventions for referring to individuals (i.e. that the listener can identify them). This infelicity suspends our judgment of the truth or falsity of the sentence: as we saw in chapter 4, it is difficult to say that *The king of France is bald* is false in the same way as *The president of France is a woman*, even though they are both not true at the time of writing this.

So we arrive at a view that all utterances constitute speech acts of one kind or another. For some the type of act is explicitly marked by their containing a verb labeling the act, *warn, bet, name, suggest, protest*, and so on; others are more implicitly signaled. Some speech acts are so universal and fundamental that their grammaticalization is the profound one of the distinction into sentence types we mentioned in section 8.1. In their cross-linguistic survey of speech acts Sadock and Zwicky (1985: 160) observe:

8.16 It is in some respects a surprising fact that most languages are similar in presenting three basic sentence types with similar functions and often strikingly similar forms. These are the declarative, interrogative, and imperative. As a first approximation, these three types can be described as follows: The declarative is used for making announcements, stating conclusions, making claims, relating stories, and so on. The interrogative elicits a verbal response from the addressee. It is used principally to gain information. The imperative indicates the speaker's desire to influence future events. It is of service in making requests, giving orders, making suggestions, and the like.

Though the authors go on to discuss the many detailed differences between the uses of these main forms in individual languages, it seems that sentence type is a basic marker of primary performative types.

This conclusion that all utterances have a speech act force has led to a widespread view that there are two basic parts to meaning: the conventional meaning of the sentence (often described as a proposition) and the speaker's intended speech act. Thus we can view our earlier examples in 8.5, repeated in 8.17 below, as divisible into propositional meaning (represented in small capitals in 8.18 below) and a sentence type marker, uniting to form a speech act as shown in 8.18 below:

8.17 a. *Siobhán is painting the anaglypta.*
b. *Is Siobhán painting the anaglypta?*
c. *Siobhán, paint the anaglypta!*
d. *If only Siobhán would paint the anaglypta!*

8.18 a. SIOBHÁN PAINT THE ANAGLYPTA + declarative = statement
b. SIOBHÁN PAINT THE ANAGLYPTA + interrogative = question
c. SIOBHÁN PAINT THE ANAGLYPTA + imperative = order
d. SIOBHÁN PAINT THE ANAGLYPTA + optative = wish

We have to remember though that the matching in 8.18 is only a typical one; we return to this question in section 8.4.

8.2.5 Three facets of a speech act

Austin proposed that communicating a speech act consists of three elements: the speaker says something, the speaker signals an associated speech act, and the speech act causes an effect on her listeners or the participants. The first element he called the **locutionary act**, by which he meant the act of saying something that makes sense in a language, that is, follows the rules of pronunciation and grammar. The second, the action intended by the speaker, he termed the **illocutionary act**. This is what Austin and his successors have mainly been concerned with: the uses to which language can be put in society. In fact the term **speech acts** is often used with just this meaning of illocutionary acts. The third element, called the **perlocutionary act**, is concerned with what follows an utterance: the effect or "take-up" of an illocutionary act. Austin gave the example of sentences like *Shoot her!* In appropriate circumstances this can have the illocutionary force of ordering, urging or advising the addressee to shoot her, but the perlocutionary force of persuading, forcing, frightening, and so on the addressee into shooting her. Perlocutionary effects are less conventionally tied to linguistic forms and so have been of less interest to linguists. We know for example that people can recognize orders without obeying them.

8.3 Categorizing Speech Acts

After Austin's original explorations of speech act theory there have been a number of works which attempt to systematize the approach. One important focus has been to categorize the types of speech act possible in languages.[6] J. R. Searle for example, while allowing that there is a myriad of language-particular speech acts, proposed that all acts fall into five main types, as in 8.19 below (1976: 10–16):

8.19 1 REPRESENTATIVES, which commit the speaker to the truth of the expressed proposition (paradigm cases: asserting, concluding);
2 DIRECTIVES, which are attempts by the speaker to get the addressee to do something (paradigm cases: requesting, questioning);
3 COMMISSIVES, which commit the speaker to some future course of action (paradigm cases: promising, threatening, offering);
4 EXPRESSIVES, which express a psychological state (paradigm cases: thanking, apologizing, welcoming, congratulating);
5 DECLARATIONS, which effect immediate changes in the institutional state of affairs and which tend to rely on elaborate extralinguistic institutions (paradigm cases: excommunicating, declaring war, christening, marrying, firing from employment).

Searle uses a mix of criteria to establish these different types, including: the act's **illocutionary point**; its "**fit**" with the world; the **psychological state** of the speaker; and the **content** of the act. The illocutionary point is the purpose or aim of the act: thus the point of directives is to get the hearer to do something. The "fit" concerns direction of the relationship between language and the world: thus speakers using representatives, for example assertions, are seeking to get their words to match the world, while users of directives, for example requests or orders, are seeking to change the world so that it matches their words. The criterion of *psychological state* relates to the speaker's state of mind: thus statements like *It's raining* reflect belief, while expressives like apologies and congratulations reveal the speaker's attitude to events. Finally, *content* relates to restrictions placed on speech acts by what they are about, their propositional content.[7] Thus one cannot properly promise or predict things that have already happened. Or for another example: one way of viewing the difference between a promise and a threat is in terms of whether the future event is beneficial or harmful to the addressee.

In distinguishing these acts, Searle further developed Austin's notion of felicity conditions into a classification of conditions that must hold for a successful speech act. Searle (1969) distinguishes between **preparatory, propositional, sincerity,** and **essential** conditions for an act. These are necessary contextual conditions that license and distinguish different speech acts. See for example 8.20 below where we give examples of his conditions for the act of *promising*:

8.20 Conditions for promising (Searle 1969: 62ff)
[where S = speaker, H = hearer, A = the future action, P = the proposition expressed in the speech act, e = the linguistic expression]
a. Preparatory 1: *H* would prefer *S*'s doing *A* to his not doing *A* and *S* believes *H* would prefer *S*'s doing *A* to not doing *A*.
b. Preparatory 2: It is not obvious to both *S* and *H* that *S* will do *A* in the normal course of events.
c. Propositional: In expressing that *P*, *S* predicates a future act *A* of *S*.
d. Sincerity: *S* intends to do *A*.
e. Essential: The utterance *e* counts as an undertaking to do *A*.

Among these conditions we might note that the second preparatory condition suggests that one does not normally promise what would happen as a matter of course. Thus saying *I'll be home at five* to one's spouse when leaving for work might not be considered a typical promise. The propositional condition, as we mentioned earlier, reflects that in a promise a future act must be predicated of the speaker, so that something that has already happened cannot be promised.

The conditions for questions include those in 8.21 below:

8.21 Conditions for questioning (Searle 1969: 66)
[where S = speaker, H = hearer, P = the proposition expressed in the speech act]
a. Preparatory 1: *S* does not know the answer, i.e. for a yes/ no question, does not know whether *P* is true or false; for an elicitative or WH-question, does not know the missing information.[8]
b. Preparatory 2: It is not obvious to both *S* and *H* that *H* will provide the information at that time without being asked.
c. Propositional: Any proposition or propositional function.
d. Sincerity: *S* wants this information.
e. Essential: The act counts as an attempt to elicit this information from *H*.

It is clear that this characterization relates to a prototypical question: it does not apply of course to rhetorical questions, nor the questions of a teacher in the classroom, a lawyer in court, and so on. Note that the propositional condition simply says that there are no semantic restrictions on the content of a question as a speech act. Searle provides felicity conditions like those in 8.20 and 8.21 for each type of speech act: we shall be satisfied for now with looking at just these two.

Elsewhere in the literature, there have been a number of taxonomies of speech act types suggested, for example Schiffer (1972), Fraser (1975), Hancher (1979), Bach and Harnish (1979), Wierzbicka (1987), Vanderveken (1990), Zaefferer (2001).[9] One assumption that seems to underlie all such classification systems, and one we have assumed so far in talking about speech acts, is that there is some linguistic marking (no doubt supported by contextual information) of a correlation between form and function. In other words we recognize a sentence type and are able to match it to a speech act. There are two problems with this: the first is how to cope with cases where what seems to be the conventional association between a sentence form and an illocutionary force is overridden. We discuss this in the next section under the heading of **indirect speech acts**. The second problem, which we discuss in section 8.5, arises from difficulties in identifying sentence types.

8.4 Indirect Speech Acts

8.4.1 Introduction

In 8.2.4 we discussed the typical matching between certain sentence types and speech acts. Thus we discussed the matching between the interrogative sentence type in English and the act of questioning. However, as we noted there, quite often this conventional matching is superseded by an extra, more immediate interpretation. The conventionally expected function is known as the **direct speech act** and the extra actual function is termed the **indirect speech act**. Thus we can find examples like those in 8.22 below:

8.22	**Utterance**	**Direct act**	**Indirect act**
	Would you mind passing me the ashtray?	question	request
	Why don't you finish your drink and leave?	question	request
	I must ask you to leave my house.	statement	order/request
	Have a nice day!	order	good wish
	Leave me and I'll jump in the river.	order and statement	threat

The problem is: how do people recognize the indirect act? There are a number of possible answers to this. We look first at Searle's (1975) approach.

The first question is whether hearers are only conscious of the indirect act, or whether they have both available and choose the indirect act as most contextually apt. Searle (1975) argues that speakers do indeed have access to both: he terms the direct use the **literal** use of the speech act and the indirect, the **nonliteral** use. He gives as examples the sentences in 8.23a–8.25a below, all of which can be requests, but none of which have the form of imperatives in the (b) versions, but instead are interrogatives and declaratives:

8.23 a. Can you pass the salt?
b. Please pass the salt.

8.24 a. I wish you wouldn't do that.
b. Please don't do that.

8.25 a. Aren't you going to eat your cereal?
b. Please eat your cereal.

Searle argues that in the cases above two speech acts are available to the hearer: the literal act is backgrounded or secondary while the nonliteral act is primary – "when one of these sentences is uttered with the primary illocutionary point of a directive, the literal illocutionary act is also performed" (1975: 70). The question he raises is: how is it that these but not all nonliteral acts will work, that is, why is it that stating *Salt is made of sodium chloride* will not work as a request like *Can you pass the salt?* (p. 75). Searle's solution relies on the system of felicity conditions mentioned in the last section. The conditions for making requests include the following:

8.26 Conditions for requesting (Searle 1975: 71)
[where *S* = speaker, *H* = hearer, *A* = the future action]
a. Preparatory condition: *H* is able to perform *A*.
b. Sincerity condition: *S* wants *H* to do *A*.
c. Propositional condition: *S* predicates a future act *A* of *H*.
d. Essential condition: Counts as an attempt by *S* to get *H* to do *A*.

Searle argues that other sentence types can only work as indirect requests when they address one of the conditions for requests. Thus sentence 8.23a *Can you pass the salt?* addresses the preparatory condition in 8.26. This example shows that an indirect request can be made by asking whether (or stating that) a preparatory condition holds.

The sentence *I wish you wouldn't do that*, in 8.24a above, forms an indirect request by addressing another felicity condition: it states that the sincerity condition in 8.26 holds.[10]

Searle's third example, *Aren't you going to eat your cereal*, in 8.25a, works by asking whether the propositional content condition holds. Perhaps we can add another example: if a teacher uses an imperative as a directive to a student: *Return that book to the library!*, the propositional content involves predicating the future act: *You will return that book to the library*. Searle's point is that a corresponding indirect directive can be made by questioning this, that is *Aren't you going to return that book to the library?* or *Are you going to return that book to the library?*

So in this view, indirect speech acts work because they are systematically related to the structure of the associated direct act: they are tied to one or another of the act's felicity conditions. This still leaves the question of how the hearer works out which of the two acts, the backgrounded direct act or the primary indirect act, is meant. We look briefly at Searle's proposal for this in 8.4.2.

8.4.2 Understanding indirect speech acts

Searle's view of how we understand indirect speech acts is that we combine our knowledge of three elements to support a chain of inference. The elements are: the felicity conditions of direct speech acts, the context of the utterance, and principles of conversational cooperation, such as the Gricean maxims of relevance, quality, and so on that we discussed in chapter 7. We can briefly sketch how these three types of knowledge are used in this chain of reasoning by looking at the example of *Can you pass the salt?* (following Searle 1975: 73–75). In an everyday situation, the context will tell the hearer that the speaker should already know that he can pass the salt, and thus he recognizes that the question violates the felicity conditions for a question. The assumption of cooperative principles however leads the hearer to search for some other point for the utterance. This is essentially the search for an indirect speech act, that is the hearer asks himself, as it were, if it can't be a genuine question, what is the purpose of this utterance? The hearer knows that a condition for requests is that the hearer can actually carry out the desired act *A* (see 8.26a above), and also recognizes that to say *yes* here is to confirm that a preparatory condition for doing *A* has been met. The hearer also knows as part of general background knowledge that passing salt around a table is a usual part of meals, so this is a reasonable goal for the speaker to entertain. From these pieces of knowledge the hearer infers that the speaker's utterance is likely to be a request.

One problem with this account is that it does not take into account the **idiomatic** quality of many indirect acts. As Searle, and others, have noted, it is not at all clear that a parallel question *Are you able to pass me the salt?* would be interpreted in the same way, even though *can* and *be able* are largely synonymous. This difference is confirmed by the different possibilities of occurrence with *please*, usually an optional marker of requests. Thus *Can you please pass me the salt?* sounds fine while *Are you able to please pass me the salt?* sounds decidedly odd.

Searle's response to this seems to be that while the account of inference we have just outlined stands, there is a certain degree of conventionality about forms like *Can you ... ?* being used as requests. Other writers strike the balance differently: Gordon and Lakoff (1975), for example, see hearers as employing shortcuts known as **conversational postulates**. These are rules that are engaged whenever the hearer is encouraged by conversational principles to search for an indirect speech act, as described above. The postulates reduce the amount of inference involved in tracing the indirect act. The relevant postulate for our present example would be as in 8.27:

8.27 Conversational postulate (Gordon and Lakoff 1975: 86)
ASK $(a, b, \text{CAN}(b, Q)) \rightarrow$ REQUEST (a, b, Q)

In their formalism, 8.27 is to be interpreted as "when a speaker *a* asks whether *b* can do *Q*, this implies a request for *b* to do *Q*." Thus these postulates can be seen as a reflection of the conventionality of some indirect acts. More generally Gordon and Lakoff agree with Searle's suggestion that stating or questioning a felicity condition of a direct act will produce an indirect version. Thus, to add to our earlier examples, if we look at the conditions for requests in 8.26 earlier, we can predict that instead of using the sentence *Please come home!*, the following indirect strategies are possible:

8.28 a. Question the preparatory condition: *Can you please come home?*
b. State the sincerity condition: *I want you to please come home.*
c. Question the propositional content condition: *Will you please come home?*

Clearly both of these accounts, by Searle and by Gordon and Lakoff, view the understanding of indirect acts as involving inference. The question remains of balance: how much of the task is inferential and how much is conventionalized into strategies or rules for forming indirect acts. A position at the opposite extreme from Searle's would be that indirect speech acts are in fact idioms and involve no inferences from a direct to an indirect act.[11] In this view an utterance like *Can you pass me the salt?* is simply recognized and interpreted as a request, with no question perceived. This position is undercut by the common-sense fact that hearers deciding to be uncooperative, or trying to be funny, can choose to address utterances like *Can you tell me the time?* as direct questions, and simply say *Yes*. There is also some psychological evidence that hearers have access to the direct act in indirect requests: Clark and Lucy (1975), for example, is a psycholinguistic study which concludes from testing subjects' responses to sentences like *Please color the circle blue*, *Why not color the circle blue?*, *I'll be very happy if you color the circle blue*, and so on that direct speech acts are understood more quickly and that hearers seem to have access to the literal meaning of indirect acts. Experiments by Clark and Schunk (1980) seem to confirm this: they suggest that the literal meaning of an indirect request is an important element in the perceived politeness of the act. Thus among indirect requests, *May I ask you what time it is?* is more polite than *Won't you tell me what time it is?* because the first sentence's literal meaning places the onus on speaker action, while the second places it on hearer action. Also, in answering *May I ask you what time it is?* the response *Yes, it's six* is more polite than just *It's six* because the former addresses both the direct and indirect speech acts, answering the question and complying with the request.

This last point raises an interesting issue: why do speakers employ these indirect acts? One motivation might be politeness, a hypothesis we examine in 8.4.3.

8.4.3 Indirect acts and politeness

Most commentators on indirect speech acts have remarked on the role of politeness. Searle (1975: 64), for example, writes:

8.29 In the field of indirect illocutionary acts, the area of directives is the most useful to study because ordinary conversational requirements of politeness normally make it awkward to issue flat imperative statements (e.g., *Leave the room*) or explicit performatives (e.g., *I order you to leave the room*), and we therefore seek to find indirect means to our illocutionary ends (e.g., *I wonder if you would mind leaving the room*). In directives, politeness is the chief motivation for indirectness.

Similarly, Ervin-Tripp's (1976) study of the social implications of indirect requests and orders in American English concludes that speakers do calculate issues of social power and politeness in framing speech acts. She suggests that indirect interrogative requests are useful because they give "listeners an out by explicitly stating some condition which would make compliance impossible" (p. 38), as in the following example of an indirect request and response (Ervin-Tripp 1976: 38):

8.30 [Daughter to father]
You ready?
Not yet.

This is even more pronounced with negative questions used indirectly as requests, for example (Ervin-Tripp 1976: 38):

8.31 [Motorist to gas station attendant]
You don't happen to have any change for the phone, do you?

Her study shows that the use of imperatives and *need* statements as directives is commoner from superiors to subordinates, for example (1976: 29):

8.32 [Doctor to nurse in hospital]
I'll need a 19 gauge needle, IV tubing, and a preptic swab.

while questions with modals like *can*, *could*, *may*, and so on as requests are commoner with superiors and non-familiars, for example (1976: 38):

8.33 [Salesman to clerk]
May I have change for a dollar?

8.34 [Employee to older employer]
May I have the salt?

Ervin-Tripp points out that, as we all know, getting the calculation right is important in maintaining social relationships: she gives the example 8.35 below (1976: 63), where the more polite form a is felt to be less appropriate than b:

8.35 [Young file clerks who have worked together for four months]
I got the applications done finally.
a. Could you take these back to Emma, please?
or
b. Take these with you.

As Ervin-Tripp remarks, "To address a familiar peer as a non-peer is to be cold and distancing" (p. 63).

The role of politeness in social interaction and conversation has been an important topic in sociology and conversational studies: we cannot hope to review this large literature here but a few remarks might shed useful light on the issue of indirect speech acts. We can begin by noting that work of the sociologist Ervin Goffman (1967, 1971, 1981)[12] on the social construction of the self, and his notion of **face** (roughly, the public image an individual seeks to project) has influenced a number of linguistic studies which have dealt with politeness, including Brown and Levinson (1978, 1987), Leech (1983) and Tannen (1984, 1986).

In Brown and Levinson's version, face is "the public self image that every member of society wants to claim for himself" (1978: 66). For them, face has two components: **positive face**, which represents an individual's desire to seem worthy and deserving of approval, and **negative face**, which represents an individual's desire to be autonomous, unimpeded by others. A kind of mutual self-interest requires that conversational participants maintain both their own face and their interactor's face. In this view, many verbal interactions are potential threats to face. Threats to negative face, which potentially damage an individual's autonomy, include orders, requests, suggestions and advice. Threats to positive face, which potentially lower an individual's self and social esteem, include expressions of disapproval, disagreements, accusations, and interruptions. Speakers can threaten their own face by their words: such self-threats to positive face include apologies and confessions.

In the continual interactive balancing of one's own and others' faces, politeness serves to diminish potential threats. In other words, speakers seek to weaken face-threatening acts by using a series of strategies, which together can be called politeness or tact. One of these strategies is the use of indirect speech acts.[13] These indirect acts can be seen to follow the distinction between positive and negative face. Negative indirectness helps to diminish the threat of orders and requests: examples would include giving an explanation for a request rather than the request itself, for example saying *It's very hot in here* instead of *Please open the window*; or as we saw earlier, querying a preparatory condition for the request, as in *Could you open the window?* Positive indirectness weakens the threat provided by disagreements, interruptions, and so on: for example, by prefacing them with apologies or explanation as in *I'm sorry but you're wrong* instead of simply *You're wrong*, or *I have to say that I don't agree* instead of *I don't agree*.

While the notion of politeness does seem to have explanatory value for the study of indirect speech acts, one important issue which it raises is cross-cultural variation. Researchers have applied the notion of politeness to a number of different languages and some have argued that the account of politeness strategies we have outlined, including the use of indirect speech acts, is too firmly based on European and North American, and particularly Anglophone, cultural norms. The notion of face, according to Brown and Levinson, is universal: every language community will have a system of politeness but the details of the system will vary because face is related to "the most fundamental cultural ideas about the nature of the social persona, honour and virtue, shame and redemption, and thus to religious concepts" (Brown and Levinson 1987: 13). Thus politeness strategies, and individual speech acts, will vary from culture to culture. This has been investigated by a number of studies containing implicit or explicit comparison with English, including Blum-Kulka (1983, 1987) on Hebrew, Wierzbicka (1985, 2003) on Polish, Matsumoto (1988, 1989), Fukishima (2003) and Haugh (2007) on Japanese, Hwang (1990) on Korean, Gu (1990) on Chinese, Sifianou (1992) on Greek, and Reiter (2000) and Felix-Brasdefer (2008) on Spanish. These studies give us insights into the politeness systems of their languages but the overall conclusion about a universal system is unclear: some have successfully applied a general system to the specific languages, while others like Matsumoto (1988) and Gu (1990) have claimed that Brown and Levinson's system does not adequately reflect conversational practices in the highly deferential societies they describe. Leech (2007) proposes a framework to overcome such cross-cultural differences in politeness strategies.

It seems safe though to conclude that both speech acts in general (thanks, apologies, compliments, invitations, etc.) and indirectness will vary from culture to culture. In terms of our current interest in indirect speech acts, comparisons have been made between requests in English and German (House and Kasper 1981) and English and Russian (Thomas 1983) which seem to suggest consistent differences, with a greater use of indirectness in English than the other two languages. However, Sifianou's (1992) study of requests in Greek and English reveals the complexity and difficulty of such comparisons. Her conclusion is that the Greek politeness system is more oriented toward positive face strategies and the (British) English to negative face, leading to different expectations of what conversational politeness is. Later research (e.g. Watts 2003, Terkourafi 2005) concentrated on the role of context rather than the form of utterances. Terkourafi's (2002) research on Cypriot Greek requests focuses on the actions of participants in matching between formulaic language and situational context to derive illocutionary force.

8.5 Sentence Types

Our final section takes us back to an issue we raised in chapter 5: how to decide whether a given grammatical category, say subjunctive, is a marker of a sentence type, or some semantic category like mood.[14] We have defined a sentence type as a conventional matching between a grammatical form and a speech act. Thus some languages have a question word which contrasts with a declarative word, as in the Somali examples 8.36a and b below, where there is also a contrast with a lack of such a word (or zero marking) for the imperative as in 8.36c:

8.36	a.	Warkii	miyaad	dhegeysatay?
		war+kii	ma+aad	dhegeysatay
		news+the	Q+you	listen.to-2sg-PAST
		"Did you listen to the news?"		
	b.	Warkii	waad	dhegeysatay.
		war+kii	waa+aad	dhegeysatay
		news+the	DECL+you	listen.to-2sg-PAST
		"You listened to the news."		
	c.	Warkii	dhegeyso!	
		news+the	listen to-2sg-IMP	
		"Listen to the news!"		

As these sentences show, the question word in 8.36a is *ma*, while *waa* in 8.36b marks a declarative; these words are called **classifiers** in Saeed (1993). Greenlandic marks a similar distinction with different verbal inflections for person, and so on (Sadock and Zwicky 1985: 167):

8.37 a. Igavoq
cook(INDIC 3SG)
"He cooks."
b. Igava
cook(Q 3SG)
"Does he cook?"

The problem however is that such marking by special words or inflections can be used for a variety of semantic distinctions. We can use some examples from Somali to show the difficulties, beginning with the lists in table 8.1, where the verb *keen* "bring" is used to show the forms.

As these tables show, the marking here is quite complicated: the system uses gaps as a marker in several places and tone is important: distinguishing the positive question word *ma* from the negative word *má*, and the optative word *há* from the negative imperative marker *ha*. Note too that the distinctions combine specific classifiers and verbal inflection.

For our current purposes, the question raised by both sections of table 8.1 is: does every classifier and negative morpheme in table 8.1 mark a distinct sentence type? The answer we would like to give is: only when it regularly and conventionally matches a corresponding speech act. Unfortunately however we do not have a pre-existing list of speech acts to help us decide this. The situation, though not clear-cut, is not totally gloomy however. Sadock and Zwicky (1985) for example suggest some rules of thumb for identifying sentence types, which we can modify slightly as follows:

Table 8.1 Possible Somali markers of sentence type

a. **Positive forms**

	Forms		
Sentence type	*Classifier*	*Verb*	*Meaning*
Declarative	*waa*	*keenaa*	"He brings it"
Interrogative	*ma*	*keenaa*	"Does he bring it?"
Imperative	–	*kèen*	"Bring (sg) it!"
Optative	*há*	*keeno*	"May he bring it!"
Potential	*shòw*	*keenee*	"Possibly he'll bring it, He may bring it"

b. **Negative forms**

	Forms			
Sentence type	*Classifier*	*Negative word*	*Verb*	*Meaning*
Declarative	–	*má*	*keenó*	"He doesn't bring it"
Interrogative	*sòw*	*má*	*keenó*	"Doesn't he bring it?"
Imperative	*ha*	–	*kéenin*	"Do not bring (sg) it!"
Optative	*yaan-u**	–	*kéenin*	"May he not bring it!"

**u* = "he"

Source: Saeed (1993: 80–81)[15]

8.38 a. The sentence types should form a system, so that there should be corresponding versions of a sentence in each type;
b. similarly, the types should be mutually exclusive, i.e. there should be no combinations of two sentence type markers in the same sentence;
c. as we have noted, there should be a conventional association with a speech act.

On the basis of rules like these, we can probably discount the **negative** morpheme *má* in table 8.1 as a marker of sentence type in Somali. Negation co-occurs with declarative and interrogative sentences, thus breaking rule 8.38b. This fact also indicates that this marker does not conventionally convey a speech act of denial in Somali, since it is used in, for example, negative questions, thus breaking rule 8.38c. The decisions are more difficult with the **optative** and **potential** markers in table 8.1. These occur in a regular correspondence with interrogative and other sentences but do not co-occur with them: no sentences are optative and interrogative, potential and declarative, and so on. Thus they seem to pass rules 8.38a and b. When it comes to 8.38c, the optative does seem a likely candidate for a sentence type because it is conventionally associated with **wishes** (like *Soomaaliya há noolaato!* "May Somalia live! Long live Somalia!"), which we know from other languages is a likely speech act. So we can add optative to interrogative, declarative and imperative as sentence types for Somali. However, the potential is a little more problematic: the type seems to pass our rules 8.38a and b since it doesn't co-occur with other markers; but note that there is no negative potential form. It is also difficult to view expressions of possibility as a distinct speech act rather than as a type of statement, differing from *waa* statements in showing a different part of the semantic range of modality.

Luckily, solving this descriptive problem is not necessary for our point here and we can leave the issue to one side. What this brief excursion into Somali sentence type marking shows us is that it is not necessarily an easy process to set up the sentence type half of the match-up between sentence type and speech act we identified in section 8.1. It also seems to indicate that markers of sentence type might have functions in other semantic systems.

8.6 Summary

In this chapter we have seen that the social function of an utterance is an important part of its meaning. We reviewed J. L. Austin's very influential theory of **speech acts**, which emphasizes the role of language in communicating social acts like requesting, questioning, promising, thanking, stating, as well as more institutional verbal acts like pronouncing sentence in court, or performing ceremonies of baptizing, marrying, and so on.

We saw that understanding the speech act force, or **illocutionary force** in Austin's terms, of an utterance involves the hearer in combining linguistic knowledge about grammatical marking with both background cultural knowledge and knowledge of the immediate local context. The determination of the linguistic marking of speech act force is in itself not a simple task: we saw that the markers may have other roles to perform in the grammar. Moreover, even when we can identify sentence types, the correlation between these and speech acts is not a steady one: the investigation of indirect speech acts reveals that inference and conversational principles play a role in hearers' recognition of a speech act. Overall the study of speech acts is a fascinating area: partly because their role is so crucial to the social interaction in a speech community (so that we have no choice but to study them) but also because they give us another glimpse of the interpretive powers that interactants routinely employ in order to communicate: unconsciously and seamlessly combining linguistic and other forms of knowledge in order to reach meaning. Speech act theory has been very influential in a wide range of disciplines from computer science (e.g. Georgila et al. 2009, Kibble 2013) to literary studies (e.g. Miller 2005) and theology (e.g. Adams 2006).

EXERCISES

8.1 In section 8.2.1 we used the ability to insert *hereby* appropriately as a test for a performative utterance. For each of the sentences below, use this as a test to decide which of the following sentences, when uttered, would count as a performative utterance, in Austin's terms:

a. I acknowledge you as my legal heir.
b. I give notice that I will stand down as chairman.
c. I'm warning you that it won't end here.
d. I think you're taking this press attention too seriously.
e. I deny all knowledge of this scandal.
f. I promised them there'd be no fuss.

8.2 Replace the following explicit performatives with corresponding implicit versions, e.g. *I predict that it will rain before teatime* → *It'll rain before teatime, mark my words.*

a. I insist that you come with us.
b. We order you to return to your unit.
c. I confess that I stole the money.
d. We invite you to join us for the weekend.
e. We request that you leave.

8.3 Given one example utterance for each of the illocutionary acts below:

a. promising
b. warning
c. requesting
d. apologizing
e. congratulating

8.4 In section 8.2.5 we noted Austin's distinction between the illocutionary act, the speech act intended by the speaker, and the perlocutionary act, the take-up by or effect upon its audience. For the following utterances try to invent a context and a plausible perlocutionary effect:

a. "Our flight is closing in five minutes!"
b. "What are you doing in here at this time?"
c. "Please turn off your mobile phone!"
d. "It's time for bed."
e. "Have you packed your malaria tablets?"

8.5 In the chapter we discussed Searle-type felicity conditions for the speech acts of **promising**, **questioning**, and **requesting**. Write similar conditions for the speech acts below, distinguishing for each between preparatory, propositional, sincerity and essential conditions:

a. Warning
b. Advising

8.6 Simple imperative sentences in English occur with the verb in the second person and with a morphologically bare form, as in *Leave the room!* The canonical direct speech act is an order. Using your own examples, give three or four other speech acts that an imperative can communicate in the right context. You might find it helpful to briefly describe the context allowing the speech act.

8.7 Interrogative sentences communicate the canonical direct speech act of questioning, as in *What is your name?* Again using your own examples give three or four other speech acts that an interrogative can communicate in the right context. Again it might be helpful to give some detail of the context allowing the speech act.

8.8 Below are some examples of statements that in context might communicate **indirect speech acts**. For each one try to identify a plausible indirect act:

a. [Customer telephoning a restaurant]
I'd like to book a table for tomorrow night.
b. [Military officer to subordinate]
You will hold this position until reinforcements arrive.
c. [Customer to barman]
I'll have the usual.
d. [Mother to child coming in from school]
I bet you're hungry.
e. [Bank manager to applicant for an overdraft]
We regret that we are unable to accede to your request.
f. [Fortune-teller to customer]
You will meet a tall dark stranger.
g. [Doorman at a nightclub to aspiring entrant]
You must be joking.

8.9 In example 8.26 in the chapter we gave a set of felicity conditions for **requesting**. Based on these, and using your own examples, try to form one indirect request for each of the following strategies:

a. by querying the preparatory condition of the direct request;
b. by stating the preparatory condition of the direct request;
c. by querying the propositional content of the direct request;
d. by stating the sincerity condition of the direct request.

8.10 Repeat exercise 8.9 for the speech act of **promising**, whose felicity conditions are given in example 8.20 in the chapter. Discuss which of the strategies in exercise 8.9 work for this speech act.

FURTHER READING

In addition to the primary sources already mentioned, speech act semantics is reviewed in Levinson (1983) and Sadock (2004). König and Siemund (2007) discuss speech acts and their grammatical forms across languages. Vanderveken and Kubo (2002) is an interdisciplinary collection of studies on speech acts. Kissine (2013) discusses the interpretation of speech acts, concentrating on constative, directive, and commissive acts. The papers in Sbisà and Turner (2013) survey recent issues in speech act theory. Ruiz de Zarobe and Ruiz de Zarobe (2012) contains articles exploring the link between speech acts and politeness across a range of languages. Kádár and Haugh (2013) provides an overview of research on politeness in communication. Searle (2007) examines the fundamental role of speech acts in human language and Searle (2010) situates speech acts in his philosophy of human social reality.

NOTES

1 These examples are in the standard Yoruba orthography, which includes the following: Tones: ´ = high tone, no mark = mid tone, ` = low tone. The subscript dot indicates distinct sounds: ọ = [ɔ], ẹ = [ɛ], ṣ = [ʃ]; and p and gb are labiovelar plosives [kp] and [gb].
2 In this approach questions and answers are an example of a more general interactional unit: the **adjacency pair**. This is a pair of utterances, which might consist of question–answer, summons–answer, compliment–acceptance/rejection, etc., which form an important structural unit in this theory's view of conversational interaction. The expectation of a response that is set up by the first part is called **conditioned relevance** by Schegloff (1972). See Levinson (1983: 226–79) and Schiffrin (1994: 232–81) for discussion.
3 See Saville-Troike (1989) for an introduction to the study of the conventions governing types of communication in different societies.
4 Such answers have been called **indirect answers** (Nofsinger 1976), **indirect responses** (Pearce and Conklin 1979), and **transparent questions** (Bowers 1982). These

studies discuss how speakers infer that such answers are equivalent to "yes" and "no," and investigate the different attitudes hearers have to such answers compared to literal answers.

5 Strawson (1964) argues for a category distinction between highly conventionalized acts like ship naming and weddings on the one hand and ordinary communicative acts like questions and requests on the other. In this view the former relies on recognizing social rituals and the latter on the recognition of a speaker's communicative intention, in the Gricean sense discussed in chapter 7.

6 We omit discussion of Austin's original five-fold classification of speech acts into *verdictives*, *exercitives*, *commissives*, *behabitives*, and *expositives* (Austin 1975: 148–64) since his proposals, which influence subsequent systems, are proposed in a very tentative way, e.g. "I distinguish five very general classes: but I am far from equally happy about all of them" (1975: 151) and "The last two classes are those which I find most troublesome, and it could well be that they are not clear or are cross-classified, or even that some fresh classification altogether is needed. I am not putting any of this forward as in the very least definitive" (1975: 152).

7 This somewhat inaccurately suggests that all speech acts have propositional content. As is well-known, some speech acts do not, for example *Sorry!* or *Excuse me!* for apologies, *Huh?* for a question, *Hello!* or *Hi!* as greetings, etc.

8 A **yes-no** (or elicitative) question seeks confirmation or denial of a proposition, and thus expects an answer yes or no, as in *Is Bill going to London?* An **elicitative** or WH-question seeks new information to augment what is already known, as in the following example, where the speaker knows that Bill is going but seeks extra information:

a. Where is Bill going?
b. When is Bill going?
c. Why is Bill going?

9 We can take a brief look at one of these as an example: Bach and Harnish (1979: 39–59) establish a general taxonomy very like Searle's in example 8.19, though they use six categories rather than five, and employ slightly different labels: **constatives** (e.g. assertions), **directives** (e.g. questions), **commissives** (e.g. promises), **acknowledgments** (e.g. greetings), and **effectives** (e.g. naming a ship) and **verdictives** (e.g. finding a defendant guilty). For their constative class, for example, which corresponds to Searle's representatives, they identify fifteen sub-types, each characterized by a description of the act performed and exemplified by English verbs. We can provide a few of their examples of constative and directive class:

1 Bach and Harnish's (1979) **constative** speech acts
[where *S* = speaker, *H* = hearer, *e* = linguistic expression, *P* = the proposition expressed in the speech act]

a. *Assertives* (simple): (affirm, allege, assert, aver, avow, claim, declare, deny (assert ... not), indicate, maintain, propound, say, state, submit)
In uttering *e*, *S* asserts that *P* if *S* expresses:
i. the belief that *P*, and
ii. the intention that *H* believe that *P*.

b. *Predictives*: (forecast, predict, prophesy)
In uttering *e*, *S* predicts that *P* if *S* expresses:
i. the belief that it will be the case that *P*, and
ii. the intention that *H* believe that it will be the case that *P*.

c. *Concessives*: (acknowledge, admit, agree, allow, assent, concede, concur, confess, grant, own)
In uttering *e*, *S* concedes that *P* if *S* expresses:
i. the belief that *P*, contrary to what he would like to believe or contrary to what he previously believed or avowed, and
ii. the intention that *H* believe that *P*.

2 Bach and Harnish's (1979) **directive** speech acts
[where S = speaker, H = hearer, e = linguistic expression, P = the proposition expressed in the speech act, A = the future action]
a. *Requestives*: (ask, beg, beseech, implore, insist, invite, petition, plead, pray, request, solicit, summon, supplicate, tell, urge)
In uttering *e*, *S* requests *H* to *A* if *S* expresses:
i. the desire that *H* do *A*, and
ii. the intention that *H* do *A* because (at least partly) of *S*'s desire.
b. *Questions*: (ask, enquire, interrogate, query, question, quiz)
In uttering *e*, *S* questions *H* as to whether or not *P* if *S* expresses:
i. the desire that *H* tell *S* whether or not *P*, and
ii. the intention that *H* tell *S* whether or not *P* because of *H*'s desire.
c. *Requirements*: (bid, charge, command, demand, dictate, direct, enjoin, instruct, order, prescribe, require)
In uttering *e*, *S* requires *H* to *A* if *S* expresses:
i. the belief that his utterance, in virtue of his authority over *H*, constitutes sufficient reason for *H* to *A*, and
ii. the intention that *H* do *A* because of *S*'s utterance.

10 Searle (1975: 72) notes that asking whether the sincerity condition holds won't work. So asking *Do I wish you wouldn't do that?* will not work as an indirect form of a request, *Please don't do that.*

11 A position close to this is adopted by Sadock (1974).

12 See Schiffrin (1994: 97–136) for a discussion of Goffman's work and its influence on conversational analysis.

13 See Brown and Levinson (1978, 1987) for a discussion of other possible strategies for performing face-threatening acts.

14 Or both: see note 15 below.

15 In Saeed (1993: 79–85) words like *waa*, *ma*, *shòw*, etc. are taken to be part of the mood system. This is because, as our discussion here hints, the two systems of modality and sentence type marking overlap in these forms. For example we can analyze the distinction between positive statements with *waa*, negative statements with *má*, and potential sentences with *shòw* as being part of the system of mood marking, i.e. marking a distinction between (for proposition *P*): certainty that-*P*, possibility that-*P*, and certainty that not-*P*. As we note here, *waa* also seems to mark the speech act of stating.

REFERENCES

Adams, Jim W. 2006. *The Performative Nature and Function of Isaiah 40–55*. New York: T & T Clark.

Akindele, Femi 1990: A sociolinguistic analysis of Yoruba greetings. *African Languages and Cultures* 3.1: 1–14.

Allan, Keith. 2006: Clause-type, primary illocution, and mood-like operators in English. *Language Sciences* 28.1: 1–50.

Alston, W. 2000: *Illocutionary Acts and Sentence Meaning*. Ithaca, NY: Cornell University Press.

Atkinson, J. Maxwell and John Heritage (eds.) 1984: *Structures of Social Action*. Cambridge: Cambridge University Press.

Austin, J. L. 1975: *How to Do Things with Words*, second edition. Oxford: Clarendon Press. (First published 1962.)

Ayer, Alfred J. (ed.) 1959: *Logical Positivism*. New York: Free Press.

Bach, Kent and Robert M. Harnish 1979: *Linguistic Communication and Speech Acts*. Cambridge, MA: MIT Press.

Blum-Kulka, Shoshana 1983: Interpreting and performing speech acts in a second language: a cross-cultural study of Hebrew and English. In Nessa Wolfson and Elliot Judd (eds.) *Sociolinguistics and Language Acquisition*, 36–55. Rowley, MA: Newbury House.

Blum-Kulka, Shoshana 1987: Indirectness and politeness in requests: same or different? *Journal of Pragmatics* 11: 131–46.

Bowers, J. W. 1982: Does a duck have antlers? Some pragmatics of "transparent questions." *Communication Monographs* 42: 63–69.

Brown, Penelope and Stephen C. Levinson 1987: *Politeness: Some Universals in Language Usage*. Cambridge: Cambridge University Press.

Clark, Herbert H. and Peter Lucy 1975: Understanding what is meant from what is said: a study in conversationally conveyed requests. *Journal of Verbal Learning and Verbal Behaviour* 14: 56–72.

Clark, Herbert H. and Dale H. Schunk 1980: Polite responses to polite requests. *Cognition* 8: 111–43.

Cole, Peter and Jerry Morgan (eds.) 1975: *Syntax and Semantics. Vol. 3: Speech Acts*. New York: Academic Press.

Croft, William 1994: Speech act classification, language typology and cognition. In S. L. Tsohatzidis (ed.) *Foundations of Speech Act Theory: Philosophical and Linguistic Perspectives*, 460–77. London: Routledge.

Dowty, David R. 1979: *Word Meaning and Montague Grammar*. Dordrecht: Reidel.

Ervin-Tripp, Susan 1976: Is Sybil there? The structure of some American English directives. *Language in Society* 5: 25–66.

Felix-Brasdefer, J. Cesar 2008: *Politeness in Mexico and the United States: A Contrastive Study of the Realization and Perception of Refusals*. Amsterdam: John Benjamins.

Fraser, Bruce 1975: Hedged performatives. In Peter Cole and Jerry Morgan (eds.) *Syntax and Semantics. Vol. 3: Speech Acts*, 187–210. New York: Academic Press.

Fukishima, Saeko 2003: *Requests and Culture: Politeness in British English and Japanese*. Bern: Peter Lang.

Gazdar, Gerald 1981: Speech act assignment. In Aaravind K. Joshi, Bonnie L. Webber and Ivan A. Sag (eds.) *Elements of Discourse Understanding*. Cambridge: Cambridge University Press.

Georgila, K., O. Lemon, J. Henderson, and J. Moore 2009: Automatic annotation of context and speech acts for dialogue corpora. *Natural Language Engineering* 15.3: 315–53.

Goffman, Erving 1967: *Interaction Ritual: Essays in Face-to-Face Behavior*. Garden City, NY: Anchor Books.

Goffman, Erving 1971: *Relations in Public*. New York: Basic Books.

Goffman, Erving 1981: *Forms of Talk*. Philadelphia: University of Pennsylvania Press.

Goodwin, Charles 1979: *Conversation Organization*. New York: Academic Press.

Gordon, David and George Lakoff 1975: Conversational postulates. In Peter Cole and Jerry Morgan (eds.) *Syntax and Semantics. Vol. 3: Speech Acts*, 83–106. New York: Academic Press.

Green, Mitchell S. 2013: Assertions. In Sbisà and Turner (eds.), 387–410.

Gu, Yueguo 1990: Politeness phenomena in Modern Chinese. *Journal of Pragmatics* 14: 237–57.

Hancher, M. 1979: The classification of cooperative illocutionary acts. *Language in Society* 8.1: 1–14.

Haugh, Michael 2007: Emic conceptualisations of (im)politeness and face in Japanese: implications for the discursive negotiation of second language learner identities. *Journal of Pragmatics* 39: 657–80.

House, Juliane and Gabriele Kasper 1981: Politeness markers in English and German. In Florian Coulmas (ed.) *Conversational Routine: Explorations in Standardized Communication Situations and Prepatterned Speech*, 157–85. The Hague: Mouton.

Hwang, Juck-Ryoon 1990: "Deference" versus "politeness" in Korean speech. *International Journal of the Sociology of Language* 82: 41–55.

Jackendoff, Ray 1983: *Semantics and Cognition*. Cambridge, MA: MIT Press.
Jucker, Andreas H. and Irma Taavitsainen (eds.) 2008: *Speech Acts in the History of English*. Amsterdam: John Benjamins.
Kádár, Dániel and Michael Haugh 2013: *Understanding Politeness*. Cambridge: Cambridge University Press.
Kibble, Rodger 2013: Speech Act Theory and intelligent software agents. In Sbisà and Turner (eds.), 313–38.
Kissine, Mikhail. 2013. *From Utterances to Speech*. Cambridge: Cambridge University Press.
König, E. and P. Siemund 2007: Speech act distinctions in grammar. In T. Shopen (ed.): *Language Typology and Syntactic Description. Volume I: Clause Structure*, 2nd edition, 276–324. Cambridge: Cambridge University Press.
Leech, Geoffrey 2007: Politeness: is there an East-West divide? *Journal of Politeness Research* 3.2: 167–206.
Leech, Geoffrey N. 1983: *Principles of Pragmatics*. London: Longman.
Levinson, Stephen C. 1983: *Pragmatics*. Cambridge: Cambridge University Press.
Matsumoto, Yoshiko 1988: Reexamination of the universality of face: politeness phenomena in Japanese. *Journal of Pragmatics* 12: 403–26.
Matsumoto, Yoshiko 1989: Politeness and conversational universals: observations from Japanese. *Multilingua* 8: 207–21.
Miller, J. Hillis 2005: *Literature as Conduct: Speech Acts in Henry James*. New York: Fordham University Press.
Nofsinger, Robert E. 1976: Answering questions indirectly. *Human Communication Research* 2: 171–81.
Pearce, W. Barnett and R. Forrest Conklin 1979: A model of hierarchical meaning in coherent conversation and a study of "indirect responses." *Communication Monographs* 46: 75–87.
Recanati, François 1987: *Meaning and Force: The Pragmatics of Performative Utterances*. Cambridge: Cambridge University Press.
Reiter, Rosina Márquez 2000: *Linguistic Politeness in Britain and Uruguay: A Contrastive Study of Requests and Apologies*. Amsterdam: John Benjamins.
Ruiz de Zarobe, Leyre and Yolanda Ruiz de Zarobe (eds.) 2012: *Speech Acts and Politeness across Languages and Cultures*. Bern: Peter Lang.
Sadock, Jerrold M. 1974: *Towards a Linguistic Theory of Speech Acts*. New York: Academic Press.
Sadock, Jerrold M. 1994: Toward a grammatically realistic typology of speech acts. In S. L. Tsohatzidis (ed.) *Foundations of Speech Act Theory: Philosophical and Linguistic Perspectives*, 393–406. London: Routledge.
Sadock, Jerrold M. 2004: Speech acts. In L. Horn and G. Ward (eds.) *The Handbook of Pragmatics*, 53–73. Oxford: Blackwell.
Sadock, Jerrold M. and Arnold M. Zwicky 1985: Speech act distinctions in syntax. In Timothy Shopen (ed.) *Language Typology and Syntactic Description*, vol. 1, 155–96. Cambridge: Cambridge University Press.
Saeed, John Ibrahim 1993: *Somali Reference Grammar*, second edition. Kensington, MD: Dunwoody Press.
Saville-Troike, Muriel 1989: *The Ethnography of Communication: An Introduction*, second edition. Oxford: Blackwell.
Sbisà, Marina and Ken Turner (eds.) 2013: *Pragmatics of Speech Actions*. Berlin: Mouton de Gruyter.
Schegloff, Emanuel A. 1972: Sequencing in conversational openings. In John J. Gumpertz and Dell Hymes (eds.) *Directions in Sociolinguistics*, 346–80. New York: Holt, Rinehart & Winston.
Schegloff, Emanuel A. 1979: The relevance of repair to syntax-for-conversation. In Talmy Givón (ed.) *Syntax and Semantics. Vol. 12: Discourse and Syntax*, 261–88. New York: Academic Press.

Schegloff, Emanuel A. and Harvey Sacks 1973: Opening up closings. *Semiotica* 7: 289–327.
Schiffer, Stephen 1972: *Meaning*. Oxford: Oxford University Press.
Schiffrin, Deborah 1994: *Approaches to Discourse*. Oxford: Blackwell.
Searle, John R. 1969: *Speech Acts*. Cambridge: Cambridge University Press.
Searle, John R. 1975: Indirect speech acts. In Peter Cole and Jerry Morgan (eds.) *Syntax and Semantics. Vol. 3: Speech Acts*, 59–82. New York: Academic Press.
Searle, John R. 1976: The classification of illocutionary acts. *Language in Society* 5: 1–23. Reprinted in *Expression and Meaning: Studies in the Theory of Speech Acts*, 1979. Cambridge: Cambridge University Press, 1–29.
Searle, John R. 1999. *Mind, Language and Society: Philosophy in the Real World*. New York: Basic Books.
Searle, John R. 2007. What is language: some preliminary remarks. In S. L. Tsohatzidis (ed.) *John Searle's Philosophy of Language: Force, Meaning, and Mind*, 15–46. Cambridge: Cambridge University Press.
Searle, John R. 2010. *Making the Social World: The Structure of Human Civilization*. Oxford: Oxford University Press.
Sifianou, Maria 1992: *Politeness Phenomena in England and Greece: A Cross-Cultural Perspective*. Oxford: Clarendon Press.
Strawson, P. 1964: Intention and convention in speech acts. *Philosophical Review* 73: 439–60.
Tannen, Deborah 1984: *Conversational Style: Analyzing Talk among Friends*. Norwood, NJ: Ablex.
Tannen, D. 1986: *That's Not What I Meant: How Conversational Style Makes or Breaks Your Relations with Others*. New York: W. Morrow and Co.
Terkourafi, Marina 2002: Politeness and formulaicity. *Journal of Greek Linguistics* 3: 179–201.
Terkourafi, Marina 2005: An argument for a frame-based approach to politeness. In R. T. Lakoff and S. Ide (eds.), *Broadening the Horizon of Linguistic Politeness*, 99–116. Amsterdam: John Benjamins.
Thomas, Jenny 1983: Cross-cultural pragmatic failure. *Applied Linguistics* 4: 91–112.
Vanderveken, D. 1990: *Meaning and Speech Acts*, 2 vols. Cambridge. Cambridge University Press.
Vanderveken, D. and S. Kubo (eds.) 2002: *Essays in Speech Act Theory*. Amsterdam: John Benjamins.
Watts, Richard 2003: *Politeness*. Cambridge: Cambridge University Press.
Wierzbicka, Anna 1985: Different cultures, different languages, different speech acts: Polish vs. English. *Journal of Pragmatics* 9: 145–78.
Wierzbicka, Anna 1987: *English Speech Act Verbs: A Semantic Dictionary*. Sydney: Academic Press.
Wierzbicka, Anna 2003: *Cross-cultural Pragmatics: The Semantics of Human Interaction*, second edition. Berlin: Mouton de Gruyter.
Zaefferer, Dietmar 2001: Deconstructing a classical classification:a typological look at Searle's concept of illocution type. *Revue Internationale de Philosophie* 217: 209–25.

part III

Theoretical Approaches

chapter 9

Meaning Components

9.1 Introduction

In chapter 3 we reviewed a range of lexical relations, including the MALE–FEMALE and ADULT–YOUNG relations in sets of words like those below:

9.1	man–woman–child	ram–ewe–lamb
	dog–bitch–pup	bull–cow–calf
	stallion–mare–foal	boar–sow–piglet

As we saw, these and other relations are characteristic of the lexicon. To explain this networking, some semanticists have hypothesized that words are not the smallest semantic units but are built up of smaller components of meaning which are combined differently (or **lexicalized**) to form different words.

Thus, to take perhaps the commonest examples in the literature, words like *woman*, *bachelor*, *spinster*, and *wife* have been viewed as being composed of elements such as [ADULT], [HUMAN] and so on:

9.2	*woman*	[FEMALE]	[ADULT]	[HUMAN]	
	bachelor	[MALE]	[ADULT]	[HUMAN]	[UNMARRIED]
	spinster	[FEMALE]	[ADULT]	[HUMAN]	[UNMARRIED]
	wife	[FEMALE]	[ADULT]	[HUMAN]	[MARRIED]

The elements in square brackets in 9.2 above are called **semantic components,** or **semantic primitives,** and this kind of analysis is often called **componential analysis** (CA for short). As we shall see in this chapter, there are three related reasons for identifying such components. The first is that they may allow an economic characterization of the lexical relations that we looked at in chapter 2, and the sentence relations we discussed in chapter 4, like the contradiction between 9.3a and b below, or the entailment between 9.4a and b:

9.3 a. Ferdinand is dead.
b. Ferdinand is alive.

9.4 a. Henrietta cooked some lamb chops.
b. Henrietta cooked some meat.

In the next section, 9.2, we discuss how semantic components might be used to capture lexical relations, and in 9.3 we look briefly at Jerrold Katz's semantic theory, a componential theory designed to capture such semantic phenomena. A second, related, justification for semantic components is that they have linguistic import outside semantics: that only by recognizing them can we accurately describe a range of syntactic and morphological processes. We look at this claim in section 9.4. The third and most ambitious claim is that in addition to these two important uses, such semantic primitives form part of our psychological architecture: that they provide us with a unique view of conceptual structure. We look at two versions of this approach when we examine the work of Ray Jackendoff in section 9.6 and James Pustejovsky in 9.7.

9.2 Lexical Relations in CA

One use for semantic components is that they might allow us to define the lexical relations we looked at earlier. Take, for example, **hyponymy** (inclusion). Below we can see that *spinster* is a hyponym of *woman*, and their components might be given as shown:

9.5	*woman*	[FEMALE]	[ADULT]	[HUMAN]	
	spinster	[FEMALE]	[ADULT]	[HUMAN]	[UNMARRIED]

We can see that by comparing the sets of components we could define hyponymy as:

9.6 A lexical item P can be defined as a hyponym of Q if all the features of Q are contained in the feature specification of P.

Similarly we might be able to deal with some kinds of antonymy, or more generally **incompatibility,** as in 9.7 below. The words *spinster, bachelor, wife* are incompatible and from a comparison of their components we might suggest a definition like 9.8:

9.7	*bachelor*	[MALE]	[ADULT]	[HUMAN]	[UNMARRIED]
	spinster	[FEMALE]	[ADULT]	[HUMAN]	[UNMARRIED]
	wife	[FEMALE]	[ADULT]	[HUMAN]	[MARRIED]

9.8 Lexical items P, Q, R . . . are incompatible if they share a set of features but differ from each other by one or more contrasting features.

Thus *spinster* is incompatible with *bachelor* by contrast of gender specification; and with *wife* by the marital specification. Note that these definitions are not exact but are meant to give a general idea of how this approach might proceed. Componential analysts also often make use of **binary features** and **redundancy rules**, which we can briefly describe.

9.2.1 Binary features

Some linguists use a binary feature format for these components, similar to that used in phonology and syntax. Our original examples will in this format be as below:

9.9	*woman*	[+FEMALE]	[+ADULT]	[+HUMAN]	
	bachelor	[−FEMALE]	[+ADULT]	[+HUMAN]	[−MARRIED]
	spinster	[+FEMALE]	[+ADULT]	[+HUMAN]	[−MARRIED]
	wife	[+FEMALE]	[+ADULT]	[+HUMAN]	[+MARRIED]

Note that this allows a characterization of antonyms by a difference of the value plus or minus a feature, and so offers a more economical format.

9.2.2 Redundancy rules

The statement of semantic components is also more economical if we include some redundancy rules which predict the automatic relationships between components. An example of such a rule is:

9.10 HUMAN → ANIMATE
ADULT → ANIMATE
ANIMATE → CONCRETE
MARRIED → ADULT
etc.

If we state these rules once for the whole dictionary, we can avoid repeating the component on the right of a rule in each of the entries containing the component on the left: so every time we enter [HUMAN], for example, we don't have to enter [ANIMATE]. With redundancy rules like 9.10, an entry like 9.11a below for *wife* might be stated more economically as in 9.11b:

9.11 a. *wife* [+FEMALE] [+HUMAN] [+ADULT] [+MARRIED] [+ANIMATE] [+CONCRETE], etc.
b. *wife* [+FEMALE] [+ADULT] [+MARRIED]

To sum up: in this approach each lexical item would be entered in the dictionary with a complex of semantic components. There will be in addition a set of redundancy rules for these components which apply automatically to reduce the number of components stated for each item. Lexical relations can then be stated in terms of the components.

9.3 Katz's Semantic Theory

9.3.1 Introduction

One of the earliest approaches to semantics within generative grammar was componential: it appeared in Katz and Fodor (1963), and was later refined, notably in Katz and Postal (1964) and Katz (1972):[1] for simplicity we will refer to it as **Katz's theory**. Two central ideas of this theory are:

1. Semantic rules have to be **recursive** for the same reasons as syntactic rules: that the number of possible sentences in a language is very large, possibly infinite.
2. The relationship between a sentence and its meaning is not arbitrary and unitary, i.e. syntactic structure and lexical content interact so that *John killed Fred* and *Fred killed John* do not have the same meaning despite containing the same lexical elements; nor do *The snake frightened Mary* and *The movie delighted Horace* despite having the same syntactic structure. In other words meaning is **compositional**. The way words are combined into phrases and phrases into sentences determines the meaning of the sentences.

Katz's theory reflects this by having rules which take input from both the syntactic component of the grammar, and from the dictionary. For these linguists the aims of the semantic component, paralleling the aims of syntax, are:

1. to give specifications of the meanings of lexical items;
2. to give rules showing how the meanings of lexical items build up into the meanings of phrases and so on up to sentences; and
3. to do this in a universally applicable metalanguage.

The first two aims are met by having two components: firstly, a dictionary which pairs lexical items with a semantic representation; and secondly, a set of **projection rules**, which show how the meanings of sentences are built up from the meanings of lexical items. The third aim is partially met by the use of semantic components. We can look at the dictionary and the projection rules in turn.

9.3.2 The Katzian dictionary

The details of the form of dictionary entries changed considerably during the development of this theory; we can risk abstracting a kind of typical entry for the most famous example: the word *bachelor* (adapted from Katz and Fodor 1963, Katz and Postal 1964):[2]

9.12 *bachelor* {N}

a. (human) (male) [one who has never been married]

b. (human) (male) [young knight serving under the standard of another knight]
c. (human) [one who has the first or lowest academic degree]
d. (animal) (male) [young fur seal without a mate in the breeding season]

The conventions for this entry are as follows. Information within curly brackets {*i*} is grammatical information; here simply that the four readings are all nouns. Our entry in 9.12 contains two types of semantic component: the first, the elements within parentheses (*i*), are **semantic markers**. These are the links which bind the vocabulary together, and are responsible for the lexical relations we looked at earlier. The second type, shown within square brackets [*i*], are **distinguishers**. This is idiosyncratic semantic information that identifies the lexical item. So Katz and his colleagues built into their theory the common-sense idea that part of a word's meaning is shared with other words, but part is unique to that word.

9.3.3 Projection rules

These rules are responsible for showing how the meaning of words combines into larger structures. Since this theory was designed to be part of a Chomskyan generative grammar, the rules interfaced with a generative syntactic component. So typically the projection rules operated on syntactic phrase markers, or "trees," as in figure 9.1. The projection rules used these trees to structure the amalgamation of word meanings into phrase meanings, and then phrase meanings into the sentence's meaning. Again we can select a standard example from Katz and Fodor (1963) in figure 9.1. In this figure the subscripts (1–4) on the syntactic labels show the order of amalgamation of semantic readings, once the individual words had been attached to the bottom of the tree. To keep the figure readable, we just include the words, not their associated dictionary entries, which are of course what is actually being amalgamated; we'll look at this fuller version a little later. Thus the projection rules begin at the bottom of the syntactic tree by amalgamating the semantic readings of *the* and *man* to give the semantics of the NP *the man.* Similarly, the rules combine the semantics of *colorful* and *ball,* then adds the semantics of *the,* to form the NP *the*

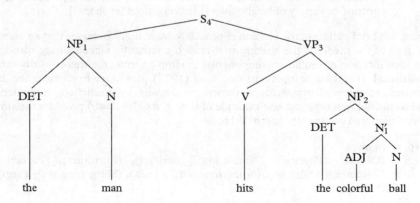

Figure 9.1 Projection rules

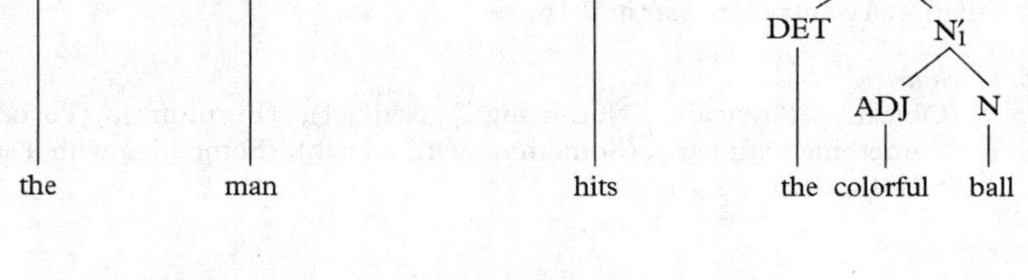

colorful ball. Thereafter the rules move up the tree combining elements until a semantic representation for the whole sentence *The man hits the colorful ball* is reached. We can see that these projection rules are clearly designed to reflect the compositionality of meaning.

The main constraint on the amalgamation processes involved in these rules is provided by **selection restrictions**. These are designed to reflect some of the contextual effects on word meaning. We can stay with the same example and look at the dictionary entries for *colorful* and *ball* in 9.13 and 9.14 below, with the selectional restrictions shown on the adjective in angle brackets < >:

9.13 **colorful** {ADJ}
- a. (color) [abounding in contrast or variety of bright colors] <(physical object) or (social activity)>
- b. (evaluative) [having distinctive character, vividness, or picturesqueness] <(aesthetic object) or (social activity)>

9.14 **ball** {N}
- a. (social activity) (large) (assembly) [for the purpose of social dancing]
- b. (physical object) [having globular shape]
- c. (physical object) [solid missile for projection by engine of war]

Thus the dictionary provides two readings for *colorful* and three for *ball*; and as we noted, the selection restrictions which restrict co-occurrence are attached to the adjective. To see how this works we can observe that by simple arithmetic the two readings for *colorful* and the three for *ball* should produce six combinations for *colorful ball*. However, some combinations are blocked by the selection restrictions: the second reading of *colorful*, being restricted to (aesthetic object) or (social activity) will not match the second or third readings for *ball*.

As the projection rules successively amalgamate readings, the selection restrictions will limit the final output. We will not spell out the process in any great detail here except to show one legal output of the amalgamation rules for figure 9.1:

9.15 *The man hits the colorful ball.*
[Some contextually definite] – (physical object) – (human) – (adult) – (male) – (action) – (instancy) – (intensity) [strikes with a blow or missile] – [some contextually definite] – (physical object) – (color) – [[abounding in contrast or variety of bright colors] [having globular shape]]

From this brief outline of the Katzian approach to meaning, we can see that an essential part of the theory is the attempt to establish a semantic metalanguage through the identification of semantic components: in simple terms, the theory is **decompositional**. It is these components that Katz (1972) uses to try to characterize the semantic relations of hyponymy, antonymy, synonymy, contradiction, entailment, and so on. We can take just one example of this: Katz (1972: 40) provides the simplified dictionary entry for *chair* in 9.16:

9.16 *chair*
(Object), (Physical), (Non-living), (Artifact), (Furniture), (Portable), (Something with legs), (Something with a back), (Something with a seat), (Seat for one)

Katz argues that the internal structure of components in 9.16 can explain the entailment relation between 9.17 below and each of 9.18a–h:

9.17 There is a chair in the room.

9.18 a. There is a physical object in the room.
b. There is something non-living in the room.
c. There is an artifact in the room.
d. There is a piece of furniture in the room.
e. There is something portable in the room.
f. There is something having legs in the room.
g. There is something with a back in the room.
h. There is a seat for one in the room.

This then is a semantic justification for meaning components: in the next section we review arguments that semantic components are necessary for the correct description of syntactic processes too.

9.4 Grammatical Rules and Semantic Components

As mentioned earlier, some linguists claim that we need semantic components to describe grammatical processes correctly, that is, it is grammatically necessary to recognize that certain units of meaning are shared by different lexical items. Thus two verbs might share a semantic concept, for example MOTION, or CAUSE. We could reflect this in two complementary ways: one is by setting up verb classes, for example of **motion verbs** or **causative verbs**; the other is to factor out the shared element of meaning and view it as a semantic component. In this section we review some components that have been proposed in the analysis of grammatical processes and we begin by looking at the basic methodology of this approach.

9.4.1 The methodology

To see the effect of these assumptions on methodology, we can look at an example from Beth Levin's study of the semantics of English verbs (Levin 1993). As part of this study, she investigates the semantic features of four English verbs by examining their grammatical behavior. The verbs are *cut*, *break*, *touch*, *hit* (Levin 1993: 5ff.). All four are transitive verbs as shown in:

9.19 a. Margaret cut the bread.
b. Janet broke the vase.
c. Terry touched the cat.
d. Carla hit the door.

Levin looks at how these four verbs interact with three different constructions which are usually seen as involving alternations of argument structure: **middle** constructions as in 9.20;[3] **conative** constructions involving *at*, as in the b sentences in 9.21 and 9.22; and what she terms **body part ascension** constructions, as in the b sentences in 9.23 and 9.24:

Middle construction:

9.20 a. These shirts wash well.
b. This car drives very smoothly.

Conative construction:

9.21 a. He chopped the meat.
b. He chopped at the meat.

9.22 a. They shot the bandits.
b. They shot at the bandits.

Body part ascension construction:

9.23 a. Mary slapped Fred's face.
b. Mary slapped Fred in the face.

9.24 a. Igor tapped Lavinia's shoulder.
b. Igor tapped Lavinia on the shoulder.

As Levin's examples in 9.25–7 below show, not all of these four verbs occur in each of these constructions:

9.25 Middle
a. The bread cuts easily.
b. Crystal vases break easily.
c. *Cats touch easily.
d. *Door frames hit easily.

9.26 Conative
a. Margaret cut at the bread.
b. *Janet broke at the vase.
c. *Terry touched at the cat.
d. Carla hit at the door.

9.27 Body part ascension
a. Margaret cut Bill's arm.
b. Margaret cut Bill on the arm.
c. Janet broke Bill's finger.
d. *Janet broke Bill on the finger.
e. Terry touched Bill's shoulder.
f. Terry touched Bill on the shoulder.
g. Carla hit Bill's back.
h. Carla hit Bill on the back.

In fact the four verbs have distinct patterns of occurrence with the three grammatical processes, as shown in 9.28 (Levin 1993: 6–7).

9.28	*touch*	*hit*	*cut*	*break*
Conative	No	Yes	Yes	No
Body part ascension	Yes	Yes	Yes	No
Middle	No	No	Yes	Yes

On the basis of this grammatical behavior, the semanticist can hypothesize that each of these verbs belongs to a different set, and indeed further investigations of this sort would confirm this. Other verbs which belong to these sets are shown in 9.29:

9.29 a. *Break* verbs: break, crack, rip, shatter, snap . . .
b. *Cut* verbs: cut, hack, saw, scratch, slash . . .
c. *Touch* verbs: pat, stroke, tickle, touch . . .
d. *Hit* verbs: bash, hit, kick, pound, tap, whack . . .

We have dealt with this example at length because it shows how verb classes can be set up within this type of approach. The next move in a decompositional approach, as we described earlier, would be to try to establish what meaning components might be responsible for this bunching of verbs into classes. Levin's conclusion, based on further analysis, is as in 9.30 (1993: 9–10):

9.30 touch is a pure verb of contact, hit is a verb of contact by motion, cut is a verb of causing a change of state by moving something into contact with the entity that changes state, and break is a pure verb of change of state.

This might provide us with the semantic components in 9.31 below, and suggests that, whatever other elements of meaning they might contain, we might analyze these four verbs as in 9.32:

9.31 CHANGE, MOTION, CONTACT, CAUSE

9.32 *cut* CAUSE, CHANGE, CONTACT, MOTION
break CAUSE, CHANGE
touch CONTACT
hit CONTACT, MOTION

So from a componential point of view, the presence of these different semantic components in these verbs causes them to participate in different grammatical rules. It follows then that correctly identifying the semantic components of a verb will help predict the grammatical processes it undergoes.

Of course the semantic components identified in 9.32 are only part of the meaning of these verbs. For a discussion of the relationship between these components and other elements of a verb's meaning, see Pinker (1989: 165ff) and his "Grammatically Relevant Subsystem" hypothesis. This hypothesis is that only some components of a word's meaning, such as those in 9.32, which are shared by a number of words, are relevant to grammatical processes; other item-specific elements are not. Pinker gives the example of the English verb *to butter* (Pinker 1989: 166):

9.33 Thus a verb like *to butter* would specify information about butter and information about causation, but only the causation part could trigger or block the application of lexical rules or other linguistic processes.

We can perhaps liken this distinction among semantic information to Katz's distinction, discussed earlier, between semantic **markers** and **distinguishers**. Components like those in 9.32 which form part of Pinker's grammatically relevant subset would correspond to Katz's markers, though Pinker's focus is on lexical rules rather than lexical relations. It is clear that Pinker, along with other writers, considers the grammatically relevant subset to be the main focus of research into language universals and language acquisition. The aim is to establish:

9.34 a set of elements that is at once conceptually interpretable, much smaller than the set of possible verbs, used across all languages, used by children to formulate and generalize verb meanings, used in specifically grammatical ways (for example, being lexicalized into closed-class morphemes), and used to differentiate the narrow classes that are subject to different sets of lexical rules. (Pinker 1989: 169)

A number of different terms have been used to make this binary distinction in the meaning of lexical items, including the following:

9.35 Grammatically relevant subsytem *versus* unrestricted conceptual representation (Pinker 1989)
Semantic structure *versus* semantic content (Grimshaw 1994)
Semantic form *versus* conceptual structure (Wunderlich 1997)
Semantic structure *versus* conceptual structure (Mohanan and Mohanan 1999)
Structural meaning *versus* conceptual meaning (Ramchand 2008).

Rappaport Hovav and Levin (2008, 2010) make a similar distinction between **event schema**, for a verb's grammatically relevant features, and **root meaning**, for the idiosyncratic component of a verb's meaning. In their approach a verb's meaning consists of a combination of both. Each verb's idiosyncratic root meaning also belongs to an ontological classification, for example state, result state, manner, instrument, and so on. Some possible combinations are shown below in 9.36, where the verb's root category is given on the left of each arrow and its role in combination with an event schema is shown to the right. Example verbs are given in italics:

9.36 Verb root and event schemas (Rappaport Hovav and Levin 2008)
a. manner → [x $\text{ACT}_{\text{manner}}$]
(e.g. *jog, run, creak, whistle*, . . .)
b. instrument → [x $\text{ACT}_{\text{instrument}}$]
(e.g. *brush, chisel, saw, shovel*, . . .)

c. container → [x CAUSE [y BECOME AT < *container* >]]
(e.g. *bag, box, cage, crate* . . .)

d. internally caused state → [x STATE]
(e.g. *bloom, blossom, decay, flower, rot, rust, sprout*, . . .)

e. externally caused, i.e. result, state →
[x [ACT] CAUSE [y BECOME < *resultstate* >]]
(e.g. *break, dry, harden, melt, open* . . .)

Obviously individual verb meanings specify the actual types of instruments, manners, states, for example that are lexicalized in the language. In the combination schemas above, elements from the essentially fixed ontology are shown as either modifiers of predicates, shown as subscripts in a–b above, or as their arguments, shown within angle brackets in c–e above. This approach thus seeks both to reflect that the lexical semantics of verbs contains both individual content and grammatically relevant semantic structure and to show something of the nature of their combination.

9.4.2 Thematic roles and linking rules

Semantic components have been used to investigate several areas of the syntax–semantics interface. It has been claimed for example that they might allow a more satisfactory account of the interaction of verbal argument structure with the **thematic roles** discussed in chapter 6. There we discussed the mapping between a verb's syntactic arguments, like subject and object, and its thematic roles like AGENT and PATIENT. One problematic area much discussed in the literature is the mapping of thematic roles in various types of what have been called **locative alternation** verbs (Rappaport and Levin 1988, Pinker 1989, Gropen et al. 1991, Levin and Rappaport Hovav 1991). In chapter 6 we discussed a subset of these, the *spray/load* verbs which allow the alternation shown below:

9.37 a. He loaded newspapers onto the van.
b. He loaded the van with newspapers.

9.38 a. She sprayed pesticide onto the roses.
b. She sprayed the roses with pesticide.

The description we proposed there is that the speaker can choose between alternate mappings, or **linkings**, between grammatical and theta-roles: in 9.37a and 9.38a the direct object represents the THEME, while in 9.37b and 9.38b it is the GOAL. As has been pointed out in the literature (e.g. Anderson 1971), however, this analysis overlooks a semantic difference between a and b sentences, namely that in the b versions there is an interpretation of completeness: the van is completely loaded with newspapers and the roses are all sprayed with pesticide. This is not true of the a sentences. The difference is not explicable in our description of alternate mappings to theta-roles.

Other problems arise when we try to characterize similar variations in other movement-to-location verbs. Rappaport and Levin (1985), Pinker (1989), and

Gropen et al. (1991) discuss locative verbs like *pour*, which describe an agent moving something into or onto a place, for example:

9.39 Adele poured oil into the pan.

In a theta-role analysis we would describe a linking pattern of AGENT, THEME, and GOAL mapping into subject, direct object, and prepositional phrase, respectively. Some verbs, like *pour*, show this linking and do not allow the GOAL to be direct object, as we can see in 9.40:

9.40 *Adele poured the pan with oil.

Other verbs, however, like *fill*, reverse this pattern:

9.41 a. Adele filled the pan with oil.
b. *Adele filled the oil into the pan.

Here the GOAL is direct object and the THEME must be in a prepositional phrase. Still other verbs, like *brush*, allow both mappings as alternatives:

9.42 a. Adele brushed oil onto the pan.
b. Adele brushed the pan with oil.

It is not clear that a simple listing of mappings to theta-roles sheds any light on these differences. We might have to simply list for each verb an idiosyncratic theta-grid. Levin, Rappaport Hovav, Pinker and other writers have argued that this approach would ignore the fact that verbs form natural classes and that we can make general statements about how these classes link to certain argument structure patterns. It is proposed that a more satisfactory account of the semantics–syntax interface requires a finer-grained analysis of verbal semantics and that a decomposition of the verb's meaning is the answer.[4]

Rappaport and Levin (1985), for example, and Pinker (1989), propose that the variation in argument structures in 9.39–42 reflects different semantic classes of verb, as in 9.43 and 9.44:

9.43 Verbs of movement with the semantic structure "X causes Y to move into/onto Z":
a. Simple motion verbs, e.g. *put*, *push*.
b. Motion verbs which specify the motion (especially manner), e.g. *pour*, *drip*, *slosh*.

9.44 Verbs of change of state with the semantic structure "X causes Z to change state by means of moving Y into/onto it," e.g. *fill*, *coat*, *cover*.

The verb class in 9.43 typically has an argument structure where the THEME argument occurs as object and the GOAL argument occurs in an *into*/*onto*-prepositional phrase as in 9.45:

9.45 a. Ailbhe pushed the bicycle into the shed.
b. Harvey pulled me onto the stage.
c. Joan poured the whiskey into the glass.

The verb class in 9.44 typically has an argument structure where the PATIENT occurs as the object and what we might call the INSTRUMENT[5] occurs in a *with*-prepositional phrase as in 9.46:

9.46 a. Joan filled the glass with whiskey.
b. Libby coated the chicken with oil.
c. Mike covered the ceiling with paint.

A third semantic class has the characteristics in 9.47:

9.47 Verbs of movement which share the semantic structure "X causes Y to move into/onto Z" with the verbs in 9.42 and thus can have the same argument structure, but which also describe a kind of motion which causes an effect on the entity Z, e.g. *spray*, *paint*, *brush*.

This third class allows the speaker a choice: either to emphasize the movement, thus giving the argument structure in 9.48a below, shared with verbs in 9.43, or to focus on the change of Z's state, giving the argument structure in 9.48b below, shared with 9.44. This choice is what has been termed locative alternation.

9.48 a. Vera sprayed paint onto the wall.
b. Vera sprayed the wall with paint.

The authors whose work we have cited here would argue that the mapping between individual verbs and particular argument structures, and phenomena like locative alternation, can only be described by investigating the internal semantic structure of the verbs.

A similar pattern occurs with locative verbs describing removal (Levin and Rappaport Hovav 1991), where we find related verbs like *clear*, *wipe*, and *remove*:

9.49 Robert cleared ashtrays from the bar.

9.50 Christy wiped the lipstick from the glasses.

9.51 Olivia removed the empties from the crate.

Once again an assumption of a canonical mapping between AGENT–subject, THEME–direct object and SOURCE–prepositional phrase will not adequately characterize the behavior of these verbs. See 9.52–54 below, for example:

9.52 Robert cleared the bar.

9.53 Christy wiped the glasses.

9.54 ?Olivia removed the crate.

In 9.52 and 9.53 *clear* and *wipe* allow the SOURCE as direct object, and the THEME to be missing; but *remove* does not allow this pattern: 9.54 is semantically different and cannot mean that Olivia took something from the crate. Another pattern allowed by *clear* also has the SOURCE as direct object but retains the THEME in an *of*-phrase:

9.55 Robert cleared the bar of ashtrays.

9.56 (?)Christy wiped the glasses of lipstick.

9.57 ?Olivia removed the crate of empties.

As we can see from 9.56, *wipe* is less acceptable with this pattern and again *remove* does not permit it: sentence 9.57 cannot mean that Olivia took empties out of the crate. Again, the proposal is that these differences in syntactic argument structure reflect three semantic classes of removal verb (Levin and Rappaport Hovav 1991: 129):

9.58 *Clear* verbs: clear, clean, empty.
Wipe verbs: buff, brush, erase, file, mop, pluck, prune, rake, rinse, rub, scour, scrape, scratch, scrub, shear, shovel, sponge, sweep, trim, vacuum, wipe, etc.
Remove verbs: dislodge, draw, evict, extract, pry, remove, steal, uproot, withdraw, wrench, etc.

Here again it seems that we might be missing something if we describe the differences between these verbs simply by listing alternate mappings between syntactic functions and theta-roles. Levin and Rappaport Hovav suggest setting up semantic verb classes, which we can represent as in 9.59–61 below.

9.59 Verbs of removal with the semantic structure "X causes Y to go away from Z," e.g. *remove*, *take*.

9.60 Verbs which share the same semantic structure "X causes Y to go away from Z" but include specification of the means of removal, either:
a. the manner of removal, e.g. *wipe*, *rub*, *scrub*; or
b. the instrument of removal, e.g. *brush*, *hose*, *mop*.

9.61 Verbs which have the semantic structure "X causes Z to change by removing Y," i.e. change of state verbs which focus on the resultant state, e.g. *clear*, *empty*, *drain*.

As we saw in our examples 9.49–57 above, each semantic class has a different pattern of syntactic argument structure. The *remove* verbs in 9.59 have the THEME as direct object and the SOURCE in a *from*-prepositional phrase, and no other pattern. The *wipe* verbs in 9.60 occur with the same pattern but can also occur with the SOURCE as direct object and no overt THEME. Finally the *clear* verbs in 9.61 allow an alternation between two patterns: the first is the argument structure shared with the other two classes, where the THEME is direct object and the SOURCE is in a *from*-prepositional phrase, and the second is where the SOURCE occurs as direct object and the THEME in an *of*-prepositional phrase. The reader can check these patterns against the sentences in 9.49–57.

Clearly there are generalizations to be made about the way that change-of-state verbs in both the *spray*-type class earlier and the *clear*-type class here allow a locative alternation; see Pinker (1989) and Levin and Rappaport Hovav (1991, 2005) for discussion. For now we can see the force of the claim that only an examination of the verb-internal semantic structure allows the analyst to correctly characterize these variations in verbal argument structure. Semantic components, it is argued, allow us to give a motivated explanation of the links between individual verbs, their argument structures, and the alternations they undergo. This general approach has been extended to other aspect of verbal semantics in, for example, Rappaport Hovav and Levin (2008, 2010) and Rappaport Hovav (2008).

9.5 Talmy's Typology of Motion Events

A similar research program of using semantic components to characterize the syntax–semantics interface has been followed by Leonard Talmy (1975, 1983, 1985, 2000), who has studied how elements of meaning are combined not only in single words but also across phrases. Talmy has for example identified semantic components associated with verbs of motion. These include the following (Talmy 1985: 60–61):

9.62	the **Figure**:	an object moving or located with respect to another object (the **Ground**);
	the **Motion**:	the presence *per se* of motion or location in the event;
	the **Path**:	the course followed or the site occupied by the Figure object with respect to the Ground object;
	the **Manner**:	the type of motion.

Thus in 9.63:

9.63 Charlotte swam away from the crocodile.

Charlotte is the Figure; the Ground is *the crocodile*; the Path is *away from*; and the verb encodes the Manner of motion: *swam*. In 9.64 below:

9.64 The banana hung from the tree.

the banana is the Figure; *the tree* is the Ground; *from* is the Path; and Manner is again expressed in the verb *hung*.

Talmy has pointed out differences between languages in how these semantic components are typically combined or **conflated** in verbs and verb phrases, comparing for example how Path and Manner information is conflated in English, as in 9.65 below, and Spanish, as in 9.66:

9.65 a. He ran out of the house.
b. He ran up the stairs.

9.66 a. Salió de la casa corriendo.
left from the house running
"He ran out of the house."

b. Subió las ecaleras corriendo.
went-up the stairs running
"He ran up the stairs."

In the English sentences in 9.65 the manner of motion, termed simply Manner, is "running" and is incorporated in the verb, while the direction of motion, or Path, is encoded in an external prepositional phrase. This strategy for the verb is schematically represented as in 9.67 below:

9.67 Conflation of Motion with Manner (Talmy 1985: 62)

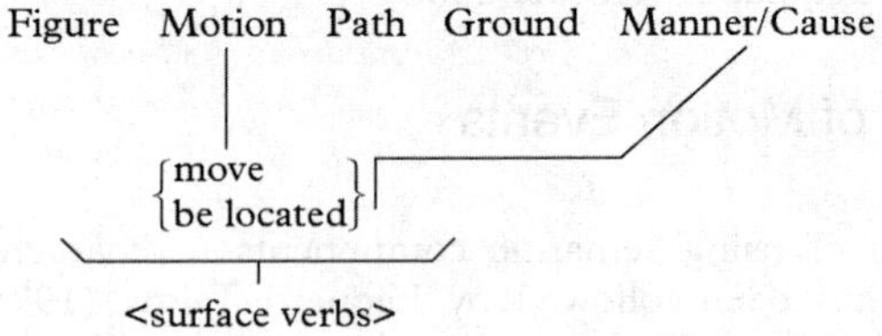

Other examples of this pattern from English are in 9.68:

9.68 a. The flag *drooped* on the mast.
b. The ball *spun* across the line.
c. She *pirouetted* out of the lecture hall.
d. They *rolled* the beer keg into the seminar.

In the Spanish sentences in 9.66 the information is differently packaged: the Path is encoded in the verb and the Manner is encoded in external phrases. The conflation in the verb can be represented as in 9.69:

9.69 Conflation of Motion with Path (Talmy 1985: 69)

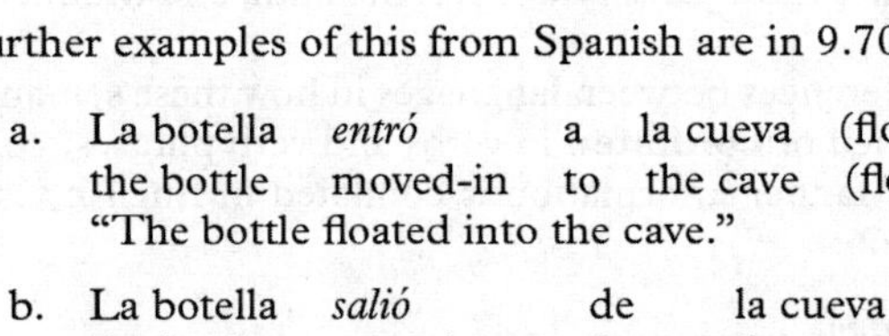

Some further examples of this from Spanish are in 9.70 (Talmy 1975, 1985):

9.70 a. La botella *entró* a la cueva (flotando).
the bottle moved-in to the cave (floating)
"The bottle floated into the cave."

b. La botella *salió* de la cueva (flotando).
the bottle moved-out from the cave (floating)
"The bottle floated out of the cave."

c. El globo *subió* por la chimenea (flotando).
the balloon moved-up through the chimney (floating)
"The balloon floated up the chimney."

d.

Metí	el barril	a	la bodega	rodandolo.
I moved in	the keg	to	the storeroom	rolling it

"I rolled the keg into the storeroom."

e.

Quité	el papel	del	paquete	cortandolo.
I moved off	the paper	from	the package	cutting it

"I cut the wrapper off the package."

A third possible pattern of conflation combines the Figure with the Motion: that is, instead of information about Manner – about *how* something is moving – being incorporated into the motion verb, as in English *running/swimming/hopping/cartwheeling and so on into the cave,* such a pattern would include information about *what* is moving. Talmy (1985) identifies the Californian Hokan language, Atsugewi as a clear instance of this pattern, and he includes the following examples (p. 73):

9.71 Atsugewi verb roots of Motion with conflated Figure

-lup-	"for a small shiny spherical object (e.g. a round candy, an eyeball, a hailstone) to move/be-located"
-t'-	"for a smallish planar object that can be functionally affixed (e.g. a stamp, a clothing patch, a button, a shingle, a cradle's sunshade) to move/be-located"
-caq-	"for a slimy lumpish object (e.g. a toad, a cow dropping) to move/be-located"
-swal-	"for a limp linear object suspended by one end (e.g. a shirt on a clothesline, a hanging dead rabbit, a flaccid penis) to move/be-located"
-qput-	"for loose dry dirt to move/be-located"
-st'aq'-	"for runny icky material (e.g. mud, manure, rotten tomatoes, guts, chewed gum) to move/be-located"

In Atsugewi, then, semantic features of the Figure are encoded in the verbs of motion. Spherical Figures, for example, occur with a different verb than small flat Figures, and so on. We can select just one of Talmy's examples of how these verb roots and other elements build into an Atsugewi verb (1985: 74):

9.72 a. Morphological elements:

locative suffix:	-ik·	"on the ground"
instrumental prefix:	uh-	"from 'gravity' (an object's own weight) acting on it"
inflectional affix-set:	'-w- -^{a}	"3rd person subject (factual mood)"

b. Combined underlying form
/'-w-uh-st'aq'-ik·-$^{a'}$/

c. Pronounced as
[w'ost'aq'ík·a]

Literal meaning:	"Runny icky material is located on the ground from its own weight acting on it"
Instantiated:	"Guts are lying on the ground"

This pattern is represented schematically as in 9.73 (Talmy 1985: 73):

9.73 Conflation of Motion with Figure

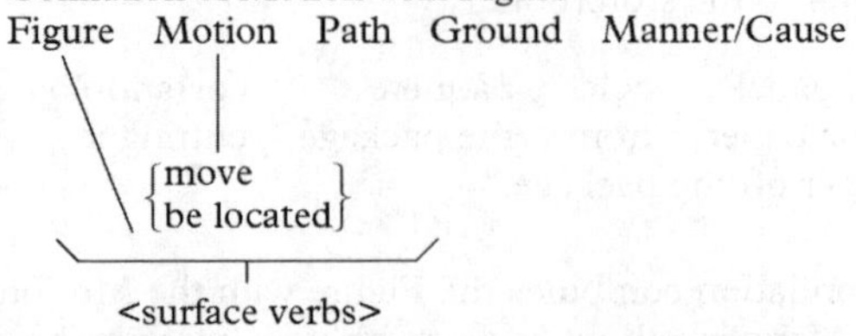

Talmy (1985) suggests that languages can be classified into different types, depending upon how their semantic components characteristically map into grammatical categories such as verbs. The word *characteristically* is used here to identify a normal or **unmarked**[6] pattern in the language:

9.74 Any language uses only one of these types for the verb in its most characteristic expression of Motion. Here, "characteristic" means that: (i) It is colloquial in style, rather than literary, stilted, etc. (ii) It is frequent in occurrence in speech, rather than only occasional. (iii) It is pervasive, rather than limited, that is, a wide range of semantic notions are expressed in this type. (Talmy 1985: 62)

The idea is that languages fall into different types on the basis of their patterns of conflation, and thus a classification or **typology** can be set up of what motion components are conflated in the verb, as in 9.75 (based on Talmy 1985, 2000):

9.75

	Language/Language family	**Verb conflation pattern**
a.	Romance (except for Latin), Semitic, Japanese, Korean, Polynesian, Nez Perce, Caddo	Motion + Path
b.	Indo-European (except for most Romance), Chinese, Finno-Ugric, Ojibwa, Warlpiri	Motion + Manner/Cause
c.	Atsugew, Navajo	Motion + Figure

Thus it is claimed that in all languages the verb expresses the Motion component but languages can be divided according to whether the verb also expresses information about the Path, Figure, or what Talmy termed the **co-event**: Manner or Cause.

Talmy (1991, 2000) proposed a second typology based on how the semantic component Path is expressed. This typology distinguishes between two main classes: languages where the path is expressed in the verb, as in the Spanish examples in 9.70 above, and languages where path is expressed by a class of **satellites**, independent elements that also carry semantic components of motion.[7] Satellites can be structurally associated with the verb (satellites proper) as in English *down* in 9.76a below or with nouns (adpositions) as in English *up* in 9.76b:

9.76 a. He knelt down.
b. They sailed up the river.

Combining the two typologies gives the chart below (Talmy 2007: 154):

9.77

	Language/Language family	Verb root	Satellite
a.	Romance Semitic Polynesian Nez Perce Caddo	Motion + Path	Manner (Figure/) Ground [Patient]
b.	Indo-European except Romance, Chinese	Motion + Manner/ Cause	Path
c.	Atsugewi	Motion + Figure	a. Path + Ground b. Cause

The two types of languages distinguished by the Path typology were termed **verb-framed** and **satellite-framed** languages, and the claim that all languages fall into these two types has generated much attention in the literature, for example Dan Slobin's and other scholars' experimental research on narrative (e.g. Berman and Slobin 1994, Slobin 2004, 2005, Strömqvist and Verhoeven 2004). This interest is partly fueled by the hypothesis that different lexicalization patterns will result in differences in the amount and type of information that speakers of these different language types will background or foreground in narratives, in particular what information will be left to the hearer/reader to infer. In Slobin (2004) wordless picture books, the Frog stories (Mayer 1969), are used to elicit narratives from preschool children, school-age children, and adult speakers of twenty-one languages.[8] The analysis of the cross-linguistic use of sentence structures and narrative techniques seems to support Talmy's proposal. For example, speakers of verb-framed languages never used a satellite to describe motion across a boundary, preferring verbs that include this meaning, unlike speakers of satellite-framed languages like English who use independent satellites like *into* and *out of*, as in extracts below from descriptions of an owl flying out from a hole in a tree in Slobin (2004: 224):

9.78 Verb-framed languages

a. Spanish

Sale	un	buho.			
exits	an	owl			

b. Italian

Da	quest'	albero	esce	un	gufo.
From	that	tree	exits	an	owl

c. Turkish

Oradan	bir	baykus	çıkıyor.
from	there	an.owl	exits

9.79 Satellite-framed languages

a. English

An owl popped out.

b. Russian

Tam	vy-skočila	sova.
There	out-jumped	owl

c. Mandarin
Fēi-chū yī zhī māotóuyīng.
Fly out one owl

The idea that narrative styles in different languages might reflect these differences in lexicalization patterns has attracted much attention. The results of Slobin's and his colleagues' research suggest that speakers of satellite-framed languages provide more information about Manner and Path in narratives, while speakers of verb-framed languages provide more information about scenes and topography, allowing for inference about Manner and Path. See Slobin (2006) for discussion.

These putative links between linguistic structure and narrative styles have been paralleled by more fundamental questions about the relationship to cognition and communication in general. Talmy's work has led to a number of studies of how these typological differences might influence language acquisition and second language learning. Comparison, for example, of how Korean-speaking and English-speaking children learn verbs (Choi and Bowerman 1992, Choi et al. 1999, Choi 2006) seems to show that Korean-speaking children learn to talk about motion events very differently from English-speaking children. Research with Turkish-speaking children has shown that they are more likely to use Path verbs and to use multiple clauses than their English-speaking equivalents (Özçalışkan and Slobin 1999, Özyürek and Özçalışkan 2000, Allen et al. 2007). Studies have also investigated the implications of this typology for second language learners, for example Filopović and Vidaković (2010) investigate learners of English and Serbian while Brown and Gulberg (2010) discuss the implications for Japanese learners of English. Other research has explored the hypothesis that speakers of these typologically distinct languages use gestures differently when speaking, for example McNeill and Duncan (2000), Kita and Ozurek (2003), and Parrill (2011). These explorations of linguistic effects on cognitive processes raise interesting questions about linguistic relativity, the notion discussed in chapter 2; see Slobin (2003) for a discussion of this point.

In the last two sections we have looked at investigations into how semantic components influence grammatical processes and grammatical structures. Next we look at work which builds on this to propose that such semantic components are part of our conceptual structure.

9.6 Jackendoff's Conceptual Structure

9.6.1 Introduction

The semanticist Ray Jackendoff has, in a series of works (e.g. 1972, 1983, 1987, 1990, 1992, 2002), developed a decompositional theory of meaning which he calls **conceptual semantics**. The central principle of this approach is that describing meaning involves describing mental representations; in Jackendoff (1987: 122) this is called the **Mentalist Postulate**:

9.80 Meaning in natural language is an information structure that is mentally encoded by human beings.

So the meaning of a sentence is a conceptual structure. Given the psychological characterization of the theory its structures should therefore align with what is independently known about perception, categorization, and language acquisition. Since Jackendoff, accepting the principle of compositionality we discussed in 9.3.1 earlier, also believes that sentence meaning is constructed from word meaning,[9] a good deal of attention is paid to lexical semantics in this approach.

A further key assumption of this approach is that meanings must serve as a basis for inference. Thus its components are motivated by their role in rules of semantic inference. Jackendoff argues, for example (1990: 39ff), that a major argument for identifying a semantic component CAUSE is economy. One of the aims of a semanticist is to explain the relationship between the sentences below:

9.81 George killed the dragon.

9.82 The dragon died.

As we saw in earlier chapters, the label **entailment** is used for this relation: to recognize a speaker's intuitions that if 9.81 is true then so 9.82 must be; or to put it another way, just from hearing 9.81, we know 9.82.[10] Jackendoff's argument is that if our analysis remains above the level of the word, all we can do for 9.81 and 9.82 above is recognize the relationship between the two words *kill* and *die*, as in 9.83:

9.83 x killed y *entails* y died

However, we then have to have similar but distinct rules for lots of other pairs, including:

9.84	a.	x lifted y	*entails*	y rose
	b.	x gave z to y	*entails*	y received z
	c.	x persuaded y that P	*entails*	y came to believe that P

Jackendoff claims that to do this is to miss a generalization: namely that all such cases share the schema:

9.85 x cause E to occur *entails* E occur

In other words, there is a semantic element CAUSE which occurs in many lexical items and which, as a result, produces many entailment relations.

Jackendoff's work also shares the aims of Levin and others, as described in section 9.4, that semantic decomposition can be used to investigate the mapping between semantics and grammatical processes. We shall see later in this section examples of conceptual structure being used to describe grammatical rules and structures.

9.6.2 The semantic components

Jackendoff's work identifies an inventory of universal semantic categories, or concepts, which include: **Event, State, Material Thing** (or **Object**), **Path, Place,** and **Property**.[11] At the level of conceptual structure a sentence is built up of these semantic categories. The two basic conceptual situations are **Event** and **State**, and if we look at examples of these, we can see something of the role of the other semantic components. We can show an example of an **Event** by looking at a sentence describing motion: 9.86 below gives first the syntactic structure, 9.86a, then the conceptual structure, 9.86b, of the same sentence *Bill went into the house* (Jackendoff 1992: 13):

9.86 a. $[_{S}\ [_{NP}\ \text{Bill}]\ [_{VP}\ [_{V}\ \text{went}]\ [_{PP}\ [_{P}\ \text{into}]\ [_{NP}\ \text{the house}]]]]$

b. $[_{Event}\ \text{GO}\ ([_{Thing}\ \text{BILL}],\ [_{Path}\ \text{TO}\ ([_{Place}\ \text{IN}\ ([_{Thing}\ \text{HOUSE}])])])]$

The structure in 9.86b concentrates on the semantics of motion and thus the entity (or "Thing") *the house* is given as an unanalyzed atom of meaning. Jackendoff is claiming here that the motion event in 9.86 has three main semantic categories: the motion itself, **Go**, which is then composed of two further categories: the entity or **Thing**, moving, and the trajectory, or **Path**, followed by the entity. This Path may have a destination or **Place**, where the motion ends. In 9.86 the motion is *went*, the Thing is *Bill*, the Path is *into the house*, and the Place is *the house*.

We can bring out the articulated nature of this semantic representation if we follow Pinker (1989) and represent 9.86 as a tree structure, where a mother node tells us the type of constituent, the leftmost daughter stands for the function and the other daughters are its arguments. This is shown in figure 9.2. Thus Jackendoff's conceptual structure has a syntax of its own: semantic categories are built up from simpler elements by rules of combination. The conceptual structure in 9.86b is formed by such rules of combination. The elements GO, TO and IN, which describe movement, direction and location, act like functions in a semantic algebra, combining elements to form the major semantic categories. Thus the overall **Event** in 9.86b is formed by GO combining a **Thing** with a **Path** to form an event of a particular type: something moving in a direction. The category **Path** is formed by the element TO, combining with a **Place** to describe the direction (or trajectory) taken by the object. Lastly, the **Place** is formed by IN, called a **place-function**, combining with an entity (or "thing") to describe an area inside the object which serves as the destination of the movement. Jackendoff paraphrases the conceptual structure in 9.86b as "Bill traverses a path that terminates at the interior of the house." (1992: 13).[12]

Figure 9.2 Conceptual structure of example 9.86 as a tree structure

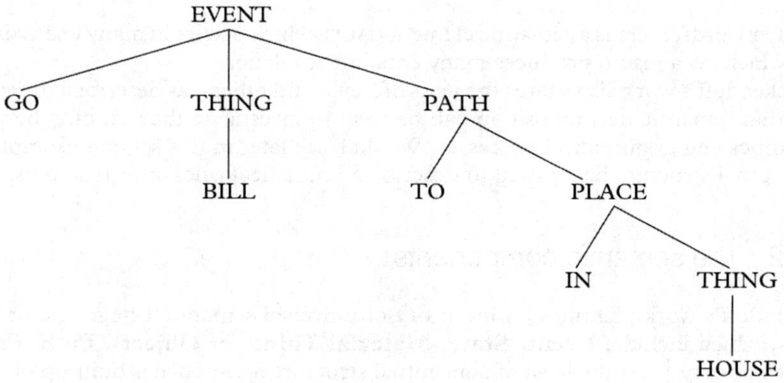

Figure 9.3 Conceptual structure of example 9.87 as a tree structure

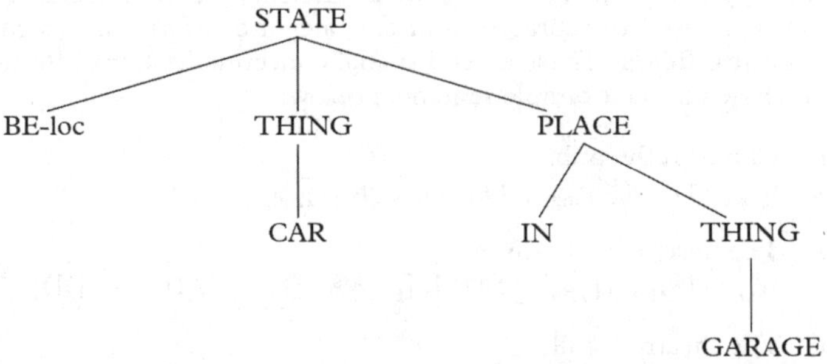

We can take 9.87a below as an example of a sentence describing a **State**, with its conceptual structure shown in 9.87b, and in tree form in figure 9.3.

9.87 a. [$_{S}$ [$_{NP}$ The car] [$_{VP}$ [$_{V}$ is] [$_{PP}$ [$_{P}$ in] [$_{NP}$ the garage]]]]
b. [$_{State}$ BE ([$_{Thing}$ CAR], [$_{Place}$ IN ([$_{Thing}$ GARAGE])])]

9.6.3 Localist semantic fields

Sentence 9.87 describes a state of being in a spatial **location**, and this is reflected in Jackendoff (1990) by giving the semantic component BE a subscript to identify this subcategory of state: BE$_{Loc}$ is used for a **locational** BE ("be in a place"), giving us the conceptual structure in 9.88:

9.88 [$_{State}$ BE$_{Loc}$ ([$_{Thing}$ CAR], [$_{Place}$ IN ([$_{Thing}$ GARAGE])])]

We can compare this with an example of a state consisting of having a **property**, which is represented by the **identifying** or **copulative** BE$_{Ident}$ in 9.89. Again figure 9.4 shows the conceptual structure in tree format.

9.89 a. [$_{S}$ [$_{NP}$ The pool] [$_{VP}$ [$_{V}$ is [$_{AP}$ [$_{ADJ}$ empty]]]]]
b. [$_{State}$ BE$_{Ident}$ ([$_{Thing}$ POOL], [$_{Place}$ AT ([$_{Property}$ EMPTY])])]

Figure 9.4 Conceptual structure of example 9.89 as a tree structure

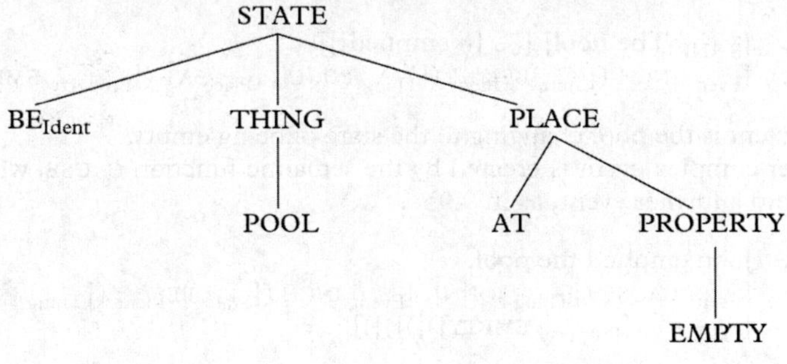

We can see that having a property is given a spatial interpretation in 9.89. This is a version of the approach which we called **localism** in chapter 7. In Jackendoff (1990) the function BE is used to represent four subcategories of STATE, which Jackendoff calls **semantic fields**. These extend spatial conceptualizations into non-spatial domains, as shown in the example sentences below:

9.90 a. Carl is in the pub.
b. [$_{State}$ BE$_{Loc}$ ([$_{Thing}$ CARL], [$_{Place}$ IN ([$_{Thing}$ PUB])])]

9.91 a. The party is on Saturday.
b. [$_{State}$ BE$_{Temp}$ ([$_{Thing}$ PARTY], [$_{Place}$ AT ([$_{Time}$ SATURDAY])])]

9.92 a. The theatre is full.
b. [$_{State}$ BE$_{Ident}$ ([$_{Thing}$ THEATRE], [$_{Place}$ AT ([$_{Property}$ FULL])])]

9.93 a. This book belongs to John.
b. [$_{State}$ BE$_{Poss}$ ([$_{Thing}$ BOOK], [$_{Place}$ AT ([$_{Thing}$ JOHN])])]

Example 9.90 shows the function BE$_{Loc}$ which represents location in space; 9.91 shows BE$_{Temp}$, which describes location in time; 9.92 shows BE$_{Ident}$ which represents the ascription of a property in locational terms; and in 9.93 we see BE$_{Poss}$ which represents possession as location. Thus the four kinds of state are given a localist interpretation.

The same four subcategories or semantic fields apply to Event functions like GO. Spatial GO$_{Loc}$ would be used to describe movement in space as in sentence 9.86, *Bill went into the house*; GO$_{Temp}$ would be used for movement in time, for example *The party has been moved from Saturday to Sunday*; GO$_{Ident}$ might be used for movement between properties, as in *Joan went from being depressed to being elated*; and GO$_{Poss}$ would represent a movement in possession like *The prize went to Kate*. So in this approach these four localist semantic fields **spatial location, temporal location, property ascription,** and **possession** cross-classify the basic ontological categories of EVENT and STATE.

9.6.4 Complex events and states

A more complicated example of an **Event** would be sentence 9.94 below, where we see the semantic component CHANGE OF STATE, or INCHOATIVE, abbreviated to INCH, which operates as a function mapping a state into an event.

9.94 a. [$_S$ [$_{NP}$ The pool] [$_{VP}$ [$_V$ emptied]]]
b. [$_{Event}$ INCH ([$_{State}$ BE$_{Ident}$ ([$_{Thing}$ POOL], [$_{Place}$ AT ([$_{Property}$ EMPTY])])])]

Here the event is the pool changing to the state of being empty.

A further complex event is created by the semantic function CAUSE, which maps an event into a further event, as in 9.95:

9.95 a. John emptied the pool.
b. [$_{Event}$ CAUSE ([$_{Thing}$ JOHN], [$_{Event}$ INCH ([$_{State}$ BE$_{Ident}$ ([$_{Thing}$ POOL], [$_{Place}$ AT ([$_{Property}$ EMPTY])])])])]

We might paraphrase 9.95 by saying that the complex event is that John caused the event of the pool changing to the state of being empty.

The structure of the events and states we have seen so far can be represented in formation rules like 9.96 below, where we collapse the various subclasses of GO and BE:

9.96
a. [EVENT] → $[_{Event}$ GO ([THING], [PATH])]
b. [STATE] → $[_{State}$ BE ([THING], [PLACE])]
c. [PATH] → [TO ([PLACE])]
d. [PLACE] → [IN ([THING])]
e. [PLACE] → [AT ([TIME])]
f. [PLACE] → [AT ([PROPERTY])]
g. [PLACE] → [AT ([THING])]
h. [EVENT] → $[_{Event}$ INCH ([STATE])]
i. [EVENT] → $[_{Event}$ CAUSE ([THING], [EVENT])]

These rules exemplify the conceptual elements identified in Jackendoff (1990). Each type of rule in 9.96 would of course need to be extended for further English examples. For example 9.96c expands PATH into a complex expression: a direction function TO and a location PLACE; other examples would require a direction function FROM. Similarly 9.96d expands PLACE into a place-function IN which defines a region of its THING argument, its interior. Other place-functions would include UNDER, OVER, AROUND, and so on which define other regions with respect to their arguments.

Having seen something of the composition of conceptual structures, we look next at one category in more detail: the category **Thing**.

9.6.5 THINGS: Semantic classes of nominals

So, to repeat, in this approach semantic components break down into smaller, simpler semantic components. We can see this clearly if we look at some properties of the category **Thing**, that is, at the semantics of nouns. We can begin with Jackendoff's semantic feature [±BOUNDED]. This distinguishes, for example, between count nouns like *banana*, or *car*, and mass nouns like *water* or *oxygen*. The idea is that count nouns are basically units: if we divide up a banana or a car, by slicing or dismantling, we don't get further instances of the basic unit. We can't call each of the pieces a *banana* or a *car*. Mass nouns, on the other hand are not units and can be divided into further instances of themselves: if you divide a gallon of water into eight pints, each of the eight pints can still be called *water*. This is reflected by describing count nouns as [+BOUNDED], or [+b], and mass nouns as [−BOUNDED], or [−b].

Plurals of count nouns, on the other hand, act like mass nouns in many ways. They occur with similar determiners, for example:

9.97 Singular count nouns
a. She offered me a banana. [with *a*]
b. I didn't get a banana. [with *a*]

9.98 Plural count and mass nouns
a. She offered me water/bananas. [with no article]
b. I didn't get any water/any bananas. [with *any*]

Count plurals can also be divided into their composite units. These plural count nouns are of course different from mass nouns in being composed of individual units and Jackendoff proposes a feature ±INTERNAL STRUCTURE to distinguish between the two types: plural count nouns are +INTERNAL STRUCTURE, or [+i], while mass nouns are −INTERNAL STRUCTURE, or [−i].

What is happening here is that nouns are being cross-classified by these two semantic features. One further type is possible: a collective noun like *the Government* contains individual units – its members – and therefore is like a plural and [+i]; however, if we do divide it, we cannot call each of the results a *government*, and thus it is bounded, [+b]. The resulting typology of semantic classes of nouns is as below:

9.99	*individuals*:	[+b, –i]	count nouns, e.g. *a banana, a car*
	groups:	[+b, +i]	collective nouns, e.g. *a government, a committee*
	substances:	[–b, –i]	mass nouns, e.g. *water, oxygen*
	aggregates:	[–b, +i]	plural nouns, e.g. *bananas, cars*

9.6.6 Cross-category generalizations

One aspect of this use of these semantic features is typical of Jackendoff's work: a feature like [BOUNDED] doesn't just cross-classify nouns: it is also used to describe situations. Thus situations which are described as ongoing processes not overtly limited in time, and are thus atelic in the terminology used in chapter 5, are analyzed as [–b], as in example 9.100 below:

9.100 John is sleeping.

Situations which are events with clearly defined beginnings and ends are classified as [+b], or telic, as in 9.101 below:

9.101 John ran into the room.

We discussed in chapter 5 the way that different verbs contribute inherent features of **situation type** to complex expressions. Here Jackendoff is making the interesting claim that there are common conceptual elements to both number in nouns and situation type in verbs.

9.6.7 Processes of semantic combination

We have already seen Jackendoff's claim for the advantages of semantic components in accounting for semantic inference. Jackendoff also employs his conceptual primitives to investigate the relationship between semantics and grammar, in a similar way to the work of the linguists described in section 9.4. We can briefly look at some examples.

When we discussed situation type in chapter 5 we noted the fact that in English some combinations of a semelfactive verb and a durative adverbial do not result in an anomalous sentence but are given instead an iterative interpretation, for example:

9.102 a. The beacon flashed.
b. The beacon flashed for two minutes.

Thus sentence 9.102a describes a single flash; however, adding the durative adverbial *for two minutes* as in 9.102b does not extend this single flash over the period but describes a series of flashes. The way Jackendoff (1992) approaches this process is to view it in terms of levels of embedding in conceptual structure. Introducing a durative adverbial is taken to have the effect of taking an unbounded event, like 9.103a below, and producing a bounded event, like 9.103b:

9.103 a. Ronan read.
b. Ronan read until 5 am.

However, in an iterative sentence like:

9.104 The beacon flashed until 5 am.

the adverbial *until 5 am* is taking an inherently bounded event and producing a further bounded, multiple event. Jackendoff describes this as involving a rule of construal that inserts a PLURAL (PL) component as an intermediate level between the two events, as in 9.105.

9.105

$$\begin{bmatrix} +\text{b} \\ \text{until}\left(\begin{bmatrix} -\text{b} \\ \text{pl}\left(\begin{bmatrix} +b \\ \text{beacon flashed} \\ \text{Event}\end{bmatrix}\right) \\ \text{Event}\end{bmatrix}, [\text{5 am}]\right) \\ \text{Event}\end{bmatrix}$$

This is a simplified version of the sentence's conceptual structure; Jackendoff (1992) gives a more formal and detailed account of this and similar analyses of situation type and aspect.

This account is part of a larger enterprise to provide a semantic account of a range of morphological and syntactic processes of combination. If we look at nouns, for example, these combinatory processes include plural formation, the construction of compounds like *chicken curry*, and the various semantic uses of *of*-constructions, as in *a grain of rice*, *a wall of the house*, *a house of bricks*, and so on. Staying with the features [±BOUNDED] and [±INTERNAL STRUCTURE], Jackendoff (1992) proposes six combinatory functions which map features of [*b*] and [*i*] together. These are divided into two types as in 9.106 below:

9.106

Including functions	Extracting functions
plural (PL)	**element of** (ELT)
composed of (COMP)	**partitive** (PART)
containing (CONT)	**universal grinder** (GR)

The headings **including** and **extracting** in 9.106 identify two different types of part–whole relation that results from the process of combination: the including functions map their arguments into a larger entity containing the argument as a part, while the extracting functions pull out a sub-entity of their arguments. We can see these characteristics if we look briefly at these functions in turn.

The **plural function**, for example, reflects the process of pluralizing nouns and changes their feature specifications for boundedness and internal structure, for example:

9.107 brick [+b, –i] → bricks [–b, +i]

The semantic representation for the plural noun *bricks* is shown in 9.108 below:

9.108
$$\begin{bmatrix} -b, +i & \\ \text{pl} & \left(\begin{bmatrix} +b, -i \\ \text{brick} \\ \text{Mat} \end{bmatrix}\right) \\ \text{Mat} & \end{bmatrix}$$

This diagram represents the fact that the plural function (PL) has overridden the original [+b, –i] specification of *brick*.

If we move to the second including function **composed of** (COMP), we can take as an example the nominal *a house of wood*, which is given the representation below:

9.109
$$\begin{bmatrix} & +b, -i & \\ & \text{house} & \\ & \text{comp} & \left(\begin{bmatrix} -b, -i \\ \text{wood} \\ \text{Mat} \end{bmatrix}\right) \\ \text{Mat} & & \end{bmatrix}$$

Here COMP links an individual entity *house*, [+b, –i], with a substance *wood*, [–b, –i], and the whole unit has the semantic features of the grammatical head of the construction, *house*. An example of where the COMP function links an individual with a plural aggregate is in 9.110 below, where the semantic structure of a *house of bricks* is shown:

9.110
$$\begin{bmatrix} +b, -i & \\ \text{house} & \\ \text{comp} & \left(\begin{bmatrix} -b, +i & \\ \text{pl} & \left(\begin{bmatrix} +b, -i \\ \text{brick} \\ \text{Mat} \end{bmatrix}\right) \\ \text{Mat} & \end{bmatrix}\right) \\ \text{Mat} & \end{bmatrix}$$

Here we can see the effect of the two semantic processes PL and COMP on the features [±b] and [±i]. Once again the construction as a whole has the features of the head, *house*. This function is also used to reflect uses where a mass noun like *coffee*, *tea*, or *beer* is used as a count noun, as for example in 9.111 below:

9.111
a. I'll have a coffee.
b. Table four want three coffees and two teas.
c. Me, drunk? I've only had three beers.

Here the interpretation of *a coffee* is of course "a unit of coffee," where the unit is some contextually appropriate one, perhaps a cup. Calling this rule which allows the counting of mass nouns **the universal packager**, Jackendoff argues for a parallel with the combination of the durative adverbial and semelfactive verb described earlier. In the case of *a cup of coffee*, the incompatibility of the indefinite article with a mass noun triggers a rule of construal, inserting the operator COMP, which causes the reading "a portion composed of coffee." The quantifiers *two* and *three* and the plural endings in 9.111b and c trigger the same process.

The third including function is **containing** (CONT), which is used to describe compound nominals like *chicken curry* or *cheese sandwich*, where the first element describes an important, identifying element of the second. In examples like *chicken curry*, the CONT function does not change the values of the features, mapping the mass nouns, that is [–b, –i], *chicken* and *curry* into the [–b, –i] compound *chicken curry*.

If we move on to the three extracting functions: **element of** (ELT) describes the semantics of phrases like *a grain of rice* and *a stick of spaghetti*, where the first noun picks out an individual from the aggregate described by the second noun, creating overall a count noun. The second function **partitive** (PART) describes the semantics of partitive constructions, N of NP, like *leg of the table* or *top of the mountain*, where the phrase identifies a bounded part (the first noun) of a larger bounded entity (the second NP). These constructions often have semantically equivalent compound nominals like *table leg* or *mountain top*. The final extracting function, with the rather strange name of **universal grinder**, is used for instances where what are usually count nouns are used to describe substances, as in Jackendoff's unpleasant example 9.112 below:

9.112 There was dog all over the road.

Here using a count noun *dog* without an article triggers a rule of construal where *dog* loses its boundedness and is construed as a substance. We can see this perhaps as the opposite process to COMP in *I'll have a coffee* where a mass noun (i.e. a substance) is interpreted as a count noun. This GR function also allows us to use animal names for their meat as in 9.113 below:

9.113 a. Have you ever eaten *crocodile*?
b. *Impala* tastes just like mutton.

From these examples we can see that Jackendoff's approach, like the work of Levin, Rappaport Hovav, Pinker, and the other writers cited in section 9.4, uses lexical decomposition to investigate the semantics–grammar interface. Jackendoff's approach in particular presents a view of semantic primitives occurring in highly articulated semantic representations. In this theory these representations are proposed as conceptual structures underlying linguistic behavior.

9.7 Pustejovsky's Generative Lexicon

James Pustejovsky (in particular 1992, 1995) has proposed a compositional account of lexical semantics which is broadly in sympathy with the Jackendoff approach described in the last section, but which both extends the compositional representation in some areas and incorporates more general or encyclopedic knowledge into the account. The central thrust of this approach is computational. Pustejovsky argues that lexical meaning is best accounted for by a dynamic approach including rules of combination and inference, rather than the essentially lexicographic tradition of listing senses of a lexeme, as we described in chapter 3. Pustejovsky (1995: 61) proposes four levels of semantic representations for lexical items, as shown below:

9.114 a. Argument structure: the semantic arguments of an item and the linking rules to syntax
b. Event structure: the situation type of an item
c. Qualia structure: a classification of the properties of an item
d. Lexical inheritance structure: how the item fits into the network of the lexicon

In our discussion we will concentrate on two of these representations and two grammatical categories: event structure and verbs, and qualia structure and nouns.

9.7.1 Event structure

Pustejovsky provides a compositional account of the situation type distinctions we discussed in chapter 5. There we reviewed several classifications systems, including Vendler's (1967) influential division into states, activities, accomplishments, and achievements. As we saw, these distinctions are viewed as part of the lexical semantics of verbs. We saw in the last section that Jackendoff includes semantic components of event structure in his representations, namely EVENT and STATE, with constituent components of CHANGE (INCHOATION) and CAUSE. These categories combine in semantic representations with other categories like THING and PLACE. As we shall see, Pustejovsky argues for finer distinctions among situation types and for a level of event structure distinct from other semantic information.

In this literature the term **event structure** is used for what we have called **situation type**, that is, for the lexically encoded aspectual distinctions in verbs. Since events in this use also include states, a more neutral term like Bach's **eventualities** (Bach 1986) might be preferable, but we will continue to use the term event structure in the present discussion. As we saw in chapter 5, a verb's event structure is modified as it combines with other elements, including noun phrases and adverbials, to build verb phrases and sentences.

A major feature of Pustejovsky's approach is the claim that events are composed of smaller events (sub-events) and that this relationship needs to be represented in an articulated way, by a form of syntax. We can briefly review from Pustejovsky (1992: 56–57) how the three main event types that he identifies are represented:

9.115 States (S) are single events that are evaluated relative to no other event, represented as:

Examples are stative verbs like *understand, love, be tall.*

9.116 Processes (P) are sequences of events identifying the same semantic expression, represented as:

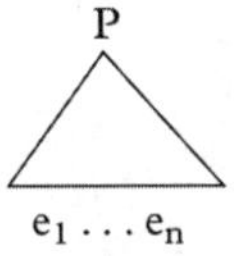

Examples are verbs like *sing*, *walk*, *swim*.

9.117 Transitions (T) are events identifying a semantic expression that is evaluated relative to its opposition, represented as follows (where E is a variable for any event type):

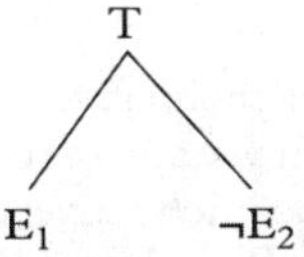

Examples are verbs like *open*, *close*, *build*.

These representations just give information about event structure. This event structure (ES) representation is united with other semantic information at two other levels: a level of logic-like predicate decomposition called LCS and an interface level which incorporates lexical semantic elements but maintains the event structure more transparently, called LCS′. The relations between can be shown in the causative/inchoative alternations *John closed the door*/*The door closed*:

9.118 a. The door closed.
b. ES:

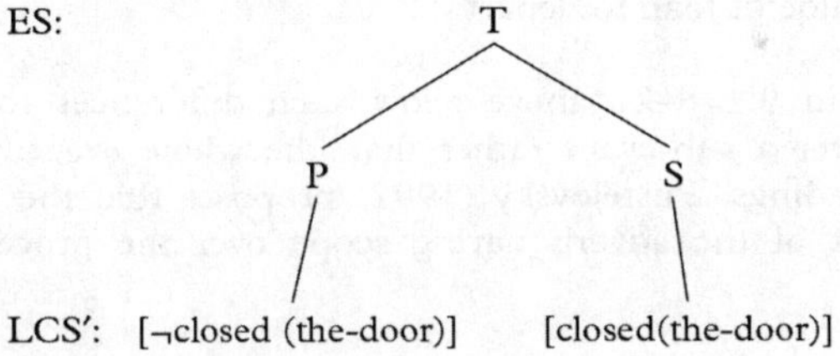

LCS: become([closed(the-door)])

9.119 a. John closed the door.
b. ES:

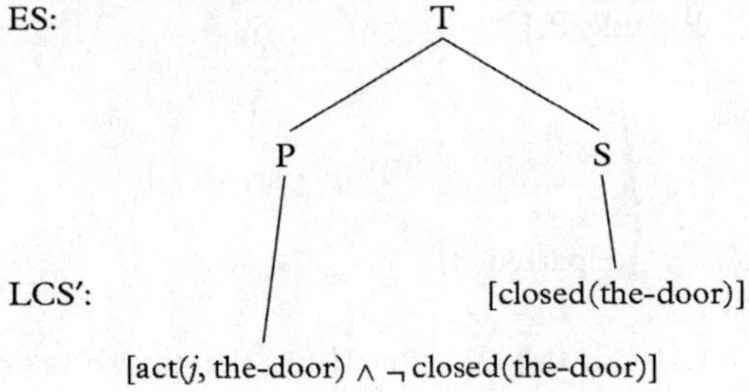

LCS: cause([act(*j*, the-door)], become([closed(the-door)]))

The corresponding state is shown in 9.120:

9.120 a. The door is closed.
b. ES:

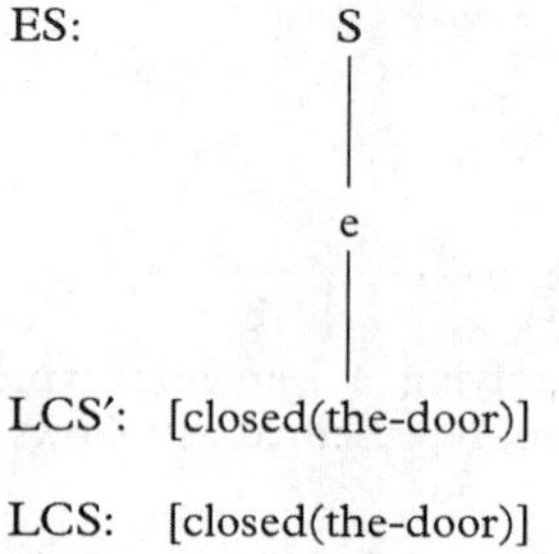

These diagrams show the claim that inchoative and causative versions of the verb *close* represent a transition from the state of being not-closed to its opposite, being closed. In Vendler terms, the inchoative *close* is an achievement and the causative *close* is an accomplishment. The difference is here recognized by the presence or absence of an agent acting on the changing entity (*John* is the agent in the example above). There is no other structural distinction between these two event types.

One main justification for this type of sub-event structural description is that it allows the recognition of regular differences in adverbial interpretation, such as the ambiguity in 9.121a, shown by the paraphrases in b and c:

9.121 a. Joan rudely departed.
b. Joan departed in a rude way.
c. It was rude of Joan to depart.

The representations in 9.118–21 above allow such differences to be analyzed as adverbial scope over a sub-event rather than the whole event: narrow-scope versus wide-scope readings. Pustejovsky (1992) proposes that the interpretation in 9.121b is a result of the adverb having scope over the process sub-event, shown below:

9.122

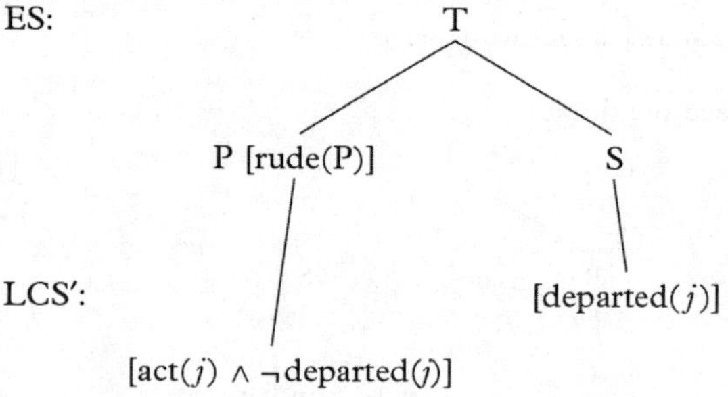

The interpretation in 9.121c on the other hand has the adverb taking wide scope over the whole event, shown as:

9.123

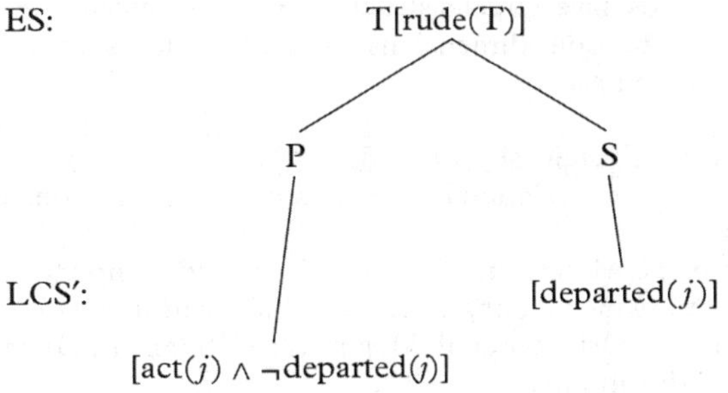

Thus the ambiguity of adverbial interpretation is given a structural account.

Another related example discussed by Pustejovsky (1992) and Alsina (1999) in this approach concerns an ambiguity of interpretation with *almost* that occurs in accomplishments but not in other event types.[13] To use Alsina's cruel example, *John almost killed the cat* has the two readings: John's action resulted in the near-death of the cat and John nearly undertook an action that would have killed the cat. In the former *almost* has scope over the resulting State, while in the latter *almost* has scope over the Process.[14] This account correctly predicts that an achievement verb like *walk* will have only one reading, the "nearly undertook the action" reading, as in *I almost walked*, because there is only one undifferentiated event constituent in the event structure (as in diagram 9.116 earlier).

The essential claim made by this approach is that a representation which does not have access to sub-events, such as the activity and state sub-events above, will lack explanatory power.

9.7.2 Qualia structure

In his treatment of nouns Pustejovsky claims that listing senses in a dictionary, making what he terms Sense Enumeration Lexicons (Pustejovsky 1995), cannot adequately account for polysemy. He discusses examples like the variation in the meaning of *good* in *a good meal*, *good soccer player*, *good book*, *good husband* or *fast* in *a fast car*, *fast driver*, *fast decision*, *fast food* and so on. As we discussed in chapter 3, there are two traditional approaches to such variation: we can decide that there are a number of related senses here or alternatively that these adjectives are simply vague, so that *good*, for example, is simply a general term of approbation whose meaning must be derived by contextual rules of inference. Pustejovsky argues for a variation of the multiple senses approach and against an explanation via general reasoning. His arguments are firstly that any inferences must rely on linguistic information in the accompanying nouns, and secondly that the variation is systematic, with different classes of items patterning together. However, rather than treating this by listing senses, Pustejovsky views the variants as products of specific rules of semantic composition, tied to systematic properties of the lexical item. These properties are called **qualia** (plural of the Latin noun *quale* "quality, nature") in this theory.

Although all types of words have a qualia structure, we concentrate our discussion on nouns. Qualia structure has four dimensions, viewed as roles, shown below with characteristic values for nominals:

9.124 Qualia Structure (Pustejovsky 1995: 85)

a. CONSTITUTIVE: the relation between an object and its constituents, or proper parts.
For example: i. Material ii. Weight iii. Parts and component elements.

b. FORMAL: that which distinguishes the object within a larger domain.
For example: i. Orientation ii. Magnitude iii. Shape iv. Dimensionality v. Color vi. Position.

c. TELIC: the purpose and function of the object
For example: i. Purpose that an agent has in performing an act. ii. Built-in function or aim which specifies certain activities.

d. AGENTIVE: factors involved in the origin or "bringing about" of an object.
For example: i. Creator ii. Artifact iii. Natural kind iv. Causal chain.

An example of the types of information represented by qualia is given below for the example of the noun *novel* discussed by Pustejovky (1995: 77–79):

9.125

$$\left[\begin{array}{l} \textbf{novel} \\ \text{QUALIA} = \left[\begin{array}{c} \text{CONSTITUTIVE} = \textbf{narrative}(x) \\ \text{FORMAL} = \textbf{book}(x) \\ \text{TELIC} = \textbf{read}(x, y) \\ \text{AGENT} = \textbf{write}(z, x) \end{array}\right] \end{array}\right]$$

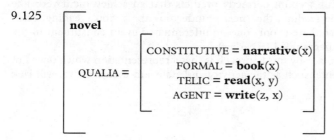

In 9.125 the CONSTITUTIVE quale says that a novel is a kind of narrative; the FORMAL quale says that within narratives a novel is a book; the TELIC quale says that its function is for someone to read it; and the AGENTIVE quale says that it is created by a process of someone writing it.

Without going into the formal detail we can sketch how the knowledge about nouns represented by qualia can be used to account for polysemy. One example is the different interpretations of *bake* in the following:

9.126 a. Joan baked the potato.
b. Joan baked the cake.

In 9.126a the verb has a change-of-state interpretation while in b it has an additional creation sense, that is, the act of baking creates a cake that didn't exist previously. For Pustejovsky this polysemy is explained by rules of combination between the verb and noun. The verb itself has only one meaning: it entails a change of state. The difference between a and b above is results from the qualia structures of the nominals. The noun *cake* will have as part of its agentive role that it is created by an act of baking by an agent, that is that it is an artifact. The verb *bake* will have as part of its agentive qualia that it describes an act of baking by an agent. When the verb and noun combine to form a verb phrase, their qualia structures merge and unite the two representations of the baking event to form the creation interpretation. In other words it is the unification of qualia structures between verb and this particular type of object that produces the creation reading. In this view an extended meaning is created by rules of composition. Hence we gain a dynamic view of polysemy which specifies the context for the extended reading. For technical details see Pustejovsky (1995: 122–25).

A further example is the variations in meanings of adjectives like *fast* and *good* mentioned earlier. Pustejovky's approach is to treat these as modifiers of events (event predicates) and therefore applicable to events represented in the qualia structure of nominals that they combine with. The noun *typist* is given the qualia structure below:

9.127

$$\begin{bmatrix} \textbf{typist} & \\ \text{ARGSTR} = & [\text{ARG1} = \textbf{x:human}] \\ \text{QUALIA} = & \begin{bmatrix} \text{FORMAL} = \textbf{x} \\ \text{TELIC} = \textbf{type(e, x)} \end{bmatrix} \end{bmatrix}$$

The combination of argument and qualia structure tells us that the activity associated with this noun is an event of a human being typing. Combining this noun with the event modifier *fast* will automatically give the reading that a fast typist types fast.

Similarly the qualia structure for *knife* is given as:

9.128

$$\begin{bmatrix} \textbf{knife} & \\ \text{ARGSTR} = & [\text{ARG1} = \textbf{x:tool}] \\ \text{QUALIA} = & \begin{bmatrix} \text{FORMAL} = \textbf{x} \\ \text{TELIC} = \textbf{cut(e, x, y)} \end{bmatrix} \end{bmatrix}$$

The telic quale tells us that a knife is used for cutting. Treating *good* as an event predicate means it can apply to this event of cutting incorporated in representation of this noun, ensuring that a good knife is one that cuts well. This of course generalizes across other adjectives and nouns, ensuring that a good driver drives well, a slow runner runs slowly, and so on. Once again variation in interpretations, this time in adjectives, is triggered by specific types of knowledge represented in the nouns with which they combine.

This sketch is necessarily only suggestive but we hope that the general approach to polysemy in this theory is clear. It is accounted for by dynamic rules of combination, unifying different forms of knowledge represented in lexical entries. It is possible to discern a distant, and dynamic, family resemblance here to the use of selectional restrictions in the Katzian semantics that we described at the beginning of this chapter.

9.8 Problems with Components of Meaning

The compositional approaches we have been looking at have been criticized in two important ways. The first concerns the identification of semantic primitives. These primitives have been attacked from both philosophical and psychological perspectives. The former (e.g. J. A. Fodor 1970, Fodor et al. 1980) claims that these semantic components are simply a variation of, and equivalent to, the necessary and sufficient conditions approach to word meaning that we discussed in chapter 2. As we saw there, it proves impossible to agree on precise definitions of word meaning. The resulting practical problems for the decompositional semanticist include knowing how to validate any proposed set of primitives, and when to stop identifying them, that is knowing what are the right features and how many is enough.

There have also been psychological criticisms, for example J. D. Fodor et al. (1975), which claim that there is no experimental evidence for semantic primitives. Though there is not a large literature on the topic, some experiments have shown little or no support for varying degrees of internal complexity in words. These studies seem to show that in processing language we appear to treat words as atoms of meaning, and therefore do not divide them into subcomponents in order to understand them.[15]

The second focus for attack has been on the use of metalanguages. As we have seen, there have been various proposals, using a range of symbols and diagrams. The criticism has been that these devices are ad hoc and unsystematic: at best another arbitrary language; at worst, a kind of garbled version of the English, French, and so on. of the writer. This criticism is related to the more serious philosophical criticism that attaching a set of primitives to a word or phrase is not a semantic analysis in the deepest sense. We can recall the point discussed in chapter 2, deriving from observations by the philosopher W. V. O. Quine, that this is in effect a form of translation into another language, a language of primitive elements which is sometimes pejoratively called **Markerese**, after Lewis (1972), by linguists making this point.. The claim is that to translate from the object language into an arbitrary invented language doesn't advance semantic analysis very far, if you then have to translate the metalanguage. If the process doesn't have an anchor in reality, the criticism goes, it is merely circular.[16] As we said earlier, the basic idea is that since the expressions of language are symbols, they must be **grounded** somehow. This grounding may be of different types: in the next chapter we shall see how **formal semanticists** attempt to ground semantic analysis in the external world; and in chapter 11 we will see an attempt by **cognitive semanticists** to ground their analyses in primitive-level concepts derived from bodily experience. But, the criticism goes, the type of componential analysis we have reviewed in this chapter begs the question of such grounding.

To decompositional semanticists, none of these attacks seems fatal. Responses to the psychological attack, for example Jackendoff (1990: 37ff), point out that we would expect words to be the relevant unit for processing, not components. After all, goes this reply, that's why semantic features are bunched into word units: because these particular bunchings have cognitive utility, that is, they are useful sizes and mixtures for thinking and talking about the world. In reply to the complaint about the never-ending identification of primitives, these linguists tend to claim that this is an empirical question, not solvable in advance by stipulation, for example:

9.129 there should eventually come a point when increasing the complexity of a semantic theory by adding new markers no longer yields enough advantage in precision and scope to warrant the increase. At that point the system of markers should reflect the systematic features of the semantic structure of the language. (Katz and Fodor 1963: 190)

Or we might note the response in Jackendoff (1990: 4) where he makes a comparison with physics, where physicists haven't worried about identifying smaller and smaller particles, if there is sufficient justification for them.

Responses to the criticism of metalanguages have varied: some semanticists agree with it and conduct their inquiry through the medium of a natural language like English; see for example Wierzbicka (1980), and Allan (1986, 1: 265–70) for discussion. This is in effect to give up the search for a neutral metalanguage. Another response is to rely more firmly on tried and tested metalanguages from other disciplines like logic, as in Dowty (1979).[17] Still others, like Jackendoff, rely on empirical justification for the formalisms they use: in this view the machinery is justified to the extent it allows the analyst to capture significant generalizations.

9.9 Summary

In this chapter we have reviewed the proposal that semantic representation should involve semantic components. These components are primitive elements which combine to form units at the level of grammar. The nature of their combination differs from author to author: from, for example, the original Katz and Fodor listings of components at the word level to the more articulated representations used by Jackendoff, where the components are arranged as functions and arguments which can be successively embedded within one another, and Pustejovsky, who proposes a syntax of event structure.

Linguists have argued that these components help characterize semantic relations: both lexical relations and sentential relations like entailment. As we have seen, they have also been used to investigate the semantic basis for morphological and syntactic processes. From the viewpoint of linguistic analysis these are claims that such components are important units at the level of semantics. From a wider perspective the question arises: are these components psychologically real? Do they form part of our cognitive structures? For some linguists, like Jackendoff, the answer is yes. These elements play a role in our thinking and by identifying them correctly we are establishing meaning.

EXERCISES

9.1 Use **semantic components** to characterize the semantic relations between the following words:

mother father daughter son sister brother grandmother grandfather granddaughter grandson uncle aunt cousin nephew niece

Discuss whether a **binary format** would be an advantage for the semantic components you decide on.

9.2 In section 9.7.1 we saw Pustejovsky's representation of the English **causative/inchoative** alternation, which we discussed earlier in chapter 6. We saw that this alternation involves a pair of verbs where the transitive is the causative version of the intransitive. The verb might signify a change of state, as in the pair of sentences *I broke the glass/The glass broke* or movement as in *She moved the car/The car moved*. As we saw in the chapter the inchoative is characterized by the absence of a causing agent. Below are some transitive verbs. Decide which may participate in the causative/inchoative alternation and classify the verb as change of state or movement:

a. The goalkeeper bounced the ball.
b. The anarchist assassinated the president.
c. The waiter melted the chocolate.
d. Charlie dug the new swimming pool.
e. The men lowered the boat.
f. The thieves destroyed the paintings.
g. Joan dried the clothes.

9.3 In chapter 6 we met the argument structure alternation in English called **Dative Alternation**, where some verbs, such as *give*, allow both of the patterns below:

a. Aideen gave the shoes to her neighbor.
   $[NP_X - V - NP_Z - \textit{to}\ NP_Y]$
b. Aideen gave her neighbor the shoes.
   $[NP_X - V - NP_Y - NP_Z]$

This alternation seems to be restricted to certain semantic subclasses of verbs. We can adapt from Pinker (1989: 110ff) an initial hypothesis to distinguish two semantic verb classes, as follows:

1	Class 1a:	the *give*-class: verbs whose semantic structure is "X causes Y to have Z," e.g. *Paul gave some money to the beggar.*
	Class 1b:	the *send*-class: verbs which share the basic semantic structure of (1a) but where the change of possession involves separation in time and/or space, which X tries to bridge by a means of transfer, e.g. *Harry sent the check to his wife.*
2	Class 2:	the *carry*-class: verbs whose semantic structure is "X moves Z to Y in a certain manner," e.g. *He carried the books to the clerk.*

The difference between classes 1 and 2 can be viewed in terms of CHANGE OF POSSESSION. In class 1a verbs this change is a necessary part of the meaning. In Class 1b verbs the change is intended though not necessary (we can say *I sent her the letter but she never got it* unlike **I gave her the money but she never got it*); while in Class 2 verbs Y's taking possession of Z is simply not part of the verb's meaning, although it may occur incidentally. We could then postulate a condition on Dative Alternation: Class 1 verbs allow Dative Alternation but Class 2 verbs do not. Thus we find *Paul gave the beggar some money*, *Harry sent his wife the check* but not **Mary carried the clerk the books*.

For the following verbs, decide which of these semantic classes they belong to and whether our prediction about Dative Alternation works. If not, discuss any further semantic qualification that might be necessary, for example, are there further classes to be set up; and if so, how would you characterize them?

mail, push, kick, pass, sell, lower, hand, push, flip, throw, bring, haul, ferry, take.

9.4 **Dative Alternation** also occurs with some verbs of communication. Once again we can set up semantic classes to try to explain which verbs show the alternation and which do not:

a. Class 3: the *tell*-class: verbs whose semantic structure is "X causes Y to cognitively possess Z," where "cognitively possess" includes Y knowing, perceiving, learning, etc. Z. For example: *Joan told the answer to Kate.*
b. Class 4: the *shout*-class: verbs whose semantic structure is "X communicates Z to Y in a certain manner," e.g. *Joan shouted the answer to Kate.*

Pinker (1989) calls Class 3 "illocutionary verbs of communication" because the verb gives information about what kind of illocutionary act the speaker intends. Thus *tell* in our example signals a **representative** act in the terminology of Searle (1976), discussed in chapter 8. Pinker (1989) and Levin (1993) follow Zwicky (1971) in calling Class 4 verbs "manner of speaking" verbs. We could claim that Class 3 verbs show the Dative Alternation, *Joan told Kate the answer*; while Class 4 verbs do not, **Joan shouted Kate the answer.*

As in the last exercise, examine the verbs below and decide which of these two semantic classes they belong to and whether our prediction about Dative Alternation works. Again, for any problematic cases, discuss whether you would add qualifications to our characterization of the classes above, or set up further semantic classes.

teach, read, whisper, mention, quote, murmur, say, show, scream, yell, cite.

9.5 **Dative Alternation** also occurs with examples like the one below:

a. She bought a car for her daughter
$[NP_X - V - NP_Z -$ *for* $NP_Y]$
b. She bought her daughter a car.
$[NP_X - V - NP_Y - NP_Z]$

These structures are called **benefactive** structures because X performs the action of the verb for the benefit of Y. Using your own examples, discuss whether this benefactive Dative Alternation exhibits the same restrictions that we saw in exercises 9.3 and 9.4, that is, is the alternation determined by a verb's membership of a semantic class?

9.6 Levin (1993), reporting on several earlier studies, notes that there seems to be a further type of lexical constraint on Dative Alternation: verbs derived from Latin roots do not undergo the alternation, even when they belong to the right semantic class. See for example 1 and 2 below which parallel verbs in exercises 9.3 and 9.4:

1 a. He gave the books to the college.
b. He gave the college the books.
c. He donated the books to the college.
d. *He donated the college the books.
2 a. He told the news to his father.
b. He told his father the news.
c. He communicated the news to his father.
d. *He communicated his father the news.

Using your own examples, investigate the range of this constraint on the semantic verb classes allowing Dative Alternation. If you find exceptions, do they form a coherent class or classes?

9.7 In this chapter we reviewed Talmy's (1985) investigations of how semantic components of motion events (Figure, Ground, Motion, Path, Manner) are conflated in verbs. Croft (1991) discusses example 1 below:

1 The boat sailed into the cave.

where the verb *sailed* conflates both the Manner and the Motion. Croft compares this with 2:

2 The boat burned into the cave.

where this cannot mean that the boat entered the cave while burning. Croft's explanation is that the Manner and the Motion can only be conflated in the same verb when the Manner causes the Motion. So in 1 sailing causes the motion into the cave; but in 2 burning does not.

Now look at the following English examples, where the verb is in bold. How many of these fit in with Croft's generalization? If any do not, try to establish what other semantic factors might be at work.

3 a. They **waltzed** onto the balcony.
b. The wind **howled** through the trees.
c. The grenade **bounced** into the bunker.
d. The ball **thudded** into his chest.
e. We **cycled** along the canal.
f. The cart **creaked** along the path.
g. The jet **flashed** across the sky.
h. The bees **swarmed** into the kitchen.

9.8 Using the format for Jackendoff's conceptual structure described in section 9.6, provide a conceptual structure for each of the following sentences:

a. Maura has a car.
b. Her birthday is on Thursday.
c. John went out of the room.
d. The house is Helen's.
e. The cat is on the roof.

9.9 Using the same format, provide a Jackendoff-style conceptual structure for the following sentences:

1 a. The window is closed.
b. The window closed.
2 a. Peg became angry.
b. Bob angered Peg.
3 a. George had the money.
b. George gave the money to Cindy.

9.10 In example 9.125 in the chapter we saw an example of Pustejovsky's qualia structure for the noun *novel*. Design a similar qualia structure for the noun *sandwich*.

FURTHER READING

A detailed discussion of Katz's semantic theory is in Allan (1986). Levin and Rappaport Hovav (2005) present a detailed overview of the role of decompositional semantic representations in analyzing the grammar of verbs. Jackendoff (1990, 2002, 2007) present his approach to semantics. For Pustejovky's notion of a generative lexicon see his (1995) book. A collection of papers on event structure, some using approaches described in this chapter, is in Tenny and Pustejovsky (2000). An example of the incorporation of a decompositional semantic representation into a grammatical theory is Role and Reference Grammar's level of logical structure; see Van Valin (2005) for discussion. For an influential attack on componential approaches see J. A. Fodor (1981).

NOTES

1 J. D. Fodor (1983) provides a good overview of Katz and Fodor's theory. See also Katz (1987) for a more recent discussion of this approach.
2 See Allan (1986, vol. 1: 274–391) for a very detailed description of the evolution of the theory and the resulting changes in dictionary entries.
3 We discussed middle constructions in chapter 6. As described there, "argument structure alternation" is a term used to describe processes which change the usual matching of semantic roles and grammatical positions. So in 9.20a we find *shirts* which would normally be the object of a verb like *wash* occurring as the subject.
4 A view shared by other writers, like Jackendoff (1990, 1992, 2002) and Pustejovsky (1995) whose work we discuss below, and Van Valin (2005), among many others.
5 Pinker (1989) calls this thematic role the "state changer" argument, while Rappaport and Levin (1985) call it the "displaced theme." These terms are used because these elements are not simple instruments but carry a role we might paraphrase as: "entities which by being moved cause a change of state in something to/from which they are moved."
6 This term **unmarked** comes from **markedness theory**. This is a theory of naturalness where the more marked an element is, the less natural it is. This notion can be applied both within a language, as in this case, or cross-linguistically, as when we say, for example, that back rounded vowels like French [u] in *tout* [tu] "all," are less marked than front rounded vowels like French [y] in *tu* [ty] "you." This implies that back rounded vowels are commoner in the languages of the world, will be learned earlier by children, are less likely to be lost in language change or in language disorders, etc. See Jakobson (1968) for discussion.
7 Subsequently some writers have modified this two-fold typological division by suggesting further language types (e.g. Zlatev and Yangklang 2003, Croft et al. 2010). But see Talmy (2009) for counterarguments.
8 The twenty-one languages were: Arrernte, Basque, Dutch, English, French, German, Hebrew, Icelandic, Italian, Mandarin, Polish, Portuguese, Russian, Serbo-Croatian, Spanish, Swedish, Tzeltal, Thai, Turkish, Warlpiri, and West Greenlandic.
9 "It is widely assumed, and I will take for granted, that the basic units out of which a sentential concept is constructed are the concepts expressed by the words in the sentence, that is *lexical* concepts." (Jackendoff 1990: 9).
10 We discussed this notion of entailment in chapter 4.
11 See Jackendoff (1990: 43, 1992: 13ff) for further details.
12 Verbs of motion have received a lot of attention in the semantics literature: see for example Miller and Johnson-Laird (1976), Talmy (1975, 1983, 1985, 2007), and Slobin (2004).
13 These and similar scope ambiguities are discussed in a formal approach by Dowty (1979).
14 Alsina (1999) in fact claims a third reading for this sentence: a wide-scope interpretation. He distinguishes this with the explanation: for example John shoots at the cat intending to kill it, but misses.
15 But see Gentner (1975, 1981) for some counter arguments and suggestions that the evidence of these earlier studies is not convincing.

16 This is reminiscent of Daniel Dennett's criticism of psychological approaches which only concern themselves with the internal state of the mind, ignoring the individual's interaction with the environment:

> The alternative of ignoring the external world and its relations to the internal machinery . . . is not really psychology at all, but just at best abstract neurophysiology – pure internal syntax with no hope of a semantic interpretation. Psychology "reduced" to neurophysiology in this fashion would not be psychology, for it would not be able to provide an explanation of the regularities it is psychology's particular job to explain: the reliability with which "intelligent" organisms can cope with their environments and thus prolong their lives. (Dennett 1987: 64)

17 But see Jackendoff (1983: 14–15) for an attack on the use of logic-based formalisms.

REFERENCES

Allan, Keith. 1986: *Linguistic Meaning*, 2 vols. London: Routledge & Kegan Paul.

Allen, S., A. Özyürek, S. Kita, A. Brown, R. Furman, T. Ishizuka, and M. Fujii 2007: Language-specific and universal influences in children's syntactic packaging of Manner and Path: A comparison of English, Japanese and Turkish. *Cognition* 102: 16–48.

Alsina, Alex 1999: On the representation of event structure. In Tara Mohanan and Lionel Wee (eds.) *Grammatical Semantics: Evidence for Structure in Meaning*, 77–122. Stanford, CA and National University of Singapore: Center for the Study of Language and Information.

Anderson, Stephen R. 1971: On the role of deep structure in semantic interpretation. *Foundations of Language* 7: 387–96.

Bach, Emmon 1986: The algebra of events. *Linguistics and Philosophy* 9: 5–16.

Berman, Ruth A. and Dan I. Slobin 1994: *Relating Events in Narrative: A Crosslinguistic Developmental Study*. Hillsdale, NJ: Lawrence Erlbaum Associates.

Boguraev, Branimir and Ted Briscoe 1989: Utilising the LDOCE grammar codes. In Branimir Boguraev and Ted Briscoe (eds.) *Computational Lexicography for Natural Language Processing*, 85–116. London: Longman.

Brown, A. and M. Gullberg 2010: Changes in encoding of path of motion after acquisition of a second language. *Cognitive Linguistics* 21.2: 263–86.

Choi, Soonja 2006: Influence of language-specific input on spatial cognition: categories of containment. *First Language* 26.2: 207–32.

Choi, Soonja and Melissa Bowerman 1992: Learning to express motion events in English and Korean: the influence of language-specific lexicalization patterns. In Beth Levin and Steven Pinker (eds.) *Lexical and Conceptual Semantics* 83–121. Oxford: Blackwell.

Choi, S, L. McDonough, M. Bowerman and J. Mandler 1999: Early sensitivity to language-specific spatial categories in English and Korean. *Cognitive Development* 14: 241–68.

Croft, William 1991: Possible verbs and the structure of events. In Savas L. Tsohatzidis (ed.) *Meanings and Prototypes: Studies on Linguistic Categorization*, 48–73. London: Routledge & Kegan Paul.

Croft, William, Jóhanna Barđdal, Willem Hollmann, Violeta Sotirova, and Chiaki Taoka 2010: Revising Talmy's typological classification of complex events construction. In Hans Boas (ed.) *Contrastive Studies in Construction Grammar*, 201–36. Amsterdam: John Benjamins.

Dennett, Daniel C. 1987: *The Intentional Stance*. Cambridge, MA: MIT Press.

Dowty, David R. 1979: *Word Meaning and Montague Grammar*. Dordrecht: Reidel.

Filipović, Luna and Ivana Vidaković 2010: Typology in the L2 classroom: second language acquisition from a typological perspective. In M. Pütz and L. Sicola (eds.) *Cognitive Processing in Second Language Acquisition*, 269–91. Amsterdam: John Benjamins.

Fodor, Janet Dean 1983: *Semantics: Theories of Meaning in Generative Grammar*. Brighton: Harvester.
Fodor, Janet Dean, Jerry A. Fodor, and Merrill F. Garrett 1975: The psychological unreality of semantic representations. *Linguistic Inquiry* 6: 515–32.
Fodor, Jerry A. 1970: Three reasons for not deriving "kill" from "cause to die." *Linguistic Inquiry* 1: 429–38.
Fodor, Jerry A. 1981: The present status of the innateness controversy. In J. A. Fodor *Representations: Philosophical Essays on the Foundations of Cognitive Science*, 257–316. Cambridge, MA: MIT Press/Bradford Books.
Fodor, Jerry A., Merrill F. Garrett, Edward C. T. Walker, and Cornelia H. Parkes 1980: Against definitions. *Cognition* 8: 263–67.
Gentner, Dedre 1975: Evidence for the psychological reality of semantic components: the verbs of possession. In Donald A. Norman and David E. Rumelhart (eds.) *Explorations in Cognition*, 211–46. San Francisco: Freeman.
Gentner, Dedre 1981: Verb structures in memory for sentences: evidence for componential representation. *Cognitive Psychology* 13: 56–83.
Grimshaw, Jane 1994: Semantic content and semantic structure. Manuscript, Rutgers University, New Brunswick, New Jersey.
Gropen, Jess, Steven Pinker, Michelle Hollander and Richard Goldberg 1991: Affectedness and direct objects: the role of lexical semantics in the acquisition of verb argument structure. In Beth Levin and Steven Pinker (eds.) *Lexical and Conceptual Semantics*, 153–95. Oxford: Blackwell.
Jackendoff, Ray 1972: *Semantic Interpretation in Generative Grammar*. Cambridge, MA: MIT Press.
Jackendoff, Ray 1983: *Semantics and Cognition*. Cambridge, MA: MIT Press.
Jackendoff, Ray 1987: *Consciousness and the Computational Mind*. Cambridge, MA: MIT Press.
Jackendoff, Ray 1990: *Semantic Structures*. Cambridge, MA: MIT Press.
Jackendoff, Ray 1992: Parts and boundaries. In Beth Levin and Steven Pinker (eds.) *Lexical and Conceptual Semantics*, 9–45. Oxford: Blackwell.
Jackendoff, Ray 2002: *Semantic Structures*. Cambridge, MA: MIT Press.
Jackendoff, Ray 2007: *Language, Consciousness, Culture: Essays on Mental Structure*. Cambridge, MA: MIT Press.
Jakobson, Roman 1968: *Child Language, Aphasia and Linguistic Universals*. The Hague: Mouton.
Katz, Jerrold J. 1972: *Semantic Theory*. New York: Harper and Row.
Katz, Jerrold J. 1987: Common sense in semantics. In Ernest Lepore (ed.) *New Directions in Semantics*, 157–233. New York: Academic Press.
Katz, Jerrold J. and Jerry A. Fodor 1963: The structure of a semantic theory. *Language* 39: 170–210.
Katz, Jerrold J. and Paul M. Postal 1964: *An Integrated Theory of Linguistic Descriptions*. Cambridge, MA: MIT Press.
Kita, Sotaro and Aslı Özyürek 2003: What does cross-linguistic variation in semantic coordination of speech and gesture reveal? Evidence for an interface representation of spatial thinking and speaking. *Journal of Memory and Language* 48.1: 16–32.
Levin, Beth 1993: *English Verb Classes and Alternations*. Chicago: University of Chicago Press.
Levin, Beth and Malka Rappaport Hovav 1991: Wiping the slate clean: a lexical semantic exploration. In Beth Levin and Steven Pinker (eds.) *Lexical and Conceptual Semantics*, 123–51. Oxford: Blackwell.
Levin, Beth and Malka Rappaport Hovav 2005: *Argument Realization*. Cambridge: Cambridge University Press.
Lewis, David K. 1972: General semantics. In Donald Davidson and Gilbert Harman (eds.) *Semantics of Natural Language*, 169–218. Dordrecht: Reidel.
McNeill, David and Susan D. Duncan 2000: Growth points in thinking-for-speaking. In D. McNeill (ed.) *Language and Gesture*, 141–61. Cambridge, MA: MIT Press.

Mayer, Mercer 1969: *Frog, Where Are You?* New York: Dial Books for Young Readers.
Miller, George A. and Philip N. Johnson-Laird 1976: *Language and Perception*. Cambridge, MA: Harvard/Belknap.
Mohanan, Tara and K. P. Mohanan 1999: On representations in grammatical semantics. In Mohanan and Wee (eds.), *Grammatical Semantics: Evidence for Structure in Meaning*, 23–75. Stanford, CA: Center for the Study of Language and Information, and Singapore: National University of Singapore.
Özçalışkan, Ş., and D. I. Slobin 1999: Learning how to search for the frog: Expression of manner of motion in English, Spanish, and Turkish. In A. Greenhill, H. Littlefield, and C. Tano (eds.) *Proceedings of the 23rd Annual Boston University Conference on Language Development*, 541–52. Boston, MA: Cascadilla Press.
Özyürek, Aslı and Şeyda Özçalışkan 2000: How do children learn to conflate manner and path in their speech and gestures? Differences in English and Turkish. In Eve V. Clark (ed.) *The Proceedings of the Thirtieth Annual Child Language Research Forum*, 77–85. Stanford, CA: CS Publications.
Parrill, Fey 2011: The relation between the encoding of motion event information and viewpoint in English-accompanying gestures. *Gesture* 11.1: 61–80.
Pinker, Steven 1989: *Learnability and Cognition: The Acquisition of Argument Structure*. Cambridge, MA: MIT Press.
Pustejovsky, James 1992: The syntax of event structure. In Beth Levin and Steven Pinker (eds.) *Lexical and Conceptual Semantics*, 47–81. Oxford: Blackwell.
Pustejovsky, James 1995: *The Generative Lexicon*. Cambridge, MA: MIT Press.
Ramchand, Gillian 2008: *Verb Meaning and the Lexicon*. Cambridge: Cambridge University Press.
Rappaport Hovav, Malka 2008: Lexicalized meaning and the internal temporal structure of events. In S. Rothstein (ed.) *Crosslinguistic and Theoretical Approaches to the Semantics of Aspect*, 13–42. Amsterdam: John Benjamins.
Rappaport, Malka and Beth Levin 1985: A case study in lexical analysis: the locative alternation. Unpublished manuscript: MIT Center for Cognitive Science.
Rappaport, Malka and Beth Levin 1988: What to do with theta-roles. In Wendy Wilkins (ed.) *Syntax and Semantics. Vol. 21: Thematic Relations*, 7–36. New York: Academic Press.
Rappaport Hovav, Malka and Beth Levin 2008: The English Dative Alternation: the case for verb sensitivity. *Journal of Linguistics* 44: 129–67.
Rappaport Hovav, Malka and Beth Levin 2010: Reflections on manner/result complementarity. In M. Rappaport Hovav, E. Doron and I. Sichel (eds.) *Syntax, Lexical Semantics, and Event Structure*, 21–38. Oxford: Oxford University Press.
Searle, John R. 1976: The classification of illocutionary acts. *Language in Society* 5: 1–23. Reprinted in *Expression and Meaning: Studies in the Theory of Speech Acts*, 1979. Cambridge: Cambridge University Press, 1–29.
Slobin, Dan I. 2003: Language and thought online: cognitive consequences of linguistic relativity. In D. Gentner and S. Goldin-Meadow (eds.) *Language in Mind: Advances in the Study of Language and Thought*, 157–92. Cambridge, MA: MIT Press.
Slobin, Dan I. 2004: The many ways to search for a frog: linguistic typology and the expression of motion events. In Sven Strömqvist and Ludo Verhoeven (eds.) *Relating Events in Narrative*, vol. 2, 219–57. Mahwah, NJ: Lawrence Erlbaum.
Slobin, Dan. I. 2005: Relating narrative events in translation. In D. Ravid and H. B. Shyldkrot (eds.) *Perspectives on Language and Language Development: Essays in Honor of Ruth A. Berman*, 115–29. Dordrecht: Kluwer.
Slobin, Dan. I. 2006: What makes manner of motion salient? Explorations in linguistic typology, discourse, and cognition. In M. Hickmann and S. Robert (eds.) *Space in Languages: Linguistic Systems and Cognitive Categories*, 59–81. Amsterdam: John Benjamins.
Strömqvist, S. and L. Verhoeven (eds.) 2004: *Relating Events in Narrative. Vol. 2: Typological and Contextual Perspectives*. Mahwah, NJ: Lawrence Erlbaum.

Talmy, Leonard 1975: Semantics and syntax of motion. In John P. Kimball (ed.) *Syntax and Semantics 4*, 181–238. London: Academic Press.
Talmy, Leonard 1983: How language structures space. In Herbert Pick and Linda Acredolo (eds.), *Spatial Orientation: Theory, Research, and Application*, 225–82. New York: Plenum Press.
Talmy, Leonard 1985: Lexicalization patterns: semantic structure in lexical forms. In Timothy Shopen (ed.) *Language Typology and Syntactic Description*, vol. 3: 57–149. Cambridge: Cambridge University Press.
Talmy, Leonard 1991: Path to realization: a typology of event conflation. In *Proceedings of the 17th Annual Meeting of the Berkeley Linguistic Society*, 480–519. Berkeley, CA: Berkeley Linguistics Society.
Talmy, Leonard. 2000: *Toward a Cognitive Semantics*, 2 vols. Cambridge, MA: MIT Press.
Talmy, Leonard. 2007: Lexical typologies. In Timothy Shopen (ed.) *Language Typology and Syntactic Description*, second edition, vol. 3, 66–168. Cambridge: Cambridge University Press.
Talmy, Leonard 2009: Main verb properties and equipollent framing. In J. Guo et al. (eds.), *Crosslinguistic Approaches to the Psychology of Language: Research in the Tradition of Dan Isaac Slobin*, 389–402. New York: Taylor & Francis.
Tenny, Carol and James Pustejovsky (eds.) 2000: *Events as Grammatical Objects: The Converging Perspectives of Lexical Semantics and Syntax*. Stanford, CA: Center for the Study of Language and Information.
Van Valin, Robert D. 2005: *Exploring the Syntax–Semantics Interface*. Cambridge: Cambridge University Press.
Vendler, Zeno 1967: *Linguistics in Philosophy*. Ithaca, NY: Cornell University Press.
Wierzbicka, Anna 1980: *Lingua Mentalis: The Semantics of Natural Language*. New York: Academic Press.
Wunderlich, Dieter 1997: Cause and the structure of verbs. *Linguistic Inquiry* 28: 27–68.
Zlatev, Jordan and Peerapat Yangklang 2003: A third way to travel: the place of Thai and serial verb languages in motion event typology. In S. Strömqvist and L. Verhoeven (eds.) *Relating Events in Narrative. Volume 2: Typological and Contextual Perspectives*, 159–90. Mahwah, NJ: Lawrence Erlbaum.
Zwicky, A. 1971: In a manner of speaking. *Linguistic Inquiry* 2: 223–33.

chapter 10

Formal Semantics

10.1 Introduction

In this chapter we look at the approach known as **formal semantics**. Although any approach might be formalized, this label is usually used for a family of denotational theories which use logic in semantic analysis. Other names which focus on particular aspects or versions of this general approach include **truth conditional semantics**, **model-theoretic semantics**, and **Montague Grammar**.[1] As we shall see, another possible label might be **logical semantics**.

This approach elaborates further the use of truth, truth conditions, and logic discussed in chapter 4. There we reviewed the strategy of borrowing from logic the notion of **truth** and the formalism of **propositional logic** to characterize semantic relations like entailment. In this chapter we shall see how further tools from logic can be used to help characterize aspects of sentence-internal semantics.

In discussing formal semantics we touch on an important philosophical divide in semantics: between **representational** and **denotational** approaches to meaning. In chapter 9 we saw examples of the representational approach: for semanticists like Jackendoff semantic analysis involves discovering the conceptual structure which underlies language. For such linguists the search for meaning is the search for mental representations. Formal semanticists on the other hand come at meaning from another angle: for them a primary function of language is that it allows us to talk about the world around us. When communicating with others and in our own internal reasoning we use language to describe, or model, facts and situations. From this perspective, understanding the meaning of an utterance is being able to match it with the situation it describes. Hence the search for meaning, from the denotational perspective, is the search for how the symbols of language relate to reality.

How is this relation characterized? Formal semanticists employ the **correspondence theory** of truth discussed in chapter 4. Speakers are held to be aware of what situation an utterance describes and to be able to tell whether the utterance and the situation match up or **correspond**. Thus knowing the meaning of an English sentence like *It's raining in Belfast* involves understanding what situation in the world this sentence would correspond to, or fit. A successful match is called **true**; an unsuccessful match is **false**. Another way of describing this is to say that the listener who understands the sentence is able to determine the **truth conditions** of the uttered sentence, that is, know what conditions in the world would make the sentence true. In the basic version of this approach used in logic there are no *almost*s or *nearly*s: an utterance either describes a situation, and is therefore true of that situation, or not, in which case it is false. See for example, the characterization from a logic text, Bradley and Swartz (1979: 11):

10.1 The account of truth which we are here espousing has been described variously as "the Correspondence Theory," "the Realist theory," or even "the Simple Theory" of truth. In effect, it says that a proposition, P, is true if and only if the (possible) states of affairs ... is as P asserts it to be. It defines "truth" as a property which propositions have just when they "correspond" to the (possible) states of affairs whose existence they assert. It is a "realist" theory insofar as it makes truth a real or objective property of propositions, i.e. not something subjective but a function of what states of affairs really exist in this or that possible world. And it is a "simple" theory of truth insofar as it accords with the simple intuitions which most of us – before we try to get too sophisticated about such matters – have about the conditions for saying that something is true or false.[2]

Some objections to this might quickly occur to a linguist seeking to borrow these notions to describe natural languages. On a practical descriptive level, this characterization seems to apply just to statements, since intuitively it is hard to see how other utterance types like questions and orders can be viewed as descriptions of situations. Yet, as we saw in our discussion of speech acts in chapter 8, many utterances are not statements. On a more general level the idea of correct or incorrect matches seems to remove the subjectivity of the speaker. We saw in chapter 5 that the certainty shown by a statement might be just one of a range of speaker attitudes to, or confidence in, a proposition. We described such ranges with terms like **modality** and **evidentiality**. In section 10.8 we discuss how formal approaches might take account of such notions.

Formal semanticists have to meet these and related objections to the extension of logical mechanisms to ordinary language. Nonetheless, this approach has become one of the most important and liveliest in the semantics literature. Why is this? We can perhaps outline at this preliminary stage a number of advantages. One great advantage comes from using logical expressions as a semantic metalanguage. It enables semanticists to import into linguistics the economy and formality of the traditional discipline of logic and the benefits of the long struggle to establish mathematics and logic on common principles.[3] Logicians try to make as explicit as possible both the relations between logical symbols and what they represent and the effects of combining symbols. Consequently logic, as a potential semantic metalanguage, has the important advantage of precision.

Denotational approaches, if successful, have another advantage: they escape the problem of circularity discussed in chapter 1. We raised the problem that if we interpret English in terms of a metalanguage, another set of symbols, then we have just translated from one language to another. This second language then needs a semantics, and so on. As we shall see, formal semanticists do translate a natural language like English into a second, logical language, but this translation is only part of the semantic analysis. This logical language is then semantically grounded by tying it to real-world situations. The aim of a denotational approach is not just to convert between representations: it seeks to connect language to the world.

There are other less obvious advantages claimed for such theories: it has been suggested, for example by Chierchia and McConnell-Ginet (2000), that denotational approaches allow us to see more clearly the connection between human languages and the simpler signs systems of other primates like vervet monkeys, baboons and chimpanzees. These systems are clearly referential: primates often have distinct conventional signs for different types of predators like eagles, snakes, or big cats.[4] Perhaps this basic matching between a symbol and entities in the environment was the starting point for human languages.

Whatever the advantages to this approach, we should mention one temporary, practical disadvantage for students new to the theory: this is a very technical and highly formalized approach. Employing the tools of logic means having to become familiar with them and this involves a substantial expenditure of time and effort. Beginners will not see a return on this investment, in terms of improved semantic analyses of real language, very quickly. For an introductory survey like this one, this poses problems of coverage. How much of this large and complicated technical apparatus can we cover in a chapter like this? Our proposal is to sketch in the basic features of the approach without too steep an immersion in mathematical formulae. In particular we will not investigate the formal proofs that a logical language must support. We mention some book-length introductions to this approach in our suggestions for further readings at the end of the chapter which will allow the interested reader to pursue these topics more fully.

10.2 Model-Theoretical Semantics

Much of the investigation of logic and natural language semantics has been conducted by philosophers, logicians and mathematicians: for example the predicate logic we describe in this chapter derives largely from the work of the logician and mathematician Gottlob Frege,[5] the notion of truth owes much to Alfred Tarski (1944, 1956), and much of the recent and contemporary debate has been undertaken by philosophers like Donald Davidson (e.g. 1980, 1984). For many linguists, interest in this approach was sparked by the work in the 1960s of the logician Richard Montague, mentioned earlier. As we shall see, an important element in this theory is a **model**, a formal structure representing linguistically relevant aspects of a situation. Consequently one term for Montague's work and similar approaches is **model-theoretical semantics**. The application of this approach to linguistic description by linguists and computer scientists has led to both further development of the model-theoretical approach and the emergence of a number of related but distinct approaches, like **situation semantics** (Barwise and Perry 1983) and **discourse representation theory** (Kamp and Reyle 1993). Since our discussion will remain at an introductory level, we begin by outlining a kind of embryonic model-theoretic approach. Our description will be influenced by **Montague Grammar** but we will not attempt an introduction to this theory here[6] (see Montague 1974, Dowty et al. 1981). In such an approach semantic analysis consists of three stages: firstly, a translation from a natural language like English into a logical language whose syntax and semantics are explicitly defined. Secondly, the establishment of a mathematical model of the situations that the language describes. Thirdly, a set of procedures for checking the mapping between the expressions in the logical language and the modeled situations. Essentially these algorithms check whether the expressions are true or false of the modeled situations. Each of these three stages can throw light on the semantic capabilities of natural languages.

We look at these stages in order: we discuss the translation in section 10.3, where we use English as our example and we concentrate on the syntax of the logical metalanguage. We discuss models and mapping algorithms in 10.4–5, where the emphasis is on adding a semantics to the metalanguage. In 10.6 we discuss word meaning in formal semantics.

Subsequently we review some key areas where this basic model has been extended to reflect more accurately the semantics of natural languages. In 10.7 we look at quantifiers in more detail; in 10.8 we discuss intensionality; and in 10.9 we look at an approach which takes account of the dynamic nature of communication, discourse representation theory (DRT).

10.3 Translating English into a Logical Metalanguage

10.3.1 Introduction

As we have said, the first stage of this semantic analysis consists of translation. The basic idea is that we can translate from a sentence in an individual language like English into an expression in a universal metalanguage. One such metalanguage is **predicate logic**. As mentioned in chapter 4, predicate logic builds on the investigation of sentence connectives in propositional logic and goes on to investigate the internal structure of sentences, for example the truth-conditional effect of certain words like the English quantifiers *all*, *some*, *one*, and so on. In chapter 4 we briefly introduced a set of logical connectives which parallel in interesting ways some uses of English expressions like *and*, *or*, *if... then*, and *not*. These connectives are summarized in 10.2 below; for each connective the table gives its symbol, an example of its syntax, that is, how it combines with sentence constants **p**, **q**, and so on, and an approximate English equivalent:

10.2 Connectives in propositional logic

Connective	Syntax	English
$\neg$	$\neg$**p**	it is not the case that **p**
$\wedge$	**p** $\wedge$ **q**	**p** and **q**
$\vee$	**p** $\vee$ **q**	**p** and/or **q**
$\vee_e$	**p** $\vee_e$ **q**	**p** or **q** but not both
$\rightarrow$	**p** $\rightarrow$ **q**	if **p**, then **q**
$\equiv$	**p** $\equiv$ **q**	**p** if and only if **q**

We will be using these connectives in our translations into predicate logic, which we begin in section 10.3.2.

10.3.2 Simple statements in predicate logic

If we begin with simple statements like 10.3 and 10.4 below:

10.3 Mulligan is sleeping.

10.4 Bill smokes.

we can identify a subject-predicate structure where the subject is a referring expression (*Mulligan*, *Bill*) and the predicate tells us something about the subject (*is asleep*, *smokes*). The predicate logic assigns different roles to these two elements: the predicate is treated as a skeletal function which requires the subject argument to be complete. Our first step is to represent the predicate by a capital **predicate letter**, for example:

10.5 is asleep: A
smokes: S

The subject argument can be represented by a lower-case letter (usually chosen from a to t and called an **individual constant**), for example:

10.6 Mulligan: m
Bill: b

The convention is that predicate logic forms begin with the predicate, followed by the subject constant. Thus our original sentences can be assigned the representations in 10.7:

10.7 Mulligan is asleep: $A(m)$
Bill smokes: $S(b)$

If we want to leave the identity of the subject unspecified we can use **variables** (lower case letters from the end of the alphabet: w, x, y, z), for example:

10.8 x is asleep: $A(x)$
y smokes: $S(y)$

As we shall see later, these variables have a special use in the analysis of quantifiers.

We have been looking at the representation of intransitive sentences. The verbs in transitive sentences like 10.9 below require more than one nominal:

10.9 Bill resembles Eddie.
Tommaso adores Libby.

These predicates are identified as relations between the arguments and represented as follows:

10.10 Bill resembles Eddie: $R(b, e)$
Tommaso adores Libby: $A(t, l)$

Other relational sentences will be represented in the same way, for example:

10.11 Pete is crazier than Ryan: $C(p, r)$

Note that the order of constant terms after the predicate letter is significant: it mirrors English sentence structure in that the subject comes before the object. Three-place relations are of course possible; we show an example with its logical translation below:

10.12 Fatima prefers Bill to Henry: $P(f, b, h)$

In our examples so far we have included the English sentence and the logical translation. Alternatively, we can keep track of what the letters in the logical form correspond to by providing a key, for example:

10.13 $P(f, b, h)$
Key: P: prefer
f: Fatima
b: Bill
h: Henry

Our notation so far can reflect negative and compound sentences by making use of the connectives shown earlier in 10.2, for example:

10.14 Máire doesn't jog: $\neg J(m)$

10.15 Fred smokes and Kate drinks: $S(f) \wedge D(k)$

10.16 If Bill drinks, Jenny gets angry: $D(b) \rightarrow A(j)$

We might also wish to translate sentences containing **relative clauses** like *(the student) who passed the exam*, *(the dress) that she wore*, and so on. We can represent complex sentences containing relative clauses by viewing them as a form of conjunction, that is by using $\wedge$ "and," as in 10.17–19 below:

10.17 Carrick, who is a millionaire, is a socialist: $M(c) \wedge S(c)$

10.18 Emile is a cat that doesn't purr: $C(e) \wedge \neg P(e)$

10.19 Jean admires Robert, who is a gangster: $A(j, r) \wedge G(r)$

In the next section we extend the logic further to cope with quantified noun phrases.

10.3.3 Quantifiers in predicate logic

One important feature of natural languages that formal semanticists have to deal with in their translation into logical form is **quantification**. All languages have strategies for allowing a proposition to be generalized over ranges or sets of individuals. In English for example quantifiers include words like *one*, *some*, *a few*, *many*, *a lot*, *most*, and *all*. We can look at a simple example. Let's say that we want to predicate the verb phrase *wrote a paper* of various members of a class of students. We could assert this predicate will be true of (at least) one member, by saying 10.20 below:

10.20 A student wrote a paper.

or vary the range of its applicability, as below:

10.21 a. A few students wrote a paper.
b. Many students wrote a paper.
c. Most students wrote a paper.
d. All students wrote a paper.
e. Every student wrote a paper.

We could also deny it applies to any of them by using:

10.22 No student wrote a paper.

The simple logical representation we have developed so far isn't able to reflect this ability to generalize statements over a set of individuals. One way to do this is to follow a proposal of Frege's that statements containing quantifiers be divided into two sections: the quantifying expression, which gives the range of the generalization; and the rest of the sentence (the generalization), which will have a place-holder element, called a **variable**, for the quantified nominal. We can show how this approach works for the quantifiers *all*, *every*, *some*, and *no*, though as we shall see in section 10.6 the other quantifiers in example 10.21 will require a different account. To show this we look first at the quantifiers *all* and *every*. Both of these English quantifiers are represented in predicate logic by the **universal quantifier**, symbolized as ∀. We can use as an example 10.21e above. This will be given the representation 10.23a below, which can be read as 10.23b:

10.23 a. $\forall x\ (S(x) \rightarrow W(x, p))$
b. For every thing *x*, if *x* is a student then *x* wrote a paper.

The universal quantifier establishes the range by fixing the value of x as every thing; the expression in parentheses is the generalization. By itself the generalization is an incomplete proposition, called an **open proposition**: until the value of x is set for some individual(s) the expression cannot be true or false. As we shall see, the quantifier serves to set the value of x and close the proposition. Expressions with the universal quantifier can be paraphrased in English by *all* or *every* as in *All students wrote a paper* or *Every student wrote a paper* in 10.23.[7]

We can see that the quantifier phrase can be associated with different positions in the predicate if we compare 10.24a and b below:

10.24 a. Every student knows the professor: $\forall x\ (S(x) \rightarrow K(x, p))$
b. The professor knows every student: $\forall x\ (S(x) \rightarrow K(p, x))$

Here the logical representations emphasize more than English does that both 10.24a and b are predicating something about all of the students. The relationship between the quantifier phrase and the rest of the formula is described in two ways: the quantifying expression is said to **bind** the variable in the predicate expression; and the predicate expression is said to be the **scope** of the quantifier.

Next we turn to the quantifier *some* in example 10.20. *Some* is represented in predicate logic by the **existential quantifier**, symbolized as ∃. We can thus translate our example as 10.25 below:

10.25 $\exists x\ (S(x) \wedge P(s, e))$
There is (at least) one thing x such that x is a student and x wrote a paper.

We can paraphrase such expressions in English by using noun phrases like *a student*, *some student*, and *at least one student*. The existential quantifier can also be associated with different positions in the predicate:

10.26 (At least) One student kissed Kylie: $\exists x\ (S(x) \wedge K(x, k))$

10.27 Kylie kissed (at least) one student: $\exists x\ (S(x) \wedge K(k, x))$

Once again the existential quantifier is said to bind the variable and the predicative expression is described as the scope of the quantifier.

The English determiner *no* can be represented by a combination of the existential quantifier and negation, as shown below:

10.28 $\neg\exists x\ (S(x) \wedge W(x, p))$
It is not the case that there is a thing x such that x is a student and x wrote a paper, There is no x such that x is a student and x wrote a paper.

This corresponds to the sentence *No student wrote a paper*. Another way of representing this is by using the material implication:

10.29 $\forall x\ (S(x) \rightarrow \neg P(x, e))$
For every thing x, if x is a student then it is not the case that x wrote a paper.

With the introduction of these quantifiers we can now summarize the syntax of the predicate logic so far. The syntax includes the vocabulary of symbols in 10.30 below and the rules for the formation of logical formulae in 10.31:

10.30 The symbols of predicate logic

Predicate letters:	*A*, *B*, *C*, etc.
Individual constants:	*a*, *b*, *c*, etc.
Individual variables:	*x*, *y*, *z*, etc.
Truth functional connectives:	$\neg, \wedge, \vee, \underline{\vee}, \rightarrow, \equiv$
Quantifiers:	$\forall, \exists$

10.31 The rules for creating logical formulae

a. Individual constants and variable are terms.

b. If A is an *n*-place predicate and $t_1 \ldots t_n$ are *n* terms, then $A(t_1 \ldots t_n)$ is a formula.[8]

c. If ϕ is a formula, then $\neg\phi$ is a formula.

d. If ϕ and ψ are formulae, then $(\phi \wedge \psi)$, $(\phi \vee \psi)$, $(\phi \underline{\vee} \psi)$, $(\phi \rightarrow \psi)$, $(\phi \equiv \psi)$ are all formulae.

e. If ϕ is a formula and *x* is a variable, then $\forall x\phi$, and $\exists x\phi$ are formulae.

We can add to these rules the convention that the outer parentheses of a complete formula can be omitted, that is, instead of writing $(\phi \wedge \psi)$, we can write $\phi \wedge \psi$.

10.3.4 Some advantages of predicate logic translation

The predicate logic we have been looking at is used by logicians to demonstrate the validity of arguments and reasoning. Thus in addition to a syntax and semantics, the logical languages requires rules of inference. This however is a topic we will not pursue here. From a linguist's perspective there are a number of advantages to the representations we have introduced. We can take as an example the way that the representation of quantifiers, as introduced above, clarifies some ambiguities found in natural languages. One of these is **scope ambiguity**, which can occur when there is more than one quantifier in a sentence. For example the English sentence 10.32a below has the two interpretations paraphrased in 10.32b and c:

10.32 a. Everyone loves someone.
b. Everyone has someone that they love.
c. There is some person who is loved by everyone.

Version 10.32b involves a many-to-many relationship of loving, while version 10.32c involves a many-to-one relationship. While the English sentence is structurally ambiguous between these two interpretations, the difference is explicitly shown in predicate logic by the ordering of the quantifiers. The interpretation in 10.32b is represented by the formula in 10.33a and that in 10.32c by 10.33b below:

10.33 a. $\forall x \exists y\ (L(x, y))$
b. $\exists y \forall x\ (L(x, y))$

The formula in 10.33a says that for every person x, there is some person y that they love. The universal quantifier comes leftmost and therefore contains the existential quantifier in its scope. This situation is described as the universal quantifier having **wide scope**. In 10.33 we have the reverse: the existential quantifier contains the universal in its scope and therefore takes wide scope. Thus the scope of one quantifier may be contained within the scope of another.

Negative words, like English *not*, also display scope over a predication and a second advantage of this type of representation is that it allows us to disambiguate some sentences which contain combinations of quantifiers and negation. The sentence *Everybody didn't visit Limerick*, for example, can have the two interpretations given in 10.34 and 10.35 below, where we give a paraphrase in b and the predicate logic translation in c:

10.34 a. Everybody didn't visit Limerick.
b. For every person x, it's not the case that x visited Limerick.
c. $\forall x \neg(V(x, l))$

10.35 a. Everybody didn't visit Limerick.
b. It's not the case that every person x visited Limerick.
c. $\neg\forall x (V(x, l))$

As we can see, the ambiguity is clearly distinguished in the predicate logic translations. In 10.34c the universal quantifier has wide scope over the negative connector $\neg$, giving a reading equivalent to *Nobody visited Limerick*, while in 10.35c the negative has wide scope over the universal quantifier, giving a reading equivalent to *Not everyone visited Limerick*. The interpretation in 10.34b–c is called the surface scope or isomorphic interpretation because the surface order reflects the scope relation, that is *every>not*. The interpretation in 10.35b–c is called the inverse scope or non-isomorphic interpretation because the surface order is reversed in the scope relation, *not>every*. Because of the mismatch in the inverse scope reading we might expect that for reasons of processing efficiency the surface scope reading would usually be preferred. However, it is clear that in certain contexts the inverse scope is preferred. This may be as a result of pragmatic issues like the influence of background knowledge. In chapter 2 we saw the example 2.27, and this is repeated as 10.36 below:

10.36 Every American doesn't drink coffee.

Here the non-isomorphic reading *Not every American drinks coffee* is likely to be preferred in most contexts to the isomorphic reading *No American drinks coffee* because of the hearers' knowledge about the world.

This discussion shows some of the advantages of semantic clarity gained by the translation into predicate logic. In fact though, as we mentioned earlier, the real purpose of this translation is to allow a denotational semantic analysis to be carried out. In the next section we look at how this logical representation is given a semantics.

10.4 The Semantics of the Logical Metalanguage

10.4.1 Introduction

As we have said, the aim of this approach is to devise a denotational semantics. Clearly our first stage alone is not such a semantic analysis. Translating from an English sentence into a logical formula is not enough: we then have to relate this second set of symbols to something outside – the situation described. To do this we need to add three further elements:

10.36
1. a **semantic interpretation** for the symbols of the predicate logic;
2. a **domain**: this is a model of a situation which identifies the linguistically relevant entities, properties and relations; and
3. a **denotation assignment function**: this is a procedure, or set of procedures, which match the logical symbols for nouns, verbs, etc. with the items in the model that they denote. This function is also sometimes called a **naming function**.

The domain and naming function are together called a **model**. We look at each of these constituents in turn.

10.4.2 The semantic interpretation of predicate logic symbols

We can adopt a simple denotational theory of reference, as discussed in chapter 2, for the units of the predicate logic. We will identify three such units for discussion: whole sentences, constant terms, and predicates, and we will use some simple **set theory** notions to help us define denotation.[9]

Sentences

Following the correspondence theory of truth we will take the denotatum of a whole sentence to be the match or lack of match with the situation it describes. A match will be called **true** (**T**), also symbolized by the numeral **1**. A mismatch will be called **false** (**F**), symbolized by the numeral **0**. So using a variable v for situations, we might say "a sentence **p** is true in situation v," and symbolize it as $[\mathbf{p}]v = \mathbf{1}$. Here we use square brackets to symbolize the denotatum of an expression, so $[x]^v$ means the denotatum of x in the situation v. Thus the notation $[\mathbf{p}]^v = \mathbf{1}$ means "the denotatum of **p** in v is **true**." By contrast the expression $[\mathbf{p}]^v = \mathbf{0}$ will be read as "the denotatum of **p** in v is **false**" or, equivalently, "the sentence **p** is false in situation v." Since, as we have acknowledged, meaning is compositional, we want the truth-value of a sentence to be determined by the semantic value of its parts: the nouns, verbs, connectives, and so on of which it is constructed.

Individual constant terms

We will assume the denotation of individual constant terms to be individuals or sets of individuals in the situation. So if we adopt as our situation the 1974 world heavyweight title fight between Muhammad Ali and George Foreman in Zaire, we could use an individual constant term *a* to denote Ali, another individual constant *f* to denote Foreman and a third, *r*, to denote the referee in this situation *v*.

Predicate constants

We will assume that predicate constants, abbreviated with capital letters, *P*, *Q*, *R*, and so on, identify sets of individuals for which the predicate holds. Thus a one-place predicate like *be standing* will pick out the set of individuals who are standing in the situation described. This can be described in a set theory notation as either $\{x \mid \ldots\}$ or $\{x: \ldots\}$, both of which can be read as "the set of all *x* such that ..." So a notation like $\{x: x \text{ is standing in } v\}$ can be read as "the set of individuals who are standing in situation *v*."

Two-place predicates identify a set of ordered pairs: two individuals in a given order. Thus the predicate *punch* will pick out an ordered pair where the first punches the second in *v* represented in set theory terms as: $\{<x, y>: x \text{ punches } y \text{ in } v\}$. Similarly a three-place predicate like *hand to* will identify a 3-tuple $\{<x, y, z>: x \text{ hands } y \text{ to } z \text{ in } v\}$.

10.4.3 The domain

The domain is a representation of the individuals and relationships in a situation, which we will continue to call *v*. Let's invent an example by imagining a situation in the Cavern Club, Liverpool in 1962 where the Beatles are rehearsing for that evening's performance. If we use this as our domain, let's say we can identify several individuals in the situation: the Beatles themselves, John, Paul, George, and Ringo, their manager Brian Epstein and one stray fan we'll call Bob. In the format we are using here we will say that the situation *v* contains a set of individuals, U, such that in this case U = {John, Paul, George, Ringo, Brian Epstein, Bob}.

10.4.4 The denotation assignment function

This function matches symbols from the logical representation with elements of the domain, according to the semantic nature of the symbols. For our simple example, we can divide its work into two parts: (a) the matching of individual constant terms with individuals in the situation *v*; and (b) the matching of predicate constants with sets of individuals in *v*.

Matching individual constant terms

The assignment is a function, which we can symbolize as *F*(*x*). This function will for any symbol *x* of the logical formula always returns its **extension** in the situation. Thus we can establish a matching for individual constant terms as follows:

10.37 Assignment of individual constant terms

F(*j*) = John
F(*p*) = Paul
F(*g*) = George
F(*r*) = Ringo
F(*e*) = Brian Epstein
F(*b*) = Bob

In other words, the individual constant *j* denotes the entity John in the situation *v*, *p* denotes Paul, and so on.

Matching predicate constants

Our function *F*(*x*) will return the extensions of predicates, as described a little earlier on for the semantics of predicates. Thus the function will return individuals, ordered pairs or 3-tuples, depending on the type of predicate. For our current example the matching will be as follows:

10.38 Assignment of predicate letters

F(*B*)	= was a Beatle	= {John, Paul, George, Ringo}
F(*M*)	= was a manager	= {Brian Epstein}
F(*F*)	= was a fan	= {Bob}
F(*S*)	= sang	= {John, Paul}
F(*G*)	= played guitar	= {John, Paul, George}
F(*D*)	= played the drums	= {Ringo}
F(*J*)	= joked with	= {<John, George>}
F(*I*)	= idolized	= {<Bob, John>, <Bob, Paul>, <Bob, George>, <Bob, Ringo>}

Thus the extension of *J* "*joked with*" in the situation is the set of the ordered pair, John and George.

At this point then we have defined the semantic (denotational) behavior of some of the logical constituents and established a model, which we take to be a combination of a domain and the assignment function. Such a model is often schematically described as $M_n = <U_n, F_n>$, where M = the model, U = the set of individuals in the situation, and F is our denotation assignment function. The subscript **n** (for 1, 2, 3 ... **n**) on each element relativizes the model to one particular situation. So we can identify our situation as $M_1 = <U_1, F_1>$. For a different situation we would need a second model, $M_2 = <U_2, F_2>$, and so on.

Next we need to have some evaluation procedure to reflect a listener's ability to evaluate a sentence's truth-value relative to a situation. Basically this means a set of algorithms to check whether a given sentence is true or not of the situation. We outline a simple informal version of this in the next section.

10.5 Checking the Truth-Value of Sentences

As we mentioned earlier, our procedures for checking the **truth-value** of a sentence must reflect the compositionality of meaning. If this is done correctly, then we will have shown something of how the constituents of a sentence contribute to the truth-value of the whole sentence. To keep our discussion within bounds, we will look at this procedure for just three basic types of sentence: a simple statement, a compound sentence with ∧ "and," and sentences with the universal and existential quantifiers, ∀ and ∃.

10.5.1 Evaluating a simple statement

If we take our model M_1, we might construct some relevant sentences in predicate logic as in 10.39 below, some of which are true of M_1 and some of which are false:

10.39 a. $D(r)$
b. $G(b)$
c. $J(e, b)$
d. $G(p)$
e. $S(j)$

The reader may routinely translate these back into English, for example, 10.39a as *Ringo played the drums*, and so on. Let's take 10.39e as an example and test its truth-value in M_1. The procedure for checking if $S(j)$ is true is based on the denotational definitions we gave earlier and can be schematized as in 10.40 below:

10.40 $[S(j)]^{M_1} = \mathbf{1}$ iff $[j]^{M_1} \in [S]^{M_1}$

This rather forbidding schema employs various elements of our notation so far and can be paraphrased in English as in 10.41:

10.41 The sentence *John sang* is true if and only if the extension of *John* is part of the set defined by *sang* in the model M_1.

Now to check this we have to check the extensions returned by the denotation assignment function for the individual constant j and the predicate constant S to see if $F_1(j) \in F_1(S)$. We know from our model and assignment that:

10.42 $F_1(j) = $ John

and we also know:

10.43 $F_1(S) = \{$John, Paul$\}$

So since it is clearly true that John $\in$ {John, Paul}, then our sentence is true, that is, schematically $[S(j)]^{M_1} = \mathbf{1}$.

10.5.2 Evaluating a compound sentence with ∧ "and"

Evaluating a compound sentence follows basically the same procedure we have just outlined. Let's take as an example sentences containing ∧ "and." We can create such sentences as 10.44 below for our model M_1:

10.44 a. $S(j) \wedge S(p)$
b. $J(j, g) \wedge J(r, b)$
c. $M(e) \wedge F(b)$
d. $S(j) \wedge I(b, e)$

Once again 10.44 contains some true and some false sentences for M_1. We can take as our example 10.44d, $S(j) \wedge I(b, e)$. To evaluate any compound sentence $\mathbf{p} \wedge \mathbf{q}$ we first establish the independent truth-value of **p** and then of **q**. Then we evaluate the effect of joining them with ∧. The truth-functional effect of ∧ was given in the form of a truth table in chapter 4: essentially a compound with ∧ is only true when **p** is true and **q** is true. In the format we are using here this behavior can be expressed as in 10.45 below:

10.45 Truth behavior of ∧
$[\mathbf{p} \wedge \mathbf{q}] = \mathbf{1}$ **iff** $[\mathbf{p}] = \mathbf{1}$ **and** $[\mathbf{q}] = \mathbf{1}$

In effect 10.45 says that both conjuncts must be true for the compound to be true. If we turn again to our example 10.44d above, we can run through the procedure for evaluating its truth-value relative to M_1. For this particular sentence and model, the behavior of ∧ can be expressed as below:

10.46 $[S(j) \wedge I(b, e)]^{M_1} = \mathbf{1}$ **iff** $[S(j)\,]^{M_1} = \mathbf{1}$ **and** $[I(b, e)]^{M_1} = \mathbf{1}$

That is, both of these conjuncts have to be true in M_1 for the sentence to be true in M_1. Well, we already know from our discussion of simple statements that $S(j)$ is true, so we can go on to evaluate $I(b, e)$ in the same way. The relevant rule is 10.47:

10.47 $[I(b, e)]^{M_1} = \mathbf{1}$ **iff** $[<b, e>]^{M_1} \in [I]^{M_1}$

We can paraphrase this in English as 10.48 below:

10.48 The sentence *Bob idolized Brian Epstein* is true if and only if the extension of *Bob* and the extension of *Brian Epstein* are an ordered pair which is part of the set defined by *idolized* in the model M_1.

Thus $I(b, e) = \mathbf{1}$ iff <Bob, Brian Epstein> ∈ $F_1(I)$. We can easily check this. The denotation assignment function will give the relevant values for this sentence as in 10.49 below:

10.49 a. $F_1(b)$ = {Bob}
b. $F_1(e)$ = {Brian Epstein}
c. $F_1(I)$ = {<Bob, John>, <Bob, Paul>, <Bob, George>, <Bob, Ringo>}

We can see that the ordered pair <Bob, Brian Epstein> is not part of the set defined by the predicate *I*, that is <Bob, Brian Epstein> ∉ {<Bob, John>, <Bob, Paul>, <Bob, George>, <Bob, Ringo>}, so our sentence $I(b, e)$ is **false**.

Since our first conjunct $S(j)$ is true and our second, $I(b, e)$, false, then by the rule in 10.46 the whole sentence $S(j) \wedge I(b, e)$ is false. This evaluation procedure may seem rather laborious as we step through it in this simple way, but the importance for semantic analysis is that the procedure is explicit, is based on our semantic definitions of logical elements and the well-proven behavior of logical connectives, and is productive: it can be applied in the same way to more and more complicated structures. The other truth-functional connectives can be treated in the same way as ∧ by reflecting their respective truth-functional behaviors, described in truth tables in chapter 4, in rules paralleling 10.45 above, thus allowing the evaluation of sentences containing ¬ "not," ∨ "or," → "if… then," and so on.

10.5.3 Evaluating sentences with the quantifiers ∀ and ∃

The same procedure can, with some modification, be used to evaluate sentences with the universal and existential quantifiers, ∀ and ∃. We won't give the step-by-step detail here but we can outline the spirit of the approach, using a different example. Let's imagine a sad situation of a house that has three cats (*Tom*, *Felix*, and *Korky*) and just one mouse (*Jerry*). Tom and Felix hunt Jerry but Korky does not. Without setting up a model for this we can see that one might say of the situation the (false) statement below:

10.50 Everyone hunts Jerry. $\forall x\ (H(x, j))$

As we saw earlier the quantifier phrase $\forall x$ expresses the range of the generalization $H(x, j)$ and the quantifier binds the variable x. The evaluation procedure can exploit this structure as follows. We reflect the meaning of ∀, *every*, by establishing the rule that a sentence with this quantifier is true if the generalization is true for **each** denotation of x, otherwise false. Thus we need to test the truth of the expression *x hunts Jerry* for each individual in the situation that x can denote.

We already have a function F_n that matches individual constant terms with their denotation in the situation; we need another function, let's call it $\mathbf{g}_n$, to do the same for variables. Such a function would successively match each individual in the situation with the variable x. In this situation the following are possible matchings:[10]

10.51 a. x = Tom
b. x = Felix
c. x = Korky

All we need to do then is test the generalization with each value for x, that is, use the procedure we used for simple statements earlier to evaluate each of the following versions:

10.52 a. x = Tom: is $H(x, j)$ true/false?
b. x = Felix: is $H(x, j)$ true/false?
c. x = Korky: is $H(x, j)$ true/false?

Once again, we won't step through the evaluation for each. Since of course 10.52a and b are true and 10.52c is false of this situation, then we know that the universal quantifier sentence $\forall x\ (H(x, j))$ is false.

Sentences containing the existential quantifier ∃ can be evaluated in the same way, except that the rule for this quantifier is that if the generalization is true of **at least one** individual in the range, the quantified sentence is true. Let's take for example, the sentence 10.53 below:

10.53 Some cat hunts Jerry. $\exists x\ (C(x) \wedge H(x, j))$

Once again the possible denotations for x are the three cats and we would evaluate the truth of $C(x) \wedge H(x, j)$ with x set for the three values in 10.51:

10.54 a. x = Tom: is $C(x) \wedge H(x, j)$ true/false?
b. x = Felix: is $C(x) \wedge H(x, j)$ true/false?
c. x = Korky: is $C(x) \wedge H(x, j)$ true/false?

The truth table for ∧ will tell us that 10.54a and 10.54b are true in our situation, while 10.54c is false. Consequently the existential quantifier rule that at least one must be true is satisfied and the sentence $\exists x\ (C(x) \wedge H(x, j))$ is true.

We have of course only sketched this evaluation procedure for quantifiers; for example we haven't given the formal detail of the function $\mathbf{g}_n$, which assigns denotations to variables. For a fuller account of this approach see Chierchia and McConnell-Ginet (2000: 126–27).

We have outlined in this section a denotational semantics for the predicate logic translations we introduced in 10.3. As we have observed, such a semantics has a number of advantages. From a methodological point of view, it has the advantages of being formal and explicit.[11] More generally it adopts the denotational program of relating utterances to specific situations. The semantics also embodies certain key features of natural languages in that it is compositional and productive; and more specifically, it allows the identification of individuals, sets of individuals and relations and, in a so far limited way, allows quantification. In the next section we look at how this approach accounts for word meaning.

10.6 Word Meaning: Meaning Postulates

As we have seen, when it comes to dealing with word meaning, the model-theoretic approach we have been looking at places great emphasis on the denotational properties of words. This is consistent with this approach's general assumption that the focus of semantic enquiry is sentence meaning: the idea is that the meaning of words is something best pursued not in isolation but in terms of their contribution to sentence meaning. Thus most formal approaches define a word's meaning as the contribution it makes to the truth-value of a sentence containing it.

However, the original structuralist position that words gain their significance from a combination of their denotation (reference) and their sense still seems to have force. We can return to our example from chapter 3: that if an English speaker hears 10.55 below, he knows 10.56:

10.55 I saw my mother just now.

10.56 The utterer saw a woman.

As we saw in chapter 3, speakers and hearers have knowledge about many kinds of sense relations between words, or what we termed **lexical relations**. The question for formal approaches is how to capture this lexical knowledge in a format compatible with the model-theoretical approach we have been looking at. One solution is to use **meaning postulates**, a term from logic (see Carnap 1952), and an approach advocated by J. D. Fodor et al. (1975) and Kintsch (1974).

The meaning postulates approach would recognize that 10.56 follows automatically from knowledge of 10.55 but rather than state this in terms of components of meaning of either word, this approach simply identifies this relationship as a form of knowledge,[12] using some basic connectives from propositional logic. These connectives are those used in our earlier discussion and are repeated below:

10.57 Logical connectives in meaning postulates

- $\rightarrow$ "if… then"
- $\wedge$ "and"
- $\neg$ "not"
- $\vee$ "or"
- $\equiv$ "if and only if"

Let's look at some lexical relations in this approach, beginning with **hyponymy**. The hyponymy relationship between, for example, *dog* and *animal* can be represented using →, the "*if… then*" connective, by writing a rule like 10.58:

10.58 $\forall x(DOG(x) \rightarrow ANIMAL(x))$

In the representation in 10.58 we use italic capitals to represent the translation of lexical items into predicate logic: 10.58 is to be read "for all *x*, if *x* is a dog, then *x* is an animal," or more simply "if something is a dog, then it is an animal." In principle, all of the lexical relations described in chapter 3 can be represented using meaning postulates. We can look at a few further examples.

Binary antonyms

Here we can use the "not" symbol (¬) as in 10.59 below:

10.59 $\forall x(DEAD(x) \rightarrow \neg ALIVE(x))$

This is to be read "if something is dead then it is not alive."

Converses

The lexical relation between the words *parent* and *child* can be captured as in 10.60:

10.60 a. $\forall x \forall y(PARENT(x, y) \rightarrow CHILD(y, x))$

b. $\forall x \forall y(PARENT(x, y) \rightarrow \neg CHILD(x, y))$

The formula in 10.60a tells us that if *x* is the parent of *y* then, *y* is the child of *x*. The second formula in 10.60b reflects the asymmetry of this relationship: if *x* is *y*'s parent, *x* cannot be *y*'s child.

Synonymy

To capture the relation of synonymy we have to use two mirror-image *if . . . then* rules, that is, both of the rules in 10.61 below for a speaker for whom *couch* and *sofa* are synonyms:

10.61 a. $\forall(COUCH(x) \rightarrow SOFA(x))$
b. $\forall x(SOFA(x) \rightarrow COUCH(x))$

If both of these are true then *couch* and *sofa* are synonymous. We can abbreviate this double implication with the symbol ≡ as in 10.62:

10.62 $\forall x\ (COUCH(x) \equiv SOFA(x))$

From these few examples we can see that this approach thus allows the formal semanticist to reflect the network of sense relations that we detect in the vocabulary of a language, in a format consistent with translation into predicate logic and interpretation via model theory.

These meaning postulates can be seen as a way of restricting or constraining denotation, for example "if something is a dog, then it is an animal" tells us something about the denotational behavior of the word *dog*. If we take the view that the source for such information is the knowledge that speakers have, then we can see meaning postulates as an example of the effect of the subject's knowledge on the denotational properties of expressions.

The version of sentence and word meaning that we have outlined so far is only the starting point for a formal semantics of natural languages. The account has to be broadened to reflect the range of semantic features we find in all languages. In the next sections we discuss some of these developments.

10.7 Natural Language Quantifiers and Higher-Order Logic

The theory of quantifiers that we have outlined so far suffers from several disadvantages as an account of quantifiers that are found in natural languages.[13] One major problem, as we mentioned earlier, is that there are some common types of quantifiers which cannot be modeled in this standard form of the predicate calculus. We can briefly show why this is so by looking at the English quantifier *most*. It is impossible to establish *most* on a par with the universal quantifier ∀ and existential quantifier ∃, using the logical connectives ∧ and →.

Neither 10.63b nor c below seems to have the same truth conditions as 10.63a:

10.63 a. Most students read a book.
b. Most $x(S(x) \wedge R(x, b))$
c. Most $x(S(x) \rightarrow R(x, b))$

The expression in b has the interpretation "For most *x*, *x* is a student and *x* reads a book" which suggests the likeliest paraphrase in English "Most things are students and read books," which is of course quite different from the meaning of 10.63a. The formula in c has the interpretation "For most *x*, if *x* is a student then *x* reads a book" which suggests "Most things are such that if they are students they read a book."

The problem here is that *most* is quantifying over all the individuals in the domain rather than over all students. We can show how this will cause a divergence from the meaning of 10.63a. First we may recall the truth table for the material implication →, given in chapter 4. We can apply this to our expression as follows:

10.64

	$S(x)$	$R(x, b)$	$(S(x) \rightarrow R(x, b))$
1.	T	T	T
2.	T	F	F
3.	F	T	T
4.	F	F	T

Next let us decide for argument's sake that *most* means more than 50 percent of the individuals concerned. So whenever the expression $(S(x) \rightarrow R(x, b))$ is true of more than 50 percent of the entities in the situation, the sentence in 10.63a will be true. However the truth table in 10.64 tells us that $(S(x) \rightarrow R\ (x, b))$ is true in a number of situations, for example when the individual is not a student (i.e. $S(x)$ is false) but does read (i.e. $R(x, b)$ is true), as in line 4 of the table. Consequently we would predict that 10.63c is true in a number of situations that do not reflect the meaning of *Most students read a book*, for example if a majority of students do not read a book but they are outnumbered by the non-students who do read a book.

What seems to be going wrong here is that our form of interpretation has quantifiers ranging over all individuals in the relevant situation whereas in noun phrases like *most students* the quantifier in determiner position seems to have its range restricted by the type of thing named by the following noun.

A second problem with our predicate logic account of quantifiers also concerns the interpretation of noun phrases. In chapter 1 we discussed the compositionality of meaning and claimed that semantic rules need to parallel the compositionality and recursion that we find in grammar. However, we can compare the following sentences and their translations into predicate logic:

10.65 a. $[_{NP}$ Ray$]$ $[_{VP}$ is hardworking$]$
b $H(r)$

10.66 a. $[_{NP}$ One student$]$ $[_{VP}$ is hardworking$]$
b. $(\exists x)(S(x) \wedge H(x))$

10.67 a. $[_{NP}$ All students$]$ $[_{VP}$ are hardworking$]$
b $(\forall x)(\ S(x) \rightarrow H(x))$

In these examples the syntactic structure is the same: a noun phrase followed by a verb phrase. While in 10.65 the noun phrase corresponds to a unit in the logical form, that is *Ray* = *r*, in the following two examples the noun phrase does not correspond to a unitary expression in the logical formulae. In 10.67 for example the English noun phrase corresponds to no single logical expression. The meaning of *all students* is split: part of the meaning is to the left of the head noun *students* in the choice of the quantifier ∀, while part occurs to the right in the choice of the connective →. The NP *one student* is similarly divided between ∃, *student* and the connective ∧. We can call this the problem of **isomorphism**.

Both of these problems can be solved by taking a different approach to the semantics of noun phrases, as described in the next sections.

10.7.1 Restricted quantifiers

One step is to express the restriction placed on quantifying determiners by their head nominals. This can be done by adopting a different notation: that of **restricted quantification**. A sentence like *All students are hardworking* would be represented in the restricted format by 10.68a below, compared to the standard format in 10.68b:

10.68 a. $(\forall x\colon S(x))\ H(x)$
b. $(\forall x)(S(x) \rightarrow H(x))$

Here the information from the rest of the noun phrase is placed into the quantifying expression as a restriction on the quantifier. Similarly *One student is hardworking* is represented in the restricted format by 10.69a below, again contrasting with the standard format in 10.69b:

10.69 a. $(\exists x\colon S(x))\ H(x)$
b. $(\exists x)(S(x) \wedge H(x))$

Restricted quantification helps solve the problem of isomorphism: it has the advantage that the logical expressions correspond more closely to natural language expressions. If we compare 10.68a and b above, for example, in a the English noun phrase *all students* has a translation into a unitary logical expression: $(\forall x{:}S(x))$. *Most students* would be represented as (Most x: $S(x)$); *few students* as (Few x: $S(x)$), and so on.

We should note that in English some quantifiers can stand alone, for example *everything*, *everybody*, *everywhere*. These will have to be translated into complex expressions in predicate logic, as in 10.70 and 10.71 below:

10.70	*everything*	every thing	$(\forall x\colon T(x))$
	everybody	every person	$(\forall x\colon P(x))$
	everywhere	every location	$(\forall x\colon L(x))$

10.71	Everything is either matter or energy:	$(\forall x\colon T(x))\ (M(x) \vee E(x))$
	Barbara hates everyone:	$(\forall x\colon P(x))\ H(b, x)$
	Everywhere is dangerous:	$(\forall x\colon L(x))\ D(x)$

As with the universal quantifier, some English words seem to incorporate an existential quantifier, for example *something*, *someone*, *somewhere*. These will be expanded in the translation into predicate logic, as shown below:

10.72	*something*	some thing	$(\exists x\colon T(x))$
	someone	some person	$(\exists x\colon P(x))$
	somewhere	some location	$(\exists x\colon L(x))$

10.7.2 Generalized quantifiers

Though restricted quantification seems to have advantages for representing the syntax–semantics interface, we still need to develop a way to provide a semantic interpretation for noun phrase formulae like (Most x: $S(x)$) *most students*, ($\forall x$: $S(x)$) *all students*, and so on. One proposal derives from an application of set theory in mathematical logic, called **generalized quantifier theory**. We can outline this approach, beginning with an example of a simple sentence like *John sang* from subsections 10.5.1–2 earlier, where we used set membership to interpret it. We used 10.73 below to claim that this sentence is true if the subject is a member of the set identified by the predicate.

10.73 a. $[S(j)]^{M_1} = \mathbf{1}$ iff $[j]^{M_1} \in [S]^{M_1}$
b. The sentence *John sang* is true if and only if the extension of *John* is part of the set defined by *sang* in the model M_1

A different approach is to reverse this and evaluate the truth of *John sang* by checking whether singing is one of the properties that are true of John in the situation. In other words we look for singing to be among the set of things John did for the sentence to be true. To do this however we need to give a new predicate–argument structure to the sentence (10.74b below) and a new semantic rule (10.74c) to replace those in 10.40 earlier:

10.74 a. John sang.
b. John(sang)
c. $[\text{John(sang)}]^{M_1} = \mathbf{1}$ iff $[\text{sang}]^{M_1} \in [\text{John}]^{M_1}$

We can paraphrase 10.74c as *John sang* is true if and only the denotation of the verb phrase *sang* is part of the denotation of the name *John* in the model M_1. To capture this procedure by a rule like 10.74c involves viewing John as a set of properties: a set of sets. For our model in sections 10.4–5 above this might include properties like "is a Beatle," "sang," "played guitar," and so on. The noun phrase *John* denotes this set of sets. This is a shift from the standard predicate logic analysis of the denotation of a noun phrase like *John* as a an individual.

This translation of a noun phrase as a set of sets was proposed by Montague (1969) and developed by Barwise and Cooper (1981) as an application of the mathematical notion of generalized quantifiers. Since sets of sets and the formula in 10.66b are not part of the predicate logic we have been using so far, this constitutes an extension into a higher-order, or second-order, logic.

In this approach the semantic interpretation of the sentence *Most students are hardworking* will interpret *most students* as a set of properties and the sentence will be judged true if the set *are hardworking* is an element of the set *most students*. The semantic rule for *most* can be given as follows:[14]

10.75 Most (A, B) = **1** iff $|A \cap B| > |A - B|$

We can paraphrase this as "*Most A are B* is true if the cardinality of the set of things that are both A and B is greater than the cardinality of the set of things which are A but not B," or more succinctly "if the members of both A and B outnumber the members of A that are not members of B." This assumes our earlier definition of *most* as more than 50 percent and therefore claims that *Most students are hardworking* is true if the number of students who are hardworking is greater than the number who aren't.

Other quantifiers can be given similar definitions in terms of relations between sets, for example:

10.76 All (A, B) = **1** iff $A \subseteq B$
All A are B is true if and only set A is a subset of set B

10.77 Some (A, B) = **1** iff $A \cap B \neq \emptyset$
Some A are B is true if and only if the set of things which are members of both A and B is not empty

10.78 No (A, B) = **1** iff $A \cap B = \emptyset$
No A are B is true if and only the set of things which are members of both A and B is empty

10.79 Fewer than seven (A, B) = **1** iff $|A \cap B| < 7$
Fewer than seven As are B is true if and only if the cardinality of the set of things which are members of both A and B is less than seven

This analysis of noun phrases as generalized quantifiers has stimulated a large literature investigating the formal properties of quantifiers in natural languages and led researchers to propose solutions to a number of descriptive problems. We cannot do justice to this literature here but in the next two sections we will select examples to illustrate this field of inquiry. The reader is referred to Keenan (2011) for an overview.

10.7.3 The strong/weak distinction and existential *there* sentences

One descriptive problem, discussed by Milsark (1977) and subsequently by Barwise and Cooper (1981), Jong (1987) and Keenan (1987), concerns the distribution of NPs in existential *there* sentences. Some examples are below:

10.80 a. There is/isn't a fox in the henhouse.
b. There are/aren't some foxes in the henhouse.
c. There are/aren't two foxes in the henhouse.
d. ?There is/isn't every fox in the henhouse.
e. ?There are/aren't most foxes in the henhouse.
f. ?There are/aren't both foxes in the henhouse.

These sentences are used to assert (or deny in negative versions) the existence of the noun phrase following *be*.[15] As can be seen, some quantifying determiners, including *every, most,* and *both,* are anomalous in this construction. The explanation proposed by Milsark (1977) is that there are two classes of noun phrases, weak and strong, and that only weak NPs can occur in these sentences. Subsequent work has sought to characterize this distinction correctly. One proposal, from Keenan (1987) uses the format of generalized quantifiers to explain the difference in terms of **symmetry**.

One group of quantifiers expresses asymmetrical relations, that is to say that the order of their set arguments is significant. We can take the example of *all* and *most.* The form *All A are B* is not equivalent to *All B are A*, so that *All my friends are cyclists* does not have the same meaning as *All cyclists are my friends*. Similarly *Most A are B* is not equivalent to *Most B are A*, so that *Most football players are male* does not mean the same as *Most males are football players*. We can schematize this pattern as below, where **det** is the quantifying determiner:

10.81 Asymmetrical quantifiers
det (A, B) ≠ **det** (B, A)

Another group expresses symmetrical relations. Here we can use *some* and *two* as examples. *Some A are B* is equivalent to *Some B are A*, so that *Some skiers are Sudanese* can describe the same situation as *Some Sudanese are skiers*. Similarly *Two Nobel prize winners are Welshmen* is equivalent to *Two Welshmen are Nobel prize winners*. These can be schematized as:

10.82 Symmetrical quantifiers
det (A, B) = **det** (B, A)

The asymmetrical class is also called **proportional** because the quantifiers express a proportion of the restricting set identified by the nominal. So for example to interpret NPs like *most foxes*, *all foxes*, *few foxes*, and so on we need access to the number of the relevant set of *foxes*. The symmetrical class is not proportional in this sense. If we say *two foxes* we don't need to know how many other foxes are in the set in order to interpret the noun phrase. This class is called, by distinction, **cardinal** quantifiers since they denote the cardinality of the intersection of the sets A and B, that is the intersection of *two* and *foxes* in our example. Some quantifiers have both a cardinal and a proportional reading, for example *many* and *few*. Compare the sentences in 10.83:

10.83 a. There are many valuable stamps in this collection.
b. Many of the stamps in this collection are valuable.

The interpretation of *many* in a is cardinal in that the sentence means that the number of valuable stamps is high. The interpretation in b is proportional since *many* is here calculated relative to the collection. It is reasonable to use b but not a if the collection is in fact a small one.

The proposal is that the asymmetrical, proportional class are strong quantifiers and create strong NPs. These strong NPs form the class of items that cannot be used in existential *there* sentences. Symmetrical, cardinal quantifiers on the other hand form weak NPs and can be used in these sentences. The theory of generalized quantifiers allows us to characterize the difference between these two types of quantifier as reflected in the English data. One possible line of explanation for the difference is that the necessity in strong NPs for access to the restriction on the domain of quantification somehow clashes with the semantic function of existential *there* sentences. In other words, when interpreting *most foxes* we have to access the whole set of foxes, including those outside the set of *most*. The idea is that accessing a presupposed set of foxes clashes with the normal assertion or denial of the existence of foxes in sentences like 10.80a–c, creating a tautology or a contradiction respectively. See Barwise and Cooper (1981) for discussion.

10.7.4 Monotonicity and negative polarity items

A further descriptive problem that has been investigated in the generalized quantifier literature is how to account for the distribution of negative polarity items like English *any*, *ever*, *yet*, which seem dependent on the presence of negation in the sentence:

10.84 a. She doesn't ever eat dessert.
b. ?She ever eats dessert.

10.85 a. I haven't seen the movie yet.
b. ?I have seen the movie yet.

However as discussed in Laduslaw (1979, 1996) and Wouden (1997), the restriction seems to be wider than strictly sentence negation. As shown below, negative polarity items are also licensed by certain quantifiers like *nobody*, *few* and adverbials like *seldom*, *rarely*, as well as other items; see Laduslaw (1996) for more examples.

10.86 a. Nobody sees any difficulty.
b. ?Everybody sees any difficulty.

10.87 a. Few people have seen the movie yet.
b. ?Many people have seen the movie yet.

10.88 a. Rarely has she ever been late.
b. ?Often has she ever been late.

An influential proposal, deriving from Laduslaw (1979), is that the licensing expressions are not simply negative but have a particular property of **monotonicity**. The term monotonicity applied to quantifiers describes patterns of entailment between sets and subsets. **Upward entailment** is characterized by entailment from a subset to a set. **Downward entailment** involves entailment from a set to a subset. Let's take as example *(NP) is driving home* which is a subset of *(NP) is driving*. By placing different quantified nominals into the subject position we can test the monotonicity of the quantifiers:

10.89 *Everyone is driving* does not entail Everyone is driving home.
Everyone is driving home does entail Everyone is driving.
Therefore: *every* involves upward entailment.

10.90 *No-one is driving* does entail No-one is driving home.
No-one is driving home does not entail No-one is driving.
Therefore: *no* involves downward entailment.

10.91 *Someone is driving* does not entail Someone is driving home.
Someone is driving home does entail Someone is driving.
Therefore: *some* involves upward entailment.

10.92 *Few people are driving* does entail Few people are driving home.
Few people are driving home does not entail Few people are driving.
Therefore: *few* involves downward entailment.

Quantifiers which trigger upward entailment are described as monotone increasing while those involving downward entailment are described as monotone decreasing. Some quantifiers are neither monotone increasing nor monotone decreasing, for example *exactly three*, since they do not trigger entailment in either direction, as in 10.93:

10.93 a. Exactly three people are driving.
b. Exactly three people are driving home.

In 10.93 neither sentence entails the other.

The specific explanatory proposal in this literature is that negative polarity items are licensed by downward entailing expressions. We can see even from our simple examples that this correctly predicts the following pattern:

10.94 a. Few people are ever driving home.
b. No-one is ever driving home.
c. ?Everyone is ever driving home.
d. ?Someone is ever driving home.

Our examples so for have been of sets and subsets identified by the right argument of the quantifier, corresponding to the VP arguments, for example *Few* (*people*, *driving*) and its subset *Few* (*people*, *driving home*). The same quantifiers may show the same or different entailment patterns in the sets and subsets in the left argument, corresponding to the NP, for example *Few* (*people*, *driving*) and its subset *Few* (*drunk people*, *driving*). The examples below show that *few* is downward entailing in the left argument as it is in the right (10.92 above) but that *every* is downward entailing in the left argument though it is upward entailing in the right (as in 10.89 above):

10.95 *Few people are driving* does entail *Few drunk people are driving.*
Few drunk people are driving does not entail *Few people are driving.*
Therefore: *few* involves downward entailment (left argument).

10.96 *Every person is driving* does entail *Every drunk person is driving.*
Every drunk person is driving does not entail *Every person is driving.*
Therefore: *every* involves downward entailment (left argument).

This difference correctly predicts that *every* licenses negative polarity items in the NP but not in the VP:

10.97 a. [Everyone who has ever driven drunk] will be ashamed of these figures.
b. ?[Everyone who has driven drunk]will ever be ashamed of these figures.

10.7.5 Section summary

In this section we have seen something of the formal investigation of quantifiers in natural language. We can identify two claims which emerge from this literature. The first is that formal models can be successfully developed to describe natural language quantifiers. The second, more ambitious, claim is that these formal models help identify and characterize features of quantifier behavior that would otherwise remain mysterious.

10.8 Intensionality

10.8.1 Introduction

As we mentioned in the introduction, section 10.1, one disadvantage of the simple version of the denotational approach is that it downplays the speaker-hearer's **subjectivity**. The procedures we have been outlining allow a mechanical-seeming matching between statements and situations. However, as we have seen in our previous chapters, it is clear that natural languages largely communicate **interpretations** between speakers and hearers. For example languages contain a whole range of verbs which describe different mental states. Instead of a flat statement **S**, we can say in English for example:

10.98 a. Frank knows that **S**.
b. Frank believes that **S**.
c. Frank doubts that **S**.
d. Frank regrets that **S**.
e. Frank suspects that **S**.
f. Frank hopes that **S**.
g. Frank imagines that **S**, etc.

As we saw in chapter 5, one way of describing this, which comes to us from the philosophy of language, is to say that in sentences like 10.98 we have a range of speaker attitudes to the proposition expressed by **S**, or more briefly that we have a set of **propositional attitudes**.

As we discussed in chapter 5, propositional attitudes are not only conveyed by embedding **S** under a higher verb. We might say that if a speaker chooses between the sentences in 10.98 below, the choice reflects a difference in propositional attitude between certainty and degrees of lack of certainty:

10.99 a. Phil misrepresented his income.
b. Phil probably misrepresented his income.
c. Phil may have misrepresented his income.

In another terminology, sentences which reveal this interpretative or cognitive behavior are said to be **intensional** and the property is called **intensionality**. More generally these terms are applied whenever linguistic behavior reveals a relation between an agent and a thought. The notion was discussed by Frege in his 1893 article "Sense and Reference" (*Über Sinn und Bedeutung*; see Frege 1980) in relation to cases where we need access to the sense of an expression as well as its denotation, as discussed in chapter 2. The classical cases are the verbs of propositional attitudes mentioned above, which in one terminology are said to form **opaque** contexts. The term opaque figuratively describes the fact that the truth or falsity of the subordinate clause seems to be independent of the truth or falsity of the whole sentences. As Quine (1980: 22–3) points out for the statements in 10.100:

10.100 a. Jones believes that Paris is in France.
b. Jones believes that Punakha is in Bhutan.

sentence 10.100a may be true and b false even though the components "Paris is in France" and "Punakha is in Bhutan" are true. Similarly for 10.101:

10.101 a. Jones believes that Punakha is in Nepal.
b. Jones believes that Paris is in Japan.

The sentence 10.101a may be true and b false even though the components "Punakha is in Nepal" and "Paris is in Japan" are both false. It's as if the subordinate clause (the belief context) is a walled-off, opaque domain, as far as the truth-value of the main sentence is concerned. It seems that in such examples we need access to the content of the subject's belief, necessitating an extra level of sense, or in a more recent terminology, intension. The notion was developed formally by Richard Montague (1974); see Dowty (1979) for discussion.

The challenge for formal semantics is to develop the semantic model to reflect the interpretation and calculation that is so central to language. One strategy has been to enrich the formal devices in certain areas where intensionality seems most clearly exhibited in natural languages. Such areas include **modality, tense, aspect** and **verbs of propositional attitude**. In each of these areas there has been research into formal semantic accounts. We cannot go into these developments in any detail here, pausing merely to sketch some of the main areas of focus and to refer the reader to the relevant literature.

10.8.2 Modality

As we saw in chapter 5, modality is often described in terms of two related aspects of meaning. The first, **epistemic modality**, concerns the resources available to the speaker to express judgment of fact versus possibility. The second, **deontic modality**, allows the expression of obligation and permission, often in terms of morality and law. All languages allow speakers a range of positions in both of these aspects. If we take epistemic modality, for example, we can quote Allan's scale of modality in 10.102 below (1986, 2: 289–90), which he views as a scale of implicatures such that each is stronger than the next about the fact of **p**:

10.102 a. I know that **p**.
b. I am absolutely certain that **p**.
c. I am almost certain that **p**.
d. I believe that **p**.
e. I am pretty certain that **p**.
f. I think that **p**.
g. I think/believe that **p** is probable.
h. I think/believe that perhaps **p**.
i. Possibly **p**.
j. I suppose it is possible that **p**.

k. It is not impossible that **p**.
l. It is not necessarily impossible that **p**.
m. It is unlikely that **p**.
n. It is very unlikely that **p**.
o. It is almost impossible that **p**.
p. It is impossible that **p**.
q. It is not the case that **p**.
r. It is absolutely certain that not-**p**.

Even if we don't agree with Allan's selection or the ordering in this list, it is clear that there is a large range of options available to the speaker. Some of these choices of degree of commitment to the truth of **p** derive from the meaning of verbs like *believe*, *know*, and so on; others from negation or from adjectives and adverbs like *possible* and *possibly*. The use of different intonation patterns can add further distinctions. In response to these facts about modality, **modal logics** were developed. The simplest approach employs a two-fold division of epistemic modality into **fact** versus **possibility**, or "situation as is" versus "situation as may be." One way of discussing this distinction between the actual and the non-actual is to talk of **possible worlds**, a phrase derived from Leibniz and formally developed by Kripke (see for example Kripke 1980). This is a difficult and controversial area in the philosophical literature but the notion has been important in formal semantics (see for example Lewis 1973, 1986). We can recognize the idea that a speaker, in moving away from certainty, can envisage two or more possible scenarios. So if we say *Fritz may be on the last train*, we entertain two situations: one where Fritz is on the train and another where he is not. Thus we imagine one situation where the statement *Fritz is on the last train* is true and another where it is not. One way of dealing with this is to see truth as being relativized to possible situations, or possible worlds, to use this terminology.[16]

To reflect this, logicians introduce two logical operators $\Diamond$ "it is possible that" and $\Box$ "it is necessary that." These can be put in front of any formula of the predicate logic, that is:

10.103 $\Diamond\phi$ = it is possible that ϕ
$\Box\phi$ = it is necessary that ϕ

The semantic definition of these relies on this new ontology of possible worlds: $\Box$ means "true in all possible worlds" (i.e. no alternatives are envisaged by the speaker) and $\Diamond$ means "true in some possible worlds" (i.e. the speaker does envisage alternative scenarios). The formal implications of this is that truth must be relativized not to one situation but to one among a series of possible situations (worlds), including the actual situation (world). This means that our model must be expanded to include this multiplicity of situations, that is now $M = \{W, U, F\}$ where, as before, U = the domain of individuals in a situation, F is the denotation assignment function, and the new element W is a set of possible worlds.

Relativizing truth to possible worlds enables one to adopt extensionally defined versions of Frege's notion of **sense** (*Sinn*), distinguished from **reference** (*Bedeutung*), as discussed in chapter 2. Using the term **intension** for sense, we can say that in this approach the intension of an expression is a function from possible worlds to its extension. In other words the function will give us the denotation of a particular linguistic expression in possible circumstances. Thus the intensions of nominals (NP), informally viewed as individual concepts, can now be viewed as functions from possible worlds to individuals; the intensions of predicates (VP), characterized as properties, can be viewed as functions from possible worlds to sets of individuals; and the intensions of sentences (S), characterized by Frege as the thoughts expressed by sentences, that is propositions, can be viewed as functions from worlds to truth-values. See Chierchia and McConnell-Ginet (2000: 257–328) for discussion.

This approaches raises interesting issues: for example, how many possible situations are relevant to a specific utterance? How are the possible situations ranked, by a combination of the linguistic expressions and background knowledge, so that some are more probable than others? We cannot pursue these issues any further here; readers are referred to Allwood et al. (1977: 108–24), Cann (1993: 263–81), and Chierchia and McConnell-Ginet (2000: 257–328) for introductory discussions.

The second type of modality, deontic modality, has been treated in a similar way: as a projection from the world as it is to the world as it should be under some moral or legal code, that is, as the speaker entertaining an idealized world. Deontic modal operators have been suggested for logic, including Oϕ "obligatorily that ϕ" and Pϕ "permitted that ϕ." The former can be interpreted denotationally as "true in all morally or legally ideal worlds" and the latter as "true in some morally or legally ideal worlds." Again see Allwood et al. (1977: 108–24) for discussion.

10.8.3 Tense and aspect

These two further important intensional categories are, as discussed in chapter 5, related to the speaker's view of time. We need not review our earlier discussion here, but in denotational terms, the speaker's ability to view propositions as timeless and eternal as in sentences like *All men are mortal*, or as fixed in relation to the time of utterance, or some other point identified in the metaphorical flow of time, clearly has truth-conditional implications. Take for example the sentences in 10.104 below:

10.104 a. The Irish punt will be replaced by the euro.
b. The Irish punt was replaced by the euro.

These sentences differ in truth-value being read by you today rather than say, in January 2002, and the only difference between them is their tense. We saw that an utterance can only be given a truth-value relative to a situation: it seems that part of the character of situations may be their location in time.

One response has been to incorporate time into model-theoretic semantics. One way to do this is to include tense operators, similar to the modal operators we have just mentioned. We might for example include three operators: **Past**(ϕ), **Present**(ϕ), and **Future**(ϕ). This would allow formulae like 10.105 below:

10.105 a. **Past**(C (t, j)) Tom chased Jerry.
b. **Present**(C (t, j)) Tom is chasing Jerry.
c. **Future**(C (t, j)) Tom will chase Jerry.
Key: C: chase
t: Tom
j: Jerry

Figure 10.1 Instants in the flow of time

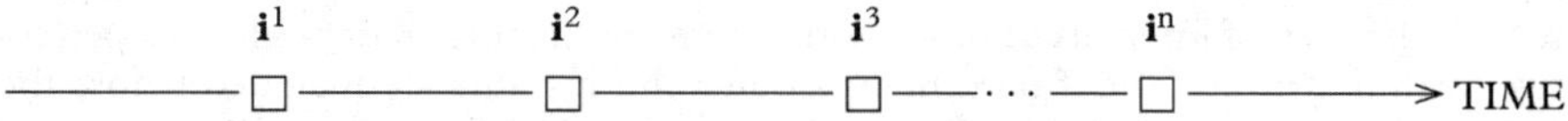

Such tense operators rely upon a division of the flow of time into a series of ordered instants, as in 10.105 below, where **i** = instant and < = before:

10.106 $\mathbf{i}^1 < \mathbf{i}^2 < \mathbf{i}^3 \ldots < \mathbf{i}^n$

or alternatively as in figure 10.1. If we select instant $\mathbf{i}^3$ in figure 10.1 as **now**, then the evaluation procedure for the formula **Past**(*C* (*t*, *j*)) in 10.102a above will state that it is true if *C*(*t*, *j*) is true at time $\mathbf{i}^n$, where $\mathbf{i}^n < \mathbf{i}^3$; that is, if it is true at a time before now. In other words the model will relativize formulae to both a situation and a time, so that our model is now $M = <W, U, F, I, <>$, where *I* are the instants in time and < is the ordering relation "before." See Gamut (1991, vol 2: 32–44) and Cann (1993: 233–51) for introductory discussions of tense logics.

We saw in chapter 5 that tense is inextricably linked to **aspect**, a speaker's choice of viewing a situation as complete or incomplete, stretched over time or punctual, depending on the aspectual parameters of the language. When we come to consider the distribution of an activity or state over time, one useful modification to our simple model of time is to allow **intervals** of time in addition to just points or instants. Intervals can be defined in terms of instants: thus we can have an interval **k** which will be a continuous series of instants stretching between an initial and final instant, say $\mathbf{i}_3$ to $\mathbf{i}_7$. We can represent this as $\mathbf{k} = [\mathbf{i}_3, \mathbf{i}_7]$. Intervals can be ordered with respect to other intervals in various ways, some of which we can show in diagram form in figure 10.2. Here interval **j** precedes interval **k**; interval **l** overlaps **k**; and **m** is contained within **k**. This treatment of intervals might allow description of stretches of time, and interrelations between times, like those in 10.107 below:

10.107 a. I studied Hausa for three years, then gave it up.
b. She was ill all last week, when the interviews took place.

Formal approaches have to cope with the various aspectual and situation type distinctions we looked at in chapter 5. Cann (1993: 251ff) proposes, for example, a

Figure 10.2 Intervals of time

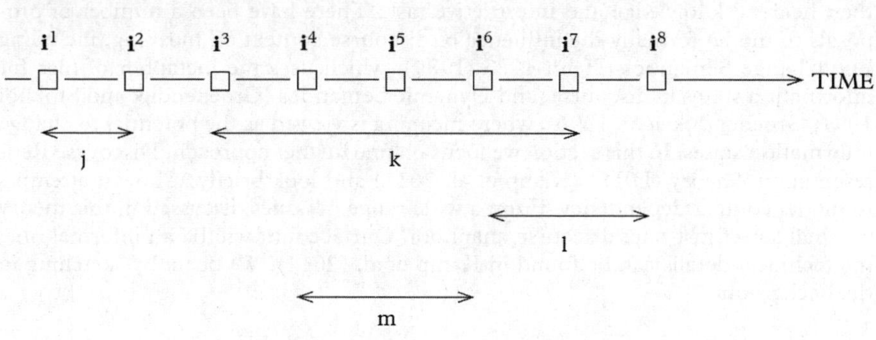

perfective aspect operator **Perf** and an imperfective operator **Impf** for predicate logic, which will further relativize the truth of logical formulae. These operators rely on the idea of intervals of time. Without giving the formal definitions, a perfective formula will be true if both the start and end instants are included before the reference time point,[17] thus reflecting the complete interpretation of the perfective aspect. An imperfective formula on the other hand will be true if the activity overflows the time interval that is being interpreted. Thus our sentence 10.105a above, repeated as 10.108a below, can be given the simple perfective interpretation as in 10.108b:

10.108 a. Tom chased Jerry.
b. **Past**(**Perf**(*C* (*t*, *j*)))

The evaluation procedures for this formula will state that it is only true if the action of chasing is complete before the time of utterance. We can compare this with the imperfective clause in 10.109a below, represented in the formula in 10.109b:

10.109 a. Tom was chasing Jerry (when I opened the door).
b. **Past**(**Impf**(*C* (*t*, *j*)))

Here the evaluation procedure will require that for 10.109b to be true the time interval for the chasing activity (*C*) should overlap the door-opening event.

These are of course only preliminary sketches of the task facing formal semanticists: to model formally the tense and aspect distinctions found in languages, some of which we saw in chapter 5. See Cann (1993: 251–62) for further discussion.

In the next section we discuss attempts to model formally the dynamism and context-dependence of language use.

10.9 Dynamic Approaches to Discourse

Our discussion of formal semantics so far has been concerned with the analysis of individual sentences. However, as we discussed in chapter 7, sentences are uttered in a context of discourse and many features of language reveal speakers' efforts to package their messages against the current context, in particular to take account of their hearers' knowledge and interpretive task. There have been a number of proposals to model formally the influence of discourse context on meaning, including File Change Semantics (Heim 1983, 1989), which uses the metaphor of files for information states in discourse, and Dynamic Semantics (Groenendijk and Stokhof 1991, Groenendijk et al. 1996), where meaning is viewed as the potential to change information states. In this section we focus on one further approach, Discourse Representation Theory (DRT) (Kamp et al. 2011) and look briefly at how it attempts to model context dependency. From a wide range of issues discussed in this theory we shall select just one: discourse anaphora. Our account will be an informal one; the technical details can be found in Kamp et al. (2011). We begin by sketching in the background.

10.9.1 Anaphora in and across sentences

In chapter 7 we discussed the anaphoric use of pronouns. Traditionally the pronoun *himself* in 10.110 below is said to gain its denotation indirectly through coreference with the preceding nominal, *James*. They are said to be coreferential, that is, denote the same entity in the situation described. As shown in a below, this can be reflected by attaching referential subscript indices; and as b shows, in predicate logic this relationship can be represented by giving each nominal the same individual constant:

10.110 a. James_i mistrusts himself_i.
b. $M(j, j)$

Since quantified nominals don't directly denote an individual, sentences like 10.111a below are given a representation like 10.111b in predicate logic, where the pronoun is treated as a variable bound by a quantifier:

10.111 a. Every thief mistrusts himself.
b. $(\forall x: T(x))\ M(x, x)$

We also discussed in chapter 7 how new entities are often introduced into a discourse by an indefinite noun phrase and thereafter referred to by a range of definite nominals varying in their informational status, including pronouns. Once again, in an example like 10.112 below the pronoun is said to be anaphorically related to the preceding indefinite NP:

10.112 Joan bought a car_i and it_i doesn't start.

In predicate logic this use of indefinite nominals can be treated as a kind of existential assertion and the pronoun again treated as a variable bound by the quantifying expression, as shown below:

10.113 $(\exists x: C(x))\ B(j, x) \wedge \neg S(x)$
Paraphrase: There is car such that Joan bought it and it doesn't start.

This parallel between indefinite NPs and quantifiers breaks down in cross-sentential anaphora. For quantifiers the representation correctly predicts that anaphoric pronouns cannot occur outside the scope of the quantifier, such as in a following sentence. See the example below, where we assume the two sentences are spoken in sequence by the same speaker:

10.114 a. Every girl_i came to the dance.
$(\forall x: G(x))\ C(x, d)$
b. ?She_i met Alexander.
$M(x, a)$

In the logical form in b the variable *x* is not bound by the quantifier in the preceding sentence and is therefore uninterpretable. This correctly predicts the fact that the pronoun *she* in b cannot refer back to *every girl* in a.

However, indefinite NPs do allow cross-sentential anaphora; see for example:

10.115 A $girl_i$ came to the dance. She_i met Alexander.

One way of reflecting this behavior of indefinite nominals is to recognize that a discourse has a level of structure above the individual sentences and to view the role of indefinite nominals as introducing entities into this discourse structure. These are called **discourse referents** (Karttunen 1976) and the idea is that they have a lifespan in the discourse during which they can be referred to by pronouns. This lifespan can be limited by semantic operators such as negation. For example a discourse referent set up by an indefinite NP under negation has its lifespan limited to the scope of that negation. See the following example, where we assume the a and b sentences are uttered in succession by the same speaker:

10.116 a. Joan can't [afford a $Ferrari_i$].
b. ?She likes it_i though.

Here the pronoun *it* cannot refer back to the indefinite NP *a Ferrari* because the latter's lifespan as a discourse referent is limited by the scope of *not*, shown by square brackets. As we shall see, Discourse Representation Theory is one way of formalizing such a notion of discourse referents.

10.9.2 Donkey sentences

Even within a single sentence there are examples where anaphora between indefinite NPs and pronouns causes problems for a quantifier-variable binding account. If we take sentence 10.117a below we can represent it in standard predicate logic as 10.117b:

10.117 a. If Joan owns a Ferrari she is rich.
b. $(\exists x\ (F(x) \wedge O(j, x))) \rightarrow R(j)$

However, applying the same translation procedure to 10.118a gives us 10.118b:

10.118 a. If a teenager owns a Ferrari he races it.
b. $(\exists x \exists y\ (T(x) \wedge F(y) \wedge O(x, y))) \rightarrow R(x, y)$

Though these two sentences seem to have the same syntactic structure, 10.118b is not a legal formula because the variables in the consequent of the implication are not correctly bound by the relevant existential quantifiers. To capture the meaning of 10.118a in a well-formed formula we have to use something like 10.119 below:

10.119 a. $\forall x \forall y\ ((T(x) \wedge F(y) \wedge O(x, y))) \rightarrow R(x, y)$
b. Paraphrase: For all *x*, all *y*: if *x* is a teenager, *y* is a Ferrari, and *x* owns *y*, then *x* races *y*

This does capture the fact that the preferred interpretation of 10.118 has universal force, that is that all teenagers who have Ferraris race them. However, the problem here is that we have translated the indefinite nominal *a Ferrari* by a universal quantifier expression in 10.119a and by an existential quantifier expression in 10.118b. This is a threat to the notion of compositionality and is another version of our isomorphism problem earlier. It seems unsatisfactory that an indefinite NP is sometimes treated as an existential quantifier and at other times as a universal quantifier, the deciding factor apparently being the presence of an anaphoric pronoun.

Examples like 10.118a are known as **donkey sentences** after Geach's (1962) discussion of this problem using examples like *If a farmer owns a donkey, he beats it* and *Every farmer who owns a donkey beats it*. In essence, the problem with the pronoun *it* in these examples is that it cannot be a referring expression, since there is no specific donkey it denotes. However, as we have seen, treating *it* as a bound variable leads to other problems.[18]

10.9.3 DRT and discourse anaphora

Discourse Representation Theory (DRT) formalizes a level of discourse structure which is updated by successive sentences and forms a representation of the discourse referents introduced so far. The discourse referents form an intermediate level between the nominals and the real individuals in the situation described. The main form of representation is a Discourse Representation Structure (DRS), usually presented in a box format, as shown below. These DRSs are built up by construction rules from the linguistic input, sentence by sentence. If we take the sentences in 10.120 below as uttered in sequence, the first sentence will trigger the construction of the DRS in 10.121:

10.120 a. Alexander met a girl$_i$.
b. She$_i$ smiled.

10.121

x y
Alexander (x) Girl (y) met (x, y)

The discourse referents are given in the top line of the DRS, called the universe of the DRS, and below them are conditions giving the properties of the discourse referents. These conditions govern whether the DRS can be embedded into the model of the current state of the discourse. A DRS is true if all of the discourse referents can be mapped to individuals in the situation described in such a way that the conditions are met. A name like *Alexander* in 10.120 denotes an individual, while an indefinite NP like *a girl* will be satisfied by any individual meeting the property of being a girl. The third condition is the relation *met (x, y)*. We can see that the truth conditions for sentence 10.120a are given here by a combination of the discourse referents and the conditions. The sentence will be true of a situation if it contains two individuals, one named Alexander, the other a girl, and if the first met the second. An important point here is that in an example like this the introduction of a discourse referent into a DRS carries an existential commitment. Thus the indefinite NP *a girl* is treated as having existential force, though there are other ways of introducing indefinite nominals which do not have this existential commitment, as we shall see below. The initial DRS is labeled K_0, the next K_1, and so on. The latest K acts as the context against which a new sentence in the discourse is interpreted.

The second sentence in 10.120 updates the discourse and adds another discourse referent, *she*. The embedding rule for pronouns will say that we must find an accessible antecedent for it. In this case gender is a factor since *she* must find a feminine antecedent. If the correct antecedent for the pronoun is identified, the result is the extended version below of the original DRS with a new reference marker and a new condition:

10.122

x y u
Alexander (x) Girl (y) met (x, y) u = y smiled (u)

A negative sentence like 10.123 below will be assigned the DRS in 10.124:

10.123 Joan does not own a Ferrari.

10.124

x Joan (x)
¬ [y | Ferrari (y), owns (x, y)]

Here the DRS contains one discourse referent and two conditions: the first is the usual naming relation, Joan (x); and the second is a second DRS embedded in the first and marked by the logical negation sign ¬. The satisfaction of this second condition is that there is not a Ferrari such that Joan owns it. This contained DRS is said to be **subordinate** to the containing DRS and is triggered by the construction rules for negation. This subordination has two effects on any discourse referents within the embedded DRS. The first, as suggested by our characterization of how the condition in 10.124 is satisfied, is that there is no existential interpretation for discourse referents in this type of subordinate DRS. Thus there is no existential commitment with the indefinite NP *a Ferrari* in this sentence, unlike *a girl* in 10.120.

The second effect follows from the existence of **accessibility rules** in DRT. Briefly, proper nouns (names) are always accessible in the subsequent discourse, that is once introduced can always be referred to by an anaphoric pronoun. The accessibility of other nominals depends on the structure of the DRSs they occur in. For negatives, the rule is that discourse referents introduced within a subordinate DRS under the scope of negation are inaccessible to pronouns in subsequent stages of the DRS.[19] This means that the discourse referent y (i.e. *a Ferrari*) in 10.124 is inaccessible to subsequent pronouns. We can look at our earlier example 10.116, repeated below, to show this.

10.125 a. Joan can't afford a Ferrari$_i$.
b. ?She likes it$_i$ though.

We can suggest 10.126 below as a DRS after the two sentences in 10.125:

10.126
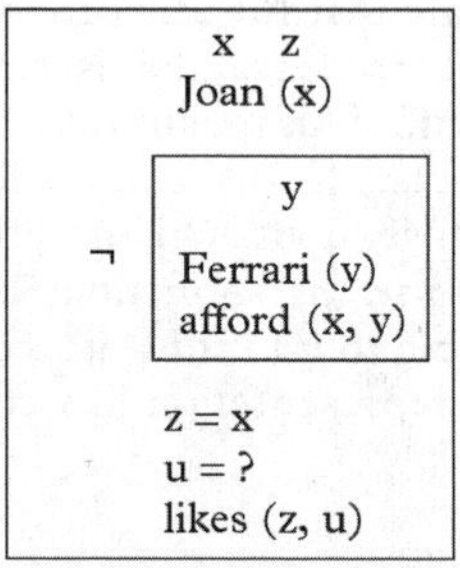

The pronoun *she* in the second sentence is successfully interpreted as anaphoric with *Joan* in the first sentence, and hence $z = x$ in the DRS conditions. However, we have written a question mark in the identification of an antecedent for u (i.e. *it*) because the only possible antecedent for y (i.e. *a Ferrari*) is not accessible since it occurs in the subordinate DRS box under negation. This explains the semantic anomaly of 10.125 above and provides a formalization of one aspect of the notion of discourse referent lifespan mentioned in section 10.9.1.

Sentences with conditionals are also represented with subordinate DRSs as conditions. The construction rules for these embed two DRSs linked by a connector ⇒, which parallels the material implication in predicate logic. The first DRS represents the antecedent and the second the consequent. Our earlier example *If Joan owns a Ferrari she is rich* would be given the complex DRS below (assuming an integration into a preceding empty DRS):

10.127
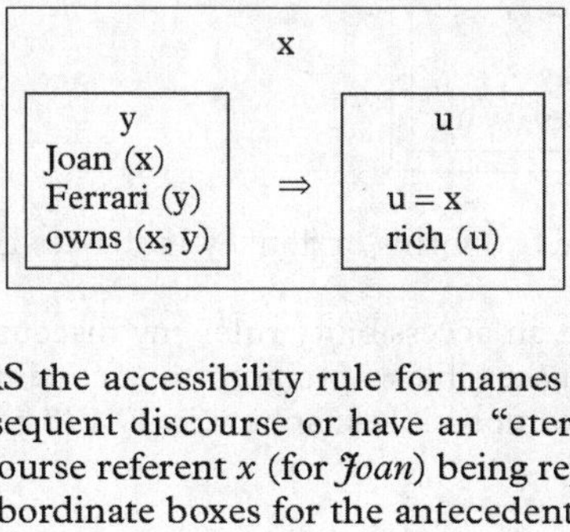

In this DRS the accessibility rule for names (that they are accessible to the whole of the subsequent discourse or have an "eternal" lifespan, so to speak) is reflected by the discourse referent x (for *Joan*) being represented in the containing DRS, outside the subordinate boxes for the antecedent and consequent.

A donkey sentence like 10.118 earlier *If a teenager owns a Ferrari he races it* would be given a DRS like the following:

10.128

x y Teenager (x) Ferrari (y) owns (x, y)	⇒	u v u = x v = y races (u, v)

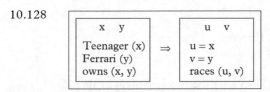

The accessibility rules for conditional sentences state that the antecedent discourse referents are accessible from the consequent but not vice versa, that is, anaphora can reach "up" and "back" but not "down" and "forward." This means that the pronoun *it* can refer anaphorically to *a Ferrari* in 10.118 because the discourse referent in the antecedent is accessible to the pronoun in the consequent. On the other hand a sentence like ?*If a teenager*$_i$ *owns it*$_k$ *he*$_i$ *races a Ferrari*$_k$ is anomalous because the indefinite nominal in the consequent is not accessible to *it* in the antecedent.

Sentences with universal quantifiers are given a representation like conditionals; 10.129 below can be given the DRS in 10.130:

10.129 Every teenager who owns a Ferrari is rich.

10.130

x y Teenager (x) Ferrari (y) owns (x, y)	⇒	rich (x)

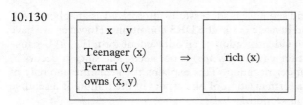

A donkey sentence with *every* like 10.131 below is therefore given the DRS 10.132, which we can compare with 10.128 above:

10.131 Every teenager who owns a Ferrari races it.

10.132

x y Teenager (x) Ferrari (y) owns (x, y)	⇒	u u = y races (x, u)

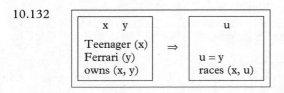

This representation brings together the two forms of donkey sentences into a structurally similar representation.

All of these conditional DRSs share an accessibility rule: any discourse referent introduced in a subordinate DRS is inaccessible to pronouns in a condition outside the subordinate DRS. This explains the impossible anaphora in 10.133 below, which would have the DRS 10.134:

10.133 Every student reads [a book on semantics]$_i$. ?It$_i$ is heavy.

10.134

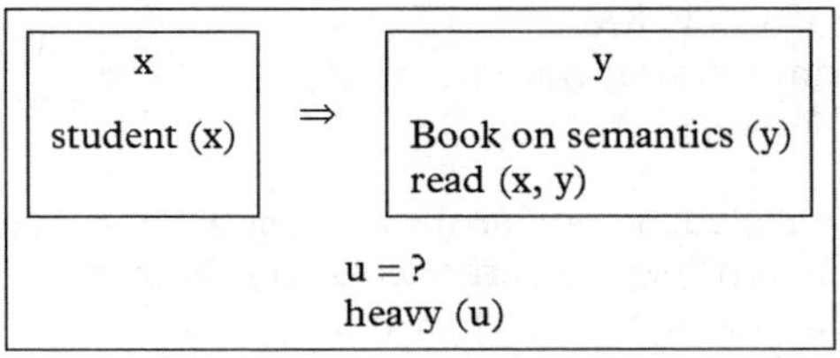

In 10.134 we again use a question mark to show that the pronoun *it* in the second sentence cannot be anaphorically related to any antecedent nominal. The discourse referent *book on semantics* is not accessible to the pronoun because it is in a subordinate DRS while the pronoun is in the superordinate DRS. This accessibility constraint explains the difference between indefinite nominals and quantified nominals in licensing a subsequent pronoun. Compare 10.133 above with 10.135 below:

10.135 A student read [a book on semantics]$_i$. It$_i$ was heavy.

In 10.135 the pronoun can be anaphorically related to the indefinite NP *a book on semantics* because the structure of the DRS involves no subordination.

We leave our brief review of DRT at this point. Our discussion has revealed that the theory has a number of advantages in the description of discourse anaphora. The theory formalizes the notion of discourse referents and provides a unified explanation for the lifespan in the discourse of different nominals. In particular we saw that DRT distinguishes between names, which are always available for subsequent anaphoric pronouns, and indefinite NPs, whose lifespan depends on the type of sentence they occur in, for example: positive assertions, negative sentences, conditional sentences, and universally quantified sentences. The theory brings out the similarity between conditional and universally quantified donkey sentences and collapses the treatment of indefinite nominals in donkey sentences to the general cases. Finally DRT's view of an incrementally adjusted discourse structure seems very appealing in the light of our discussion in chapter 7. This structure can be viewed as one facet of the kind of knowledge representation that we described in chapter 7 as being cooperatively managed by participants in discourse.

DRT has influenced other dynamic models of discourse structure. One example is Segmented Discourse Representation Theory (SDRT; Asher and Lascarides 2005), which combines ideas from DRT and dynamic semantics with Rhetorical Structure Theory (Mann and Thompson 1988, Mann et al.1992), a theory of text organization which identifies relationships between parts of a text, such as Background, Elaboration, Contrast, Summary, which make the text coherent. SDRT views a discourse as being segmented into constituents related to each other by such rhetorical relations. The claim is that this rhetorical structure affects the updating of reference, tense and other semantic relations. For example the expected availability of anaphoric relations may blocked by rhetorical structure. Asher and Lascarides (2005: 60) give the following example:

10.136 a. John had a great evening last night.
b. He had a great meal.
c. He ate salmon$_i$.

d. He devoured lots of cheese.
e. He won a dancing competition.
f. ?It$_i$ was a beautiful pink.

In the absence of operators like quantifiers or negation nothing in standard DRT would prevent the pronoun *it* in (f) being interpreted as coreferential with *salmon* in (c). The unnaturalness of this, in the SDRT view, comes from the rhetorical structure, which sees the sequence (b–e) as an elaboration of (a), which thus forms a discourse subordination structure, a kind of descent or digression into greater detail. When the narration resumes at a more general level the nominals are in some sense blocked off from subsequent anaphoric relations.

In other cases the rhetorical structure allows anaphora where strictly grammatical accounts would not predict it, as with the pronoun *it* in bold in 10.137d:

10.137 a. The room was cold.
b. The wine was poor.
c. The turkey was overcooked.
d. **It** was a disaster.

In examples like this, SDRT allows each line to be seen as a continuation of an implicit topic, something like *the dinner*, and the last line can be rhetorically connected to that topic, which allows *it* to refer either to the turkey in c or the whole dinner, implicit in a–c. This move within formal approaches toward dynamic accounts and modeling information states marks a shift in orientation from a denotational to a representational approach, as attention moves to the participants' mental models of the ongoing discourse.

10.10 Summary

In this chapter we have attempted an outline of how a formal semantic analysis might proceed. We have looked at how English sentences might be translated into a logical metalanguage, the predicate logic, and how this logic can be given a denotational semantics via model theory. We began with the translation and interpretation of simple statements. We then looked at quantification by discussing sentences with the universal quantifier ∀ and the existential quantifier ∃, and looked at compound sentences, using the example of the connective ∧ "and." We then turned briefly to word meaning in this approach. Having sketched in this basic formal model, we began to look at how it has been extended to reflect important features of natural language semantics. We began by looking at how the treatment of quantifiers in first-order predicate logic has to be extended to reflect natural language quantifiers. We saw how the notion of generalized quantifiers has been applied to solve descriptive problems in English quantifiers. We turned then to the treatment of pronominal anaphora and looked at how Discourse Representation Theory models anaphora within and between sentences by establishing a dynamic model of discourse structure.

In the simple model *M1* we concentrated on the extensions of expressions like nominals, predicates, and sentences. We have seen, however, that in a number of different ways we need to expand such a model to take account of intensional features of language. The developments we have touched on – possible worlds, models of time and aspect – are mechanisms introduced to reflect this intensionality. It is at this point – intensions – that we can perhaps see denotational approaches coming into contact with representational approaches. For the latter will ask the essentially psychological question about intensions: how is it that speakers identify a relationship between a word and its extension? If we look back to our model *M1* we can see that we used a function F_1 to return the denotations of constants and predicates in the situation. It is this function, relating the logical translation of nouns like *cat* and *dog* to the entities in the situation, for which representational approaches will seek a psychological explanation. It might thus be possible to view the different traditions of denotational and representational semantics as complementary lines of enquiry, concerning themselves with two related aspects of meaning.

EXERCISES

10.1 Translate the following sentences into predicate logic. For compound sentences use the truth-functional connectives we employed in this chapter. Some symbols are provided for your use:

[Symbols: a = Arthur, m = Merlin, g = Guinevere, l = Lancelot, e = the sword Excalibur, $K(x)$ = x was a king, $Q(x)$ = x was a queen, $W(x)$ = x was a wizard, $A(x, y)$ = x advised y, $P(x, y)$ = x possessed y, $L(x, y)$ = x loved y]

a. Arthur was a king and Merlin was a wizard.
b. If Arthur was a king, then Guinevere was a queen.
c. Arthur, who was a king, possessed the sword Excalibur.
d. Merlin did not advise Lancelot.
e. Either Lancelot loved Guinevere or Guinevere loved Lancelot.

10.2 Translate the following sentences into predicate logic, using the restricted format for ∃ and ∀, the existential and universal quantifiers, as necessary. Note which sentences, if any, allow two interpretations.

[Symbols: l = Lancelot, m = Merlin, h = the Holy Grail, $D(x)$ = x is a dragon, $P(x)$ = x is a person, $N(x, y)$ = x was nervous of y, $K(x, y)$ = x was keen on y, $H(x, y)$ = x hated y, $S(x, y)$ = x searched for y]

a. Lancelot hated all dragons.
b. Every dragon was nervous of Lancelot.
c. Every dragon wasn't keen on Merlin.
d. Not everyone searched for the Holy Grail.

10.3 For the following exercise, assume the model M_3 specified below:

U_3 = {Lancelot, Gawaine, Elaine, Igraine, dragon}

$F_3(l)$ = Lancelot, $F_3(g)$ = Gawaine, $F_3(e)$ = Elaine, $F_3(i)$ = Igraine, $F_3(d)$ = dragon

$F_3(M)$ = was a maiden = {<Elaine>, <Igraine>}
$F_3(K)$ = was a knight = {<Lancelot>, <Gawaine>}
$F_3(D)$ = was a dragon = {<dragon>}
$F_3(L)$ = loved = {<Elaine, Lancelot>, <Igraine, Gawaine>, <Gawaine, Igraine>}
$F_3(C)$ = captured = {<dragon, Elaine>, <dragon, Igraine>}
$F_3(S)$ = slew = {<Lancelot, dragon>}
$F_3(F)$ = freed = {<Lancelot, Elaine>, <Lancelot, Igraine>}

Calculate the truth-value of the following sentences with respect to M_3:

a. $L(g, i)$
b. $C(d, i)$
c. $(\forall x{:}\ M(x))\ L(x, g)$
d. $(\exists x{:}\ M(x))\ L(x, g)$
e. $S(l, d) \wedge \neg(\exists x{:}\ K(x))\ L(x, e)$
f. $(\forall x{:}\ D(x))\ S(l, x) \wedge (\forall y{:}\ M(y))\ F(l, y)$

10.4 Assuming the truth tables for the connectives given in 1a–c below, evaluate the truth of the sentences in 2 with respect to the same model M_3 above:

1 a.

p	**q**	$\mathbf{p \vee q}$
T	T	T
T	F	T
F	T	T
F	F	F

b.

p	**q**	$\mathbf{p \underline{\vee} q}$
T	T	F
T	F	T
F	T	T
F	F	F

c.

p	**q**	$\mathbf{p \rightarrow q}$
T	T	T
T	F	F
F	T	T
F	F	T

2 a. $F(l, e) \vee F(l, i)$
b. $F(l, e) \underline{\vee} F(l, i)$
c. $S(l, d) \rightarrow F(l, e)$
d. $L(g, i) \rightarrow F(g, i)$

10.5 Use the formulae of meaning postulates to represent the semantic relations between the following pairs of words:

sweater/jumper

true/false

gun/weapon

open/shut (of a door)

uppercut/punch (in boxing)

car/automobile

10.6 In section 10.8.1 we used verbs of propositional attitude like *believe* to show the phenomenon of opaque contexts. Try to come up with four or five sentences where the truth or falsity of the subordinate clause seems to be independent of the truth or falsity of the whole sentences.

10.7 In section 10.7.3 we discussed the symmetry of quantifiers. For each of the quantifiers below decide whether it is symmetrical or symmetrical:

a. many (in its cardinal use)
b. few (in its cardinal use)
c. every
d. (at least) four

10.8 In section 10.7.4 we discussed the monotonicity of quantifiers. For each of the quantifiers below use your own examples to decide whether they are (a) upward or downward entailing in the right argument; or (b) non-monotone:

a. most
b. many
c. (exactly) two

10.9 Below is a mini-discourse of two sentences. Assume that there is no preceding context. Give a DRT Discourse Representation Structure (DRS) for the first sentence and a second updated DRS after the second is embedded:

A man bought a donkey. He fed it.

10.10 Using the DRT accessibility rules discussed in the chapter, try to identify which NPs in the following sentences introduce discourse referents that are accessible for coreference with pronouns in subsequent sentences.

a. If Carl drinks a beer he is happy.
b. Maura does not own a scanner.

FURTHER READING

There are several very good introductions to logic and the choice depends on the reader's taste. Allwood et al. (1977), and McCawley (1981) are intended for a linguistics audience. Other more general introductions are Guttenplan (1986), and McKay (1989).

There are a number of good introductions to formal semantics: Chierchia and McConnell-Ginet (2000) and Cann (1993) both provide in-depth descriptions of the kind of model-theoretic semantics outlined in this chapter. De Swart (1998) and Portner (2005) provide concise and accessible introductions, while Bach (1989) is an engaging and non-technical introduction in lecture format. Lappin (1996) is a comprehensive collection of papers which review topics of contemporary research in formal semantics. Portner and Partee (2002) present an important selection of primary articles. Gamut (1991) consists of two volumes: the first is an introduction to logic; the second deals with intensional logics and formal semantics, and includes an introduction to Montague Grammar. The original basic reference for Discourse Representation Theory is Kamp and Reyle (1993); Kamp et al. (2011) provides a comprehensive update, and van Eijck and Kamp (2011) is a more compact overview.

NOTES

1 This term describes the studies in formal semantics which have followed the work of Richard Montague. As mentioned in chapter 4, Montague hypothesized that the methods of logic could be used to analyze the semantics of English and other natural languages: "There is in my opinion no important theoretical difference between natural languages and the artificial languages of logicians: indeed, I consider it possible to comprehend the syntax and semantics of both kinds of language within a single, natural and mathematically precise theory" (Montague 1974: 222, cited in Cann 1993: 2). For introductions to Montague semantics see Dowty et al. (1981) and Cann (1993).

2 This quotation refers to **possible states of affairs**. This another way of referring to the notion of **possible worlds**. We met this notion briefly in chapter 5 when we discussed modality; we come back to it again later in this chapter.

3 See Haack (1978) for an accessible description of the development of modern logic, and its philosophical background.

4 For an introductory discussion of animal communication systems, see Akmajian et al. (1984: 9–45).

5 For a modern translation of Frege's work into English, see Frege (1980). Frege's work on the logic of quantifiers seems to have been independently paralleled in the investigations of the logician Charles Sanders Peirce. See Haack (1978: 39ff.).

6 For example, we shall not deal with the fundamental relationship between syntactic rules and semantic rules that is characteristic of Montague Grammar.

7 Note that though the universal quantifier sets up a range of applicability for the generalization, it does not carry any existential commitment. Our expression in 10.23 is equivalent to saying that if there were students, then they wrote a paper (or more opaquely perhaps, there is no such thing as a student who didn't write a paper). Because of the truth behavior of material implication, discussed in chapter 4, if there are no students, then our sentence is vacuously true. So, rather counter-intuitively, *Every student wrote a paper* is held to be true when there are no students. We can show this with the following truth table (based on the table for → described in 4.28 in chapter 4):

	Sx	$W(x, p)$	$(Sx \rightarrow W(x, p))$
1	T	T	T
2	T	F	F
3	F	T	T
4	F	F	T

If there are no students (no thing is a student) then lines 3 and 4 of this table apply and in both the whole expression is true. Clearly though, it would be very odd to say *Every student wrote a paper* when there were no students and therefore no papers. One way of explaining this is to say that it is because the universal quantifier is quantifying over the universe of individuals, whether they are students or not. In section 10.7.1 below we discuss proposals to restrict the range of the quantifier to the type of things named by the nominal, here students. The existential quantifier ∃ described below in the text does carry an existential commitment.

8 As we noted earlier, some predicates only require one argument, e.g. *Fred smokes S(f)*, others two, *Pat resembles Beethoven R(p, b)*, or three, *Giovanni gave the cello to Mike G(g, c, m)*. In logic any number of arguments is theoretically possible; in English, of course, the normal requirements for a verb would be one, two, or three arguments (with a few verbs like *bet* having four).

9 We will assume the following set theory notion and representations:
   1 A **set** {..}, which can be identified by listing the members, e.g. {Mercury, Mars, Earth, ... } or by describing an attribute of the members, e.g. {*x*: *x* is a planet in the solar system}.
   2 **Set membership, x ∈ A**, e.g. Mercury ∈ {*x*: *x* is a planet in the solar system}.
   3 **Subset, A ⊆ B**, where every member of **A** is a member of **B**, e.g. {Venus, Jupiter} ⊆ {*x*: *x* is a planet in the solar system}.
   4 **Intersection** of sets, **A ∩ B**, which is the set consisting of the elements which are members of both **A** and **B**, e.g. {Venus, Mars, Jupiter, Saturn) ∩ {Mars, Jupiter, Uranus, Pluto} = {Mars, Jupiter}.
   5 **Ordered pair,** <*a*, *b*>, where the ordering is significant, e.g. <Mercury, Venus> ≠ <Venus, Mercury>.
   6 **Ordered n-tuple,** $<a_1, a_2, a_3 \ldots a_n>$, e.g. the 4-tuple <Mercury, Venus, Earth, Mars>.
   7 **Cardinality** of **A**, |**A**|, which is the number of members in **A**.
   8 |**A**| = five, the cardinality of **A** is five, i.e. **A** has five members.
   9 |**A**| > |**B**|, the cardinality of **A** is greater than **B**; i.e. **A** has more members than **B**.
   10 |**A**| ≥ |**B**|, the cardinality of **A** is greater than or equal to **B**; i.e. **A** has the same or more members than **B**.
   11 **A – B, A** minus **B**, the set of members of A that are not also members of **B**.
   12 **Ø** is the empty set.

10 We ignore here the logic possibility but murine improbability that Jerry hunts himself.

11 Of course, in our informal presentation here we necessarily take on trust these advantages of formality and explicitness: we have not investigated the formal nature of sets, functions, relations, and the logics. For an excellent introduction to the mathematical foundations of these notions, see Partee et al. (1990).

12 Note that since meaning postulates express relationships between the **extensions** of linguistic expressions, they constitute knowledge about the world rather than about words.

13 We restrict our discussion to nominal quantifiers, usually called determiner quantifiers (D-quantifiers) since they have this grammatical role in English. This includes English words such as *each, every, all, some, most* in noun phrases like *each man, some foxes*, etc. These quantifiers communicate properties of entities. However, there are other types of quantifiers, for example adverbial quantifiers (A-quantifiers) like English *always, usually,*

never that communicate properties of events. See Bach et al. (1995) and Matthewson (2008) for studies of types of quantifiers across languages.

14 This formulation is described as the **relational** view of quantifying determiners since it treats the determiner as a two-place predicate taking sets as arguments, i.e. as denoting a relation between sets. An alternative is the **functional** view where the determiner is a function that maps a common noun denotation onto a noun phrase, which is the generalized quantifier. The generalized quantifier then takes a VP denotation as an argument to build propositions. See Keenan (1996) for discussion and Chierchia and McConnell-Ginet (2000: 501–02) for an introductory description.

15 This existential *there* construction must be distinguished from other sentences beginning with *there*, for example the use of *there* to introduce lists, as in A: *Which paintings do you have left?* B: *Well, there's the Picasso, the Rembrandt, and the Klee.* This construction behaves differently, allowing for example: *There's most of the Impressionists, and there's both Kandinskys.*

16 For a discussion of the application of possible world semantics to the issue of fictional entities and worlds that we discussed in chapter 2, see Lewis (1978).

17 As we saw in chapter 5, the reference time point may be the time of utterance as in the perfective in 1 below; or a time in the future or past of the time of utterance, as in the perfectives in 2 and 3:

1 He has served three presidents.
2 By next year, he will have served three presidents.
3 By 1992, he had served three presidents.

18 Seuren (1994: 1060) points out another problem for a bound variable analysis: that is, our translation via the universal quantifier ∀ in 10.119 lacks generality because a similar scope problem occurs in sentences like *If it's a good thing that Smith owns a donkey, it's a bad thing that he beats it* and *Either Smith no longer owns a donkey or he still beats it*. For discussion of donkey sentences see Kamp (1981), Reinhart (1986), Heim (1990), and Seuren (1994).

19 For a discussion of counterexamples to this generalization, and a proposal for a solution, see Krahmer (1998: 65–66).

REFERENCES

Akmajian, Adrian, Richard A. Demers and Robert M. Harnish 1984: *Linguistics*, second edition. Cambridge, MA: MIT Press.

Allan, Keith. 1986: *Linguistic Meaning*, 2 vols. London: Routledge & Kegan Paul.

Allwood, Jens, Lars-Gunnar Andersson, and Östen Dahl 1977: *Logic in Linguistics*. Cambridge: Cambridge University Press.

Asher, Nicholas and Alex Lascarides 2005: *Logics of Conversation*. Cambridge: Cambridge University Press.

Bach, Emmon, Eloise Jelinek, Angelika Kratzer, and Barbara H. Partee (eds.) 1995: *Quantification in Natural Languages*. Dordrecht: Kluwer.

Barwise, Jon and Robin Cooper 1981: Generalized quantifiers and natural language. *Linguistics and Philosophy* 4: 159–219.

Barwise, Jon and John Perry 1983: *Situations and Attitudes*. Cambridge, MA: MIT Press.

Bradley, Raymond and Norman Swartz 1979: *Possible Worlds: An Introduction to Logic and Its Philosophy*. Oxford: Blackwell.

Cann, Ronnie 1993: *Formal Semantics*. Cambridge: Cambridge University Press.

Carnap, Rudolf 1952: Meaning postulates. *Philosophical Studies* 3: 65–73.

Chierchia, Gennaro and Sally McConnell-Ginet 2000: *Meaning and Grammar: An Introduction to Semantics*, second edition. Cambridge, MA: MIT Press. (First edition 1990.)

Davidson, Donald 1980: *Essays on Actions and Events*. Oxford: Clarendon Press.

Davidson, Donald 1984: *Inquiries into Truth and Interpretation*. Oxford: Oxford University Press.
de Swart, Henriëtte 1998: *Introduction to Natural Language Semantics*. Stanford: Center for the Study of Language and Information.
Dowty, David R. 1979: *Word Meaning and Montague Grammar*. Dordrect: Reidel.
Dowty, David, Robert E. Wall, and Stanley Peters 1981: *Introduction to Montague Semantics*. Dordrecht: Reidel.
Fodor, Janet Dean, Jerry A. Fodor, and Merrill F. Garrett 1975: The psychological unreality of semantic representations. *Linguistic Inquiry* 6: 515–32.
Frege, Gottlob 1980: *Translations from the Philosophical Writings of Gottlob Frege*, edited by Peter Geach and Max Black. Oxford: Blackwell.
Gamut, L. T. F. 1991: *Logic, Language, and Meaning*, 2 vols. Chicago: University of Chicago Press.
Geach, Peter Thomas 1962: *Reference and Generality*. Ithaca, NY: Cornell University Press.
Groenendijk, Jeroen, and Martin Stokhof 1991: Dynamic predicate logic. *Linguistics and Philosophy* 14: 39–100.
Groenendijk, Jeroen, Martin Stokhof, and Frank Veltman 1996: Coreference and modality. In Shalom Lappin (ed.) *The Handbook of Contemporary Semantic Theory*, 179–213. Oxford: Blackwell.
Guttenplan, Samuel 1986: *The Languages of Logic*. Oxford: Blackwell.
Haack, Susan 1978: *Philosophy of Logics*. Cambridge: Cambridge University Press.
Heim, Irene 1983: On the projection problem for presupposition. In Michael Barlow, Daniel P. Flickinger, and Michael T. Westcoat (eds.) *Proceedings of the West Coast Conference on Formal Linguistics*, vol. 2, 114–26. Stanford, CA: Stanford Linguistics Association.
Heim, Irene 1989: *The Semantics of Definite and Indefinite NPs*. New York: Garland Press.
Heim, Irene 1990: E-type pronouns and the donkey anaphora. *Linguistics and Philosophy* 13: 137–77.
Jong, Franciska de 1987: The compositional nature of (in)definiteness. In Eric Reuland and Alice ter Meulen (eds.) *The Representation of (In)definiteness*, 170–85. Cambridge, MA: MIT Press.
Kamp, Hans 1981: A theory of truth and semantic representation. In J. Groenendijk, T. Janssen, and M. Stokhof (eds.) *Formal Methods in the Study of Language*, 277–322. Amsterdam: Mathematisch Centrum.
Kamp, Hans and Uwe Reyle 1993: *From Discourse to Logic: Introduction to Modeltheoretic Semantics of Natural Language, Formal Logic and Discourse Representation Theory*. Dordrecht: Kluwer.
Kamp, Hans, Josef van Genabith, and Uwe Reyle 2011: Discourse Representation Theory. In D. Gabbay and F. Guenthner (eds.) *Handbook of Philosophical Logic*, 125–394. Dordrecht: Springer.
Karttunen, Lauri 1976: Discourse referents. In James D. McCawley (ed.) *Syntax and Semantics. Vol. 7: Notes from the Linguistic Underground*, 363–85. New York: Academic Press.
Keenan, Edward L. 1987: A semantic definition of "indefinite NP." In Eric Reuland and Alice ter Meulen (eds.) *The Representation of (In)definiteness*, 286–317. Cambridge, MA: MIT Press.
Keenan, Edward L. 1996: The semantics of determiners. In Shalom Lappin (ed.) *The Handbook of Contemporary Semantic Theory*, 41–63. Oxford: Blackwell.
Keenan, Edward 2011: Quantifiers. In K. von Heusinger, C. Maienborn, and P. Portner (eds.) *Semantics: An International Handbook of Natural Language Meaning*, vol. 2, 1058–87. Berlin: Mouton de Gruyter.
Kintsch, Walter 1974: *The Representation of Meaning in Memory*. Hillsdale, NJ: Lawrence Erlbaum.
Krahmer, Emiel 1998: *Presupposition and Anaphora*. Stanford: Center for the Study of Language and Information.

Kripke, Saul 1980: *Naming and Necessity*. Oxford: Blackwell.
Laduslaw, William A. 1979: Polarity sensitivity as inherent scope relations. PhD dissertation, University of Texas at Austin.
Laduslaw, William A. 1996: Negation and polarity items. In Shalom Lappin (ed.) *The Handbook of Contemporary Semantic Theory*, 321–41. Oxford: Blackwell.
Lappin, Shalom (ed.) 1996: *The Handbook of Contemporary Semantic Theory*. Oxford: Blackwell.
Lewis, David K. 1973: *Counterfactuals*. Oxford: Blackwell.
Lewis, David K. 1978: Truth in fiction. *American Philosophical Quarterly* 15: 37–46.
Lewis, David K. 1986: *The Plurality of Worlds*. Oxford: Blackwell.
McCawley, James D. 1981: *Everything that Linguists Have Always Wanted to Know about Logic**. Oxford: Blackwell.
McKay, Thomas J. 1989: *Modern Formal Logic*. London: Macmillan.
Mann, William C. and Sandra A. Thompson 1988: Rhetorical Structure Theory: toward a functional theory of text organization. *Text* 8.3: 243–81.
Mann, William C., Christian M. I. M. Matthiessen, and Sandra A. Thompson 1992: Rhetorical Structure Theory and text analysis. In W. C. Mann and S. A. Thompson. (eds.) *Discourse Description: Diverse Linguistic Analyses of a Fund-Raising Text*, 39–78. Amsterdam: John Benjamins.
Matthewson, Lisa (ed.) 2008: *Quantification: A Cross-Linguistic Perspective*. Bingley: Emerald.
Milsark, G. 1977: Toward an explanation of certain peculiarities of the existential construction in English. *Linguistic Analysis* 3: 1–29.
Montague, Richard 1969: On the nature of certain philosophical entities. *The Monist* 53: 159–94. Reprinted in R. Montague 1974, 119–47.
Montague, Richard 1974: *Formal Philosophy: Selected Papers of Richard Montague*. Edited and with an introduction by Richmond H. Thomason. New Haven: Yale University Press.
Partee, Barbara H., Alice ter Meulen and Robert E. Wall 1990: *Mathematical Models in Linguistics*. Dordrecht: Kluwer.
Portner, Paul H. 2005: *What is Meaning? Fundamentals of Formal Semantics*. Malden, MA: Blackwell.
Portner, Paul H. and Barbara H. Partee (eds.) 2002: *Formal Semantics: The Essential Readings*. Oxford: Blackwell.
Quine, W. V. 1980: *Elementary Logic*, revised edition. Cambridge, MA: MIT Press.
Reinhart, Tanya 1986: On the interpretation of "donkey" sentences. In Elizabeth Closs Traugott, Alice ter Meulen, Judith Snitzer Reilly, and Charles A. Ferguson (eds.) *On Conditionals*, 103–22. Cambridge: Cambridge University Press.
Seuren, Peter A. M. 1994: Donkey sentences. In Ronald Asher (ed.) *Encyclopedia of Language and Linguistics*, vol. 2, 1059–60. Oxford: Pergamon Press.
Tarski, Alfred 1944: The semantic conception of truth. *Philosophy and Phenomenological Research* 4: 341–75. Reprinted in Aloysius Martinich (ed.) 1985: *The Philosophy of Language*. Oxford: Oxford University Press.
Tarski, Alfred 1956: *Logic, Semantics, Metamathematics: Papers from 1923 to 1938*. Translated by J. H. Woodger. Oxford: Oxford University Press.
van Eijck, Jan and Hans Kamp 2011: Discourse representation in context. In J. van Benthem and A. ter Meulen (eds.) *Handbook of Logic and Language*, second edition, 181–252. Amsterdam: Elsevier.
Wouden, A. van der 1997: *Negative Contexts: Collocation, Polarity and Multiple Negation*. London: Routledge.

chapter 11

Cognitive Semantics

11.1 Introduction

In this chapter we look at semantics within the approach known as *cognitive semantics*. As is often the case with labels for theories,[1] this might be objected to as being rather uninformative: in this instance because, as we have seen, in many semantic approaches it is assumed that language is a mental faculty and that linguistic abilities are supported by special forms of knowledge. Hence for many linguists semantics is necessarily a part of the inquiry into cognition. However, as we shall see, writers in the general approach called *cognitive linguistics*, and other scholars who are broadly in sympathy with them, share a particular view of linguistic knowledge. This view is that there is no separation of linguistic knowledge from general thinking or cognition. Contrary to the influential views of the philosopher Jerry Fodor or of Noam Chomsky,[2] these scholars see linguistic behavior as another part of the general cognitive abilities which allow learning, reasoning, and so on. So perhaps we can take the label *cognitive linguistics* as representing the slogan "linguistic knowledge is part of general cognition." As we shall see, this slogan does fit work in semantics in this approach.

We can begin by outlining some of the main principles behind this general approach. Cognitive linguists often point to a division between **formal** and **functional** approaches to language. Formal approaches, such as **generative grammar** (Chomsky 1988), are often associated with a certain view of language and cognition: that knowledge of linguistic structures and rules forms an autonomous module (or faculty), independent of other mental processes of attention, memory, and reasoning. This external view of an independent linguistic module is often combined with a view of internal modularity: that different levels of linguistic analysis, such as phonology, syntax and semantics, form independent modules. In this view, the difference between modules is one of kind: thus externally, it is good practice to investigate linguistic principles without reference to other mental faculties; and internally, to investigate, say, syntactic principles without reference to semantic content. This characterization of formal approaches concentrates on epistemological implications. Formalism also implies the desirability and possibility of stating the autonomous principles in ways that are formally elegant, conceptually simple, and mathematically well-formed.[3]

Functionalism, with which cognitive linguists identify themselves, implies a quite different view of language: that externally, principles of language use embody more general cognitive principles; and that internally, explanation must cross boundaries between levels of analysis. In this view the difference between language and other mental processes is possibly one of degree but is not one of kind. Thus it makes sense to look for principles shared across a range of cognitive domains. Similarly, it is argued that no adequate account of grammatical rules is possible without taking the meaning of elements into account.

This general difference of approach underlies specific positions taken by cognitive linguists on a number of issues: in each case their approach seeks to break down the abstractions and specializations characteristic of formalism, many of which we have met in earlier chapters. Thus studies in cognitive semantics have tended to blur, if not ignore, the commonly made distinctions between linguistic knowledge and encyclopedic, real-world knowledge – a topic we touched on earlier and return to in the next section; and between literal and figurative language, as we shall see. Similarly, cognitive linguists share the functionalist view that distinguishing linguistic levels of analysis, while a useful ploy for practical description, is potentially harmful to our conceptions of language, since syntax, for example, can never be autonomous from semantics. Ultimately, this view goes, the explanation of grammatical patterns cannot be given in terms of abstract syntactic principles but only in terms of the speaker's intended meaning in particular contexts of language use.

A further distinction that is reassessed in this framework is the traditional structuralist division between, to use Ferdinand de Saussure's (1974) terms, **diachronic** (or historical) linguistics and **synchronic** linguistics. In his foundational lectures, Saussure, attempting to free linguistics from etymological explanation, proposed his famous abstraction: a synchronic linguistics, where considerations of historical change might be ignored, as if in describing a language we could factor out or "freeze" time.[4] Such an idealization has been accepted in many linguistic theories, but is currently questioned in functional approaches. Linguistic structures, in a functionalist perspective, have evolved through long periods of use and the processes of change are evident in and relevant to an understanding of the current use of the language. Thus processes of **grammaticalization**, for example, where lexical categories may over time develop into functional categories and independent words become inflections, can provide evidence of general linguistic and cognitive principles, as discussed by Heine and Kuteva (2002).[5]

If we turn to meaning, a defining characteristic of cognitive semantics is the rejection of what is termed **objectivist semantics**. George Lakoff (1988: 123–24), for example, assigns to objectivism the basic metaphysical belief that categories exist in objective reality, together with their properties and relations, independently of consciousness. Associated with this is the view that the symbols of language are meaningful because they are associated with these objective categories. This gives rise to a particular approach to semantics which Lakoff characterizes under three "doctrines":

11.1 Objectivist semantics (adapted from Lakoff 1988: 125–26)
- a. The doctrine of truth-conditional meaning: Meaning is based on reference and truth.
- b. The "correspondence theory" of truth: Truth consists in the correspondence between symbols and states of affairs in the world.
- c. The doctrine of objective reference: There is an "objectively correct" way to associate symbols with things in the world.

In rejecting these views, cognitive semanticists place themselves in opposition to the formal semantics approach described in chapter 10. Cognitive semanticists take the view that we have no access to a reality independent of human categorization and that therefore the structure of reality as reflected in language is a product of the human mind. Consequently they reject the **correspondence theory of truth**, discussed in chapters 4 and 10. For these writers, linguistic truth and falsity must be relative to the way an observer construes a situation, based on his or her conceptual framework.[6] The real focus of investigation should, in this view, be these conceptual frameworks and how language use reflects them. In the rest of this chapter we examine this line of inquiry; we might begin here by asking of this approach our deceptively simple question: what is meaning? One answer in the cognitive semantics literature is that meaning is based on conventionalized conceptual structures. We begin to explore what this means in the next section where we discuss the cognitive semantics approach to conceptual categories, and in particular how this influences the approach to lexical meaning. In subsequent sections we see how this account deals with the phenomenon of **polysemy**, which we have touched on in earlier chapters. We then move on to **metaphor**, which has received special attention in this framework because it brings together many fundamental issues. Cognitive linguists agree with the proposal by Lakoff and Johnson (1980), Lakoff (1987, 1993), and Johnson (1987) that metaphor is an essential element in our categorization of the world and our thinking processes. Examples from this literature, such as the LIFE AS A JOURNEY metaphor where birth is arrival, death is departure, and life's problems are seen as obstacles, have been extremely influential. We review this work on metaphor in section 11.4.

A consequence of this cognitively based view of language is that the study of semantics, and linguistics, must be an interdisciplinary activity. One result is that scholars working within this and related frameworks tend to stray across intra- and inter-disciplinary boundaries more easily than most. Cognitive semanticists have, for example, examined not only the relationship of grammar and semantics, but also historical linguistics (Sweetser 1990, Geeraerts 1997, Blank and Koch 1999,

Winters et al. 2010), categories of thought (Lakoff 1987), literary language (Turner 2006), philosophy (Lakoff and Johnson 1999, Johnson 2008), mathematics (Lakoff and Núñez 2000), music (Gärdenfors 1988), rhetoric (Turner 1987), and ethics (Johnson 1993), among other areas.

11.2 Categorization

A central view in cognitive semantics is that semantic structure, along with other cognitive domains, reflects the mental categories which people have formed from their experience of growing up and acting in the world. This view has several consequences: the first is a rejection of classical theories of categories, the second is the acceptance of embodiment theories, and the third is to dissolve the distinction between linguistic and encyclopedic knowledge in the use of lexical categories. We look at each of these in turn.

11.2.1 The rejection of classical categories

In chapter 2 we discussed problems with the attempt to define categories by sets of necessary and sufficient condition, an approach we described as **the definitional theory**. Cognitive linguists trace this approach back to Aristotle's attempts, in for example the *Metaphysics* (Charles 2002), to distinguish between the essence of a thing and its *accidents*, which are possible but not defining features. So in this distinction it is essential for a bachelor to be unmarried but his hair color is accidental. The essential features define the category. The key implications of this theory, from a cognitive linguistics perspective, are as below:

11.2 Implications of classical theory (Taylor 2003, 2008)
a. Word meanings can be defined in terms of sets of features
b. The features are individually necessary and jointly sufficient
c. Categories have clear boundaries
d. All members of a category have equal status
e. The features are binary

In the cognitive semantics literature such an approach is identified with formal approaches to language, as outlined in the last section. The classical theory is rejected for a number of reasons, with two in particular being important. Firstly, as we discussed in chapter 2, it proves impossible to establish the set of defining features that is shared by all members of a lexical category. Secondly, and vitally for a cognitive approach, the theory is psychologically implausible given the evidence of protypicality effects, where for example, speakers' behavior seems to show that they view some members of a category as better examples than others. This rejection is prefigured by philosophical attacks on classical categories such as Wittgenstein's (1953) demonstration that various members of the category *game* (represented by the word *Spiel* in German) do not share a set of common properties which allow games to be clearly distinguished from non-games. Features like *played for enjoyment* or *competition between players* are not shared by all games. The boundaries are fuzzy and Wittgenstein used the analogy of family resemblance to characterize the overlapping sets of features that link the category. However, the most powerful influence has been from the work by Eleanor Rosch and her co-workers (Rosch 1973, 1975, Rosch and Mervis 1975, Rosch et al. 1976, Mervis and Rosch 1981) on prototypes, as discussed briefly in chapter 2. The claims of this theory can be summarized as below:

11.3 Prototype model of categories
- a. Categories have fuzzy boundaries
- b. There are central and peripheral members of a category
- c. Categories have marginal examples whose membership is doubtful
- d. Category members do not all share the same discrete features
- e. Attributes are not all binary features but may be from a range of mental representations including images, schemas, exemplars, etc.

Other work in psychology (e.g. Murphy and Medin 1985) suggests that categories are not objectively present in the environment but evolve from experience, belief systems and their utility in forming explanatory inferences.

These ideas have been incorporated into cognitive semantics in various ways. Lakoff (1987) suggested that lexical items form a type of complex category called **radial categories**. Radial categories have a prototypical sense and the structure of the category is represented by links to other related senses. The links are conventionalized and therefore learned rather than inferred in context. In this view lexemes are stored as complex categories that show typicality effects. We shall see some examples in section 11.3.1 when we discuss the application of this idea to prepositional polysemy. Lakoff makes the point that such categories are culturally specified, discussing for example categories corresponding to English *mother*:

11.4 There is no general rule for generating kinds of mothers. They are culturally defined and have to be learned. They are by no means the same in all cultures. In the Trobriands, a woman who gives birth often gives the child to an old woman to raise. In traditional Japanese society, it was common for a woman to give her child to her sister to raise. Both of these are cases of kinds of mothers that we don't have an exact equivalent of. (Lakoff 1987: 84)

Lakoff is here arguing that categories are related to bodies of real-world knowledge, which themselves are conceptual structures. These he characterized as **idealized cognitive models (ICMs)**, which represent belief systems and theories about the world that underpin linguistic communication.[7] Lakoff (1987: 74–76) describes the category *mother* as being interpreted against a number of culturally based linked domains of knowledge, or ICMs, about birth, marriage, genetics, nurture, genealogy, and so on with the prototypical sense showing the following links:

11.5	BIRTH:	the person giving birth is the mother
	GENETIC:	the female who contributed the genetic material is the mother
	NURTURANCE:	the female adult who nurtures and raises the child is the mother of that child

MARITAL: the wife of the father is the mother
GENEALOGICAL: the closest female ancestor is the mother

Clearly the noun *mother* may be applied in senses that deviate from the prototype's position relative to the ICMs, as can be reinforced by the use of complex expressions such as *adoptive mother*, *stepmother*, *foster mother*, *birth mother*, *surrogate mother*, and so on.

These two notions, ICMs and radial categories, are important elements in the cognitive semantic account of categorization and central to their approach to metaphor and metonymy, as we shall see later in this chapter.

11.2.2 Embodiment and image schemas

An important assumption of cognitive semantics is that conception is embodied (Anderson 2003). The basic idea is that because of our physical experience of being and acting in the world – of perceiving the environment, moving our bodies, exerting and experiencing force, and so on – we form basic conceptual structures which we then use to organize thought across a range of more abstract domains.[8] An important proposal for embodied conceptual structure is the **image schema.** In Johnson (1987), whose proposals we will examine in this section, these image schemas are proposed as a primitive level of conceptual category underlying metaphor and which provide a link between bodily experience and higher cognitive domains such as language. We can look at some examples of image schemas, beginning with the **Containment schema**.

Containment schema

Johnson (1987: 21ff) gives the example of the schema of Containment, which derives from our experience of the human body itself as a container; from experience of being physically located ourselves within bounded locations like rooms, beds, and so on; and also of putting objects into containers. The result is an abstract schema, of physical containment, which can be represented by a very simple image like figure 11.1, representing an entity within a bounded location.

Such a schema has certain experientially based characteristics: it has a kind of natural logic, including for example the "rules" in 11.6:

Figure 11.1 Containment

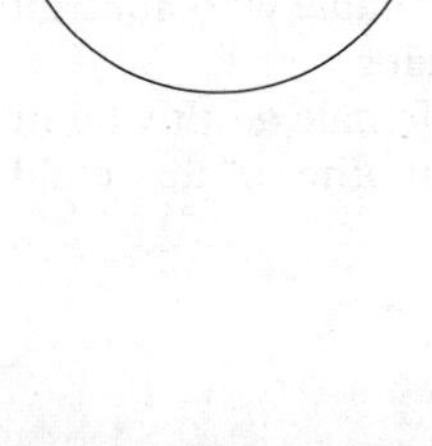

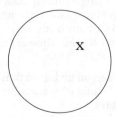

Source: Johnson (1987: 23)

11.6 a. Containers are a kind of disjunction: elements are either inside or outside the container.
b. Containment is typically transitive: if the container is placed in another container the entity is within both, as Johnson says: "If I am *in* bed, and my bed is *in* my room, then I am *in* my room."

The schema is also associated with a group of implications, which can be seen as natural inferences about containment. Johnson calls these "entailments" and gives examples like the following (adapted from Johnson 1987: 22):

11.7 a. Experience of containment typically involves protection from outside forces.
b. Containment limits forces, such as movement, within the container.
c. The contained entity experiences relative fixity of location.
d. The containment affects an observer's view of the contained entity, either improving such a view or blocking it (containers may hide or display).

The fact that a schema has parts which "hang together" in a way that is motivated by experience leads Johnson to call them **gestalt structures** (1987: 44):

11.8 I am using the term "gestalt structure" to mean an organized, unified whole within our experience and understanding that manifests a repeatable pattern or structure. Some people use the term "gestalt" to mean a mere form or shape with no internal structure. In contrast to such a view, my entire project rests on showing that experiential gestalts have internal structure that connects up aspects of our experience and leads to inferences in our conceptual structure.

Though we have represented this schema in a static image like figure 11.1, it is important to remember that these schemas are in essence neither static nor restricted to images. The schema may be dynamic, as we shall see shortly with path and force schemas, which involve movement and change.

This schema of containment can be extended by a process of metaphorical extension into abstract domains. Lakoff and Johnson (1980) identify CONTAINER as one of a group of **ontological** metaphors, where our experience of non-physical phenomena is described in terms of simple physical objects like substances and containers. For example the visual field is often conceived as a container, as in examples like: *The ship is coming into view*; *He's out of sight now*; *There's nothing in sight* (p. 30). Similarly, activities can be viewed as containers: *I put a lot of energy into washing the windows*; *He's out of the race* (p. 31), *She's deep in thought.* States can be viewed in the same way: *He's in love*; *He's coming out of the coma now* (p. 32), *She got into a rage*, *We stood in silence.* For Lakoff and Johnson these examples are typical and reveal the important role of metaphor in allowing us to conceptualize experience.

Some other schemas identified by Johnson (1987) include *Path*, *Links*, *Forces*, *Balance*, *Up–Down*, *Front–Back*, *Part–Whole*, and *Center–Periphery*. We might briefly look at the **Path** schema, and some of his examples of **Force** schemas, since these have been used in a number of linguistic studies.

Figure 11.2 Path schema

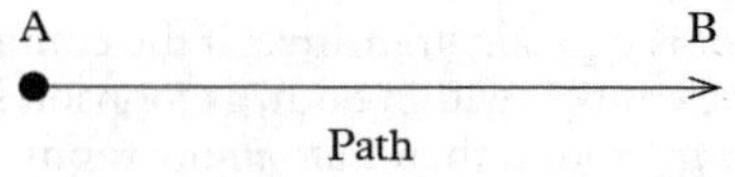

Source: Johnson (1987: 114)

Path schema

The Path schema can be shown as in figure 11.2. Johnson claims that this schema reflects our everyday experience of moving around the world and experiencing the movements of other entities. Our journeys typically have a beginning and an end, a sequence of places on the way and direction. Other movements may include projected paths, like the flight of a stone thrown through the air. Based on such experiences the path schema contains a starting point (marked A in figure 11.2), an end point (marked B), and a sequence of contiguous locations connecting them (marked by the arrow). This schema has a number of associated implications, as listed in 11.9:

11.9 a. Since A and B are connected by a series of contiguous locations, getting from A to B implies passing through the intermediate points.
b. Paths tend to be associated with directional movement along them, say from A to B.
c. There is an association with time. Since a person traversing a path takes time to do so, points on the path are readily associated with temporal sequence. Thus an implication is that the further along the path an entity is, the more time has elapsed.

These implications are evidenced in the metaphorical extension of this schema into abstract domains: we talk, for example, of achieving purposes as paths, as in 11.10 below:

11.10 a. He's writing a PhD thesis and he's nearly there.
b. I meant to finish painting it yesterday, but I got sidetracked.

We shall see in section 11.4 examples of more elaborate metaphors that derive from this schema, such as LIFE IS A JOURNEY.

Force schemas

The Force schemas include the basic force schema of **Compulsion**, which can be shown as in figure 11.3, where a force vector **F** acts on an entity u. In this diagram the essential element is movement along a trajectory: the dashed line represents the fact that the force may be blocked or may continue.

Figure 11.3 Compulsion

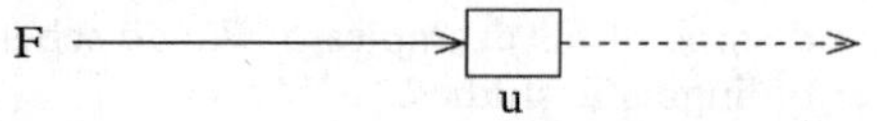

Figure 11.4 Blockage

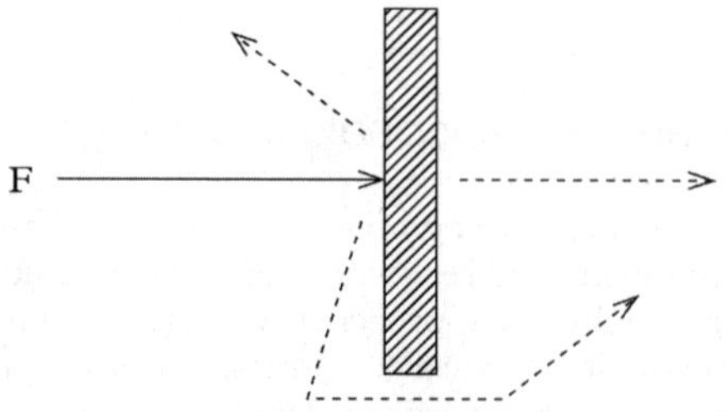

In figure 11.4 we see represented the more specific schema of **Blockage**, where a force meets an obstruction and acts in various ways: being diverted, or continuing on by moving the obstacle or passing through it.

Figure 11.5 represents the related schemas of **Removal of Restraint**, where the removal (by another cause) of a blockage allows an exertion of force to continue along a trajectory.

These force schemas, like other image schemas, are held to arise from our everyday experiences as we grew as children, of moving around our environment and interacting with animate and inanimate entities. This schema also extended by a process of metaphorical extension into more abstract domains. Emotions are commonly conceptualized in terms of forces, as in the examples in 11.11 below:

11.11 a. She was moved by the recital.
b. He kept his anger in check.
c. Anxiety pushed him deeper into depression.
d. So many men are emotionally blocked.

As with other image schemas force schemas they are held to be pre-linguistic and to shape the form of our linguistic categories. These schemas also underlie metaphors, for example Compulsion in 11.12a below and Blockage in b:

11.12 a. She pushed me into getting a new job.
b. He has been trying to convince her but he can't get through to her.

Figure 11.5 Removal of restraint

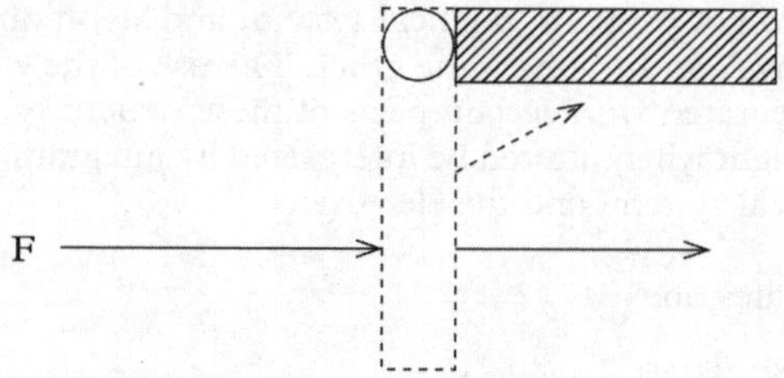

Source: Adapted from Johnson (1987: 47)

In the section 11.3 we discuss an important application of these schemas: to describe polysemy.

11.2.3 Linguistic and encyclopedic knowledge

As mentioned in the last section, cognitive linguists have sought to dismantle the rigid barrier between linguistic and real-world, or encyclopedic, knowledge that they see as a central principle of formal approaches to language. This has been an important area of enquiry in cognitive lexical semantics. An assumption that follows from the theory's basic principles is that words are labels for conceptual categories. Cognitivists reject the traditional idea of a **mental lexicon** which is an independent level of information about the meanings of words that is stored separately from the speaker's knowledge about the world. However, this view raises questions about the relations between these labeled concepts, which we can term **lexical concepts**, and other conceptual representations. One approach (Langacker 1987: 161–67) is to identify lexical concepts as points of access to other non-linguistic conceptual domains. This suggests that meaning is constructed in context by the process of accessing and integrating knowledge. A similar idea is Allwood's (1999) **meaning potential** of a lexical concept, which only becomes determinate in context. The meaning potential combines all kinds of knowledge, including memory of previous uses.

The idealized cognitive models described above are an example of the interaction between lexical concepts and other knowledge. A commonly used example is the English word *bachelor* (Fillmore 1982; Lakoff 1987; Taylor 2003), which as we saw in the discussion of Katz's semantic theory in chapter 9 might traditionally be defined as an adult human male who has never been married. However, Lakoff, echoing Fillmore, points out that the term is not applied to various individuals who fit this definition, most notably the Pope. As we discussed in chapter 2, Lakoff's point is that in use the word is interpreted against the ICM of marriage in our culture. The Pope is not usually referred to as a bachelor because the ICM excludes Catholic priests.

Evans (2009) suggests an account of how lexical concepts and encyclopedic knowledge interact in his theory of lexical concepts and cognitive models (LCCM theory). In this approach meaning is a property of individual uses of words in context rather than of the lexical concepts themselves. The latter drive processes, akin to Langacker's activation, which integrate lexical and general knowledge into a once-off situated meaning. Evans (2009: 253–70) uses the example of the name *France*, which will potentially license activation of a number of cognitive models associated with it, including the political entity and the geographical area. These contain conceptual structures related to government, political system, and so on on the one hand and physical terrain, travel, and so on on the other. The use of the word in context may activate and be integrated with certain parts of these structures, so that a sentence like 11.13 below might when uttered be interpreted by integrating knowledge about the state, the political system, and the electorate:

11.13 France votes no.

On the other hand sentence 11.14 below might exploit encyclopedic knowledge about the physical landmass:

11.14 France is beautiful.

The same approach is applied to common nouns like *book*, where cognitive models include information about books as physical entities, abstract entities, acts of reading and writing and so on. The integration of this encyclopedic knowledge with the lexical concept allows the specific interpretations below:

11.15	a.	The book wouldn't fit on the shelf.	(physical object)
	b.	The book was made into a movie.	(content)
	c.	A book is handy on a long flight.	(activity of reading)

In this theory lexical concepts are conceptual structures designed for communication, that is, to interact with other forms of knowledge to create meaning in individual speech events. As such they have specific qualities, including being language specific, associated with certain linguistic forms, showing collocation effects, combining with other lexical concepts, and so on. See Evans (2009) for discussion.

The investigation of how the selective activation of conceptual information is organized is an important topic in psychology and neuroscience; see Yee et al. (2013) and Mahon and Caramazza (2013) for overviews. We will look at further proposals for conceptual structures in the rest of this chapter, including Fauconnier's (1994) notion of **mental spaces**, which are mental structures that speakers set up to manipulate reference to entities. Such mental spaces underlie the process of **conceptual blending** (Fauconnier and Turner 2002), where speakers develop extended analogies which selectively combine existing domains of knowledge to create new scenarios. Cognitive linguists also investigate the conceptual processes which reveal the importance of the speaker's construal of a scene: processes such as **viewpoint shifting, figure-ground shifting,** and **profiling**. We look at these structures and processes in successive sections later.

11.3 Polysemy

In this section we look at how two of the conceptual structures we have seen so far, image schemas and radial categories, have together with the notion of metaphorical extension been used to characterize **polysemy**: the phenomenon discussed in chapter 3 where we find a group of related but distinct meanings attached to a word. We can look at two examples of this phenomenon from English: prepositions and modal verbs.

11.3.1 Prepositions

The schema of Containment has been use to investigate the semantics of spatial prepositions in a number of languages including the Cora language of Mexico (Langacker and Cassad 1985), English (Herkovits 1986), French (Vandeloise 1991) and Korean (Choi 2006). These studies use schemas to explore the typical polysemy of prepositions: the fact that we can for example use the English preposition *in* in a number of related but distinct ways, as in the examples below given by Herkovits (1986):

11.16 a. the water in the vase
b. the crack in the vase
c. the crack in the surface
d. the bird in the tree
e. the chair in the corner
f. the nail in the box
g. the muscles in his leg
h. the pear in the bowl
i. the block in the box
j. the block in the rectangular area
k. the gap in the border
l. the bird in the field

It is easy to see the different relationships between the entity and the container in these examples. The water is likely to be entirely contained in the vase in 11.16a but the pear in 11.16h could easily be sitting on top of a pile of fruit and thus protrude beyond the top edge of the bowl. Similarly the bird in 11.16d might be inside a hole in the tree-trunk but equally, might be sitting on a branch which if "inside" anything is inside our projection of the tree's shape. Meanwhile in 11.16l the bird might be flying or hovering several feet above the field. Herkovits's point is that such extended uses are typical and regular, that is, not idiomatic. This seems to be supported by the fact that the studies of other languages mentioned above come up with similar examples. Herkovits (1986: 48) claims that these uses are most satisfactorily described by viewing them as extensions from a central, ideal containment schema which she describes in words as "the inclusion of a geometric construct in a one-, two-, or three-dimensional geometric construct."

There are two important points to make about this polysemy from a cognitive semantics perspective: the first is that the various and varying real-world situations are described in language in a way that is essentially metaphorical in nature, relating them all to an underlying schema of containment. The second is that the relationship between the various senses is not arbitrary but systematic and natural. We can see the latter point if we look briefly at Brugman and Lakoff's (1988) description of the preposition *over*. They argue that the polysemous nature of this and other prepositions cannot be accurately described using semantic features or definitions but instead requires an essentially topographical approach, that is a description employing spatial models. They claim (1988: 479):

11.17 Topological concepts are needed in order to account for how prepositions can be used to characterize an infinity of visual scenes.

The polysemous nature of *over* can be shown, as we did for *in* earlier, by a set of examples (Brugman and Lakoff 1988):

11.18 a. The plane is flying over the hill.
b. Sam walked over the hill.
c. The bird flew over the yard.

d. The bird flew over the wall.
e. Sam lives over the hill.
f. The painting is over the mantel.
g. The board is over the hole.
h. She spread the tablecloth over the table.
i. The city clouded over.
j. The guards were posted all over the hill.
k. Harry still hasn't gotten over his divorce.

Brugman and Lakoff propose a complex structure for the meanings of *over*: the preposition has a number of related senses, of which we can identify four, termed the **above-across** sense, the **above** sense, the **covering** sense, and the **reflexive** sense. Each of these senses is then structured as a radial category with extensions from a central prototype. Let us take the **above-across** sense first. This sense of *over* is described in terms of a **Path** image schema: using the terms **trajector** (TR) for a moving entity and **landmark** (LM) for the background against which movement occurs.[9] Following Brugman and Lakoff's work, diagrams are commonly used to represent these schemas and the above-across sense would be as in figure 11.6, which would fit for example 11.18a, *The plane is flying over the hill.* In this approach several other senses of *over* can be systematically related to this central schema by a number of basic processes, for example by adding information to the schema or by metaphorical extension. In the first type of process the central schema may alter along a number of parameters: for example there may be contact between the trajector and the landmark as in 11.18b *Sam walked over the hill*, shown schematically in figure 11.7. Other information may be added about the landmark, which may be viewed as different geometric shapes: as an extended area as in 11.18c, or as a vertical form as in 11.18d. Alternatively the focus may be on the end point of the path as in 11.18e. In the second type of process the preposition can be used metaphorically, where it interacts with the metaphorical structures available to the language users. Thus in 11.18k we see a version of the LIFE AS A JOURNEY metaphor mentioned earlier, where problems are seen as obstacles.

Figure 11.6 Prototypical **above-across** sense of *over*

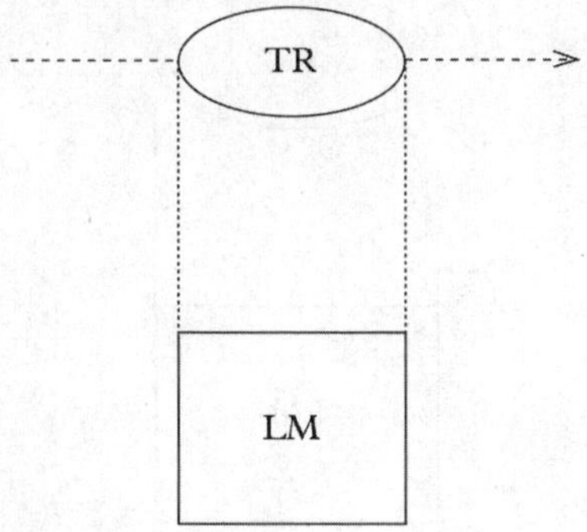

Source: Brugman and Lakoff (1988: 482)

Figure 11.7 Sam walked over the hill

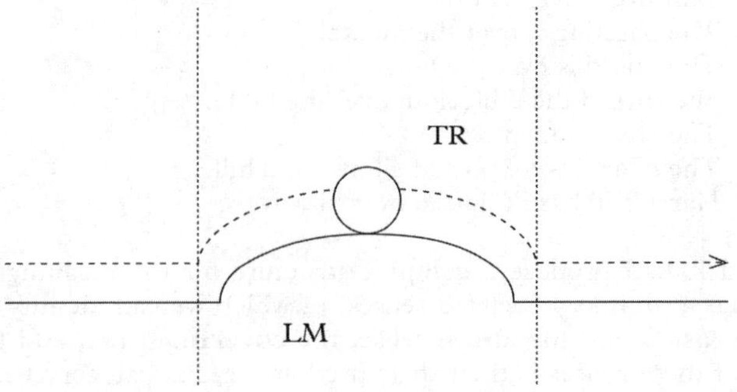

Source: Brugman and Lakoff (1988: 483)

A second major sense of *over* is the **above** sense, as in 11.18f above: *The painting is over the mantel.* This sense is stative and has no path element. It can be represented by the schema in figure 11.8. Since this schema does not include a path element it has no meaning of **across**. It also differs from the first sense in that there are no restrictions on the shape of the landmark, nor can there be contact between trajector and landmark. If there is contact we are more likely to use another preposition, such as *on* as in *The painting is on the mantel.*

Our third sense, or group of senses, of *over* is the **covering** sense, which can be represented in figure 11.9. The schema in this figure corresponds to sentence 11.17g above: *The board is over the hole.* This schema may have a path element depicting the motion of the trajector into its position over the landmark as in 11.18h *She spread the tablecloth over the table* or 11.18i *The city clouded over.* In this schema the use of a quantifier like *all* changes the nature of the trajector, as for example in sentence 11.17j: *The guards were posted all over the hill.* Here the trajector is what Brugman and Lakoff call a **multiplex** trajector, made up of many individual elements. A further variant has a multiplex path as in *I walked all over the hill.*

Figure 11.8 The **above** sense of *over*

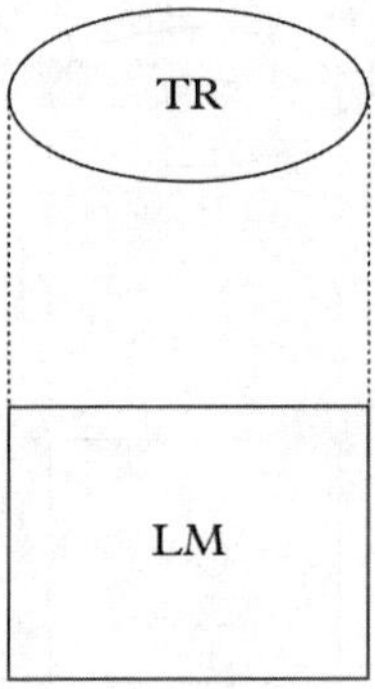

Source: Brugman and Lakoff (1988: 487)

Figure 11.9 The **covering** sense of *over*

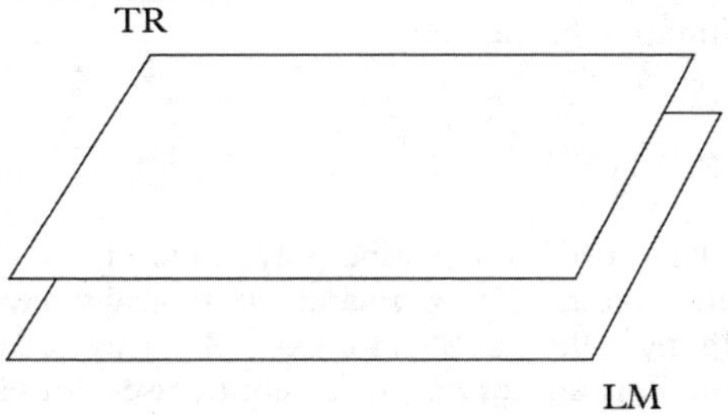

Source: Brugman and Lakoff (1988: 489)

The fourth sense of over is the **reflexive** sense as in *The fence fell over*, which can be represented as in figure 11.10. The repetitive sense of *over* as in *They watch the same film over and over again* can be seen as an extension of this reflexive sense.

We have looked at four of the major sense groups of *over* identified in this analysis. In each sense group there is a prototypical schema which is related to a number of extended senses, thus exhibiting the radial category structure we mentioned earlier. This prototypicality also extends to the relationship between the sense groups: see Brugman and Lakoff (1988) for arguments that our first sense group, the **above-across** sense, is the prototypical group for *over*.

An important element of this analysis is the claim that the processes which extend senses from a central prototype to form a radial category are systematic and widespread. Brugman and Lakoff (1988) claim, for example, that any path schema will allow a focus on the end point, as we saw for *over* in 11.18e. We can see this with the prepositions in 11.19–21 below:

11.19 a. He walked across the road.
b. He works across the road.

11.20 a. You go around the corner.
b. She lives around the corner.

11.21 a. Walk through the atrium and turn to the left.
b. His office is through the atrium and to the left.

Figure 11.10 Reflexive sense of *over*

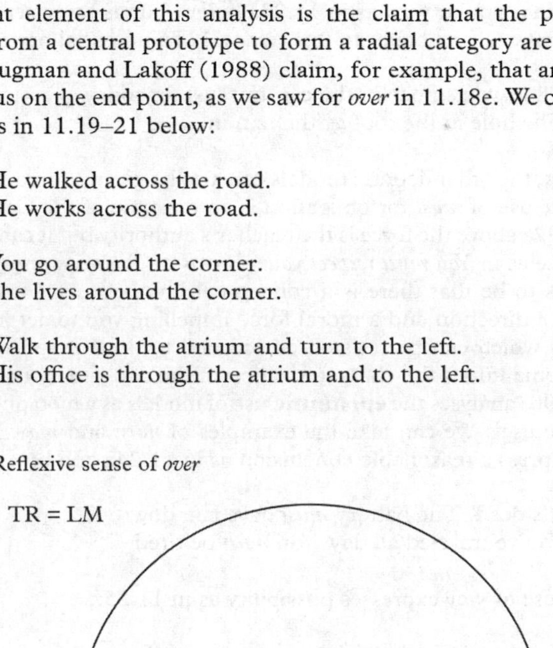

Each of the prepositions in 11.19–21 shows this ability to support a motion variant in the a sentence and a stative variant in the b sentence, where the latter identifies the end point or destination of the path.

11.3.2 Modal verbs

Force schemas have been used to describe polysemy in modal verbs. As we saw in chapter 5, modal verbs like English *may* and *can* typically have both **deontic** and **epistemic** senses. Talmy (1985, 1988), for example, uses force schemas to analyze modal verbs like *must*, *may*, and *can* in their deontic uses: for example *must* used to express obligation as in 11.22a below, *may* used for permission as in 11.22b and *can* used for ability as in 11.22c;

11.22 a. You *must* hand in your term essay before the end of this week.
b. You *may* enter the studio when the light goes out.
c. She *can* swim much better than me.

Talmy analyzes these deontic uses in terms of forces and barriers. He proposes, for example, that a typical use of *may* as permission is an example of removing a barrier or keeping back a potential but absent barrier. Thus in 11.22b some potential barrier to entering the studio is identified as being negated.

Sweetser (1990) adopts and extends this analysis of *may*. She observes that the normal use of *may* is when the barrier is a social one (deriving from authority). The verb *let* is used in a similar way, as in 11.23a below, but as Sweetser notes, with this verb there are physical analogues to this removal of a potential barrier as in 11.23b:

11.23 a. I'll *let* you smoke in the car, but just for today.
b. The hole in the roof *let* the rain in.

In this approach, the other deontic modals can also be given a force schema analysis: for example, the use of *must* for obligation is an example of the Compulsion Force schema. In 11.22a above the force is the teacher's authority but it can also be a moral or religious force as in *You must respect your parents* or *You must pray five times a day*. The idea seems to be that there is a conceptual link between someone physically pushing you in a direction and a moral force impelling you to act in a certain way. Both are forces which can be resisted or acceded to; in this approach a common conceptual schema unites the characterization of the two situations.

Sweetser (1990) analyses the **epistemic** use of modals as a metaphorical extension of these deontic uses. We can take the examples of *must* and *may*. In its epistemic use *must* can express a reasonable conclusion as in 11.24a and b:

11.24 a. It's dead. The battery *must* have run down.
b. You've traveled all day. You *must* be tired.

The epistemic use of *may* expresses possibility as in 11.25:

11.25 a. You *may* feel a bit sick when we take off.
b. He *may not* last out the whole game.

Sweetser argues that such uses of modals for rational argument and judgment are derived from their uses for the real world of social obligation and permission. This derivation follows the usual metaphorical extension from the external concrete world to the internal world of cognition and emotion. Thus to take the example of *may*, the epistemic use is again taken to represent a lack of barrier. Here though the barrier is to the line of reasoning leading to the conclusion expressed. Thus a sentence like 11.26a below can be paraphrased as 11.26b:

11.26 a. You may be right.
b. There is no evidence preventing the conclusion that you are right.

Thus an overt parallel is drawn in this account between barriers in social action and barriers in mental reasoning.

In a similar way epistemic *must* is interpreted as the Compulsion Force schema extended to the domain of reasoning. So 11.27a below is paraphrased as 11.27b:

11.27 a. You must have driven too fast.
b. The evidence forces my conclusion that you drove too fast.

Thus Sweetser is arguing that evidence is conceptualized as a force analogous to social pressure and laws, moving a person's judgment in a certain direction.

This type of analysis is extended to other modals but we need not follow the analysis further: we can identify from these few examples her claim that the relationship between the deontic and epistemic use of each modal is not accidental but a further example of polysemy: that is, the different uses are semantically related. What relates them, in this view, is the metaphorical extension of the force and barriers schemas from the social world to our inner reasoning.

So to conclude this section, we have seen that polysemy in both prepositions and modal verbs is characterized in this approach by the image schemas we introduced in section 11.2.2 as experientially based conceptual constructs by which we characterize, for example, spatial relations. These can be metaphorically extended across a range of domains, typically shifting from the external and concrete to the internal and abstract. Such schemas are seen as the building blocks of metaphor, allowing us to conceive of emotional states as containers (*She's in love*), evidence as compulsion (*He must be guilty*), or purposes as paths (A: *Have you finished the book?* B: *I'm getting there*). Polysemy is the result of this extension of schemas to form radial categories and is seen as a natural and ubiquitous phenomenon in language. In the next section we look in more detail at what has been an important element in the cognitive account of polysemy, **metaphor**.

11.4 Metaphor

11.4.1 Introduction

We have mentioned the interaction of metaphor with a number of the conceptual structures and processes identified so far in this chapter. The cognitive semantics approach to metaphor is central to this theory of language and has been very influential in a number of disciplines. In particular the cognitive approach stands in contrast to traditional views of metaphor where it is seen as the most important form of **figurative** language use, and is usually seen as reaching its most sophisticated forms in literary or poetic language. We can, however, begin with a couple of examples from journalism. Both are from reports on films: 11.28 about US box office sales and 11.29 about the Hollywood film awards, the "Oscars":

11.28 Next weekend's action release *Need for Speed* may apply the brakes to a degree, but that movie's largely unknown cast and brand may struggle to stop *Rise of an Empire* from holding on to pole position for a second weekend.

11.29 But my, how ill-fitting the crown of best picture seems to fit on the recent pretenders to that throne: The Artist, Argo, The King's Speech.[10]

As we can see, in 11.28 the competition for sales is portrayed in terms of motor sport, while in 11.29 the image is of a coronation. There are many explanations of how metaphors work but a common idea is that metaphor is somewhat like **simile** (e.g. *Reading that essay was like wading through mud*) in that it involves the identification of resemblances, but that metaphor goes further by causing a transference, where properties are transferred from one concept to another. This transference has some interesting properties, as we will see later.

To begin we can introduce some terminology. The two concepts involved in a metaphor are referred to in various ways in the literature. We can select two: the starting point or described concept (in 11.28 above US movie sales; in 11.29 the Oscar awards) is often called the **target** domain, while the comparison concept or the analogy (in our two examples, car racing and coronations) is called the **source** domain. In I. A. Richards's (1936) terminology the former is called the **tenor** and the latter, the **vehicle**. Both sets of terms are commonly used in the literature; we will adopt the former: target and source.

There are two traditional positions on the role of metaphor in language. The first, often called the **classical** view since it can be traced back to Aristotle's writings on metaphor, sees metaphor as a kind of decorative addition to ordinary plain language; a rhetorical device to be used at certain times to gain certain effects. This view portrays metaphor as something outside normal language which requires special forms of interpretation from listeners or readers. A version of this approach is often adopted in the **literal language theory** we described in chapter 1. In this view metaphor is often seen as a departure from literal language, detected as anomalous by the hearer, who then has to employ some strategies to construct the speaker's intended meaning. We can take as an example of this general approach Searle (1979: 114) who describes the start of the process thus (where a contextual assumption is that Sam is a person):

11.30 Suppose he hears the utterance, "Sam is a pig." He knows that cannot be literally true, that the utterance, if he tries to take it literally, is radically defective. And, indeed, such defectiveness is a feature of nearly all the examples that we have considered so far. The defects which cue the hearer may be obvious falsehood, semantic nonsense, violations of the rules of speech acts, or violations of conversational principles of communication.

> This suggests a strategy that underlies the first step: *Where the utterance is defective if taken literally, look for an utterance meaning that differs from sentence meaning* [author's italics].

We won't go into details of the various proposals that have been made for the next steps that the hearer uses to repair the "defective" utterance; see Ortony (ed. 1993) for some proposals.

The second traditional approach to metaphor, often called the **Romantic** view since it is associated with eighteenth- and nineteenth-century Romantic views of the imagination, takes a very different view of metaphor. In this view, metaphor is integral to language and thought as a way of experiencing the world. In this view metaphor is evidence of the role of the imagination in conceptualizing and reasoning, and it follows that all language is metaphorical. In particular, there is no distinction between literal and figurative language.[11]

11.4.2 Conceptual Metaphor Theory

An important characteristic of cognitive semantics is the central role in thought and language assigned to metaphor. Lakoff and his colleagues (e.g. Lakoff and Johnson 1980, 1999, Lakoff 1987, 1993, Johnson 1987, Lakoff and Turner 1989) proposed an approached termed **Conceptual Metaphor Theory** (CMT). Given the classical/Romantic opposition we have described, CMT can be seen as an extension of the Romantic view.[12] Cognitivists argue that metaphor is ubiquitous in ordinary language, though they pull back a little from the strong Romantic position that all language is metaphorical. While metaphor is seen as a very important mode of thinking and talking about the world, it is accepted that there are also non-metaphorical concepts:

11.31 Metaphors allow us to understand one domain of experience in terms of another. To serve this function, there must be some grounding, some concepts that are not completely understood via metaphor to serve as source domains. (Lakoff and Turner 1989: 135)

In emphasizing the important role of metaphor in ordinary language, Lakoff and his colleagues identified a large number of common metaphors. One group, for example, they describe as **spatial** metaphors, for example the many metaphors associated with an UP–DOWN orientation. These include the following, where we select a few of their examples (Lakoff and Johnson 1980: 14–21):

11.32 a. HAPPY IS UP; SAD IS DOWN
I'm feeling *up*. My spirits *rose*. You're in *high* spirits. I'm feeling *down*. I'm *depressed*. He's really *low* these days. My spirits *sank*.

b. CONSCIOUS IS UP; UNCONSCIOUS IS DOWN
Wake *up*. He *fell* asleep. He *dropped* off to sleep. He's *under* hypnosis. He *sank* into a coma.

c. HEALTH AND LIFE ARE UP; SICKNESS AND DEATH ARE DOWN
He's at the *peak* of health. He's in *top* shape. He *fell* ill. He's *sinking* fast. He came *down* with the flu. His health is *declining*.

d. HAVING CONTROL OR FORCE IS UP; BEING SUBJECT TO CONTROL OR FORCE IS DOWN
I have control *over* her. He's at the *height* of his powers. He's in a *superior* position. He ranks *above* me in strength. He is *under* my control. He *fell* from power. He is my social *inferior*.

e. GOOD IS UP; BAD IS DOWN
Things are looking *up*. We hit a *peak* last year, but it's been *downhill* ever since. Things are at an all-time *low*. He does *high*-quality work.

f. VIRTUE IS UP; DEPRAVITY IS DOWN
He is *high*-minded. She has *high* standards. She is an *upstanding* citizen. That was a *low* trick. Don't be *underhanded*. I wouldn't *stoop* to that. That was a *low-down* thing to do.

As the authors point out, these metaphors seem to be based on our bodily experiences of lying down and getting up and their associations with consciousness, health, and power, that is of verticality in human experience. These then support the experiential basis of meaning described in section 11.2. For now we can see that Lakoff and Johnson's point is that in using language like this, speakers are not adding rhetorical or poetical flourishes to their language: this is how we conceive of happiness, health, and so on. As a result metaphors are conceptual structures which pervade ordinary language. In the next section we look at some of the features of metaphor identified in Conceptual Metaphor Theory.

11.4.3 Features of metaphor

Cognitive semanticists argue that, far from being idiosyncratic anomalies, metaphors exhibit characteristic and systematic features. We can look at some of these characteristics under the headings of conventionality, systematicity, asymmetry, and abstraction. The first, **conventionality**, raises the issue of the novelty of the metaphor: we could say, for example, that the first of our two examples in 11.28 and 11.29 is less novel than the second. As we discussed in chapter 1, some writers would claim that some metaphors have become fossilized or **dead** metaphors. In the literal language theory this means that they have ceased to be metaphors and have passed into literal language, as suggested by Searle (1979: 122):

11.33 *Dead metaphor*. The original sentence meaning is bypassed and the sentence acquires a new literal meaning identical with the former metaphorical meaning. This is a shift from the metaphorical utterance . . . to the literal utterance.

Cognitive semanticists argue against this approach, pointing out that even familiar metaphors can be given new life, thus showing that they retain their metaphorical status. If we take, for example the UP–DOWN metaphor, we might consider an instance like *My spirits rose* to be a dead metaphor, yet this general metaphor is continually being extended: it is no accident in this view that stimulant recreational drugs were called *uppers* and tranquillizers, *downers*.

The second feature, **systematicity**, refers to the way that a metaphor does not just set up a single point of comparison: features of the source and target domain are joined so that the metaphor may be extended, or have its own internal logic. We can take an example from a *Science* magazine article about genetic research on the history of European peoples, where genetic contacts are metaphorically viewed as a cookery recipe:

11.34 How do you make a modern European? For years, the favored recipe was this: Start with DNA from a hunter-gatherer whose ancestors lived in Europe 45,000 years ago, then add genes from an early farmer who migrated to the continent about 9,000 years ago.

This metaphor is part of an extended metaphorical structure which surfaces through the rest of this article; see the following extracts, which continue the mapping:

11.35 a. An extensive study of ancient DNA now points to a third ingredient for most Europeans: blood from an Asian nomad who blew into central Europe perhaps only about 4,000 or 5,000 years ago…
b. But if the genomicists are right, the chief components of the latest European recipe will endure…[13]

This systematicity has been an important focus in cognitive semantic views of metaphor: Lakoff and Turner (1989) discuss, for example, the metaphor mentioned earlier, LIFE IS A JOURNEY, which pervades our ordinary way of talking. Thus birth is often described as arrival as in *The baby is due next week*, or *She has a baby on the way*; and death is viewed as a departure as in *She passed away this morning* or *He's gone*. Lakoff and Turner (1989: 3–4) identify systematicity in this mapping between the two concepts:

11.36 LIFE IS A JOURNEY

- The person leading a life is a traveler.
- His purposes are destinations.
- The means for achieving purposes are routes.
- Difficulties in life are impediments to travel.
- Counselors are guides.
- Progress is the distance traveled.
- Things you gauge your progress by are landmarks.
- Material resources and talents are provisions.

Their point is that we use this mapping every day in ordinary speech as when we use expressions like: *Giving the children a good start in life*; *He's over the hill*; *I was bogged down in a dead-end job*; *Her career is at a standstill*; *They're embarking on a new career*; *He's gone off the rails*; *Are you at a cross-roads in your life?*; *I'm past it (= I'm too old)*; *He's getting on (= he's aging)*, and so on.

Another example comes from the role of metaphor in the creation of new vocabulary: the coining of the term *computer virus* for a specific type of harmful program; see Fauconnier (1997: 19ff) for discussion. This coining is based on a conceptual model of biological viruses which is generalized or schematized away from the biological details:

11.37 Biological virus schema (Fauconnier 1997: 19)
a. *x* is present, but unwanted; it comes in, or is put in, from the outside; it does not naturally belong;

b. *x* is able to replicate; new tokens of *x* appear that have the same undesirable properties as the original *x*;
c. *x* disrupts the "standard" function of the system;
d. the system should be protected against *x*; this might be achieved if the system were such that *x* could not come into it, or if other elements were added to the system that would counteract the effects of *x*, or eject *x*, or destroy *x*.

This schema is transferred to the general aspects of the computer situation; it provides a way of characterizing the new domain. The schema in 11.37 is itself based on lower-level schemas like the image schemas of Container and Path discussed earlier in this chapter, and force dynamics of entry, resistance and so on (Talmy 2000, 1: 409–69).

This metaphorical mapping between a health schema and a computer domain can be viewed as a form of **analogical mapping** (Gentner 1983, Holyoak and Thagard 1995). It licenses a whole system of lexical innovations so that files can be said to be "infected"; files downloaded from the internet might be "contagious"; the anti-virus programs are said to "disinfect" programs, and may place them in special areas of memory called "quarantine."

The importance of the process of metaphorical extension of the vocabulary can be seen from the following list of conventionalized mappings from parts of the human body:

11.38 Conventionalized metaphors of body parts in English (Ungerer and Schmid 2006: 117)

head	of department, of state, of government, of a page, of a queue, of a flower, of a beer, of stairs, of a bed, of a tape recorder, of a syntactic construction
face	of a mountain, of a building, of a watch
eye	of a potato, of a needle, of a hurricane, of a butterfly, in a flower, hooks and eyes
mouth	of a hole, of a tunnel, of a cave, of a river
lip	of a cup, of a jug, of a crater, of a plate
nose	of an aircraft, of a tool, of a gun
neck	of land, of the woods, of a shirt, bottleneck
shoulder	of a hill or mountain, of a bottle, of a road, of a jacket
arm	of a chair, of the sea, of a tree, of a coat or jacket, of a record player
hands	of a watch, of an altimeter/speedometer

Our third feature, **asymmetry**, refers to the way that metaphors are **directional**. They do not set up a symmetrical comparison between two concepts, establishing points of similarity. Instead they provoke the listener to transfer features from the source to the target. We can take the metaphor LIFE IS A JOURNEY as an example: this metaphor is asymmetrical and the mapping does not work the other way around. We do not conventionally describe journeys in terms of life, so that it sounds odd to say *Our flight was born* (*i.e. arrived*) *a few minutes early* or *By the time we got there, the boat had died* (*i.e. gone*). Even if we are able to set up such a metaphor, it is clear that the meaning would be different from that of the original structure.

Our final feature, **abstraction**, is related to this asymmetry. It has often been noted that a typical metaphor uses a more concrete source to describe a more abstract target. Again the LIFE IS A JOURNEY metaphor exhibits this feature: the common, everyday experience of physically moving about the earth is used to characterize the mysterious (and unreported) processes of birth and death, and the perhaps equally mysterious processes of ageing, organizing a career, and so on. This pattern reflects the embodiment of conceptual structures discussed earlier. This is not a necessary feature of metaphors: the source and target may be equally concrete or abstract, but as we shall see, this typical viewing of the abstract through the concrete is seen in cognitive semantics as allowing metaphor its central role in the categorizing of new concepts, and in the organization of experience.

11.4.4 The influence of metaphor

Cognitivists argue that because of their presence in speakers' minds, metaphors exert influence over a wide range of linguistic behaviors. Sweetser (1990), for example, identifies a cross-linguistic metaphor MIND-AS-BODY, as when in English we speak of *grasping* an idea or *holding* a thought. She identifies this metaphorical viewing of the mental in terms of the physical as an important influence in the historical development of **polysemy** and of cognate words in related languages. Thus in English the verb *see* has two meanings: the basic physical one of "perceiving with the eyes" and the metaphorically extended one of "understanding" as in *I see what you mean.* Sweetser discusses how over time verbs of sense perception in Indo-European languages have shown a consistent and widespread tendency to shift from the physical to the mental domain. Her claim is that this basic underlying metaphor underlies the paths of semantic change in many languages so that words of seeing come to mean understanding, words of hearing to mean obeying, and words of tasting to mean choosing, deciding or expressing personal preferences. Some of her examples are given below (1990: 32ff):

11.39 a. seeing →understanding

Indo-European root **weid-* "see":[14]
Greek *eîdon* "see," perfective *oîdoa* "know" (> English *idea*)
English *wise, wit*
Latin *video* "see"
Irish *fios* "knowledge"

b. hearing → paying attention to, obeying

Indo-European root **k'leu-s-* "hear, listen"
English *listen*
Danish *lystre* "obey"

c. tasting → choosing, expressing preferences

possible Indo-European root **g'eus* "taste"
Greek *geúomai* "taste"

Latin *gustare* "taste"
Gothic *kiusan* "try"
Old English *ceosan* "choose"
Sanskrit *jus-* "enjoy"[15]

Sweetser's point is that historical semantic change is not random but is influenced by such metaphors as MIND-AS-BODY. Thus metaphor, as one type of cognitive structuring, is seen to drive lexical change in a motivated way, and provides a key to understanding the creation of polysemy and the phenomenon of semantic shift. See also Heine et al. (1991) who provide a wide range of examples to support their own version of the same thesis: that metaphor underlies historical change.

In this section we have looked briefly at cognitivist investigations of the role of metaphor in language. Next we turn to a related process: metonymy.

11.5 Metonymy

We discussed metonymy in chapter 7 as a referential strategy, describing it in traditional terms as identifying a referent by something associated with it. This reflects the traditional definition in terms of **contiguity**. For cognitive semanticists metonymy shows many of the same features as metaphor: they are both conceptual processes; both may be conventionalized; both are used to create new lexical resources in language and both show the same dependence on real-world knowledge or cognitive frames. The same terminology of target and source can be used. The distinction between them is made in this literature (Lakoff and Johnson 1980, Lakoff 1987, Lakoff and Turner 1989) in terms of these cognitive frames. Metaphor is viewed as a mapping across conceptual domains, for example disease and computers in our example above of *computer virus*. Metonymy establishes a connection within a single domain. The traditional notion of contiguity can be expressed in cognitive terms using Lakoff's idealized cognitive models (ICMs) discussed earlier. The source may support a link to the target when they both belong to the same ICM. Thus in 11.40 below the British Prime Minister's office and residence and Downing Street in London are part of the same ICM of the UK government. Other writers describe metonymy as highlighting (Croft 1993) or activating (Barcelona 2011) different elements of an ICM for special purposes.

Various taxonomies of metonymic relations have been proposed including those by Lakoff and Johnson (1980), Fass (1991), Nunberg (1995), Kövecses and Radden (1998), and Ruiz de Mendoza and Díez (2002). We give some typical strategies below, with examples (and traditional terms in parentheses):

11.40 Types of metonymic relation

PART FOR WHOLE (synecdoche)
There are a lot of new faces in the squad.
WHOLE FOR PART (synecdoche)
Germany won the world cup.
CONTAINER FOR CONTENT

I don't drink more than two bottles.

MATERIAL FOR OBJECT

She needs a glass.

PRODUCER FOR PRODUCT

She always wears Stella McCartney.

PLACE FOR INSTITUTION

Downing Street has made no comment.

INSTITUTION FOR PEOPLE

The Senate isn't happy with this bill.

PLACE FOR EVENT

Hiroshima changed our view of war.

CONTROLLED FOR CONTROLLER

All the hospitals are on strike.

CAUSE FOR EFFECT

His native tongue is Hausa.

As with metaphor, metonymy is a productive way of creating new vocabulary. We can give just two conventionalized examples from the PRODUCER FOR PRODUCT relation: *shrapnel* from the English general who invented the type of shell, and *silhouette* from the French finance minister who designed the technique.

There have been attempts to account for the particular choice of metonymic reference points. Some choices seem more common and natural than others, for example to use *tongue* for *language* rather than *throat*, or *head* or *face* for a person rather than, say *waist*. Langacker (1993: 30) suggested a general notion of salience, where items are graded for relative salience, for example (where > = more salient): human > non-human, whole > part, visible > non-visible, and concrete > abstract. Kövecses and Radden (1998) develop this idea further by appealing to experiential and in particular perceptual motivation for principles governing the choice of metonymic reference point.

We have now seen something of the related processes of metaphor and metonymy. In the next section we look at a proposal for a cognitive theory of meaning construction: mental spaces.

11.6 Mental Spaces

Mental spaces are conceptual structures, originally proposed by Fauconnier (1994, 1997), to describe how language users assign and manipulate reference, including the use of names, definite descriptions, and pronouns. Fauconnier's structures are set up in the light of a particular view of meaning: that when we study linguistic meaning we are studying the way that language provides a patchy and partial trigger for a series of complex cognitive procedures. In this view meaning is not "in" language; rather, language is like a recipe for constructing meaning, a recipe which relies on a lot of independent cognitive activity. Moreover, this process of meaning construction is a discourse-based process, implying that typically a single sentence is only a step in the recipe and cannot be clearly analyzed without recognizing its relationship to and dependency on earlier sentences.

So Fauconnier's focus is on the cognitive processes triggered during discourse by linguistic structures. Within this, a particular topic of investigation has been the management of reference: the issue of how speakers and hearers keep track of the entities referred to in the language. The central idea is that when we are involved in using language, for example in conversation, we are continually constructing domains, so that if we talk about, say, Shakespeare's play *Julius Caesar*, we might maintain several relevant domains, or mental spaces. One domain is the world of the play, while another might be the real world, where Julius Caesar is a historical figure. Our referential practices make use of such divisions into domains so that we can use the same name *Julius Caesar* to talk about the historical person and the character in the play. Between our different uses of the name there are nevertheless links: we might want to say for example that Shakespeare's character is meant to describe the historical figure. Such processes can be quite complicated: we might go to see a performance of the play and afterwards say *Julius Caesar was too young*, referring now to the actor playing the part. Or if we saw some children running off with the foyer's life-size figure of the actor in costume, we might say *Hey, they're stealing Julius Caesar*. So we can use the same name to refer to a historical person, a role in a play written about him, an actor playing that role and a figure of that actor playing the role. Fauconnier's point is that such flexibility is inherent in our use of referring expressions: his mental spaces are an attempt to explain such behavior.

Mental spaces can be seen as a cognitive parallel to the notion of possible worlds in formal semantics, as discussed in chapter 10, since it is assumed that speakers can partition off and hold separate domains of reference. Some of these might be very complex: we might for example be talking of the world of Charles Dickens's *A Tale of Two Cities* and refer to individuals in that novel, like *Charles Darnay* and *Sydney Carton*. Or the domain might be very sparsely furnished, provoked just by a counterfactual as in *If I were you, I'd go on a diet*, where once the shift from the real to the non-real domain is made in the first clause, the *I* in the second clause identifies not the speaker but the addressee. Here, however, any further implications of this domain, or mental space, are not explored and it remains a local, minimal space.

11.6.1 Connections between spaces

One important issue is what links there might be between mental spaces. What, for example, allows us to use the name *Julius Caesar* as we did, for a historical person, a role in a play, an actor, and so on? Fauconnier (1994), building on work by Jackendoff (1975), and Nunberg (1978, 1979) discusses the way that speakers can make reference to entities by a number of indirect strategies. We can for example refer to a representation of someone by their name: so that looking at a photograph of a friend I might say *Graham looks really young*, where *Graham* refers to the picture of Graham (who in reality might look far from young). Fauconnier uses the terms **trigger** and **target** here: the name of the real Graham is the trigger and the target (what I want to describe) is the image. Clearly photographs and the people in them are related by the viewer's recognition of resemblance, but similar strategies are widespread. We can refer, for example, to a book or books by the author's name and say sentences like

Shakespeare's on the top shelf. Similarly, a nurse might say *The gall bladder in the end bed is awake*; or in a favourite type of example in this literature, a waiter might say *The ham omelette wants his bill*. As we have seen, this phenomenon has traditionally been termed **metonymy**. Fauconnier employs an **identification principle** which allows speakers to use such referential shifts; one version is in 11.41 below (Fauconnier 1994: 3):

11.41 If two objects (in the most general sense), *a* and *b*, are linked by a pragmatic function *F* ($b = F(a)$), a description of *a*, d_a, may be used to identify its counterpart *b*.

So since in our photograph example real Graham (*a*) and photo Graham (*b*) are linked by the pragmatic function IMAGE, a description of real Graham (his name, d_a) can be used to identify his photographic image (*b*). It is assumed that there might be a number of such pragmatic functions, as we shall see.

We can look at some more complicated examples of this referential shifting by looking at Fauconnier's account of Jackendoff's (1975) example in 11.42 below:

11.42 In Len's painting, the girl with blue eyes has green eyes.

Let us take as an interpretation of this sentence the situation where the speaker knows the identity of the artist's model, knows that she has blue eyes and is pointing out that the painter has decided to give her green eyes in the picture. The proposal is that here two mental spaces are set up: one is the real world (as the speaker knows it) which has in it a girl with blue eyes; the other the space of the painting which has a girl with green eyes. The sentence 11.42 explicitly connects these two girls, saying in effect they are in the image–person relationship we discussed for our hypothetical friend Graham earlier. This can be represented in figure 11.11, which shows the connection (our image relationship) as an arrow.

Fauconnier, following Jackendoff (1975), makes the point that this can be likened to the relationship between beliefs and reality: thus, paralleling 11.42 above we can say 11.43 and 11.44 below:

11.43 Len believes that the girl with blue eyes has green eyes.

11.44 Len wants the girl with blue eyes to have green eyes.

Here Len's belief and wish are at odds with reality as known by the speaker. In the semantics literature such examples are often described as instances of **belief contexts**. In this theory they are viewed as a mental parallel to the image relation,

Figure 11.11 Person–image connector

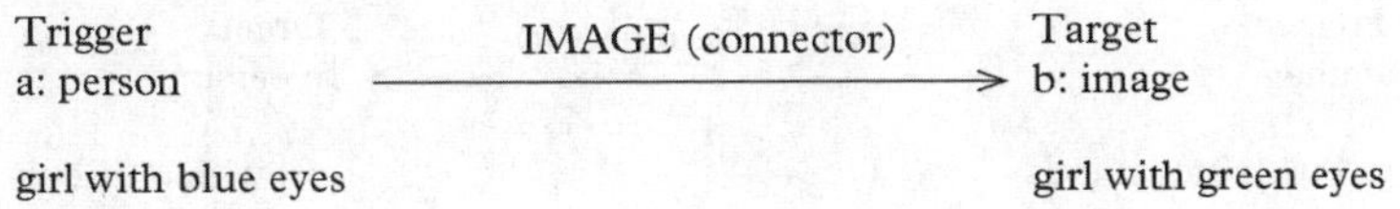

Source: Based on Fauconnier (1994)

Figure 11.12 World–mind connector

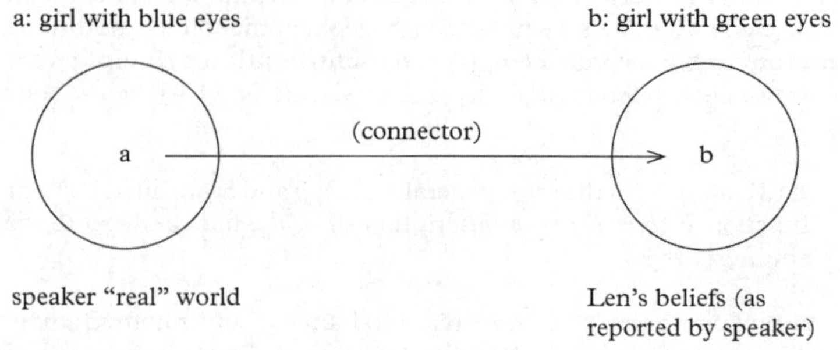

Source: Based on Fauconnier (1994)

and are represented by similar diagrams, using a belief or MIND connector, as in figure 11.12. As Fauconnier points out, the speaker can work such relationships in the other direction. Taking the image relationship as an example, a speaker might say, looking at a picture: *In reality, the girl with brown eyes has blue eyes.* Here the trigger is the image and the target is the real girl, as shown in figure 11.13.

These examples are of mental spaces created by talking of paintings and a person's beliefs and wishes. There are in fact a whole range of linguistic elements which serve as triggers for setting up mental spaces, which Fauconnier calls **spacebuilders**. These include adverbials of location and time like *in Joan's novel, in Peter's painting, when she was a child, after we find the crash site*, and so on. They also include adverbs like *possibly* and *really*; connectives like *if. . . then*; and certain verbs like *believe, hope*, and *imagine*. The context in which a sentence is uttered will provide the anchoring or background mental space. Where spaces are stacked inside one another, the including space is referred to as the **parent** space. Often of course the default (unmarked) highest parent space will be reality, or more accurately the current speaker's assessment of reality. Take for example, a speaker uttering the sentences in 11.45 below:

11.45 Barry's in the pub. His wife thinks he's in the office.

Here the initial space is the speaker's reality (*R*) where Barry is in the pub, then the phrase *his wife thinks* sets up a new mental space (*M*) in which his counterpart Barry2 is in the office. The speaker can then develop either space, talking about what Barry1 is doing in *R* or what Barry2 is (supposedly) doing in *M*.

Figure 11.13 Image–person connector

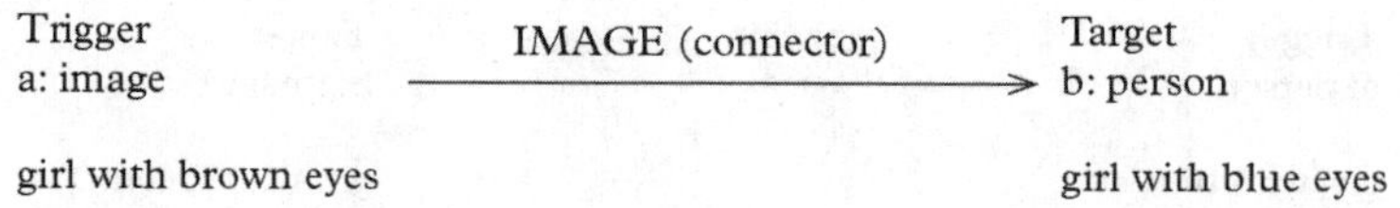

Source: Based on Fauconnier (1994)

11.6.2 Referential opacity

One important advantage to this idea of mental spaces and links between them is that it can be used to explain the phenomenon of **referential opacity**. This is the traditionally problematic area where, as we discussed in chapter 2, knowledge interacts with reference. Let's take, for example, sentence 11.46 below to be true of a policeman called Jones:

11.46 Jones believes that the leader of the Black Gulch Gang is a sociopath.

If Jones does not know that his wife is the leader of the Black Gulch Gang we can also take the sentence 11.47 below to be true at the same time:

11.47 Jones doesn't believe his wife is a sociopath.

Because of what Jones knows, we are not ascribing contradictory beliefs to him, even though the nominals *his wife* and *the leader of the Black Gulch Gang* denote the same individual. This is a typical effect of belief contexts and in chapter 2 we saw that such examples have been used to argue that there must be more to meaning than simply denotation.

As we discussed in chapter 10, sentences like 11.46 are described as **opaque contexts**. In this type of example the opacity is associated with embedded clauses under verbs of propositional attitudes like *believe*, *want*, *suspect*, *hope*, and so on. To give another example, a sentence like 11.48 below can have two distinct interpretations:

11.48 The Captain suspects that a detective in the squad is taking bribes.

If we take 11.48 to mean that the Captain suspects a particular detective, this is called the **specific** or **transparent** reading. If on the other hand we take 11.48 to mean that the Captain suspects that one of the detectives is involved but doesn't know which one, this is called the **non-specific** or **opaque** reading. In another terminology used in logic, the transparent reading (the captain knows which individual) is given the Latin label the *de re* interpretation (meaning roughly "of the thing") while the opaque reading is called the *de dicto* interpretation (roughly "of what is said").

In the mental spaces approach these two interpretations do not arise from any ambiguity in the sentence but from two different space-connecting strategies that hearers may use. Nor are opaque contexts restricted to verbs of propositional attitude: they are a regular consequence of referential strategies. To show this, we might go back to an example of identifying actors and parts. Suppose for example a speaker says 11.49 below:

11.49 In the film, Michelle is a witch.

This sentence sets up two spaces which we can identify as speaker's reality (*R*) and the film (*F*). The name *Michelle* can be used to refer in two ways. In the first there is the kind of referential shifting we described earlier: *Michelle* is the name of a person in *R*, but the speaker uses her name to describe the film images of her acting the role of a witch (here of course the film images may or may not resemble real-life Michelle). We could call this connector ACTOR. We can represent this interpretation

Figure 11.14 First interpretation of *In the film, Michelle is a witch.*

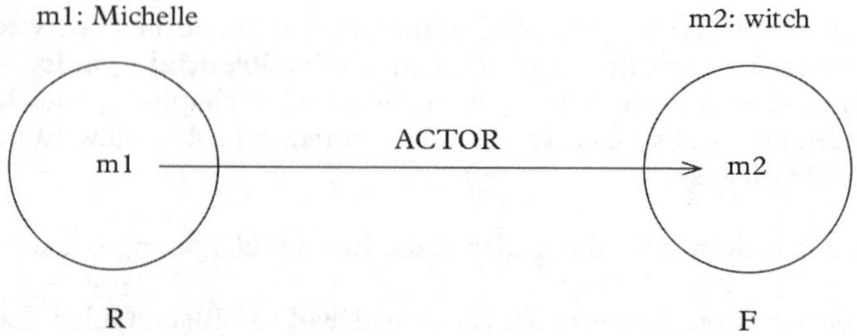

in figure 11.14. We can roughly describe this as: real-life Michelle plays the film part of a witch. In the second interpretation there is no referential shifting between the two mental spaces: *Michelle* is the name of a character in the film space and we predicate of this character that she is a witch. This interpretation can be represented as in figure 11.15. We can roughly describe this as: in the film the character Michelle is a witch.

These two interpretations are predicted to be regular options whenever two spaces are set up like this and this same behavior is used to explain the examples of referential opacity we have been looking at. If we go back to example 11.46 *Jones believes that the leader of the Black Gulch Gang is a sociopath,* the verb *believe* is a spacebuilder which adds the space of Jones's belief (call it space *B*) to the parent space, which we can take to be the speaker's reality (call this space *R*), although of course our sentence could easily be embedded in a story or someone else's belief. The transparent reading of this sentence will be where Jones knows the identity of the gang leader in reality and sets up a belief space where he describes the gang leader as a sociopath. There is therefore a referential link between the gang leader in reality and the gang leader in Jones's belief, shown by the connector arrow in figure 11.16. We can roughly describe this as: Jones knows the identity of the gang leader in *R* and in his belief space *B* the gang leader is a sociopath.

The opaque reading of this sentence will be where Jones doesn't know the identity of the gang leader in *R* but has a belief about this person in *B*: here there is no referential link between the reality space and the belief space, as we show in figure 11.17. We can roughly describe this as: Jones doesn't know the identity of the gang leader in reality but in his belief the gang leader is a sociopath.

Figure 11.15 Second interpretation of *In the film, Michelle is a witch.*

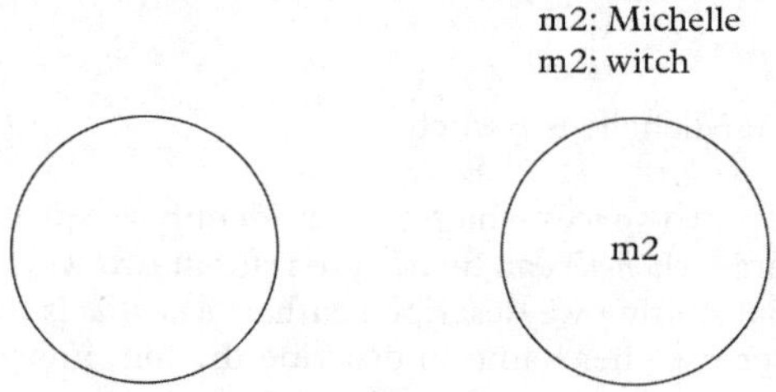

Figure 11.16 Transparent reading of example 11.46

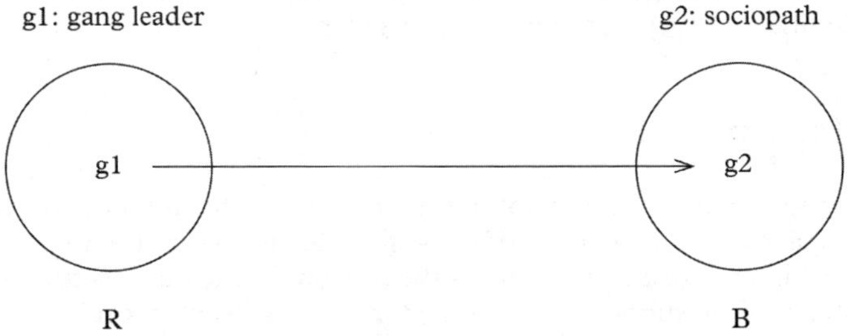

In this approach any spacebuilder can trigger such ambiguities of interpretation so that a time adverbial like *in 1966* can trigger two readings for the sentence 11.50 below:

11.50 In 1966 my wife was very young.

Here two time spaces are established: the "now" of the speaker and the time 1966. The reference to the nominal *my wife* can be interpreted in two ways. The first simply identifies a wife in the 1966 time space and is consistent with the speaker either having the same wife in the "now" space or not. The second interpretation is that the person who is the speaker's wife now was not his wife in 1966, but is referred to as *my wife* by a shift linking the mental spaces. On this type of reading there is nothing odd about the sentence *In 1966 my wife was a baby*. As Fauconnier points out, this ability to connect or not connect spaces allows the transparent non-contradictory readings for his examples in 11.51 and 11.52 below:

11.51 In Canadian football, the 50-yard line is 55 yards away.

11.52 In this new Californian religion, the devil is an angel.

In this approach then the regular system of establishing mental spaces predicts these types of referential flexibility and the prediction naturally includes referential opacity.

Figure 11.17 Opaque reading of example 11.46

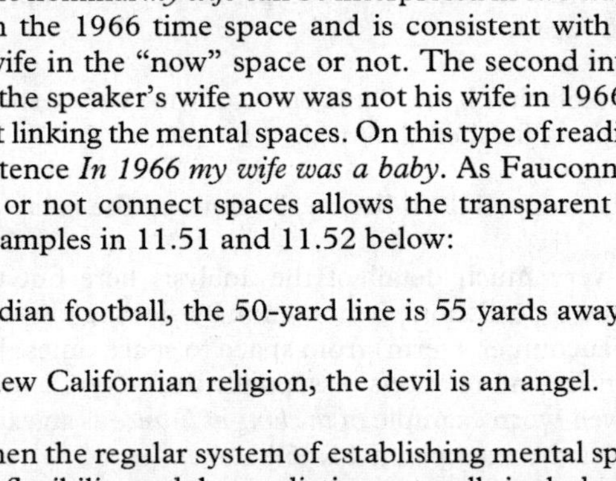

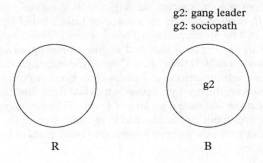

The advantage over traditional accounts, perhaps, is that this approach moves the phenomenon center-stage, so to speak, in the study of reference and predicts that such ambiguities are very widespread and regular.

11.6.3 Presupposition

One further advantage of the mental spaces approach is that it unifies the account of referential opacity with an analysis of **presupposition**. In our discussion of presupposition in chapter 4 we saw that one of the problematic features is the defeasibility or cancelability of presuppositions. Thus, for example, sentence 11.53a below has the presupposition 11.53b, but this is canceled in 11.53c by the added clause:

11.53 a. John hasn't stopped smoking.
b. John used to smoke.
c. John hasn't stopped smoking, because he never smoked.

We saw that presuppositions can be canceled by various kinds of contextual information, including general background knowledge. We used examples like 11.54 and 11.55 below, where the presupposition trigger *before* in 11.54a produces the presupposition in 11.54b, while in 11.55 no such presupposition is produced because of what we know about death:

11.54 a. Aunt Lola drank the whole bottle of wine before she finished the meal.
b. Aunt Lola finished the meal.

11.55 Aunt Lola dropped dead before she finished the meal.

We won't go into very much detail of the analysis here but the mental spaces approach explains the cancellation phenomenon by viewing presuppositions as moving ("floating" in Fauconnier's term) from space to space unless blocked by contradiction with the entities and relations (essentially the facts) identified in a space.

We can take the well-worn example of *the king of France* as an example. Fauconnier (1994: 101) discusses the example in 11.56 below:

11.56 Luke believes that it is probable that the king of France is bald, even though in fact there is no king of France.

Here we have three mental spaces: we begin with the first parent space of the speaker's reality *R*; then *believe* sets up a space of Luke's belief *B*; and *probable* sets up another space *P*. The presupposition *There is a king of France* originates in *P* from the sentence *The king of France is bald* and is thus a presupposition of *It is probable that the king of France is bald.* It then "floats" up to the encompassing parent space *B* and thus becomes a presupposition of *Luke believes that it is probable that the king of France is bald.* However, the presupposition is blocked from floating into the space *R* by the explicit clause *in fact there is no king of France.* The advantage of this analysis is that though the presupposition is blocked in *R* and therefore for the sentence as a whole, the analysis shows how it remains associated with parts of the sentence which relate to other spaces.

The floating or sharing of presuppositions between spaces is possible because of a general similarity principle, or laziness principle, of space creation, which Fauconnier calls optimization, as defined below:

11.57 Optimization (Fauconnier 1994: 91)
When a daughter space *M* is set up within a parent space *R*, structure *M* implicitly so as to maximize similarity with *R*. In particular, in the absence of explicit contrary stipulation, assume that
a. elements in *R* have counterparts in *M*,
b. the relations holding in *R* hold for the counterparts in *M*, and
c. background assumptions in *R* hold in *M*.

Though this is only an initial stab at such a principle, we can see that it must operate in all space building and thus not only explains the sharing of presuppositions across mental spaces but also explains why in counterfactuals like 11.58 below:

11.58 If I were rich, I'd move from Ireland to a Caribbean island.

we assume in the hypothetical space that the world is pretty much the same as in reality except for the speaker's increased wealth. We don't assume for example that Caribbean islands change to acquire Ireland's climate.[16]

Given such a principle and the mechanism of presupposition floating, it is a straightforward prediction of this approach that all kinds of knowledge about a parent space, say reality, can cancel an incompatible presupposition.

11.6.4 Conceptual integration theory

Conceptual integration theory, or **conceptual blending**, is a development of mental spaces theory which, taking on board aspects of the notion of conceptual metaphor, seeks to account for speakers' abilities to create and develop extended analogies. In cognitive semantic terms this ability involves speakers taking knowledge from different domains of experience, viewed as mental spaces, and combining them to create a new analogy. Conceptual blending involves the creation of a relationship between four or more mental spaces. In the simplest case two of them are input spaces which combine conceptual structures that will contribute to resulting output structure. A third space, the generic space, represents a schematic structure abstracted from both input spaces. The bringing together of these spaces creates an output, the blended space that contains new conceptual structure. This can be represented in a diagram like figure 11.18, where the solid lines represent the cross-space correspondences that constitute the mapping between the input spaces, and the dotted lines represent projections between spaces. The pattern of links shows that some elements of the input spaces correspond to each other in the blended space while other elements project independently from the input spaces to the blended space.

Fauconnier and Turner (2002) discuss an application of this, the counterfactual example below:

11.59 If Clinton had been the *Titanic*, the iceberg would have sunk.

Figure 11.18 Conceptual integration network

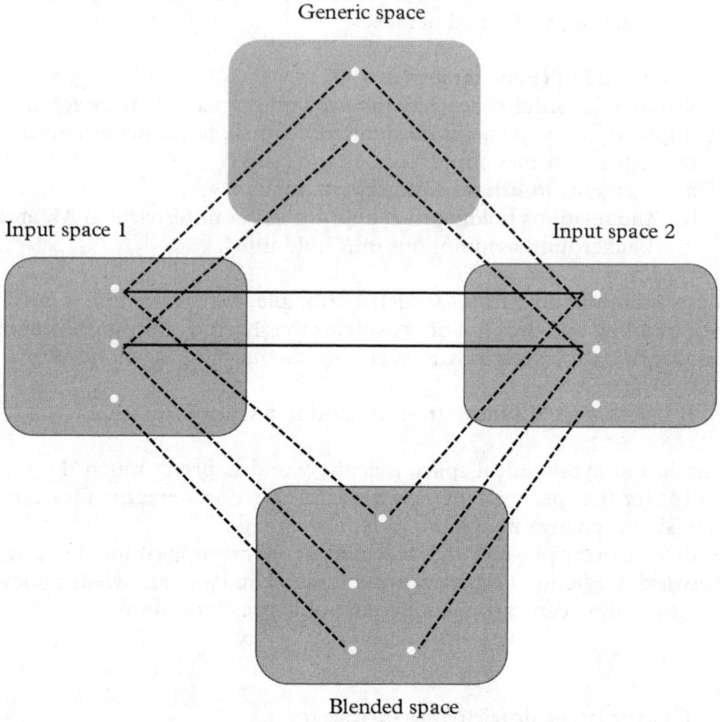

This example from the time of US president Clinton's administration is a joke that works by linking knowledge about the scandals of the Clinton years with the well-known episode of the sinking of the ship, the *Titanic*. These two domains of knowledge are characterized as mental spaces that act as input to the created blend where Clinton becomes the counterpart of the *Titanic*, and the scandals the iceberg. In this blend the first input space contains knowledge about Clinton, threatened by scandals but surviving; the second contains knowledge about the sinking of the *Titanic*. The generic space contains a schema about an entity experiencing threats. The blended space links elements from these domains to create a new scenario, where, far from being harmed, the Clinton-*Titanic* sinks the scandal-iceberg, reversing the causal relationship between the ship and the iceberg (Fauconnier and Turner 2002: 222). An important feature of blends such as this is that they create material that is not in any of the input spaces; and speakers can elaborate the blend as far as they wish. This is often referred to as the blend's emergent structure.

Fauconnier and Turner (1998) propose a number of principles that constrain the creation of conceptual blends. Grady et al. (2007: 425–26) describe them as follows:

11.60 Principles of Conceptual Integration

a. Integration:
The scenario in the blended space should be a well-integrated scene.

b. Web:
Tight connections between the blend and the inputs should be maintained, so that an event in one of the input spaces, for instance, is construed as implying a corresponding event in the blend.
c. Unpacking:
It should be easy to reconstruct the inputs and the network of connections, given the blend.
d. Topology:
Elements in the blend should participate in the same sorts of relations as their counterparts in the inputs.
e. Good reason:
If an element appears in the blend, it should have meaning.
f. Metonymic tightening:
Relations between elements from the same input should become as close as possible in the blend.

Grady et al. (2007: 426) suggest that these principles are flexible and combine under tension in the creation of a blend. They reflect the cohesion and dynamism of successful blends.

Example (11.59) above is taken to be merely a striking and original example of a much more general process.[17] Fauconnier and Turner (1996, 1998) discuss another example: of a present-day philosophy professor positioning his views relative to Immanuel Kant's by an imaginary debate:

11.61 I claim that reason is a self-developing capacity. Kant disagrees with me on this point. He says it's innate, but I answer that that's begging the question, to which he counters, in *Critique of Pure Reason*, that only innate ideas have power. But I say to that, what about neuronal group selection? He gives no answer.

This is taken as a more everyday example of conceptual integration. The input spaces contribute information about the speaker on the one hand, and Kant on the other, but the blended space has its own emergent features. These include the debate, particularly the fact that the contemporary philosopher and Kant, who lived 1734–1804 and wrote his works in German, are engaging with each other at the same point in time and using the same language, English.

Conceptual blending theory has been applied to a variety of linguistic processes from the formation of lexical blends, such as *hacktivist* and *infobesity*, and lexical compounds, such as *bank deserts* and *digital wildfire*, to the creation of proverbs (Andersson 2013), for example, *Necessity is the mother of invention*, jokes (Coulson 2001), advertisements (Joy et al. 2009), fiction (Dancygier 2012) and literary language in general (Turner 2006). There is a growing literature on blending as cognitive semanticists have sought to identify the sub-processes involved in the creation of blends. These include processes of composition, where the speaker creates links between spaces, in our example by links of identity; of completion, where speakers can bring in and rely on knowledge from the relevant spaces; and of elaboration, where the blend's innovative structure is developed and new inferences formed (Fauconnier and Turner 2008). As with metaphor earlier, blending is proposed as a cognitive process that is more general than language: blending has been identified in non-linguistic areas such as rituals (Sweetser 2000).

11.6.5 Section summary

At this point we must leave our discussion of mental spaces. From our brief view of this theory, we can see that in proposing these mental structures, Fauconnier has created a procedural view of the creation of meaning, where very simple processes of space formation and linking are triggered by the linguistic input and combine to allow the participants considerable flexibility in the manipulation of reference and knowledge about domains. The diagrams we have seen in this section are a form of notation which helps us to view these various referential strategies as a unified phenomenon. As such, of course, these are still linguistic tools, which presumably must be translated into realistic psychological models. As we have seen, one advantage of this approach is that it firmly situates referential opacity and belief contexts in a family of regular linguistic processes. Thus they are not seen as irregular or exceptional features of languages but as part of the wonderful referential flexibility allowed to speakers by the semantic structures of their languages. The theory has been applied to a variety of other areas including tense, mood, and counterfactuals; see Fauconnier (1997) for details. An important development is conceptual blending theory, a dynamic model of how speakers selectively integrate elements of input spaces to create novel blended spaces; this is applied to a wide range of linguistic and cognitive processes in Fauconnier and Turner (2002). In the next section we look briefly at Ronald W. Langacker's theory of Cognitive Grammar, which identifies a range of other cognitive processes important in language.

11.7 Langacker's Cognitive Grammar

Ronald W. Langacker (especially 1987, 1991, 1999, 2002, 2008, 2009) has proposed a theory called Cognitive Grammar that has been very influential in the development of the cognitive linguistics approach. As we have noted at several points, this theory makes no distinction between grammar and semantics. The lexicon, morphology and syntax are all seen as symbolic systems. A linguistic sign is in this view a mapping or correspondence between a semantic structure and a phonological structure. This is a familiar view of lexical items but Langacker views grammar in the same light. Grammatical categories and constructions are also symbols. This may sound no different than the basic assumption of all linguists who rely on the notion of compositionality: sentences are articulated groupings of words, which are sound–meaning mappings. However, Langacker differs from the structuralist and formalist grammatical traditions, in viewing larger structures as directly symbolic in the same way as words. Moreover, in a departure from the traditional view of levels of analysis, items at all levels of the grammar are characterized in the same conceptual terms. This is a view we shall see developed further in section 11.8 when we discuss Construction Grammar.

We can outline some important features of this approach, beginning by looking at how the categories of noun and verb are characterized in semantic/conceptual terms, and related to a cognitive account of clause structure. Thereafter we move on to look at the importance of construal in this theory.

11.7.1 Nouns, verbs, and clauses

In this theory linguistic categories reflect conceptual models, such as the idealized cognitive models (ICMs) we discussed in section 11.2.1. Among such models Langacker identifies a naive world-view that he calls the **billiard-ball model**. This is a view or theory of reality that incorporates concepts of space, time, energy, and matter. He describes it as follows:

11.62 These elements are conceived as constituting a world in which discrete objects move around in space, make contact with one another, and participate in energy interactions. Conceptually, objects and interactions present a maximal contrast, having opposite values for such properties as domain of instantiation (space vs. time), essential constituent (substance vs. energy transfer), and the possibility of conceptualizing one independently of the other (autonomous vs. dependent). Physical objects and energetic interactions provide the respective prototypes for the noun and verb categories, which likewise represent a polar opposition among the basic grammatical classes. (Langacker 1991: 283)

Thus the linguistic categories of noun and verb are characterized in terms of a cognitive model, a conceptual partitioning of reality. Though the quotation above identifies physical objects as the prototypical nouns, the crucial cognitive process is the bounding of a portion of experience to create a thing distinct from its surroundings. So nouns may describe time-stable states and of course may describe processes or "interactions" normally identified by verbs, as in *his arrival among us* or *dieting is bad for you*. This characterization emphasizes that the conditions for something being a noun are not objectively out in the world but a product of cognitive processes and a communicative decision.

The model in 11.62 extends naturally to the characterization of the prototypical transitive clause. Langacker describes this from the viewpoint of a speaker wanting to communicate a description of an event or scene. The initial identification of a scene is described (1987: 6) as the "chunking into discrete events of temporally contiguous clusters of interactions observed within a setting." The tasks of a describer in this account include distinguishing between the occurrence and the setting, establishing a vantage point, determining what types of entities are to be interpreted as participants and identifying their forms of interaction. A schema of a canonical transitive event is given in figure 11.19.

In this schema the viewer, shown as V, is outside the setting and thus is not a participant, making this a third-person report of an event. The viewer identifies three elements in an **action chain**: an asymmetrical relationship where energy is transmitted from one entity to a second entity, and in this case on to a third. In figure 11.19 the energy transfer is shown as a double-shafted arrow, and the wavy arrow in the PATIENT represents the change of state within this entity caused by the interaction. This schema describes a prototypical case where energy originates with an AGENT and ends with a PATIENT, via an intermediate entity the INSTRUMENT.

Figure 11.19 Prototypical event schema

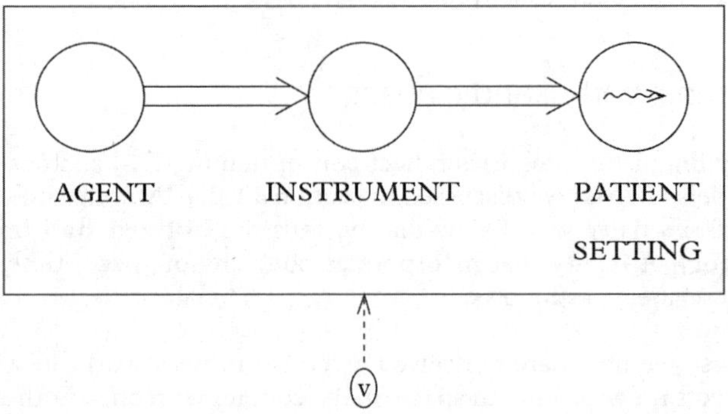

Source: Based on Langacker (1990: 209ff.)

Thereafter, in choosing to talk about this scene the speaker is faced with a number of choices. An important emphasis in this theory is on the speaker's active characterization of scenes, employing the conventional conceptualizations of language and a range of cognitive processes. A general term for these processes is **construal**: as we mentioned earlier, a basic tenet of cognitive linguistics is that speakers can construe a scene in alternative ways. We will now discuss some aspects of this choice of construal.

11.7.2 Construal

One type of construal discussed by Langacker is **profiling**: within the action chain the speaker can choose to profile certain segments of the chain. We can use Langacker's (2008: 369) example of *Floyd broke the glass with a hammer* to illustrate the possibilities below, where each sentence profiles a different part of the depicted action chain:

11.63 a. Floyd broke the glass with a hammer. $\mathbf{AG_S} \Rightarrow \mathbf{INSTR} \Rightarrow \mathbf{PAT_O} \rightarrow$
b. The hammer broke the glass. $AG_S \Rightarrow \mathbf{INSTR_S} \Rightarrow \mathbf{PAT_O} \rightarrow$
c. The glass broke. $AG_S \Rightarrow INSTR \Rightarrow \mathbf{PAT_S} \rightarrow$

We can see here Langacker proposing his own version of the mapping hierarchies we saw in chapter 6 proposed by Dowty (1991) to relate thematic roles, grammatical relations and syntactic structure. This is a characterization of subjects based on the focal prominence of agents. For discussion, the reader is referred to Langacker (2008: 366–82).

Another important notion is **perspective**, which in Langacker (1987) is taken to include the notions of **viewpoint** and **focus**. This notion of perspective is a reflection of the importance that cognitivists attach to the role of the observer in scenes: in particular, the selection of the observer's viewpoint and the choice of elements to focus on. We can take as a simple example of the former the choice between external and internal viewpoints of a container, as reflected in the two interpretations of the preposition *around* in sentence 11.64 below:

11.64 The children ran around the house.

If we choose an external viewpoint of the house as a container, this sentence describes a scene where the children's motion circles the outside of the house, whereas if we choose an internal viewpoint, the children are moving around within the house's internal space.

We saw something of the linguistic implications of focus in chapter 7 and again in chapter 9, when we discussed Leonard Talmy's analysis of motion events into features including **Figure** and **Ground**, as in for example Talmy (1975, 1985). We saw there that the Figure (which Langacker terms the **trajector**) is an entity chosen to stand out in some way from the background, the Ground (called the **landmark** by Langacker). In the case of motion events, the entity which is moving with respect to stationary surroundings tends to be chosen as the Figure. The choice to focus on either Figure or Ground in a scene can have lexical significance: Talmy (1985) describes the choice in English between the verbs *emanate* and *emit* in 11.65 and 11.66 below:

11.65 The light emanated from a beacon.

11.66 The beacon emitted light.

The verb *emanate* requires the Figure as subject; while *emit* requires the Ground as subject. Talmy argues therefore that choosing the former reflects a choice of focus on the Figure; and the latter, focus on the Ground. As we saw in earlier chapters, sometimes the choice of focus involves not separate verbs but different argument structures for the same verb, as in the pairs below:

11.67 a. The bees swarmed in the field.
b. The field swarmed with bees.

11.68 a. The ice glistened in the moonlight.
b. The moonlight glistened on the ice.

For Langacker the trajector/landmark distinction is fundamental to all relational expressions, including the subject/object distinction, spatial distinctions such as X *is above* Y or Y *is below* X, and the semantics of motions verbs like *come*, *go*, *leave*, and *enter*.

There are other related processes of construal proposed in this theory, for example **scanning** (Langacker 1987: 101–05), by which speakers are able to structure a scene in order to form a description. Langacker makes a distinction between **sequential** and **summary** scanning. These are different ways that a reporter may construe a scene. Sequential scanning is a way of viewing a process as a sequence of component sub-events. Summary scanning is a way of viewing a process as a complete unit where all its sub-events are viewed as an integrated whole. Langacker proposes that this difference is reflected in grammar in a number of ways including a speaker's decision to use a noun or a verb to describe an event. So someone going into a room or falling off a cliff can be viewed in sequential mode and described verbally as in the a sentences in 11.69–70 below, or be viewed in summary mode and described with nominals as in the b versions:

11.69 a. Keegan entered the room.
b. Keegan's entrance into the room

11.70 a. Wheeler fell off the cliff.
b. Wheeler's fall from the cliff

Langacker uses an analogy to bring out the difference between these modes: sequential scanning is like viewing a motion picture sequence while summary scanning is like viewing a still photograph.

These examples of viewpoint, focusing, profiling and scanning reveal the importance attached in this theory, and in cognitive linguistics generally, to the role of the speaker's construal of a situation in determining meaning.

11.8 Construction Grammar

Construction Grammar (CG) developed from work by cognitive linguists such as Lakoff (1987), Fillmore et al. (1988), Langacker (1987, 1991) and is a cognitive theory (or group of theories) that began with the recognition that grammatical constructions may map to semantic or conceptual representations in a similar way to lexical items. Fillmore et al. (1988) discussed a number of English constructions such as the comparative construction *the X-er the Y-er* as in 11.71 below and analyzed in great detail the coordination construction with *let alone*, schematically *X A Y let alone B* as in 11.72 (where the capitals show intonational focus):

11.71 a. The more carefully you do your work, the easier it will be.
b. The bigger they come, the harder they fall.

11.72 a. I was too young to serve in World War TWO let alone World War ONE.
b. I barely got up in time to EAT LUNCH let alone COOK BREAKFAST.

These constructions cause problems for standard views of syntax where the verb projects the argument structure for the clause, as in the thematic role grids discussed in chapter 6. Fillmore et al.'s analysis of the meaning of such constructions shows that they have a conventional meaning that is not dependent on the verbs that occur in them. In traditional terms this would be nonstandard semantic composition. This might suggest that these constructions be treated as a form of idiom. However Jackendoff (1990, 1997) and Goldberg (1995) discuss other English constructions such as the caused-motion construction in 11.73 below, which has the schematic syntactic form SUBJ V OBJ PP and means "X causes Y to move along a path represented by the PP," and the sound-motion construction in 11.74 which has the form V PP and means "go PP while emitting sound of type W":

11.73 a. She sneezed the powder off the table.
b. The audience laughed him off the stage.

11.74 a. The car screeched around the corner.
b. The two planes roared into the night sky.

These cause the same problems for a traditional view of verb-projected argument structure. The verb *sneeze* in 11.73 a, for example, is normally intransitive, not normally causative, nor selects a Path argument. Thus the syntactic and semantic characteristics of the verb do not seem to be licensing the structure of the clause in the predictable way. In fact the verb seems to be adding a Manner component to a motion event. We could account for this by simply adding the additional senses and syntax to the specification of the verb but this would suffer the disadvantage of obliging us to do this for all verbs that can occur in this construction, and other similar ones, and also leave us with no explanation for the apparent disjunctions in meaning. The alternative strategy of treating the constructions as unanalyzable idioms is undercut both by the fact that there do seem to be semantic regularities in their construction, for instance for the examples in 11.73 the causation and motion elements of what Goldberg (1995) characterizes as a caused-motion scene, and by the productivity of these constructions. The Construction Grammar solution is to allow constructions to have meaning in themselves and thus to license argument structure.

Other constructions identified in the literature include the **resultative** in 11.75 below (Goldberg and Jackendoff 2004), which, as the schematic syntactic form SUBJ V OBJ X-COMP and means "X causes Y to become Z"; and the time-away construction in 11.76, which has the form V –NP[time period] *away*, and means "spend NP V-ing"

11.75 Isabel combed her hair dry.

11.76 Alexander danced the night away.

Here again the constructions contribute their own element of meaning instead of being entirely the compositional result of the meanings of their words.

Rather than viewing these constructions as an alternative form of mapping between form and meaning, Goldberg (2006) argues for a general **constructionist** view of language that covers all form–meaning relations. In this view all linguistic expressions from words to clauses exhibit form–meaning correspondences. In constructions larger than words the meaning is a combination of word meaning and construction meaning. Goldberg (2009: 95–96) uses the example of the verb *cook* in a range of syntactic constructions as in 11.77 below (where the constructions are named in parentheses):

11.77	a.	The chicken cooked all night.	(intransitive inchoative)
	b.	Pat cooked the steaks.	(transitive)
	c.	Pat cooked the steak well-done.	(resultative)
	d.	Pat cooks.	(deprofiled object)
	e.	Pat cooked Chris some dinner.	(ditransitive)
	f.	Pat cooked her way into the Illinois State bake-off.	(*way* construction)

Goldberg suggests that the verb *cook* adds a consistent meaning to each of these examples, of preparing food by heating, while the constructions contribute individual elements of meaning: of change of state in a; someone acting on something in b; someone causing something to change state in c; someone acting generically in d; someone intending to cause someone to receive something in e; and someone (metaphorically) moving somewhere in f. The task then is to characterize the semantic interaction between verbs and constructions that license their co-occurrence. Goldberg (1995) suggests that this involves the creation of a semantic link between the event denoted by the verb and the event denoted by the construction. Such links include semantic categories of means, manner, and result. These links allow the combination of the arguments licensed by both verb and construction. So in 11.73a the verb *sneeze* contributes manner information to the caused motion construction and while only licensing a single subject argument it occurs with two additional arguments, a direct object and a prepositional phrase that indicates the Path of the motion.

There are a number of varieties of Construction Grammar in the literature, including the Cognitive Construction Grammar we have been discussing (Goldberg 1995, 2006, 2009), the typologically oriented Radical Construction Grammar (Croft 2002) and computationally oriented Embodied Construction Grammar (Bergen and Chang 2005). A central claim of all these accounts is that there is no strict division between grammar and the lexicon: form and meaning are associated in similar ways with units of all sizes from words to sentences. As we saw in the last section, Langacker (e.g. 2008) calls these **symbolic units**; he proposes that they are arranged on a continuum of schematicity, or conversely specificity. Units at one pole are more phonologically and semantically specific, such as words, while at the other they are more abstract and schematic, such as constructions. However, the same form–meaning relation holds for all and they can be characterized in the same way.

11.9 Summary

In this chapter we have reviewed the approach known as cognitive semantics. We have seen that it includes a group of theoretical approaches that, influenced by cognitive psychology, rejects many of the assumptions and methods of what they characterize as the formal approach to language, arguably the dominant paradigm of the twentieth century. Cognitive linguists propose that linguistic structure is not qualitatively distinct from general cognitive structures and processes. In rejecting the classical theory of categories they adopt an experientialist basis for meaning. Cognitive semanticists propose that the common human experience of maturing and interacting in society motivates basic conceptual structures which make understanding and language possible. They propose a range of structures that are characterized by positing no distinction between linguistic knowledge and general or encyclopedic knowledge. These include Johnson's (1987) pre-linguistic **image schemas** and Lakoff's (1987) **radial categories** that seek to explain the polysemy of words. These notions have been developed in the subsequent literature and have been central to the description of **metaphor** and **metonymy**, both seen as general cognitive process rather than linguistic devices. We saw in Fauconnier's (1994, 1997) theory of **mental spaces** a mechanism for explaining how participants in a discourse maintain referential links, set up referential domains and regulate knowledge sharing between them. **Conceptual integration theory** (Coulson 2000, Fauconnier and Turner

2002), often called **blending** for short, seeks to account for a speaker's abilities to integrate conceptual structures in dynamic and novel ways.

In the final sections we turned to how this conceptual theory impacts on the understanding of grammar. We saw the importance in Langacker's (2008) Cognitive Grammar of the cognitive processes which underpin the speaker's construal of a scene, for example by determining **perspective**, selecting **viewpoint**, establishing **Figure-Ground focus, profiling**, and **scanning**. In Construction Grammar we saw the claim that linguistic expressions larger than words show the same form–meaning relations as words themselves. The result is the complete integration of grammar and meaning, with these form–meaning pairings being termed **symbolic assemblies** (Langacker 2008) or **constructions** (Goldberg 2006).

In earlier chapters we discussed the claim that semantic representations have to be grounded in some way, if semantic analysis is not to be simply a form of translation. In chapter 10 we saw that in formal semantics this is done by establishing denotational links with the external non-linguistic world. In this chapter we have seen that in cognitive semantics a similar grounding is sought but, not directly in reality (which in this view is not directly accessible) but in conceptual structures derived from the experience of having human bodies and of sharing in social conventions, and all that this implies.

EXERCISES

11.1 In this chapter we discussed the tendency for prepositions to exhibit **polysemy**. As we saw, within cognitive semantics this is described in terms of extension from a prototypical image schema. Below we give examples of three English prepositions: *on*, *under*, and *over*. For each set of examples discuss any differences you detect in how the preposition leads you to conceive of the spatial relations. Discuss how you could informally capture the shared meaning. Then try to use schemas like the diagrams we saw in section 11.3 to capture the distinctions you identify. (Similar examples are discussed in Lakoff 1987, Brugman 1988, and Vandeloise 1991.)

a. *on*

The camera is on the table.
The fly is on the ceiling.
The painting is on the wall.
The shoe is on my foot.
The leaves are on the tree.
The house is on fire.

b. *under*

The mechanic is under the car.
Under the wallpaper the plaster is very damp.

Our next goal is to explore under the oceans.
It can breathe under water.
We have the house under surveillance.
Try looking under "Crime Novels."

c. *over*

The horse jumped over the fence.
The boys walked over the hill.
The hawk hovered over the field.
The bridge stretches over the highway.
The runner looked over her shoulder at the following group.
He's over the worst.

11.2 In a cognitive semantic approach the uses of language in the examples below are seen as metaphorical. For each example try to identify the underlying **image schema** from the list of Containment, Path, Compulsion, and Blockage:

a. She's fallen out of love with him.
b. The director didn't let us deviate from the script.
c. They leaned on him to take a loan.
d. You can't get out of this contract if you change your mind.
e. The meeting ran smoothly to its conclusion.
f. You will have to learn how to push past the pain barrier.
g. He was blown away by her performance.
h. She's definitely headed for stardom.
i. The minimum wage will not obstruct job creation.
j. We saw a man who appeared to have stepped out of the last century.

11.3 Give example sentences in English, or any other language you know, of the **metaphors** LOVE IS A JOURNEY, IDEAS ARE OBJECTS, and TIME IS MOTION.

11.4 For the metaphors you gave in exercise 11.3, try to establish some of the systematic correspondences between the two concepts.

11.5 For any two languages you know discuss similarities and differences in conventionalized metaphors of body parts (e.g. head of a bed, hand of a watch).

11.6 Discuss the types of **metonymic relationship** involved in the use of the nominals in bold in the examples below:

a. **The BMW** is waiting for his ticket.
b. The gallery has just bought **a Monet.**
c. The demonstrators saw **Iraq** as another **Vietnam**.
d. **Brighton** welcomes careful drivers.
e. **The piano** upstairs keeps waking the baby.
f. We do all the stuff **the back office** don't do.

11.7 Provide your own examples of the following metonymic strategies:

a. CONTAINER FOR CONTENTS
b. WHOLE FOR PART
c. PART FOR WHOLE
d. CONTROLLER FOR CONTROLLED
e. OBJECT USED FOR USER

11.8 Clearly different prepositions allow different characterizations of spatial relations. However, if we compare two prepositions, say English *on* and *in*, we may find different conceptualizations chosen between individual speakers or between dialects. For example in Irish English, some people, speaking of an item of news, might say *It was* ***on*** *the newspaper yesterday*, while others might say ***in*** *the newspaper*. How would you describe the two different metaphorical strategies in this example? Below are pairs of sentences differing only in the choice of *on* and *in*. Discuss the meaning relationship between the sentences in each pair. Once again discuss whether diagrammatic schemas would help your analysis.

1 a. I heard it on the radio.
b. I heard it in the radio.
2 a. I heard it on the news.
b. I heard it in the news.
3 a. He lay on his bed.
b. He lay in his bed.
4 a. He lay on his deathbed.
b. He lay in his deathbed.
5 a. I put a new engine on the car.
b. I put a new engine in the car.
6 a. I put a new set of tires on the car.
b. I put a new set of tires in the car.
7 a. The children on the bus need to be counted.
b. The children in the bus need to be counted.

11.9 Using the theory of **mental spaces, spacebuilders,** and **referential connectors** outlined in this chapter, discuss the referential interpretations of the items in bold in the sentences below:

a. In the novel, **Hitler** wins **World War II**.
b. If **I** were **you I**'d ask **myself** "Why?"

c. On Sundays **the 8 a.m. bus** leaves an hour later.
d. In 1947 **the president** was a child.
e. In Andy Warhol's prints **Marilyn Monroe's face** keeps changing color.

11.10 Discuss the **conceptual blends** in the examples below:

a. Let's respect our Mother Earth.
b. They're digging their graves with their teeth.
c. Edinburgh is the Athens of the North.
d. Ireland is the poster child of austerity.
e. If department stores are the cathedrals of commerce, Christmas windows are the stained glass that lifts the spirits of the faithful.[18]

FURTHER READING

A lively introduction to cognitive semantics is Lakoff (1987), which has been very influential in the development of this approach. Kövecses (2002) is a book-length introduction to Conceptual Metaphor Theory. Gibbs (2008) includes an interdisciplinary collection of essays on metaphor. Benczes et al. (2011) contains articles on cognitive approaches to metonymy. Fauconnier and Turner (2002) discusses the theory of conceptual blending. Oakley and Hougard (2008) contains articles on mental spaces and conceptual integration. Langacker (2008) provides an overview of his Cognitive Grammar. There are a number of good general introductions to cognitive linguistics, in particular Croft and Cruse (2004), Ungerer and Schmid (2006), and Evans and Green (2006). Geeraerts (2006) and Evans et al. (2007) provide important selections of primary readings. Evans (2014) presents the general case for the cognitive linguistic view of language.

NOTES

1 The label *cognitive* is used in this approach in a number of related ways. Ronald W. Langacker uses the term *cognitive grammar* to describe his own and close colleagues' work, in for example Langacker (1987, 2008). George Lakoff (1988) uses *cognitive semantics* as a cover term for the work of a number of scholars including Langacker, Lakoff himself, Claudia Brugman, Mark Johnson, Gilles Fauconnier, Leonard Talmy, and Eve Sweetser, among others. References to work by these authors can be found in the end-of-chapter references. As we note, this a very varied group of scholars, working on different topics and not always sharing the same interests. However, there are unifying factors: there is an International Cognitive Linguistics Association, which publishes a journal *Cognitive Linguistics*, holds an annual conference, and links researchers who share the basic outlook we describe here. In this chapter we will use the term *cognitive semantics* in the spirit of Lakoff (1988) as a loose, inclusive term for scholars who, while they may not form a tight, coherent school of thought, do share some basic assumptions about the direction a semantic theory must take.

2 For such views see J. A. Fodor (1983) and Chomsky (1988).

3 For discussion of these aims, and a rejection of them as premature for linguistics, see Fauconnier (1994: xxviii–xlvi).
4 See Saussure (1974) for discussion.
5 Heine et al. (1991) discuss examples of such processes of grammaticalization. These include full lexical nouns becoming pronouns, e.g. (p. 35) "Latin *homo* 'person, man' to French *on* (impersonal subject pronoun), German *Mann* 'man' to *man* (impersonal subject pronoun), and Latin *persona* 'person' to French *personne* (negative pronoun, negation marker)." Another example (p. 131) is of nouns for parts of the body becoming spatial adverbs and prepositions, as in the example of Swahili, where what was historically a noun **mbele* "breast" became a noun *mbele* "front" and then an adverb "in front" as shown below:

    Gari liko mbele
    car is front
    "The car is in front, ahead."

Similar processes have been identified for a number of African languages; see Heine et al. (1991) for discussion.
6 This of course leaves open the question of the "fit" between human categorization and what is really out there in the world. The cognitivist position is consistent with a range of views. The point perhaps is that from a linguistic perspective, it is the mapping between language and conceptual structure that is crucial. Clearly conceptual structure is intimately related to perception: for example we don't have words in our ordinary vocabulary for the light wavelengths we cannot see as color, or to describe the sound waves we cannot hear. The perceptual and experiential basis of conceptual categories is an important topic of inquiry in cognitive semantics. See the relations identified in Mark Johnson (1987) for example, which we discuss in section 11.2.2.
7 A similar notion is that of *frames* in Frame Semantics (Fillmore 1985, Fillmore and Atkins 1992), which are bodies of real-world knowledge against which words are interpreted and which influenced the notion of *scripts* discussed in chapter 7.
8 Our discussion concentrates on what might be termed *corporeal* embodiment, that is the effect that characteristics of the human body may have on language, and *experiential* embodiment, the influences of the experiences an individual has had. The cognitive semantics literature also discusses *neural* embodiment, the influence of how the brain is structured, and *social* embodiment, the effects of the social purposes to which language is put and the social contexts in which it is used. See Rohrer (2007) for discussion.
9 These are equivalent to the terms **Figure** and **Ground** we met in chapter 9 in our discussion of Leonard Talmy's description of motion events (e.g. Talmy 1985).
10 Example 11.2 is from the article *300: Rise of an Empire action film assaults US box office* by Jeremy Kay in the British newspaper *The Guardian*, Monday March 10, 2014. Example 11.3 is from the article *Oscars 2014: is any director strong enough to unite the Academy?* by Tom Shone in *The Guardian*, Tuesday February 25, 2014.
11 For a discussion of this distinction between classical and Romantic views of metaphor, see the accessible overview in Hawkes (1972), and the more extended discussions in Black (1962), Ortony (1979) and Kittay (1987).
12 Given what we have already said about the cognitivist rejection of objectivist semantics, it is interesting to read the remarks of the English Romantic poet Samuel Taylor Coleridge in a letter to James Gillman, written in 1827 (cited in Hawkes 1972: 54–55):

> It is the fundamental mistake of grammarians and writers on the philosophy of grammar and language to suppose that words and their syntaxis are the immediate representatives of *things*, or that they correspond to *things*. Words correspond to thoughts, and the legitimate order and connection of words to the *laws* of thinking and to the acts and affections of the thinker's mind.

13 From *Science* magazine, volume 345, no. 6201, pp. 1106–07, September 5, 2014: "Three-part ancestry for Europeans" by Ann Gibbons.

14 The symbol * is used in example 11.39, as in historical linguistics, to identify a hypothetical reconstructed form.

15 We could of course add modern Indo-European examples like French *goûter* "taste," Spanish *gustar* "please," *gustarse* "like," etc.

16 This principle can be seen as a cognitive parallel to the notion in formal semantics of **resemblance** or **similarity** between possible worlds; see Stalnaker (1968) and Lewis (1973) for discussion.

17 This blend was striking and memorable enough to be quoted later by Clinton's successor, president George W. Bush, at the dedication of the Clinton Presidential Center in Little Rock, Arkansas (Press Release, November 18, 2004, Office of the Press Secretary, The White House, Washington DC).

18 Imogen Fox, *The Guardian* newspaper, November 9, 2007, G2, p. 18.

REFERENCES

Allwood, Jens 1999: Semantics as meaning determination with semantic-epistemic operations. In: J. Allwood and P. Gärdenfors (eds.) *Cognitive Semantics*, 1–18. Amsterdam: John Benjamins.

Anderson, M. 2003: Embodied cognition: A field guide. *Artificial Intelligence* 149: 91–130.

Andersson, Daniel 2013: Understanding figurative proverbs: a model based on conceptual blending. *Folklore* 124.1: 28–44.

Barcelona, Antonio 2011: Reviewing the properties and prototype structure of metonymy. In Benczes et al. (eds.), 7–60.

Benczes, Réka, Antonio Barcelona, and Francisco José Ruiz de Mendoza Ibáñez (eds.) 2011: *Defining Metonymy in Cognitive Linguistics: Towards a Consensus View*. Amsterdam: John Benjamins.

Bergen, Benjamin K. and Nancy Chang 2005: Embodied Construction Grammar in simulation-based language understanding. In J.-O. Östman and M. Fried (eds.), *Construction Grammar(s): Cognitive and Cross-Language Dimensions*, 147–90. Amsterdam: Johns Benjamins. (Reprinted in Evans et al. (eds.) 2007.)

Black, Max 1962: *Models and Metaphors*. Ithaca, NY: Cornell University Press.

Blank, Andreas and Peter Koch (eds.) 1999: *Historical Semantics and Cognition*. Berlin: Mouton de Gruyter.

Brugman, Claudia 1988: *The Story of Over: Polysemy, Semantics and the Structure of the Lexicon*. New York: Garland.

Brugman, Claudia and George Lakoff 1988: Cognitive topology and lexical networks. In S. Small, G. Cottrell, and M. Tanenhaus (eds.) *Lexical Ambiguity Resolution: Perspectives from Psycholinguistics, Neuropsychology and Artificial Intelligence*, 477–508. San Mateo, CA: Morgan Kaufmann.

Charles, David 2002: *Aristotle on Meaning and Essence*. Oxford: Clarendon Press.

Choi, Soonja 2006: Influence of language-specific input on spatial cognition: categories of containment. *First Language* 26.2: 207–32.

Chomsky, Noam 1988: *Language and Problems of Knowledge. The Managua Lectures*. Cambridge, MA: MIT Press.

Coulson, Seana 2000: *Semantic Leaps*. Cambridge: Cambridge University Press.

Coulson, Seana 2001: What's so funny? Conceptual blending in humorous examples. In V. Herman (ed.). *The Poetics of Cognition: Studies of Cognitive Linguistics and the Verbal Arts*. Cambridge: Cambridge University Press.

Croft, William 1993: The role of domains in the interpretation of metaphors and metonymies. *Cognitive Linguistics* 4.4: 335–70.

Croft, William 2002: *Radical Construction Grammar: Syntactic Theory in Typological Perspective.* Oxford: Oxford University Press.
Croft, William and D. Alan Cruse 2004: *Cognitive Linguistics*. Cambridge: Cambridge University Press.
Dancygier, Barbara 2012: *The Language of Stories: A Cognitive Account*. Cambridge: Cambridge University Press.
Dowty, David R. 1991: Thematic proto-roles and argument selection. *Language* 67: 574–619.
Evans, Vyvyan 2009: *How Words Mean: Lexical Concepts, Cognitive Models, and Meaning Construction*. Oxford: Oxford University Press.
Evans, Vyvyan 2014: *The Language Myth: Why Language is Not an Instinct*. Cambridge: Cambridge University Press.
Evans, Vyvyan and Melanie Green 2006: *Cognitive Linguistics: An Introduction*. Edinburgh: Edinburgh University Press.
Evans, Vyvyan, Benjamin K. Bergen and Jörg Zinken (eds.) 2007: *The Cognitive Linguistics Reader*. London: Equinox.
Fass, Dan 1991: met*: A method for discriminating metonymy and metaphor by computer. *Computational Linguistics* 17.1: 49–90.
Fauconnier, Gilles 1994: *Mental Spaces: Aspects of Meaning Construction in Natural Language*, second edition. Cambridge: Cambridge University Press.
Fauconnier, Gilles 1997: *Mappings in Thought and Language*. Cambridge: Cambridge University Press.
Fauconnier, Gilles and Mark Turner 1996: Blending as a central process of grammar. In A. Goldberg (ed.) *Conceptual Structure, Discourse, and Language*, 113–30. Stanford, CA: Center for the Study of Language and Information.
Fauconnier, Gilles and Mark Turner 1998: Conceptual integration networks. *Cognitive Science* 22.2: 133–87.
Fauconnier, Gilles and Mark Turner 2002: *The Way We Think: Conceptual Blending and the Mind's Hidden Complexities*. New York: Basic Books.
Fauconnier, Gilles and Mark Turner 2008: Rethinking metaphor. In Gibbs (ed.), 53–66.
Fillmore, Charles J. 1982: Frame semantics. In Linguistic Society of Korea (ed.), *Linguistics in the Morning Calm*, 111–38. Seoul: Hanshin.
Fillmore, Charles J. 1985: Frames and the semantics of understanding. *Quaderni di Semantica* 6.2: 222–54.
Fillmore, Charles J. and B. T. Atkins 1992: Towards a Frame-based organization of the lexicon: the semantics of RISK and its neighbors. In Adrienne Lehrer and Eva Kittay (eds.) *Frames, Fields, and Contrasts: New Essays in Semantics and Lexical Organization*, 75–102. Hillsdale, NJ: Lawrence Erlbaum.
Fillmore, Charles J., Paul Kay and Catherine O'Connor 1988: Regularity and idiomaticity in grammatical constructions: the case of *let alone*. *Language* 64: 501–38.
Fodor, Jerry A. 1983: *The Modularity of Mind*. Cambridge, MA: MIT Press.
Gärdenfors, P. 1988: Semantics, conceptual spaces and the dimensions of music. In V. Rantala, L. Rowell, and E. Tarasti (eds.), *Essays on the Philosophy of Music* (Acta Philosophica Fennica, vol. 43), 9–27. Helsinki: Philosophical Society of Finland.
Geeraerts, Dirk 1997: *Diachronic Prototype Semantics: A Contribution to Historical Lexicology.* Oxford: Clarendon Press.
Geeraerts, Dirk (ed.) 2006: *Cognitive Linguistics: Basic Readings*. Berlin: Mouton de Gruyter.
Gentner, Dedre 1983: Structure-mapping: a theoretical framework for analogy. *Cognitive Science* 7: 155–70.
Gibbs, Ronald W. (ed.) 2008: *The Cambridge Handbook of Metaphor and Thought*. Cambridge: Cambridge University Press.
Goldberg, Adele E. 1995: *Constructions: A Construction Grammar Approach to Argument Structure*. Chicago: University of Chicago Press.

Goldberg, Adele E. 2006: *Constructions at Work: The Nature of Generalization in Language*. Oxford: Oxford University Press.

Goldberg, Adele E. 2009: The nature of generalization in language. *Cognitive Linguistics* 20.1: 93–127.

Goldberg, Adele E. and Ray Jackendoff 2004: The English resultative as a family of constructions. *Language* 80: 532–68.

Grady, Joseph E., Todd Oakley, and Seana Coulson 2007: Blending and metaphor. In V. Evans, B. K. Bergen and J. Zinken (eds.) *The Cognitive Linguistics Reader*, 420–40. London: Equinox.

Hawkes, Terence 1972: *Metaphor*. London: Methuen.

Heine, Bernd and Tania Kuteva 2002: *World Lexicon of Grammaticalization*. Cambridge: Cambridge University Press.

Heine, Bernd, Ulrike Claudi and Friederike Hünnemeyer 1991: *Grammaticalization: A Conceptual Framework*. Chicago: University of Chicago Press.

Herkovits, Annette 1986: *Language and Spatial Cognition: An Interdisciplinary Study of the Prepositions in English*. Cambridge: Cambridge University Press.

Holyoak, Keith J. and Paul Thagard (1995). *Mental Leaps: Analogy in Creative Thought*. Cambridge, MA: MIT Press.

Jackendoff, Ray 1975: On belief contexts. *Linguistic Inquiry* 6.1: 53–93.

Jackendoff, Ray 1990: *Semantic Structures*. Cambridge, MA: MIT Press.

Jackendoff, Ray 1997: Twistin' the night away. *Language* 73: 534–59.

Johnson, Mark 1987: *The Body in the Mind: The Bodily Basis of Meaning, Imagination, and Reason*. Chicago: University of Chicago Press.

Johnson, Mark 1993: *Moral Imagination: Implications of Cognitive Science for Ethics*. Chicago: University of Chicago Press.

Johnson, Mark 2008: Philosophy's debt to metaphor. In Gibbs (ed.), 39–52.

Joy, Annamma, John F. Sherry, and Jonathan Deschenes 2009: Conceptual blending in advertising. *Journal of Business Research* 62: 39–49.

Kittay, Eva F. 1987: *Metaphor: Its Cognitive Force and Linguistic Structure*. New York: Oxford University Press.

Kövecses, Zoltán 2002: *Metaphor: A Practical Introduction*. Oxford: Oxford University Press.

Kövecses, Zoltán and Günter Radden 1998: Metonymy: developing a cognitive linguistic view. *Cognitive Linguistics* 9.1: 37–77.

Lakoff, George 1987: *Women, Fire, and Dangerous Things: What Categories Reveal about the Mind*. Chicago: University of Chicago Press.

Lakoff, George 1988: Cognitive semantics. In Umberto Eco, Marco Santambrogio and Patrizia Violi (eds.), *Meaning and Mental Representations*, 119–54. Bloomington and Indianapolis: Indiana University Press.

Lakoff, George 1993: The contemporary theory of metaphor. In Andrew Ortony (ed.), 202–51.

Lakoff, George and Mark Johnson 1980: *Metaphors We Live By*. Chicago: University of Chicago Press.

Lakoff, George and Mark Johnson 1999: *Philosophy in the Flesh: The Embodied Mind and its Challenge to Western Thought*. New York: Basic Books.

Lakoff, George and Rafael Núñez 2000: *Where Mathematics Comes From: How the Embodied Mind Brings Mathematics into Being*. New York: Basic Books.

Lakoff, George and Mark Turner 1989: *More than Cool Reason: A Field Guide to Poetic Metaphor*. Chicago: University of Chicago Press.

Langacker, Ronald W. 1987: *Foundations of Cognitive Grammar, Vol 1: Theoretical Prerequisites*. Stanford, CA: Stanford University Press.

Langacker, Ronald W. 1991: *Foundations of Cognitive Grammar. Vol. 2: Descriptive Applications*. Stanford, CA: Stanford University Press.

Langacker, Ronald W. 1993: Reference-point constructions. *Cognitive Linguistics* 4: 1–38.

Langacker, Ronald W. 1999: *Grammar and Conceptualization*. Berlin: Mouton de Gruyter.
Langacker, Ronald W. 2002: *Concept, Image, Symbol: The Cognitive Basis of Grammar*, second edition. Berlin: Mouton de Gruyter.
Langacker, Ronald W. 2008: *Cognitive Grammar: A Basic Introduction*. Oxford: Oxford University Press. 2008
Langacker, Ronald W. 2009: *Investigations in Cognitive Grammar*. Berlin: Mouton de Gruyter.
Langacker, Ronald W. and Eugene H. Cassad 1985: "Inside" and "outside" in Cora grammar. *International Journal of American Linguistics* 51: 247–81.
Lewis, David K. 1973: *Counterfactuals*. Oxford: Blackwell.
Mahon, Bradford Z. and Alfonso Caramazza 2013: Organization of conceptual knowledge of objects in the human brain. In Kevin N. Ochsner and Stephen Kosslyn (eds.) *The Oxford Handbook of Cognitive Neuroscience. Volume 1: Core Topics*, 554–77. Oxford: Oxford University Press.
Mervis, Carolyn. B. and Eleanor Rosch 1981: Categorization of Natural Objects. *Annual Review of Psychology* 32: 89–115.
Murphy, Gregory L. and Douglas L. Medin 1985: The role of theories in conceptual coherence. *Psychological Review* 92: 289–316.
Nunberg, Geoffrey 1978: *The Pragmatics of Reference*. Bloomington, Indiana: Indiana University Linguistics Club.
Nunberg, G. 1979: The non-uniqueness of semantic solutions: polysemy. *Linguistics and Philosophy* 3.2: 143–84.
Nunberg, G. 1995: Transfers of meaning. *Journal of Semantics* 12.2: 109–32.
Oakley, Todd and Anders Hougard (eds.) 2008: *Mental Spaces in Discourse and Interaction*. Amsterdam: John Benjamins.
Ortony, Andrew (ed.) 1979: *Metaphor and Thought*. Cambridge: Cambridge University Press.
Richards, I. A. 1936: *The Philosophy of Rhetoric*. London: Oxford University Press.
Rohrer, Tim 2007: Embodiment and experientialism. In D. Geeraerts and H. Cuyckens (eds.) *The Oxford Handbook of Cognitive Linguistics*, 25–47. Oxford: Oxford University Press.
Rosch, Eleanor 1973: Natural categories. *Cognitive Psychology* 4: 328–50.
Rosch, Eleanor 1975: Cognitive reference points. *Cognitive Psychology* 7: 532–47.
Rosch, Eleanor and Carolyn Mervis 1975: Family resemblances: studies in the internal structure of categories. *Cognitive Psychology* 7: 573–605.
Rosch, Eleanor, Carolyn Mervis, Wayne Gray, David Johnson and Penny Boyes-Braem 1976: Basic objects in natural categories. *Cognitive Psychology* 8: 382–439.
Ruiz de Mendoza Ibañez, F. J. and O. I. Díez Velasco 2002: Patterns of conceptual interaction. In R. Pörings and R. Dirven, *Metaphor and Metonymy in Comparison and Contrast*, 501–46. Berlin: Mouton de Gruyter.
Saussure, Ferdinand de 1974: *Course in General Linguistics*. Edited by Charles Bally and Albert Sechehaye, translation by Wade Baskin. Glasgow: Fontana/Collins. (First published 1915 as *Cours de Linguistique Générale*. Paris: Pyot.)
Searle, John R. 1979: Metaphor. In Andrew Ortony (ed.), 92–123.
Stalnaker, Robert 1968: A theory of conditionals. In Nicholas Rescher (ed.) *Studies in Logical Theory*. Oxford: Blackwell.
Sweetser, Eve E. 1990: *From Etymology to Pragmatics*. Cambridge: Cambridge University Press.
Sweetser, Eve E. 2000: Blended spaces and performativity. *Cognitive Linguistics* 11.3–4: 305–33.
Talmy, Leonard 1975: Semantics and syntax of motion. In John P. Kimball (ed.) *Syntax and Semantics 4*, 181–238. London: Academic Press.
Talmy, Leonard 1985: Lexicalization patterns: semantic structure in lexical forms. In Timothy Shopen (ed.) *Language Typology and Syntactic Description*, vol. 3: 57–149. Cambridge: Cambridge University Press.
Talmy, Leonard. 2000: *Toward a Cognitive Semantics*, 2 vols. Cambridge, MA: MIT Press.

Taylor, John R. 2003: *Linguistic Categorization*, third edition. Oxford: Oxford University Press.

Taylor, John R. 2008. Prototypes in cognitive linguistics. In P. Robinson and N. Ellis (eds.) *Handbook of Cognitive Linguistics and Second Language Acquisition*, 39–65. London: Routledge.

Turner, Mark 1987: *Death is the Mother of Beauty: Mind, Metaphor, Criticism*. Chicago: University of Chicago Press.

Turner, Mark 2006: *The Literary Mind*. Oxford: Oxford University Press.

Ungerer, Friedrich and Hans-Jörg Schmid 2006: *An Introduction to Cognitive Linguistics*, second edition. London: Longman.

Vandeloise, Claude 1991: *Spatial Prepositions: A Case Study from French*. Chicago: University of Chicago Press.

Winters, Margaret E., Heli Tissari and Kathryn Allan (eds.) 2010: *Historical Cognitive Linguistics*. Berlin: Mouton de Gruyter.

Wittgenstein, Ludwig 1953: *Philosophische Untersuchungen/ Philosophical Investigations*. (Translated by G. E. M. Anscombe). Oxford: Blackwell.

Yee, Eiling, Evangelia G. Chrysikou, and Sharon L. Thompson-Schill 2013: Semantic memory. In Kevin N. Ochsner and Stephen Kosslyn (eds.) *The Oxford Handbook of Cognitive Neuroscience. Volume 1: Core Topics*, 353–74. Oxford: Oxford University Press.

Solutions to Exercises

Many of the chapter exercises ask readers to reflect on their own language use and to imagine scenarios involving verbal communication. As a result we can predict a lot of variation in responses. The solutions that follow should therefore be taken as illustrative and representative rather than exclusively the correct ones.

CHAPTER 1

1.1 We can divide the compounds into two groups:

Semantically transparent	**Semantically non-transparent**
businessman	agony aunt
bus stop	blackmail
climate change	boyfriend
daydream	eye candy
doormat	firsthand
foxhound	flea market
horseshoe	gravy train
houseboat	greenhouse
human being	hotdog
mailbox	housewife
mousetrap	monkey business

Semantically transparent	**Semantically non-transparent**
shopping list	nightmare
speed limit	redhead
sunglasses	software
video game	spin doctor
	sweatshop
	taste bud

You may not agree with this division: it depends on your own judgment. One important issue is whether the compound is being used literally or not. For example *doormat* can be used literally for a mat at the door, where it seems transparent, or figuratively for a passive person, where it does not.

For the transparent group, we can suggest a couple of structures: one is of qualifier-head, Y–X, where the compound is *a type of X used for/as Y*. So *houseboat* is a type of boat used like a house, for living in. *Mailbox* is a type of box for mail. This pattern also seems to apply to *bus stop, doormat, foxhound, horseshoe, mousetrap, shopping list*, and *sunglasses*. Another similar pattern is where the qualifier Y assigns an attribute to X that subdivides X, i.e. *an X that is Y*. This seems to fit compounds like *human being, climate change, daydream, speed limit*, and *video game*, which we could say identify specific types of the head noun. This leaves *businessman*, which is a part of an occupational group with *businesswoman, postman, policeman*, etc., which does not quite fit either of these two suggested patterns. These compounds, where both Y and X are nouns, have three main patterns: (a) where X works in or controls Y (*businessman, fireman, gasman, postman*); (b) where X sells, delivers or makes Y (*milkman, newspaperman*); and (c) where X belongs to a professional group named by Y (*policeman, seaman, clergyman*). These are part of a larger and very old system of English compounds ending in *–man*; see Peitsara (2006) for more details.

1.2 This exercise just asks you to provide a definition for each word. My definition for *sabre*, for example, would simply be *a kind of sword*. This wouldn't help me distinguish between it and the other type of sword, *rapier*. To do any better I would have to use a dictionary. This might tell me that a sabre is a heavy sword with a curved blade, while a rapier is a sword with a long slender blade. Similarly my definitions of *yew* "dark-green evergreen tree" and *oak* "large deciduous tree," based on local species, are not very informative. My definition of *copper* is an orange-colored metal and *bronze* is an alloy that contains copper, though I would need to look up the other metal(s) involved. *Vodka* and *gin* are separated in my personal knowledge base by the juniper used to flavor gin and associations with different countries. *Hay* is used for feeding animals and *straw* for bedding or flooring but their plant origins are rather a mystery to me, as an urban dweller. The conclusion we might draw is that speakers may use words without having much encyclopedic knowledge about their extensions.

1.3 a. *This schedule is crazy*: when this sentence is uttered, the nominal *this schedule* would typically be a referring expression, because the speaker would be identifying a specific schedule. The referring expressions in b are *she, herself* and *the party*. In c: *a policeman, your car*. In d: *the script*. In e: *you, this*.

1.4 a. Context is required to select the intended sense of *shot*, which among its senses could relate to firing a gun, a scoring attempt in a sport like soccer or golf, a view from a specific camera angle, a small glass of strong alcoholic drink, etc. The selected sense of *shot* determines the meaning of *take*. So contextual knowledge is required to disambiguate the words.

b. Although in print the capital letters give a clue that *Tigers* and *Bulldogs* are names, this would not be evident in speech. Even so, situational knowledge is needed to identify the referents of these expressions, such as college football teams.

c. As with the last example, contextual knowledge is needed to determine who the name *Isabel* is being used to identify. In addition *tall* is a gradable adjective that needs some kind of contextual scale to be evaluated: is Isabel tall for a child or an adult basketball player?

d. Contextual knowledge is needed to determine the location identified by the adverb *here*. The expression *too hot*, containing the gradable adjective *hot*, has to be evaluated against a contextually assumed purpose. This could simply be "too hot to be comfortable" but could be any assumed activity.

e. As with gradable adjectives, quantifiers need some contextual modification based on the knowledge of the participants. *Everyone* is clearly not intended to mean everyone in the world and so must be understood relative to a group known to the speaker and audience.

1.5 Each of these examples involves a metaphorical use of language.

a. The expression *glass ceiling* is a metaphorical way of referring to covert barriers to promotion or advancement, introduced originally with reference to women but used subsequently for other groups. The metaphor has been used since the 1970s so is relatively conventionalized.

b. Metaphors characterizing economic issues as war are frequent (for example *trade wars*). Here a future economic crisis is metaphorically viewed as a bomb, specifically a time bomb, suggesting the threat is already present and inexorable. The metaphor sets up a chronological parallel between the aging process and the bomb's timing device.

c. Here the metaphor creates an analogy between the passage of a parliamentary bill and childbirth. The choice of metaphor is given an extra dimension by the fact that the bill is related to laws governing abortion in Ireland.

d. *In the dock* is an idiomatic way of describing being on trial in (an English-style) court. It is a conventional metaphor for being subject to critical scrutiny.

e. The nautical metaphor *throw a lifeline* is conventionalized for helping someone. In chapter 11 we discuss the idea that metaphors can become conventionalized to the point that they lose their figurative value and become dead metaphors. This example also includes metonymy, where the European Commission is identified by its location, Brussels, and *Spain* is used for the Spanish government.

CHAPTER 2

2.1 a. *We waited for twelve hours at* ***Nairobi airport***. If this sentence is spoken, the speaker would be using the expression *Nairobi airport* to refer, since she would be using it to identify a specific place.

b. *No food* is non-referring.

c. *A pair of shoes* is being used as a referring expression.
d. *A cake* is non-referring.
e. *A whirlwind* is non-referring.
f. *A bus* is used as a referring expression.
g. *An army of volunteers* is non-referring.

2.2 a. *The Senator paid a visit to* ***the Ukrainian capital***. We could replace the nominal in bold with an alternative, the name *Kiev*. The sentence *The Senator paid a visit to Kiev* could be used to describe the same event.
b. In 2015, David Cameron.
c. December 25th.
d. The capital of the United States.
e. Mount Everest.

2.3 The following are basically mass nouns: *milk, weather, warmth, blood.*
Milk and *blood* can be used with implicit units of measurement as in ordering *two milks* in a café, or doctors *taking bloods* in a hospital.
The count nouns are: *table, dog, hand, word.*
Two nouns seem to be equally used as mass and count nouns: *difficulty* (*We experienced difficulty/many difficulties*) and *talk* (*There was too much talk/We attended several talks*).

2.4 a. Leaving aside any cooks who might be reading this, the uninitiated might wish to distinguish *cake* from *biscuit* (British)/*cookie* (US) by attributes of shape, size and consistency. Typically a biscuit or cookie is flatter, harder and usually smaller than a cake; and perhaps drier or crisper. A *cracke*r might be an especially thin and crispy biscuit. Some are sweet, others not. Thereafter, though we each might have a considerable history of eating these items, further necessary and sufficient conditions might prove hard to determine. These words are of course subject to wide regional variation across the English-speaking world.
b. You might decide that these cooking terms can be divided according to **heating medium**: air (*bake, grill, roast*); water (*boil, simmer*) and oil/fat (*fry, sauté*); **direction of heat**: from below, i.e. up (*boil, fry, sauté, simmer*), above, i.e. down, (*grill*, at least in some uses, up in others); and surrounding, i.e. around, (*bake, roast*); and **intensity**: differing amounts of heat in *boil* vs. *simmer* and *sauté vs. fry*. These features work to some extent, but cannot distinguish between *bake* and *roast*. You might try to come up with features to distinguish these. Nor does the feature **intensity** work very well: sautéing implies high heat, short duration and relatively little fat, which is a poor parallel to the *boil/simmer* distinction. The feature does not seem to apply in a binary way to the other terms, which can have variable heat without changing the term. Thus even a small set of related terms seems difficult to define precisely with necessary and sufficient conditions.

2.5 a. A possible list of characteristic features for the prototype of the concept FRUIT might be: PRODUCED BY FLOWERS OF PLANTS, CONTAINS SEEDS, TASTES SWEET. More typical members might be: orange, apple, peach, and cherry. Less typical members might be: tomatoes, olives, and avocadoes.

b. MAMMAL: ANIMAL, WARM-BLOODED, HAIRY/FURRY, FEEDS MILK TO YOUNG. More typical: dog, cat, sheep, mouse. Less typical: dolphin, whale.
c. FOOD: SUBSTANCE, PEOPLE AND ANIMALS CONSUME IT, GIVES ENERGY, HELPS GROWTH. Typicality: In chapter 11 we will see convincing arguments that all conceptual categories are conditioned by culture. This seems especially true of the category of food, where we would expect that typicality judgments would vary across cultures. Thus, for some groups insects would be less typical members of this category.
d. TOY: ARTIFACT, FOR CHILDREN'S PLAY, SMALL. More typical: dolls, soft animal figures, blocks, model vehicles. Less typical: ant farms, executive toys.
e. SPORT: ACTIVITY, INVOLVES EXERCISE, INVOLVES SKILL, INVOLVES COMPETITION, NOT INTENTIONALLY HARMFUL. More typical: football, basketball, athletics. Less typical: chess, billiards, ballooning.

CHAPTER 3

3.1 In this exercise speakers have to balance their intuitions about semantic relatedness with what they know, or might guess, about the history of these words. As a result, speakers differ in grouping the senses into lexical entries. In some cases editorial policy means that dictionaries will differ too.

a. In judging the **port** examples, speakers readily group **port**^{1} and **port**^{2} together; and may perhaps feel that **port**^{4} stands alone. Speakers who know Portuguese or Latin may use **port**^{4} to raise the issue of the role of loan words in a language since *o porto* means "the port" in Portuguese and derives from Latin *portus* "harbor, port," which is also the source of **port**^{1} and **port**^{2}. Many dictionaries identify four lexical entries: 1 **port**^{1} and **port**^{2}; 2 **port**^{3}; 3 **port**^{4}; 4 **port**^{5} and **port**^{6}.
b. **Mold**: Typically three separate entries.
c. **Pile**: Typically three entries: 1 **pile**^{1} and **pile**^{3}; 2 **pile**^{2} and **pile**^{5}; 3 **pile**^{4} and **pile**^{6}.
d. **Ear**: Typically two entries: 1 **ear**^{1} and **ear**^{2}; 2 **ear**^{3}.
e. **Stay**: Some dictionaries have three entries: 1 **stay**^{1} and **stay**^{2}; 2 **stay**^{3}; 3 **stay**^{4} and **stay**^{5}. Others select **stay**^{5} as a separate fourth entry.

3.2 a. The pair *safe/secure*. An example of a difference in predicative use is: *His seatbelt is secure* has a different meaning than *His seatbelt is safe*. Another example might be: *The beach is safe* versus *The beach is secure*. An attributive example might be: *a secure lock* versus *a safe lock*.
b. *quick/fast*. Collocation: *Fast food* vs. *quick food*.
c. *near/close*. Attributive vs. predicate: *His close friends/His friends are close. It was a near miss. The miss was near.* Collocation: *Close friends* vs. *near friends. A near miss* vs. *?a close miss*.
d. *dangerous/perilous*. Collocation: *A dangerous animal* vs. *a perilous animal*.
e. *wealthy/rich*. Collocation: The temptation here is to move to one of the different senses of *rich*: *rich food, rich colors, rich soil*, etc. It is only in its meaning of having much money (rather than taste, etc.) that *rich* is a synonym of *wealthy*. Example: *get-rich-quick* vs. *get-wealthy-quick*.

f. *fake/false*. Collocation: these are not close synonyms, since *fake* has an association with deceit, e.g. *a fake diamond* vs. *a false diamond* and *false eyelashes* vs. *fake eyelashes*. Also *false teeth* vs. *fake teeth*.
g. *sick/ill*. Collocation: *sick building* vs. *ill building*; *sick room* vs. *ill room*.
h. *light/bright*. Collocation: these are not close synonyms, each having a distinct range of senses, overlapping in examples like *light as day/bright as day*.
i. *mad/insane*. Collocation: *insane* has more formal uses, hence *insane asylum* vs. *mad asylum*; *legally insane* vs. *legally mad*.
j. *correct/right*. Collocation: where their senses overlap, *correct* is more formal, hence *Is this sentence grammatically correct?* vs. *Is this sentence grammatically right?* Also *correct language* vs. *right language*.

3.3 **Case (noun):**

1 Ellipsis: *be so* identity. Example: *Jim was given a new case and so was his partner*. This exercise uses verb phrase ellipsis to test for ambiguity. If we imagine that Jim and his partner are police detectives, it wouldn't be usual to understand by this sentence that, for example, Jim got a new briefcase and his partner got a new crime to investigate. We rule out of course the speaker consciously punning. So *case* seems to be ambiguous between at least these two readings.
2 Sense relations. Using the same example, *case* has a sense that might be replaced by *bag* and another that might be replaced by *investigation*. *Bag* and *investigation* are unrelated suggesting two distinct senses for *case*.
3 Zeugma: a new example provides both zeugma and a further sense for *case*: *Jim got a case of beer and of homicide*.

Fair (adjective):

1 Ellipsis: for adjectives, *be so* identity. Example: *Helen was fair and so were all her children*. If the hair- and skin-color sense of *fair* is selected for Helen it must be also for her children; and the same if the just and honourable sense is selected.
2 Sense relations: *fair* has a sense that might be replaced by *blonde* and another that might be replaced by *just*, suggesting that *fair* is ambiguous.
3 Zeugma: *The judge's hair, and her judgments, are fair*.

File (verb):

1 Ellipsis: *do so* identity. Example: *George filed for an hour and so did Brian*. Leaving aside word play again, we don't easily interpret this as one person putting documents in a file and the other smoothing something with a metal file.
2 Sense relations: *file* has a sense that can be replaced by *sort* and another by *smooth*, suggesting ambiguity.
3 Zeugma: *She filed her nails and her tax records*.

3.4 In these examples, it is helpful to think of a specific context since the lexical relation may vary across contexts. Additionally, some examples may belong to more than one word class and this may also affect our decision. For example the pair *clean/dirty* may be adjectives or verbs. The adjectives are gradable antonyms, but what about the verbs? Similarly *open/shut* are complementary antonyms as adjectives but reverses as verbs.

Complementary antonyms: temporary/permanent; open/shut, present/absent

Gradable antonyms: strong/weak; messy/neat; clean/dirty

Reverses: advance/retreat; assemble/dismantle

Converses: monarch/subject; buyer/seller

Taxonomic sisters: tea/coffee; boot/sandal

3.5 It might be useful to recall that hyponymy can be characterized as a "IS A (KIND OF)" relation. So *tulip* IS A (KIND OF) *flower* and *tulip* is therefore a hyponym of *flower*. Hyponymy like other lexical relations is sensitive to context, so it's possible that a word might be in several hyponymic relations at the same time. So, for example, if we're thinking of the animal kingdom *dog* is a hyponym of *mammal*. However, in another context it is also a hyponym of *pet*. We can perhaps think figuratively of acts of identifying hyponymy as lighting up relations in the semantic network associated with lexical concepts. For nouns it seems that between four and six levels of inclusion are generally identifiable in ordinary language, for example: *poodle* → *dog* → *mammal* → *animal*. Another example: *tangerine* → *orange* → *fruit* → *plant* (or → *food*).

3.6 The depth of inclusion for verbs is much shallower than nouns: we find examples like: *whisper* → *speak* or *jog* → *run*. In many cases the "IS A (KIND OF)" relation we find with nouns in verbs corresponds to a "IS A MANNER OF" So jogging is a way of running, whispering is a way of speaking, etc. Fellbaum (1998) describes how, because of this, a distinct term **troponymy** is used for verbal hyponymy in the WordNet project.

3.7 An intransitive meronymy might be *handle* → *door* → *house*. A handle is a part of a door and a door is part of a house, but this chain lacks transitivity because it would sound odd to say that a house has handles. Similarly *arm* → *hand* → *finger* → *nail* where we might hesitate to say that arms have nails. A transitive meronymy is *car* → *wheel* → *tire*.

3.8 An important issue in this exercise is semantic transparency. While it should be possible to call something that chokes a *choker*, in fact this word is in use for a necklace, or ribbon worn around the neck. This probably derives historically from the agentive noun, used as slang, as a humorous description of a neckerchief worn high around the throat. However, this may no longer be evident to speakers. Similarly *blinker* has one transparent sense, something or someone who blinks, but the use for something that flashes light on and off is less predictable and is listed in dictionaries. Another sense of *blinker*, side flap on a horse's bridle to restrict its view, is not semantically transparent and derivable by rule. So we have three classes:

Not identifiably agentive: author, blazer, debtor, loner, mentor

Agentive nouns with both transparent and non-transparent meanings: choker, blinker

Agentive nouns with plausibly rule-derived meanings: crofter, reactor, roller

3.9 The nouns in group a are regularly related to nouns ending in *-ism*, e.g. *socialist: socialism*. So an *X-ist* holds the beliefs of *X-ism*. We find other examples like *pacifist* and *nationalist*. There is also an extended use where the beliefs involve discrimination against particular groups of people, e.g. *racism* and *sexism*. The nouns in group b are split between regular forms where *X-ist* means *person who produces X*, i.e. *artist, novelist, satirist* and *scientist*, and a second group that are not semantically transparent: *chemist* and *dentist*. This is because these words were borrowed from French: *dentist* from *dentiste* (from *dent* "tooth") and *chemist* in the sixteenth century from *chimiste*, from earlier Latin *alchimisa* (itself borrowed from Arabic).

3.10 1 The verb in b, *rise* is inchoative, describing a change of state. The verb *raise* is the corresponding causative verb, meaning "to cause to rise."
2 The verbs *send* and *receive* are converses.
3 In normal conversational contexts saying sentence a, *Ethel tried to win the cookery contest,* communicates the negative of sentence b, i.e. that she didn't succeed in winning it. In chapter 7 we will see attempts to view this meaning as a kind of contextual inference.
4 *Tie* and *untie* are reverses.
5 *Damage* and *repair* are in an opposition that is reminiscent of reverses but doesn't strictly entail the same processes. Cruse (1986) names this kind of opposition *restitutive*, as in other pairs like *remove/replace*. One term, the restitutive (here *repair*), seems to presume the action of the other, the degrading term (here *damage*).
6 *Fear* and *frighten* describe a similar relationship from opposite viewpoints or angles so we can call them converses.
7 The meaning of *show* can be described as a causative version of *see*, i.e. as *cause to see*. Interestingly French has a compound verb *faire voir* "show" that is literally "make see."

CHAPTER 4

4.1 The truth table for ∧ is:

p	**q**	**p ∧ q**
T	T	T
T	F	F
F	T	F
F	F	F

The truth table below shows the corresponding values of **p ∧ q** in the four situations:

	p	**q**	**p ∧ q**
S1	T	F	F
S2	T	T	T
S3	F	T	F
S4	F	F	F

So **r** is false in S1, true in S2, false in S3 and false in S4.

4.2 a. This example shows that English *and* may have a sequential interpretation. We can show this by reversing the order of the clauses. *He saw on TV that he had won the lottery and woke up* describes (sadly) a different situation than *He woke up and saw on TV that he had won the lottery.*
b. Again *and* has an interpretation of sequence.
c. Here the coordinate structure with *and* has an interpretation of the second clause being a consequence or result of the first.
d. Here *and* is not simply linking an order and a statement: this structure conventionally carries the meaning of a conditional warning: If you move, I'll shoot.

4.3 This exercise asks you to make four computations for logical form (a) and four for (b). Using the two relevant truth tables in the chapter, we can show the results for (a) in the table below, determining the value of ¬ (**p** ∨ **q**) in the situations S1–S4:

	p	**q**	**p ∨ q**	**¬(p ∨ q)**
S1	T	F	T	F
S2	T	T	T	F
S3	F	T	T	F
S4	F	F	F	T

The results for the logical form (b) in the situations S1–S4 are shown in the table below:

	p	**q**	**¬p**	**¬p ∨ q**
S1	T	F	F	F
S2	T	T	F	T
S3	F	T	T	T
S4	F	F	T	T

4.4 a. This sentence seems to have an inclusive meaning, since it suggests we swim or sunbathe or do both. Assuming disjunction reduction is a little problematic with this example (though perhaps not as much as with some later examples) because the fuller version, *We spend the afternoons swimming or we spend the afternoons sunbathing* seems for some speakers to tilt towards an exclusive meaning.
b. Exclusive disjunction.
c. Inclusive disjunction.
d. Exclusive disjunction.
e. Inclusive disjunction.
f. This example does not seem to correspond to either form of disjunction: the *or* construction here conveys approximation or uncertainty.
g. In this example assuming disjunction reduction does not correctly portray the meaning of the sentence, i.e., it is not equivalent to *He doesn't smoke or he drinks.* The negation in the first clause operates over the whole sentence not just the first clause. In one interpretation it is equivalent to the

disjunction *It is not the case that he smokes or drinks*, i.e. ¬ [p∨q], which is the negation of an inclusive disjunction. A second interpretation is equivalent to conjunction: *He doesn't smoke and he doesn't drink*, i.e. [¬p] ∧ [¬q]. The latter is equivalent to the English sentence *He neither smokes nor drinks*.

h. This use of *or* does not correspond to either form of disjunction. It is used here as a marker of reformulation, to provide an alternative name.

i. As in exercise 4.2d above, here we have a conventionalized way of forming a conditional warning. This time what on the surface seems to be the disjunction of an order and a statement is in fact a warning with a negative condition equivalent to *If you do not stop I will shoot.* In chapter 8 we will discuss examples like these as indirect speech acts in Speech Act Theory.

4.5 a. If it rains, we'll get wet. This sentence is not analytically true because it is possible to think of a situation where it would not be true: for example we might be inside for the whole time it is raining.

b. Analytically true since it covers all possibilities.

c. Analytically true.

d. Analytically true because of the hyponymy relationship between *deer* and *animal.*

e. Not analytically true because the truth of this sentence does not arise from the meaning of the sentence but from the facts of the world.

f. Not analytically true: to know if this is true we have to check the facts of the world.

4.6 1 a. Olivia passed her driving test/b. Olivia didn't fail her driving test. To decide if a entails b we can use the composite truth table in the chapter:

Composite truth table for entailment

p		**q**
T	→	T
F	→	T or F
F	←	F
T or F	←	T

From this we can see that sentence a entails sentence b. Let's work it out line by line. If it is true that she passed the test, it is true that she didn't fail. If it is false that she passed her test, we can't say anything about the truth of sentence b. This is because she may not have taken the test: in this scenario it's not true that she passed, but it is also true that she hasn't failed. If it's false that she didn't fail (i.e. she failed) then she didn't pass the test; and finally if it's true that she didn't fail, then we can't say anything about the truth of the a sentence. Using the same procedure we get the following decisions:

2 a entails b.

3 a does not entail b. Here the verb tense is crucial.

4 a does not entail b unless you use the verb *poison* to mean "kill by poisoning."

5 a entails b.
6 a does not entail b because a is true when no-one likes the show. However, even though this is not entailment by our truth tests, if these sentences are uttered in normal conversational usage, b might be assumed after a because the speaker of a didn't say *No-one will like the show.* We discuss such assumptions in chapter 7 under the notion of implicature.

4.7 We can use the negation test to identify the factitive predicates in the list. For example: *He realized that it was raining* presupposes *It was raining.* If we negate the presupposing sentence to get *He didn't realize it was raining,* it still presupposes *It was raining.* Thus *realize* is factive.

Using this test the following predicates are factive:

be aware, be glad, realize, be sorry, know

4.8 1 Again we can use the negation test to identify presupposition. Both *Dave knows that Jim crashed the car* and *Dave doesn't know that Jim crashed the car* presuppose the b sentence, *Jim crashed the car.* This suggests that a presupposes b. This behavior doesn't fit the truth table for entailment, as will be clear from later examples in this exercise.
2 a entails b.
3 a presupposes b.
4 a entails b.
5 a presupposes b.

CHAPTER 5

5.1 The verb *seem* is a stative verb: we can't use it in the progressive as in "It is seeming to be raining" or "He is seeming happy." Typically, using this test the following verbs emerge as stative: *possess, resemble, lack, comprise.* The verb *think* has two senses. One, which means "have an opinion," is a stative verb. For instance, one cannot use the progressive in this example, Q: "Are you going to go to the party?" A: ? "I am not thinking so" (for "I don't think so"). The second, meaning "to perform the action of thinking" is dynamic and does occur in the progressive: Q: "What are you doing?" A: "I'm thinking." It may be possible to identify dynamic uses for the other verbs, for example *possess* when meaning "controlled by a demon or spirit."

5.2 *Admire*: An example of the stative use is "He admires courage in a woman." The dynamic use is shown in "She was admiring my new portrait." The former might be paraphrased as "have an attitude of respect or esteem toward something"; the latter as "look at or view something in an approving way."

Equal: Two and two equals four; She is equaling the record.

Appear: It appears to be raining; She is appearing in the show twice weekly.

Hold: The tank holds eight liters; He was holding his son.

Contain: Water contains oxygen; He is containing his emotions.

Reach: The spire reaches 120 meters in the air; They reached the top of the mountain.

Cost: This brand costs too much; They are costing the job.

Smell: This cheese smells bad; We smelled the flowers.

5.3 *Read* is not a punctual verb: "I was reading for an hour" usually suggests that I continued the same activity of reading for an hour. On the other hand, the verb *ring* in "The phone was ringing for an hour" suggests an iterative interpretation. Following this, the clearly punctual verbs in this group are: *tap, sigh, twitch.*

5.4 The verb phrase *ate oranges* is unbounded. This is why *Isabel ate oranges for an hour* sounds fine but *Isabel ate oranges in an hour* sounds odd. We can change this value by having as the object *an orange* instead of *oranges*: *Isabel ate an orange* is bounded. Thus *Isabel ate an orange in an hour* is fine while *Isabel ate an orange for an hour* sounds strange. The other unbounded examples are: *swim, put out fires, direct movies.* The bounded examples are: *ripen, walk to the station. Swim* can be part of a bounded predicate in examples like *swim to the buoy.*

5.5 The terminology used for these verb forms differs across different grammatical traditions and scholars. So the terms we use here are not definitive. Standard reference grammars like Quirk et al. (1985) and Huddleston and Pullum (2002) have comprehensive treatments of these.

a. Simple past.
b. Past progressive.
c. Simple present.
d. Present perfect.
e. Simple future.
f. Present progressive.
g. Future perfect.
h. Present progressive.

5.6 1 The verb in *My brother works in France* is in the simple present form, here signifying habitual action. The interpretation will be that this is the usual place for the speaker's brother to work. The verb in *My brother is working in France* is in the present progressive. It emphasizes the present moment and in the right context can imply that the situation is temporary.

2 The present progressive is the usual form for the proximate future. The simple present is used to emphasize a link between the future event and the present, for example with planned itineraries, timetables and schedules.

3 Here the simple present is the usual form with a stative verb like *look* for a state holding at the time of speaking. As mentioned earlier the progressive has features of dynamism and change which, depending on context, could mean here that the state is viewed as temporary, for example contrasted with the past, or the speaker is emphasizing the immediacy of the effect.

4, 5 These examples display aspects of the general distinction between the habitual or permanent nature of the simple present versus the temporary or dynamic quality of the progressive.

6 Here the progressive adds a dynamic link to the present moment so that in context sentence b can be used for emphasis, for example a complaint.

5.7 a. Strictly speaking the verb *could* in *This could be our bus now* signifies belief in the possibility of the situation described. In chapter 7 we discuss the ideas of Paul Grice, whose theory of conversational cooperation suggests that speakers will try to be as helpful as possible, for example, by making the strongest statement they can. In this case, the speaker's use of *could* can imply that since he or she can't offer anything stronger than possibility, there is some uncertainty in the speaker. In context this then can be a weaker form of "I think that's our bus now."

b. *Would* marks a confident prediction about a potential situation.

c. *Must* marks a conclusion based on some evidence.

d. *Should* marks a prediction, i.e. epistemic modality. However, a possible reading here is of a statement of obligation to rules, perhaps a timetable, which can be viewed as deontic modality.

e. *Might* marks a judgment of possibility.

f. *Will* marks the speaker's strong confidence, but not certain knowledge, about the situation.

5.8 a. In the epistemic reading of the sentence *Alcohol may not be served to persons under twenty-one* the speaker is expressing this as a possibility. A context for this might be where there are two age limits for alcohol consumption, 18 years and 21 years. The speaker could use this sentence to show they are not sure whether the upper limit will apply. In its deontic reading, this sentence might be an order or instruction. A context for this could be where it is used by the management to servers of alcohol to ensure they apply the age limit.

b. An epistemic reading is possibility; a deontic reading is permission.

c. An epistemic reading is a future possibility; a deontic reading is past permission.

d. An epistemic reading is strong commitment to a future prediction; a deontic reading is a prohibition.

e. An epistemic reading is a weak commitment to a future prediction; a deontic reading is a statement of obligation or duty.

5.9 *Urge* may occur in both the subjunctive form, *He urged that the prisoner be released*, and with the modal verb, *He urged that the prisoner should be released.* The other verbs that can be used in this way are: *demand, beg, command, insist, request, suggest.*

5.10 a. In *Apparently Fred doesn't like skiing* the evidential is *apparently*. The most likely use is probably as hearsay evidence, if for example I'm reporting what somebody has told me about Fred's attitude to skiing. It can also be used in cases of induction, where the speaker has reached this conclusion from

some unspecified evidence. Despite the meaning of the related adjective *apparent*, this evidential is unlikely to be used for direct visual evidence.
b. The marker is *should*; the source is deduction.
c. The marker is *look like*; the source is sensory evidence.
d. The marker is *evidently*; the source is induction.
e. The marker is *sounds*; the source can be sensory or hearsay, depending on context.
f. The marker is *must*; the source can be induction or deduction, depending on context.
g. The marker is *allegedly*; the source is hearsay.
h. The marker is *I suppose*; the source is belief.

CHAPTER 6

6.1 a. *Helen* is an AGENT; and *the party* is a GOAL argument.
b. *he*: AGENT, *the fly*: PATIENT, *a newspaper*: INSTRUMENT.
c. *baboon*: THEME, *roof of my car*: LOCATION
d. *Joan*: AGENT, *yard of ale*: PATIENT
e. *Campbell*: EXPERIENCER, *the gun*: STIMULUS.
f. *George*: AGENT, *the doorman*: RECIPIENT; *a tip*: THEME.

6.2 a. Harold felt the heat of the sun.
b. The wall collapsed under the pressure.
c. The ball flew over the fence.
d. The knife cut the rope.
e. Jaime accepted the prize from the Dean.

6.3 a. The protesters destroyed the fence.
b. Bill threw the frisbee into the air.
c. Joan baked her mother a cake.
d. John gave his wife a diamond ring.
e. The team heard the cheering.

6.4 a. AGENT and GOAL: Helen accepted the Oscar.
b. PATIENT and THEME: Regina crushed her cigarette into the lawn.
c. AGENT and SOURCE: The referee tossed the ball to the goalkeeper.
d. AGENT and THEME: Miguel bungee-jumped off the bridge.

6.5 In sentence a the subject *the butler* is a typical AGENT, combining properties of volition, sentience, causing and movement, as predicted by Dowty's model. The object *the silverware* is also as predicted, a typical PATIENT, undergoing change of state by an incremental process, causally affected by another, and stationary. In b *the dogs* is a less typical subject, lacking (at least) volition and causation while *the food* is an untypical object, lacking change of state, and not being affected by the other participant(s). In c *the train* is also a less typical subject, lacking agency, while *the cow* is a typical object. For the problem cases:

1 These two sentences have the same types of argument showing up as both subject and object, with different verbs. We saw in 6.79 in the chapter that

the first corollary of the Argument Selection Principle suggested that: "If two arguments of a relation have (approximately) equal numbers of entailed Proto-Agent and Proto-Patient properties, then either or both may be lexicalized as the subject (and similarly for objects)." This might explain how we could say both *She married him* and *He married her* to describe the same situation, where the difference could be explained pragmatically by the conversational context. However, this doesn't seem to work here because a person, *he,* should presumably always have more Proto-Agent properties than a disease. The conclusion one might make is that the principles might be considered as a default that can be overridden by a particular verb's requirements for arguments.

2 Here both arguments of the same verb have equal numbers of entailments so the Principle cannot explain the difference. This is one of viewpoint or perspective and is context dependent.

3 This is similar to 1. The buyer and seller in a transaction will plausibly have the same numbers of Proto-Agent and Proto-Patient properties, so the subject selection depends on the semantics of the individual verbs *buy* and *sell,* which allow different viewpoints on the same situation.

6.6 This exercise focuses on the interaction between the English passive rule and the rule of Dative Alternation, or Dative Shift. There are differences between dialects of English in how this operates and you will need to see which sound fine to you. The symbol * is used for versions predicted as ungrammatical for all major varieties of English.

a. Emma was fined five hundred francs by the court.
b. I was abducted in the middle of my examination by aliens. This sentence is grammatically fine though if in context the aliens are of higher salience a speaker might prefer: I was abducted by aliens in the middle of my examination.
c. The answer was mailed to the student by the professor.
d. *To the student was mailed the answer by the professor/*The student was mailed the answer to by the professor. The problem here is that non-subject argument is in a prepositional phrase, which is not covered by our proposed rule.
e. The student was mailed the answer by the professor.
f. The answer was mailed to the student by the professor. This construction is rejected by some speakers, but accepted by others.

6.7 There is some variation in speakers' use of these verbs but a characteristic distribution is below:

Causative-inchoative alternation verbs: break, open, melt, bend, dissolve, dry, tilt

Inchoative only: disappear, erupt, decay

Causative only: dirty, mow, crush

6.8 The following verbs typically allow an understood reflexive object: *undress, strip* (i.e. oneself of clothes), *bathe,* and *shave,* e.g. *He undressed.* In contrast the sentences *He brushed, He soaped, He toweled,* and *He lathered* seem incomplete, except where the context allows ellipsis, for example in a list of actions. Speakers seem to vary in whether the verb *shampoo* can be used with an understood reflexive object.

6.9 We assume that theta-grids specify required arguments of the verb. This means, for example, deciding whether prepositional phrases in specific sentence are arguments or adjuncts. For the purposes of this exercise we can simply ignore these decisions and simply list all the phrases as part of the grid.

a. *report:* V: <AGENT, THEME, GOAL>
b. *fall:* V: <THEME, SOURCE>
c. *remain:* V: <THEME, LOCATION>
d. *receive:* V: <RECIPIENT, THEME, SOURCE>
e. *notice:* V: <EXPERIENCER, STIMULUS>

CHAPTER 7

7.1 a. Two shorthand expressions: 1. "Let me have two plain and two onion, please" when ordering bagels at a stall only selling bagels. 2. "I'll take red" when requesting a glass of wine at a reception.
b. Metonymy: 1. Berlin seeks privacy rules in trade pact. Here *Berlin* is used to refer to the German government. 2. She married money. Here *money* is used for a wealthy person or people.
c. Synecdoche: 1. There are a few new faces on the team. Here the part *face* is used for a person. 2. "Nice threads" used for "nice clothes".

7.2 a. She is sitting over there. *Over there* is an example of spatial deixis. In the context where the speaker and/or addressee can see the person referred to, *she* would an example of person deixis.
b. This is the biggest room in the house. *This* is spatial deixis.
c. Bring him in whenever you're ready. *Bring* contains a deictic element (toward the speaker) in its meaning; *him* can be person deixis if used to indicate someone present; *you* is person deixis.
d. I'll see you tomorrow. *I* and *you* are person deixis. The future tense of the verb and the adverbial *tomorrow* reflect time deixis.
e. They were here, looking at this painting. *They* can be person deixis if the referents are physically present or observable. *Here* and *this* are spatial deixis.

7.3 a. Hyponymy. *Dog* is a hyponym of *animal.*
b. Anaphora.
c. Inference.
d. Meronymy.
e. Meronymy.
f. Hyponymy.
g. Inference.

7.4 1 The best continuation is:
a. No, Fred brought the groceries in.
2 Sentence a. Sentence d is possible in context where the car had been described earlier.
3 Sentence a. Sentence b is also possible, depending on the intonation used.
4 Sentence a. Sentence d is possible if we assume the narration shifts to give Kelly's thoughts.

7.5 As discussed in the chapter, conversational implicature is context dependent and so the answers to this question will depend on the imagined scenarios.

a. One possible implicature is that B is refusing the offer. This might be in the context that B is obeying typical family behavior. The reason for using implicature might be politeness, to defuse the force of the refusal by giving the reason for declining. Of course in another context, the implicature might be an acceptance, where B is humorously giving an additional motivation for going out to the pub.
b. Possible implicature: United didn't play well or as would be expected of the team. Motivation: possibly humor or scorn.
c. Possible implicature: Don't do it. Motivation: humor.
d. The implicature depends on the specific contextual assumptions. If the speaker (and hearer) assume that the activity that seems to be assumed in this exchange is one where new trousers wouldn't be worn, the implicature is no. If the opposite, the implicature is yes.
e. Possible implicature: You are not helping my anxiety with that comment. Motivation: reproof.
f. Possible implicature: It does bother me. Motivation: politeness.
g. Possible implicature: I am not going to tell you where I am going. Motivation: softened rejection of the question perhaps because of the authority of questioner or a parent–child relationship.
h. Possible implicature: The answer is obviously yes. Motivation: Humour, by breaking constraints of respect for figures of authority in a now conventionalized way.

7.6 a. The hedge *I may have got it all wrong but I thought…* might be used to show that the speaker anticipates violating the maxim of quality: she is suggesting that what she is about to say might not be accurate.
b. Maxim of manner.
c. Maxim of quality.
d. Maxim of quantity.
e. Maxim of relevance.

7.7 a. <always, sometimes>
We can use the three tests for scales discussed in the chapter. Firstly, in normal use the sentence *He sometimes chooses pizza* would implicate *He doesn't always choose pizza.* Secondly, the hypothetically stronger term *always* does seem to entail the weaker, *sometimes.* So *He always chooses pizza* entails *He sometimes chooses pizza*, i.e. if the first is true the second is automatically true. Thirdly the implicature can be canceled without anomaly: thus *He*

sometimes, no always, chooses pizza is not a semantically odd sentence, unlike ?*He sometimes, no never, chooses pizza*. So this does seem to be a valid Horn scale.

b. A valid Horn scale.

c. A valid Horn scale.

d. This question rests on what you consider to be the meaning of *as many as*. If we restrict ourselves to its use with a cardinal number, e.g. *As many as 1000 people filled in the questionnaire*, the question is what meaning is added to that of the number? One possible answer for this example is that *as many as* approximately equates the amount of responders to the cardinal number and emphasizes its size. If so this scale would operate like the cardinal number scale in e below. If you consider part of the meaning of *as many as* to be identifying the top of the range then this does not form a scale with *more than*.

e. Cardinal numbers are traditionally understood to form a scale so that a number *n* Q-implicates *not n+1*, *not n+2*, etc. A number of scholars, for example Carston (1998), have suggested that the interpretation of cardinal numbers is context dependent, so that a cardinal number *n* may have one of three intended interpretations: (a) exactly *n* as in *He had six huskies but one died so now he has five*, (b) at most *n* as in *Undergraduates may borrow six books from the library*, and (c) at least *n* as in *She needs to reach thirty meters to make the final*. Interpretations (a) and (b), but not (c), would correspond to the scalar implicature not more than *n*.

f. This is a valid Horn scale, a negative scale which means that *not all* Q-implicates *some*, i.e. *not none*.

7.8 a. I haven't eaten since breakfast this morning. I'm starving.
b. There's a thousand different ways out of this city.
c. A sharp blow to the base of the head is a painless way to kill a rabbit.
d. You're a genius. I could never get that printer to work properly.
e. Louisiana is flat.

7.9 a. It was a good Christmas dinner but the bird was a bit overcooked.
b. "It is obvious today that America has defaulted on this promissory note in so far as her citizens of color are concerned." (Martin Luther King, Jr. "I Have a Dream" speech, August 28, 1963)
c. We all hate people who brag that they have money.
d. You need to tone up your arms and your body.
e. She has a certain reputation.

CHAPTER 8

8.1 a. This sentence seems to work with *hereby*: *I hereby acknowledge you as my legal heir*. So this can be uttered as a performative. One problem with this test is that *hereby* is rather formal and so might sound strange with clearly informal uses of language, even though we might want to say they are performative. So for example *I hereby promise you to come home straight after school* might sound strange from a child to a parent.

b. Performative.
c. Performative.
d. Not performative.
e. Performative.
f. Not performative.

8.2 a. You have to come with us or You must come with us.
b. Return to your unit!
c. I stole the money.
d. Please join us for the weekend.
e. Please leave.

8.3 The question leaves it open to use explicit, implicit or indirect speech acts, so the solutions below mix these.

a. I'll be there, I promise.
b. Don't leave after dark!
c. I would be grateful if you left your dog outside.
d. I apologize for the noise.
e. Well done on winning the competition!

8.4 a. A possible context: airport coffee shop or bookstore. The illocutionary act is one of warning and the perlocutionary effect could be to cause the listener to hurry to the gate.
b. Possible context: co-worker to colleague long after normal hours. Perlocutionary effect: persuading colleague to go home.
c. Possible context: theatre auditorium during performance. Perlocutionary act: reminding audience member to turn off the phone.
d. Possible context: parent to child. Perlocutionary act: convincing the child to go to bed.
e. Possible context: packing for a tropical holiday. Perlocutionary effect: reminding the listener to pack the tablets.

8.5 1 Felicity conditions for warning
[where *S* = speaker, *H* = hearer, *E* = the future event, *P* = the proposition expressed in the speech act, *e* = the linguistic expression]
a. Preparatory 1: *S* thinks *E* will occur and is not in *H*'s interest.
b. Preparatory 2: *S* thinks it is not obvious to *H* that *E* will occur.
c. Propositional: In expressing that *P*, *S* predicates a future event *E*.
d. Sincerity: *S* believes *E* is not in *H*'s best interest.
e. Essential: the utterance *e* counts as an undertaking that *E* is not in *H*'s best interest.

2 Felicity conditions for advising
[where *S* = speaker, *H* = hearer, *A* = the future act, *P* = the proposition expressed in the speech act, *e* = the linguistic expression]
a. Preparatory 1: *S* has some reason to believe *A* will benefit *H*.
b. Preparatory 2: It is not obvious to both *S* and *H* that *H* will do *A* in the normal course of events.
c. Propositional: In expressing that *P*, *S* predicates a future act *A* of *H*.

d. Sincerity: *S* believes *A* will benefit *H*.
e. Essential: the utterance *e* counts as an undertaking to the effect that *A* is in *H*'s best interest.

8.6 Imperatives can be used for the following speech acts:

a. Warnings: Don't try it. You'll be sorry.
b. Wishes: Get well soon.
c. Permission: [Context: Can I try this cake?] Help yourself.
d. Advice: [Context: Where's the railway station?] Take the next left and continue straight on.

8.7 Interrogatives can be used for the following speech acts:

a. Requests: Can't you be quiet for a minute?
b. Exclamations: [Context: speaker's team loses by conceding an own goal in the last minute] How unlucky is that? This use can be reflected by the use of an exclamation rather than a question mark: How unlucky is that!
c. Statement of opinion (in this case an insult): Why are you so stupid?
d. Seeking agreement or permission: Okay?
Other examples of indirect uses of interrogative: What is the point of this endless bickering? Who asked for your opinion? These are often termed rhetorical questions to reflect their non-questioning force.

8.8 The indirect acts are: a. request; b. order; c. request; d. offer; e. refusal; f. prediction and g. refusal.

8.9 The strategies result in the following sentences:

a. Will you be able to bring your guitar along to the party?/Can you bring your guitar along to the party?
b. You can bring your guitar to the party.
c. Will you bring your guitar to the party?
d. I want you to bring your guitar to the party.

Each of these seems like a possible candidate for an indirect request given appropriate contexts.

8.10 The strategies result in the following sentences:

a. Would you like me to return your books?/Isn't it obvious that I'll return your books?
b. I believe you would prefer me to return your books.
c. Shall I return your books?
d. I intend to return your books.

Of these only d seems clearly to work as an indirect promise, though some speakers may accept the second alternative under certain contextual conditions.

CHAPTER 9

9.1 Anthropologists, faced with the task of describing kinship systems in different cultures, have used componential analysis; see for example, Goodenough, (1956, 1964), and Lounsbury (1956, 1964) for early accounts. Since kinship terms are relative to a specific person we can assume for our exercise that this is the speaker. Anthropologists then design tree diagrams to show the relationships between the speaker and his or her relations for which lexical terms are used. A simple example is the diagram below, where a triangle denotes a male relative and a circle, a female relative. For brevity this exercise adopts a simple dualistic view of gender that may not reflect cultural realities. Assuming that S represents the speaker, the English words for the positions are then: 1 = father; 2 = mother; 3 = brother; and 4 = sister.

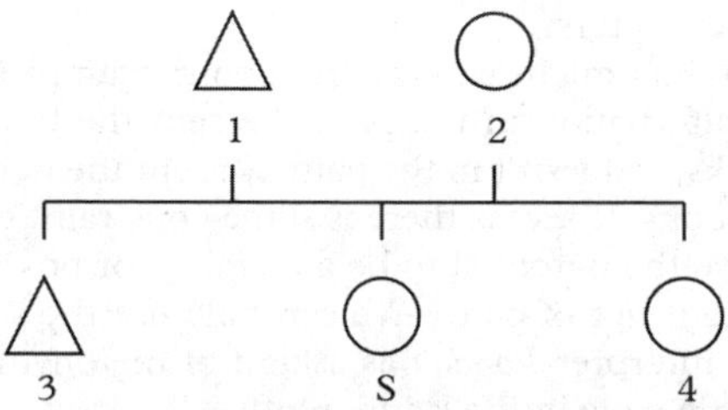

The nouns used to identify a person in the genealogical tree are defined by generation, gender and the genealogical connection to the speaker. The words for these relations may be identified as semantic components.

For this exercise you need to draw a big enough genealogy tree diagram to include all the English terms given, then use features such as these to uniquely identify each position in the tree. Following traditional anthropological linguistics we could posit three basic features for the terms in this exercise: GENERATION, where the level of the self (or *ego*) is 0, ancestors go +1, +2, +3 etc. and descendants go –1, –2, –3, etc.; GENDER, masculine, feminine, or unspecified; and LINEALITY, lineal (direct) and collateral. If we included relatives by marriage we would have to include a feature CONSANGUINITY. So some feature analyses are:

brother	[GENERATION 0, GENDER masculine, LINEALITY lineal]
sister	[GENERATION 0, GENDER feminine, LINEALITY lineal]
father	[GENERATION +1, GENDER masculine, LINEALITY lineal]
mother	[GENERATION +1, GENDER feminine, LINEALITY lineal]
uncle	[GENERATION +1, GENDER masculine, LINEALITY collateral]
aunt	[GENERATION +1, GENDER feminine, LINEALITY collateral]
cousin	[GENERATION 0, GENDER unspecified, LINEALITY collateral]

The other terms follow the same pattern.

9.2 a. *Bounce* participates in the alternation: *The goalkeeper bounced the ball/The ball bounced.* Motion.
b. Does not participate.

c. Participates; change of state.
d. Does not participate.
e. Participates; motion.
f. Does not participate.
g. Participates; change of state.

9.3 There seems to be some variation among speakers in which verbs allow Dative Shift, in particular among the class that Rappaport and Levin (2008) call *throw* verbs (including throw, toss, slap, shoot, fling, flip, kick). You may not therefore agree with the following decisions. For some speakers the following verbs seem to belong to Class 1 and undergo the alternation: mail, kick, pass, sell, hand, throw, bring, take. The following verbs seem to belong to Class 2 and do not undergo the alternation: lower, push, flip, haul, ferry. If your intuitions depart radically from the predictions you may conclude that Pinker's hypothesis is incorrect or is missing some other factors.

Some further semantic constraints might emerge from your examples. For example while *send* allows the alternation in the pair: We sent the books to George/We sent George the books, it doesn't in the pair: We sent the books to London/?We sent London the books. It seems there is some constraint on the Goal argument that it has to have the potential to be a recipient or possessor, something we expect of people but not of cities. We can only use the second alternant in this example, if we interpret *London* as a kind of metonymy, for example, for something like "the people in the London office."

9.4 The following verbs seem to belong to Class 3 and allow the alternation: teach, read, quote, show, cite

The following seem to belong to Class 4 and not undergo the alternation: whisper, mention, murmur, say, scream, yell

9.5 One important distinction is between cases where the nominal after *for* becomes the owner of something, i.e. a recipient; and cases where *for* means "on behalf of." The latter do not undergo the alternation. The example given is of the former: She bought a car for her daughter/She bought her daughter a car. An example of the latter would be: She parked a car for her daughter/*She parked her daughter a car. One problem with identifying verb classes that undergo benefactive shift is that the requirement for an intended recipient sometimes distinguishes between uses of the same verb, for example the contrast between Open me a beer, would you? and *Open me the door, would you? This suggests that it is not just the verb and its class that are determining the construction; see Goldberg (2002) for discussion. Another problem is that there is some elasticity in the notion of recipient: in some examples the recipient does not actually possess anything, as in: Please call me a taxi.

9.6 The main point of this exercise is to find Latinate verbs that follow the proposed restrictions and others that do not. You shouldn't expect to find a neat way of classifying the exceptions. There have been a number of suggestions: some are based on other factors, for example that the Latinate verbs may have a lower frequency, and tend to have more syllables, than corresponding native English verbs. So, the argument goes, the truer this is of a particular verb, the less likely it is to participate in the Dative Alternation. See Boguraev and Briscoe

(1989: 113ff) for discussion. Pinker (1989: 216) identifies a semantic class of verbs that are an exception to the Latinate constraint: verbs that express a future possession, including assign, bequeath, and guarantee. This may explain examples like: They will manufacture you a whole new kitchen.

9.7 The following verbs seem to fit the generalization: waltz, bounce, cycle, swarm. The verbs howl, thud, creak and flash do not fit this generalization, leading us to set up a class of verbs of sound or light emission that can conflate with motion.

9.8 a. $[_{State}\ \mathrm{BE}_{Poss}\ ([_{Thing}\ \mathrm{CAR}], [_{Place}\ \mathrm{AT}\ ([_{Thing}\ \mathrm{MAURA}])])]$
b. $[_{State}\ \mathrm{BE}_{Temp}\ ([_{Thing}\ \mathrm{BIRTHDAY}], [_{Place}\ \mathrm{AT}\ ([_{Time}\ \mathrm{THURSDAY}])])]$
c. $[_{Event}\ \mathrm{GO}\ ([_{Thing}\ \mathrm{JOHN}], [_{Path}\ \mathrm{FROM}\ [_{Place}\ \mathrm{IN}\ ([_{Thing}\ \mathrm{ROOM}])])]]$
d. $[_{State}\ \mathrm{BE}_{Poss}\ ([_{Thing}\ \mathrm{HOUSE}], [_{Place}\ \mathrm{AT}\ ([_{Thing}\ \mathrm{HELEN}])])]$
e. $[_{State}\ \mathrm{BE}_{Loc}\ ([_{Thing}\ \mathrm{CAT}], [_{Place}\ \mathrm{ON}\ ([_{Thing}\ \mathrm{ROOF}])])]$

9.9 1a. $[_{State}\ \mathrm{BE}_{Ident}\ ([_{Thing}\ \mathrm{WINDOW}], [_{Place}\ \mathrm{AT}\ ([_{Property}\ \mathrm{CLOSED}])])]$
1b. $[_{Event}\ \mathrm{INCH}\ ([_{State}\ \mathrm{BE}_{Ident}\ ([_{Thing}\ \mathrm{WINDOW}], [_{Place}\ \mathrm{AT}\ ([_{Property}\ \mathrm{CLOSED}])])])]$
2a. $[_{Event}\ \mathrm{INCH}\ ([_{State}\ \mathrm{BE}_{Ident}\ ([_{Thing}\ \mathrm{PEG}], [_{Place}\ \mathrm{AT}\ ([_{Property}\ \mathrm{ANGRY}])])])]$
2b. $[_{Event}\ \mathrm{CAUSE}\ ([_{Thing}\ \mathrm{JOHN}], [_{Event}\ \mathrm{INCH}\ ([_{State}\ \mathrm{BE}_{Ident}\ ([_{Thing}\ \mathrm{PEG}], [_{Place}\ \mathrm{AT}\ ([_{Property}\ \mathrm{ANGRY}])])])])]$
3a. $[_{State}\ \mathrm{BE}_{Poss}\ ([_{Thing}\ \mathrm{MONEY}], [_{Place}\ \mathrm{AT}\ ([_{Thing}\ \mathrm{GEORGE}])])]$
3b. $[_{Event}\ \mathrm{CAUSE}\ ([_{Thing}\ \mathrm{GEORGE}], [_{Event}\ \mathrm{INCH}\ ([_{State}\ \mathrm{BE}_{Poss}\ ([_{Thing}\ \mathrm{MONEY}], [_{Place}\ \mathrm{AT}\ ([_{Thing}\ \mathrm{CINDY}])])])])]$

9.10 The labels for the functions in the diagram below might vary since they link to other items in the respective domains, not present for our isolated example. So for example the FORMAL feature could be **artifact** (x) instead of the more specific feature below. The structure below should give the general idea.

sandwich

QUALIA = [CONSTITUTIVE = **bread** (x)
FORMAL = **meal** (x)
TELIC = **eat** (x, y)
AGENT = **prepare** (z, x)]

CHAPTER 10

10.1 a. $K(a) \wedge W(m)$
b. $K(a) \rightarrow Q(g)$
c. $K(a) \wedge P(a, e)$
d. $\neg A(m, l)$
e. $L(l, g) \vee L(g, l)$

10.2 a. $(\forall x: D(x))\ H(l, x)$
b. $(\forall x: D(x))\ N(x, l)$
c. This sentence is ambiguous in English. It could correspond to $(\forall x: D(x))\ \neg K(d, m)$, i.e. No dragon was keen on Merlin or $\neg\ (\forall x: D(x))\ K(d, m)$ i.e. It's not the case that all dragons were keen on Merlin.
d. $\neg\ (\forall x; P(x))\ S(x, h)$

10.3 a. The matchings for the individual constant terms are: $F_3(g)$ = Gawain; and
$F_3(i)$ = Igraine. The assignment of the predicate letter is:
$F_3(L)$ = loved = {<Elaine, Lancelot>, <Igraine, Gawaine>, <Gawaine, Igraine>}

To check the truth of the sentence we have to check the extensions of the individual constants and the predicate constant in this model to see if the ordered pair (g, i) is part of the set defined by $[L]$. Schematically the rule is: $[L(g, i)]\ M_3 = \mathbf{1}$ iff $[\langle g, i\rangle]\ M_3 \in [L]\ M_3$

In English this says: *Gawain loved Igraine* is true if and only if the extension of *Gawaine* and the extension of *Igraine* are an ordered pair which is part of the set defined by *loved* in the model M_3. We can see that this is true so $L(g, i)$ is **true** in this model.
b. False
c. False
d. True
e. True
f. True

10.4 a. True
b. False
c. True
d. False

10.5 sweater/jumper : $\forall x$(SWEATER (x) ≡ JUMPER (x))
true/false: $\forall x$(TRUE (x) → ¬ FALSE (x))
gun/weapon: $\forall x$(GUN (x) → WEAPON (x))
open/shut (of a door): $\forall x$(OPEN (x) → ¬ SHUT (x))
uppercut/punch (in boxing): $\forall x$(UPPERCUT (x) → PUNCH (x))
car/automobile: $\forall x$(CAR (x) ≡ AUTOMOBILE (x))

10.6 Remember that subordinate clauses under propositional attitude verbs are opaque contexts because inserting different referring expressions into them, even when these refer to the same entity, may affect the truth conditions of the whole sentence (when uttered). So an example would be the pair: *Bruce wants to climb the third-highest mountain in the world* and *Bruce wants to climb Kanchenjunga*. These two sentences may in certain contexts have two different truth values. The first may be true when Bruce has yet to learn the identity of his target mountain, so that the second would be false in that context. Another example: *The Commissioner believes that Batwoman is an assassin*/*The Commissioner believes that Kate Kane is an assassin*, where unknown to the Commissioner they are one and the same.

10.7 a. The quantifier *many* in its cardinal use is symmetrical, since from the example *Many Americans have won gold medals* it allows the "switched" version *Many gold medal winners are American.* Compare this with the asymmetrical quantifier *all,* where such switching is not possible: *All Americans watch football matches* ↔**All football watchers are Americans.*

b. Symmetrical

c. Asymmetrical

d. Symmetrical

10.8 a. For this exercise we need to remember that upward entailment is from a subset to a set; and downward is from a set to a subset. Using the same example as in the chapter, we can test *most* in the right argument position of the quantifier (i.e. the VP) with the set *most (people, driving)* and its subset, *most (people, driving home)*:

Most people are driving does not entail *Most people are driving home.*

Most people are driving home does entail *Most people are driving.*

Therefore: *most* involves upward entailment in the right argument.

b. Upward entailment in the right argument.

c. Non-monotone.

10.9 1.

x y
Man (x) Donkey (y) bought (x, y)

2.

x y u
Man (x) Donkey (y) bought (x, y) v = x u = y fed (v, u)

10.10 a. Names are always accessible in the subsequent discourse, so the name *Carl* in sentence a will be accessible for later coreference.

b. As above, the name *Maura* will be accessible for later coreference. The noun phrase *a scanner* is introduced in a negative subordinate DRS and so will not be accessible for later coreference.

CHAPTER 11

11.1 The different examples show different conceptualizations of the relationship between the trajector (TR) and landmark (LM), for example their relative positions, whether there is contact or a relation of inclusion, etc. There

Figure 12.1 The camera is on the table

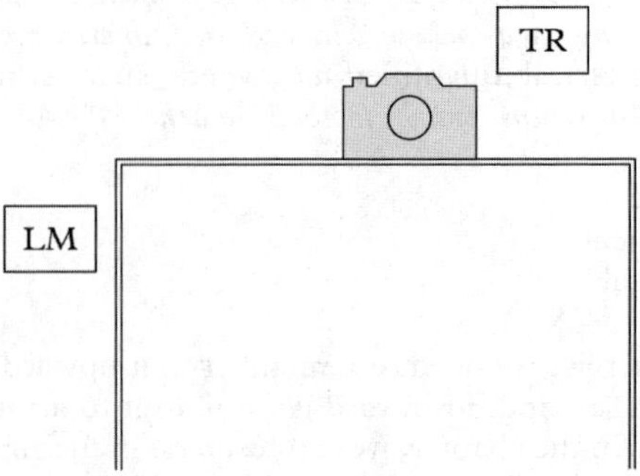

may also be differences in the conceptualizations of the landmark, as a two-dimensional surface or a three-dimensional medium. In some cases you might be able to detect metaphorical extensions of the schema.

a. The *camera, fly*, and *painting* are trajectors whose position relative to their landmarks is different. We can assume the prototypical relation as in figure 12.1 with other relations describable in a similar format. The *shoe* example shows a covering sense of *on*, as in other examples like *The helmet was on his head*. The *leaves* example shows a multiplex trajector. The *house* example can be seen as a metaphorical extension.
b. The *mechanic* and *wallpaper* examples reflect different relationships between trajector and landmark, while the *ocean* and *water* examples seem to show different aspects of bodies of water being conceptualized as a landmark. The *house* and *novels* examples might be seen as metaphorical extensions.
c. The *horse*, *boys*, and *hawk* examples show different relations between landmark and trajector as discussed in the chapter. The *bridge* example is sometimes called "fictive motion" (Talmy 2000), where static spatial relations are metaphorically characterized as dynamic motion. The *shoulder* example can be seen as a metaphoric spatial characterization of an act of looking. The *worst* example is a metaphorical extension that we can see as part of the LIFE IS A JOURNEY metaphor discussed in this chapter.

11.2 a. Containment.
b. Path.
c. Compulsion.
d. Containment.
e. Path.
f. Blockage.
g. Compulsion.
h. Path.
i. Blockage.
j. Containment.

11.3 LOVE IS A JOURNEY: This relationship is going nowhere. Their marriage is on the rocks.

IDEAS ARE OBJECTS: I can't grasp this argument. Her explanation went right over my head.

TIME IS MOTION: You may find useful Kövecses' (2002: 33–34) distinction between two subtypes of the metaphor TIME IS MOTION in English: TIME PASSING IS MOTION OF AN OBJECT (e.g. *Christmas is coming*) and TIME PASSING IS AN OBSERVER'S MOTION OVER A LANDSCAPE (e.g. *We're coming up to Christmas*).

11.4 a. Suggested correspondences for LOVE IS A JOURNEY:

Source: Journey		Target: Love
travelers	→	lovers
the vehicle	→	the relationship
distance covered	→	progress in relationship
physical obstacles	→	difficulties in relationship

b. IDEAS ARE OBJECTS

Source: Physical Objects		Target: Ideas
objects	→	ideas
container	→	mind
movement in space	→	communication
grasping object	→	understanding idea

c. TIME IS MOTION. This depends on which conceptualization is involved, for example, for TIME PASSING IS MOTION OF AN OBJECT:

Source: Motion of Physical Objects		Target: Time
observer's physical location	→	present time
objects	→	times
motion toward observer	→	passage of time
in front of observer	→	future time
behind observer	→	past time

11.5 Some French versus English examples:
French uses *pied* "foot" for mountains and beds, as does English. But for the foot of stairs French has *bas*. Similarly French has *tête* "head" for queues and pins, as in English, but for the head of a bed the French word is *chevet* and the head of a river is *extrémité*. Interestingly, while both English and French use *head/tête* for a unit of garlic, French uses *pied* "foot" where English has *head* for a unit of celery.

11.6 a. *The BMW is waiting for his ticket*. We can imagine a possible context as a car-parking situation. Here the name of the make of car, BMW, is used to refer to its driver. We could informally label this relation POSSESSION FOR OWNER. Additionally you might want to consider whether using the nominal BMW for the car is another example of metonymy, or a **shorthand**, as discussed in chapter 7.

b. PRODUCT FOR PRODUCER
c. PLACE FOR EVENT
d. PLACE FOR PEOPLE, if we take *Brighton* to refer to the population rather than the city authorities.
e. CONTROLLED FOR CONTROLLER, like Lakoff and Johnson's (1980) example, *The buses are on strike*.
f. PLACE FOR PEOPLE

11.7 a. CONTAINER FOR CONTENTS: The kettle is boiling. He drank two glasses then left. She's read the whole library.
b. WHOLE FOR PART: The police are at the door. It's time to light the Christmas tree.
c. PART FOR WHOLE: She has a lot of mouths to feed. We need some new blood in the organization.
d. CONTROLLER FOR CONTROLLED: Bush invaded Iraq. I hit the car in front.
e. OBJECT USED FOR USER: this can be seen as a subpart of CONTROLLED FOR CONTROLLER, e.g. The lead guitar quit. I won't talk to the newspapers.

11.8 1 The first example shows that the products of electronic mass communication are typically conceptualized in English as two-dimensional surfaces. Thus we say: *on the radio, on television, on the internet.* Using the preposition *in* is incompatible with this and causes the interpretation to shift to the concrete three-dimensional object (*the radio, television*) and we therefore assume the speaker means a noise inside the box, not connected to the usual sound production. We can compare this with related languages. In Dutch, the conceptualization is also as a surface, giving: *op de radio, op de televisie, op het internet*; while in German the conceptualization is of three-dimensional media, thus employing the position *im* "in": *im Radio, im Fernsehen, im Internet.*
2 The first example follows the pattern mentioned above. The second conceptualizes news broadcasts as containers of information.
3 In this pair the bedcovers transform the bed from a surface to a container. So someone *in* bed is under the covers.
4 In contrast to the last example, the bed in which someone dies is conventionally conceptualized as a surface so that a is more typical than b.
5 These two sentences can describe the same situation, reflecting two different ways of conceiving the relationship between the engine and the car. The more typical is b, reflecting the real-world location of an engine.
6 In contrast to the last example these two sentences describe different situations and locations for the tires.
7 The contrast here is a subtle one, reflecting different contexts of use. The more typical case is probably a, where the bus is conceptualized as a surface as usual, so we say *Get on the bus!* or *Board the bus!* The b sentence focuses on the bus as a container so might be used to contrast that set of children with the children not on the bus.

11.9 a. *In the novel, Hitler wins World War II.* In this example we are invited to manipulate two mental spaces. The space builder is the adverbial phrase *in the novel*, which identifies a story as a new space, distinct from the (assumed) real space of the context of utterance. The real domain and the novel space both contain *Hitler* and *World War II*, each pair connected by naming. The event in the novel space is counterfactual since it is at odds with historical fact in the real domain. The present tense of *wins* is a further signal that this is a non-real event. The use of the present tense for the past is common when describing plots of novels, films etc. This can be seen as identifying them as not located as events in real time, and potentially re-enactable.

b. In this counterfactual the two spaces are reality and an imaginary space where the speaker and addressee swap identities. The space-builder is the grammatical construction of the hypothetical conditional, involving *if* and the subjunctive form of the verb.

c. The two spaces here are a typical weekday, in which a bus leaves at 8 a.m., and Sunday, where a corresponding bus leaves at 9 a.m. The connection is made by using the name of the weekday bus for the Sunday bus. This comparative merger allows a non-contradictory reading of the sentence, in a way that motivated conceptual blending theory.

d. The space-builder is the temporal adverbial *in 1947*, which sets up a new space additional to the time of the utterance. The link is between two counterparts: *the president* in the current space and *a child* in the 1947 space. The copula verb *was* connects the two, identifying them as the same individual. This allows the title *the president* to be used to refer to a child.

e. The space builder is the phrase *in Andy Warhol's prints*, which sets up a new referential space. The connector IMAGE connects Marilyn Monroe in the real-world space to her image in the Warhol space, allowing the name to be used to refer to the image.

11.10 a. This example has two input spaces: firstly, mothers and motherhood, and secondly, the planet Earth. The generic space here contains the image schemas that support the general aspects required for personification, for example agency. The blend-space contains the fusing of Mother and Earth to create an image of a powerful but caring female who has given life to us all; in the blend space, the human populations are her children. From the first input space are projected the structures that say "children should respect their mother," and so the blend supports the exhortation: Let's respect our Mother Earth.

b. This example has grave-digging and eating food input spaces and develops a blended space where not only do people unusually dig their own graves but do so with their teeth instead of spades.

c. The input spaces are Edinburgh, capital of modern Scotland, and Athens in the classical Greek world. In the blend Edinburgh merges with Athens, with the blended city exhibiting Athens's importance and intellectual achievements in a much later northern European setting.

d. This blend draws on two domains of knowledge: Ireland's economic relations with the European Union following the 2008 financial crash and the tradition of charities campaigning for funds using posters picturing children in need. In the blend Ireland becomes emblematic of the EU's austerity policy, which takes on the associations of a cause for good. Perversely Ireland becomes an ideal and advocate of the policy.

e. The input spaces are Christian worship in cathedrals and retail activity in department stores. The blend merges shopping with worship at the shared highpoint of Christmas. In the blended space shop windows take on the cathedral windows' role of educating and uplifting the viewer.

REFERENCES

Boguraev, Branimir and Ted Briscoe 1989: Utilising the LDOCE grammar codes. In Branimir Boguraev and Ted Briscoe (eds.) *Computational Lexicography for Natural Language Processing*, 85–116. London: Longman.

Carston, Robyn 1998: Informativeness, relevance and scalar implicature. In R. Carston and S. Uchida (eds.), *Relevance Theory: Applications and Implications*, 179–238. Amersterdam: John Benjamins.

Cruse, D. Alan 1986: *Lexical Semantics*. Cambridge: Cambridge University Press.

Fellbaum, Christiane (ed.) 1998: *WordNet: An Electronic Lexical Database*. Cambridge, MA: MIT Press.

Goldberg, Adele E. 2002: Surface generalizations: an alternative to alternations. *Cognitive Linguistics* 13.4: 327–56.

Goodenough, Ward H. 1956: Componential Analysis and the study of meaning. *Language* 32: 195–216.

Goodenough, Ward H. (ed.) 1964: *Explorations in Cultural Anthropology: Essays in Honor of George Peter Murdock*. New York: McGraw-Hill.

Huddleston, Rodney and Geoffrey K. Pullum 2002: *The Cambridge Grammar of the English Language*. Cambridge: Cambridge University Press.

Kövecses, Zoltán 2002: *Metaphor: A Practical Introduction*. Oxford: Oxford University Press.

Lakoff, George and Mark Johnson 1980: *Metaphors We Live By*. Chicago: University of Chicago Press.

Lounsbury, Floyd 1956: Semantic analysis of Pawnee kinship usage. *Language* 32: 158–94.

Lounsbury, Floyd 1964: A formal account of the Crow- and Omaha-type kinship terminologies. In Ward H. Goodenough (ed.) *Explorations in Cultural Anthropology: Essays in Honor of George Peter Murdock*, 351–94. New York: McGraw-Hill. Reprinted in Stephen A. Tyler (ed.) 1969: *Cognitive Anthropology*, 212–45. New York: Holt, Rinehart & Winston.

Peitsara, Kirsti 2006: MAN-compounds in English. In R. W. McConchie et al. (eds.) *Selected Proceedings of the 2005 Symposium on New Approaches in English Historical Lexis* (HEL-LEX), 113–22. Somerville, MA: Cascadilla Proceedings Project. Available at http://www.lingref.com/cpp/hel-lex/2005/paper1352.pdf, accessed April 15, 2015.

Pinker, Steven 1989: *Learnability and Cognition: The Acquisition of Argument Structure*. Cambridge, MA: MIT Press.

Quirk, Randolph, Sidney Greenbaum, Geoffrey Leech, and Jan Svartvik 1985: *A Comprehensive Grammar of the English Language*. London: Longman.

Rappaport Hovav, Malka and Beth Levin 2008: The English Dative Alternation: the case for verb sensitivity. *Journal of Linguistics* 44: 129–67.

Talmy, Leonard. 2000: *Toward a Cognitive Semantics*, 2 vols. Cambridge, MA: MIT Press.

Glossary

Accommodation: see **presupposition failure**.

Accomplishment: A situation type that is dynamic, durative and telic, i.e. has an inherent end point, e.g. *The president walked to the podium*.

Achievement: A situation type that is dynamic and telic and non-durative, i.e. a point event, e.g. *He recognized his assailant*.

Acknowledgments: In Bach and Harnish's (1979) classification of speech acts, this class includes apologizing, condoling, congratulating, greeting, thanking, accepting.

Action chain: In Langacker's (2008) *Cognitive Grammar*, an event involving energy transfer, for example one entity acting on and affecting another. The actor is assumed to be more salient for linguistic encoding.

Active voice: A grammatical category that reflects a specific relationship between a verb and its thematic roles, distinct from **passive** and **middle** voices. With a transitive verb, for example, in active voice the **agent thematic role** is construed as most salient and occurs in subject position. In many language descriptions the active voice is taken as the basic form or canonical template for the verb.

Activity: A situation type that is dynamic, durative and atelic, i.e. a process that does not have an inherent end point, e.g. *Ciara was dancing*.

Actor: A generalized thematic role that includes AGENT and non-volitional instigators of actions.

Ad hoc concept: Where speakers form novel categories relevant to their current interest, such as *previous winners of the Nobel Peace Prize.*

Adjunct: A **non-obligatory clause participant**.

Agent: A thematic role, the volitional instigator of an action.

***Aktionsarten*:** A German-language term for **situation type**.

Ambiguity: Where an expression has more than one possible meaning. Since all expressions show some variation in context the problem for semanticists is to identify true ambiguity, where the same form can give rise to different specific and distinct meanings. An example of lexical ambiguity is the noun *bark*, which can mean "hard outer covering of a tree" or "sound made by a dog."

Ambiguous: See **ambiguity**.

Analogical mapping: The cognitive process of linking two entities by analogy, which in cognitive semantics is viewed as the process underlying the construction and comprehension of metaphors.

Analytic truth: Another term for **linguistic truth**.

Anaphora: A referential relationship where further expressions are used to refer to the same entity, as in *I invited John and he came* when *John* and *he* identify the same individual. In this example *he* is an anaphoric use of a pronoun and *John* is termed the antecedent.

Anaphoric pronoun: See **anaphora**.

Animacy hierarchy: The proposal that linguistic systems reflect a semantic and conceptual grading of entities according to how sentient or alive they are.

Antecedent: See **anaphora**.

Antonymy: Words in a semantic opposition, including **complementary**, **gradable**, **relational**, and **reverse antonyms**.

***A posteriori* truth:** Truth that is known from experience or evidence.

Approximation: Another term for **broadening**.

***A priori* truth:** Truth that is known independently of experience or evidence.

Argument: In grammar, a syntactic phrase that is associated with a verb to form a clause. In semantics, entities coded as participants in a situation, represented as grammatical arguments. See **thematic role**.

Argument structure alternation: Where the same verb allows different configurations of thematic roles and their associated syntactic frames, like the English dative alternation *I sent Mary the parcel/I sent the parcel to Mary*.

Aspect: A semantic system, marked in grammar, which allows speakers different viewpoints on the time profile of an event or situation, e.g. by choosing between a **perfective** and **imperfective** verb form.

Atelic: A feature of situation types where the process has no inherent end point.

Attributive use of adjective: Where syntactically the adjective occurs inside a noun phrase and semantically qualifies the head noun, for example *black* in *the black book*.

Auxiliary verbs: Verbs which co-occur with other verbs and primarily convey grammatical information, e.g. **tense, aspect**, or **modality**.

Benefactive: The grammatical marking on nouns (typically by case) or verbs (typically by affixes) indicating the entity for whose benefit something is done.

Beneficiary: A **thematic role**, the entity for whose benefit the action was performed.

Bi-conditional: In logic, a **logical connective** represented by ↔ or ≡. An expression A ↔ B is only true if both A and B are true or both are false. It is often identified with the English phrase *if and only if*.

Binary antonym: See **complementary antonym**.

Binary features: Features that can only have two values, + or –.

Binding: A term used in logic and semantics for the relation between **variables** and **quantifiers** or other operators upon which they are dependent.

Blending: The process of creating and understanding **blends**.

Blends: A term from conceptual integration theory, an extensive and dynamic analogical structure in which new meaning is created.

Blockage: A type of **image schema**.

Body part ascension construction: An argument structure alternating with a transitive clause including a prepositional phrase, as in English *She slapped his face/She slapped him in the face*.

Bounded: Another term for **telic**.

Broadening: A process where the concept expressed by use of a lexical item is more general than that usually assumed to be linguistically encoded.

Cardinal (quantifiers)**:** Used to express the number of individuals in a set.

Category extension: A type of **broadening** that allows names to denote wider categories, for example when a brand name like *Kleenex* is used as a generic for paper tissues.

Causal theory of names: A theory of how we use names that focuses on the social inheritance of names, based on historical first uses.

Causative: A semantic and grammatical category that identifies a causal role of a referent in relation to an event or state described by a verb.

Causative-inchoative alternation: An argument structure alternation, as in English *Fred snapped the branch/The branch snapped*. The first alternant identifies a causer of the change of state; the second just the change of state.

Classical category: The result of a view of categories that they are defined by singly necessary and jointly sufficient features.

Classifiers: Morphemes that reflect conceptual categories of nominal referents, such as number, shape or function.

Cognates: Words that share a common etymological origin, for example *uomo* "man" in Italian and *homme* in French.

Collocation: This is used in two ways. The first simply describes expressions occurring together grammatically and semantically in a well-formed way, i.e. regular combination. The second describes the semantic effects on expressions of frequently occurring together, e.g. becoming routinized like *whisper softly* rather than *whisper quietly*, or *high mountains* rather than *tall mountains*.

Commissives: In Bach and Harnish's (1979) classification of speech acts, this class includes agreeing, guaranteeing, inviting, offering, promising, swearing, volunteering.

Common ground: A term used by Stalnaker (1974) for the set of assumptions shared by participants at a particular point in a conversation. The notion has been important in accounts of **presupposition**.

Complementary antonyms: A type of oppositeness where terms divide a domain into two mutually exclusive subdomains so that something must be one or the other but not both, for example *hit* or *miss* a target. Also called binary antonyms.

Componential analysis: An approach that identifies semantic elements (also called components or primitives) smaller than a word that combine to form the meanings of words.

Compositional: Where the meaning of a complex meaning is predictable from its parts.

Compound: A lexeme formed from two or more other lexemes, such as the compound noun *infill* or the compound verb *overflow*.

Compulsion: A type of **image schema**.

Conative alternation: A correspondence between two verb phrase patterns exemplified by *Joan chopped the meat* (basic) and *Joan chopped at the meat* (conative). The conative alternant usually has interpretations of unsuccessful or repeated action, as in the pair *Mario kicked the ball/Mario kicked at the ball.*

Conceptual blending: An alternative term for **blending**.

Conceptual integration theory: An alternative term for **blending**.

Conceptual metaphor theory: The account of metaphor given in cognitive linguistic approaches, where metaphor is seen as part of a general process of analogical mapping between cognitive domains rather than a strictly linguistic strategy.

Conceptual semantics: In general terms, the theory that meanings of linguistic expressions are concepts. Also the label for a theory proposed by Ray Jackendoff (e.g. Jackendoff 2002).

Conjunction: In grammar a word that joins words, phrases, and clauses, e.g. *and*. In logic a **logical connective**, symbolized by ∧ (or &), with a specific binary truth-function. The expression with ∧ is true only when all of its parts are true; it is false otherwise. Its function is narrower than many uses of natural language conjunctions like *and*.

Conjuncts: Linguistic expressions joined together, usually by a linking device such as a coordinating conjunction like English *and, or, but*. In semantics these are often conjoined clauses representing conjoined propositions, for example *Rob plays golf and Róisín drives cars*.

Constant reference: The idea that some names are consistently used to pick out the same referent, for example *Malaysia, Nelson Mandela, the Atlantic Ocean*, while other names and nouns have variable reference, so that they are used in different contexts to identify different referents, for example *John, the cat, the President*.

Constative: In Speech Act Theory an utterance that has the performative force of stating, usually via a declarative sentence, for example, *The thief is stealing Joan's bicycle*. Originally J. L. Austin (1975) distinguished between **performative** utterances, representing social acts, and constatives, which were truth-bearing descriptions of states of affairs. Subsequently constatives were themselves viewed as a particular kind of act and therefore performative. In Bach and Harnish's (1979) classification of speech acts, constatives are a class that includes affirming, alleging, announcing, answering, attributing, claiming, classifying, concurring, confirming, conjecturing, denying, disagreeing, disclosing, disputing, identifying, informing, insisting, predicting, ranking, reporting, stating, stipulating.

Construal: A speaker's choices in characterizing a situation for communication.

Construction: In linguistics this is traditionally a string of words that form a unit for grammatical rules. In cognitive semantics any form–meaning pairing, including words.

Containment schema: A type of **image schema**.

Contingent truth: Something that depends on facts and that could conceivably be true or false; sometimes used as equivalent to **empirical truth**.

Contradiction: A sentence that is false by virtue of its meaning, irrespective of context.

Contradictory: The relation between two sentences where the truth of one entails the falseness of the other and vice versa.

Conventional implicature: In Grice's theory of inferential communication, an inference conventionally communicated by an expression, i.e. not dependent on context though cancelable by additional correction.

Conversational implicature: In Grice's theory of inferential communication, an inference designed to be understood by a combination of linguistic form and contextual knowledge. It crucially depends on the hearer using contextual information to arrive at the intended inference.

Conversational maxims: In Grice's theory of inferential communication, principles that speakers and hearers expect each other to follow. They are assumed to be of different types, including quality, quantity, relevance, and manner maxims.

Converses: A lexical relation between two words that describe a relationship between two entities from alternate viewpoints, for example *parent/child*.

Cooperative principle: Grice's proposal that the exploitation of inference in conversation depends on an implicit guarantee of shared communicative assumptions.

Coreference: When two linguistic expressions are used to refer to the same entity.

Correspondence theory of truth: A traditional theory that says that truth is a relationship between a proposition and a corresponding fact or state of the world.

Counterfactual conditionals: Sentences that describe the hypothetical consequences of non-factual events or situations, for example, "If you had left yesterday, you would have missed the strike."

Count nouns: Nouns denoting an entity that can be counted.

Dative alternation: An argument structure alternation which under certain conditions allows a transposition of direct and indirect object, e.g. *I gave a book to Frank/I gave Frank a book.*

Dead metaphor: The idea that metaphorical expressions lose their novelty over time, become conventionalized, and are no longer recognized as metaphoric.

Decompositional semantics: Strictly speaking, analyses that break expressions into their constituent parts; commonly applied to analyses that identify sub-word components of meaning.

Defeasible: This term is used in semantics and pragmatics to mean cancelable or capable of being overridden in a context. It is claimed to be a feature of some inferences, such as **implicature**, but not others, such as **entailment**.

Definite descriptions: A term from the philosophy of language describing nominal expressions used to refer to individuals. The typical examples begin in English with *the*, e.g. *the Secretary-General of the United Nations*. However, possessive expressions (*my head of department*) and other expressions have also been included. In linguistics these expressions have been described as **presupposition triggers**.

Deictic center: The point around which the deictic systems orient, typically the position in space and time of the current speaker.

Deixis, deictic expressions: Linguistic expressions that in order to be understood rely on a link to the act of speaking or writing. So adverbs like *here* and *there* relate to the location of the speaker, *now* to the time of the utterance, and pronouns like *I* and *you* to the identities of the current speaker and addressee(s).

Denotation: The relation between a linguistic expression and its **extension**.

Denotational approach: An approach to meaning that focuses on the correspondences between linguistic expressions and language-external entities.

Denotatum: Another term for **extension**.

Deontic modality: A linguistic system allowing the speaker to communicate attitudes toward social obligation, permission, and prohibition. In English the modal verbs *may, must, can*, etc. express choices in this system.

Directives: In Bach and Harnish's (1979) classification of speech acts, this class includes advising, admonishing, asking, begging, dismissing, excusing, forbidding, instructing, ordering, permitting, requesting, requiring, suggesting, urging, warning.

Discourse: A connected series of utterances by one or more speakers (less commonly used for writing).

Disjunction: In logic a **logical connective** with a specific binary truth-function. The expression is true if at least one of the parts is true and it is false otherwise. It is represented by the logical operator $\vee$. In language it is often used for a complex expression with parts linked by a set of connectives including English *or*. The parallels between the logical operator and the meaning of natural language connectives like *or* are only partial.

Durative: A situation type that extends over a period of time.

Dynamic: A feature of situation types, and by extension of verbs, where a situation is portrayed as involving change over a period conceived as a succession of phases. Dynamic situation types are opposed to **states**.

Empirical truth: Truth that derives from correspondence to a set of affairs, gained by experience.

Encyclopedic knowledge: General knowledge that an individual has about the world. In mainstream linguistics it is contrasted with linguistic knowledge, the unconscious knowledge speakers exhibit in using their language.

Entailment: A relation between sentences where the truth of one guarantees the truth of the other, so *John broke the window* entails *The window broke.*

Epistemic modality: A linguistic system allowing the speaker to communicate attitudes toward the possibilities that a proposition is true. Typically a speaker has choices between certainty and a range of weaker positions, for example: *She is leaving* vs. *She may be leaving.* In English the choices are often communicated by modal verbs such as *may, might, can, could.*

Event: This term has a number of uses related to **situation type** (ST). In one use it is a dynamic ST opposed to processes by being telic. In another it includes all dynamic STs as opposed to states. In a third it is used for all STs, as in **event structure**.

Event structure: Like **event**, this has a number of uses. One is equivalent to **situation type**. Another, in decompositional approaches to meaning, is a representation that involves sub-events and semantic features such as agency, motion, and causation.

Eventuality: An alternative term for **situation type**.

Evidentiality: A semantic system that allows speakers to communicate their attitudes toward the source of information conveyed in their propositions. In some languages this is an obligatory feature represented by morphological marking, often on the verb. Typically such systems distinguish between types of direct knowledge, from witnessing something, and other, indirect forms, including inference and being told.

Exclusive or: This is a logical operator with a specific binary truth-function. A complex expression containing it is only true if just one of its disjuncts is true, otherwise it is false. It can be represented by the abbreviation **XOR** or the symbol $\underline{\vee}$.

Exemplar theory of categories: A version of the *prototype theory* of categories where category membership is determined by similarity to previously encountered real examples.

Existential quantifier: A logical operator, one of the two quantifiers in predicate logic. Represented by the symbol $\exists$, it expresses that the formula following it is true of at least one entity in a domain. The expression $\exists x P(x)$ can be translated into English as "There exists an x such that $P(x)$" or "There is at least one x such that $P(x)$."

Experiencer: A thematic role, the entity who is aware of the action or state described by the predicate but is not in control of it.

Explicatures: In Relevance theory, the level of meaning representation that results from listeners recovering the explicit content of an utterance by processes such as working out what entities are being referred to by names and nouns, resolving ambiguity, and filling in gaps. A further interpretive step occurs when listeners combine explicatures with contextual information to produce **implicatures**.

Extension: A thing or set of things that a linguistic expression can be used to refer to.

Face, positive and negative: Terms used in the study of politeness phenomena in conversation. Positive face is the desire to signal engagement with others; negative face is the desire to avoid offending others.

Felicitous: See **felicity conditions**.

Felicity conditions: In speech act semantics the social conventions governing the appropriate performance of a speech act. An appropriately performed act is termed **felicitous** while an unsuccessful act is **infelicitous**.

Figurative language: Traditionally, using figurative language, also described as employing figures of speech, involves communicating something by an intended deviation from **literal meaning**, for example by using **metaphor, irony**, or **hyperbole**.

Figure: An entity that stands out against some background. In cognitive approaches the background is often termed the **Ground**, giving a Figure/Ground distinction.

Flouting: In Grice's theory of **conversational implicature**, a speaker's overt breaking of **conversational maxims** in order to create special effects, for example by saying something obviously untrue to communicate **irony**.

Focus: This is used in several ways. In information structure it can refer to new information that is marked as most salient by the particular mechanisms of a language, e.g. intonation, syntactic structure, or specific morphemes. In the semantics of color terms it refers to the best example of the color to which a term applies.

Generalization: Another term for **broadening**.

Generalized conversational implicatures: In Grice's theory of **conversational implicature**, a type of conversational implicature that, though context-dependent, ranges over contexts and acts like a default, which holds unless canceled. For example *some* generally implicates *not all*, so that "Some of his students came to the talk" implicates "Not all of his students came to the talk." However, this generalized implicature can be canceled without anomaly, as in "Some, in fact all, of his students came to the talk."

Generalized quantifier theory: An approach in formal semantics that characterizes quantifiers in terms of set theory. Nominals are viewed as sets of properties, which themselves are viewed as sets. Quantifiers in language are then described by the usual set theory operations. So *All men are mortal* is true if the set of men is a subset of the set of mortal things. *Some men are mortal* is true if the set of things that are members of both the set of men and the set of mortal things is not empty, and so on.

Goal: A thematic role, the entity toward which something moves.

Gradable antonyms: A type of oppositeness where terms are on a scale of some variable property, e.g. *hot* vs. *cold*. There are other terms on the scale, e.g. *cool*, and the terms can be made comparative, e.g. *hotter*.

Ground: The background against which an entity stands out. In cognitive approaches the latter is often termed the **Figure**, giving a Figure/Ground distinction.

Hedges: Expressions used to weaken the impact of an utterance. They may signal a speaker's uncertainty, acknowledge a lack of evidence, or reduce the speaker's responsibility or authority. English examples include *I think, kind of, sort of, perhaps*.

Holonym: See **meronymy**.

Homographs: Distinct lexemes sharing spelling but not pronunciation, e.g. *row* "line" and *row* "loud argument."

Homonymy: The relation between words that are identical in form but belong to different lexemes, e.g. *bark* "cry of a dog" and *bark* "outer covering of a tree."

Homophones: A term for a subclass of **homonymy** where the words are pronounced the same but spelled differently, for example *cent* "monetary unit" and *scent* "pleasant smell."

Hyperbole: A traditional label for exaggeration viewed as a rhetorical figure of speech.

Hypernym (Hyperonym): In the lexical relation of **hyponymy** or inclusion, the hypernym is the more general or including term. So *dog* is a hypernym of *poodle*.

Hyponym: See **hyponymy**.

Hyponymy: A relationship of inclusion in the lexicon between more specific and more general terms. The more specific term is the *hyponym* and the more general term is either called the superordinate or the *hypernym*. So *poodle* is a hyponym of *dog*.

Idealized cognitive model (ICM): A theoretical proposal by linguist George Lakoff (e.g. 1987) to characterize structured domains of knowledge that underpin the use of language.

Ideophones: Words that evoke sensory events. The class includes sound-based **onomatopoeia** but also words like English *twinkle* and *bling* that cross sense modalities.

Idiolect: The speech of a particular individual.

Idioms: Multi-word expressions that are non-compositional and therefore have to be learned as semantic units, e.g. *pass away* meaning "die."

Illocutionary act: In Speech Act Theory, an instance of a speech act type, carrying meaning and a particular **illocutionary force**.

Illocutionary force: In Speech Act Theory, the type of speech act that an utterance performs, e.g. promising, warning, threatening.

Image schema: In cognitive semantics, a theoretical proposal made by Mark Johnson (e.g. 1987) for very basic conceptual categories that are experientially based and that underlie higher-level cognitive processes such as **metaphor**. Well-known examples include CONTAINER and PATH.

Imperfective aspect: An aspectual category that allows an internal view of a dynamic situation type, identifying internal temporal structure. Typically there is no identified end point. An example is the English progressive in *Henry was rowing the boat*. It contrasts in many languages with **perfective aspect**.

Impersonal passive: A construction containing an overtly passive verb and no subject, e.g. the German *Gerstern wurde getanzt* "Yesterday there was dancing" (literally "Yesterday (it) was danced").

Implicature: In Grice's theory of inferential communication, implicatures are inferences understood by the hearer to be intentionally communicated by an utterance.

Implicit performatives: See **performative**.

Inchoative: A semantic and grammatical category in verbs that identifies a change of state in an entity.

Indirect speech act: In Speech Act Theory a speech act communicated through a non-typical linguistic form, as when a question is used to make a request, e.g. *Will you lend me your bike?*

Infelicitous: See **felicity conditions**.

Inference: In general terms this is the process of deriving conclusions from assumptions and evidence. In linguistics an important focus of interest is the idea, in for example Grice's work, that speakers routinely exploit or predict future inferences by their hearers in order to convey meaning. This confidence in inference drawing allows speakers to communicate more than they explicitly say and emphasizes the importance of context in meaning.

Information structure: The linguistic marking of a speaker's assumptions about the knowledge surrounding a conversation, in particular the distinction between shared assumptions and new information. This distinction is sometimes termed given versus new information. Another distinction in information structure is between **focus** and **topic**.

Instrument: A thematic role, the means by which an action is performed or something comes about.

Intension: In the study of reference, the properties something has to have to count as a member of a category and be identified by a linguistic expression. Some writers view this as a concept. Others relate it to Frege's use of the term **sense**.

Intensional/intensionality: In logic and semantics an intensional context is one where the substitution of a referentially equivalent expression into a sentence does not automatically preserve the truth-value. This is also termed **referential opacity**.

Intentionality: A philosophical term that refers to the nature of relations between mental states and objects outside the individual mind. In semantics it is often used for features of language that reflect the speaker's subjectivity, e.g. a selection of options in the tense, aspect, and modality systems or expressing attitudes to propositions.

Irony: More narrowly verbal irony, is traditionally a type of **figurative language** where the speaker for purposes of humor or mockery communicates the opposite of what is literally said, for example saying *That went well* to a colleague after a disastrous meeting.

Iterative interpretation: Where a **punctual** situation type interpreted as a series of repetitions, for example, *He sneezed for ten minutes.*

Landmark: See **trajector**.

Language of thought hypothesis: The proposal that thinking is done in a mental language that is distinct from individual spoken languages.

Lemma: a form of a lexeme used to identify it, for example as the citation form in a dictionary entry, so in an English dictionary *sing* might be the lemma for *sings, sang, singing*, etc.

Levels of analysis: The idea that the structural organization of language motivates separate subfields of study, including phonology, morphology, syntax, and semantics.

Lexeme: A semantic word; the basic unit of lexical semantics.

Lexical ambiguity: Where a word form is associated with more than one distinct sense or concept.

Lexical aspect: An alternative term for **situation type**.

Lexical causatives: Verbs that specify as their subject the causer of an action but require no causative morphological affix or separate verb, for example English *kill.*

Lexical concepts: Concepts that equate to a single **lexeme**.

Lexical entry: The grouping of related senses of a word in a published dictionary; or a hypothetical organizational level of lexemes in a mental lexicon.

Lexical relations: The semantic relations between lexemes in the same language, such as **synonymy, antonymy, hyponymy**, etc.

Lexical semantics: The study of word meaning and meaning relations between words.

Lexical typology: The search for cross-linguistic generalizations about word meaning and **lexical relations**.

Lexicon: Another term for dictionary. In some semantic theories the mental lexicon is a speaker's linguistic knowledge about individual morphemes and words.

Linguistic knowledge: See **encyclopedic knowledge**.

Linguistic relativity: The idea, associated in different forms with Sapir (1949) and Whorf (1956), that the semantic and grammatical categories of a language determine thought.

Linguistic truth: Truth that derives from linguistic meaning, regardless of context.

Literal language theory: See **literal meaning**.

Literal meaning: The hypothesis that there is a regular, transparent use of sentences and words, which is different from and more basic than non-literal or figurative uses like **metaphor, metonymy**, etc.

Litotes: A traditional term for understatement, viewed as a figure of speech.

Localism: The view that in grammar and semantics expressions of location are more basic than other systems, as when time is viewed as characterized in spatial terms relative to the speaker.

Location: A thematic role, the place in which something is situated or an action takes place.

Locative alternation: An argument structure alternation, as in English *She sprayed red paint onto the wall/She sprayed the wall with red paint.* The first alternant is the locative and is said by Levin and Rappaport Hovav (1991) to emphasize the motion while the second, the *with* alternant, emphasizes the change of state.

Locutionary act: In Speech Act Theory the basic act of a speaker saying something meaningful in a language, considered independently of any intended function.

Logical form: A meaning representation assigned to a sentence that identifies its qualities in a specific type of logic, for example predicate logic.

Logical connectives: Elements of logical formulae (also called logical operators) that allow the description of truth relations between propositions. They include: $\wedge$ (also symbolized by &) (conjunction); $\vee$ (inclusive disjunction); $\underline{\vee}$ (exclusive disjunction); $\neg$ (negation); and $\rightarrow$ (material implication).

Logical words: Words in a natural language, like English *and, or, not*, that have been likened to **logical connectives**.

Macro-roles: The term is used for two generalized thematic roles, an agent-like role, termed Actor, and a patient-like role, termed Undergoer.

Marked(ness) (theory): A notion used in various areas of linguistics, particularly in linguistic typology, that identifies an asymmetry between forms. In one use, some forms are said to be more basic than others. The more basic are termed less marked and may be more widespread, productive, learned earlier by children or resistant to loss over time.

Material implication: A logical operator symbolized as $\rightarrow$ or $\supset$. $P \rightarrow Q$ can be translated into English *If P then Q* but is probably more accurately represented by *It is never the case that P is true and Q is false* (i.e. not both *p* and not-*q*).

Meaning postulates: The use of logical rules to represent lexical relations. For example **hyponymy** can be represented by using **material implication**, so that the hyponym between *animal* and *dog* can be shown as $\forall x\ (DOG\ (x) \rightarrow ANIMAL\ (x))$, i.e. "for all *x*, if *x* is a dog then *x* is an animal."

Medio-passive: A cover term for **middle** and **passive** voices.

Mentalese: A name sometimes used for the mental language assumed in the **language of thought hypothesis**.

Mental lexicon: The notional store of known words in the minds of speakers. Traditionally this is seen as containing all the idiosyncratic information about lexemes. Different models have been proposed for the relationship between semantic information and related phonological, morphological, and orthographic features.

Meronymy: The lexical relation of part–whole. So English *knuckle* is a meronym of *finger* and *finger* a meronym of *hand*. The whole is sometimes called the holonym.

Metalanguage: A language used in the description of another language, where the latter is called the **object** language. In formal semantics logics are used as metalanguages for natural languages.

Metalinguistic negation: When a speaker, rather than denying an assertion, rejects the assertion's assumptions or implications.

Metaphor: In traditional terms, a figurative use of language based on an implicit identification of resemblance or analogy. In cognitive linguistics it is seen as a linguistic reflection of a more general and systematic psychological process of analogical mapping between two domains of knowledge, one being a source domain and the other a target domain. So in one interpretation of *He and his wife have called a truce* the target domain would be a marital dispute and the source domain would be war.

Metonymy: In traditional terms, a figurative use of language where reference is achieved by identifying something associated with, or contiguous with, the referent. So place-names like *Moscow* and *Washington* can be used to refer to governments, as in *Moscow and Washington are still at odds over Iran's role*. In cognitive linguistics it is seen, like metaphor, as a mapping, but within a single domain of knowledge. The expression used (e.g. *Washington*) is called the vehicle and the intended referent, the target (the US government).

Middle alternation: An argument structure alternation in English when a normally transitive verb as *Evelyn sells this wine* may occur in an alternant with the THEME argument as subject: *This wine sells well*.

Middle voice: A grammatical category in some languages that reflects specific relationships between a verb and its thematic roles, distinct from **active** and **passive** voices. It may be marked by verb morphology and/or argument selection. Its typical meanings include reflexivity, actions involving the subject's body, and uncontrolled processes in the subject.

Modality: A semantic system, or systems, that allow speakers to express varying degrees of commitment to a proposition. It is typically divided into **deontic** modality, relating to judgments of social obligation, permission, and prohibition, and **epistemic** modality, relating to judgments of fact.

Modal logics: Logics that include operators to express **modality**.

Modal verbs: Verbs used to convey judgments of modality, for example English *can, may, must, should, will, would.*

***Modes d'action*:** A French-language term for **situation type**.

Modus ponens: A form of valid logical argument where, given a conditional claim in one line, the antecedent to the condition in the second line, you can deduce the consequent in the third, e.g. (i) A → B; (ii) A; (iii) B.

Modus tollens: A form of valid logical argument where, given a conditional claim in one line, the denial to its consequent in the second line, you can deduce the denial of the antecedent in the third, e.g. (i) A → B; (ii) Not B; (iii) Not A.

Monotonicity: a term from mathematics used in logic. In logic it is a feature of **entailment** in some systems where statements remain true when further assumptions are added. In formal semantics it is a feature of quantifiers in **generalized quantifier theory**, where it reflects patterns of entailments between sets and subsets.

Mood: A grammatical system marked on verbs. In one use it describes a distinction between sentence types grammatically distinguished by their function, for example between indicative (or declarative), interrogative, and imperative. Some languages have a subjunctive mood, with a range of uses including marking subordinate clauses and descriptions of hypothetical or unreal situations. In descriptions of some languages, the term mood is used for distinctions of **modality** and **evidentiality**.

Morpheme: Traditionally the minimum form–meaning unit in language. It is sometimes equivalent to a word, as in English *real,* or to a smaller unit as with the morpheme *un-* in *unreal.*

Morphological causatives: Verbs where, unlike in **lexical causatives**, the identification of a causer argument results from a morphological process, such as affixation.

Motion: A semantic component of motion events, the presence of motion or location in an event.

Multi-word unit: Semantic unit consisting of more than one word whose meaning is not compositional, e.g. phrasal verbs like *give up* or an idiomatic expression like *kick the bucket* for "die."

Narrowing: A process where the concept expressed by use of a lexical item is more specific than that usually assumed to be linguistically encoded. For example when *drink* in *She doesn't drink* is interpreted to mean *drink alcohol.*

Natural kinds: A term from philosophy for categories of things that are assumed to exist independently of human thought and, particularly, independently of naming in a particular language.

Necessary and sufficient conditions: In the classical theory of categories these are conditions on membership of a category that constitute a definition of that category. So the features ADULT, FEMALE, and HUMAN might in this view be proposed for the concept *woman.* Each of these features is individually necessary for something to be a woman and they are also jointly sufficient, since anything with all of them will be a woman.

Necessary truth: A truth that cannot be denied without altering our view of reality. Put another way, denying a necessary truth causes a contradiction. Often opposed to **contingent truth**.

Negation: In linguistics the lexical or grammatical means a language has for denying a proposition or reversing the meaning of words, for example English *not* in *It is not raining*, and prefixes *un-* and *-in* in words like *unfashionable* or *incomplete*. In logic, a **logical connective**, symbolized by ¬, with a specific binary truth-function. The addition of ¬ reverses the truth-value of an expression, so if *P* is true, then ¬*P* is false and *vice versa*.

Non-literal meaning: The hypothesis that there are figurative uses of language like **metaphor, metonymy**, etc. that are distinct from the regular, transparent use of sentences and words, which is termed literal meaning. Traditionally non-literal meaning is seen as requiring extra effort to understand.

Noun classes: Grammatically marked classifications of nouns based partially or historically on semantic classifications. Gender systems are an example of a small noun class system.

Object language: See **metalanguage**.

Onomatopoeia: A quality of words whose sounds imitate those made by their denotation, e.g. English *cuckoo* or Swahili *pikipiki* "motorcycle." Some resemble the sounds they denote, such as English *ping* or French *boum* "bang." Onomatopoeic words are a subclass of **ideophones**.

Ontology: The term has different uses in linguistics. In decompositional semantics it is used for basic classes of concepts such as EVENT, MATERIAL THING, QUALITY, PLACE, etc. In computational lexical semantics it is used for relational classifications of concepts.

Opaque contexts: See **referential opacity**.

Optative: A grammatical **mood** used to express wishes or hopes.

Ostensive definition: The theory that one acquires the meaning of words by being directed to examples in the world.

Paraphrases: Sentences with different forms but the same meaning. Sometimes described as, when uttered, having the same truth conditions.

Participant role: See **thematic role**.

Particularized conversational implicatures: In Grice's theory of **conversational implicature**, a type of conversational implicature that is strictly bound to a specific context of communication.

Passive voice: A grammatical category that reflects a specific relationship between a verb and its thematic roles, distinct from **active** and **middle** voices. It may be marked by a change both in verb morphology and in the verb's argument selection compared with the canonical active voice template. Typically it involves downgrading or omission of the agent argument and promotion to subject of another thematic role, such as patient, as in *The escaped convicts were captured.*

Path: a semantic component of motion events, the course followed or the site occupied by the **Figure** object with respect to the **Ground**.

Patient: a thematic role, the entity undergoing the effect of an action, often undergoing a change of state.

Perfective aspect: An aspectual category that allows an external view of a dynamic situation type, with no identification of internal temporal structure. It typically portrays an event as a complete unit. An example is the English simple past in *Henry built a boat.* It contrasts in many languages with **imperfective aspect**.

Performative: In Speech Act Theory a performative utterance, if used appropriately, represents an action in itself. Thus *I promise to be home early* is, under the right conditions (called **felicity conditions** in this theory), a promise. Since it contains a performative verb, *promise*, this is an explicit performative. Using *I'll be home early* as a promise would be an implicit performative. Other performatives include requests, warnings, and apologies.

Periphrastic causatives: Causative expressions formed from multiple rather than single verbs, for example with English *make* as in *She made them leave.*

Perlocutionary act: In Speech Act Theory the act of producing an effect in the listener by successfully communicating a performative utterance. It identifies a change effected in the listener(s).

Polysemous, polysemy: These terms are used when a word has distinct but related meanings.

Possible world semantics: An approach in formal semantics that relativizes truth to a number of alternative situations or worlds that differ in at least one respect from the actual world. This notion seeks to reflect speakers' ability to express **modality**.

Pragmatics: In theories that separate subfields of semantic and pragmatics, pragmatics is typically concerned with the contribution to meaning of contextual assumptions and processes. The nature of this division varies across different theoretical approaches.

Predicate: In the traditional linguistic distinction between subject and predicate, the predicate contains the verb and perhaps other elements that give information about the subject. In predicate logic the predicate is a function that requires (at least) a subject argument to be complete. Predicates are represented by capital letters, *A*, *B*, etc.

Predicate logic: This, together with **propositional logic**, is one of the two basic forms of logic used in formal semantics. It allows analysis of propositions into arguments and predicates and via a number of **logical connectives** allows more complex expressions to be created. Two of these operators allow features of quantification to be described: the **universal quantifier**, symbolized by $\forall$ and the **existential quantifier**, symbolized by $\exists$.

Predicative use of adjective: where syntactically the adjective occurs in the predicate as a complement of the subject, for example *black* in *The book is black.*

Premise: In logic the premises of an argument are those propositions in it that are intended to provide the support or evidence for its conclusion.

Presupposition: A proposition assumed by a speaker when making an assertion. So a speaker saying *Harry has stopped sending his ex-wife Christmas cards* presupposes that Harry used to send his ex-wife Christmas cards. Traditionally this was viewed as a semantic relationship between two propositions but the assumption's sensitivity to context has led some scholars to view it as a pragmatic phenomenon, reflecting participants' management of shared assumptions in a conversation.

Presupposition failure: This is an extreme case of infelicitous use of presuppositions: when a speaker communicates an assumption that is not or cannot be shared by the addressee(s). Some cases can be rescued by accommodation, where the addressee(s) supply the missing assumptions, e.g. if someone says *My wife is ill* when you didn't know they were married. Others cannot, e.g., if they clash with known reality, as the famous example *The King of France is bald* uttered when there is no king of France. The philosophical use of the term presupposition failure is restricted to these latter cases.

Presupposition trigger: A linguistic element that signals the speaker's presuppositions, such as lexical items like the English factive verbs *realize* or *regret*, and constructions like clefts, such as *It was the butler who murdered the guests*, which presupposes somebody murdered the guests.

Proposition: Part of the meaning of a sentence that describes some state of affairs. The same proposition can be expressed in various sentences, which can then be spoken or written as utterances. Some philosophers describe propositions as communicable beliefs that are capable of being judged true or false.

Propositional attitudes: A term from philosophy for mental states held about a proposition. These are typically represented in language by verbs that take sentential complements, for example English *believe, think, expect, hope.*

Propositional logic: This, together with **predicate logic**, is one of the two basic forms of logic used in formal semantics. It allows the analysis of the truth effects of combining propositions by using a set of **logical connectives**, including **negation** (symbolized by $\neg$), **conjunction** (symbolized by $\wedge$ or &), **disjunction** ($\vee$), and **material implication** ($\rightarrow$).

Prototype theory: A theory, associated particularly with the cognitive psychologist Eleanor Rosch, in which concepts have a complex structure containing a central prototype and other more marginal elements which may be more or less similar.

Punctual: Feature of situation types that are thought of as happening in an instant, e.g. *Emmet sneezed.*

Qualia structure: In Pustejovsky's Generative Lexicon theory this is a classification of the properties of a lexical item. These properties reflect prototypical information associated with the entities and events denoted by the lexical item. They are organized into four types: agentive, constitutive, formal, and telic.

Quantifiers: In linguistics, expressions that indicate a quantity of something, though usually distinguished from enumerating by numerals. Quantifiers may constitute a special class of determiners like English *all, every, no, most, many*, etc., or in other languages belong to other grammatical categories such as adjectives. In predicate logic there are two quantifiers: the **universal** and **existential quantifiers**.

Radial category: A theoretical proposal by linguist George Lakoff (e.g. 1987) for the organization of lexical categories that reflects **prototype** theory. Radial categories have a prototypical sense and the structure of the category is represented by conventional links to other related senses.

Realis/irrealis: A distinction of **modality** in some languages that differentiates between two classes of situations: actual and non-actual. The latter may include wishes, intentions, predictions, hypothetical statements, etc. Irrealis modality is reflected in a range of moods across languages, including **subjunctive**, conditional, **optative**.

Refer: See **reference**.

Reference: The act of using of linguistic expressions to identify things in the world.

Referent: The thing identified by an act of reference.

Referential opacity: A construction is referentially opaque when the substitution of one coreferential expression for another in that context does not always preserve the truth-value of the whole. An example is: *John wants to meet Aoibhinn's father* may be true and *John wants to meet the Prime Minister* false, even though Aoibhinn is the Prime Minister's daughter, for example if John doesn't know the latter fact.

Register: A term describing a variety of language specific to certain social situations or purposes.

Representational approach: An approach to meaning that focuses on the relationship between linguistic expressions and mental representations.

Restricted quantification: A representation for quantifiers in predicate logic that brings the logical formulae into closer alignment with natural language syntax.

Reverse relation: A lexical relation between two words where they describe movement or change in opposite directions, for example *ascend/descend*, *rise/fall*, *heat/cool*.

Rheme: See **theme**.

Satellite: In Talmy's typology of motion events, an element independent of the verb that also carries semantic components of motion, like English *up* and *down*.

Satellite-framed language: In Talmy's typology of motion events, a language where the path component of motion is expressed by a class of **satellites**, independently of the verb, as in English.

Scalar implicature: A type of implicature that depends on expressions being ordered on a scale of values. Such a scale from strong to weak is English <*all, most, many, some*>. Implicatures follow from the assumption that speakers will make their utterances as informative as required and will therefore not use a weaker term if a stronger applies. So typically a use of *some* will implicate *not all*.

Scanning: In Langacker's (2008) Cognitive Grammar this is a process through which speakers construe a scene, for example choosing to view a process as a series of stages or as a complete unit. The choice influences grammatical decisions, for example, the use of nouns or verbs to represent actions.

Scope: See **scope ambiguity**.

Scope ambiguity: Scope is the range or limit of dependency of one item upon another in a structure, for example of a quantifier and a variable in logic or a negative word in a sentence. Scope ambiguity occurs when two or more ranges can be identified, giving rise to different readings. For example, *All the winners wanted to watch one show* has ambiguity in interpretation of the relative scope of the quantifiers *all* and *one*: if *all* is given wide scope over *one*, then there may be as many shows as winners; if *one* has scope over *all* then they all want to see the one show.

Scripts: Representations of knowledge associated with specific social situations.

Selection restrictions: A method, for example in Katz's semantic theory, of capturing the combinatorial possibilities of words.

Semantic components, or semantic primitives: Sub-word atoms of meaning that are held to combine to form words, so woman = [+FEMALE] [+ADULT] [+HUMAN].

Semantic role: Another term for **thematic role**.

Semantic typology: The systematic comparison of languages at the level of meaning.

Semelfactive: A situation type that is dynamic, non-durative and atelic, i.e. a single instantaneous event, e.g. *The guard blinked.*

Semiotics: The general study of signs, including both linguistic and non-linguistic signs.

Sense: This term is used in various ways in semantics. One important use is as a translation of Frege's (1892) German term *Sinn.* Here it is used for the knowledge that allows a speaker to match successfully a linguistic expression with its extension and thus use it to refer. This use relates sense to the thought expressed by a linguistic expression such as a word. Sense is used in lexical semantics to identify the distinct lexemes linked by homonymy, so an ambiguous word like *bark* is said to have more than one sense. Similarly the related meaning distinctions identified in polysemy are also called senses, so a polysemous word like the noun *run* (a fast pace, a race, an errand, continuous production, sequence of cards, score in cricket, etc.) is also said to have multiple senses.

Signification: The relationship created by the cognitive process of allowing one entity to stand for another in communication, thus creating **signs**.

Signifier/signified: Saussure's (1974) distinction of parts of a **sign**, where for a linguistic sign the signifier is the linguistic expression and the signified is the concept. Saussure emphasized the arbitrariness of the relation between the two.

Simile: In traditional terms, a figurative use of language based on an explicit identification of resemblance or analogy. In English it is associated with the word *like*, for example *Reading this paper is like wading through mud.*

Simple antonym: See **complementary antonym**.

Sincerity conditions: In speech act semantics a subclass of **felicity conditions** that govern the speaker's attitude to the act.

Situation type: A categorization of events and situations encoded in the lexical items of a language, allowing distinctions, for example, between **states** and dynamic types, and within the latter between **durative** and **punctual**. One influential classification distinguishes between **accomplishments, activities, achievements,** and **semelfactives.**

Social deixis: deictic expressions, such as pronouns, that in a conversation reflect the participants' relative social status and intimacy.

Source: Used in several senses, including:(a) a thematic role, the entity from which something moves, and (b) in the analysis of **metaphor** and **metonymy**, the comparison concept or analogy.

Speech acts: A term used by Austin (1975) to describe utterances in interpersonal communication as types of action.

States: Situation types that portray a situation as unchanging and with no internal sequence of temporal phases.

Stative verb: A verb whose situation type conveys a constant state with no element of change.

Subject hierarchy: A cross-linguistic generalization about the preference for thematic roles occurring in subject position.

Subjunctive: A mood whose functions vary across languages but is typically associated with irrealis modality and syntactic subordination.

Superordinate: A term describing an element higher in a hierarchy than another. In lexical relations it is used as an equivalent to **hypernym.**

Syllogism: In logic, a form of deductive reasoning that involves a major **premise,** a minor premise, and a conclusion.

Synchronic linguistics: A term introduced by Saussure (1974) as part of the distinction between synchronic and diachronic linguistics. The latter studies change over time while the former idealizes that at a particular time (of study) a language is in a timeless and unchanging state.

Synecdoche: A traditional label for PART FOR WHOLE and WHOLE FOR PART metonymies.

Synonymy: Having the same meaning; sometimes defined as two sentences entailing one another.

Synthetic truth: A proposition true by correspondence to a set of affairs.

Target: See **metaphor** and **metonymy**.

Tautology: In logic, a statement that cannot be denied without contradiction. It is true under any interpretation.

Taxonomic sisters: Items at the same level in a **taxonomy**

Taxonomy: In lexical semantics a grouping of lexical items in a classificatory hierarchy that can be represented as a tree diagram, such as animals or plants.

Telic: A feature of situation types where the event or process has an inherent end point.

Tenor: In some writing on **metaphor** the term tenor is used for the intended referent, or **target**, while **vehicle** is used for the comparison or **source**.

Tense: A semantic and grammatical system that allows speakers to situate events in time. Tense is deictic since it relates fundamentally to the time of an act of speaking or writing.

Thematic role: A semantic relation an argument takes in relation to a verb, such as **agent**, **patient**, **theme**, **instrument**, **location**, **source**, **goal**, etc.

Thematic role grid: A representation of a verb's required arguments in terms of their thematic role.

Theme: This term has two uses: (a) a thematic role, the entity which is moved by an action, or whose location is described; and (b) in opposite to theme, a division of a sentence's information structure, comparable to **topic/comment structure**.

Theta-Criterion: A proposal that thematic roles and syntactic arguments must be in a one-to-one relationship.

Topic: This term has several uses in linguistics. In information structure it is used at sentence level for a sentence constituent in languages that mark a topic/focus or a **topic/comment** distinction by syntactic structure or special morphemes. At a higher level the term is used for a unifying element in the unfolding structure of discourse, the discourse topic, which is what participants understand the discourse or conversation to be about.

Topic/comment structure: The proposal that some languages, e.g. Chinese, Japanese, present a sentence structure that distinguishes between a topic, which is what the sentence is about and that links to the previous discourse, and the comment about the topic, which is new information. Some writers see the traditional subject-predicate sentence division as a subset of this distinction.

Trajector: In Langacker's (2008) Cognitive Grammar, the opposition trajector versus landmark identifies a relation where one item (the **trajector**) is of higher salience than the other (the **landmark**). In motion events it is similar to the **figure/ground** distinction of other writers but it also covers other semantic areas, e.g. spatial relations (*X is above Y* versus *Y is below X*) and the relationship between thematic roles (AGENT versus PATIENT).

Transitivity: In lexical semantics this term is used for a relation passing unchanged across a sequence of terms. Typically hyponymy is transitive: if A (*poodle*) is a hyponym of B (*dog*), and B (*dog*) a hyponym of C (*animal*), then A (*poodle*) is a hyponym of C (*animal*). In syntax transitivity describes the number of arguments a verb takes, typically distinguishing between intransitive (subject only), transitive (subject and object), and ditransitive (subject, direct object, indirect object). These patterns reflect semantic differences of **situation type** and **thematic** roles.

Truth-conditional semantics: An approach to semantics that holds that knowing the meaning of a sentence is equivalent to knowing the conditions (in the world) under which it could be used to express a true proposition.

Truth-table: A table that shows how logical connectives affect the truth-value of complex propositions.

Truth-value: Being true or false; the value of a declarative sentence in a given context.

Truth-value gap: In logic and semantics, a truth-value of neither true or false.

Typology: The subfield of linguistics that explores regularities in cross-linguistic variation. Its goal is to describe and explain both common properties and diversity among the world's languages.

Unbounded: another term for **atelic**.

Undergoer: A generalized thematic role that includes PATIENT, THEME, and other entities affected by the action described by the verb but not in control of it.

Underspecification: The idea, in for example lexical semantics, that conventional stored meanings are insufficient to explain what is understood by a word, and that further specification of meaning has to be supplied by the context. The extent of underspecification varies across theories.

Universal quantifier: A logical operator, one of the two quantifiers in predicate logic. Represented by the symbol ∀ it expresses that the formula following it is true of all entities in a domain. The expression $\forall x P(x)$ can be translated into English as "For all x, $P(x)$ is true" or "For every x, $P(x)$ is true."

Utterance: a spoken or written piece of language.

Vagueness: Variability in the meaning of a lexeme that is due to lack of specificity rather than ambiguity. Typical examples are gradable adjectives like *young* and *tall*.

Variable reference: See **constant reference**.

Variables: In logic and formal linguistics these are symbols that can represent any one of a specified range of values. They are often represented by letters, such as x, y, z in **predicate logic**.

Vehicle: See **metonymy**.

Verb-framed languages: In Talmy's (2000) typology of motion events, a language where the path component of motion is expressed in the verb, as in Spanish.

Voice: A grammatical category representing a particular configuration between a verb and the thematic roles and grammatical roles of its arguments, for example **passive** and **middle voice**.

Zeugma: the simultaneous evoking of distinct senses of a word in the same sentence, usually by conjunction of phrases or clauses, for example *Her kitchen and her son are very bright*. In this use it is also called syllepsis.

REFERENCES

Austin, J. L. 1975: *How to Do Things with Words*, second edition. Oxford: Clarendon Press. (First published 1962.)

Bach, Kent and Robert M. Harnish 1979: *Linguistic Communication and Speech Acts*. Cambridge, MA: MIT Press.
Frege, Gottlob 1892: Über Sinn und Bedeutung. *Zeitschrift für Philosophie und philosophische Kritik* 100: 25–50. Translated as "On sense and reference" in P. Geach and M. Black (eds.) 1980: *Translations from the Philosophical Writings of Gottlob Frege*, third edition, 56–78. Oxford: Blackwell.
Jackendoff, Ray 2002: *Semantic Structures*. Cambridge, MA: MIT Press.
Johnson, Mark 1987: *The Body in the Mind: The Bodily Basis of Meaning, Imagination, and Reason*. Chicago: University of Chicago Press.
Lakoff, George 1987: *Women, Fire, and Dangerous Things: What Categories Reveal about the Mind*. Chicago: University of Chicago Press.
Langacker, Ronald W. 2008: *Cognitive Grammar: A Basic Introduction*. Oxford: Oxford University Press.
Levin, Beth and Malka Rappaport Hovav 1991: Wiping the slate clean: a lexical semantic exploration. In Beth Levin and Steven Pinker (eds.) *Lexical and Conceptual Semantics*, 123–51. Oxford: Blackwell.
Sapir, Edward 1949: *Language: An Introduction to the Study of Speech*. New York: Harcourt Brace. (First published 1921.)
Saussure, Ferdinand de 1974: *Course in General Linguistics*. Edited by Charles Bally and Albert Sechehaye, translation by Wade Baskin. Glasgow: Fontana/Collins. (First published 1915 as *Cours de Linguistique Générale*. Paris: Pyot.)
Stalnaker, Robert 1974: Pragmatic presuppositions. In Milton K. Munitz and Peter K. Unger (eds.) *Semantics and Philosophy*, 197–213. New York: New York University Press.
Talmy, Leonard 2000: *Toward a Cognitive Semantics*, 2 vols. Cambridge, MA: MIT Press.
Whorf, Benjamin Lee 1956: *Language, Thought, and Reality: Selected Writings of Benjamin Lee Whorf*. Edited by John B. Carroll. Cambridge, MA: MIT Press.

Index